OTHER BOOKS BY ANN FAGAN GINGER

Human Rights & Peace Law in the United States (course materials) (1997)

Peace Law Almanac (1997)

Human Rights & Peace Law Docket: 1945-1993 (1995)

Carol Weiss King: Human Rights Lawyer 1895-1952 (1993)

The National Lawyers Guild: From Roosevelt through Reagan (with Eugene M. Tobin) (1988)

The Cold War Against Labor (with David Christiano) (2 vols.) (1987)

Jury Selection in Civil & Criminal Trials (2 vols.) (1984, 1985)

The International Juridical Association Bulletin 1932-1942 (editor) (3 vols., reprint edition) (1982)

Human Rights Docket U.S. 1979 (1979)

The Law, the Supreme Court and the People's Rights (1974, 1977)

The Relevant Lawyers (1972)

Civil Liberties Docket 1968-69 (1970)

Minimizing Racism in Jury Trials (1968)

The New Draft Law: A Manual for Lawyers and Counselors (1965, 1969)

Civil Rights & Liberties Handbook: Pleadings & Practice (2 vols.) (1963)

NUCLEAR WEAPONS
ARE ILLEGAL

The Historic Opinion
of the World Court and
How It Will Be Enforced

edited with an
introduction by
Ann Fagan Ginger

The Apex Press
New York

Published by The Apex Press, an imprint of the

Council on International and Public Affairs,

777 United Nations Plaza, Suite 3C,

New York, NY 10017 (800/316-2739)

Published in cooperation with the Meiklejohn Civil

Liberties Institute, Berkeley, California

Library of Congress Cataloging-in-Publication Data:

Nuclear weapons are illegal : the historic opinion of the World Court
    and how it will be enforced   /   edited with an introduction by Ann
    Fagan Ginger.
        p.   cm.
    Includes bibliographical references and index.
        ISBN 0-945257-87-2 (hardcover : alk. paper). — ISBN 0-945257-86-4
(pbk. : alk. paper)
        1. Nuclear disarmament.   2. Nuclear weapons (International law)
    I. Ginger, Ann Fagan.
    KZ5665.N83   1998   98-13533
    341.7'34—dc21   CIP

Typesetting by Carol Marino

Cover design by Warren Hurley; photo from Alyn Ware,

Lawyers' Committee on Nuclear Policy

Printed in the United States of America

CONTENTS

Preface   *ix*

PART ONE

A Court Opinion to Help Change the Course of History,   1
   by Ann Fagan Ginger

PART TWO

Legality of the Threat or Use of Nuclear Weapons
   (Advisory Opinion of the International Court of Justice)   23

PART THREE

Declarations, Separate and Dissenting
   Opinions of the Judges

   Declaration of President Mohammed Bedjaoui   79

   Dissenting Opinion of Vice-President Stephen M.
      Schwebel   89

   Dissenting Opinion of Judge Mohamed Shahabuddeen   111

   Declaration of Judge Shi Jiuyong   170

   Declaration of Judge Vladlen S. Vereshchetin   172

   Dissenting Opinion of Judge Abdul G. Koroma   176

   Separate Opinion of Judge Carl-August Fleishhauer   207

   Declaration of Judge Geza Herczegh   215

   Declaration of Judge L. Ferrari Bravo   218

   Individual Opinion of Judge Gilbert Guillaume   225

   Dissenting Opinion of Judge Christopher Gregory
      Weeramantry   234

   Individual Opinion of Judge Raymond Ranjeva   376

Dissenting Opinion of Judge Rosalyn Higgins   389
Dissenting Opinion of Judge Shigeru Oda   403

PART FOUR

The Opinion on Illegality of Nuclear Weapons Is Being
    Enforced, by Ann Fagan Ginger   455

The World Court Project: How a Citizen Network Can
    Influence the United Nations, by Kate Dewes and
    Commdr. Robert Green RN (Retired)   473

PART FIVE: APPENDICES

Study Guide with Questions for Discussion   496
Glossary of Latin and Legal Words and Phrases   507
Texts of Relevant Documents   513
Table of Cases   532
Table of Treaties, Resolutions, Conventions and Charters   538

Index   549

This book is dedicated to:

Mary Kaufman
who taught me the Nuremberg Principles (1912-1995)

Frank Newman
who taught me that the UN Charter is a treaty (1917-1996)

Haywood Burns
who taught me that brotherhood is powerful (1940-1996)

Thomas Jefferson Ginger
who taught me that Mississippi is part of my United States
(1951-1996)

Ernest Goodman
who taught me that South Africa is part of my world (1907-1997)

Bella Abzug
who taught me that sisterhood is global (1920-1998)

PREFACE

When human beings rise to our highest potential, when we take all that we have learned from the past and start using it to ensure the future, when we feel empowered to face the end of the world and say "No," it is cause for celebration.

This book is the celebration of such an event. As a body, the International Court of Justice rose to the challenge of looking straight into the fiery inferno — the radiating center of the stockpiles of nuclear bombs — and carefully analyzed what the bombs are made of and how they can be prevented from destroying us all.

And the ICJ judges as individuals, beginning from their own cultures, histories and legal training, built a structure to contain and ultimately to destroy all of the thousands of nuclear weapons now hidden in stockpiles around the globe.

A common thread runs through the opinion of the Court and the opinions of several of the judges — the thread of the traditional/customary/common law. The reader eventually comes to feel the strength of rules made in every culture over many centuries, rules limiting what a people or government can do to another people or government, and to their own people, without feeling shame or facing punishment.

Some of the witnesses who experienced the use of nuclear bombs in so-called testing in so-called isolated areas presented testimony to the Court in the oral tradition people have used since the beginning of civilization to pass down legendary lessons from one generation to the next. They called forth our duty to search our souls and consciences as human beings, rising far beyond nation states and governments. Sometimes reading the opinions one can almost hear folk songs being fiddled and strummed all over the world, hear the talking drums around the fires to ward off the evil spirits encased in nuclear bombs.

Rejecting egotism and a false sense of their own power, the judges wrote an opinion based on material reality, on the limited power of judges to enforce their opinions, based on their duty to enunciate where the power of enforcement rests. Some of the judges mentioned the work of Non-Governmental Organizations in bringing the issue before them. They all made clear that the duty of enforcement lies with national governments, spurred to action by the opinion (and, some suggested, by the insistence of their citizens).

Several of the judges expressed their faith in the elemental ability of human beings to actually abolish nuclear weapons that were created by their scientific communities with the massive assistance of their military/industrial complexes. The judges expressed their reliance on rules of law enunciated by individual scholars working out of their law libraries and by representatives of many nations meeting in conferences to face the man-made catastrophes of war over many centuries. Judges obviously prefer standing on safer ground in deciding most cases — citing Article X of section (w) in the Code of (A) and the case of *P v. D* in the Supreme Court of Z. But the judges on the World Court in this case, after citing articles and sections of constitutions and treaties and case law, rose to their responsibility to go deeper and wider to touch the elemental gulf stream of law flowing around the surviving nations of the world.

I hope this book makes the World Court opinion accessible to many people in the United States and in other nuclear and non-nuclear weapons states. I frankly tried to construct this book so that many more people would decide to take the awful plunge into thinking about nuclear weapons in their daily lives.

Once a person takes this fateful step, they are forever changed. Once the nuclear weapons genie enters one's consciousness, one can never again feel really secure or happy. One must somehow work for nuclear disarmament whenever possible as one realizes that security depends on the abolition of nuclear weapons, and that happiness will be possible when the end of nuclear weapons releases the resources of the world to meet all other human needs. Yet one sees that the steps in that direction seem very small and far between.

The fact that 14 judges from all over the world sitting as the International Court of Justice in a dignified quiet room heard reasoned and passionate words about nuclear weapons — this gives a feeling of security. The fact that all 14 of the judges voted for the abolition of nuclear weapons is a cause for happiness. The beginning of references to the opinion by legislators, administrators, activists, lawyers, judges and juries is a cause for hope.

The judges decided the question posed to them by the legislative body of our international system of governance, by the General Assembly of the United Nations, and then placed the duty of enforcement on the government of every nation and on each and all of the peoples of the world.

I am grateful to Ward Morehouse of The Apex Press for quickly agreeing to the idea for this book; to Cynthia T. Morehouse for her conscientious editing, as well as to Carol Marino for her careful work on the manuscript; to Mary Fagan Bates, my sister, for selecting illustrations to make the awful facts real and accessible; to Jim Ginger, my son, and Gooby Herms and Pante'a Javidan, for their help on the Index; to Doris Brin Walker for her suggestions; and to Selma Brackman for her help with the photographs.

December 1997   Ann Fagan Ginger

The International Court of Justice, Outside and Inside

Japanese delegation of World Court Project in front of International Court of Justice, The Hague, Netherlands, 1995. Photo from Alyn Ware, Lawyers' Committee on Nuclear Policy.

Credit: UN Photo 186867/A. Brizzi

In session, 1993. Photo courtesy of Freelance Photographers Guild (FPG).

PART ONE

A COURT OPINION TO HELP CHANGE THE COURSE OF HISTORY

Ann Fagan Ginger

This Opinion Is Vitally Important to Each of Us

Nuclear weapons are the first man-made weapons that can destroy everything on this planet. They are the greatest immediate man-made threat to the future of all human beings. They continue to maim and kill long after they explode in a test or in a war. In the process, they kill budget items for education, food, housing and medical care for hundreds of millions of people in at least ten countries.

On July 8, 1996, the World Court ruled that the use or threat of use of nuclear weapons is subject to the rules of international law applicable to armed conflict and to the rules of humanitarian law, which nuclear weapons cannot satisfy.

The Court unanimously announced its opinion that: "There exists an obligation to pursue in good faith and bring to a conclusion negotiations leading to nuclear disarmament in all its aspects under strict and effective international control." (¶ 105 (2)F)*

This opinion may be the most important opinion by a court in the history of the world. It was issued at the request of the United Nations General Assembly, which is the congress or parliament of our existing

---

* All citations to the Court's opinion are to numbered paragraphs in Part Two. All citations to material in the opinions of the individual judges are to paragraphs or sections by name of judge in Part Three. (Boldface highlighting is by the editor.)

1

system of world governance. The advisory opinion is based on evidence, scientific studies and law. It directly contradicts the legal arguments of the nuclear weapons states.

This opinion is based on evidence presented to the Court in oral and written statements by government officials and legal scholars:

- Pacific Island women saw totally deformed "monster babies" resembling jellyfish emerge from the bodies of civilian women exposed to radiation from peacetime nuclear weapons tests conducted by the United States in the South Pacific before the mothers were born. (Weeramantry § II(h))

- The mayors of Hiroshima and Nagasaki see daily reminders in the 1990s of the continuing effects of the atomic bombs dropped in wartime on their Japanese civilian cities in 1945 — citizens who had their eyes, noses and mouths burned away and their ears melted off. (Weeramantry § I.6)

And this opinion is based on scientific studies by physicists, physicians and other scholars from many geographic regions on the effect of the use of atom smashing to create bombs, and on studies of the bombs dropped on Hiroshima and Nagasaki and speculative scenarios of the effects of the larger bombs developed subsequently. The legal counsel of our international health department, the World Health Organization, presented studies of the effects of ionizing radiation, the effects of nuclear war and the legality of the use of nuclear weapons that led to data after the 1945 bombings and from nuclear accidents at Rocky Flats and Chernobyl. WHO "envisaged three possible scenarios: the use of a single bomb, a limited war and a total war. The number of dead in each of these scenarios varied from one million to one thousand million, to which the same number of people injured was to be added."[1]

Finally, this opinion is based on the law developed over centuries and especially in the last 150 years. The law was developed largely by means of treaties negotiated and signed by the leaders of powerful nations to prevent their own destruction. In the last 50 years, the law was developed by treaties drafted in conferences convened by a UN body, and by opinions of the International Court of Justice (ICJ) established by the United Nations and of its predecessor court established by the League of Nations.

Every man and woman and child who has suffered from nuclear weapons being used in war or in testing has a right to read and a need to understand what the Court decided. So does every mother and father and grandparent in every nation who suffers from the fear that an accident will trigger a nuclear explosion and nuclear winter, or that nuclear weapons will be used and so destroy the next generation. This fear of nuclear weapons is well-founded. They unleash the kind of terror unleashed by a military junta that causes the disappearance of individuals and groups without regard to their ages, political beliefs, ethnic origins or individual characteristics. The nuclear terror is indiscriminate, massive, global.

Many people in the world live with this terror without knowing much about the work of the World Court in the past 50 years to bring to an end actions by governments that violate the rights of other governments and of the peoples of the world. The opinion on nuclear weapons is part of this work of the Court.

This book presents the opinion on the legality or illegality of nuclear weapons by the International Court of Justice, also called our World Court, with the goal that it will be published widely so every woman and man and child will be able to use this opinion in their daily lives.

This goal will be carried out by presenting the complete opinion of the Court and the separate opinions of each of the members of the Court who come from many regions of the world and from many distinct cultures. The opinion of the Court and the declarations and opinions of each of the 14 judges are rich in history, custom and law. Many of the opinions are beautifully written. Together they provide an unparalleled text for studies of society, law, political science, nonviolence and conflict resolution, war, international relations, international business, international organizations and of global peace.

This opinion is must reading for every thinking and feeling person, whether activist, government official, career military personnel, corporate executive, citizen, lawyer, judge, student or scholar. The opinion belongs on the shelves of every public and university and law library, and in the boardrooms of every transnational corporation, international labor union, non-governmental organization (NGO), and in every Army canteen, nuclear weapons bunker, veterans hospital and ship library.

This opinion is must reading for the CEOs of every corporation engaged in any aspect of the nuclear weapons industry. It should be read by administrators and civil servants and policy-makers in the Departments of State, Defense, Energy, Justice and Education in all countries. It has a place in instructional manuals and law books in academies for the Army, Navy, Marine Corps, Air Corps, Coast Guard, and in many business and law school courses from Environmental Law to Peace Law.

This Law Is Not for Lawyers

The opinion of the International Court of Justice was not made for lawyers. The opinion was made for all of the peoples of the world living under the United Nations Charter (which, of course, *includes* lawyers), and for each of the 178 national governments that are members of the United Nations committed to upholding the opinions of the International Court.

For 50 years the majority of nations in the UN General Assembly had voted for resolutions against nuclear weapons as the stockpiles kept growing. Finally, the General Assembly passed a resolution asking its judicial body, the World Court, to answer the question: whether the threat or use of nuclear weapons is legal or illegal.

The Court did answer this question.

Of course, the opinion of the Court was written by lawyers using the tools of lawyers, i.e., writings by judges in opinions of previous courts, and by lawyers in treaties (agreements, protocols, covenants and conventions), and in briefs to courts and in textbooks for law students. Few of these sources of law are written in the day-to-day language of the peoples of any country. They are written in legal language. And an opinion by the International Court of Justice is written from the perspective, as well as in the languages of the members of the Court, then translated into English.

This opinion is presented here in a format for easy use.[2] The full opinions of the 14 judges are included in Part Three (although the order has been changed from the official report). For more interesting reading, some paragraphs have been set in different typefaces to *highlight testimony given to the Court* and **important conclusions by the judges.** (Some outlines and subheads have been added by the editor within boxes or brackets to make the longer opinions more readable. As well, editor changes/additions to text are indicated by boldface brackets.) How the opinion is being enforced, how it will be enforced and how the case got to the World Court are discussed in Part Four. Part Five includes questions for class and group discussions and also a Glossary that defines all phrases and words in Latin, French, German and legal English. Illustrations add another dimension. The Table of Cases lists all cases, while the Table of Treaties, Resolutions, Conventions and Charters lists all treaties, resolutions, agreements, constitutions, conventions, charters and statutes.

In this Part One, we will consider:

1. How Did This Question Arise?
2. Who Presented This Question to the World Court?
3. Why the General Assembly Asked the World Court for an Advisory Opinion.
4. What Questions the Court Considered.
5. From What Regions of the World Did the Judges Come?
6. Where Did the Court Look for Answers?
7. What Are *Non Liquet* and *Lex Lata* and *"Corfu Channel"*?
8. What the Court Decided in Its Opinion.
9. What the Court Decided Unanimously.
10. What the Court Decided by Divided Votes.
11. How the Judges from the Nuclear Weapons States Voted.
12. What the President of the Court Said Is the Meaning of ¶ 105 (2)E.
13. How the Opinion Will Be Enforced.
14. How Not to Read the Opinion.
15. What Next?

1. How Did This Question Arise?

Nuclear scientists working for the U.S. Government made three attempts to stop the use of the first nuclear bomb against Japan in 1945. James Franck, Leo Szilard and five other nuclear scientists raised the issue of the *political and economic problems* for the first nation to use nuclear weapons when they wrote to the U.S. Secretary of War before the U.S. dropped the first nuclear bomb on Hiroshima.

The scientists also raised the issue of the *need for effective international control* of nuclear weapons.[3]

The issue of the *legality or illegality* of nuclear weapons was raised immediately in the note of protest by Japan of August 10, 1945, after the United States dropped the bombs on Hiroshima and then on Nagasaki.[4]

The issue of the *immorality* of those acts was raised almost as soon as the world became aware of the effects of these bombs.

The very first resolution of the UN General Assembly, adopted unanimously by the representatives of national governments at the London session of the new world body on January 24, 1946, set up a commission to make specific proposals for "The elimination from national armaments of atomic weapons and of all other major weapons adaptable to mass destruction." (¶ 101) The General Assembly, as it grew from 51 to 185 member countries, adopted many similar resolutions from 1961 to 1991. (¶ 1; Oda, Part Two)

Fifty years after its first resolution, the General Assembly considered a resolution asking the Court for an advisory opinion on the legality or illegality of nuclear weapons in 1994. (¶ 1)

This resolution was the outcome of years of effort by some government officials of some anti-nuclear weapons states; by massive work through governmental and non-governmental channels by an international network of non-governmental organizations spearheaded by the NGOs that launched the World Court Project: the International Association of Lawyers Against Nuclear Arms, the International Peace Bureau and the International Physicians for Prevention of Nuclear War; the massive anti-nuclear movement in Japan; and many others. The UN General Assembly ultimately voted to bring this issue to the Court, which brought it to the attention of the media and the general public, against the votes of the nuclear weapons states (as summarized in the Court's opinion in ¶ 15, and discussed in several of the opinions of the judges).

The forces opposing this resolution are not listed or described as clearly. They are part of what is now being called the military/industrial kudzu that is spreading worldwide. (Kudzu, planted in alien soil to solve the problem of soil erosion, is now covering and killing plants and trees, seeking to engulf highways and houses, resisting all efforts to limit its harmful effects in Mississippi, U.S.A., and other regions.) U.S. General and President Eisenhower warned us about the military/industrial complex in 1960. It is now out of control, covering and killing the very institutions it was organized to protect.

Several groups of people played important roles in the struggles over the legality or illegality of nuclear weapons. The roles of ambassadors and officials of many governments in negotiating a series of international and regional treaties outlawing nuclear weapons is described in the Court opinion (¶¶ 58-60), and in opinions of several judges.

The roles of international law experts in formulating the laws of war and the humanitarian law of war and all of the other laws and legal principles involved in this dispute are set forth in the opinions of the several judges.

The roles of scientists, physicians, physicists, lawyers, concerned citizens of the globe, environmentalists, of local and regional governments and of NGOs are mentioned in some of the opinions of the judges. A more complete picture of the role of concerned citizens and of NGOs working through the World Court Project is in Part Four and in "Introduction to the Draft Memorial in support of the Application of the World Health Organization for an Advisory Opinion by the International Court of Justice . . .".[5]

2. Who Presented This Question to the World Court?

On December 15, 1994, the General Assembly took a vote on whether to send to the World Court the question of the legality or illegality of the threat or use of nuclear weapons and to ask the Court to issue an advisory opinion. Seventy-nine countries instructed their ambassadors to vote Yes, the Court should decide the question. Ninety-nine countries did not instruct their ambassadors to vote Yes. Forty-three voted No (including the U.S., UK, France, Russia, that is, countries that openly say they have nuclear weapons). Thirty-eight Abstained (including Kazakhstan, Ukraine and Belarus which have/had nuclear weapons) and 18 were Absent (including China which has nuclear weapons). The number of countries that voted Yes for sending the case was more than twice as many as voted No, although the number of countries that voted Yes was less than the number who did not vote Yes:

Yes		79
Not Voting Yes		99
No	43	
Abstained	38	
Absent	18	

Finally, the General Assembly sent this question to the World Court "urgently," that is, on an expedited basis, for an Advisory Opinion that is "non-binding."

3. Why the General Assembly Asked the World Court for an Advisory Opinion

No non-nuclear weapons state would file suit against a nuclear weapons state charging it with threatening to use nuclear weapons in what is called a "contentious" lawsuit. And the General Assembly did not file a lawsuit against the nuclear weapons states. Instead, the congress of the United Nations asked the judicial branch to issue an advisory opinion on a legal question. This procedure is permitted in the rules or statutes of the World Court[6] and has led to important opinions on important questions that one nation could not/would not raise in a suit directly against another nation.

The Registrar of the Court gave notice to all the nations permitted to appear before the Court that they could make presentations on this question to the Court in writing. (¶ 3) Then the Court decided to hold public sittings to hear oral statements.

34 national governments filed written statements

22 nations presented oral statements from government officials and professors of law

23 nations participated that had voted to have the case heard

9 nations participated that had abstained in the vote

4 nuclear countries participated in the case

2,000,000 individuals from 25 countries signed petitions submitted to the Court (*See* Weeramantry § II.1)

Corporations involved in the nuclear weapons industry did not appear directly in the proceedings.

4. What Questions the Court Considered

In order to answer the question asked, the Court considered many issues. (These are listed in a box at the beginning of the Court's opinion in Part Two.)

The issues are questions of fact, including:

- What has happened to people who reside near nuclear weapons test sites in the United States, in the Pacific and in other nations? (*See* Koroma § 3)

- Are there any "clean nuclear bombs" now in existence that will not violate the "humanitarian laws of war"? (*See* ¶ 94)

The issues are questions of law, including:

- What is the "humanitarian law of war"? (¶ 78)

- Does it supersede "military necessity"? (*See* ¶ 96)

The issues are questions of government policy, including:

- "What is the status of compliance with the Nuclear Non-Proliferation Treaty by nuclear nations? (*See* ¶¶ 99-103)

5. From What Regions of the World Did the Judges Come?

The 15 judges on the International Court of Justice are selected from the top international law scholars on all of the continents to reflect the world's principal cultural traditions. They come to the Court as individual jurists, not as ambassadors or representatives of the governments in the countries where they live. Each is approved by a majority vote of the General Assembly and the Security Council and they serve for a term of nine years and may be reappointed. At the time that the nuclear weapons case came before the Court, one of the judges (from Latin America) who had just died had not been replaced, so the President of the Court had the authority to break a tie by voting twice. By custom, six of the 15 judges came from each of the nuclear weapons states (the United States, United Kingdom, France, Russia and China) and Japan; in 1996, the other eight sitting judges came from Africa (3), Asia (1), Latin America (1), and Europe (3).

6. Where Did the Court Look for Answers?

The Court first had to look at the *facts* before them on the effects of the use and of the testing of nuclear weapons, presented in written and oral statements. The judges heard the statements in the Court's imposing and beautiful chambers in the Hague on the effects of nuclear weapons use and testing in several countries since 1945.

Several lawyers and representatives of governments described the horrors of the use, the testing, the stockpiling and the threat of use of nuclear weapons. They were specific about the effects they had seen with their own eyes on their own peoples. They were eloquent. No briefs filed in opposition discredited this evidence. Several of the judges mentioned these statements and their effect on their opinions. Judge Weeramantry summed up the testimony:

> "Nuclear weapons cause death and destruction; induce cancers, leukemia, keloids and related afflictions; cause gastro intestinal, cardiovascular and related afflictions; continue for decades after their use to induce the health-related problems mentioned above; damage the environmental rights of future generations; cause congenital deformities, mental retardation and genetic damage; carry the potential to cause a nuclear winter; contaminate and destroy the food chain; imperil the ecosystem; produce lethal levels of heat and blast; produce radiation and radioactive fall-out; produce a disruptive electromagnetic pulse; produce social disintegration; imperil all

civilization; threaten human survival; wreak cultural devastation; span a time range of thousands of years; threaten all life on the planet; irreversibly damage the rights of future generations; exterminate civilian populations; damage neighboring States; produce psychological stress and fear syndromes — *as no other weapons do.*" (Weeramantry § 2.4)

Then the Court looked at the *existing law* covering the use of such weapons. The Court opinion refers to many types of sources: laws, treaties, agreements, declarations; previous opinions by this International Court of Justice and its predecessor, the International Court of Permanent Justice; and maxims or principles set down by international law experts from many countries over many centuries. Many of the judges in their separate opinions refer to these sources; some add moral and religious precepts of many cultures and faiths over many centuries, and quote classic literary works.

As Judge Weeramantry said in his opinion: "Humanitarian law and custom have a very ancient lineage. They reach back thousands of years. They were worked out in many civilizations." (§ I.5)

The judges referred to the recognition of the origins of the basic laws of war in Hindu, Buddhist, Chinese, Judaic, Islamic, African and modern European cultural traditions. They made clear that the humanitarian rules of warfare cannot be regarded as a new sentiment, invented in the nineteenth century and so slenderly rooted in universal tradition that they may be lightly overridden.

The judges had to deal with all of the very strong legal arguments presented by the nuclear weapons states, by the anti-nuclear weapons states, and by the non-nuclear weapons states.

Finally the Court looked at the *present weapons policies* of the nuclear weapons states and the would-be nuclear weapons states, and the present status of treaty negotiations to limit nuclear weapons.

7. What Are *Non Liquet* and *Lex Lata* and *"Corfu Channel"*?

These and other words and phrases in Latin and French and the names of important cases are used by many of the judges. They are clearly defined in the Glossary. It only takes a minute to look them up and avoid the frustration of not being able to understand what the judges mean.

8. What the Court Decided in Its Opinion

The Court issued its opinion in 105 numbered paragraphs. (The topics covered are listed at the beginning of Part Two by the editor.)

First the Court decided to decide the question (on the legality or illegality of nuclear weapons)[7] by a vote of 13-1, with Judge Oda from Japan dissenting (¶ 105). Other holdings leap out from the pages:

- "The exercise of legitimate self-defense is subject to the rule of law." (¶ 40)

- "Thus it would be illegal for a State to threaten force to secure territory from another State, or to cause it to follow or not to follow certain political or economic paths." (¶ 47)

- "The Court recognizes that the environment is under daily threat and that the use of nuclear weapons could constitute a catastrophe for the environment. The Court also recognizes that the environment is not an abstraction but represents the living space, the quality of life and the very health of human beings, including generations unborn." (¶ 29)

- ". . . Respect for the environment is one of the elements that go to assessing whether an action is in conformity with the principles of necessity and proportionality." (¶ 30)

- ". . . [T]he long-promised complete nuclear disarmament appears to be the most appropriate means of achieving that result [of ending the difference about the legal status of nuclear weapons]." (¶ 98)

The Court decided not to decide several important questions that it held were not necessary to the main opinion or on which they held they did not have sufficient factual information. (¶¶ 94-95, 97)

9. What the Court Decided Unanimously

The Judges were unanimous in the dispositif, that is, in the answer to the question asked by the General Assembly (in ¶ 105) that:

(2)A "There is in **neither customary nor conventional international law** any specific **authorization of the threat or use of nuclear weapons.**"

(2)C "**A threat or use of force by means of nuclear weapons that is contrary to** Article 2, paragraph 4, of **the United Nations Charter** and that fails to meet all the requirements of Article 51,

is unlawful." (See Charter Articles quoted in Part Five.)

(2)D "**A threat or use of nuclear weapons should also be compatible with** the requirements of **international law applicable in armed conflict, particularly** those of the principles and **rules of international humanitarian law, as well as with specific obligations under treaties** and other undertakings which expressly deal with nuclear weapons."

The Court had already spelled out the pertinent rules of humanitarian law. They prohibit the use of any weapon:

- that is likely to cause unnecessary suffering to combatants (¶ 78 and *see* ¶¶ 92, 95);

- that is incapable of distinguishing between civilian and military targets (¶¶ 95, 78);

- that kills people in a neutral state (as through nuclear winter) (*See* ¶ 78);

- that is not a proportional response to an attack (¶ 78);

- that does permanent damage to the environment.(¶¶ 32-33, 35).

No testimony was presented that any nuclear weapon can meet these requirements. (*See* ¶¶ 91, 94-95)

The Court completed its task of answering the question put to it by the UN General Assembly composed of members representing national governments. The Court announced in ¶ 105 (2)F that enforcement of this opinion must be made urgently by all of the nations by means of negotiations by their heads of state: "**There exists an obligation to pursue in good faith and bring to a conclusion negotiations leading to nuclear disarmament in all its aspects under strict and effective international control.**"

That is, the judicial branch of the United Nations ruled that enforcement of its opinion must be urgently undertaken by the member states of the General Assembly through their executive and legislative branches responsible for making and enforcing treaties. Member states must deal with the nuclear weapons makers in military/industrial complexes in their nations. (Part Four describes early steps toward enforcement of this opinion.)

10. What the Court Decided by Divided Votes

The Court also ruled in the dispositif, by a vote of 7-7:[8]

¶ 105 (2)E clause 1: **"It follows from the above-mentioned requirements that the threat or use of nuclear weapons would generally be contrary to the rules of international law applicable in armed conflict, and in particular the principles and rules of humanitarian law;"**

¶ 105 (2)E clause 2: **"However, in view of the current state of international law, and of the elements of fact at its disposal, the Court cannot conclude definitively whether the threat or use of nuclear weapons would be lawful or unlawful in an extreme circumstance of self-defence, in which the very survival of a State would be at stake."**

The Court opened a seeming hole by saying: (1) that the threat or use is "generally" illegal and (2) that they could not say that there would never be an attack on a country that threatened its very existence to which nuclear weapons would be a legal response. But they had already built a steel wall by ruling unanimously that nuclear weapons must obey the humanitarian law of war (¶ 105 (2)D), which nuclear weapons cannot do because they always kill civilians and people from neutral countries and harm the environment (¶¶ 78, 92, 93, 95). So clause 2 is merely a hole in a partition wall leading to an impenetrable wall of steel.

The President of the Court said the same thing about ¶ 105 (2)E:

"I cannot sufficiently emphasize the fact that the Court's inability to go beyond this statement of the situation can in no manner be interpreted to mean it is leaving the door ajar to recogition of the legality of the threat or use of nuclear weapons." (Bedjaoui ¶ 11)

(In an opinion by lawyers, not by concerned citizens, we must settle for this sentence that takes four negatives to make a positive.)

As to the votes on the two clauses, in effect the vote on clause 1 was ten for and four against (not 7-7) because the three judges who wanted an absolute statement on illegality and wanted to leave out the word "generally" supported this first clause and opposed the second clause. The vote on clause 2 was 11-3 because the four judges who opposed the first clause and wanted an absolute permission for the threat or use of nuclear weapons in some circumstances supported this clause. Judge Higgins wrote that this was a *non liquet* (i.e., a refusal to rule) because, on the basis of the facts before the Court, it found the law to be "not clear." President Bedjaoui emphatically disagreed.

11. How the Judges from the Nuclear Weapons States Voted

Of the five judges from nuclear weapons states, two supported all of the dispositif or opinion, including both sentences in ¶ 105 (2)E, and wrote short declarations — Judge Shi Jiuyong from China and Judge Vladlen S. Vereshchetin from Russia.

Judge Shi, coming from the nuclear weapons state with the world's largest population, wrote the shortest opinion. In one paragraph, he stated directly that "the policy of nuclear deterrence should be a subject of regulation by law, not *vice versa.* . . .":

"'. . . [T]he appreciable section of the international community' adhering to the policy of deterrence is composed of certain nuclear weapon States and those States that accept the protection of the 'nuclear umbrella.' No doubt, these States are important and powerful members of the international community and play an important role on the stage of international politics. However, the Court, as the principal judicial organ of the United Nations, cannot view this 'appreciable section of the international community' in terms of material power. The Court can only have regard to it from the standpoint of international law. Today the international community of States has a membership of over 185 States. The appreciable section of this community to which the Opinion refers by no means constitutes a large proportion of that membership, and the structure of the international community is built on the principle of sovereign equality. Therefore, any undue emphasis on the practice of this 'appreciable section' would not only be contrary to the very principle of sovereign equality of States, but would also make it more difficult to give an accurate and proper view of the existence of a customary rule on the use of the weapon."

Judge Vladlen S. Vereshchetin from the Russian Federation wrote the clearest statement of the reality the Court faced in his declaration:

"If I may be allowed the comparison, the construction of a

solid edifice for the total prohibition on the use of nuclear weapons is not yet complete. This, however, is not because of the lack of building materials, but rather because of the unwillingness and objections of a sizeable number of the builders of this edifice. If this future edifice is to withstand the test of time and the vagaries of the international climate, it is the States themselves — rather than the Court with its limited building resources — that must shoulder the burden of the construction to completion. At the same time, the Court has clearly shown that the edifice of the total prohibition on the threat or use of nuclear weapons is being constructed and a great deal has already been achieved."

Vice-President of the Court, Stephen M. Schwebel from the United States, Judge Gilbert Guillaume from France and Judge Rosalyn Higgins from the United Kingdom all voted No on ¶ 105 (2)E. Judge Schwebel wrote in his dissenting opinion:

"It cannot be accepted that the use of nuclear weapons on a scale which would — or could — result in the deaths of many millions in indiscriminate inferno and by far-reaching fall-out have profoundly pernicious effects in space and time, and render uninhabitable much or all of the earth, could be lawful." (§ 6)

12. What the President of the Court Said Is the Meaning of ¶ 105 (2)E

The President of the Court, in his declaration, wrote:

"Nuclear weapons, the ultimate evil, destabilize humanitarian law, which is the law of the lesser evil. Thus, the very existence of nuclear weapons is a great challenge to humanitarian law itself, not to mention their long-term damage to the human environment, respect for which is required for the right to life to exert itself. Unless science can succeed in developing a 'clean' nuclear weapon which would strike the combatant while sparing the non-combatant, it is clear that the nuclear weapon has indiscriminate effects and constitutes an absolute challenge to humanitarian law." (Bedjaoui ¶ 20)

". . . [O]ne would lack the most elementary prudence if one placed, without hesitation, the survival of the State above all other considerations, especially above the survival of humanity itself. " (Bedjaoui ¶ 22)

"[T]he ultimate goal of all action in the domain of nuclear weapons will always remain nuclear disarmament, a goal that is no longer utopian and that it is the duty of all to seek more actively than ever. Human fate depends on the will to enter into this commitment, for, as Albert Einstein wrote [in *How I See the World*, Paris: Flammarion, p. 84], 'the fate of humanity will be that which it deserves.'" (Bedjaoui ¶ 24)

13. How This Opinion Will Be Enforced

Everyone who hears about this opinion by the World Court immediately asks: But how will it be enforced? Or they assume it will not be enforced.

The Court answered that question clearly as realist jurists. With the end of the cold war period, it is possible to conclude a meaningful treaty to end the nuclear threat, after decades of cold war theories of Mutual Assured Destruction (MAD), then "extended deterrence," followed by the end-of-the-cold-war theory of "minimal deterrence." The Court ruled unanimously in ¶ 105 (2)F that: **"There exists an obligation to pursue in good faith and bring to a conclusion negotiations leading to nuclear disarmament in all its aspects under strict and effective international control."**

In other words, the Court ruled that enforcement of the opinion must be made urgently by all of the nations by means of negotiations through their executive and legislative officers. This is the only way the court of the United Nations could answer this question.

The judges undoubtedly wrote in the secure knowledge that their decisions against the apartheid regime in South Africa[9] had been one factor, along with the early and frequent actions by the General Assembly, in helping the heroic, determined people of South Africa in mounting an internal and international campaign against a governmental/economic structure that seemed intractable.

How this opinion will be enforced cannot be discussed adequately in one paragraph or in one page. (See the discussion in Part Four, and the questions for group discussion in Part Five.)

14. How Not to Read the Opinion

What is important in this case is the actual opinion of the Court, both the numbered paragraphs 24 to 104 and the paragraphs of the decision and reply to the question asked, ¶ 105 (2)A through (2)F. The opinion clearly states that ¶¶ 1-104 are to be read with ¶ 105. The judges carried out their function and reached an opinion on the law. They explained how and why they came to that decision in the Court opinion. Each judge voted on each paragraph and the votes are recorded.

The additional statements of each judge, whether labeled declarations, separate opinions or dissenting opinions on one or more points, are simply that — additional statements. They are not the holding of the Court, although the language they insisted on affected the language the Court used in the Court opinion. The statements are interesting for what they reveal about the thinking of the individual judges, and for the insights they provide on the points of view that led to the specific wording of the dispositif of the Court.

While readers will appreciate the UN system of numbering paragraphs in Court opinions, which makes them much easier to find and cite, readers from different countries will find many different frustrations in reading these opinions.

On the simplest level, many words, e.g., "self-defence" and "colour," are given the English rather than the American spelling. And even the meanings of some words are different, e.g., the word "State" means nation or country, not a state in the United States or Australia; and New Zealanders use the word "tabled" to mean a motion is put on the table for discussion, whereas Americans use the word to mean a motion is taken off the table and will not be discussed. Also the same document will be referred to in many different ways. For example, the San Francisco Agreement is another name for the UN Charter, and an important legal principle is called the Martens clause or the de Martens clause. (All of the names for each of the documents are listed separately in the Table of Cases and Table of Treaties, etc., as well as in the Index for the reader's convenience.)

On a more important level, readers will realize that the International Court of Justice is not the U.S. Supreme Court or the highest court of any other nation and so does not follow their procedures, although each court has limited powers of enforcement.[10] (See discussion in Part Four.)

It is also fascinating for students of the work of the U.S. Supreme Court to discover how similar this opinion of the World Court is to the decision by the U.S. Supreme Court on school desegregation,[11] including early criticisms from all sides moving to ultimate acceptance of the opinions as masterpieces of realistic judicial decision-making on issues going to the heart of organized society.

15. What Next?

In the end, the 14 judges from all of the regions and cultures of the world did their share of the work needed to place on all of the heads of state of the world the duty to end every aspect of nuclear weaponry at the earliest possible moment. They did not assign to themselves the ability to write a law to be enforced throughout the world. They did not pretend that they have an army to enforce their opinion, or that they have police officers to arrest or prisons in which to incarcerate all leaders of governments who violate this ruling. They did not suggest that they have an attorney general to lift the charters of all corporations that continue nuclear weapons work in the face of this ruling. Or that they have an administrative staff to cut the budgets for nuclear weapons being proposed in the congresses or parliaments of every nuclear weapons or would-be nuclear weapons state. Or that they have a scientific staff to judge whether proposals for "scientific research" are really covert nuclear weapons projects.

The judges *did* insist, in language that is sometimes direct and sometimes in double negatives, that all of the governments that joined the United Nations agreed in the Charter that the goal of each and all nations is to live in peace and not to destroy the world in the interest of any one country or group of countries.

The judges were clearly aware that the UN was founded by war-weary nations after the first atomic bombs had been dropped and most of the regions of the world were struggling to rise from the ashes of fascism and war to defend and reassert the principles of humanity. The Court wrote for the peoples of the world to uphold the Charter they wrote in 1945.

In the end, the peoples of the world must now require their heads of state to read and study the law, to publicize it and then to obey it. People living in nuclear weapons states have a particularly heavy responsibility, having participated (tacitly, actively or unwillingly) in the building and using and testing and stockpiling of nuclear weapons, and having experienced the resultant affirmative and negative effects on our incomes, sense of security, environment and hope for the future.

We can work with hope as we observe that the rights enunciated by the General Assembly in the Universal Declaration of Human Rights in 1948 are now recognized in every nation. They are being enforced in many nations, and nations violating these rights are being required to report their violations to UN committees and to face the condemnation of nations and peoples throughout the world. We can work with hope as we observe that previous decisions of the World Court have been enforced, as the judges frequently described in their opinions.

Judges, government leaders, NGOs and individuals began to enforce the World Court opinion as soon as it was handed down. Their efforts are described in Part Four. The military-industrial complex did nothing.

NOTES

[1] From the WHO report on the *Effects of Nuclear War on Health and Health Services* (1984, 2d ed. 1987) in testimony (CR 95/22 [trans.], p. 14.).

[2] I have drawn on everything I have learned as a lawyer teaching this law to judges when I represented nuclear weapons protesters and as a professor of peace law testifying as an expert witness, as a member of the Berkeley, California City Commission on Peace and Justice (which administers a Nuclear Free Zone Ordinance adopted by initiative vote), as the wife of a veteran of World War II, as the mother of a son who filed as a conscientious objector in the Vietnam War, and as a one-time printshop typesetter.

[3] *See* the Franck Committee Report in *Genius in the Shadows: A Biography of Leo Szilard, the Man Behind the Bomb* by William Lanouette (New York: Scribners, 1992), pp. 259-280.

[4] *The Japanese Annual of International Law*, Vol. 8, 1964, p. 252.

[5] Peter Weiss, Burns H. Weston, Richard A. Falk and Saul H. Mendlovitz, *Transnational Law & Contemporary Problems* 4:709 (1994).

[6] This procedure is not permitted in the United States. The U.S. Supreme Court is specifically forbidden to file advisory opinions and will only hear cases in which one side sues another side. Modern law in the United States does encourage negotiation, conciliation and arbitration to come to conclusions on some matters without litigation.

[7] At the same session, the Court ruled 11-3 not to hear the case brought by the World Health Organization, *Legality of the Use by a State of Nuclear Weapons in Armed Conflict*, and presented to the Court in the same sessions as the General Assembly case. The majority held that, although the WHO is duly authorized under the UN Charter to request advisory opinions from the Court and the opinion requested concerned a legal question, the request submitted by the WHO did not relate to a question arising within the scope of the activities of that organization as required by UN Charter Art. 96(2). Judges

Weeramantry, Shahabuddeen and Koroma dissented. Judges Ranjeva and Ferrari Bravo filed declarations. Judge Oda filed a separate opinion (ICJ No. 93, July 8, 1996).

[8]The President of the Court broke the 7-7 tie caused by the death of the 15th judge on the Court, as permitted under the statutes of the Court.

[9]See *Legal Consequences for States of the Continued Presence of South Africa in Namibia (South West Africa) notwithstanding Security Council Resolution 276 (1970)(Advisory Opinion), I.C.J. Report 1971* 1, p. 27.

[10]It is worthwhile for students of the U.S. judicial system to remember that nothing in the U.S. Constitution gave the U.S. Supreme Court the power to declare unconstitutional acts of Congress or executive orders of the President. *See Marbury v. Madison*, 1 Cranch 137, 2 L.Ed. 60 (1803).

[11]*Brown v. Board of Education*, 347 U.S. 483 (1954) and 349 U.S. 294 (1955). There is a vast literature attacking, praising and finally evaluating the opinions in this case, which is certainly the most important opinion of the U.S. Supreme Court in the last 50 years and perhaps in the twentieth century.

Nuclear Weapons Kill Everything

Credit: UN Photo 14948/Yosuke Yamahata

Charred remains of young boy from 1945 Nagasaki blast about 100 meters from hypocenter.

Credit: UN Photo 14936/Mitsuga Kishida

Smouldering ruins of Hiroshima about 450 meters from hypocenter. Photos courtesy of FPG.

Nuclear Weapons Leave Lasting Scars

Six years after Hiroshima, one of many destroyed buildings (left), and survivor Kiyashi Yoshitawa finally leaving hospital (right). Photos courtesy of FPG.

PART TWO

LEGALITY OF THE THREAT OR USE OF NUCLEAR WEAPONS

INTERNATIONAL COURT of JUSTICE
YEAR 1996　　8 July, General List No. 95

EDITOR'S LIST OF ISSUES IN COURT OPINION

* Procedure to Bring Question to Court ¶ 1

Nations and Scholars Participating in Case ¶ 9

* Jurisdiction to Give Reply ¶ 10

Must Relate to a Legal Question ¶ 13

* Court May Give Advisory Opinion ¶ 14

Arguments against Giving Opinion ¶ 15

Conclusion ¶ 19

* Problem with Formulation of the Question ¶ 20

* Relevant Applicable Law ¶ 23

* Human Rights and Genocide Treaties ¶ 24

* Environmental Protection Norms ¶ 27

* Conclusion ¶ 34

* Unique Characteristics of Nuclear Weapons ¶ 35

* UN Charter Provisions ¶ 37

Threat or Use of Force, Article 2.4 ¶ 38

Self-Defense When Armed Attack, Article 51 ¶ 40

Necessity and Proportionality ¶ 41

Reprisals ¶ 46

Threat ¶ 47

Possession as Threat ¶ 48

Internal Use ¶ 50
* Law re Armed Conflict 51
* No Specific Law ¶ 52
* Conventional Prohibition
    ¶ 53
Poisoned Weapons ¶ 54
Weapons Declared Illegal
    by Treaties ¶ 57
Specific Treaties against
    Nuclear Weapons ¶ 58
Arguments against Legality
    ¶ 60
Arguments against Illegal-
    ity ¶ 61
Anti-Nuclear Treaties Fore-
    shadow General Prohibi-
    tion ¶ 62
        Conclusion ¶ 63
* Customary International
    Law ¶ 64
Arguments against Legality
    ¶ 65
Arguments for Legality ¶ 66
General Assembly
    Resolutions ¶ 68
        Conclusions ¶ 73
* International Humanitarian
    Law re Armed Conflict
    ¶¶ 74, 83-87

Hague Law and Geneva
    Law ¶ 75
Cardinal Principles of
    Humanitarial law ¶ 78
Nuremberg International
    Military Tribunal ¶ 80
Martens Clause ¶¶ 84, 78
        Conclusion ¶¶ 86-87
* Principle of Neutrality ¶ 88
        Conclusion ¶ 89
* Conclusions from Applica-
    bility of Humanitarian
    Law ¶ 90
For Legality ¶ 91
Against Legality ¶ 92
"Clean" Nuclear Weapons
    ¶ 94
Law of Armed Conflict ¶ 95
Self-Defense ¶ 96
        Conclusion ¶ 97
* Complete Nuclear
    Disarmament ¶ 98
Nuclear Non-Proliferation
    Treaty Obligations ¶ 99
        Conclusion ¶ 103
* Totality of the Legal
    Grounds ¶ 104
* Dispositif, Decision and
    Replies to Question Put
    ¶¶ 91, 105

*Asterisks indicate divisions in the Opinion marked by the Court. Editor's additions to orig-
inal text are indicated by bracketed headings or boldface brackets.

ADVISORY OPINION

Present: *President* BEDJAOUI; *Vice-President* SCHWEBEL; *Judges* ODA, GUILLAUME, SHAHABUDDEEN, WEERAMANTRY, RANJEVA, HERCZEGH, SHI, FLEISCHHAUER, KOROMA, VERESHCHETIN, FERRARI BRAVO, HIGGINS; *Registrar* VALENCIA-OSPINA.

On the legality of the threat or use of nuclear weapons,
THE COURT,
composed as above,
gives the following Advisory Opinion:

[Procedure to Bring Question to Court]

1. The question upon which the advisory opinion of the Court has been requested is set forth in resolution 49/75 K adopted by the General Assembly of the United Nations (hereinafter called the "General Assembly") on 15 December 1994. By a letter dated 19 December 1994, received in the Registry by facsimile on 20 December 1994 and filed in the original on 6 January 1995, the Secretary-General of the United Nations officially communicated to the Registrar the decision taken by the General Assembly to submit the question to the Court for an advisory opinion. Resolution 49/75 K, the English text of which was enclosed with the letter, reads as follows:

"The General Assembly,

Conscious that the continuing existence and development of nuclear weapons pose serious risks to humanity,

Mindful that States have an obligation under the Charter of the United Nations to refrain from the threat or use of force against the territorial integrity or political independence of any State.

Recalling its resolutions 1653 (XVI) of 24 November 1961, 33/71 B of 14 December 1978, 34/83 G of 11 December 1979, 35/152 D of 12 December 1980, 36/92 1 of 9 December 1981, 45/59 B of 4 December 1990 and 46/37 D of 6 December 1991, in which it declared that the use of nuclear weapons would be a violation of the Charter and a crime against humanity,

Welcoming the progress made on the prohibition and elimination of weapons of mass destruction, including the Convention on the Prohibition of the Development, Production and Stockpiling of Bacteriological (Biological) and Toxic Weapons and on Their Destruction[1] and the Convention on the Prohibition of the Development, Production, Stockpiling and Use of Chemical Weapons and on Their Destruction,[2]

Convinced that the complete elimination of nuclear weapons is the only guarantee against the threat of nuclear war,

Noting the concerns expressed in the Fourth Review Conference of the Parties to the Treaty on the Non-Proliferation of Nuclear Weapons that insufficient progress had been made towards the complete elimination of nuclear weapons at the earliest possible time,

Recalling that, convinced of the need to strengthen the rule of law in international relations, it has declared the period 1990-1999 the United Nations Decade of International Law,[3]

Noting that Article 96, paragraph 1, of the Charter empowers the General Assembly to request the International Court of Justice to give an advisory opinion on any legal question,

Recalling the recommendation of the Secretary-General, made in his report entitled 'An Agenda for Peace',[4] that United Nations organs that are authorized to take advantage of the advisory competence of the International Court of Justice turn to the Court more frequently for such opinions,

Welcoming resolution 46/40 of 14 May 1993 of the Assembly of the World Health Organization, in which the organization requested the International Court of Justice to give an advisory opinion on whether the use of nuclear weapons by a State in war or other armed conflict would be a breach of its obligations under international law, including the Constitution of the World Health

---

[1]Resolution 2826 (XXVI), Annex.
[2]See Official Records of the 47th Session of the General Assembly, Supplement No. 27 (A/47/27), Appendix I.
[3]Resolution 44/23.
[4]A/47/277-S/24111.

Organization,

Decides, pursuant to Article 96, paragraph 1, of the Charter of the United Nations, to request the International Court of Justice urgently to render its advisory opinion on the following question: 'Is the threat or use of nuclear weapons in any circumstance permitted under international law?'"

2. Pursuant to Article 65, paragraph 2, of the Statute, the Secretary-General of the United Nations communicated to the Court a dossier of documents likely to throw light upon the question.

3. By letters dated 21 December 1994, the Registrar, pursuant to Article 66, paragraph 1, of the Statute, gave notice of the request for an advisory opinion to all States entitled to appear before the Court.

4. By an Order dated 1 February 1995 the Court decided that the States entitled to appear before it and the United Nations were likely to be able to furnish information on the question, in accordance with Article 66, paragraph 2, of the Statute. By the same Order, the Court fixed, respectively, 20 June 1995 as the time-limit within which written statements might be submitted to it on the question, and 20 September 1995 as the time-limit within which States and organizations having presented written statements might submit written comments on the other written statements in accordance with Article 66, paragraph 4, of the Statute. In the aforesaid Order, it was stated in particular that the General Assembly had requested that the advisory opinion of the Court be rendered "urgently"; reference was also made to the procedural time-limits already fixed for the request for an advisory opinion previously submitted to the Court by the World Health Organization on the question of the *Legality of the use by a State of nuclear weapons in armed conflict*.

On 8 February 1995, the Registrar addressed to the States entitled to appear before the Court and to the United Nations the special and direct communication provided for in Article 66, paragraph 2, of the Statute.

5. Written statements were filed by the following States: Bosnia and Herzegovina, Burundi, Democratic People's Republic of Korea, Ecuador, Egypt, Finland, France, Germany, India, Ireland, Islamic Republic of Iran, Italy, Japan, Lesotho, Malaysia, Marshall Islands, Mexico, Nauru, Netherlands, New Zealand, Qatar, Russian Federation,

Samoa, San Marino, Solomon Islands, Sweden, United Kingdom of Great Britain and Northern Ireland, and United States of America. In addition, written comments on those written statements were submitted by the following States: Egypt, Nauru and Solomon Islands. Upon receipt of those statements and comments, the Registrar communicated the text to all States having taken part in the written proceedings.

6. The Court decided to hold public sittings, opening on 30 October 1995, at which oral statements might be submitted to the Court by any State or organization which had been considered likely to be able to furnish information on the question before the Court. By letters dated 23 June 1995, the Registrar requested the States entitled to appear before the Court and the United Nations to inform him whether they intended to take part in the oral proceedings; it was indicated, in those letters, that the Court had decided to hear, during the same public sittings, oral statements relating to the request for an advisory opinion from the General Assembly as well as oral statements concerning the above-mentioned request for an advisory opinion laid before the Court by the World Health Organization, on the understanding that the United Nations would be entitled to speak only in regard to the request submitted by the General Assembly, and it was further specified therein that the participants in the oral proceedings which had not taken part in the written proceedings would receive the text of the statements and comments produced in the course of the latter.

7. By a letter dated 20 October 1995, the Republic of Nauru requested the Court's permission to withdraw the written comments submitted on its behalf in a document entitled "Response to submissions of other States". The Court granted the request and, by letters dated 30 October 1995, the Deputy-Registrar notified the States to which the document had been communicated, specifying that the document consequently did not form part of the record before the Court.

8. Pursuant to Article 106 of the Rules of Court, the Court decided to make the written statements and comments submitted to the Court accessible to the public, with effect from the opening of the oral proceedings.

[Nations and Scholars Participating in Case]

9. In the course of public sittings held from 30 October 1995 to 15 November 1995, the Court heard oral statements in the following order

by:

For the Commonwealth of Australia:	Mr. Gavan Griffith, Q.C., Solicitor-General of Australia, Counsel; The Honourable Gareth Evans, Q.C., Senator, Minister for Foreign Affairs, Counsel;
For the Arab Republic of Egypt:	Mr. George Abi-Saab, Professor of Intenational Law, Graduate Institute of International Studics, Geneva, member of the Institute of International Law;
For the French Republic:	Mr. Marc Perrin de Brichambaut, Director of Legal Affairs. Ministry of Foreign Affairs; Mr. Alain Pellet, Professor of International Law, University of Paris X and Institute of Political Studies, Paris;
For the Federal Republic of Germany:	Mr. Hartmut Hillgenberg, Director-General of Legal Affairs, Ministry of Foreigh Affairs;
For Indonesia:	H.E. Mr. Johannes Berchmans Soedarmanto Kardarisman, Ambassador of Indonesia to the Netherlands;
For Mexico:	H.E. Mr. Sergio González Gálvez, Ambassador, Under Secretary of Foreign Relations;
For the Islamic Republic of Iran:	H.E. Mr. Mohammad J. Zarif, Deputy Minister, Legal and International Affairs, Ministry of Foreign Affairs;
For Italy:	Mr. Umberto Leanza, Professor of International Law at the Faculty of Law at the University of Rome "Tor Vergata", Head of the Diplomatic Legal Service at the Ministry of Foreign Affairs;
For Japan:	H.E. Mr. Takekazu Kawamura, Ambassador, Director General for Arms Control and Scientific Affairs, Ministry of Foreign Affairs; Mr. Takashi Hiraoka, Mayor of Hiroshima; Mr. Iccho Itoh, Mayor of Nagasaki;
For Malaysia:	H.E. Mr. Tan Sri Razali Ismail, Ambassador, Permanent Representative of Malaysia to the United Nations; Dato' Mohtar Abdullah, Attorney-General;
For New Zealand:	The Honourable Paul East, Q.C., Attorney-General of New Zealand; Mr. Allan Bracegirdle, Deputy Director of Legal Division of the New Zealand Ministry for Foreign Affairs and Trade;
For the Philippines:	H.E. Mr. Rodolfo S. Sanchez, Ambassador of the Philippines to the Netherlands; Professor Merlin N. Magallona, Dean, College of Law, University of the Philippines;

For Qatar: H.E. Mr. Najeeb ibn Mohammed Al-Nauimi

For the Russian   Mr. A. G. Khodakov, Director, Legal Department,
*   Federation:*   Ministry of Foreign Affairs;

For San Marino: Mrs. Federica Bigi, Embassy Counsellor, Political
                                    Directorate, Department of Foreign Affairs;

For Samoa: H.E. Mr. Neroni Slade, Ambassador and Permanent,
                                    Representative of Samoa to the United Nations;
                                Mrs. Laurence Boisson de Chazournes, Assistant
                                    Professor, Graduate Institute of International Studies,
                                    Geneva;
                                Mr. Roger S. Clark, Distinguished Professor of Law,
                                    Rutgers Univeristy School of Law, Camden, New Jersey;

For the Marshall   The Honourable Theodore G. Kronmiller, Legal Counsel,
*   Islands:*   Embassy of the Marshall Islands to the United States of
                                    America;
                                Mrs. Lijon Eknilang, Council Member, Rongelap Atoll
                                    Local Government;

For the Solomon   The Honorourable Victor Ngele, Minister of Police and
*   Islands:*   National Security;
                                Mr. Jean Salmon, Professor of Law, *Université libre de*
                                    Bruxelles;
                                Mr. Eric David, Professor of Law, *Université libre de*
                                    Bruxelles;
                                Mr. Philippe Sands, Lecturer in Law, School of Oriental
                                    and African Studies, London University, and Legal
                                    Director, Foundation for International Environmental
                                    Law and Development;
                                Mr. James Crawford, Whewell Professor International
                                    Law, University of Cambridge;

For Costa Rica: Mr. Carlos Vargas-Pizarro, Legal Counsel and Special
                                    Envoy of the Government of Costa Rica;

For the United   The Rt. Honourable Sir Nicholas Lyell, Q.C., M.P., Her
*   Kingdom and*   Majesty's Attorney-General;
*   Northern Ireland:*

For the United States   Mr. Conrad K. Harper, Legal Adviser, US Department of
*   of America:*   State;
                                Mr. Michael Matheson, Principal Deputy Legal Adviser,
                                    US Department of State;
                                Mr. John H. McNeill, Senior Deputy General Counsel,
                                    U.S. Department of Defense;

For Zimbabwe: Mr. Jonathan Wutawunashe, Chargé d'affaires a.i., Em-
                                    bassy of the Republic of Zimbabwe in the Netherlands.

Questions were put by Members of the Court to particular participants in the oral proceedings, who replied in writing, as requested,

within the prescribed time-limits; the Court having decided that the other participants could also reply to those questions on the same terms, several of them did so. Other questions put by Members of the Court were addressed, more generally, to any participant in the oral proceedings; several of them replied in writing, as requested, within the prescribed time-limits.

*

*   *

[Jurisdiction to Give Reply]

10. The Court must first consider whether it has the jurisdiction to give a reply to the request of the General Assembly for an Advisory Opinion and whether, should the answer be in the affirmative, there is any reason it should decline to exercise any such jurisdiction.

The Court draws its competence in respect of advisory opinions from Article 65, paragraph 1, of its Statute. Under this Article, the Court

"may give an advisory opinion on any legal question at the request of whatever body may be authorized by or in accordance with the Charter of the United Nations to make such a request".

11. For the Court to be competent to give an advisory opinion, it is thus necessary at the outset for the body requesting the opinion to be "authorized by or in accordance with the Charter of the United Nations to make such a request". The Charter provides in Article 96, paragraph 1, that:

"The General Assembly or the Security Council may request the International Court of Justice to give an advisory opinion on any legal question."

Some States which oppose the giving of an opinion by the Court argued that the General Assembly and Security Council are not entitled to ask for opinions on matters totally unrelated to their work. They suggested that, as in the case of organs and agencies acting under Article 96, paragraph 2, of the Charter, and notwithstanding the difference in wording between that provision and paragraph 1 of the same Article, the General Assembly and Security Council may ask for an advisory opinion on a legal question only within the scope of their activities.

In the view of the Court, it matters little whether this interpretation of Article 96, paragraph 1, is or is not correct; in the present case, the General Assembly has competence in any event to seise the Court. Indeed, Article 10 of the Charter has conferred upon the General Assembly a competence relating to "any questions or any matters" within the scope of the Charter. Article 11 has specifically provided it with a competence to "consider the general principles . . . in the maintenance of international peace and security, including the principles governing disarmament and the regulation of armaments". Lastly, according to Article 13, the General Assembly "shall initiate studies and make recommendations for the purpose of . . . encouraging the progressive development of international law and its codification".

12. The question put to the Court has a relevance to many aspects of the activities and concerns of the General Assembly including those relating to the threat or use of force in international relations, the disarmament process, and the progressive development of international law. The General Assembly has a long-standing interest in these matters and in their relation to nuclear weapons. This interest has been manifested in the annual First Committee debates, and the Assembly resolutions on nuclear weapons; in the holding of three special sessions on disarmament (1978, 1982 and 1988) by the General Assembly, and the annual meetings of the Disarmament Commission since 1978; and also in the commissioning of studies on the effects of the use of nuclear weapons. In this context, it does not matter that important recent and current activities relating to nuclear disarmament are being pursued in other fora.

Finally, Article 96, paragraph 1, of the Charter cannot be read as limiting the ability of the Assembly to request an opinion only in those circumstances in which it can take binding decisions. The fact that the Assembly's activities in the above-mentioned field have led it only to the making of recommendations thus has no bearing on the issue of whether it had the competence to put to the Court the question of which it is seised.

[Must Relate to a Legal Question]

13. The Court must furthermore satisfy itself that the advisory opinion requested does indeed relate to a "legal question" within the meaning of its Statute and the United Nations Charter.

The Court has already had occasion to indicate that questions

"framed in terms of law and rais[ing] problems of international law . . . are by their very nature susceptible of a reply based on law . . . [and] appear . . . to be questions of a legal character" (*Western Sahara, Advisory Opinion, I.C.J. Reports 1975*, p. 18, para. 15).

The question put to the Court by the General Assembly is indeed a legal one, since the Court is asked to rule on the compatibility of the threat or use of nuclear weapons with the relevant principles and rules of international law. To do this, the Court must identify the existing principles and rules, interpret them and apply them to the threat or use of nuclear weapons, thus offering a reply to the question posed based on law.

The fact that this question also has political aspects, as, in the nature of things, is the case with so many questions which arise in international life, does not suffice to deprive it of its character as a "legal question" and to "deprive the Court of a competence expressly conferred on it by its Statute" (*Application for Review of Judgement No. 158 of the United Nations Administrative Tribunal, Advisory Opinion, I.C.J. Reports 1973*, p. 172, para. 14). Whatever its political aspects, the Court cannot refuse to admit the legal character of a question which invites it to discharge an essentially judicial task, namely, an assessment of the legality of the possible conduct of States with regard to the obligations imposed upon them by international law (cf. *Conditions of Admission of a State to Membership in the United Nations (Article 4 of the Charter), Advisory Opinion, I.C.J. Reports 1947-1948*, pp. 61-62; *Competence of the General Assembly for the Admission of a State to the United Nations, Advisory Opinion, I.C.J. Reports 1950*, pp. 6-7; *Certain Expenses of the United Nations (Article 17, paragraph 2, of the Charter), Advisory Opinion, I.C.J. Reports 1962*, p. 155).

Furthermore, as the Court said in the Opinion it gave in 1980 concerning the *Interpretation of the Agreement of 25 March 1951 between the WHO and Egypt*:

"Indeed, in situations in which political considerations are prominent it may be particularly necessary for an international organization to obtain an advisory opinion from the Court as to the legal principles applicable with respect to the matter under debate . . ." (*Interpretation of the Agreement of 25*

March 1951 between the WHO and Egypt, Advisory Opinion, I.C.J. Reports 1980, p. 87, para. 33.)

The Court moreover considers that the political nature of the motives which may be said to have inspired the request and the political implications that the opinion given might have are of no relevance in the establishment of its jurisdiction to give such an opinion.

*

[Court May Give Advisory Opinion]

14. Article 65, paragraph 1, of the Statute provides: "The Court *may* give an advisory opinion . . ." (Emphasis added.) This is more than an enabling provision. As the Court has repeatedly emphasized, the Statute leaves a discretion as to whether or not it will give an advisory opinion that has been requested of it, once it has established its competence to do so. In this context, the Court has previously noted as follows:

> "The Court's Opinion is given not to the States, but to the organ which is entitled to request it; the reply of the Court, itself an 'organ of the United Nations', represents its participation in the activities of the Organization, and, in principle, should not be refused." (*Interpretation of Peace Treaties with Bulgaria, Hungary and Romania, First Phase, Advisory Opinion, I.C.J. Reports 1950*, p. 71; see also *Reservations to the Convention on the Prevention and Punishment of the Crime of Genocide, Advisory Opinion, I.C.J. Reports 1951*, p. 19; *Judgments of the Administrative Tribunal of the ILO upon Complaints Made against Unesco, Advisory Opinion, I.C.J. Reports 1956*, p. 86; *Certain Expenses of the United Nations (Article 17, paragraph 2, of the Charter), Advisory Opinion, I.C.J. Reports 1962*, p. 155; and *Applicability of Article VI, Section 22, of the Convention on the Privileges and Immunities of the United Nations, Advisory Opinion, I.C.J. Reports 1989*, p. 189.)

The Court has constantly been mindful of its responsibilities as "the principal judicial organ of the United Nations" (Charter, Art. 92). When considering each request, it is mindful that it should not, in principle, refuse to give an advisory opinion. In accordance with the consistent jurisprudence of the Court, only "compelling reasons" could lead it to such a refusal *(Judgments of the Administrative Tribunal of the ILO upon Complaints Made against Unesco, Advisory Opinion, I.C.J. Reports 1956*, p. 86; *Certain Expenses of the United Nations (Article 17, paragraph 2, of the Charter), Advisory Opinion, I.C.J. Reports 1962*, p. 155; *Legal Consequences for States of the Continued Presence of South Africa in Namibia (South West Africa) notwithstanding Security Council Resolution 276 (1970), Advisory Opinion, I.C.J. Reports 1971*, p. 27; *Application for Review of Judgement No. 158 of the United Nations Administrative Tribunal, Advisory Opinion, I.C.J. Reports 1973*, p. 183; *Western Sahara, Advisory Opinion, I.C.J. Reports 1975*, p. 21; and *Applicability of Article VI, Section 22, of the Convention on the Privileges and Immunities of the United Nations, Advisory Opinion, I.C.J. Reports 1989*, p. 191). There has been no refusal, based on the discretionary power of the Court, to act upon a request for advisory opinion in the history of the present Court; in the case concerning the *Legality of the Use by a State of Nuclear Weapons in Armed Conflict*, the refusal to give the World Health Organization the advisory opinion requested by it was justified by the Court's lack of jurisdiction in that case. The Permanent Court of International Justice took the view on only one occasion that it could not reply to a question put to it, having regard to the very particular circumstances of the case, among which were that the question directly concerned an already existing dispute, one of the States parties to which was neither a party to the Statute of the Permanent Court nor a Member of the League of Nations, objected to the proceedings, and refused to take part in any way *(Status of Eastern Carelia, P.C.I.J., Series B, No. 5)*.

[Arguments against Giving Opinion]

15. Most of the reasons adduced in these proceedings in order to persuade the Court that in the exercise of its discretionary power it should decline to render the opinion requested by General Assembly resolution 49/75K were summarized in the following statement made by one State in the written proceedings:

> "The question presented is vague and abstract, addressing complex issues which are the subject of consideration among interested States and within other bodies of the United Nations which have an express mandate to address these matters. An opinion by the Court in regard to the question presented would provide no practical assistance to the General Assembly in car-

rying out its functions under the Charter. Such an opinion has the potential of undermining progress already made or being made on this sensitive subject and, therefore, is contrary to the interest of the United Nations Organization." (United States of America, Written Statement, pp. 1-2; cf. pp. 3-7, II. See also United Kingdom, Written Statement, pp. 9-20, paras. 2.23-2.45; France, Written Statement, pp. 13-20, paras. 5-9; Finland, Written Statement, pp. 1-2; Netherlands, Written Statement, pp. 3-4, paras. 6-13; Germany, Written Statement, pp. 3-6, para. 2*(b)*.)

In contending that the question put to the Court is vague and abstract, some States appeared to mean by this that there exists no specific dispute on the subject-matter of the question. In order to respond to this argument, it is necessary to distinguish between requirements governing contentious procedure and those applicable to advisory opinions. The purpose of the advisory function is not to settle — at least directly — disputes between States, but to offer legal advice to the organs and institutions requesting the opinion (cf. *Interpretation of Peace Treaties, I.C.J. Reports 1950*, p. 71). The fact that the question put to the Court does not relate to a specific dispute should consequently not lead the Court to decline to give the opinion requested.

Moreover, it is the clear position of the Court that to contend that it should not deal with a question couched in abstract terms is "a mere affirmation devoid of any justification", and that "the Court may give an advisory opinion on any legal question, abstract or otherwise" (*Conditions of Admission of a State to Membership in the United Nations (Article 4 of the Charter), Advisory Opinion, 1948, I.C.J. Reports 1947-1948*, p. 61; see also *Effect of Awards of Compensation Made by the United Nations Administrative Tribunal, Advisory Opinion, I.C.J. Reports 1954*, p. 51; and *Legal Consequences for States of the Continued Presence of South Africa in Namibia (South West Africa) notwithstanding Security Council Resolution 276 (1970), Advisory Opinion, I.C.J. Reports 1971*, p. 27, para. 40).

Certain States have however expressed the fear that the abstract nature of the question might lead the Court to make hypothetical or speculative declarations outside the scope of its judicial function. The Court does not consider that, in giving an advisory opinion in the present case, it would necessarily have to write "scenarios", to study various types of nuclear weapons and to evaluate highly complex and controversial technological, strategic and scientific information. The

Court will simply address the issues arising in all their aspects by applying the legal rules relevant to the situation.

16. Certain States have observed that the General Assembly has not explained to the Court for what precise purposes it seeks the advisory opinion. Nevertheless, it is not for the Court itself to purport to decide whether or not an advisory opinion is needed by the Assembly for the performance of its functions. The General Assembly has the right to decide for itself on the usefulness of an opinion in the light of its own needs.

Equally, once the Assembly has asked, by adopting a resolution, for an advisory opinion on a legal question, the Court, in determining whether there are any compelling reasons for it to refuse to give such an opinion, will not have regard to the origins or to the political history of the request, or to the distribution of votes in respect of the adopted resolution.

17. It has also been submitted that a reply from the Court in this case might adversely affect disarmament negotiations and would, therefore, be contrary to the interest of the United Nations. The Court is aware that, no matter what might be its conclusions in any opinion it might give, they would have relevance for the continuing debate on the matter in the General Assembly and would present an additional element in the negotiations on the matter. Beyond that, the effect of the opinion is a matter of appreciation. The Court has heard contrary positions advanced and there are no evident criteria by which it can prefer one assessment to another. That being so, the Court cannot regard this factor as a compelling reason to decline to exercise its jurisdiction.

18. Finally, it has been contended by some States that in answering the question posed, the Court would be going beyond its judicial role and would be taking upon itself a law-making capacity. It is clear that the Court cannot legislate, and, in the circumstances of the present case, it is not called upon to do so. Rather its task is to engage in its normal judicial function of ascertaining the existence or otherwise of legal principles and rules applicable to the threat or use of nuclear weapons. The contention that the giving of an answer to the question posed would require the Court to legislate is based on a supposition that the present *corpus juris* is devoid of relevant rules in this matter. The Court could not accede to this argument; it states the existing law

and does not legislate. This is so even if, in stating and applying the law, the Court necessarily has to specify its scope and sometimes note its general trend.

[Conclusion]

19. In view of what is stated above, the Court concludes that it has the authority to deliver an opinion on the question posed by the General Assembly, and that there exist no "compelling reasons" which would lead the Court to exercise its discretion not to do so.

An entirely different question is whether the Court, under the constraints placed upon it as a judicial organ, will be able to give a complete answer to the question asked of it. However, that is a different matter from a refusal to answer at all.

*

*   *

[Problem with Formulation of the Question]

20. The Court must next address certain matters arising in relation to the formulation of the question put to it by the General Assembly. The English text asks: "Is the threat or use of nuclear weapons in any circumstance permitted under international law?" The French text of the question reads as follows: *"Est-il permis en droit international de recourir à la menace ou à l'emploi d'armes nucléaires en toute circonstance?"* It was suggested that the Court was being asked by the General Assembly whether it was permitted to have recourse to nuclear weapons in every circumstance, and it was contended that such a question would inevitably invite a simple negative answer.

The Court finds it unnecessary to pronounce on the possible divergences between the English and French texts of the question posed. Its real objective is clear: to determine the legality or illegality of the threat or use of nuclear weapons.

21. The use of the word "permitted" in the question put by the General Assembly was criticized before the Court by certain States on the ground that this implied that the threat or the use of nuclear weapons would only be permissible if authorization could be found in a treaty provision or in customary international law. Such a starting point, those States submitted, was incompatible with the very basis of international law, which rests upon the principles of sovereignty and

consent; accordingly, and contrary to what was implied by use of the word "permitted", States are free to threaten or use nuclear weapons unless it can be shown that they are bound not to do so by reference to a prohibition in either treaty law or customary international law. Support for this contention was found in dicta of the Permanent Court of International Justice in the *"Lotus"* case that "restrictions upon the independence of States cannot . . . be presumed" and that international law leaves to States "a wide measure of discretion which is only limited in certain cases by prohibitive rules" (*P.C.I.J., Series A, No. 10*, pp. 18 and 19). Reliance was also placed on the dictum of the present Court in the case concerning *Military and Paramilitary Activities in and against Nicaragua (Nicaragua v. United States of America)* that:

> "in international law there are no rules, other than such rules as may be accepted by the State concerned, by treaty or otherwise, whereby the level of armaments of a sovereign State can be limited" (*I.C.J. Reports 1986*, p. 135, para. 269).

For other States, the invocation of these dicta in the *"Lotus"* case was inapposite; their status in contemporary international law and applicability in the very different circumstances of the present case were challenged. It was also contended that the above-mentioned dictum of the present Court was directed to the *possession* of armaments and was irrelevant to the threat or use of nuclear weapons.

Finally, it was suggested that, were the Court to answer the question put by the Assembly, the word "permitted" should be replaced by "prohibited".

22. The Court notes that the nuclear-weapon States appearing before it either accepted, or did not dispute, that their independence to act was indeed restricted by the principles and rules of international law, more particularly humanitarian law (see below, paragraph 86), as did the other States which took part in the proceedings.

Hence, the argument concerning the legal conclusions to be drawn from the use of the word "permitted", and the questions of burden of proof to which it was said to give rise, are without particular significance for the disposition of the issues before the Court.

*　　*

[Relevant Applicable Law]

23. In seeking to answer the question put to it by the General Assembly, the Court must decide, after consideration of the great corpus of international law norms available to it, what might be the relevant applicable law.

*

[Human Rights and Genocide Treaties]

24. Some of the proponents of the illegality of the use of nuclear weapons have argued that such use would violate the right to life as guaranteed in Article 6 of the International Covenant on Civil and Political Rights, as well as in certain regional instruments for the protection of human rights. Article 6, paragraph 1, of the International Covenant provides as follows:

> "Every human being has the inherent right to life. This right shall be protected by law. No one shall be arbitrarily deprived of his life."

In reply, others contended that the International Covenant on Civil and Political Rights made no mention of war or weapons, and it had never been envisaged that the legality of nuclear weapons was regulated by that instrument. It was suggested that the Covenant was directed to the protection of human rights in peacetime, but that questions relating to unlawful loss of life in hostilities were governed by the law applicable in armed conflict.

25. The Court observes that the protection of the International Covenant of Civil and Political Rights does not cease in times of war, except by operation of Article 4 of the Covenant whereby certain provisions may be derogated from in a time of national emergency. Respect for the right to life is not, however, such a provision. In principle, the right not arbitrarily to be deprived of one's life applies also in hostilities. The test of what is an arbitrary deprivation of life, however, then falls to be determined by the applicable *lex specialis*, namely, the law applicable in armed conflict which is designed to regulate the conduct of hostilities. Thus whether a particular loss of life, through the use of a certain weapon in warfare, is to be considered an arbitrary deprivation of life contrary to Article 6 of the Covenant, can

only be decided by reference to the law applicable in armed conflict and not deduced from the terms of the Covenant itself.

26. Some States also contended that the prohibition against genocide, contained in the Convention of 9 December 1948 on the Prevention and Punishment of the Crime of Genocide, is a relevant rule of customary international law which the Court must apply. The Court recalls that, in Article II of the Convention genocide is defined as

> "any of the following acts committed with intent to destroy, in whole or in part, a national, ethnical, racial or religious group, as such:
>
> *(a)*　Killing members of the group;
>
> *(b)*　Causing serious bodily or mental harm to members of the group;
>
> *(c)*　Deliberately inflicting on the group conditions of life calculated to being about its physical destruction in whole or in part;
>
> *(d)*　Imposing measures intended to prevent births within the group;
>
> *(e)*　Forcibly transferring children of the group to another group."

It was maintained before the Court that the number of deaths occasioned by the use of nuclear weapons would be enormous; that the victims could, in certain cases, include persons of a particular national, ethnic, racial or religious group; and that the intention to destroy such groups could be inferred from the fact that the user of the nuclear weapon would have omitted to take account of the well-known effects of the use of such weapons.

The Court would point out in that regard that the prohibition of genocide would be pertinent in this case if the recourse to nuclear weapons did indeed entail the element of intent, towards a group as such, required by the provision quoted above. In the view of the Court, it would only be possible to arrive at such a conclusion after having taken due account of the circumstances specific to each case.

*

[Environmental Protection Norms]

27. In both their written and oral statements, some States furthermore argued that any use of nuclear weapons would be unlawful by reference to existing norms relating to the safeguarding and protection of the environment, in view of their essential importance.

Specific references were made to various existing international treaties and instruments. These included Additional Protocol I of 1977 to the Geneva Conventions of 1949, Article 35, paragraph 3, of which prohibits the employment of "methods or means of warfare which are intended, or may be expected, to cause widespread, long-term and severe damage to the natural environment"; and the Convention of 18 May 1977 on the Prohibition of Military or Any Other Hostile Use of Environmental Modification Techniques, which prohibits the use of weapons which have "widespread, long-lasting or severe effects" on the environment (Art. 1). Also cited were Principle 21 of the Stockholm Declaration of 1972 and Principle 2 of the Rio Declaration of 1992 which express the common conviction of the States concerned that they have a duty "to ensure that activities within their jurisdiction or control do not cause damage to the environment of other States or of areas beyond the limits of national jurisdiction". These instruments and other provisions relating to the protection and safeguarding of the environment were said to apply at all times, in war as well as in peace, and it was contended that they would be violated by the use of nuclear weapons whose consequences would be widespread and would have transboundary effects.

28. Other States questioned the binding legal quality of these precepts of environmental law; or, in the context of the Convention on the Prohibition of Military or Any Other Hostile Use of Environmental Modification Techniques, denied that it was concerned at all with the use of nuclear weapons in hostilities; or, in the case of Additional Protocol I, denied that they were generally bound by its terms, or recalled that they had reserved their position in respect of Article 35, paragraph 3, thereof.

It was also argued by some States that the principal purpose of environmental treaties and norms was the protection of the environment in time of peace. It was said that those treaties made no mention of nuclear weapons. It was also pointed out that warfare in general, and nuclear warfare in particular, were not mentioned in their texts and that it would be destabilizing to the rule of law and to confidence in international negotiations if those treaties were now interpreted in such a way as to prohibit the use of nuclear weapons.

29. The Court recognizes that the environment is under daily threat and that the use of nuclear weapons could constitute a catastrophe for the environment. The Court also recognizes that the environment is not an abstraction but represents the living space, the quality of life and the very health of human beings, including generations unborn. The existence of the general obligation of States to ensure that activities within their jurisdiction and control respect the environment of other States or of areas beyond national control is now part of the corpus of international law relating to the environment.

30. However, the Court is of the view that the issue is not whether the treaties relating to the protection of the environment are or not applicable during an armed conflict, but rather whether the obligations stemming from these treaties were intended to be obligations of total restraint during military conflict.

The Court does not consider that the treaties in question could have intended to deprive a State of the exercise of its right of self-defence under international law because of its obligations to protect the environment. Nonetheless, States must take environmental considerations into account when assessing what is necessary and proportionate in the pursuit of legitimate military objectives. Respect for the environment is one of the elements that go to assessing whether an action is in conformity with the principles of necessity and proportionality.

This approach is supported, indeed, by the terms of Principle 24 of the Rio Declaration, which provides that:

"Warfare is inherently destructive of sustainable development. States shall therefore respect international law providing protection for the environment in times of armed conflict and cooperate in its further development, as necessary."

31. The Court notes furthermore that Articles 35, paragraph 3, and 55 of Additional Protocol I provide additional protection for the environment. Taken together, these provisions embody a general obligation to protect the natural environment against widespread, long-term and severe environmental damage; the prohibition of methods and means of warfare which are intended, or may be expected, to cause such damage; and the prohibition of attacks against the natural envi-

ronment by way of reprisals.

These are powerful constraints for all the States having subscribed to these provisions.

32. General Assembly resolution 47/37 of 25 November 1992 on the Protection of the Environment in Times of Armed Conflict, is also of interest in this context. It affirms the general view according to which environmental considerations constitute one of the elements to be taken into account in the implementation of the principles of the law applicable in armed conflict: it states that "destruction of the environment, not justified by military necessity and carried out wantonly, is clearly contrary to existing international law". Addressing the reality that certain instruments are not yet binding on all States, the General Assembly in this resolution "*[a]ppeals* to all States that have not yet done so to consider becoming parties to the relevant international conventions."

In its recent Order in the *Request for an Examination of the Situation in Accordance with Paragraph 63 of the Court's Judgment of 20 December 1974 in the Nuclear Tests (New Zealand v. France) Case*, the Court stated that its conclusion was "without prejudice to the obligations of States to respect and protect the natural environment" (*Order of 22 September 1995, I.C.J. Reports 1995*, p. 306, para. 64). Although that statement was made in the context of nuclear testing, it naturally also applies to the actual use of nuclear weapons in armed conflict.

33. The Court thus finds that while the existing international law relating to the protection and safeguarding of the environment does not specifically prohibit the use of nuclear weapons, it indicates important environmental factors that are properly to be taken into account in the context of the implementation of the principles and rules of the law applicable in armed conflict.

*

[Conclusion]

34. In the light of the foregoing the Court concludes that the most directly relevant applicable law governing the question of which it was seised, is that relating to the use of force enshrined in the United Nations Charter and the law applicable in armed conflict which regulates the conduct of hostilities, together with any specific treaties on nuclear

weapons that the Court might determine to be relevant.

*　　*

[Unique Characteristics of Nuclear Weapons]

35. In applying this law to the present case, the Court cannot however fail to take into account certain unique characteristics of nuclear weapons.

The Court has noted the definitions of nuclear weapons contained in various treaties and accords. It also notes that nuclear weapons are explosive devices whose energy results from the fusion or fission of the atom. By its very nature, that process, in nuclear weapons as they exist today, releases not only immense quantities of heat and energy, but also powerful and prolonged radiation. According to the material before the Court, the first two causes of damage are vastly more powerful than the damage caused by other weapons, while the phenomenon of radiation is said to be peculiar to nuclear weapons. These characteristics render the nuclear weapon potentially catastrophic. The destructive power of nuclear weapons cannot be contained in either space or time. They have the potential to destroy all civilization and the entire ecosystem of the planet.

The radiation released by a nuclear explosion would affect health, agriculture, natural resources and demography over a very wide area. Further, the use of nuclear weapons would be a serious danger to future generations. Ionizing radiation has the potential to damage the future environment, food and marine ecosystem, and to cause genetic defects and illness in future generations.

36. In consequence, in order correctly to apply to the present case the Charter law on the use of force and the law applicable in armed conflict, in particular humanitarian law, it is imperative for the Court to take account of the unique characteristics of nuclear weapons, and in particular their destructive capacity, their capacity to cause untold human suffering, and their ability to cause damage to generations to come.

*

*　　*

[UN Charter Provisions]

37. The Court will now address the question of the legality or illegality of recourse to nuclear weapons in the light of the provisions of the Charter relating to the threat or use of force.

[Threat or Use of Force, Article 2.4]

38. The Charter contains several provisions relating to the threat and use of force. In Article 2, paragraph 4, the threat or use of force against the territorial integrity or political independence of another State or in any other manner inconsistent with the purposes of the United Nations is prohibited. That paragraph provides:

> "All Members shall refrain in their international relations from the threat or use of force against the territorial integrity or political independence of any State, or in any other manner inconsistent with the Purposes of the United Nations."

This prohibition of the use of force is to be considered in the light of other relevant provisions of the Charter. In Article 51, the Charter recognizes the inherent right of individual or collective self-defence if an armed attack occurs. A further lawful use of force is envisaged in Article 42, whereby the Security Council may take military enforcement measures in conformity with Chapter VII of the Charter.

39. These provisions do not refer to specific weapons. They apply to any use of force, regardless of the weapons employed. The Charter neither expressly prohibits, nor permits, the use of any specific weapon, including nuclear weapons. A weapon that is already unlawful *per se*, whether by treaty or custom, does not become lawful by reason of its being used for a legitimate purpose under the Charter.

[Self-Defense When Armed Attack, Article 51]

40. The entitlement to resort to self-defence under Article 51 is subject to certain constraints. Some of these constraints are inherent in the very concept of self-defence. Other requirements are specified in Article 51.

[Necessity and Proportionality]

41. The submission of the exercise of the right of self-defence to the conditions of necessity and proportionality is a rule of customary international law. As the Court stated in the case concerning *Military and Paramilitary Activities in and against Nicaragua (Nicaragua v. United States of America) (I.C.J. Reports 1986*, p. 94, para. 176): "there is a specific rule whereby self-defence would warrant only measures which are proportional to the armed attack and necessary to respond to it, a rule well established in customary international law". This dual condition applies equally to Article 51 of the Charter, whatever the means of force employed.

42. The proportionality principle may thus not in itself exclude the use of nuclear weapons in self-defence in all circumstances. But at the same time, a use of force that is proportionate under the law of self-defence, must, in order to be lawful, also meet the requirements of the law applicable in armed conflict which comprise in particular the principles and rules of humanitarian law.

43. Certain States have in their written and oral pleadings suggested that in the case of nuclear weapons, the condition of proportionality must be evaluated in the light of still further factors. They contend that the very nature of nuclear weapons, and the high probability of an escalation of nuclear exchanges, mean that there is an extremely strong risk of devastation. The risk factor is said to negate the possibility of the condition of proportionality being complied with. The Court does not find it necessary to embark upon the quantification of such risks; nor does it need to enquire into the question whether tactical nuclear weapons exist which are sufficiently precise to limit those risks: **it suffices for the Court to note that the very nature of all nuclear weapons and the profound risks associated therewith are further considerations to be borne in mind by States believing they can exercise a nuclear response in self-defence in accordance with the requirements of proportionality.**

44. Beyond the conditions of necessity and proportionality, Article 51 specifically requires that measures taken by States in the exercise of the right of self-defence shall be immediately reported to the Security Council; this article further provides that these measures shall not in any way affect the authority and responsibility of the Security Coun-

cil under the Charter to take at any time such action as it deems necessary in order to maintain or restore international peace and security. These requirements of Article 51 apply whatever the means of force used in self-defence.

45. The Court notes that the Security Council adopted on 11 April 1995, in the context of the extension of the Treaty on the Non-Proliferation of Nuclear Weapons, resolution 984 (1995) by the terms of which, on the one hand, it

> "*[t]akes note* with appreciation of the statements made by each of the nuclear-weapon States (S/1995/261, S/1995/262, S/1995/263, S/1995/264, S/1995/265), in which they give security assurances against the use of nuclear weapons to non-nuclear-weapon States that are Parties to the Treaty on the Non-Proliferation of Nuclear Weapons,"

and, on the other hand, it

> "*[w]elcomes* the intention expressed by certain States that they will provide or support immediate assistance, in accordance with the Charter, to any non-nuclear-weapon State Party to the Treaty on the Non-Proliferation of Nuclear Weapons that is a victim of an act of, or an object of a threat of, aggression in which nuclear weapons are used".

[Reprisals]

46. Certain States asserted that the use of nuclear weapons in the conduct of reprisals would be lawful. The Court does not have to examine, in this context, the question of armed reprisals in time of peace, which are considered to be unlawful. Nor does it have to pronounce on the question of belligerent reprisals save to observe that in any case any right of recourse to such reprisals would, like self-defence, be governed *inter alia* by the principle of proportionality.

[Threat]

47. In order to lessen or eliminate the risk of unlawful attack, States sometimes signal that they possess certain weapons to use in self-defence against any State violating their territorial integrity or political independence. Whether a signalled intention to use force if certain events occur is or is not a "threat" within Article 2, paragraph 4,

of the Charter depends upon various factors. **If the envisaged use of force is itself unlawful, the stated readiness to use it would be a threat prohibited under Article 2, paragraph 4. Thus it would be illegal for a State to threaten force to secure territory from another State, or to cause it to follow or not follow certain political or economic paths.** The notions of "threat" and "use" of force under Article 2, paragraph 4, of the Charter stand together in the sense that if the use of force itself in a given case is illegal — for whatever reason — the threat to use such force will likewise be illegal. In short, if it is to be lawful, the declared readiness of a State to use force must be a use of force that is in conformity with the Charter. For the rest, no State — whether or not it defended the policy of deterrence — suggested to the Court that it would be lawful to threaten to use force if the use of force contemplated would be illegal.

[Possession as Threat]

48. Some States put forward the argument that possession of nuclear weapons is itself an unlawful threat to use force. Possession of nuclear weapons may indeed justify an inference of preparedness to use them. In order to be effective, the policy of deterrence, by which those States possessing or under the umbrella of nuclear weapons seek to discourage military aggression by demonstrating that it will serve no purpose, necessitates that the intention to use nuclear weapons be credible. Whether this is a "threat" contrary to Article 2, paragraph 4, depends upon whether the particular use of force envisaged would be directed against the territorial integrity or political independence of a State, or against the Purposes of the United Nations or whether, in the event that it were intended as a means of defence, it would necessarily violate the principles of necessity and proportionality. In any of these circumstances the use of force, and the threat to use it, would be unlawful under the law of the Charter.

49. Moreover, the Security Council may take enforcement measures under Chapter VII of the Charter. From the statements presented to it the Court does not consider it necessary to address questions which might, in a given case, arise from the application of Chapter VII.

[Internal Use]

50. The terms of the question put to the Court by the General

Assembly in resolution 49/75K could in principle also cover a threat or use of nuclear weapons by a State within its own boundaries. However, this particular aspect has not been dealt with by any of the States which addressed the Court orally or in writing in these proceedings. The Court finds that it is not called upon to deal with an internal use of nuclear weapons.

*

*   *

[Law re Armed Conflict]

51. Having dealt with the Charter provisions relating to the threat or use of force, the Court will now turn to the law applicable in situations of armed conflict. It will first address the question whether there are specific rules in international law regulating the legality or illegality of recourse to nuclear weapons *per se*; it will then examine the question put to it in the light of the law applicable in armed conflict proper, i.e. the principles and rules of humanitarian law applicable in armed conflict, and the law of neutrality.

*   *

[No Specific Law]

52. The Court notes by way of introduction that international customary and treaty law does not contain any specific prescription authorizing the threat or use of nuclear weapons or any other weapon in general or in certain circumstances, in particular those of the exercise of legitimate self-defence. Nor, however, is there any principle or rule of international law which would make the legality of the threat or use of nuclear weapons or of any other weapons dependent on a specific authorization. State practice shows that the illegality of the use of certain weapons as such does not result from an absence of authorization but, on the contrary, is formulated in terms of prohibition.

*

[Conventional Prohibition]

53. The Court must therefore now examine whether there is any

prohibition of recourse to nuclear weapons as such; it will first ascertain whether there is a conventional prescription to this effect.

[Poisoned Weapons]

54. In this regard, the argument has been advanced that nuclear weapons should be treated in the same way as poisoned weapons. In that case, they would be prohibited under:

(a)   the Second Hague Declaration of 29 July 1899, which prohibits "the use of projectiles the object of which is the diffusion of asphyxiating or deleterious gases";

(b)   Article 23 (a) of the Regulations respecting the laws and customs of war on land annexed to the Hague Convention IV of 18 October 1907, whereby "it is especially forbidden: . . . to employ poison or poisoned weapons"; and

(c)   the Geneva Protocol of 17 June 1925 which prohibits "the use in war of asphyxiating, poisonous or other gases, and of all analogous liquids, materials or devices".

55. The Court will observe that the Regulations annexed to the Hague Convention IV do not define what is to be understood by "poison or poisoned weapons" and that different interpretations exist on the issue. Nor does the 1925 Protocol specify the meaning to be given to the term "analogous materials or devices". The terms have been understood, in the practice of States, in their ordinary sense as covering weapons whose prime, or even exclusive, effect is to poison or asphyxiate. This practice is clear, and the parties to those instruments have not treated them as referring to nuclear weapons.

56. In view of this, it does not seem to the Court that the use of nuclear weapons can be regarded as specifically prohibited on the basis of the above-mentioned provisions of the Second Hague Declaration of 1899, the Regulations annexed to the Hague Convention IV of 1907 or the 1925 Protocol (see paragraph 54 above).

[Weapons Declared Illegal by Treaties]

57. The pattern until now has been for weapons of mass destruction to be declared illegal by specific instruments. The most recent such instruments are the Convention of 10 April 1972 on the Prohibition of

the Development, Production and Stockpiling of Bacteriological (Biological) and Toxic Weapons and on Their Destruction — which prohibits the possession of bacteriological and toxic weapons and reinforces the prohibition of their use — and the Convention of 13 January 1993 on the Prohibition of the Development, Production, Stockpiling and Use of Chemical Weapons and on Their Destruction — which prohibits all use of chemical weapons and requires the destruction of existing stocks. Each of these instruments has been negotiated and adopted in its own context and for its own reasons. The Court does not find any specific prohibition of recourse to nuclear weapons in treaties expressly prohibiting the use of certain weapons of mass destruction.

[Specific Treaties against Nuclear Weapons]

58. In the last two decades, a great many negotiations have been conducted regarding nuclear weapons; they have not resulted in a treaty of general prohibition of the same kind as for bacteriological and chemical weapons. However, a number of specific treaties have been concluded in order to limit:

(a)   **the acquisition, manufacture and possession of nuclear weapons (Peace Treaties of 10 February 1947; State Treaty for the Re-establishment of an Independent and Democratic Austria of 15 May 1955; Treaty of Tlatelolco of 14 February 1967 for the Prohibition of Nuclear Weapons in Latin America, and its Additional Protocols; Treaty of 1 July 1968 on the Non-Proliferation of Nuclear Weapons; Treaty of Rarotonga of 6 August 1985 on the Nuclear-Weapon-Free Zone of the South Pacific, and its Protocols; Treaty of 12 September 1990 on the Final Settlement with respect to Germany);**

(b)   **the deployment of nuclear weapons (Antarctic Treaty of 1 December 1959; Treaty of 27 January 1967 on Principles Governing the Activities of States in the Exploration and Use of Outer Space, including the Moon and Other Celestial Bodies; Treaty of Tlatelolco of 14 February 1967 for the Prohibition of Nuclear Weapons in Latin America, and its Additional Protocols; Treaty of 11 February 1971 on the Prohibition of the Emplacement of Nuclear Weapons and Other Weapons of Mass Destruction on the Sea-Bed and the Ocean Floor and in the Subsoil Thereof; Treaty of Rarotonga of 6 August 1985**

on the Nuclear-Weapon-Free Zone of the South Pacific, and its Protocols); and

(c)   the testing of nuclear weapons (Antarctic Treaty of 1 December 1959; Treaty of 5 August 1963 Banning Nuclear Weapon Tests in the Atmosphere, in Outer Space and under Water; Treaty of 27 January 1967 on Principles Governing the Activities of States in the Exploration and Use of Outer Space, including the Moon and Other Celestial Bodies; Treaty of Tlatelolco of 14 February 1967 for the Prohibition of Nuclear Weapons in Latin America, and its Additional Protocols; Treaty of Rarotonga of 6 August 1985 on the Nuclear-Weapon-Free Zone of the South Pacific, and its Protocols).

59. Recourse to nuclear weapons is directly addressed by two of these Conventions and also in connection with the indefinite extension of the Treaty on the Non-Proliferation of Nuclear Weapons of 1968:

(a)   the Treaty of Tlatelolco of 14 February 1967 for the Prohibition of Nuclear Weapons in Latin America prohibits, in Article 1, the use of nuclear weapons by the Contracting Parties. It further includes an Additional Protocol II open to nuclear-weapon States outside the region, Article 3 of which provides:

> "The Governments represented by the undersigned Plenipotentiaries also undertake not to use or threaten to use nuclear weapons against the Contracting Parties of the Treaty for the Prohibition of Nuclear Weapons in Latin America."

The Protocol was signed and ratified by the five nuclear-weapon States. Its ratification was accompanied by a variety of declarations. The United Kingdom Government, for example, stated that "in the event of any act of aggression by a Contracting Party to the Treaty in which that Party was supported by a nuclear-weapon State", the United Kingdom Government would "be free to reconsider the extent to which they could be regarded as committed by the provisions of Additional Protocol II". The United States made a similar statement. The French Government, for its part, stated that it "interprets the undertaking made in article 3 of the Protocol as being without prejudice to the full exercise of the right of self-defence confirmed by Article 51 of the Charter". China reaffirmed its commitment not to be the first to make use of nuclear weapons. The Soviet Union reserved "the right to review" the obligations imposed upon it by Additional Protocol II, particularly in the event of an attack by a State party either "in support of a nuclear-weapon State or jointly with that State". None of these statements drew comment or objection from the parties to the Treaty of Tlatelolco.

(b)   **the Treaty of Rarotonga of 6 August 1985 establishes a South Pacific Nuclear Free Zone in which the Parties undertake not to manufacture, acquire or possess any nuclear explosive device (Art. 3). Unlike the Treaty of Tlatelolco, the Treaty of Rarotonga does not expressly prohibit the use of such weapons. But such a prohibition is for the States parties the necessary consequence of the prohibitions stipulated by the Treaty.** The Treaty has a number of protocols. Protocol 2, open to the five nuclear-weapon States, specifies in its Article 1 that:

> "Each Party undertakes not to use or threaten to use any nuclear explosive device against:
>
> *(a)* Parties to the Treaty; or
>
> *(b)* any territory within the South Pacific Nuclear Free Zone for which a State that has become a Party to Protocol 1 is internationally responsible."

China and Russia are parties to that Protocol. In signing it, China and the Soviet Union each made a declaration by which they reserved the "right to reconsider" their obligations under the said Protocol; the Soviet Union also referred to certain circumstances in which it would consider itself released from those obligations. France, the United Kingdom and the United States, for their part, signed Protocol 2 on 25 March 1996, but have not yet ratified it. On that occasion, France declared, on the one hand, that no provision in that Protocol "shall impair the full exercise of the inherent right of self-defence provided for in Article 51 of the . . . Charter" and, on the other hand, that "the commitment set out in Article 1 of [that] Protocol amounts to the negative security assurances given by France to non-nuclear-weapon States which are parties to the Treaty on . . . Non-Proliferation", and that "these assurances shall not apply to States which are not parties" to that Treaty. For its part, the United Kingdom made a declaration setting out the precise circumstances in which it "will not be bound by [its] undertaking under Article 1" of the Protocol.

(c) as to the Treaty on the Non-Proliferation of Nuclear Weapons, at the time of its signing in 1968 the United States, the United Kingdom and the USSR gave various security assurances to the non-nuclear-weapon States that were parties to the Treaty. In resolution 255 (1968) the Security Council took note with satisfaction of the intention expressed by those three States to

> "provide or support immediate assistance, in accordance with the Charter, to any non-nuclear-weapon State Party to the Treaty on the Non-Proliferation . . . that is a victim of an act of, or an object of a threat of, aggression in which nuclear weapons are used".

On the occasion of the extension of the Treaty in 1995, the five nuclear-weapon States gave their non-nuclear-weapon partners, by means of separate unilateral statements on 5 and 6 April 1995, positive and negative security assurances against the use of such weapons. All the five nuclear-weapon States first undertook not to use nuclear weapons against non-nuclear-weapon States that were parties to the Treaty on the Non-Proliferation of Nuclear Weapons. However, these States, apart from China, made an exception in the case of an invasion or any other attack against them, their territories, armed forces or allies, or on a State towards which they had a security commitment, carried out or sustained by a non-nuclear-weapon State party to the Non-Proliferation Treaty in association or alliance with a nuclear-weapon State. Each of the nuclear-weapon States further undertook, as a permanent Member of the Security Council, in the event of an attack with the use of nuclear weapons, or threat of such

attack, against a non-nuclear-weapon State, to refer the matter to the Security Council without delay and to act within it in order that it might take immediate measures with a view to supplying, pursuant to the Charter, the necessary assistance to the victim State (the commitments assumed comprising minor variations in wording). The Security Council, in unanimously adopting resolution 984 (1995) of 11 April 1995, cited above, took note of those statements with appreciation. It also recognized

"that the nuclear-weapon State permanent members of the Security Council will bring the matter immediately to the attention of the Council and seek Council action to provide, in accordance with the Charter, the necessary assistance to the State victim";

and welcomed the fact that

"the intention expressed by certain States that they will provide or support immediate assistance, in accordance with the Charter, to any non-nuclear-weapon State Party to the Treaty on the Non-Proliferation of Nuclear Weapons that is a victim of an act of, or an object of a threat of, aggression in which nuclear weapons are used."

[Arguments against Legality]

60. Those States that believe that recourse to nuclear weapons is illegal stress that the conventions that include various rules providing for the limitation or elimination of nuclear weapons in certain areas (such as the Antarctic Treaty of 1959 which prohibits the deployment of nuclear weapons in the Antarctic, or the Treaty of Tlatelolco of 1967 which creates a nuclear-weapon-free zone in Latin America), or the conventions that apply certain measures of control and limitation to the existence of nuclear weapons (such as the 1963 Partial Test-Ban Treaty or the Treaty on the Non-Proliferation of Nuclear Weapons) all set limits to the use of nuclear weapons. In their view, these treaties bear witness, in their own way, to the emergence of a rule of complete legal prohibition of all uses of nuclear weapons.

[Arguments against Illegality]

61. Those States who defend the position that recourse to nuclear weapons is legal in certain circumstances see a logical contradiction in reaching such a conclusion. According to them, those Treaties, such as the Treaty on the Non-Proliferation of Nuclear Weapons, as well as Security Council resolutions 255 (1968) and 984 (1995) which take note of the security assurances given by the nuclear-weapon States to the non-nuclear-weapon States in relation to any nuclear aggression against the latter, cannot be understood as prohibiting the use of nuclear weapons, and such a claim is contrary to the very text of those instruments. For those who support the legality in certain circumstances of recourse to nuclear weapons, there is no absolute prohibition against the use of such weapons. The very logic and construction of the Treaty on the Non-Proliferation of Nuclear Weapons, they assert, confirm this. This Treaty, whereby, they contend, the possession of nuclear weapons by the five nuclear-weapon States has been accepted, cannot be seen as a treaty banning their use by those States; to accept the fact that those States possess nuclear weapons is tantamount to recognizing that such weapons may be used in certain circumstances. Nor, they contend, could the security assurances given by the nuclear-weapon States in 1968, and more recently in connection with the Review and Extension Conference of the Parties to the Treaty on the Non-Proliferation of Nuclear Weapons in 1995, have been conceived without its being supposed that there were circumstances in which nuclear weapons could be used in a lawful manner. For those who defend the legality of the use, in certain circumstances, of nuclear weapons, the acceptance of those instruments by the different non-nuclear-weapon States confirms and reinforces the evident logic upon which those instruments are based.

[Anti-Nuclear Treaties Foreshadow General Prohibition]

62. The Court notes that the treaties dealing exclusively with acquisition, manufacture, possession, deployment and testing of nuclear weapons, without specifically addressing their threat or use, certainly point to an increasing concern in the international community with these weapons; the Court concludes from this that these treaties could therefore be seen as foreshadowing a future general prohibition of the use of such weapons, but they do not constitute such a prohibition by themselves. As to the treaties of Tlatelolco and Rarotonga and their Protocols, and also the declarations made in connection with the indef-

inite extension of the Treaty on the Non-Proliferation of Nuclear Weapons, it emerges from these instruments that:

   (a)   a number of States have undertaken not to use nuclear weapons in specific zones (Latin America; the South Pacific) or against certain other States (non-nuclear-weapon States which are parties to the Treaty on the Non-Proliferation of Nuclear Weapons);

   (b)   nevertheless, even within this framework, the nuclear-weapon States have reserved the right to use nuclear weapons in certain circumstances; and

   (c)   these reservations met with no objection from the parties to the Tlatelolco or Rarotonga Treaties or from the Security Council.

[Conclusion]

63. These two treaties, the security assurances given in 1995 by the nuclear-weapon States and the fact that the Security Council took note of them with satisfaction, testify to a growing awareness of the need to liberate the community of States and the international public from the dangers resulting from the existence of nuclear weapons. The Court moreover notes the signing, even more recently, on 15 December 1995, at Bangkok, of a Treaty on the Southeast Asia Nuclear-Weapon-Free Zone, and on 11 April 1996, at Cairo, of a treaty on the creation of a nuclear-weapons-free zone in Africa. It does not, however, view these elements as amounting to a comprehensive and universal conventional prohibition on the use, or the threat of use, of those weapons as such.

*

[Customary International Law]

64. The Court will now turn to an examination of customary international law to determine whether a prohibition of the threat or use of nuclear weapons as such flows from that source of law. As the Court has stated, the substance of that law must be "looked for primarily in the actual practice and *opinio juris* of States" (*Continental Shelf (Libyan Arab Jamahiriya/Malta), Judgment, I.C.J. Reports 1985*, p. 29, para. 27).

[Arguments against Legality]

65. States which hold the view that the use of nuclear weapons is illegal have endeavoured to demonstrate the existence of a customary rule prohibiting this use. They refer to a consistent practice of non-utilization of nuclear weapons by States since 1945 and they would see in that practice the expression of an *opinio juris* on the part of those who possess such weapons.

[Arguments for Legality]

66. Some other States, which assert the legality of the threat and use of nuclear weapons in certain circumstances, invoked the doctrine and practice of deterrence in support of their argument. They recall that they have always, in concert with certain other States, reserved the right to use those weapons in the exercise of the right to self-defence against an armed attack threatening their vital security interests. In their view, if nuclear weapons have not been used since 1945, it is not on account of an existing or nascent custom but merely because circumstances that might justify their use have fortunately not arisen.

67. The Court does not intend to pronounce here upon the practice known as the "policy of deterrence". It notes that it is a fact that a number of States adhered to that practice during the greater part of the Cold War and continue to adhere to it. Furthermore, the members of the international community are profoundly divided on the matter of whether non-recourse to nuclear weapons over the past fifty years constitutes the expression of an *opinio juris*. Under these circumstances the Court does not consider itself able to find that there is such an *opinio juris*.

[General Assembly Resolutions]

68. According to certain States, the important series of General Assembly resolutions, beginning with resolution 1653 (XVI) of 24 November 1961, that deal with nuclear weapons and that affirm, with consistent regularity, the illegality of nuclear weapons, signify the existence of a rule of international customary law which prohibits recourse to those weapons. According to other States, however, the resolutions in question have no binding character on their own account and are not declaratory of any customary rule of prohibition of nuclear weapons; some of these States have also pointed out that this series

of resolutions not only did not meet with the approval of all of the nuclear-weapon States but of many other States as well.

69. States which consider that the use of nuclear weapons is illegal indicated that those resolutions did not claim to create any new rules, but were confined to a confirmation of customary law relating to the prohibition of means or methods of warfare which, by their use, overstepped the bounds of what is permissible in the conduct of hostilities. In their view, the resolutions in question did no more than apply to nuclear weapons the existing rules of international law applicable in armed conflict; they were no more than the "envelope" or *instrumentum* containing certain pre-existing customary rules of international law. For those States it is accordingly of little importance that the *instrumentum* should have occasioned negative votes, which cannot have the effect of obliterating those customary rules which have been confirmed by treaty law.

70. The Court notes that General Assembly resolutions, even if they are not binding, may sometimes have normative value. They can, in certain circumstances, provide evidence important for establishing the existence of a rule or the emergence of an *opinio juris*. To establish whether this is true of a given General Assembly resolution, it is necessary to look at its content and the conditions of its adoption; it is also necessary to see whether an *opinio juris* exists as to its normative character. Or a series of resolutions may show the gradual evolution of the *opinio juris* required for the establishment of a new rule.

71. Examined in their totality, the General Assembly resolutions put before the Court declare that the use of nuclear weapons would be "a direct violation of the Charter of the United Nations"; and in certain formulations that such use "should be prohibited". The focus of these resolutions has sometimes shifted to diverse related matters; however, several of the resolutions under consideration in the present case have been adopted with substantial numbers of negative votes and abstentions; thus, although those resolutions are a clear sign of deep concern regarding the problem of nuclear weapons, they still fall short of establishing the existence of an *opinio juris* on the illegality of the use of such weapons.

72. The Court further notes that the first of the resolutions of the General Assembly expressly proclaiming the illegality of the use of

nuclear weapons, resolution 1653 (XVI) of 24 November 1961 (mentioned in subsequent resolutions), after referring to certain international declarations and binding agreements, from the Declaration of St. Petersburg of 1868 to the Geneva Protocol of 1925, proceeded to qualify the legal nature of nuclear weapons, determine their effects, and apply general rules of customary international law to nuclear weapons in particular. That application by the General Assembly of general rules of customary law to the particular case of nuclear weapons indicates that, in its view, there was no specific rule of customary law which prohibited the use of nuclear weapons; if such a rule had existed, the General Assembly could simply have referred to it and would not have needed to undertake such an exercise of legal qualification.

[Conclusion]

73. Having said this, the Court points out that the adoption each year by the General Assembly, by a large majority, of resolutions recalling the content of resolution 1653 (XVI), and requesting the member States to conclude a convention prohibiting the use of nuclear weapons in any circumstance, reveals the desire of a very large section of the international community to take, by a specific and express prohibition of the use of nuclear weapons, a significant step forward along the road to complete nuclear disarmament. The emergence, as *lex lata*, of a customary rule specifically prohibiting the use of nuclear weapons as such is hampered by the continuing tensions between the nascent *opinio juris* on the one hand, and the still strong adherence to the practice of deterrence on the other.

*   *

[International Humanitarian Law re Armed Conflict]

74. The Court not having found a conventional rule of general scope, nor a customary rule specifically proscribing the threat or use of nuclear weapons *per se*, it will now deal with the question whether recourse to nuclear weapons must be considered as illegal in the light of the principles and rules of international humanitarian law applicable in armed conflict and of the law of neutrality.

[Hague Law and Geneva Law]

75. A large number of customary rules have been developed by the

practice of States and are an integral part of the international law relevant to the question posed. The "laws and customs of war" — as they were traditionally called — were the subject of efforts at codification undertaken in The Hague (including the Conventions of 1899 and 1907), and were based partly upon the St. Petersburg Declaration of 1868 as well as the results of the Brussels Conference of 1874. This "Hague Law" and, more particularly, the Regulations Respecting the Laws and Customs of War on Land, fixed the rights and duties of belligerents in their conduct of operations and limited the choice of methods and means of injuring the enemy in an international armed conflict. One should add to this the "Geneva Law" (the Conventions of 1864, 1906, 1929 and 1949), which protects the victims of war and aims to provide safeguards for disabled armed forces personnel and persons not taking part in the hostilities. These two branches of the law applicable in armed conflict have become so closely interrelated that they are considered to have gradually formed one single complex system, known today as international humanitarian law. The provisions of the Additional Protocols of 1977 give expression and attest to the unity and complexity of that law.

76. Since the turn of the century, the appearance of new means of combat has — without calling into question the longstanding principles and rules of international law — rendered necessary some specific prohibitions of the use of certain weapons, such as explosive projectiles under 400 grammes, dum-dum bullets and asphyxiating gases. Chemical and bacteriological weapons were then prohibited by the 1925 Geneva Protocol. More recently, the use of weapons producing "non-detectable fragments", of other types of "mines, booby traps and other devices", and of "incendiary weapons", was either prohibited or limited, depending on the case, by the Convention of 10 October 1980 on Prohibitions or Restrictions on the Use of Certain Conventional Weapons Which May Be Deemed to Be Excessively Injurious or to Have Indiscriminate Effects. The provisions of the Convention on "mines, booby traps and other devices" have just been amended, on 3 May 1996, and now regulate in greater detail, for example, the use of anti-personnel land mines.

77. All this shows that the conduct of military operations is governed by a body of legal prescriptions. This is so because "the right of belligerents to adopt means of injuring the enemy is not

unlimited" as stated in Article 22 of the 1907 Hague Regulations relating to the laws and customs of war on land. The St. Petersburg Declaration had already condemned the use of weapons "which uselessly aggravate the suffering of disabled men or make their death inevitable". The aforementioned Regulations relating to the laws and customs of war on land, annexed to the Hague Convention IV of 1907, prohibit the use of "arms, projectiles, or material calculated to cause unnecessary suffering" (Art. 23).

[Cardinal Principles of Humanitarian Law]

78. The cardinal principles contained in the texts constituting the fabric of humanitarian law are the following. The first is aimed at the protection of the civilian population and civilian objects and establishes the distinction between combatants and non-combatants; States must never make civilians the object of attack and must consequently never use weapons that are incapable of distinguishing between civilian and military targets. According to the second principle, it is prohibited to cause unnecessary suffering to combatants: it is accordingly prohibited to use weapons causing them such harm or uselessly aggravating their suffering. In application of that second principle, States do not have unlimited freedom of choice of means in the weapons they use.

The Court would likewise refer, in relation to these principles, to the Martens Clause, which was first included in the Hague Convention II with Respect to the Laws and Customs of War on Land of 1899 and which has proved to be an effective means of addressing the rapid evolution of military technology. A modern version of that clause is to be found in Article 1, paragraph 2, of Additional Protocol I of 1977, which reads as follows:

> "In cases not covered by this Protocol or by other international agreements, civilians and combatants remain under the protection and authority of the principles of international law derived from established custom, from the principles of humanity and from the dictates of public conscience."

In conformity with the aforementioned principles, humanitarian law, at a very early stage, prohibited certain types of weapons either because of their indiscriminate effect on combatants and civilians or because of the unnecessary suffering caused to combatants, that is to say, a harm greater than that unavoidable to achieve legitimate military objectives. If an envisaged use of weapons would not meet the requirements of humanitarian law, a threat to engage in such use would also be contrary to that law.

79. It is undoubtedly because a great many rules of humanitarian law applicable in armed conflict are so fundamental to the respect of the human person and "elementary considerations of humanity" as the Court put it in its Judgment of 9 April 1949 in the *Corfu Channel* case (*I.C.J. Reports 1949*, p. 22), that the Hague and Geneva Conventions have enjoyed a broad accession. Further these fundamental rules are to be observed by all States whether or not they have ratified the conventions that contain them, because they constitute intransgressible principles of international customary law.

[Nuremberg International Military Tribunal]

80. The Nuremberg International Military Tribunal had already found in 1945 that the humanitarian rules included in the Regulations annexed to the Hague Convention IV of 1907 "were recognized by all civilized nations and were regarded as being declaratory of the laws and customs of war" (International Military Tribunal, *Trial of the Major War Criminals*, 14 November 1945–1 October 1946, Nuremberg, 1947, Vol. 1, p. 254).

81. The Report of the Secretary-General pursuant to paragraph 2 of Security Council resolution 808 (1993), with which he introduced the Statute of the International Tribunal for the Prosecution of Persons Responsible for Serious Violations of International Humanitarian Law Committed in the Territory of the Former Yugoslavia since 1991, and which was unanimously approved by the Security Council (resolution 827 (1993)), stated:

> "In the view of the Secretary-General, the application of the principle *nullum crimen sine lege* requires that the international tribunal should apply rules of international humanitarian law which are beyond any doubt part of customary law. . . .
> The part of conventional international humanitarian law which has beyond doubt become part of international customary law is the law applicable in armed conflict as embodied in: the Geneva Conventions of 12 August 1949 for the Protection of War Victims; the Hague Convention (IV) Respecting the

Laws and Customs of War on Land and the Regulations annexed thereto of 18 October 1907; the Convention on the Prevention and Punishment of the Crime of Genocide of 9
December 1948; and the Charter of the International Military
Tribunal of 8 August 1945."

82. The extensive codification of humanitarian law and the extent
of the accession to the resultant treaties, as well as the fact that the
denunciation clauses that existed in the codification instruments have
never been used, have provided the international community with a
corpus of treaty rules the great majority of which had already become
customary and which reflected the most universally recognized humanitarian principles. These rules indicate the normal conduct and behaviour expected of States.

83. It has been maintained in these proceedings that these principles and rules of humanitarian law are part of *jus cogens* as defined in
Article 53 of the Vienna Convention on the Law of Treaties of 23 May
1969. The question whether a norm is part of the *jus cogens* relates to
the legal character of the norm. The request addressed to the Court by
the General Assembly raises the question of the applicability of the
principles and rules of humanitarian law in cases of recourse to nuclear
weapons and the consequences of that applicability for the legality of
recourse to these weapons. But it does not raise the question of the
character of the humanitarian law which would apply to the use of
nuclear weapons. There is, therefore, no need for the Court to pronounce on this matter.

[Martens Clause]

84. Nor is there any need for the Court [to] elaborate on the question of the applicability of Additional Protocol I of 1977 to nuclear
weapons. It need only observe that while, at the Diplomatic Conference of 1974-1977, there was no substantive debate on the nuclear
issue and no specific solution concerning this question was put forward, Additional Protocol I in no way replaced the general customary
rules applicable to all means and methods of combat including nuclear
weapons. In particular, the Court recalls that all States are bound by
those rules in Additional Protocol I which, when adopted, were merely
the expression of the pre-existing customary law, such as the Martens
Clause, reaffirmed in the first article of Additional Protocol I. The fact
that certain types of weapons were not specifically dealt with by the

1974-1977 Conference does not permit the drawing of any legal conclusions relating to the substantive issues which the use of such weapons would raise.

85. Turning now to the applicability of the principles and rules of
humanitarian law to a possible threat or use of nuclear weapons, the
Court notes that doubts in this respect have sometimes been voiced on
the ground that these principles and rules had evolved prior to the
invention of nuclear weapons and that the Conferences of Geneva of
1949 and 1974-1977 which respectively adopted the four Geneva Conventions of 1949 and the two Additional Protocols thereto did not deal
with nuclear weapons specifically. Such views, however, are only held
by a small minority. In the view of the vast majority of States as well
as writers there can be no doubt as to the applicability of humanitarian
law to nuclear weapons.

[Conclusion]

86. The Court shares that view. Indeed, nuclear weapons were
invented after most of the principles and rules of humanitarian law
applicable in armed conflict had already come into existence; the Conferences of 1949 and 1974-1977 left these weapons aside, and there is
a qualitative as well as quantitative difference between nuclear weapons and all conventional arms. However, it cannot be concluded from
this that the established principles and rules of humanitarian law applicable in armed conflict did not apply to nuclear weapons. Such a
conclusion would be incompatible with the intrinsically humanitarian
character of the legal principles in question which permeates the entire
law of armed conflict and applies to all forms of warfare and to all
kinds of weapons, those of the past, those of the present and those of
the future. In this respect it seems significant that the thesis that the
rules of humanitarian law do not apply to the new weaponry, because
of the newness of the latter, has not been advocated in the present
proceedings. On the contrary, the newness of nuclear weapons has
been expressly rejected as an argument against the application to them
of international humanitarian law:

> "In general, international humanitarian law bears on
> the threat or use of nuclear weapons as it does of other
> weapons.
>
> International humanitarian law has evolved to meet
> contemporary circumstances, and is not limited in its ap-
> plication to weaponry of an earlier time. The fundamental

principles of this law endure: to mitigate and circumscribe
the cruelty of war for humanitarian reasons." (New Zealand, Written Statement, p. 15, paras. 63-64.)

None of the statements made before the Court in any way advocated a freedom to use nuclear weapons without regard to humanitarian constraints. Quite the reverse; it has been explicitly stated,

"Restrictions set by the rules applicable to armed conflicts in respect of means and methods of warfare definitely
also extend to nuclear weapons" (Russian Federation, CR
95/29, p. 52);

"So far as the customary law of war is concerned, the
United Kingdom has always accepted that the use of nuclear weapons is subject to the general principles of the *jus
in bello*" (United Kingdom, CR 95/34, p. 45); and

"The United States has long shared the view that the
law of armed conflict governs the use of nuclear weapons
— just as it governs the use of conventional weapons"
(United States of America, CR 95/34, p. 85).

87. Finally, the Court points to the Martens clause, whose continuing existence and applicability is not to be doubted, as an affirmation
that the principles and rules of humanitarian law apply to nuclear
weapons.

*

[Principle of Neutrality]

88. The Court will now turn to the principle of neutrality which
was raised by several States. In the context of the advisory proceedings brought before the Court by the WHO concerning the *Legality of
the Use by a State of Nuclear Weapons in Armed Conflict*, the position
was put as follows by one State:

"The principle of neutrality, in its classic sense, was aimed
at preventing the incursion of belligerent forces into neutral
territory, or attacks on the persons or ships of neutrals. Thus:
'the territory of neutral powers is inviolable' (Article 1 of the
Hague Convention (V) Respecting the Rights and Duties of
Neutral Powers and Persons in Case of War on Land, con-

cluded on 18 October 1907); 'belligerents are bound to respect the sovereign rights of neutral powers . . .' (Article 1 to the Hague Convention (XIII) Respecting the Rights and Duties of Neutral Powers in Naval War, concluded on 18 October 1907), 'neutral states have equal interest in having their rights respected by belligerents . . .' (Preamble to Convention on Maritime Neutrality, concluded on 20 February 1928). It is clear, however, that the principle of neutrality applies with equal force to transborder incursions of armed forces and to the transborder damage caused to a neutral State by the use of a weapon in a belligerent State." (*Legality of the Use by a State of Nuclear Weapons in Armed Conflict*, Nauru, Written Statement (I), p. 35, IV E.)

The principle so circumscribed is presented as an established part of the customary international law.

[Conclusion]

89. The Court finds that as in the case of the principles of humanitarian law applicable in armed conflict, international law leaves no doubt that the principle of neutrality, whatever its content, which is of a fundamental character similar to that of the humanitarian principles and rules, is applicable (subject to the relevant provisions of the United Nations Charter), to all international armed conflict, whatever type of weapons might be used.

*

[Conclusions from Applicability of Humanitarian Law]

90. Although the applicability of the principles and rules of humanitarian law and of the principle of neutrality to nuclear weapons is hardly disputed, the conclusions to be drawn from this applicability are, on the other hand, controversial.

[For Legality]

91. According to one point of view, the fact that recourse to nuclear weapons is subject to and regulated by the law of armed conflict does not necessarily mean that such recourse is as such prohibited. As one State put it to the Court:

"Assuming that a State's use of nuclear weapons meets the requirements of self-defence, it must then be considered whether it conforms to the fundamental principles of the law of armed conflict regulating the conduct of hostilities" (United Kingdom, Written Statement, p. 40, para. 3.44);

"[T]he legality of the use of nuclear weapons must therefore be assessed in the light of the applicable principles of international law regarding the use of force and the conduct of hostilities, as is the case with other methods and means of warfare" (United Kingdom, Written Statement, p. 75, para. 4.2(3)); and

"The reality . . . is that nuclear weapons might be used in a wide variety of circumstances with very different results in terms of likely civilian casualties. In some cases, such as the use of a low yield nuclear weapon against warships on the High Seas or troops in sparsely populated areas, it is possible to envisage a nuclear attack which caused comparatively few civilian casualties. It is by no means the case that every use of nuclear weapons against a military objective would inevitably cause very great collateral civilian casualties." (United Kingdom, Written Statement, p. 53, para. 3.70; see also United States of America, Oral Statement, CR 95/34, pp. 89-90.)

[Against Legality]

92. Another view holds that recourse to nuclear weapons could never be compatible with the principles and rules of humanitarian law and is therefore prohibited. In the event of their use, nuclear weapons would in all circumstances be unable to draw any distinction between the civilian population and combatants, or between civilian objects and military objectives, and their effects, largely uncontrollable, could not be restricted, either in time or in space, to lawful military targets. Such weapons would kill and destroy in a necessarily indiscriminate manner, on account of the blast, heat and radiation occasioned by the nuclear explosion and the effects induced; and the number of casualties which would ensue would be enormous. The use of nuclear weapons would therefore be prohibited in any circumstance, notwithstanding the absence of any explicit conventional prohibition. That view lay at the basis of the assertions by certain States before the Court that nuclear weapons are by their nature illegal under customary international law,

by virtue of the fundamental principle of humanity.

93. A similar view has been expressed with respect to the effects of the principle of neutrality. Like the principles and rules of humanitarian law, that principle has therefore been considered by some to rule out the use of a weapon the effects of which simply cannot be contained within the territories of the contending States.

["Clean" Nuclear Weapons]

94. The Court would observe that none of the States advocating the legality of the use of nuclear weapons under certain circumstances, including the "clean" use of smaller, low yield, tactical nuclear weapons, has indicated what, supposing such limited use were feasible, would be the precise circumstances justifying such use; nor whether such limited use would not tend to escalate into the all-out use of high yield nuclear weapons. This being so, the Court does not consider that it has a sufficient basis for a determination on the validity of this view.

[Law of Armed Conflict]

95. Nor can the Court make a determination on the validity of the view that the recourse to nuclear weapons would be illegal in any circumstance owing to their inherent and total incompatibility with the law applicable in armed conflict. Certainly, as the Court has already indicated, the principles and rules of law applicable in armed conflict — at the heart of which is the overriding consideration of humanity — make the conduct of armed hostilities subject to a number of strict requirements. Thus, methods and means of warfare, which would preclude any distinction between civilian and military targets, or which would result in unnecessary suffering to combatants, are prohibited. In view of the unique characteristics of nuclear weapons, to which the Court has referred above, the use of such weapons in fact seems scarcely reconcilable with respect for such requirements. Nevertheless, the Court considers that it does not have sufficient elements to enable it to conclude with certainty that the use of nuclear weapons would necessarily be at variance with the principles and rules of law applicable in armed conflict in any circumstance.

[Self-Defense]

96. Furthermore, the Court cannot lose sight of the fundamental

right of every State to survival, and thus its right to resort to self-defence, in accordance with Article 51 of the Charter, when its survival is at stake.

Nor can it ignore the practice referred to as "policy of deterrence", to which an appreciable section of the international community adhered for many years. The Court also notes the reservations which certain nuclear-weapon States have appended to the undertakings they have given, notably under the Protocols to the Treaties of Tlatelolco and Rarotonga, and also under the declarations made by them in connection with the extension of the Treaty on the Non-Proliferation of Nuclear Weapons, not to resort to such weapons.

[Conclusion]

97. Accordingly, in view of the present state of international law viewed as a whole, as examined above by the Court, and of the elements of fact at its disposal, the Court is led to observe that it cannot reach a definitive conclusion as to the legality or illegality of the use of nuclear weapons by a State in an extreme circumstance of self-defence, in which its very survival would be at stake.

*

*   *

[Complete Nuclear Disarmament]

98. Given the eminently difficult issues that arise in applying the law on the use of force and above all the law applicable in armed conflict to nuclear weapons, the Court considers that it now needs to examine one further aspect of the question before it, seen in a broader context.

In the long run, international law, and with it the stability of the international order which it is intended to govern, are bound to suffer from the continuing difference of views with regard to the legal status of weapons as deadly as nuclear weapons. It is consequently important to put an end to this state of affairs: the long-promised complete nuclear disarmament appears to be the most appropriate means of achieving that result.

[Nuclear Non-Proliferation Treaty Obligations]

99. In these circumstances, the Court appreciates the full importance of the recognition by Article VI of the Treaty on the Non-

Proliferation of Nuclear Weapons of an obligation to negotiate in good faith a nuclear disarmament. This provision is worded as follows:

> "Each of the Parties to the Treaty undertakes to pursue negotiations in good faith on effective measures relating to cessation of the nuclear arms race at an early date and to nuclear disarmament, and on a treaty on general and complete disarmament under strict and effective international control."

The legal import of that obligation goes beyond that of a mere obligation of conduct; the obligation involved here is an obligation to achieve a precise result — nuclear disarmament in all its aspects — by adopting a particular course of conduct, namely, the pursuit of negotiations on the matter in good faith.

100. This twofold obligation to pursue and to conclude negotiations formally concerns the 182 States parties to the Treaty on the Non-Proliferation of Nuclear Weapons, or, in other words, the vast majority of the international community.

Virtually the whole of this community appears moreover to have been involved when resolutions of the United Nations General Assembly concerning nuclear disarmament have repeatedly been unanimously adopted. Indeed, any realistic search for general and complete disarmament, especially nuclear disarmament, necessitates the co-operation of all States.

101. Even the very first General Assembly resolution, unanimously adopted on 24 January 1946 at the London session, set up a commission whose terms of reference included making specific proposals for, among other things, "the elimination from national armaments of atomic weapons and of all other major weapons adaptable to mass destruction". In a large number of subsequent resolutions, the General Assembly has reaffirmed the need for nuclear disarmament. Thus, in resolution 808 A (IX) of 4 November 1954, which was likewise unanimously adopted, it concluded

> ". . . that a further effort should be made to reach agreement on comprehensive and co-ordinated proposals to be embodied in a draft international disarmament convention providing for: . . . *(b)* The total prohibition of the use and manufacture

of nuclear weapons and weapons of mass destruction of every type, together with the conversion of existing stocks of nuclear weapons for peaceful purposes."

The same conviction has been expressed outside the United Nations context in various instruments.

102. The obligation expressed in Article VI of the Treaty on the Non-Proliferation of Nuclear Weapons includes its fulfilment in accordance with the basic principle of good faith. This basic principle is set forth in Article 2, paragraph 2, of the Charter. It was reflected in the Declaration on Friendly Relations between States (resolution 2625 (XXV) of 24 October 1970) and in the Final Act of the Helsinki Conference of 1 August 1975. It is also embodied in Article 26 of the Vienna Convention on the Law of Treaties of 23 May 1969, according to which "[e]very treaty in force is binding upon the parties to it and must be performed by them in good faith".

Nor has the Court omitted to draw attention to it, as follows:

"One of the basic principles governing the creation and performance of legal obligations, whatever their source, is the principle of good faith. Trust and confidence are inherent in international co-operation, in particular in an age when this co-operation in many fields is becoming increasingly essential." (*Nuclear Tests (Australia v. France), Judgment of 20 December 1974, I.C.J. Reports 1974*, p. 268, para. 46.)

[Conclusion]

103. In its resolution 984 (1995) dated 11 April 1995, the Security Council took care to reaffirm "the need for all States Parties to the Treaty on the Non-Proliferation of Nuclear Weapons to comply fully with all their obligations" and urged

"all States, as provided for in Article VI of the Treaty on the Non-Proliferation of Nuclear Weapons, to pursue negotiations in good faith on effective measures relating to nuclear disarmament and on a treaty on general and complete disarmament under strict and effective international control which remains a universal goal".

The importance of fulfilling the obligation expressed in Article VI of the Treaty on the Non-Proliferation of Nuclear Weapons was also reaffirmed in the final document of the Review and Extension

Conference of the parties to the Treaty on the Non-Proliferation of Nuclear Weapons, held from 17 April to 12 May 1995.

In the view of the Court, it remains without any doubt an objective of vital importance to the whole of the international community today.

*
*   *

[Totality of the Legal Grounds]

104. At the end of the present Opinion, the Court emphasizes that its reply to the question put to it by the General Assembly rests on the totality of the legal grounds set forth by the Court above (paragraphs 20 to 103), each of which is to be read in the light of the others. Some of these grounds are not such as to form the object of formal conclusions in the final paragraph of the Opinion; they nevertheless retain, in the view of the Court, all their importance.

*
*   *

[Dispositif, Decision and Replies to Question Put]

105. For these reasons,

THE COURT,

(1) **By thirteen votes to one,**

   Decides **to comply with the request for an advisory opinion;**

IN FAVOUR: *President* Bedjaoui; *Vice-President* Schwebel; *Judges* Guillaume, Shahabuddeen, Weeramantry, Ranjeva, Herczegh, Shi, Fleischhauer, Koroma, Vereshchetin, Ferrari Bravo, Higgins;

AGAINST: *Judge* Oda.

(2) *Replies* **in the following manner to the question put by the General Assembly:**

A. Unanimously,

There is in neither customary nor conventional international law any specific authorization of the threat or use of nuclear weapons;

B. By eleven votes to three,

There is in neither customary nor conventional international law any comprehensive and universal prohibition of the threat or use of nuclear weapons as such;

IN FAVOUR: *President* Bedjaoui; *Vice-President* Schwebel; *Judges* Oda, Guillaume, Ranjeva, Herczegh, Shi, Fleischhauer, Vereshchetin, Ferrari Bravo, Higgins;

AGAINST: *Judges* Shahabuddeen, Weeramantry, Koroma.

C. Unanimously,

A threat or use of force by means of nuclear weapons that is contrary to Article 2, paragraph 4, of the United Nations Charter and that fails to meet all the requirements of Article 51, is unlawful;

D. Unanimously,

A threat or use of nuclear weapons should also be compatible with the requirements of the international law applicable in armed conflict, particularly those of the principles and rules of international humanitarian law, as well as with specific obligations under treaties and other undertakings which expressly deal with nuclear weapons;

E. By seven votes to seven, by the President's casting vote,

It follows from the above-mentioned requirements that the threat or use of nuclear weapons would generally be contrary to the rules of international law applicable in armed conflict, and in particular the principles and rules of humanitarian law;

However, in view of the current state of international law, and of the elements of fact at its disposal, the Court cannot conclude definitively whether the threat or use of nuclear weapons would be lawful or unlawful in an extreme circumstance of self-defence, in which the very survival of a State would be at stake;

IN FAVOUR: *President* Bedjaoui; *Judges* Ranjeva, Herczegh, Shi, Fleischhauer, Vereschetin, Ferrari Bravo;

AGAINST: *Vice-President* Schwebel; *Judges* Oda, Guillaume, Shahabuddeen, Weeramantry, Koroma, Higgins.

   F. Unanimously,

   There exists an obligation to pursue in good faith and bring to a conclusion negotiations leading to nuclear disarmament in all its aspects under strict and effective international control.

Done in English and in French, the English text being authoritative, at the Peace Palace, The Hague, this eighth day of July, one thousand nine hundred and ninety-six, in two copies, one of which will be placed in the archives of the Court and the other transmitted to the Secretary-General of the United Nations.

                              (Signed) Mohammed BEDJAOUI, President

                              (Signed) Eduardo VALENCIA-OSPINA, Registrar

   President BEDJAOUI, Judges HERCZEGH, SHI, VERESHCHETIN and FERRARI BRAVO append declarations to the Advisory Opinion of the Court.
   Judges GUILLAUME, RANJEVA and FLEISCHHAUER append separate opinions to the Advisory Opinion of the Court.

   Vice-President SCHWEBEL, Judges ODA, SHAHABUDDEEN, WEERAMANTRY, KOROMA and HIGGINS append dissenting opinions to the Advisory Opinion of the Court.

(Initialled) M. B.   *(Initialled)* E. V. O.

The Bombs Hit the Enemy

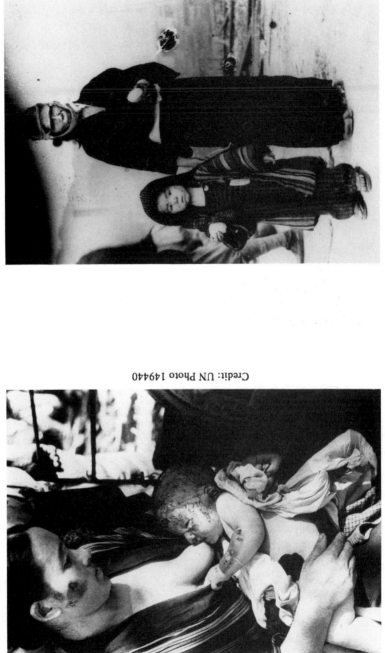

Credit: UN Photo 149449/Youske Yamahata

Credit: UN Photo 149440

Mothers and daughters after Hiroshima (left), and Nagasaki (right) holding boiled rice balls distributed by emergency relief. Photos courtesy of FPG.

**People
Determined
to Stop
Nuclear
Bombs**

One of a delegation of "Hibakusha" (nuclear blast survivors), Yasuko Ohta traveled the U.S. in 1986 to end nuclear war. Drawing by Mary Fagan Bates.

Demonstrators knelt on the tracks of the Burlington and Northern Railroad to stop the nuclear "white train" in Fort Collins, Colorado, March 1983. Photo by Ken Levine.

PART THREE

DECLARATIONS, SEPARATE AND DISSENTING OPINIONS OF THE JUDGES

DECLARATION OF PRESIDENT BEDJAOUI

President of the International Court of Justice,
appended to the Advisory Opinion on the
Legality of the Threat or Use of Nuclear Weapons,
delivered on 8 July 1996

EDITOR'S OUTLINE OF BEDJAOUI DECLARATION*

2. Fear of Nuclear War/Star Wars, Then Détente/Ending of Cold War
6. Nuclear Blackmail
9. Moral Dilemma
11. ¶ 105 (2)E 2 Does Not Leave Door Ajar
12. *Lotus* Case Distinguished
13. Globalization
17. Court Going as Far as Elements at Its Disposal Permit
18. Why I Supported ¶ 105 (2)E 2
19. International Humanitarian Law an Exacting Corpus of Rules
20. Nuclear Weapons Destabilize Humanitarian Law

22. Self-Defense and "Intransgressible" Norms
23. ¶ 105 (2)F: Twofold General Obligation
24. Legal Reality and Ultimate Goal: Nuclear Disarmament

*Editor's additions to original text are indicated by bracketed headings or boldface brackets.

1. I have never been much in favour of declarations and other individual or dissenting opinions. I have therefore very rarely had recourse to them. However, the adoption by the Court of operative paragraph E of this Opinion by my casting vote as President, in accordance with Article 55 of the Statute, is in itself a sufficiently exceptional event to prompt me to abandon my usual reticence in this matter. Moreover, I regard my recourse to this Declaration less as the exercise of a mere option than as the discharge of a real duty, both on account of the responsibility which I have thus been led to assume in the normal exercise of my functions as President and in the light of the implications of the aforementioned paragraph.

*   *

*

[Fear of Nuclear War/Star Wars, Then Détente/ Ending of Cold War]

2. With nuclear weapons, humanity is living on a kind of suspended sentence. For half a century now these terrifying weapons of mass destruction have formed part of the *human condition*. Nuclear weapons have entered into all calculations, all scenarios, all plans. Since Hiroshima, on the morning of 6 August 1945, fear has gradually become man's first nature. His life on earth has taken on the aspect of what the Koran calls " long nocturnal journey", a nightmare whose end he cannot yet foresee.

3. **However the Atlantic Charter did promise to deliver mankind from fear and the San Francisco Charter to "save succeeding generations from the scourge, of war". Much still remains to be done to exorcise this new terror hanging over man, reminiscent of the terror of his ancestors, who feared being struck by a thunderbolt from the leaden, storm-laden skies. But twentieth-century**

man's situation differs in many ways from that of his ancestors: he is armed with knowledge; he lays himself open to self-destruction by his own doing; and his fears are better founded. Although endowed with reason, man has never been so unreasonable; his destiny is uncertain; his conscience is confused; his vision is clouded and his ethical co-ordinates are being shed, like dead leaves from the tree of life.

4. However, it must be acknowledged that man has made some attempts to emerge from the blackness of his night. Mankind seems, today at any rate, more at ease than in the 1980s, when it subjected itself to the threat of "star wars". In those years the mortal blast of a space war, a war which would be total, highly sophisticated and would rend our planet asunder, was more likely than ever before to unfurl itself upon humanity. Missiles orbiting close to the Earth could train their infernal nuclear warheads on our globe, while military satellites — for reconnaissance, observation, surveillance or communication — proliferated. The *lethal system* was about to be established. The "*universal government of death*", the "*thanatocracy*", as the French historian and philosopher of science Michel Serres once called it, said it was ready to set up its batteries in the furthest reaches of the planet. But luckily détente, followed by the ending of the cold war, put a stop to these terrifying preparations.

5. Nevertheless, the proliferation of nuclear weapons has still not been brought under control, despite the existence of the Non-Proliferation Treaty. Fear and folly may still link hands at any moment to perform a final dance of death. Humanity is all the more vulnerable today for being capable of mass producing nuclear missiles.

*   *

*

[Nuclear Blackmail]

6. Humanity is subjecting itself to a perverse and unremitting nuclear blackmail. The question is how to put a stop to it. The Court had a duty to play its part, however small, in this rescue operation for humanity; it did so in all conscience and all humility, bearing in mind the limits imposed upon it by both its Statute and by the applicable international law.

7. Indeed, the Court has probably never subjected the most complex elements of a problem to such close scrutiny as it did when considering the problem of nuclear weapons. In the drafting of this Opinion the Court was guided by a sense of its own particular responsibilities and by its wish to state the law as it is, seeking neither to denigrate nor embellish it. Its aim was to avoid any temptation to create new law and it certainly did not overplay its role by urging States to legislate as quickly as possible to complete the work which they have done so far.

8. This very important question of nuclear weapons proved alas to be an area in which the Court had to acknowledge that there is no immediate and clear answer to the question put to it. It is to be hoped that the international community will give the Court credit for having carried out its mission — even if its reply may seem unsatisfactory — and will endeavour as quickly as possible to correct the imperfections of an international law which is ultimately no more than the creation of the States themselves. The Court will at least have had the merit of pointing out these imperfections and calling upon international society to correct them.

[Moral Dilemma]

9. As its Advisory Opinion shows, at no time did the Court lose sight of the fact that nuclear weapons constitute a potential means of destruction of all mankind. Not for a moment did it fail to take into account this eminently crucial factor for the survival of mankind. The moral dilemma which confronted individual consciences finds many a reflection in the present Opinion. But the Court could obviously not go beyond what the law says. It could not say what the law does not say.

10. Accordingly, at the end of its Opinion, the Court limited itself to stating the situation, finding itself unable to do any more than this. There are some who will inevitably interpret operative paragraph E as contemplating the possibility of States having recourse to nuclear weapons in exceptional circumstances. For my part, and in the light of the foregoing, I feel obliged in all honesty to construe this paragraph differently, and this has enabled me to give my support to the text. My explanation of this follows.

*   *
*

[¶ 105 (2)E 2 Does Not Leave Door Ajar]

11. I cannot sufficiently emphasize the fact that the Court's inability to go beyond this statement of the situation can in no manner be interpreted to mean that it is leaving the door ajar to recognition of the legality of the threat or use of nuclear weapons.

[*Lotus* Case Distinguished]

12. The Court's decision in the *Lotus* case, which some people will inevitably resurrect, should be understood to be of very limited application in the particular context of the question which is the subject of this Advisory Opinion. It would be to exaggerate the importance of that decision of the Permanent Court and to distort its scope were it to be divorced from the particular context, both judicial and temporal, in which it was taken. No doubt this decision expressed the *spirit of the times*, the spirit of an international society which as yet had few institutions and was governed by an international law of strict co-existence, itself a reflection of the vigour of the principle of State sovereignty.

[Globalization]

13. It scarcely needs to be said that the fact of contemporary international society is much altered. Despite the still limited emergence of "*supra-nationalism*", the progress made in terms of the institutionalization, not to say integration and "*globalization*", of international society cannot be denied. Witness the proliferation of international organizations, the gradual substitution of an international law of co-operation for the traditional international law of co-existence, the emergence of the concept of "*international community*" and its sometimes successful attempts at subjectivization. A testimony to all these developments is provided by the place which international law now accords to concepts such as obligations *erga omnes*, rules of *jus cogens*, or the common heritage of mankind. The resolutely positivist, voluntarist approach of international law which still held sway at the beginning of the century — and to which the Permanent Court also

gave its support in the aforementioned judgment[1] — has been replaced
by an objective conception of international law, a law more readily
seen as the reflection of a collective juridical conscience and as a response to the social necessities of States organized as a community.
Added to the evolution of international society itself, there is also the
progress made in the technological sphere, thanks to which the total
and virtually instantaneous eradication of the human race is now possible.

14. Furthermore, apart from the time and context factors, there is
everything to distinguish the decision of the Permanent Court from the
Advisory Opinion of the present Court: the nature of the problem posed,
the implications of the Court's pronouncement, and the underlying philosophy of the submissions upheld. In 1927, the Permanent Court,
when considering a much less important question, in fact concluded
that behaviour not expressly prohibited by international law was au-
thorised by that fact alone.[2] In the present Opinion, on the contrary.
the Court does not find the threat or use of nuclear weapons to be either
legal or illegal; from the uncertainties surrounding the law and the
facts it does not infer any freedom to take a position. Nor does it suggest that such licence could in any way whatever be deduced therefrom.

Whereas the Permanent Court gave the green light of authorization, having found in international law no reason for giving the red
light of prohibition, the present Court does not feel able to give a signal
either way.

---

[1]"International law governs relations between independent States. The rules of
law binding upon States therefore emanate from their own free will as expressed in
conventions or by usage generally accepted as expressing principles of law and
established in order to regulate the relations between these co-existing independent
communities or with a view to the achievement of common aims," *Lotus* case,
Judgement No. 9 of 7 September 1927, P.C.I.J., Series A, No. 10, p. 18.

[2]"The Court therefore must, in any event, ascertain whether or not there exists a
rule of international law limiting the freedom of States to extend the criminal
jurisdiction of their courts to a situation uniting the circumstances of the present case"
(*ibid.*, p. 21); and the Court concluded: "It must therefore be held that there is no
principle of international law, within the meaning of Article 15 of the Convention of
Lausanne of July 24, 1923, which precludes the institution of the criminal proceedings
under consideration. Consequently, Turkey, by instituting, in virtue of the discretion
which international law leaves to every sovereign State, the criminal proceedings in
question, has not, in the absence of such principles, acted in a manner contrary to the
principles of international law within the meaning of the special agreement" (*ibid.*, p.
31).

15. Thus, the Court, in this Opinion, is showing much more circumspection than its predecessor in the *Lotus* case in asserting today that what is not expressly prohibited by international law is not therefore authorized.

16. While not finding either in favour of or against the legality of the threat or use of nuclear weapons, the Court takes note, in its Opinion, the existence of a very advanced process of change in the relevant international law or, in other words, of a current trend towards the replacement of one rule of international law by another, where the first is already defunct and its successor does not yet exist. Once again, if the Court as a judicial body felt that it could do no more than register this fact, States should not, in my view, see in this any authorization whatever to act as they please.

[Court Going as Far as Elements at Its Disposal Permit]

17. The Court is obviously aware that, at first sight, [its] reply to the General Assembly is unsatisfactory. However, while the Court may leave some people with the impression that it has left the task assigned to it half completed, I am on the contrary persuaded that it has discharged its duty by going as far, in its reply to the question put to it, as the elements at its disposal would permit.

[Why I Supported ¶ 105 (2)E 2]

18. In the second sentence of operative paragraph E of the Advisory Opinion, the Court indicates that it has reached a point in its reasoning beyond which it cannot proceed without running the risk of adopting a conclusion which would go beyond what seems to it to be legitimate. That is the position of the Court as a judicial body. Some of the Judges supported this position, though no doubt each with an approach and an interpretation of their own. **It will certainly have been noted that the distribution of the votes, both for and against paragraph E, was in no way consistent with any geographical split; this is a mark of the independence of the Members of the Court which I am happy to emphasize.** Having thus explained the construction which I believe should be put on the Court's pronouncement, I would now like to revert briefly to the substantive reasons which induced me to support it.

[International Humanitarian Law an Exacting Corpus of Rules]

19. International humanitarian law is a particularly exacting corpus of rules, and these rules are meant to be applied in all circumstances. The Court has fully recognized this fact.

[Nuclear Weapons Destabilize Humanitarian Law]

20. **Nuclear weapons can be expected — in the present state of scientific development at least — to cause indiscriminate victims among combatants and non-combatants alike, as well as unnecessary suffering among both categories.** *The very nature of this blind weapon therefore has a destabilizing effect on humanitarian law which regulates discernment in the type of weapon used. Nuclear weapons, the ultimate evil, destabilize humanitarian law which is the law of the lesser evil. The existence of nuclear weapons is therefore a challenge to the very existence of humanitarian law,* **not to mention their long-term effects of damage to the human environment, in respect to which the right to life can be exercised. Until scientists are able to develop a "clean" nuclear weapon which would distinguish between combatants and non-combatants, nuclear weapons will clearly have indiscriminate effects and constitute an absolute challenge to humanitarian law.** *Atomic warfare and humanitarian law therefore appear to me mutually exclusive: the existence of the one automatically implies the non-existence of the other.*

21. I have no doubt that most of the principles and rules of humanitarian law and, in any event, the two principles, one of which prohibits the use of weapons with indiscriminate effects and the other use of arms causing unnecessary suffering, are a part of *jus cogens*. The Court raised this question in the present Opinion; but it nevertheless stated that it did not have to reach a finding on the point since the question of the nature of humanitarian law applicable to nuclear weapons did not fall within the framework of the request addressed to it by the General Assembly of the United Nations. Nonetheless, the Court expressly stated the view that these fundamental rules constitute

"intransgressible principles of international customary law."[3]

[Self-Defense and "Intransgressible" Norms]

22. A State's right to survival is also a fundamental law, similar in many respects to a "natural" law. However, self-defence — if exercised in extreme circumstances in which the very survival of a State is in question — cannot engender a situation in which a State would exonerate itself from compliance with the *"intransgressible"* norms of international humanitarian law. In certain circumstances, therefore, a relentless opposition can arise, a head-on collision of fundamental principles, neither one of which can be reduced to the other. The fact remains that the use of nuclear weapons by a State in circumstances in which its survival is at stake risks in its turn endangering the survival of all mankind, precisely because of the inextricable link between terror and escalation in the use of such weapons. It would thus be quite foolhardy unhesitatingly to set the survival of a State above all other considerations, in particular above the survival of mankind itself.

*   *

*

[¶ (2)F: Twofold General Obligation]

23. As the Court has acknowledged, the obligation to negotiate in good faith for nuclear disarmament concerns the 182 or so States parties to the Non-Proliferation Treaty. I think one can go beyond that conclusion and assert that there is in fact a twofold *general obligation*, opposable *erga omnes*, to negotiate in good faith and to achieve the desired result. Indeed, it is not unreasonable to think that, considering

---

[3]See paragraph 79 of the Advisory Opinion, which reads: "It is undoubtedly because a great many rules of humanitarian law applicable in armed conflict are so fundamental to the respect of the human person and 'elementary considerations of humanity' as the Court put it in its Judgment of 9 April 1949 in the *Corfu Channel* case (*I.C.J. Reports 1949*, p. 22) that the Hague and Geneva Conventions have enjoyed a broad accession. Further these fundamental rules are to be observed by all States whether or not they have ratified the conventions that contain them, because they constitute intransgressible principles of international customary law."

the at least formal unanimity in this field, this twofold obligation to negotiate in good faith and achieve the desired result has now, 50 years on, acquired a *customary character*. For the rest, I fully share the Court's opinion as to the legal scope of this obligation. I would merely stress once again the great importance of the goal to be attained, particularly in view of the uncertainties which still persist. The Court patently had to say this. Owing to the, by the nature of things, very close link between this question and the question of the legality [or] illegality of the threat or use of nuclear weapons, the Court cannot be reproached for having reached a finding *ultra petita*, a notion which in any event is alien to the advisory procedure.

*   *

*

[Legal Reality and Ultimate Goal: Nuclear Disarmament]

24. The solution arrived at in this Advisory Opinion frankly states the legal reality, while faithfully expressing and reflecting the hope, shared by all, peoples and States alike, *that nuclear disarmament will always remain the ultimate goal of all action in the field of nuclear weapons, that the goal is no longer utopian and that it is the duty of all to seek to attain it more actively than ever*. The destiny of man depends on the will to enter into this commitment, for as Albert Einstein wrote, *"Man's destiny will be the one he deserves"*.[4]

(*Signed*) Mohammed BEDJAOUI

[Original: French]   [Algeria]

---

[4]Albert Einstein, *How I See the World* (tr. into French by Colonel Cros), Paris: Flammarion, p. 84.

DISSENTING OPINION OF VICE-PRESIDENT SCHWEBEL

EDITOR'S OUTLINE OF SCHWEBEL OPINION*

Introduction
    Titanic Tension between State Practice and Legal Principle
State Practice
The Nuclear Non-Proliferation Treaty
    Deterrence: Threat to Use
Negative and Positive Security Assurances Endorsed by the
        Security Council
    Security Council Resolution 984 (1995)
    Contemplation of the Use of Nuclear Weapons
Other Nuclear Treaties
Resolutions of the General Assembly
Principles of International Humanitarian Law
    "Countervalue" Use
    "Counterforce" Use
    Proportionality
    ¶ 105 (2)E 1
Extreme Circumstances of Self-Defense and State Survival
    ¶ 105 (2)E 2
Desert Storm
    Threat of Use of Nuclear Weapons Deterred Iraqi Use of
        Biological or Chemical Weapons
    Belligerent Reprisal Using Outlawed Weapons
Article VI of the Nuclear Non-Proliferation Treaty

*Editor's additions to original text are indicated by bracketed headings or boldface brackets.

[Introduction]

[Titanic Tension between State Practice and Legal Principle]

More than any case in the history of the Court, this proceeding presents a titanic tension between State practice and legal principle. It is accordingly the more important not to confuse the international law we have with the international law we need. In the main, the Court's Opinion meets that test. I am in essential though not entire agreement with much of it, and shall, in this opinion, set out my differences. Since however I profoundly disagree with the Court's principal and ultimate holding, I regret to be obliged to dissent.

The essence of the problem is this. Fifty years of the practice of States does not debar, and to that extent supports, the legality of the threat or use of nuclear weapons in certain circumstances. At the same time, principles of international humanitarian law which antedate that practice govern the use of all weapons including nuclear weapons, and it is extraordinarily difficult to reconcile the use — at any rate, some uses — of nuclear weapons with the application of those principles.

One way of surmounting the antinomy between practice and principle would be to put aside practice. That is what those who maintain that the threat or use of nuclear weapons is unlawful in all circumstances do. Another way is to put aside principle, to maintain that the principles of international humanitarian law do not govern nuclear weapons. That has not been done by States, including the nuclear-weapon States, in these proceedings nor should it be done. These principles — essentially proportionality in the degree of force applied, discrimination in the application of force as between combatants and civilians, and avoidance of unnecessary suffering of combatants — evolved in the pre-nuclear age. They do not easily fit the use of weaponry having the characteristics of nuclear weapons. At the same time, it is the fact that the nuclear Powers and their allies have successfully resisted applying further progressive development of humanitarian law to nuclear weapons; the record of the conferences that concluded the Geneva Conventions of 1949 and its Additional Protocols of 1977 establishes that. Nevertheless to hold that inventions in weaponry that post-date the formation of such fundamental principles are not governed by those principles would vitiate international humanitarian law. Nor is it believable that in fashioning these principles the international community meant to exclude their application to post-invented weaponry. The Martens Clause implies the contrary.

Before considering the extent to which the chasm between practice and principle may be bridged — and is bridged by the Court's Opinion — observations on their content are in order.

State Practice

State practice demonstrates that nuclear weapons have been manufactured and deployed by States for some 50 years; that in that deployment inheres a threat of possible use; and that the international community, by treaty and through action of the United Nations Security Council, has, far from proscribing the threat or use of nuclear weapons in all circumstances, recognized in effect or in terms that in certain circumstances nuclear weapons may be used or their use threatened.

Not only have the nuclear Powers avowedly and for decades, with vast effort and expense, manufactured, maintained and deployed nuclear weapons. They have affirmed that they are legally entitled to use nuclear weapons in certain circumstances and to threaten their use. They have threatened their use by the hard facts and inexorable implications of the possession and deployment of nuclear weapons; by a posture of readiness to launch nuclear weapons 365 days a year, 24 hours of every day; by the military plans, strategic and tactical, developed and sometimes publicly revealed by them; and, in a very few international crises, by threatening the use of nuclear weapons. In the very doctrine and practice of deterrence, the threat of the possible use of nuclear weapons inheres.

This nuclear practice is not a practice of a lone and secondary persistent objector. This is not a practice of a pariah Government crying out in the wilderness of otherwise adverse international opinion. This is the practice of five of the world's major Powers, of the permanent Members of the Security Council, significantly supported for almost 50 years by their allies and other States sheltering under their nuclear umbrellas. That is to say, it is the practice of States — and a practice supported by a large and weighty number of other States — that together represent the bulk of the world's military and economic and financial and technological power and a very large proportion of its population. This practice has been recognized, accommodated and in some measure accepted by the international community. That measure of acceptance is ambiguous but not meaningless. It is obvious that the alliance struc-

tures that have been predicated upon the deployment of nuclear weapons accept the legality of their use in certain circumstances. But what may be less obvious is the effect of the Non-Proliferation Treaty and the structure of negative and positive security assurances extended by the nuclear Powers and accepted by the Security Council in pursuance of that Treaty, as well as of reservations by nuclear Powers adhering to regional treaties that govern the possession, deployment and use of nuclear weapons.

The Nuclear Non-Proliferation Treaty

The Treaty on the Non-Proliferation of Nuclear Weapons, concluded in 1968 and indefinitely extended by 175 States Parties in 1995, is of paramount importance. By the terms of Article I, "Each nuclear-weapon State Party to the Treaty undertakes not to transfer to any recipient whatsoever nuclear weapons . . . or control over such weapons" nor to assist "any non-nuclear weapon State to manufacture or otherwise acquire nuclear weapons . . .". By the terms of Article II, each non-nuclear weapon State undertakes not to receive nuclear weapons and not to manufacture them. Article III provides that each non-nuclear-weapon State shall accept safeguards to be negotiated with the International Atomic Energy Agency with a view to preventing diversion of nuclear energy from peaceful uses to nuclear weapons. Article IV preserves the right of all Parties to develop peaceful uses of nuclear energy, and Article V provides that potential benefits from peaceful applications of nuclear explosions will be made available to non-nuclear weapon States Party. Article VI provides:

> "Each of the Parties to the Treaty undertakes to pursue negotiations in good faith on effective measures relating to cessation of the nuclear arms race at an early date and to nuclear disarmament, and on a treaty on general and complete disarmament under strict and effective international control."

Article VII provides:

> "Nothing in this Treaty affects the right of any group of States to conclude regional treaties in order to assure the total absence of nuclear weapons in their respective territories."

Article VIII is an amendment clause. Article IX provides that the Treaty shall be open to all States and that, for the purposes of the Treaty, "a nuclear-weapon State is one which has manufactured and exploded a nuclear weapon or other nuclear explosive device prior to 1 January 1967". Article X is an extraordinary withdrawal clause which also contains provision on the basis of which a conference of the Parties may be called to extend the Treaty.

The NPT is thus concerned with the possession rather than the use of nuclear weapons. It establishes a fundamental distinction between States possessing, and States not possessing, nuclear weapons, and a balance of responsibilities between them. It recognizes the possibility of the presence of nuclear weapons in territories in which their total absence has not been prescribed. Nothing in the Treaty authorizes, or prohibits, the use or threat of use of nuclear weapons. However, the Treaty recognizes the legitimacy of the possession of nuclear weapons by the five nuclear Powers, at any rate until the achievement of nuclear disarmament. In 1968, and in 1995, that possession was notoriously characterized by the development, refinement, maintenance and deployment of many thousands of nuclear weapons. If nuclear weapons were not maintained, they might be more dangerous than not; if they were not deployed, the utility of possession would be profoundly affected. Once a Power possesses, maintains and deploys nuclear weapons and the means of their delivery, it places itself in a posture of deterrence.

[Deterrence: Threat to Use]

What does the practice of such possession of nuclear weapons thus import? Nuclear Powers do not possess nuclear arms to no possible purpose. They develop and maintain them at vast expense; they deploy them in their delivery vehicles; and they made and make known their willingness to use them in certain circumstances. They pursue a policy of deterrence, on which the world was on notice when the NPT was concluded and is on notice today. The policy of deterrence differs from that of the threat to use nuclear weapons by its generality. But if a threat of possible use did not inhere in deterrence, deterrence would not deter. If possession by the five nuclear Powers is lawful until the achievement of nuclear disarmament; if possession is the better part of deterrence; if deterrence is the better part of threat, then it follows that the practice of States — including their treaty practice — does not absolutely debar the threat or use of nuclear weapons.

Thus the regime of the Non-Proliferation Treaty constitutes more than acquiescence by the non-nuclear States in the reality of possession of nuclear weapons by the five nuclear Powers. As the representative of the United Kingdom put it in the oral hearings, "The entire structure of the Non Proliferation Treaty . . . presupposes that the parties did not regard the use of nuclear weapons as being proscribed in all circumstances." To be sure, the acquiescence of most non-nuclear weapon States in the fact of possession of nuclear weapons by the five nuclear Powers — and the ineluctable implications of that fact — have been accompanied by vehement protest and reservation of rights, as successive resolutions of the General Assembly show. It would be too much to say that acquiescence in this case gives rise to *opinio juris* establishing the legality of the threat or use of nuclear weapons. What it — and the State practice described — does do is to abort the birth or survival of *opinio juris* to the contrary. Moreover, there is more than the practice so far described and the implications of the Nuclear Non-Proliferation Treaty to weigh.

Negative and Positive Security Assurances Endorsed by the Security Council

[Security Council Resolution 984 (1995)]

In connection with the conclusion of the Treaty in 1968 and its indefinite extension in 1995, three nuclear Powers in 1968 and five in 1995 extended negative and positive security assurances to the non-nuclear States Parties to the NPT. In resolution 984 (1995), co-sponsored by the five nuclear Powers, and adopted by the Security Council on 11 April 1995 by unanimous vote,

"The Security Council, . . .

Recognizing the legitimate interest of non-nuclear-weapon States Parties to the Treaty on the Non-Proliferation of Nuclear Weapons to receive security assurances, . . .

Taking into consideration the legitimate concern of non-nuclear weapon States that, in conjunction with their adherence to the Treaty on the Non-Proliferation of Nuclear Weapons, further appropriate measures be undertaken to safeguard their security, . . .

Considering further that, in accordance with the relevant provisions of the Charter of the United Nations, any aggression with the use of nuclear weapons would endanger international peace and security,

1. Takes note with appreciation of the statements made by

each of the nuclear-weapon States . . ., in which they give security assurances against the use of nuclear weapons to non-nuclear weapon States that are Parties to the Treaty on the Non-Proliferation of Nuclear Weapons;

2. Recognizes the legitimate interest of non-nuclear-weapon States Parties to the Treaty on the Non-Proliferation of Nuclear Weapons to receive assurances that the Security Council, and above all its nuclear-weapon State permanent members, will act immediately in accordance with the relevant provisions of the Charter of the United Nations, in the event that such States are the victim of an act of, or object of a threat of, aggression in which nuclear weapons are used;

3. Recognizes further that, in case of aggression with nuclear weapons or the threat of such aggression against a non-nuclear-weapon State Party to the Treaty on the Non-Proliferation of Nuclear Weapons, any State may bring the matter immediately to the attention of the Security Council to enable the Council to take urgent action to provide assistance, in accordance with the Charter, to the State victim of an act of, or object of a threat of, such aggression; and recognizes also that the nuclear-weapon State permanent members of the Security Council will bring the matter immediately to the attention of the Council and seek Council action to provide, in accordance with the Charter, the necessary assistance to the State victim; . . .

7. Welcomes the intention expressed by certain States that they will provide or support immediate assistance, in accordance with the Charter, to any non-nuclear weapon State Party to the Treaty on the Non-Proliferation of Nuclear Weapons that is a victim of an act of, or an object of a threat of, aggression in which nuclear weapons are used; . . .

9. Reaffirms the inherent right, recognized under Article 51 of the Charter, of individual and collective self-defence if an armed attack occurs against a member of the United Nations, until the Security Council has taken measures necessary to maintain international peace and security; . . ."

It is plain — especially by the inclusion of operative paragraph 9 in its context — that the Security Council, in so taking note "with appreciation" in operative paragraph 1 of the negative security assurances of the nuclear Powers, and in so welcoming in operative paragraph 7 "the intention expressed" by the positive security assurances of the nuclear Powers, accepted the possibility of the threat or use of nuclear weapons, particularly to assist a non-nuclear-weapon State that, in the words of paragraph 7 — "is a victim of an act of, or an object of a threat of, aggression in which nuclear weapons are used".

[Contemplation of the Use of Nuclear Weapons]

This is the plainer in view of the terms of the unilateral security assurances made by four of the nuclear-weapon States which are, with the exception of those of China, largely concordant. They expressly contemplate the use of nuclear weapons in specified circumstances. They implicitly do not debar the use of nuclear weapons against another nuclear Power (or State not party to the NPT), and explicitly do not debar their use against a nuclear-non-weapon State Party that acts in violation of its obligations under the NPT.

For example, the United States reaffirms that it will not use nuclear weapons against non nuclear weapon States Parties to the NPT

> "except in the case of an invasion or other attack on the United States . . . its armed forces, its allies, or on a State towards which it has a security commitment, carried out or sustained by such a non-nuclear-weapon State in association or alliance with a nuclear-weapon State".

The exception clearly contemplates the use of nuclear weapons in the specified exceptional circumstances. The United States assurances add: "parties to the Treaty on the Non-Proliferation of Nuclear Weapons must be in compliance" with "their obligations under the Treaty" in order to be "eligible for any benefits of adherence to the Treaty". The United States further "affirms its intention to provide or support immediate assistance" to any non-nuclear-weapon State "that is a victim of an act of, or an object of a threat of, aggression in which nuclear weapons are used". It reaffirms the inherent right of individual or collective self-defence under Article 51 of the Charter "if an armed attack, including a nuclear attack, occurs against a Member of the United Nations . . .". Such affirmations by it — and their unanimous acceptance by the Security Council — demonstrate that nuclear Powers have asserted the legality and that the Security Council has accepted the possibility of the threat or use of nuclear weapons in certain circumstances.

Other Nuclear Treaties

As the Court's Opinion recounts, a number of treaties in addition to the NPT limit the acquisition, manufacture, and possession of nuclear weapons; prohibit their deployment or use in specified areas; and regulate their testing. The negotiation and conclusion of these treaties only makes sense in the light of the fact that the international community has not comprehensively outlawed the possession, threat or use of nuclear weapons in all circumstances, whether by treaty or through customary international law. Why conclude these treaties if their essence is already international law, indeed, as some argue, *jus cogens?*

The fact that there is no comprehensive treaty proscribing the threat or use of nuclear weapons in all circumstances is obvious. Yet it is argued that the totality of this disparate treaty making activity demonstrates an emergent *opinio juris* in favour of the comprehensive outlawry of the threat or use of nuclear weapons; that, even if nuclear weapons were not outlawed decades ago, they are today, or are on the verge of so becoming, by the cumulation of such treaties as well as resolutions of the United Nations General Assembly.

The looseness of that argument is no less obvious. Can it really be supposed that, in recent months, nuclear Powers have adhered to a protocol to the Treaty of Raratonga establishing a nuclear free zone in the South Pacific because they believe that the threat or use of nuclear weapons already is outlawed in all circumstances and places, there as elsewhere? Can it really be believed that as recently as 15 December 1995, at Bangkok, States signed a Treaty on the South-East Asia Nuclear Weapon-Free Zone, and on 11 April 1996 the States of Africa took the considerable trouble to conclude at Cairo a treaty for the creation of a nuclear-weapons-free zone in Africa, on the understanding that by dint of emergent *opinio juris* customary international law already requires that all zones of the world be nuclear-free?

On the contrary, the various treaties relating to nuclear weapons confirm what the practice described above imports: the threat or use of nuclear weapons is not — certainly, not yet — prohibited in all circumstances, whether by treaty or customary international law. This is the clearer in the light of the terms of the Treaty of Tlatelolco for the Prohibition of Nuclear Weapons in Latin America of 14 February 1967 and the declarations that accompanied adherence to an Additional Protocol under the Treaty of the five nuclear-weapon States. All of the five nuclear-weapon States in so adhering

undertook not to use or threaten to use nuclear weapons against the Contracting Parties to the Treaty. But they subjected their undertakings to the possibility of the use of nuclear weapons in certain circumstances, as recounted above in paragraph 59 of the Court's Opinion. None of the Contracting Parties to the Tlatelolco Treaty objected to the declarations of the five nuclear-weapon States, which is to say that the Contracting Parties to the Treaty recognized the legality of the use of nuclear weapons in certain circumstances.

Resolutions of the General Assembly

In its opinion, the Court concludes that the succession of resolutions of the General Assembly on nuclear weapons "still fall short of establishing the existence of an *opinio juris* on the illegality of the use of such weapons". In my view, they do not begin to do so. The seminal resolution, resolution 1653 (XVI) of 24 November 1961, declares that the use of nuclear weapons is "a direct violation of the Charter of the United Nations" and "is contrary to the rules of international law and to the laws of humanity", and that any State using nuclear weapons is to be considered "as committing a crime against mankind and civilization". It somewhat inconsistently concludes by requesting consultations to ascertain views on the possibility of convening a conference for signing a convention on the prohibition of the use of nuclear weapons for war purposes. Resolution 1653 (XVI) was adopted by a vote of 55 to 20, with 26 abstentions. Four of the five nuclear Powers voted against it. Succeeding resolutions providing, as in resolution 36/92 I, that "the use or threat of use of nuclear weapons should . . . be prohibited . . .", have been adopted by varying majorities, in the teeth of strong, sustained and qualitatively important opposition. Any increase in the majority for such resolutions is unimpressive, deriving in some measure from an increase in the membership of the Organization. The continuing opposition, consisting as it does of States that bring together much of the world's military and economic power and a significant percentage of its population, more than suffices to deprive the resolutions in question of legal authority.

The General Assembly has no authority to enact international law. None of the General Assembly's resolutions on nuclear weapons are declaratory of existing international law. The General Assembly can adopt resolutions declaratory of international law only if those resolutions truly reflect what international law is. If a resolution purports to be declaratory of international law, if it is adopted unanimously (or virtually so, qualitatively as well as quantitively) or by consensus, and if it corresponds to State practice, it may be declaratory of international law. The resolutions of which resolution 1653 is the exemplar conspicuously fail to meet these criteria. While purporting to be declaratory of international law (yet calling for consultations about the possibility of concluding a treaty prohibition of what is so declared), they not only do not reflect State practice, they are in conflict with it, as shown above. Forty-six States voted against or abstained upon the resolution, including the majority of the nuclear Powers. It is wholly unconvincing to argue that a majority of the Members of the General Assembly can "declare" international law in opposition to such a body of State practice and over the opposition of such a body of States. Nor are these resolutions authentic interpretations of principles or provisions of the United Nations Charter. The Charter contains not a word about particular weapons, about nuclear weapons, about *jus in bello*. To declare the use of nuclear weapons a violation of the Charter is an innovative interpretation of it, which cannot be treated as an authentic interpretation of Charter principles or provisions giving rise to obligations binding on States under international law. Finally, the repetition of resolutions of the General Assembly in this vein, far from giving rise, in the words of the Court, to "the nascent *opinio juris*", rather demonstrates what the law is not. When faced with continuing and significant opposition, the repetition of General Assembly resolutions is a mark of ineffectuality in law formation as it is in practical effect.

Principles of International Humanitarian Law

While it is not difficult to conclude that the principles of international humanitarian law — above all, proportionality in the application of force, and discrimination between military and civilian targets — govern the use of nuclear weapons, it does not follow that the application of those principles to the threat or use of nuclear weapons "in any circumstance" is easy. Cases at the extremes are relatively clear; cases closer to the centre of the spectrum of possible uses are less so.

["Countervalue" Use]

At one extreme is the use of strategic nuclear weapons in quantities against enemy cities and industries. This so-called "countervalue" use (as contrasted with "counterforce" uses directly only against enemy nuclear forces and installations) could cause an enormous number of deaths and injuries, running in some cases into the millions; and, in addition to those immediately affected by the heat and blast of those weapons, vast numbers could be affected, many fatally, by spreading radiation. Large-scale "exchanges" of such nuclear weaponry could destroy not only cities but countries, and render continents, perhaps the whole of the earth, uninhabitable, if not at once then through longer-range effects of nuclear fallout. **It cannot be accepted that the use of nuclear weapons on a scale which would — or could — result in the deaths of many millions in indiscriminate inferno and by far-reaching fallout, have profoundly pernicious effects in space and time, and render uninhabitable much or all of the earth, could be lawful.**

["Counterforce" Use]

At the other extreme is the use of tactical nuclear weapons against discrete military or naval targets so situated that substantial civilian casualties would not ensue. For example, the use of a nuclear depth-charge to destroy a nuclear submarine that is about to fire nuclear missiles, or has fired one or more of a number of its nuclear missiles, might well be lawful. By the circumstance of its use, the nuclear depth-charge would not give rise to immediate civilian casualties. It would easily meet the test of proportionality; the damage that the submarine's missiles could inflict on the population and territory of the target State would infinitely outweigh that entailed in the destruction of the submarine and its crew. The submarine's destruction by a nuclear weapon would produce radiation in the sea, but far less than the radiation that firing of its missiles would produce on and over land. Nor is it as certain that the use of a conventional depth-charge would discharge the mission successfully; the far greater force of a nuclear weapon could ensure destruction of the submarine whereas a conventional depth-charge might not.

[Proportionality]

An intermediate case would be the use of nuclear weapons to destroy an enemy army situated in a desert. In certain circumstances, such a use of nuclear weapons might meet the tests of discrimination and proportionality; in others not. The argument that the use of nuclear weapons is inevitably disproportionate raises troubling questions, which the British Attorney General addressed in the Court's oral proceedings in these terms:

"If one is to speak of 'disproportionality', the question arises: disproportionate to what? The answer must be 'to the threat posed to the victim State'. It is by reference to that threat that proportionality must be measured. So one has to look at all the circumstances, in particular the scale, kind and location of the threat. To assume that any defensive use of nuclear weapons must be disproportionate, no matter how serious the threat to the safety and the very survival of the State resorting to such use, is wholly unfounded. Moreover, it suggests an overbearing assumption by the critics of nuclear weapons that they can determine in advance that no threat, including a nuclear, chemical or biological threat, is ever worth the use of any nuclear weapon. It cannot be right to say that if an aggressor hits hard enough, his victim loses the right to take the only measure by which he can defend himself and reverse the aggression. That would not be the rule of law. It would be an aggressor's charter."

[¶ 105 (2)E 1]

For its part, the body of the Court's Opinion is cautious in treating problems of the application of the principles of international humanitarian law to concrete cases. It evidences a measure of uncertainty in a case in which the tension between State practice and legal principle is unparalleled. It concludes, in Paragraph 2E of the *dispositif,* that,

"It follows from the above-mentioned requirements that the threat or use of nuclear weapons would generally be contrary to the rules of international law applicable in armed conflict, and in particular the principles and rules of international humanitarian law."

That conclusion, while imprecise, is not unreasonable. The use of nuclear weapons is, for the reasons examined above, exceptionally difficult to reconcile with the rules of international law applicable in armed conflict, particularly the principles and rules of international humanitarian law. But that is by no means to say that the use of nuclear weapons, in any and all circumstances, would necessarily and invariably conflict with those rules of international law. On the contrary, as the *dispositif* in effect acknowledges, while they might "generally" do so, in specific cases they might not. It all depends upon the facts of the case.

Extreme Circumstances of Self-Defence and State Survival

[¶ 105 (2)E 2]

The just-quoted first paragraph of Paragraph 2E of the holdings is followed by the Court's ultimate, paramount — and sharply controverted — conclusion in the case, narrowly adopted by the President's casting vote:

> "However, in view of the current state of international law, and of the elements of fact at its disposal, the Court cannot conclude definitively whether the threat or use of nuclear weapons would be lawful or unlawful in an extreme circumstance of self-defence, in which the very survival of a State would be at stake."

This is an astounding conclusion to be reached by the International Court of Justice. Despite the fact that its Statute "forms an integral part" of the United Nations Charter, and despite the comprehensive and categorical terms of Article 2, paragraph 4, and Article 51 of that Charter, the Court concludes on the supreme issue of the threat or use of force of our age that it has no opinion. In "an extreme circumstance of self-defence, in which the very survival of a State would be at stake", the Court finds that international law and hence the Court have nothing to say. After many months of agonizing appraisal of the law, the Court discovers that there is none. When it comes to the supreme interests of State, the Court discards the legal progress of the Twentieth Century, puts aside the provisions of the Charter of the United Nations of which it is "the principal judicial organ", and proclaims, in terms redolent of *Realpolitik*, its ambivalence about the most important provisions of modern international law. If this was to be its ultimate holding, the Court would have done better to have drawn on its undoubted discretion not to render an Opinion at all.

Neither predominant legal theory (as most definitively developed by Lauterpacht in *The Function of Law in the International Community*, 1933) nor the precedent of this Court admit a holding of *non liquet*, still less a holding — or inability to hold — of such a fundamental character. Lauterpacht wrote most pertinently (and, as it has turned out, presciently):

"There is not the slightest relation between the content of the right to self-defence and the claim that it is above the law and not amenable to evaluation by law. Such a claim is self-contradictory, inasmuch as it purports to be based on legal right, and as, at the same time, it dissociates itself from regulation and evaluation by the law. Like any other dispute involving important issues, so also the question of the right of recourse to war in self-defence is in itself capable of judicial decision . . ." (At p. 180.)

Indeed, the drafters of the Statute of the Permanent Court of International Justice crafted the provisions of Article 38 of its Statute — provisions which Article 38 of the Statute of this Court maintains — in order, in the words of the President of the Advisory Committee of Jurists, to avoid "especially the blind alley of *non liquet*". To do so, they adopted the Root-Phillimore proposal to empower the Court to apply not only international conventions and international custom but "the general principles of law recognized by civilized nations". (Permanent Court of International Justice, Advisory Committee of Jurists, *Procès-Verbaux of the Proceedings of the Committee*, June 16th-July 24th, 1920, The Hague, 1920, pp. 332, 344. See also pp. 296 ("A rule must be established to meet this eventuality, to avoid the possibility of the Court declaring itself incompetent (*non liquet*) though lack of applicable rules"); 307-320, and 336 (the reference to general principles "was necessary to meet the possibility of a *non-liquet*").

Moreover, far from justifying the Court's inconclusiveness, contemporary events rather demonstrate the legality of the threat or use of nuclear weapons in extraordinary circumstances.

Desert Storm

The most recent and effective threat of the use of nuclear weapons took place on the eve of "Desert Storm". The circumstances merit exposition, for they constitute a striking illustration of a circumstance in which the perceived threat of the use of nuclear weapons was not only eminently lawful but intensely desirable.

Iraq, condemned by the Security Council for its invasion and annexation of Kuwait and for its attendant grave breaches of international humanitarian law, had demonstrated that it was prepared to use weapons of mass destruction. It had recently and repeatedly used gas in large quantities against the military formations of Iran, with substantial and perhaps decisive effect. It had even used gas against its own Kurdish citizens. There was no ground for believing that legal or humanitarian scruple would prevent it from using weapons of mass destruction — notably chemical, perhaps bacteriological or nuclear weapons — against the coalition forces arrayed against it. Moreover, it was engaged in extraordinary efforts to construct nuclear weapons in violation of its obligations as a Party to the Non-Proliferation Treaty.

General Norman Schwarzkopf stated on 10 January 1996 over national public television in the United States on *"Frontline"*:

> "My nightmare scenario was that our forces would attack into Iraq and find themselves in such a great concentration that they became targeted by chemical weapons or some sort of rudimentary nuclear device that would cause mass casualties.
>
> That's exactly what the Iraqis did in the Iran-Iraq war. They would take the attacking masses of the Iranians, let them run up against their barrier system, and when there were thousands of people massed against the barrier system, they would drop chemical weapons on them and kill thousands of people." (*Frontline*, Show #1408, "The Gulf War," *Transcript of Journal Graphics, Inc., Part II*, p. 5.)

[Threat of Use of Nuclear Weapons Deterred Iraqi Use of Biological or Chemical Weapons]

To exorcise that nightmare, the United States took action as described by then Secretary of State James A. Baker in the following terms, in which he recounts his climactic meeting of 9 January 1990 in Geneva with the then Foreign Minister of Iraq, Tariq Aziz:

> "I then made a point 'on the dark side of the issue' that Colin Powell had specifically asked me to deliver in the plainest possible terms. 'If the conflict involves your use of chemical or biological weapons against our forces,' I warned, 'the American people will demand vengeance. We have the means to exact it. With regard to this part of my presentation, that is not a threat, it is a promise. If there is any use of weapons like that, our objective won't just be the liberation of Kuwait, but the elimination of the current Iraqi regime, and anyone responsible for using those weapons would be held accountable.'
>
> "The President had decided, at Camp David in December, that the best deterrent of the use of weapons of mass destruction by Iraq would be a threat to go after the Ba'ath regime

itself. He had also decided that U.S. forces would not retaliate with chemical or nuclear response if the Iraqis attacked with chemical munitions. There was obviously no reason to inform the Iraqis of this. In hope of persuading them to consider more soberly the folly of war, I purposely left the impression that the use of chemical or biological agents by Iraq could invite tactical nuclear retaliation. (We do not really know whether this was the reason there appears to have been no confirmed use by Iraq of chemical weapons during the war. My own view is that the calculated ambiguity how we might respond has to be part of the reason.)" *(The Politics of Diplomacy — Revolution, War and Peace, 1989-1992* by James A. Baker III, 1995, p. 359.)

In "Frontline", Mr. Baker adds:

"The president's letter to Saddam Hussein, which Tariq Aziz read in Geneva, made it very clear that if Iraq used weapons of mass destruction, chemical weapons, against United States forces that the American people would — would demand vengeance and that we had the means to achieve it." *(Loc. cit., Part I,* p. 13.)

Mr. Aziz is then portrayed on the screen immediately thereafter as saying:

"I read it very carefully and then when I ended reading it, I told him, 'Look, Mr. Secretary, this is not the kind of correspondence between two heads of state. This is a letter of threat and I cannot receive from you a letter of threat to my president,' and I returned it to him." *(Ibid.)*

At another point in the programme, the following statements were made:

"NARRATOR: The Marines waited for a chemical attack. It never came.

TARIQ AZIZ: We didn't think that it was wise to use them. That's all what I can say. That was not — was not wise to use such kind of weapons in such kind of a war with — with such an enemy." *(Loc. cit.,* Part II, p. 7.)

In *The Washington Post* of 26 August 1995, an article datelined United

Nations, 25 August was published as follows:

"Iraq has released to the United Nations new evidence that it was prepared to use deadly toxins and bacteria against U.S. and allied forces during the 1991 Persian Gulf War that liberated Kuwait from its Iraqi occupiers, U.N. Ambassador Rolf Ekeus said today.

"Ekeus, the chief U.N. investigator of Iraq's weapons programs, said Iraqi officials admitted to him in Baghdad last week that in December 1990 they loaded three types of biological agents into roughly 200 missile warheads and aircraft bombs that were then distributed to air bases and a missile site.

"The Iraqis began this process the day after the U.N. Security Council voted to authorize using 'all necessary means' to liberate Kuwait, Ekeus said. He said the action was akin to playing 'Russian roulette' with extraordinarily dangerous weapons on the eve of war.

"U.S. and U.N. officials said the Iraqi weapons contained enough biological agents to have killed hundreds of thousands of people and spread horrible diseases in cities or military bases in Israel, Saudi Arabia or wherever Iraq aimed the medium range missiles or squeaked a bomb-laden aircraft through enemy air defenses.

"Ekeus said Iraqi officials claimed they decided not to use the weapons after receiving a strong but ambiguously worded warning from the Bush administration on Jan. 9, 1991, that any use of unconventional warfare would provoke a devastating response.

"Iraq's leadership assumed this meant Washington would retaliate with nuclear weapons, Ekeus said he was told. U.N. officials said they believe the statement by Iraqi Deputy Prime Minister Tariq Aziz is the first authoritative account for why Iraq did not employ the biological or chemical arms at its disposal. . . .

"Iraqi officials said the documents were hidden by Hussein Kamel Hassan Majeed, the director of Iraq's weapons of mass destruction program who fled to Jordan on Aug. 7 and whose defection prompted Iraq to summon Ekeus to hear the new disclosures . . .

"Iraq admitted to filling a total of 150 aircraft bombs with botulinum toxin and bacteria capable of causing anthrax disease, each of which is among the most deadly substances known and can kill in extremely small quantities, Ekeus said. It also claimed to have put the two agents into 25 warheads to be carried by a medium range rocket.

"According to what Aziz told Ekeus on Aug. 4, then-Secretary of State James A. Baker III delivered the U.S. threat of grievous retaliation that caused Iraq to hold back during a tense, four-hour meeting in Geneva about five weeks before the beginning of the U.S.-led Desert Storm military campaign. Baker hinted at a U.S. response that would set Iraq back years by reducing its industry to rubble.

"Ekeus said that Aziz told him Iraq 'translated' the warning into a threat that Washington would respond with nuclear arms. In fact, then-Joint Chiefs of Staff Chairman Colin L. Powell and other U.S. military leaders had decided early on that nuclear weapons were not needed and no such retaliatory plans existed." (*The Washington Post*, 26 August 1995, p. A1. See also the report in *The New York Times*, 26 August 1995, p. 3.) For a contrasting contention by Iraq that "authority to launch biological and chemical war-heads was pre-delegated in the event that Baghdad was hit by nuclear weapons during the Gulf war", see the 8th Report to the Security Council by the Executive Chairman of the Special Commission (Ambassador Ekeus), U.N. document S/1995/864 of 11 October 1996, p. 11. That Report continues: "This pre-delegation does not exclude the alternative use of such capability and therefore does not constitute proof of only intentions concerning second use." (*Ibid.*)

Finally, there is the following answer by Ambassador Ekeus to a question in the course of testimony in hearings on global proliferation of weapons of mass destruction of 20 March 1996:

". . . I have had conversation with the Deputy Prime Minister of Iraq, Tariq Aziz, in which he made references to his meeting with Secretary of State James Baker in Geneva just before the outbreak of war. He, Tariq Aziz, says that Baker told him to the effect that if such [chemical or biological] weapons were applied there would be a very strong reaction from the United States.

"Tariq Aziz did not imply that Baker mentioned what type of reaction. But he told me that the Iraqi side took it for

granted that it meant the use of maybe nuclear weapons against
Baghdad, or something like that. And that threat was decisive
for them not to use the weapons.

"But this is the story he, Aziz, tells. I think one should be
very careful about buying it. I don't say that he must be wrong,
but I believe there are strong reasons that this may be an explanation he offers of why Iraq lost the war in Kuwait. This is
the story which they gladly tell everyone who talks to them.
So I think one should be cautious at least about buying that
story. I think still it is an open question." (Testimony of Ambassador Rolf Ekeus before the Senate Permanent Subcommit-
tee on Investigations of the Committee on Governmental
Affairs of the United States Senate, *Hearings on the Global
Proliferation of Weapons of Mass Destruction*, in press.)

**Thus there is on record remarkable evidence indicating that an
aggressor was or may have been deterred from using outlawed
weapons of mass destruction against forces and countries arrayed
against its aggression at the call of the United Nations by what the
aggressor perceived to be a threat to use nuclear weapons against
it should it first use weapons of mass destruction against the forces
of the coalition. Can it seriously be maintained that Mr. Baker's
calculated — and apparently successful — threat was unlawful?
Surely the principles of the United Nations Charter were sustained
rather than transgressed by the threat. "Desert Storm" and the
resolutions of the Security Council that preceded and followed it
may represent the greatest achievement of the principles of collective security since the founding of the League of Nations. The defeat of this supreme effort of the United Nations to overcome an
act of aggression by the use of weapons of mass destruction against
coalition forces and countries would have been catastrophic, not
only for coalition forces and populations, but for those principles
and for the United Nations. But the United Nations did triumph,
and to that triumph what Iraq perceived as a threat to use nuclear
weapons against it may have made a critical contribution. Nor is
this a case of the end justifying the means. It rather demonstrates
that, in some circumstances, the threat of the use of nuclear weapons — as long as they remain weapons unproscribed by international law — may be both lawful and rational.**

[Belligerent Reprisal Using Outlawed Weapons]

Furthermore, had Iraq employed chemical or biological weapons — prohibited weapons of mass destruction — against coalition forces, that would have been a wrong in international law giving rise to the right of belligerent reprisal. Even if, *arguendo,* the use of nuclear weapons were to be treated as also prohibited, their proportionate use by way of belligerent reprisal in order to deter further use of chemical or biological weapons would have been lawful. At any rate, this would be so if the terms of a prohibition of the use of nuclear weapons did not debar use in reprisal or obligate States "never under any circumstances" to use nuclear weapons, as they will be debarred by those terms from using chemical weapons under Article I of the Convention on the Prohibition of the Development, Production, Stockpiling and Use of Chemical Weapons and on Their Destruction of 1993, should it come into force. In paragraph 46 of its Opinion, the Court states that, on the question of belligerent reprisals, "any" right of such recourse would, "like self-defence, be governed *inter alia* by the principle of proportionality." The citation of that latter principle among others is correct, but any doubt that the Court's reference may raise about the existence of a right of belligerent reprisal is not. Such a doubt would be unsupported not only by the customary law of war and by military manuals of States issued in pursuance of it, which have long affirmed the principle and practice of belligerent reprisal, but by the terms of the Geneva Conventions and its Additional Protocols, which prohibit reprisals not generally but in specific cases (against prisoners-of-war, the wounded, civilians, certain objects and installations, etc.) The far-reaching additional restrictions on reprisals of Protocol I, which bind only its Parties, not only do not altogether prohibit belligerent reprisals; those restrictions as well as other innovations of Protocol I were understood at the time of their preparation and adoption not to govern nuclear weapons.

There is another lesson in this example, namely, that as long as what are sometimes styled as "rogue States" menace the world (whether they are or are not Parties to the NPT), it would be imprudent to set policy on the basis that the threat or use of nuclear weapons is unlawful "in any circumstance". Indeed, it may not only be rogue States but criminals or fanatics whose threats or acts of terrorism conceivably may require a nuclear deterrent or response.

Article VI of the Nuclear Non-Proliferation Treaty

Finally, I have my doubts about the Court's last operative conclusion in Paragraph 2F: "There exists an obligation to pursue in good faith and bring to a conclusion negotiations leading to nuclear disarmament in all its aspects under strict and effective international control." If this obligation is that only of "Each of the Parties to the Treaty" as Article VI of the Non-Proliferation Treaty states, this is another anodyne asseveration of the obvious, like those contained in operative Paragraphs 2A, 2B, 2C and 2D. If it applies to States not party to the NPT, it would be a dubious holding. It would not be a conclusion that was advanced in any quarter in these proceedings; it would have been subjected to no demonstration of authority, to no test of advocacy; and it would not be a conclusion that could easily be reconciled with the fundamentals of international law. In any event, since Paragraph 2F is not responsive to the question put to the Court by the General Assembly, it is to be treated as *dictum*.

(Signed) Stephen M. SCHWEBEL

[United States]

[Original: English]

DISSENTING OPINION OF JUDGE SHAHABUDDEEN

EDITOR'S OUTLINE OF SHAHABUDDEEN OPINION*

Introduction: Problems with Specific Paragraphs of *Dispositif*

PART I. Introductory and Miscellaneous Matters

1. The Main Issue
2. The Charter Assumes that Mankind and Its Civilisation Will Continue
3. The Use of Nuclear Weapons Is Unacceptable to the International Community
4. Neutrality
5. Belligerent Reprisal
6. There Is No *Non Liquet*
7. The General Assembly's Call for a Convention

PART II. Whether the Court Could Hold that States Have a Right to Use Nuclear Weapons, Having Regard to the General Principles which Determine When a State Is to Be Considered as Having a Power (*Lotus* Case)

PART III. Whether the Court Could Hold that the Use of Nuclear Weapons Is Prohibited by Humanitarian Law

1. The Methods or Means of Warfare (*Shimoda* Case)
2. Unnecessary Suffering
3. The Martens Clause

PART IV. Whether a Prior Prohibitory Rule, If It Existed, Was Modified or Rescinded by the Emergence of a Subsequent Rule.

1. The Position as at the Commencement of the Nuclear Age
2. The Position Subsequent to the Commencement of the Nuclear Age

PART V. The Denuclearization Treaties and the NPT

PART VI. Conclusion

---

*Editor's additions to original text are indicated by bracketed headings or boldface brackets.

[Introduction: Problems with Specific Paragraphs of *Dispositif*]

The Charter was signed on 26 June 1945. A less troubled world was its promise. But the clash of arms could still be heard. A new weapon was yet to come. It must first be tested. The date was 12 July 1945; the place Alamogordo. The countdown began. The moment came: "The radiance of a thousand suns." That was the line which came to the mind of the leader of the scientific team. He remembered also the end of the ancient verse: "I am become death, *The Shatterer of Worlds*".[1]

By later standards, it was a small explosion. Bigger bombs have since been made. Five declared nuclear-weapon States possess them. The prospect of mankind being destroyed through a nuclear war exists. The books of some early peoples taught that the use of a super weapon which might lead to excessively destructive results was not allowed. What does contemporary international law have to say on the point?

That, in substance, is the General Assembly's question. The question raises the difficult issue as to whether, in the special circumstances of the use of nuclear weapons, it is possible to reconcile the imperative need of a State to defend itself with the no less imperative need to

---

[1]Peter Michelmore, *The Swift Years, The Robert Oppenheimer Story* (New York, 1969), p. 110. Oppenheimer could read the verse in the original Sanskrit of the *Bhagavad-Gita*.

ensure that, in doing so, it does not imperil the survival of the human species. If a reconciliation is not possible, which side should give way? Is the problem thus posed one of law? If so, what lines of legal inquiry suggest themselves?

*

Overruling preliminary arguments, the Court, with near unanimity, decided to comply with the General Assembly's request for an advisory opinion on the question whether "the threat or use of nuclear weapons [is] in any circumstance permitted under international law". By a bare majority, it then proceeded to reply to the General Assembly's question by taking the position, on its own showing, that it cannot answer the substance of the question. I fear that the contradiction between promise and performance cannot, really, be concealed. With respect, I am of the view that the Court should and could have answered the General Assembly's question — one way or another.

*

From the point of view of the basic legal principles involved, the reply of the Court, such as it is, is set out in the first part of subparagraph E of paragraph (2) of the operative paragraph of its Advisory Opinion. Subject to a reservation about the use of the word "generally", I agree with the Court "that the threat or use of nuclear weapons would generally be contrary to the rules of international law applicable in armed conflict, and in particular the principles and rules of humanitarian law".

My difficulty is with the second part of subparagraph E of paragraph (2) of the operative paragraph of the Court's Advisory Opinion. If the use of nuclear weapons is lawful, the nature of the weapon, combined with the requirements of necessity and proportionality which condition the exercise of the inherent right of self-defence, would suggest that such weapons could only be lawfully used "in an extreme circumstance of self-defence, in which the very survival of a State would be at stake"; and this, I think, notwithstanding variations in formulation and flexible references to "vital security interests", is the general theme underlying the position taken by the nuclear weapon States. That in turn must be the main issue presented for consideration by the Court. But this is exactly the issue that the Court says it cannot decide, with the result that the General Assembly has not received an answer to the substance of its question.

I have the misfortune to be unable to subscribe to the conclusion so reached by the Court, and the more so for the reason that, when that conclusion is assessed by reference to the received view of the "Lotus" case, the inference could be that the Court is saying that there is a possibility that the use of nuclear weapons could be lawful in certain circumstances and that it is up to States to decide whether that possibility exists in particular circumstances, a result which would give me difficulty. In my respectful view, "the current state of international law, and . . . the elements of fact at its disposal" permitted the Court to answer one way or another.

As the two parts of subparagraph E cannot be separated for the purpose of voting, I have been regretfully constrained to withhold support from this subparagraph. Further, as the point of disagreement goes to the heart of the case, I have elected to use the style "Dissenting Opinion", even though voting for most of the remaining items of the operative paragraph.

A second holding which I am unable to support is subparagraph B of paragraph (2) of the operative paragraph. The specificity conveyed by the words "as such" enables me to recognize that "[t]here is in neither customary nor conventional international law any comprehensive and universal prohibition of the threat or use of nuclear weapons as such". But the words "as such" do not outweigh a general suggestion that there is no prohibition at all of the use of nuclear weapons. The circumstance that there is no "comprehensive and universal prohibition of the threat or use of nuclear weapons as such" in customary or conventional international law does not conclude the question whether the threat or use of such weapons is lawful; more general principles have to be consulted. Further, for reasons to be given later, the test of prohibition does not suffice to determine whether there is a right to do an act with the magnitude of global implications which would be involved in such use. Finally, the holding in this subparagraph is a step in the reasoning; it does not properly form part of the Court's reply to the General Assembly's question.

*

As remarked above, I have voted for the remaining items of the operative paragraph of the Court's Advisory Opinion. However, a word of explanation is appropriate. The Court's voting practice does not always allow for a precise statement of a judge's position on the elements of a *dispositif* to be indicated through his vote; how he votes would depend on his perception of the general direction taken by such an element and of any risk of his basic position being misunderstood. A declaration, separate opinion or dissenting opinion provides needed opportunity for explanation of subsidiary difficulties. This I now give below in respect of those parts of the operative paragraph for which I have voted.

As to subparagraph A of paragraph (2) of the operative paragraph, I take the view, to some extent implicit in this subparagraph, that, at any rate in a case of this kind, the action of a State is unlawful unless it is authorized under international law; the mere absence of prohibition is not enough. In the case of nuclear weapons, there is no authorization, whether specific or otherwise. However, subparagraph A is also a step in the reasoning; it is not properly part of the Court's reply to the General Assembly's question.

As to subparagraph C of paragraph (2) of the operative paragraph, there is an implication here that a "threat or use of force by means of nuclear weapons that is contrary to Article 2, paragraph 4, of the United Nations Charter" may nevertheless be capable of complying with some or all of the requirements of Article 51 and would in that event be lawful. I should have thought that something which was "contrary" to the former was *ipso facto* illegal and not capable of being redeemed by meeting any of the requirements of the latter. Thus, an act of aggression, being contrary to Article 2, paragraph 4, is wholly outside of the framework of Article 51, even if carried out with antiquated rifles and in strict conformity with humanitarian law. Further, it is difficult to see how the Court can allow itself to be suggesting here that there are circumstances in which the threat or use of nuclear weapons is lawful in view of the fact that in subparagraph E of paragraph (2) of the operative paragraph it has not been able to come to a definitive conclusion on the main issue as to whether the threat or use of such weapons is lawful or unlawful in the circumstances stated there.

As to subparagraph D of paragraph (2) of the operative paragraph, the statement that a "threat or use of nuclear weapons should also be compatible with the requirements of the international law applicable in armed conflict . . . " suggests the possibility of cases of compatibility and consequently of legality. As mentioned above, it is difficult to see how the Court can take this position in view of its inability to decide the real issue of legality. The word "should" is also out of place in a finding as to what is the true position in law.

As to subparagraph F of paragraph (2) of the operative paragraph,

I have voted for this as a general proposition having regard to the character of nuclear weapons. The particular question as to the legal implications of Article VI of the Treaty on the Non-Proliferation of Nuclear Weapons (" NPT") is not before the Court; it does not form part of the General Assembly's question. It could well be the subject of a separate question as to the effect of that Article of the NPT, were the General Assembly minded to present one.

Going beyond the operative paragraph, I have hesitations on certain aspects of the *consideranda* but do not regard it as convenient to list them all. I should however mention paragraph 104 of the Advisory Opinion. To the extent that this reproduces the standing jurisprudence of the Court, I do not see the point of the paragraph. If it ventures beyond, I do not agree. The operative paragraph of the Court's Advisory Opinion has to be left to be interpreted in accordance with the settled jurisprudence on the point.

*

Returning to subparagraph E of paragraph (2) of the operative paragraph of the Court's Advisory Opinion, I propose to set out below my reasons for agreeing with this holding in so far as I agree with it and for disagreeing with it in so far as I disagree. **The limited objective will be to show that, contrary to the Court's major conclusion, "the current state of international law, and . . . the elements of fact at its disposal" were sufficient to enable it to "conclude definitively whether the threat or use of nuclear weapons would be lawful or unlawful in an extreme circumstance of self-defence, in which the very survival of a State would be at stake".** With this end in view, I propose, after noticing some introductory and miscellaneous matters in Part I, to deal, in Part II, with the question whether States have a right to use nuclear weapons having regard to the general principles which determine when States are to be considered as having a power, and, in Part III, with the position under international humanitarian law. In Part IV, I consider whether a prohibitory rule, if it existed at the commencement of the nuclear age, was modified or rescinded by the emergence of a subsequent rule of customary international law. I pass on in Part V to consider denuclearization treaties and the NPT. The conclusion is reached in Part VI.

PART I. INTRODUCTORY AND
MISCELLANEOUS MATTERS

1. *The Main Issue*

The commencement of the nuclear age represents a legal bench-mark for the case in hand. One argument was that, at that point of time, the use of nuclear weapons was not prohibited under international law, but that a prohibitory rule later emerged, the necessary *opinio juris* developing under the twin influences of the general prohibition of the use of force laid down in Article 2, paragraph 4, of the Charter and of growing appreciation of and sensitivity to the power of nuclear weapons. In view of the position taken by the proponents of the legality of the use of nuclear weapons ("proponents of legality") over the past five decades, it will be difficult to establish that the necessary *opinio juris* later crystallised, if none existed earlier. That argument was not followed by most of the proponents of the illegality of the use of nuclear weapons ("proponents of illegality").

The position generally taken by the proponents of illegality was that a prohibitory rule existed at the commencement of the nuclear age, and that subsequent developments merely evidenced the continuing existence of that rule. For their part, the proponents of legality took the position that such a prohibitory rule never existed, and that what subsequent developments did was to evidence the continuing non-existence of any such rule and a corresponding right to use nuclear weapons. There was no issue as to whether, supposing that a prohibitory rule existed at the commencement of the nuclear age, it might have been reversed or modified by the development of a later rule in the opposite direction;[2] supposing that that had been argued, the position taken by the proponents of illegality would bar the development of the *opinio juris* necessary for the subsequent emergence of any such permissive rule, and more particularly so if the earlier prohibitory rule had the quality of *ius cogens*. This would have been the case if any humanitarian principles on which the earlier prohibitory rule was based themselves had the quality of *ius cogens*, a possibility left open by paragraph 83 of the Court's Advisory Opinion.

---

[2] For the possibility of a rule of customary international law being modified by later inconsistent State practice, see *Military and Paramilitary Activities in and against Nicaragua, Merits, I. C. J. Reports 1986,* p. 109, para. 207.

State practice is important. But it has to be considered within the framework of the issues raised. Within the framework of the issues raised in this case, State practice subsequent to the commencement of the nuclear age does not have the decisive importance suggested by the focus directed to it during the proceedings: it is not necessary to consider it in any detail beyond and above what is reasonably clear, namely, that the opposition shown by the proponents of legality would have prevented the development of a prohibitory rule if none previously existed, and that the opposition shown by the proponents of illegality would have prevented the development of a rescinding rule if a prohibitory rule previously existed. In either case, the legal situation as it existed at the commencement of the nuclear age would continue in force. The question is, what was that legal situation?

The real issue, then, is whether at the commencement of the nuclear age there was in existence a rule of international law which prohibited a State from creating effects of the kind which could later be produced by the use of nuclear weapons. If no such rule then existed, none has since come into being, and the case of the proponents of legality succeeds; if such a rule then existed, it has not since been rescinded, and the case of the proponents of illegality succeeds.

2. *The Charter Assumes that Mankind and Its Civilisation Will Continue*

International law includes the principles of the law of armed conflict. These principles, with roots reaching into the past of different civilizations, were constructed on the unspoken premise that weapons, however destructive, would be limited in impact, both in space and in time. That assumption held good throughout the ages. New and deadlier weapons continued to appear, but none had the power to wage war on future generations or to threaten the survival of the human species. Until now.

Is a legal problem presented? I think there is; and this for the reason that, whatever may be the legal position of the individual in international law, if mankind in the broad is annihilated, States disappear and, with them, the basis on which rights and obligations exist within the international community. How might the problem be approached?

Courts, whether international or national, have not had to deal with the legal implications of actions which could annihilate man-

kind. Yet in neither system should there be difficulty in finding an answer; both systems must look to the juridical foundations on which they rest. What do these suggest?

In his critical study of history, Ibn Khaldûn referred to "the explanation that laws have their reason in the purposes they are to serve". Continuing, he noted that "the jurists mention that . . . injustice invites the destruction of civilization with the necessary consequence that the species will be destroyed", and that the laws "are based upon the effort to preserve civilization".[3] Thus, the preservation of the human species and of civilization constitutes the ultimate purpose of a legal system. In my opinion, that purpose also belongs to international law, as this is understood today.

This conclusion is not at variance with the Charter of the United Nations and the Statute of the Court, by which the Court is bound. The first preambular paragraph of the Charter recorded that "the Peoples of the United Nations" were "[d]etermined to save succeeding generations from the scourge of war, which twice in our lifetime has brought untold sorrow to mankind . . .". A world free of conflict was not guaranteed; but, read in the light of that and other statements in the Charter, Article 9 of the Statute shows that the Court was intended to serve a civilized society. **A civilized society is not one that knowingly destroys itself, or knowingly allows itself to be destroyed. A world without people is a world without States. The Charter did not stipulate that mankind would continue, but it at least assumed that it would; and the assumption was not the less fundamental for being implicit.**

3. *The Use of Nuclear Weapons Is Unacceptable to the International Community*

It is necessary to consider the character of nuclear weapons. It was said on the part of the proponents of legality that there are "tactical", "battlefield", "theatre" or "clean" nuclear weapons which are no more destructive than certain conventional weapons. Supposing that this is so, then ex hypothesi the use of nuclear weapons of this kind would be as lawful as the use of conventional weapons. It was in issue, however, whether the material before the Court justified that hypothesis, the argument of the proponents of illegality being that the use of any nu-

---

[3]Ibn Khaldûn, *The Muqaddimah, An Introduction to History*, tr. Franz Rosenthal, edited and abridged by N.J. Dawood (Princeton, 1981), p. 40.

clear weapon, even if directed against a lone nuclear submarine at sea
or against an isolated military target in the desert, results in the emission of radiation and nuclear fall-out and carries the risk of triggering
a chain of events which could lead to the annihilation of the human
species. The eleventh preambular paragraph of the 1968 NPT, which
was extended "indefinitely" in 1995, records that the States parties
desired "the liquidation of all their existing stockpiles, and the elimination from national arsenals of nuclear weapons . . . ". Presumably
the elimination so foreshadowed comprehended all "nuclear weapons"
and, therefore, "tactical", "battlefield", "theatre" or "clean" nuclear
weapons also. The parties to the NPT drew no distinction. On the material before it, the Court could feel less than satisfied that the suggested exceptions exist.

The basic facts underlying the resolutions of the General Assembly
as to the nature of a nuclear war, at least a full-scale one, are difficult
to controvert. Since 1983 the technology has advanced, but the position
even at that stage was put thus by the Secretary-General of the United
Nations, Mr. Javier Pérez de Cuéllar:

> **"The world's stockpile of nuclear weapons today is
> equivalent to 16 billion tons of TNT. As against this, the
> entire devastation of the Second World War was caused by
> the expenditure of no more than 3 million tons of muni-
> tions. In other words, we possess a destructive capacity of
> more than 5,000 times what caused 40 to 50 million deaths
> not too long ago. It should suffice to kill every man, woman
> and child 10 times over."**[4]

Thus, nuclear weapons are not just another type of explosive weapons, only occupying a higher position on the same scale: their destructive power is exponentially greater. Apart from blast and heat, the
radiation effects over time are devastating. To classify these effects as
being merely a byproduct is not to the point; they can be just as extensive as, if not more so than, those immediately produced by blast and
heat. They cause unspeakable sickness followed by painful death, affect the genetic code, damage the unborn, and can render the earth
uninhabitable. These extended effects may not have military value for
the user, but this does not lessen their gravity or the fact that they result

---

[4]Javez Pérez de Cuéllar, Statement at the University of Pennsylvania, 24 March
1983, in *Disarmament*, Vol. VI, No. 1, p. 91.

from the use of nuclear weapons. This being the case, it is not relevant for present purposes to consider whether the injury produced is a by-product or secondary effect of such use.

Nor is it always a case of the effects being immediately inflicted but manifesting their consequences in later ailments; nuclear fall-out may exert an impact on people long after the explosion, causing fresh injury to them in the course of time, including injury to future generations. The weapon continues to strike for years after the initial blow, thus presenting the disturbing and unique portrait of war being waged by a present generation on future ones — on future ones with which its successors could well be at peace.

The first and only military use of nuclear weapons which has so far been made took place at Hiroshima on 6 August 1945 and at Nagasaki on 9 August 1945. A month later, the International Committee of the Red Cross ("ICRC") considered the implications of the use of newly developed weapons. In a circular letter to national Red Cross committees, dated 5 September 1945 and signed by Mr. Max Huber as acting President, the ICRC wrote this:

> "Total warfare has brought new techniques into being. Must it be accepted therefore that the individual will cease to be legally protected and will no longer be taken into consideration except as a mere element of warring collectivities? That would mean the collapse of the principles underpinning international law, which is about the physical and spiritual protection of the individual. Even in time of war a strictly egoistical and utilarian law founded only on the interests of the moment could never offer lasting security. If it denies human beings their worth and their dignity, war will move irresistibly towards limitless destruction, for the human mind, which is seizing control of the forces of the universe, seems through its creations to be stepping up this devastating momentum."

Do the rules stand set aside? Or do they still apply to protect the individual? If they do not, the seizure by man of the forces of the universe propels war irresistibly and progressively in the direction of destruction without limit, including the extinction of the human species. In time, the nuclear-weapon States ("NWS") and most of the non-nuclear-weapon States ("NNWS") would subscribe to statements acknowledging the substance of this result.

The concerns raised by the ICRC did not go unechoed. As was pointed out by several States, four months later the General Assembly unanimously adopted a resolution by which it established a commission charged with the responsibility of making "specific proposals . . . (c) for the elimination from national armaments of atomic weapons and of all other major weapons adaptable to mass destruction" (G.A. res. 0101, para. 5 of 24 January 1946). It is too limited a view to restrict the significance of the resolution to the mere establishment of the commission; the bases on which the commission was established are also important.

In line with this, on 20 September 1961 an agreement, known as "The McCloy-Zorin Accords", was signed by representatives of the United States of America and the Soviet Union, the two leading NWS. The Accords recommended eight principles as guidance for disarmament negotiations. The fifth principle read: "Elimination of all stockpiles of nuclear, chemical, bacteriological, and other weapons of mass destruction, and cessation of the production of such weapons." On 20 December 1961 that agreement was unanimously welcomed by the General Assembly on the joint proposition of those two States (General Assembly resolution 1722 (XVI) of 20 December 1961).

The first preamble to the 1968 NPT refers to "the devastation that would be visited upon all mankind by a nuclear war . . . ". The preamble to the NPT (inclusive of that statement) was reaffirmed in the first paragraph of the preamble to Decision No. 2 adopted by the 1995 Review and Extension Conference of the Parties to the Treaty on the Non-Proliferation of Nuclear Weapons. The overwhelming majority of States are parties to these instruments.

The Final Document adopted by consensus in 1978 by the Tenth Special Session of the General Assembly (on the subject of disarmament) opened with these words: "Alarmed by the threat to the very survival of mankind posed by the existence of nuclear weapons and the continuing arms race . . . ". Paragraph 11 stated:

"Mankind today is confronted with an unprecedented threat of self-extinction arising from the massive and competitive accumulation of the most destructive weapons ever produced. Existing arsenals of nuclear weapons alone are more than sufficient to destroy all life on earth . . . "

Paragraph 47 of the Final Document noted that "[n]uclear weapons pose the greatest danger to mankind and to the survival of civilization". All of these words, having been adopted by consensus, may be regarded as having been uttered with the united voice of the international community.

Important regional agreements also testify to the character of nuclear weapons. See the Agreement of Paris of 23 October 1954 on the entry of the Federal Republic of Germany into the North Atlantic Treaty Organization, Article 1(*a*) of Annex II to Protocol No. III on the Control of Armaments, indicating that nuclear weapons are weapons of mass destruction. The preamble to the 1967 Treaty of Tlatelolco, Additional Protocol II of which was signed and ratified by the five NWS, declared that the Parties were convinced

> "That the incalculable destructive power of nuclear weapons has made it imperative that the legal prohibition of war should be strictly observed in practice if the survival of civilization and of mankind itself is to be assured.
>
> That nuclear weapons, whose terrible effects are suffered, indiscriminately and inexorably, by military forces and civilian population alike, constitute, through the persistence of the radioactivity they release, an attack on the integrity of the human species and ultimately may even render the whole earth uninhabitable."

The first two preambular paragraphs of the 1985 South Pacific Nuclear Free Zone Treaty (the Treaty of Rarotonga), Protocol 2 of which has been signed and ratified by two of the five NWS and signed by the remaining three, likewise recorded that the Parties were

> "Gravely concerned that the continuing nuclear arms race presents the risk of nuclear war which would have devastating consequences for all people;
>
> Convinced that all countries have an obligation to make every effort to achieve the goal of eliminating nuclear weapons, the terror which they hold for humankind and the threat which they pose to life on earth."

The Court has also referred to the more recently signed treaties on nuclear-free zones relating to South-East Asia and Africa.

A position similar in principle to those mentioned above was taken in agreements between two of the NWS. In the preamble to a 1971 Agreement on Measures to Reduce the Risk of Outbreak of Nuclear War, the United States of America and the Soviet Union stated that they were "[t]aking into account the devastating consequences that nuclear war would have for all mankind". The substance of that statement was repeated in later agreements between those States, namely, in the 1972 Anti-Ballistic Missile Treaty, in a 1973 Agreement on the Prevention of Nuclear War, in a 1979 Treaty on the Limitation of Strategic Offensive Arms, and in the 1987 Intermediate-Range and Shorter-Range Missiles Treaty.

It was argued by some States that the purpose of possessing nuclear weapons is, paradoxically, to ensure that they are never used, and that this is shown by the circumstance that it has been possible to keep the peace, as among the NWS, during the last fifty years through policies of nuclear deterrence. Other States doubted the existence of the suggested link of causation, attributing that result to luck or chance, pointing to occasions when such weapons were nearly used, and adverting to a number of wars and other situations of armed conflict which have in fact occurred outside of the territories of the NWS. Assuming, however, that such a link of causation can be shown, a question which remains is why should policies of nuclear deterrence have kept the peace as among the NWS. A reasonable answer is that each NWS itself recognized that it faced the risk of national destruction. The record before the Court indicates that that destruction will not stop at the frontiers of warring States, but can extend to encompass the obliteration of the human species.

Other weapons are also members of the category of weapons of mass destruction to which nuclear weapons belong. However, nuclear weapons are distinguishable in important ways from all other weapons, including other members of that category. In the words of the Court:

> "[N]uclear weapons are explosive devices whose energy results from the fusion or fission of the atom. By its very nature, that process, in nuclear weapons as they exist today, releases not only immense quantities of heat and energy, but also powerful and prolonged radiation. According to the material before the Court, the first two causes of damage are vastly more powerful than the damage caused by other weapons, while the phenomenon of radiation is said to be peculiar to nuclear weapons. These characteristics render the nuclear weapon potentially catastrophic. The destructive power of nuclear weapons cannot be contained in space or time. They have the potential to destroy all civilisation and the entire ecosystem of the planet." (Advisory Opinion, para. 35.)

And a little later:

> "[I]t is imperative for the Court to take account of the

unique characteristics of nuclear weapons, and in particular their destructive capacity, their capacity to cause untold human suffering, and their ability to cause damage to generations to come." (Advisory Opinion, para. 36.)

Even if it is possible that, scientifically considered, other weapons of mass destruction, such as biological and chemical weapons, can also annihilate mankind, the question is not merely whether a weapon can do so, but whether the evidence shows that the international community considers that it can. The evidence was not specifically directed to this purpose in the case of other weapons; in the case nuclear weapons, it was, however, directed to that purpose and, the Court could find, successfully so directed. Similar remarks would apply to other weapons, such as flame-throwers and napalm, which, though not capable of annihilating mankind, can undoubtedly cause shocking harm. Unlike the case of nuclear weapons, there was no material before the Court to suggest that, however appalling may be the effects produced by the use of such other weapons, the international community was on record as considering their use to be repugnant to its conscience.

It may be added that, once it is shown that the use of a weapon could annihilate mankind, its repugnance to the conscience of the international community is not materially diminished by showing that it need not have that result in every case; it is not reasonable to expect that the conscience of the international community will, both strangely and impossibly, wait on the event to see if the result of any particular use is the destruction of the human species. The operative consideration is the risk of annihilation. That result may not ensue in all cases, but the risk that it can inheres in every case. The risk may be greater in some cases, less in others; but it is always present in sufficient measure to render the use of nuclear weapons unacceptable to the international community in all cases. In my view, the answer to the question of repugnance to the conscience of the international community governs throughout.

In sum, the Court could conclude, in accordance with its findings in paragraph 35 of its Advisory Opinion, that the international community as a whole considers that nuclear weapons are not merely weapons of mass destruction, but that there is a clear and palpable risk that their use could accomplish the destruction of mankind, with the result that any such use would be repugnant to the conscience of the community. What legal consequences follow will be examined later.

4. *Neutrality*

A question was raised as to whether damage resulting to a neutral State from use of nuclear weapons in the territory of a belligerent State is a violation of the former's neutrality. I accept the affirmative answer suggested in Nauru's statement in the parallel case brought by the World Health Organization, as set out in paragraph 88 of the Court's Advisory Opinion. A number of incidents collected in the books does not persuade me to take a different view.[5]

The principle, as stated in Article 1 of Hague Convention No. 5 of 1907 Regarding the Rights and Duties of Neutral Powers and Persons in Case of War on Land, is that "[t]he territory of neutral powers is inviolable". The principle has not been understood to guarantee neutral States absolute immunity from the effects of armed conflict; the original purpose, it is said, was to preclude military invasion or bombardment of neutral territory, and otherwise to define complementary rights and obligations of neutrals and belligerents.

It is difficult, however, to appreciate how these considerations can operate to justify the use of nuclear weapons where the radiation effects which they emit extend to the inhabitants of neutral States and cause damage to them, their off-spring, their natural resources, and possibly put them under the necessity to leave their traditional homelands. The statement of an inhabitant of the Marshall Islands left little to be imagined. Considered in relation to the more dramatic catastrophe immediately produced and the military value to the user State, these effects may be spoken of as by-products of the main event; but, as argued above, that classification is without legal pertinence. The "by-products" are not remote economic or social consequences. Whether direct or indirect effects, they result from the use of nuclear weapons, for it is a property of such weapons that they emit radiation; their destructive effect on the enemy is largely due to their radiation effects. Such radiation has a high probability of transboundary penetration.

To say that these and other transboundary effects of the use of nuclear weapons do not violate the neutrality of third States in the absence of belligerent incursion or transboundary bombardment is to

---

[5]See, for example, Roberto Ago, Addendum to the Eighth Report on State Responsibility, para. 50, in *Yearbook of the International Law Commission*, 1980, Vol. II, Part I, pp. 35-36.

cast too heavy a burden on the proposition that neutrality is not an absolute guarantee of immunity to third States against all possible effects of the conduct of hostilities. The Fifth Hague Convention of 1907 does not define inviolability; nor does it say that the territory of a neutral State is violated only by belligerent incursion or bombardment. Accepting nevertheless that the object of the architects of the provision was to preclude military incursion or bombardment of neutral territory, it seems to me that that purpose, which was related to the then state of warfare, does not conclude the question whether, in terms of the principle, "the territory of neutral powers" is violated where that territory and its inhabitants are physically harmed by the effects of the use elsewhere of nuclear weapons in the ways in which it is possible for such harm to occur. The causes of the consequential suffering and the suffering itself are the same as those occurring in the zone of battle.

It was said, no doubt correctly, that no case was known in which a belligerent State had been held responsible for collateral damage in neutral territory for lawful acts of war committed outside of that territory. It may be recalled, however, that the possibilities of damage by nuclear fall-out did not previously exist; because of technological limitations, damage on neutral territory, as a practical matter, could only be committed by incursion or bombardment, in which cases there would be acts of war committed on the neutral territory itself. To the extent that the *Trail Smelter* type of situation was likely to be a significant consequence of acts of war, the occurrence of concrete situations in the pre-nuclear period has not been shown to the Court. Thus, while no case may have occurred in which a belligerent State has been held responsible for collateral damage in neutral territory for lawful acts of war committed outside of that territory, that is decisive of the present case only if it can be shown that there is no responsibility even where substantial physical effects of acts of war carried out elsewhere demonstrably extend to neutral territory. That cannot be persuasively shown; principle is against it. The causative act of war would have had the consequence of physically violating the territory of the neutral State. The 1907 Hague principle that the territory of a neutral State is inviolable would lose much of its meaning if in such a case it was not considered to be breached.

5. *Belligerent Reprisal*

The question was argued whether, assuming that the use of nuclear weapons was otherwise unlawful, such use might nevertheless be lawful for the exceptional purposes of belligerent reprisal (i.e., as distinguished from reprisals in situations other than those of armed conflict). It seems to me, however, that there is not any necessity to examine this aspect in an opinion devoted to showing that "the current state of international law, and . . . the elements of fact at its disposal" did not prevent the Court from concluding "definitively whether the threat or use of nuclear weapons would be lawful or unlawful in an extreme circumstance of self-defence, in which the very survival of a State would be at stake". The use of nuclear weapons in belligerent reprisal, if lawful, would be equally open to an aggressor State and to a State acting in self-defence. This being so, an inquiry into the lawfulness of the use of such weapons in belligerent reprisal would not materially promote analysis of the question whether they may be lawfully used in self-defence, this being the question presented by the Court's holding.

6. *There Is No* Non Liquet

The commentators suggest that some decisions of the Court could be understood as implying a non liquet. It is possible that the second part of subparagraph E of paragraph (2) of the operative paragraph of the Court's Advisory Opinion will be similarly interpreted. If that is the correct interpretation, I respectfully differ from the position taken by the Court.

To attract the idea of a *non liquet* in this case, it would have to be shown that there is a gap in the applicability of whatever may be the correct principles regulating the question as to the circumstances in which a State may be considered as having or as not having a right to act.

If, as it is said, international law has nothing to say on the subject of the legality of the use of nuclear weapons, this necessarily means that international law does not include a rule prohibiting such use. On the received view of the "*Lotus*" decision, absent such a prohibitory rule, States have a right to use nuclear weapons.

On the other hand, if that view of "*Lotus*" is incorrect or inadequate in the light of subsequent changes in the international legal structure, then the position is that States have no right to use such weapons unless international law authorises such use. **If international law has nothing to say on the subject of the use of nuclear weapons, this necessarily means that international law does not include a rule authorising such use. Absent such authorisation, States do not have a right to use nuclear weapons.**

It follows that, so far as this case at any rate is concerned, the principle on which the Court acts, be it one of prohibition or one of authorization, leaves no room unoccupied by law and consequently no space available to be filled by the *non liquet* doctrine or by arguments traceable to it. The fact that these are advisory proceedings and not contentious ones makes no difference; the law to be applied is the same in both cases.

7. *The General Assembly's Call for a Convention*

Putting aside the question of the possible law-making effect or influence of General Assembly resolutions, did its resolutions on this matter really take the position that the use of nuclear weapons was contrary to existing law? Arguing that that was not the position taken, some States point to the fact that the resolutions also called for the conclusion of a convention on the subject.

However, as the case of the Genocide Convention shows, the General Assembly could well consider that certain conduct would be a crime under existing law and yet call for the conclusion of a convention on the subject. Its resolution 96 (I) of 11 December 1946, which called for the preparation of "a draft convention on the crime of genocide", also affirmed "that genocide is a crime under international law . . . " It was likewise that, in its resolution of 14 December 1978, the General Assembly declared "that

  (a) The use of nuclear weapons will be a violation of the
      Charter of the United Nations and a crime against hu-
      manity;
  (b) The use of nuclear weapons should therefore be prohib-
      ited, pending nuclear disarmament."

It was on this basis that the resolution then passed on to mention the future discussion of an international convention on the subject.

A convention may be useful in focusing the attention of national bodies on the subject, particularly in respect of any action which may have to be taken by them; it may also be helpful in clarifying and settling details required to implement the main principle, or more generally for the purpose of laying down a regime for dealing with the illegality in question. A call for a convention to prohibit a particular kind of conduct does not necessarily imply that the conduct was not already forbidden.

A further argument is that some of the later General Assembly

resolutions adopted a more qualified formulation than that of earlier
ones (see paragraph 71 of the Advisory Opinion). I do not assign much
weight to this as indicative of a resiling from the position taken in
earlier General Assembly resolutions to the effect that such use was
contrary to existing international law. The later resolutions proceeded
on the basis that that position had already and sufficiently been taken;
they therefore contented themselves with simply recalling the primary
resolution on the subject, namely, resolution 1653 (XVI) of 1961. Thus,
while the language employed in the resolutions has varied from time
to time, it is to be observed that in resolution 47/53 of 9 December
1992 the General Assembly reaffirmed "that the use of nuclear weapons would be a violation of the Charter of the United Nations and a
crime against humanity, as declared in its resolutions 1653 (XVI) of
24 November 1961," and other cited resolutions.

The General Assembly's resolutions may reasonably be interpreted
as taking the position that the threat or use of nuclear weapons was
forbidden under pre-existing international law. The question is whether
there is a sufficiency of fact and law to enable the Court to decide
whether the position so taken by the General Assembly was correct.
To the giving of an answer I proceed below.

PART II. WHETHER THE COURT COULD HOLD THAT STATES HAVE A RIGHT TO USE NUCLEAR WEAPONS HAVING REGARD TO THE GENERAL PRINCIPLES WHICH DETERMINE WHEN A STATE IS TO BE CONSIDERED AS HAVING A POWER
[*Lotus* Case]

The General Assembly's question presents the Court, as a World
Court, with a dilemma: to hold that States have a right to use nuclear
weapons is to affirm that they have a right to embark on a course of
conduct which could result in the extinction of civilization, and indeed
in the dissolution of all forms of life on the planet, both flora and
fauna. On the other hand, to deny the existence of that right may seem
to contradict the "*Lotus*" principle, relied on by some States, to the
effect that States have a sovereign right to do whatever is not prohibited under international law, in this respect it being said that there is
no principle of international law which prohibits the use of such weap-

ons. The dilemma[6] was the subject of close debate. In my view, it was open to the Court to consider four possible solutions.

*

The first possible solution proceeds on the basis of the *"Lotus"* principle that a State has a right to do whatever is not prohibited, but it argues that an act which could lead to the extinction of mankind would necessarily involve the destruction of neutral States. This being so, the act cannot be justified under the rubric of self-defence. There-fore, even if, *quod non*, it is otherwise admissible under the ius in bello, the Court could hold that it is not covered by the *ius ad bellum* and is prohibited under Article 2, paragraph 4, of the Charter. The question of neutrality is dealt with in Part I, section 4, above.

*

The second possible solution also proceeds on the basis of the *"Lotus"* principle. However, it argues that, due effect being given to the Charter and the Statute of the Court thereto annexed, by both of which the Court is bound, these instruments are not consistent with a State having a right to do an act which would defeat their fundamental assumption that civilization and mankind would continue: the Court could hold that, by operation of law, any such inconsistent act stands prohibited by the Charter.

*

The third possible solution also proceeds on the basis of the *"Lotus"* principle that a State has a right to do whatever is not prohib-ited under international law, but (as anticipated in Part I, section 2, above) it argues that, even in the absence of a prohibition, that residual

---

[6]The dilemma recalls that which confronted the learned judges of Persia when, asked by King Cambyses whether he could marry his sister, they made prudent answer "that though they could discover no law which allowed brother to marry sister, there was undoubtedly a law which permitted the king of Persia to do what he pleased". See *Herodotus, The Histories*, tr. Aubrey de Sélincourt (Penguin Books, 1959), p. 187. So here, an affirmative answer to the General Assembly's question would mean that, while the Court could discover no law allowing a State to put the planet to death, there is undoutedly a law which permits the State to accomplish the same result through an exercise of its sovereign powers.

right does not extend to the doing of things which, by reason of their essential nature, cannot form the subject of a right, such as actions which could destroy mankind and civilization and thus bring to an end the basis on which States exist and in turn the basis on which rights and obligations exist within the international community.

There is not any convincing ground for the view that the "Lotus" Court moved off on a supposition that States have an absolute sovereignty which would entitle them to do anything however horrid or repugnant to the sense of the international community, provided that the doing of it could not be shown to be prohibited under international law. The idea of internal supremacy associated with the concept of sovereignty in municipal law is not neatly applicable when that concept is transposed to the international plane. The existence of a number of sovereignties side by side places limits on the freedom of each State to act as if the others did not exist. These limits define an objective structural framework within which sovereignty must necessarily exist;[7] the framework, and its defining limits, are implicit in the reference in "*Lotus*" to "co-existing independent communities" (*P.C.I.J., Series A, No. 10*, p. 18), an idea subsequently improved on by the Charter, a noticeable emphasis on cooperation having been added.

Thus, however far-reaching may be the rights conferred by sovereignty, those rights cannot extend beyond the framework within which sovereignty itself exists; in particular, they cannot violate the framework. The framework shuts out the right of a State to embark on a course of action which would dismantle the basis of the framework by putting an end to civilization and annihilating mankind. It is not that a State is prohibited from exercising a right which, but for the prohibition, it would have; a State can have no such right to begin with.

So a prior question in this case is this: even if there is no prohibition, is there anything in the sovereignty of a State which would entitle it to embark on a course of action which could effectively wipe out the existence of all States by ending civilization and anni-

---

[7]The idea is evoked by the following remark of one writer: "For some writers the existence of a *corpus juris* regulating a decentralized and horizontal society is something of a miracle. I would rather say that it is something of a necessity. It is not in spite of but because of the heterogeneity of the States living side by side in a society that international law was created and developed. If international law did not exist, it would have to be invented". Prosper Weil, *Le Droit international en quête de son identité*, General course on public international law, Recueil des cours, Vol. 237 (1992-VI), p. 36.

hilating mankind? An affirmative answer is not reasonable; that sovereignty could not include such a right is suggested by the fact that the acting State would be one of what the Permanent Court of International Justice, in the language of the times, referred to as "co-existing independent communities", with a consequential duty to respect the sovereignty of other States. It is difficult for the Court to uphold a proposition that, absent a prohibition, a State has a right in law to act in ways which could deprive the sovereignty of all other States of meaning.

*

The fourth possible solution is this: if the "*Lotus*" principle leaves a State free to embark on any action whatsoever provided it is not prohibited — a proposition strongly supported by some States and as strenuously opposed by others — then, for the purposes of these proceedings at any rate, that case may be distinguished. The case did not relate to any act which could bring civilization to an end and annihilate mankind. It does not preclude a holding that there is no right to do such an act unless the act is one which is authorized under international law.

This fourth solution calls for fuller consideration than the others. It will be necessary to take account of three developments which bear on the extent to which modes of legal thought originating in an earlier age are applicable in today's world. First, as set out in Article 2, paragraph 4, of the Charter, and following on earlier developments, the right of recourse to force has come under a major restriction. This is a significant movement away from the heavy emphasis on individual sovereignty which marked international society as it earlier existed. The point was stressed by the Philippines and Samoa.

Second, there have been important developments concerning the character of the international community and of inter-State relations. While the number of States has increased, international relations have thickened; the world has grown closer. In the process, there has been a discernible movement from a select society of States to a universal international community. Thus it was that in 1984 a Chamber of the Court could speak of "the co-existence and vital co-operation of the members of the international community" (*Maritime Delimitation of the Gulf of Maine Area, I.C.J. Reports 1984*, p. 299, para. 111). The earlier legal outlook has not lost all relevance. It is reasonably clear, however, that the previous stress on the individual sovereignty of each State considered as *hortus conclusus* has been inclining before a new awareness of the responsibility of each State as a member of a more cohesive and comprehensive system based on cooperation and interdependence.

These new developments have in part been consecrated by the Charter, in part set in motion by it. Their effect and direction were noticed by Judge Alvarez (*Conditions of Admission of a State to Membership in the United Nations (Article 4 of the Charter), I.C.J. Reports 1947-1948*, p. 68, separate opinion). Doubts about his plea for a new international law did not obscure the fact that he was not alone in his central theme. Other judges observed that it was

> "an undeniable fact that the tendency of all international activities in recent times has been towards the promotion of the common welfare of the international community with a corresponding restriction of the sovereign power of individual States" (*Reservations to the Convention on the Prevention and Punishment of the Crime of Genocide, I.C.J. Reports 1951*, p. 46, joint dissenting opinion of Judges Guerrero, McNair, Read and Hsu Mo).

Though elsewhere critical of "the theory which reduces the rights of States to competences assigned and portioned by international law",[8] Judge De Visscher, for his part, observed that "[t]he Charter has created an international system", and added:

> "[I]n the interpretation of a great international constitutional instrument, like the United Nations Charter, the individualistic concepts which are generally adequate in the interpretation of ordinary treaties, do not suffice." (*International Status of South West Africa, I.C.J. Reports 1950*, p. 189, dissenting opinion.)

The Charter did not, of course, establish anything like world government; but it did organise international relations on the basis of an "international system"; and fundamental to that system was an assumption that the human species and its civilization would continue.

But, third, there have been developments working in the opposite direction, in the sense that it now, and for the first time, lies within the power of some States to destroy the entire system, and all mankind with it.

---

[8]Charles De Visscher, *Theory and Reality in Public International Law*, rev. ed., tr. P.E. Corbett, ([Princeton], 1968), p. 104.

What lesson is to be drawn from these developments, the third being opposed to the first and the second?

The notions of sovereignty and independence which the *"Lotus"* Court had in mind did not evolve in a context which visualised the possibility that a single State could possess the capability of wiping out the practical existence both of itself and of all other States. The Court was dealing with a case of collision at sea and the criminal jurisdiction of States in relation thereto — scarcely an earth-shaking issue. Had its mind been directed to the possibility of the planet being destroyed by a minority of warring States, it is not likely that it would have left the position which it took without qualification. No more than this Court would have done when in 1986 it said that

> "in international law there are no rules, other than such rules as may be accepted by the State concerned, by treaty or otherwise, whereby the level of armaments of a sovereign State can be limited, and this principle is valid for all States without exception" (*Military and Paramilitary Activities in and against Nicaragua, I.C.J. Reports 1986*, p. 135, para. 269).

The situation did not relate to the use of nuclear weapons; the Court's statement was directed to the right of a State to possess a level of armaments about the use of which no issue of legality had been raised. Caution needs to be exercised in extending the meaning of a judicial dictum to a field which was not in contemplation. The fact that he was dissenting does not diminish the value of Judge Badawi Pasha's reminder of problems which could arise "when a rule is removed from the framework in which it was formed, to another of different dimensions, to which it cannot adapt itself as easily as it did to its proper setting" (*Reparation for Injuries Suffered in the Service of the United Nations, I.C.J.Reports 1949*, p. 215).

It is worth remembering, too, that, in his dissenting opinion in "Lotus", Judge Finlay understood the compromis to present an issue not as to whether there was "a rule forbidding" the prosecution, but as to "whether the principles of international law authorize" it. (P.C.I.J., Series A, No. 10, p. 52.) In the early post-Charter period, Judge Alvarez specifically challenged the principle that States have "the right . . . to do everything which is not expressly forbidden by international law". In his view, "This principle, formerly correct, in the days of absolute sovereignty, is no longer so at the present day" (*Fisheries, I.C.J. Reports 1951*, p. 152, separate opinion).

I do not consider now whether so general a challenge is maintainable. This is because it appears to me that there is a particular area in which *"Lotus"* is distinguishable. On what point does this limited distinction turn? It is this. Whichever way the issue in *"Lotus"* was determined, the Court's determination could be accommodated within the framework of an international society consisting of "co-existing independent communities". Not so as regards the issue whether there is a right to use nuclear weapons. Were the Court to uphold such a right, it would be upholding a right which could be used to destroy that framework and which could not therefore be accommodated within it. However extensive might be the powers available to a State, there is not any basis for supposing that the Permanent Court of International Justice considered that, in the absence of a prohibition, they included powers the exercise of which could extinguish civilization and annihilate mankind and thus destroy the framework of the international community; powers of this kind were not in issue. To the extent that a course of action could be followed by so apocalyptic a consequence, the case is distinguishable; it does not stand in the way of this Court holding that States do not have a right to embark on such a course of action unless, which is improbable, it can be shown that the action is authorized under international law.

It is the case that the formulations (and in particular the title) employed in various draft conventions appended to a number of General Assembly resolutions on the subject of nuclear weapons were cast in the terminology of prohibition. However, assuming that the correct theory is that authorisation under international law has to be shown for the use of nuclear weapons, this would not prevent States from concluding a formal prohibitory treaty; the fact that the draft conventions were directed to achieving a prohibition does not invalidate the view that authorisation has to be shown.

The terminology of prohibition is also to be found in the reasoning of the Tokyo District Court in *Shimoda v. The State* (*The Japanese Annual of International Law,* Vol. 8, 1964, p. 212, at p. 235). I do not consider that much can be made of this. The Tokyo District Court, being satisfied that the dropping of the bombs was prohibited under international law, was not called upon to consider whether, if there was no prohibition, it was necessary for an authorisation to be shown; the received statement of the law being, in its view, sufficient for a holding of unlawfulness, a sense of judicial economy could make it unnecessary for the Court to inquire whether the same holding could be sustained on another basis.

Can the required authorisation be shown in this case? It seems not. The Court is a creature of the Charter and the Statute. If it finds, as it should, that both the Charter and the Statute posit the continued existence of civilization and of mankind, it is difficult to see how it can avoid a holding that international law does not authorise a State to embark on a course of action which could ensue in the destruction of civilization and the annihilation of mankind.

PART III. WHETHER THE COURT COULD HOLD THAT THE USE OF NUCLEAR WEAPONS IS PROHIBITED BY HUMANITARIAN LAW

I propose now to consider the question of the legality of the use of nuclear weapons from the standpoint of some of the leading principles of humanitarian law (a term now generally used) which were in force at the commencement of the nuclear age. These principles relate to the right to choose means of warfare, the unnecessary suffering principle, and the Martens Clause.

1. The Methods or Means of Warfare [*Shimoda* Case]

This customary international law principle is restated in Article 35, paragraph 1, of Protocol Additional I of 1977 to the Geneva Conventions of 1949 as follows: "In any armed conflict, the right of the Parties to the conflict to choose methods or means of warfare is not unlimited." The principle has come under pressure from the continuing emergence of weapons with increasing destructive power, the tendency being to accept higher levels of destructiveness with growing powers of destruction. Its value would be further eroded if, as it is sometimes argued, all it does is to leave open the possibility that a weapon may be banned under some law other than that setting out the principle itself; but that argument cannot be right since, if it is, the principle would not be laying down a norm of State conduct and could not therefore be called a principle of international law. Paragraph 77 of the Court's Advisory Opinion recognizes that the principle is one of international law; it is not meaningless. Nor is it spent; its continuing existence was attested to by General Assembly resolution 2444 (XXIII), adopted unanimously on 19 December 1968. By that resolution the General Assembly affirmed

"resolution XXVIII of the XXth International Conference of
the Red Cross held at Vienna in 1965, which laid down, inter
alia, the following principles for observance by all governmental and other authorities responsible for action in armed conflicts:

(a) That the right of the parties to a conflict to adopt means
    of injuring the enemy is not unlimited;
(b) That it is prohibited to launch attacks against the civilian
    populations as such;
(c) That distinction must be made at all times between persons
    taking part in the hostilities and members of the civilian
    population to the effect that the latter be spared as much
    as possible."

As is suggested by subparagraph (a), the principle limiting the
right to choose means of warfare subsists. Notwithstanding an impression of non-use, it is capable of operation. In what way? The principle
may be interpreted as intended to exclude the right to choose some
weapons. What these might be was not specified, and understandably
so. Yet, if, as it seems, the principle can apply to bar the use of some
weapons, it is difficult to imagine how it could fail to bar the use of
nuclear weapons; difficulties which may exist in applying the rule in
less obvious cases disappear as more manifest ones appear. But, of
course, imagination is not enough; a juridical course of reasoning has
to be shown. How?

A useful beginning is to note that what is in issue is not the existence of the principle, but its application in a particular case. Its application does not require proof of the coming into being of an *opinio
juris* prohibiting the use of the particular weapon; if that were so, one
would be in the strange presence of a principle which could not be
applied without proof of an *opinio juris* to support each application.

But how can the principle apply in the absence of a stated criterion? If the principle can operate to prohibit the use of some means
of warfare, it necessarily implies that there is a criterion on the basis
of which it can be determined whether a particular means is prohibited.
What can that implied criterion be? As seems to be recognised by the
Court, humanitarian considerations are admissible in the interpretation
of the law of armed conflict (see paras. 86 and 92 of the Court's Advisory Opinion). Drawing on those considerations, and taking an approach based on the principle of effectiveness, it is reasonable to
conclude that the criterion implied by the principle in question is set

by considering whether the use of the particular weapon is acceptable to the sense of the international community; it is difficult to see how there could be a right to choose a means of warfare the use of which is repugnant to the sense of the international community.

In relation to some weapons, it may be difficult to establish, with evidential completeness, what is the sense of the international community. But the use of nuclear weapons falls, as it were, at the broad end of a range of possibilities, where difficulties of that kind evaporate. Unlike the case of conventional weapons, the use of nuclear weapons can result in the annihilation of mankind and of civilization. As it has been remarked, if all the explosive devices used throughout the world since the invention of gunpowder were to detonate at the same time, they could not result in the destruction of civilization; this could happen if recourse were made to the use of nuclear weapons, and with many to spare. The principle limiting the right to choose means of warfare assumed that, whatever might be the means of warfare lawfully used, it would continue to be possible for war to be waged on a civilized basis in future. Thus, however free a State may be in its choice of means, that freedom encounters a limiting factor when the use of a particular type of weapon could ensue in the destruction of civilization.

It may be added that, in judging of the admissibility of a particular means of warfare, it is necessary, in my opinion, to consider what the means can do in the ordinary course of warfare, even if it may not do it in all circumstances. A conclusion as to what nuclear weapons can do in the ordinary course of warfare is not speculative; it is a finding of fact. In advisory proceedings, the Court can make necessary determinations of fact (*Legal Consequences for States of the Continued Presence of South Africa in Namibia (South West Africa) notwithstanding Security Council Resolution 276 (1970), I.C.J. Reports 1971*, p. 27). For the reasons given, there is no difficulty in making one in this case.

In making a finding as to what is the sense of the international community, it is of course essential for the Court to consider the views held by States, provided that, for the reasons given above, there is no slippage into an assumption that, so far as concerns the particular principle in question, it is necessary to establish an *opinio juris* supportive of the existence of a specific rule prohibiting the use of nuclear weapons.

The views of States are available. The first General Assembly resolution, which was unanimously adopted on 24 January 1946, bears the interpretation that the General Assembly considered that the use of nuclear weapons is unacceptable to the international community; it is referred to above. Also there are the 1968 NPT and associated arrangements, dealt with more fully below. The Court may interpret these as amounting to a statement made both by the NWS and the NNWS to the effect that the actual use of nuclear weapons would be unacceptable to the international community, and that it is for this reason that efforts should be made to contain their spread under arrangements which committed all parties to work, in good faith, towards their final elimination. If the actual use of nuclear weapons is acceptable to the international community, it is difficult to perceive any credible basis for an arrangement which would limit the right to use them to some States, and more particularly if the latter could in some circumstances exercise that right against States not enjoying that exclusive right.

In the year following the conclusion of the NPT, the Institute of International Law, at its 1969 session in Edinburgh, had occasion to note that "existing international law prohibits the use of all weapons" (nuclear weapons being understood to be included) "which, by their nature, affect indiscriminately both military objectives and non-military objects, or both armed forces and civilian population". Whatever may be said of other such weapons, that view, expressed with near unanimity, is helpful not only for its high professional value, but also for its independent assessment of the unacceptability to the international community of the use of nuclear weapons. That assessment accurately reflected the basis on which the NPT arrangements had been concluded in the preceding year.

Other weapons share with nuclear weapons membership of the category of weapons of mass destruction. As mentioned above, however, it is open to the Court to take the view that the juridical criterion is not simply how destructive a weapon is, but whether its destructiveness is such as to cause the weapon to be considered by the international community to be unacceptable to it. The material before the Court (some of which was examined in Part I, section 3, above) is sufficient to enable the Court to conclude that, in the case of nuclear weapons, the revulsion of the international community is an established fact. Thus, the legal consequences in the specific case of nuclear weapons need not be the same for other weapons of mass destruction not already banned by treaty.

In *Shimoda v. The State* the plaintiffs' claims were dismissed on grounds not now material; the case remains the only judicial decision, national or international, in the field. It was decided by the Tokyo

District Court on 7 December 1963. Though not of course binding, it ranks as a judicial decision under Article 38, paragraph 1(*d*), of the Statute of the Court; it qualifies for consideration. A judicial conclusion different from that reached by the Tokyo District Court would need to explain why the reasoning of that Court was not acceptable.

The Tokyo District Court was deliberating over the proposition (based on expert legal opinion) "that the means which give unnecessary pain in war and inhumane means are prohibited as means of injuring the enemy" (The Japanese Annual of International Law, Vol. 8, 1964, p. 240). The proposition reflected two grounds invoked by Japan in its Note of protest of 10 August 1945, in which it said:

> "It is a fundamental principle of international law in time of war that a belligerent has not an unlimited right in choosing the means of injuring the enemy, and should not use such weapons, projectiles, and other material as cause unnecessary pain; and these are each expressly stipulated in the annex of the Convention respecting the Laws and Customs of War on Land and articles 22 and 23(e) of the Regulations respecting the Laws and Customs of War on Land" (ibid., p. 252).

Article 22 of those Regulations concerned the right to adopt means of injuring the enemy, while Article 23 (*e*) concerned the unnecessary suffering principle.

The Tokyo District Court's reasoning dealt with both branches of the proposition before it, on an inter-related basis. It accepted that "international law respecting war is not formed only by humane feelings, but it has as its basis both military necessity and efficiency and humane feelings, and is formed by weighing these two factors" (*ibid.*, p. 240). Consequently, "however great the inhumane result of a weapon may be, the use of the weapon is not prohibited by international law, if it has a great military efficiency" (*ibid.*, p. 241). Nevertheless, the Tokyo District Court thought that it could "safely see that besides poison, poison gas and bacterium the use of the means of injuring the enemy which causes at least the same or more injury is prohibited by international law" (*ibid.*).

The Tokyo District Court confined itself to the issue whether the particular use of atomic weapons at Hiroshima and Nagasaki was lawful, noticing but not deciding "an important and very difficult question", namely, "whether or not an atomic bomb having such a character and effect is a weapon which is permitted in international law as a so-called nuclear weapon . . . " (*ibid.*, p. 234). Nevertheless, it is clear that in deciding the former issue, relating to the particular use, the Court's reasoning flowed from its consideration of the latter issue, relating to the legal status of such weapons. Thus, although the Tokyo District Court did not so decide, it followed from its reasoning that nuclear weapons would not be an admissible means of warfare. It is the reasoning of the Tokyo District Court that this Court is concerned with.

The material before this Court is sufficient to enable it to make a finding of fact that the actual use of nuclear weapons is not acceptable to the sense of the international community; on the basis of such a finding of fact, it would lie within its judicial mission to hold that such weapons are not admissible "means of warfare" within the meaning of the law.

2. *Unnecessary Suffering*

Then as to the customary international law prohibition of superfluous and unnecessary suffering. As restated in Article 35, paragraph 2, of the 1977 Protocol Additional I to the 1949 Geneva Conventions, the principle reads: "It is prohibited to employ weapons, projectiles and material and methods of warfare of a nature to cause superfluous injury or unnecessary suffering". The case of a weapon, such as the "dum-dum" bullet,[9] which is deliberately crafted so as to cause unnecessary suffering, does not exhaust the interpretation and application of the prohibition. That may be regarded as a particular instance of the working of a broader underlying idea that suffering is superfluous or unnecessary if it is materially in excess of the degree of suffering which is justified by the military advantage sought to be achieved. A mechanical or absolute test is excluded: a balance has to be struck between the degree of suffering inflicted and the military advantage in view. The greater the military advantage, the greater will be the willingness to tolerate higher levels of suffering. And, of course, the balance has to be struck by States. The Court cannot usurp their judgment; but, in this case, it has a duty to find what that judgment is. In appreciating what is the judgment of States as to where the balance is to be struck, the Court may properly consider that, in striking the balance, States them-

---

[9]"[T]he projectile known under the name of 'dum-dum' was made in the arsenal of that name near Calcutta". See *The Proceedings of the Hague Peace Conferences, The Conference of 1899* (Oxford, 1920), p. 277, *per* General Sir John Ardagh.

selves are guided by the public conscience. The Court has correctly held that "the intrinsically humanitarian character of the legal principles in question . . . permeates the entire law of armed conflict and applies to all forms of warfare and to all kinds of weapons . . . " (Advisory Opinion, para. 86). It is not possible to ascertain the humanitarian character of those principles without taking account of the public conscience.

It was thus open to the Court to take the view that the public conscience could consider that no conceivable military advantage could justify the degree of suffering caused by a particular type of weapon. Poison gas was, arguably, a more efficient way of deactivating the enemy in certain circumstances than other means in use during the First World War. That did not suffice to legitimise its use; the prohibition rested on an appreciation, as set out in the first preamble to the 1925 Geneva Gas Protocol, that "the use in war of asphyxiating, poisonous or other gases has been justly condemned by the general opinion of the civilized world". In effect, the use of a weapon which caused the kind of suffering that poison gas caused was simply repugnant to the public conscience, and so unacceptable to States whatever might be the military advantage sought to be achieved. That reasoning has not given birth to a comprehensive and universal prohibitory treaty provision in this case; it is nonetheless helpful in estimating the acceptability to the public conscience of the suffering that could be inflicted by the use of nuclear weapons on both combatants and civilians, on distant peoples, and on generations yet unborn.

On the material before it, the Court could reasonably find that the public conscience considers that the use of nuclear weapons causes suffering which is unacceptable whatever might be the military advantage derivable from such use. On the basis of such a finding, the Court would be entitled, in determining what in turn is the judgment of States on the point, to proceed on the basis of a presumption that the judgment of States would not differ from that made by the public conscience.

The "unnecessary suffering" principle falls within the framework of principles designed for the protection of combatants. If the use of nuclear weapons would violate the principle in relation to them, that is sufficient to establish the illegality of such use. However, is it possible that the principle, when construed in the light of developing military technology and newer methods of waging war, has now come to be regarded as capable of providing protection for civilians also?

In the "expanding" bullet phase in which the principle made its appearance in the second half of the nineteenth century, it was no doubt visualised that "unnecessary suffering" would only be inflicted on soldiers in the battlefield; the effects of the use of weapons which could then cause such suffering would not extend to civilians. But the framework of military operations is now different: if nuclear weapons can cause unnecessary suffering to soldiers, they can obviously have the same effect on civilians within their reach. The preamble to the Treaty of Tlatelolco correctly declared that the "terrible effects [of nuclear weapons] are suffered, indiscriminately and inexorably, by military forces and civilian population alike . . . "

It may be said that the substance of the principle of unnecessary suffering operates for the benefit of civilians through the medium of other principles, such as that which prohibits indiscriminate attacks, but that the principle itself does not operate in relation to them. What, however, is the position where it is contended that an apparently indiscriminate attack on civilians is validated by recourse to the collateral damage argument? In a case in which the collateral damage principle (whatever its true scope) would justify injury to civilians, the contradictory result of confining the unnecessary suffering principle to combatants would be that such injury may be prohibited by that principle in respect of combatants but not in respect of civilians who are equally affected; thus, an act which causes injury to combatants and non-combatants equally may be unlawful in relation to the former but lawful in relation to the latter. If combatants and non combatants are both victims of the same act, it is difficult to see why the act should be unlawful in the former case but lawful in the latter.

In Shimoda, *the Tokyo District Court said, "[I]t is not too much to say that the pain brought by the atomic bombs is severer than that from poison and poison-gas, and . . . that the act of dropping such a cruel bomb is contrary to the fundamental principle of the laws of war that unnecessary pain must not be given"* (The Japanese Annual of International Law, *No. 8, 1964, pp. 241-242). So, in this part of its reasoning, the Tokyo District Court relied on the "fundamental principle" of "unnecessary pain"; it did so in relation to injuries caused to civilians. Assisted by three experts who were professors of international law, as well as by a full team of advocates for the parties in a closely contested case, the Court did not seem to be aware of a view that the principle of unnecessary suffering was restricted to injuries caused to combatants. And yet that view, if correct, should have been central to a case which concerned injury to civilians. However, even if the unnecessary suffering principle is restricted to combatants, the question remains whether the principle is breached in so far as com-*

batants are affected by the use of nuclear weapons. For the reasons given above, the Court could hold that it is.

3. *The Martens Clause*

Some States argued that the Martens Clause depends on proof of the separate existence of a rule of customary international law prohibiting the use of a particular weapon, and that there is no such prohibitory rule in the case of nuclear weapons. The proposition is attractive.

However, an initial difficulty is this. As is recognized in paragraphs 78 and 84 of the Court's Advisory Opinion, it is accepted that the Martens Clause is a rule of customary international law. That means that it has a normative character — that it lays down some norm of State conduct. It is difficult to see what norm of State conduct it lays down if all it does is to remind States of norms of conduct which exist wholly dehors the Clause. The argument in question would be directed not to ascertaining the field of application of an acknowledged rule, but to denying the existence of any rule. Would an argument which produces this infirmity be right?

As set out in the 1899 Hague Convention Respecting the Laws and Customs of War on Land, the Martens Clause came at the end of a preambular passage reading as follows:

"According to the view of the high contracting Parties, these provisions, the wording of which has been inspired by the desire to diminish the evils of war, so far as military requirements permit, are intended to serve as a general rule of conduct for the belligerents in their mutual relations and in their relations with the inhabitants.

It has not, however, been found possible at present to concert regulations covering all the circumstances which arise in practice.

On the other hand, the high contracting Parties clearly do not intend that unforeseen cases should, in the absence of a written undertaking, be left to the arbitrary judgment of military commanders.

Until a more complete code of the laws of war has been issued, the High Contracting Parties deem it expedient to declare that, in cases not included in the Regulations adopted by them, the inhabitants and the belligerents remain under the protection and the rule of the principles of the law of nations, as they result from the usages estab-

**lished among civilized peoples, from the laws of humanity,
and the dictates of the public conscience."**

These statements support an impression that the Martens Clause was
intended to fill gaps left by conventional international law and to do
so in a practical way. How?

The Martens Clause bears the marks of its period; it is not easy of
interpretation. One acknowledges the distinction between usages and
law.[10] However, as the word "remain" shows, the provision implied
that there were already in existence certain principles of the law of
nations which operated to provide practical protection to "the inhabitants and the belligerents" in the event of protection not being available
under conventional texts. In view of the implications of that word, the
Clause could not be confined to principles of the law of nations waiting, uncertainly, to be born in future. The reference to the principles
of the law of nations derived from the mentioned sources was descrip-
tive of the character of existing principles of the law of nations and
not merely a condition of the future emergence of such principles. It
may be added that, in its 1977 formulation, the relevant phrase now
reads, "derived from established custom, from the principles of humanity and from the dictates of public conscience". Since "established
custom" alone would suffice to identify a rule of customary international law, a cumulative reading is not probable. It should follow that
"the principles of international law" (the new wording) could also be
sufficiently derived "from the principles of humanity and from the
dictates of public conscience"; as mentioned above, those "principles
of international law" could be regarded as including principles of international law already derived "from the principles of humanity and
from the dictates of public conscience".

In effect, the Martens Clause provided authority for treating the
principles of humanity and the dictates of public conscience as principles of international law, leaving the precise content of the standard
implied by these principles of international law to be ascertained in the
light of changing conditions, inclusive of changes in the means and
methods of warfare and the outlook and tolerance levels of the international community. The principles would remain constant, but their
practical effect would vary from time to time: they could justify a

---

[10]For "usages of war" maturing into rules of customary international law, see L.
Oppenheim, *International Law, A Treastise*, Vol II, 7th ed. by H. Lauterpacht (London,
1952), p. 226, para. 67, and p. 231, para. 69.

method of warfare in one age and prohibit it in another. In this respect, M. Jean Pictet was right in emphasising, according to Mr. Sean Mc Bride, "that the Declarations in the *Hague Conventions* . . . by virtue of the de Martens Clause, imported into humanitarian law principles that went much further than the written convention; it thus gave them a dynamic dimension that was not limited by time".[11]

Nor should this be strange. Dealing with the subject of "Considerations of Humanity" as a source of law, Sir Gerald Fitzmaurice remarked that "all the implications of this view — i.e. in exactly what circumstances and to what extent considerations of humanity give rise in themselvesto obligations of a legal character — remain to be worked out" (Sir Gerald Fitzmaurice, *The Law and Procedure of the International Court of Justice*, Vol. 1 (Cambridge, 1986), p. 17, note 4, emphasis as in the original. And see, *ibid.*, p. 4). The reservation does not neutralise the main proposition that "considerations of humanity give rise in *themselves* to obligations of a legal character". The substance of the proposition seems present in the judgment given in 1948 in *Krupp's* case, in which the United States Military Tribunal sitting at Nuremberg said:

> "The Preamble [of Hague Convention No. IV of 1907] is much more than a pious declaration. It is a general clause, making the usages established among civilized nations, the laws of humanity and the dictates of public conscience into the legal yardstick to be applied if and when the specific provisions of the Convention and the Regulations annexed to it do not cover specific cases occurring in warfare, or concomitant to warfare." (*Annual Digest and Reports of Public International Law Cases*, 1948, p. 622.)

A similar view of the role of considerations of humanity appears in the *Corfu Channel* case. There Judge Alvarez stated that the "characteristics of an *international delinquency* are that it is an act contrary to the sentiments of humanity" (*I.C.J. Reports 1949*, p. 45, separate opinion); and the Court itself said that Albania's "obligations are based, not on the Hague Convention of 1907, No. VIII, which is applicable in time of war, but on certain general and well-recognised prin-

---

[11]Sean McBride, "The Legality of Weapons for Societal Destruction", in Christophe Swinarski (ed.), *Studies and Essays on International Humanitarian Law and Red Cross Principles in Honour of Jean Pictet* (Geneva, 1984), p. 402.

ciples, namely: elementary considerations of humanity, even more exacting in peace than in war; . . . " (*I.C.J. Reports 1949*, p. 22). Thus, Albania's obligations were "based . . . on . . . elementary considerations of humanity . . . ", with the necessary implication that those considerations can themselves exert legal force. In 1986 the Court considered that "the conduct of the United States may be judged according to the fundamental general principles of humanitarian law"; and it expressed the view that certain rules stated in common Article 3 of the 1949 Geneva Conventions were "rules which, in the Court's opinion, reflect what the Court in 1949 called 'elementary considerations of humanity' (*Corfu Channel, Merits, I.C.J. Reports 1949*, p. 22)" (*Military and Paramilitary Activities in and against Nicaragua, Merits, I.C.J. Reports 1986*, pp. 113-114, para. 218). Consistent with the foregoing is the earlier observation by the Naulilaa Tribunal that the right of reprisals "est *limitée* par les expériences de l'humanité . . . " (*Reports of International Arbitral Awards*, Vol. 2, p. 1026).

I am not persuaded that the purpose of the Martens Clause was confined to supplying a humanitarian standard by which to interpret separately existing rules of conventional or customary international law on the subject of the conduct of hostilities; the Clause was not needed for that purpose, for considerations of humanity, which underlie humanitarian law, would in any event have supplied that service (see para. 86 of the Court's Advisory Opinion). It is also difficult to accept that all that the Martens Clause did was to remind States of their obligations under separately existing rules of customary international law. No doubt, the focus of the Clause in the particular form in which it was reproduced in the 1949 Geneva Conventions was on reminding States parties that denunciation of these humanitarian treaties would not relieve them of the obligations visualised by the Clause; but the Clause in its more usual form was not intended to be a mere reminder.[12] The basic function of the Clause was to put beyond challenge the existence of principles of international law which residually served, with current effect, to govern military conduct by reference to "the principles of humanity and . . . the dictates of public conscience". It was in this sense that "civilians and combatants (would) remain under the protection and authority of the principles of international law de-

---

[12]For differences between the 1949 Martens Clause and its classical formulation, see Georges Abi-Saab, "The Specificities of Humanitarian Law", in Christophe Swinarski (ed.), *Studies and Essays on International Humanitarian Law, op. cit.*, p. 275.

rived . . . from the principles of humanity and from the dictates of public conscience". The word "remain" would be inappropriate in relation to "the principles of humanity and . . . the dictates of public conscience" unless these were conceived of as presently capable of exerting normative force to control military conduct.

Thus, the Martens Clause provided its own self-sufficient and conclusive authority for the proposition that there were already in existence principles of international law under which considerations of humanity could themselves exert legal force to govern military conduct in cases in which no relevant rule was provided by conventional law. Accordingly, it was not necessary to locate elsewhere the independent existence of such principles of international law; the source of the principles lay in the Clause itself.

This was probably how the matter was understood at the Hague Peace Conference of 1899. After Mr. Martens's famous declaration was adopted, the "senior delegate from Belgium, Mr. Beernaert, who had previously objected to the adoption of Articles 9 and 10 (1 and 2 of the new draft), immediately announced that he could because of this declaration vote for them".[13] The senior Belgian delegate, as were other delegates, was not satisfied with the protection guaranteed by the particular provisions of the draft (see the *Krupp* case, *supra*, p. 622). Eventually, he found himself able to vote for the provisions. Why? Not because the required additional protection was available under independently existing customary international law; such protection would be available in any case. The reason he was able to vote for the provisions was because he took the view, not dissented from by other delegates, that the Martens Clause would itself be capable of exerting normative force to provide the required additional protection by appropriately controlling military behaviour.

"One is entitled to test the soundness of a principle by the consequences which would flow from its application" (*Barcelona Traction, Light and Power Co. Ltd., I.C.J. Reports 1970*, p. 220, para. 106, Judge Jessup, separate opinion). Hence, it is useful to consider the implications of the view that the Martens Clause is not by itself relevant to the issue of legality of the use of nuclear weapons. It is clear that the use of nuclear weapons could result, even in the case of neutral

---

[13]*The Proceedings of the Hague Peace Conferences, The Conference of 1899* (Oxford, 1920), pp. 54 and 419.

countries, in destruction of the living, in sickness and forced migration of survivors, and in injury to future generations to the point of causing serious illness, deformities and death, with the possible extinction of all life. If nothing in conventional or customary international law forbids that, on the view taken by the proponents of legality of the meaning of the *"Lotus"* case, States would be legally entitled to bring about such cataclysmic consequences. It is at least conceivable that the public conscience may think otherwise. But the "dictates of public conscience" could not translate themselves into a normative prohibition unless this was possible through the Martens Clause.

It is not, I think, a question of the Court essaying to transform public opinion into law: that would lead to "government by judges", which, as Judge Gros rightly observed, "no State would easily accept".[14] Existing international law, in the form of the Martens Clause, has already established the necessary legal norm. The Court does not have to find whether there is an *opinio juris*. Its task is that of evaluating a standard embodied in an existing principle by way of making a finding as to what it is that the "principles of humanity and . . . the dictates of public conscience" require of military conduct in a given situation. In the last analysis, the answer will depend on what are the views of States themselves; but, so far as the Martens Clause is concerned, the views of States are relevant only for their value in indicating the state of the public conscience, not for the purpose of determining whether an *opinio juris* exists as to the legality of the use of a particular weapon.

The task of determining the effect of a standard may be difficult, but it is not impossible of performance; nor is it one which a court of justice may flinch from undertaking where necessary. The law is familiar with instances in which a court has to do exactly that, namely, to apply a rule of law which embodies a standard through which the rule exerts its force in particular circumstances.[15]

Some appreciation of a factual nature may be required. The stan-

---

14 *The Gulf of Maine, I.C.J. Reports 1984*, p. 385, para. 41, dissenting opinion. But see *I. C. J. Pleadings, Northern Cameroons, 1963*, p. 352, M. Weil, " . . . il est parfois bon, pour exorxiser les démons, de les appeler par leur nom", i.e., "le spectre du gouvernement des juges".

15 See *I.C.J. Pleadings, South West Africa*, Vol. VIII, p. 258, argument of Mr. Gross; *Fisheries Jurisdiction, I.C.J. Reports 1974*, pp. 56-57, footnote 1, separate opinion of Judge Dillard; and Julius Stone, *Legal System and Lawyers' Reasonings* (Stanford, 1964), at pp. 59, 68, 263-264, 299, 305-306, 320 and 346.

dard being one which is set by the public conscience, a number of pertinent matters in the public domain may be judicially noticed. This is apart from the fact that the Court is not bound by the technical rules of evidence found in municipal systems; it employs a flexible procedure. That, of course, does not mean that it may go on a roving expedition; it must confine its attention to sources which speak with authority. Among these there is the General Assembly. Reference has already been made to its very first resolution of 24 January 1946. That resolution, unanimously adopted, may fairly be construed by the Court as expressive of the conscience of the international community as to the unacceptability of the use of nuclear weapons. So too with the Final Document adopted by consensus in 1978 by the Tenth Special Session of the General Assembly on the subject of disarmament. A number of related General Assembly resolutions preceded and followed that Final Document. In one, adopted in 1983, the General Assembly stated that it "[r]esolutely, unconditionally and for all time condemns nuclear war as being contrary to human conscience and reason . . . " (G.A. res. 38/75 of 15 December 1983). Though not unanimously adopted, the resolution was validly passed by the General Assembly, acting within its proper province in the field of disarmament. Whatever may be the position as regards the possible law-making effects or influence of General Assembly resolutions, the Court would be correct in giving weight to the Assembly's finding on the point of fact as to the state of "human conscience and reason" on the subject of the acceptability of the use of nuclear weapons, and more particularly in view of the fact that that finding accords with the general tendency of other material before the Court.

The Court may look to another source of evidence of the state of the public conscience on the question of the acceptability of the use of nuclear weapons. It may interpret the NPT to mean that the public conscience, as demonstrated in the positions taken by all parties to that treaty, considers that the use of nuclear weapons would involve grave risks, and that these risks would make such use unacceptable in all circumstances. The better view, I think, is that the Court cannot correctly interpret the treaty to mean that it was agreed by all parties that those risks may be both effectively and responsibly managed by five States but not by others. Nor could it be the case that the public conscience, as manifested in the positions taken by the parties to that treaty, *now* says that, after final elimination has been achieved, nuclear weapons could not be used, while *now* also saying that they could be acceptably used until final elimination has been achieved. On a matter touching the survival of mankind, the public conscience could not at one and the same time be content to apply one standard of acceptability as of now and another as of a later time. That would involve a contradiction in its views as to the fundamental unacceptability of the weapon as a means of warfare which could destroy civilization. No basis appears for ascribing such a contradiction to the public conscience; there is not much merit in prohibiting civilization from being destroyed in the future, while at the same time accepting that it may, with impeccable legality, be destroyed now.

If the above is correct, the Martens Clause helps to meet the objection, raised by the proponents of legality, that the General Assembly's question would require the Court to speculate on a number of matters. The Court could not say in advance what would be the exact effect of any particular use of nuclear weapons. Examples of possible situations relate to proportionality, the duty to discriminate between combatants and civilians, escalation of conflict, neutrality, genocide and the environment. The Court could however find, and find as a fact, that the use of nuclear weapons involves real risks in each of these areas. It could then look to the public conscience for its view as to whether, in the light of those risks, the use of such weapons is acceptable in any circumstances; the view of the public conscience could in turn be found to be that, in the light of those risks, such use is unacceptable in all circumstances. The public conscience thus has a mediating role through which it enjoys a latitude of evaluation not available to the Court.

In the result, on the basis of what the Court finds to be the state of the public conscience, it will be able to say whether the Martens Clause operates to prohibit the use of nuclear weapons in all circumstances. On the available material, it would be open to the Court to hold that the Clause operates to impose such a prohibition.

PART IV. WHETHER A PRIOR PROHIBITORY RULE, IF IT EXISTED, WAS MODIFIED OR RESCINDED BY THE EMERGENCE OF A SUBSEQUENT RULE

1. *The Position as at the Commencement of the Nuclear Age*

Underlying the Court's holding in the second part of subparagraph E of paragraph (2) of the operative paragraph of its Advisory Opinion that it "cannot conclude definitively" on the issue there referred to, is a contention by some States that the Court was being invited by the General Assembly's question to speculate on possible "scenarios". If that means that the Court could not decide on the basis of conjectures, I would uphold the contention. But I would not feel able to go the further step of accepting (if this other proposition was also intended) that there are no circumstances in which the Court may properly have recourse to the use of hypotheses. It would not, I think, be correct to say, as it is sometimes said, that the interpretation and application of the law always abjures hypotheses. Within reasonable limits, a hypothesis, as in other fields of intellectual endeavour, may be essential to test the limits of a theory or to bring out the true meaning of a rule. When, in a famous statement, it was said *"hypotheses non fingo"*, that only excluded propositions going beyond actual data. The actual data may themselves suggest possibilities which need to be explored if the correct inference is to be drawn from the data.[16]

The position as it stood immediately before the commencement of the nuclear age was that, since nuclear weapons did not exist, *ex hypothesi* there was, and could have been, no rule in conventional or customary international law which prohibited the use of nuclear weapons "as such". But it cannot be a serious contention that the effects produced by the use of nuclear weapons, when they were later invented, were beyond the reach of the pre-existing law of armed conflict (see paragraphs 85-86 of the Advisory Opinion and *Shimoda, supra,* pp. 235-236); the "novelty of a weapon does not by itself convey with it a legitimate claim to a change in the existing rules of war" (L. Oppenheim, *International Law, A Treatise,* Vol. II, 7th edition by H. Lauterpacht, p. 469, para. 181a).

Thus, if, immediately before the commencement of the nuclear age, the question was asked whether effects of the kind that would be later produced by the use of nuclear weapons would constitute a breach of the law of armed conflict, the Court could well hold that the answer would inevitably have been in the affirmative. If the effects so produced would have been forbidden by that law, it follows that nuclear

---

[16]For whatever is not deduced from the phaenomena, is to be called an hypothesis". See Sir Isaac Newton, *The Mathematical Principles of Natural Philosophy.* book III, Vol. II, tr. Andrew Motte (London, 1968), p. 392; and Derek Gjertsen, *The Newton Handbook* (London, 1986), p. 266.

weapons, when they later materialised, could not be used without violating that law — not, that is to say, unless that law was modified by the subsequent evolution of a law operating in the opposite direction, a point considered below.

2. The Position Subsequent to the Commencement of the Nuclear Age

A "froward retention of custom is as turbulent a thing as an innovation", says Bacon.[17] So, on the assumption that a prohibitory rule existed at the commencement of the nuclear age, it would remain to consider whether that rule was later modified or reversed by the emergence of a new rule operating in the opposite direction: would the "froward retention" of the previous prohibition of the use of nuclear weapons have been judged a "turbulent" thing?

It is necessary to have regard to the structure of the debate. The argument of some States is that there is not and never was a rule prohibitory of the use of nuclear weapons. In determining the issue so raised, a useful benchmark is the commencement of the nuclear age. The position as at that time has to be determined by reference to the law as it then stood. Subsequent developments do not form part of any process creative of any rule on the subject as at that time. If a correct finding is that, on the law as it existed at the commencement of the nuclear age, a prohibitory rule then existed, evidence of subsequent State practice cannot serve to contradict that finding by showing that, contrary to that finding, no prohibitory rule then existed. What subsequent State practice can do is to create an *opinio juris* supportive of the emergence of a new rule modifying or reversing the old rule. But it has not been suggested that, if a prohibitory rule existed at the commencement of the nuclear age, it was modified or reversed by the emergence of a later rule operating in the opposite direction. This being the case, it follows that if a prohibitory rule existed at the commencement of the nuclear age, that rule continues in force.

The same conclusion is reached even if it were in fact argued that any prior prohibitory rule was reversed by the emergence of a later rule operating in the opposite direction. The substantial and long standing opposition within the ranks of the NNWS to the proposition that there is a right in law to use nuclear weapons would have sufficed to prevent

---

[17]"Of Innovations", in J. Spedding, R.L. Ellis and D.D. Heath (eds.), *The Works of Francis Bacon* (London, 1890),Vol. VI, p. 433.

the evolution of the *opinio juris* required to support the birth of any such new rule, and more particularly so if the earlier rule had the status of ius cogens. This would have been the case if the humanitarian principles on which the earlier rule was based had that status, a possibility left open by paragraph 83 of the Advisory Opinion.

One last point. Argument was made that the NWS were "States whose interests are specially affected" within the meaning of the principle relating to the creation of customary international law, as enunciated by the Court in 1969 (*North Sea Continental Shelf Cases, I.C.J. Reports 1969*, p. 43, para. 74), and that, indeed, "in the present case, a practice involving the threat or use of nuclear weapons could proceed only from States recognized as possessing the status of nuclear weapon States" (C.R. 95/24, p. 3, translation). The argument is interesting, but not persuasive. Where what is in issue is the lawfulness of the use of a weapon which could annihilate mankind and so destroy all States, the test of which States are specially affected turns not on the ownership of the weapon, but on the consequences of its use. From this point of view, all States are equally affected, for, like the people who inhabit them, they all have an equal right to exist.

For these reasons, granted the prior existence of a prohibitory rule, it was open to the Court to hold that the position taken by a considerable number of the NNWS, if not the majority, would have operated to bar the development of the *opinio juris* necessary to support the creation of a new rule rescinding the old. The old prohibitory rule would therefore have continued up to the present time.

PART V. THE DENUCLEARIZATION TREATIES AND THE NPT

Some States rely on regional denuclearization treaties and on the NPT and associated arrangements as State practice evidencing the nonexistence of a prohibitory rule. Those arrangements, they argue, are only explicable on the assumption that the use of nuclear weapons was regarded by the negotiating States as lawful. They emphasize that for fifty years the NWS have been openly possessing and deploying nuclear weapons under one form or another of a policy of nuclear deterrence; that it is well known that several NNWS have been sheltering under the nuclear umbrella of a NWS; that the NWS and other States sheltering under a nuclear umbrella constitute a substantial and important part of the international community; that elements of the negative and positive security assurances given by the NWS necessarily imply recognition by the NNWS that nuclear weapons may be lawfully used; that Security Council resolution 984 (1995) expressed the Council's appreciation of the statements through which the NWS gave those assurances; and that no NNWS protested against those assurances or with the appreciation thus expressed. How should these matters be evaluated?

The position as at the beginning of the nuclear age was either that there was no rule prohibiting States from producing effects of the kind which could later be produced by nuclear weapons, or that there was such a prohibitory rule. If there was no such prohibitory rule, it is not necessary to consider in detail whether subsequent State practice introduced one, for the known position of the NWS and those of the NNWS sheltering under a nuclear umbrella, representing a substantial and important part of the international community, would have prevented the crystallisation of the *opinio juris* required to create such a rule: the non-existence of a prohibitory rule would continue to this day, and the case of the proponents of legality succeeds.

On the opposite view that there was a prior prohibitory rule, there is equally no need to consider subsequent State practice in any detail. As has been argued, if, on the basis of the law as it stood at the commencement of the nuclear age, it is found that there then existed a prohibitory rule, that finding as to what was the then state of the law cannot be contradicted by later developments. Later developments may only be considered for the purpose of determining whether they represented a State practice which brought into being a new rule modifying or rescinding the prior prohibitory rule. But then the known position of the majority of the NNWS, also representing a substantial and important part of the international community, would have barred the development of the *opinio juris* required for the creation of a modifying or rescinding rule: the prior prohibitory rule would thus continue to this day, and the case of the proponents of illegality succeeds.

On either view, it is accordingly not necessary to consider later developments in any detail. As there has been much debate over regional denuclearization treaties and the NPT, I shall nevertheless say something about these. In my opinion, the Court could hold that they do not show that the proponents of illegality accepted the legality of the use of nuclear weapons.

*   *

First, as to the regional denuclearization treaties. It will be convenient to deal with one only, namely, the Treaty of Tlatelolco of 1967. The preamble to this treaty stated that "the proliferation of nuclear weapons" seemed "inevitable unless States, in the exercise of their sovereign rights, impose restrictions on themselves in order to prevent it". The treaty being concerned with both possession and use, there is force in the argument that that statement recognized that there was a sovereign right in law to use such weapons. That inference does not however necessarily follow when regard is had to the fact that the preamble also said that the use of such a weapon could result in "an attack on the integrity of the human species and ultimately may even render the whole earth uninhabitable". The better interpretation of the treaty is that it was, objectively, directed to the establishment of a regime to ensure that Latin America would be nuclear-free, given that nuclear weapons in fact existed and might in fact be used; the treaty did not rest on an assumption that there existed a right in law to use weapons which could "render the whole earth uninhabitable." Reservations or declarations made by the NWS on signing or ratifying Protocol II to the treaty did rest on an assumption that there was a right of use; but it is risky to infer that, by remaining silent, States parties to the treaty acquiesced in that assumption in the light of the fact that, both before and after the conclusion of the treaty, many of them were on record as affirming through the General Assembly and otherwise that the use of such weapons would be a crime.

* *

Next as to the NPT. This calls for fuller discussion; the arguments were more intense. Some States, or one or another of them, argued that a right to use nuclear weapons formed part of the inherent right of self-defence; that the inherent right of self-defence was inalienable; that it had a fundamental and overriding character; that it was the most fundamental right of all; but that it could be restricted by express treaty provisions. It followed that some States could retain their right to use nuclear weapons, while others could competently agree to forego it. The argument adds that acceptance of a right to possess such weapons under the NPT implies acknowledgment of a right of use.

*

These arguments are weighty; they demand careful consideration. A difficulty lies, however, in the characterization of a right to use nuclear weapons as being a part of the right of self-defence. If the characterization is correct, it is not easy to appreciate how the proponents of illegality, which were parties to the NPT, would have intended voluntarily to forego an important part of their inherent right of self-defence whilst agreeing that the right would be retained in full by the NWS. The third preambular paragraph of the NPT showed that the treaty was concluded in "conformity with resolutions of the United Nations General Assembly calling for the conclusion of an agreement on the prevention of wider dissemination of nuclear weapons". Those resolutions would include General Assembly resolution 2028 (XX) of 19 November 1965, paragraph 2 (*b*) of which laid it down that a non-proliferation treaty "should embody an acceptable balance of mutual responsibilities and obligations of the nuclear and non-nuclear Powers". It is hard to see how that prescription could find an acceptable reflection in an asymmetrical enjoyment of so fundamental a right as the inherent right of self-defence.

There would be difficulty also in following how it is that what is inalienable for some States is alienable for others. It is an attribute of sovereignty that a State may by agreement restrain the exercise of its competence; yet how far it may do so without losing its status as a State is another question.[18] Since the right of self-defence is "inherent" in a State, it is not possible to conceive of statehood which lacks that characteristic. See the illustration in General Assembly resolution 49/10 of 3 November 1994, "[r]eaffirming . . . that as the Republic of Bosnia and Herzegovina is a sovereign, independent State and a Member of the United Nations, it is entitled to all rights provided for in the Charter of the United Nations, including the right to self-defence under Article 51 thereof". Arrangements for the exercise of the right of self-defence are a different matter. But, so far as the right itself is concerned, if the right includes a right to use nuclear weapons, the latter is not a small part of the former. It was no doubt for this reason that, in the parallel case brought by the World Health Organization, it was argued that to "deny the victim of aggression the right to use the only weapons which might save it would be to make a mockery of the inherent right of self-defence".[19] The argument is understandable,

---

[18]See argument of M. Yassen in *I.C.J. Pleadings, Interpretation of the Agreement of 25 March 1951 between WHO and Egypt*, pp. 298-299.

[19]Statement of the Government of the United Kingdom, in *Legality of the Use by a State of Nuclear Weapons in Armed Cnnflict (Request for Advisory Opinion)*, para. 24.

granted the premise that the right to use nuclear weapons is part of the inherent right of self-defence. The question is whether the premise is correct. For, if it is correct, then, by the same token, there is difficulty in seeing how the NNWS which were parties to the NPT could have wished to part with so crucially important a part of their inherent right of self-defence.

It is possible to see the NNWS agreeing that, because of the dangers represented by nuclear weapons, they would not acquire such weapons, on the basis that the NWS, which already had such weapons, would take steps to eliminate them. It is less easy to see how the NNWS would, on the ground of such dangers, agree to deprive themselves of the opportunity of using such weapons in exercise of their inherent right of self-defence whilst nevertheless agreeing that such weapons, notwithstanding the same dangers, could be legally used by the NWS in exercise of their own inherent right of self-defence and used in some circumstances against the NNWS. The Court could not uphold so unbalanced a view of the scheme of the NPT without endorsing the controversial thesis that its real thrust was not so much to prevent the spread of a dangerous weapon, as to ensure that enjoyment of its use was limited to a minority of States. The difference in perceived objectives is material to the correctness of the interpretation to be placed on the treaty.

A further area of nuclear weapon discrepancy could arise as between non-NPT States and the NNWS which are parties to the NPT. On the argument for legality, the former would have a right in law to use nuclear weapons in self-defence, whereas the latter would have foregone the exercise of that right even in relation to the former. For, since a NNWS, which is a party to the NPT, cannot possess nuclear weapons without breaching the treaty, it follows that it cannot threaten or use nuclear weapons even in relation tonon-parties to the treaty, although the latter, not being bound by the treaty, may have gone on to develop, acquire and possess such weapons. In the result, a NNWS which is a party to the NPT would be prevented by the treaty from exercising the full measure of its inherent right of self-defence under Article 51 of the Charter, notwithstanding that the non-party to the treaty would be entitled to use such weapons in exercise of its own inherent right of self-defence under that Article.

*

These difficulties suggest that it is necessary to distinguish between the inherent right of self-defence and the means by which the right is exercisable. A State using force in self-defence is acting legally under the *ius ad bellum*. But, whether a State is acting legally or illegally under the *ius ad bellum*, if it is in fact using force it must always do so in the manner prescribed by the *ius in bello*. It is the *ius in bello* which lays down whether or not a particular means of warfare is permissible. Thus, where the use of a particular weapon is proscribed by the *ius in bello*, the denial of the use of that weapon is not a denial of the right of self-defence of the attacked State: the inherent right of self-defence spoken of in Article 51 of the Charter simply does not comprehend the use of the weapon in question. The legal answer to the possible plight of the victim State is given by the principle, as enunciated by the United States Military Tribunal at Nuremburg on 19 February 1948, that "the rules of international law must be followed even if it results in the loss of a battle or even a war. Expediency or necessity cannot warrant their violation . . . ".[20]

A reasonable view is that the proponents of illegality which were parties to the NPT did not consider that they were contracting away an important part of their inherent right of self-defence, but that they acted on the view that a State's inherent right of self-defence did not include a right to use nuclear weapons. If they considered that a right to use nuclear weapons was an integral part of so fundamental a right as the inherent right of self-defence, it is difficult to see why they should have intended to agree that such weapons could be used only by some, and not by all. On the other hand, if they acted on the basis that a right to use such weapons was not part of the inherent right of self-defence, this governs, or at any rate qualifies and explains, the NPT arrangements, inclusive of the 1995 extension, the positive and negative assurances, and the Security Council statements set out in its resolution 984 (1995). As was pointed out by Solomon Islands, all of these arrangements formed part of a declared process for eliminating nuclear weapons; it is not persuasive to interpret them as implying acceptance by the NNWS of the legality of the use of such weapons. Answering an argument that, through the NPT, the "nuclear-weapon States were being given a legal basis for the maintenance of their nu-

---

[20]The *List* case, *Trials of War Criminals Before the Nuremberg Military Tribunals Under Control Council Law No. 10* (Washington, 1950), Vol. XI, p. 1272; and see, *ibid.*, pp. 1236 and 1254. See also the remarks of the United States Military Tribunal at Nuremberg in *Krupp's* case, *Annual Digest and Reports on Public International Law Cases*, 1948, p. 628.

clear arsenals", *New Zealand submitted, correctly in my view, that*

> *"the very* raison d'être *of the Treaty . . . is based on a recognition that nuclear weapons are different. The judgment made was that, in view of the uniquely destructive potential of such weapons, and human nature being what it is, the only option for humanity was to rid itself of these weapons entirely. The threat that the weapons represent hangs over the security of the whole international community. They also constitute a threat, and a challenge, to the international legal order." (CR 95/28, p. 36.)*

In the light of the foregoing, the Court could read the NPT this way. As stated in the preamble, all parties, both the NWS and the NNWS, recognized "the devastation that would be visited upon all mankind by a nuclear war . . . ". The spread of nuclear weapons should therefore be halted, and States which, by their own declarations, already possessed them should eliminate them. As this would take time, the NWS would of necessity continue in possession until final elimination. This was recognition of a fact which could not suddenly be wished away, and tolerance of that fact transitionally; it was not acquiescence in a right of use. Such an acknowledgment would have been at variance with the repeated affirmation by many NNWS, through General Assembly resolutions and otherwise, and made both before and after the conclusion of the NPT, that the use of such weapons would be contrary to the Charter, to the rules of international law and the laws of humanity, and a crime against mankind and civilization.

*

It remains to consider whether this conclusion is impaired by the security assurances given by the NWS to the NNWS. In contrast with the reservations made by four of the five NWS in their negative assurances of a right to use nuclear weapons against the NNWS in certain circumstances, the positive assurances did not include a commitment to use nuclear weapons in defence of a NNWS attacked with nuclear weapons and therefore did not imply a claim to a right to use nuclear weapons. A claim to a right to use nuclear weapons is however clearly implied in the negative assurances; that need not be discussed. The question is whether the claim to such a right has been accepted by the international community.

It will be convenient to take, first, the reaction of the Security

Council. Paragraph 1 of its resolution 984 (1995), adopted unanimously, recorded that the Council

> "[t]akes note with appreciation of the statements made by each of the nuclear-weapon States (S/1995/261, S/1995/262, S/1995/263, S/1995/264, S/1995/265), in which they give security assurances against the use of nuclear weapons to non-nuclear weapon States that are Parties to the Treaty on the Non-Proliferation of Nuclear Weapons".

It is argued that the "appreciation" with which the Security Council noted the statements made by each of the NWS implied an acknowledgment by it of a right in law to use nuclear weapons, and more particularly in the light of a reaffirmation in paragraph 9 of the resolution of the inherent right of self-defence under Article 51 of the Charter. The argument, which is a forceful one, makes it necessary to consider what it was that the Council's "appreciation" referred to.

Viewed in context and in particular in the light of the preamble to the resolution, the focus of paragraph 1 of the resolution was directed to the objective fact that negative security assurances had been given in the cited statements; the paragraph referred to the statements of the NWS as statements "in which they give security assurances against the use of nuclear weapons to non-nuclear-weapon States . . . ". The resolution did not refer to the statements as statements in which the NWS "reserved a right to use nuclear weapons against the NNWS in certain circumstances", as it could have done had the Council intended to indicate that its expression of appreciation extended thus far. The Council could not say so in respect of all five of the NWS because one of them, namely, China, did not reserve such a right (see paragraph 59 (*c*) of the Court's Advisory Opinion). On the contrary, in paragraph 2 of its statement, China said, "China undertakes not to use or threaten to use nuclear weapons against non-nuclear-weapon States or nuclear weapon-free zones at any time or under any circumstances"; this was the opposite of the reservation of such a right. It may be argued that the statement nonetheless implied the existence of a right to use nuclear weapons. The question, however, is how was the Security Council's expression of "appreciation" to be understood. The Court could not reasonably say that the Council's "appreciation" was to be understood as extending to the reservations made by four of the five NWS of a right to use nuclear weapons against the NNWS without also saying that it extended to China's under-

taking, to the opposite effect, not to use nuclear weapons against the NNWS "at any time or under any circumstances".

In the result, the proponents of illegality, reading the text of the resolution, would not have thought that the "appreciation" expressed by the Security Council extended to those aspects of the statements in which four of the five NWS reserved a right to use nuclear weapons against the NNWS in certain circumstances, which included a situation in which there was no prior use of nuclear weapons against the NWS reserving and exercising such a right. On its part, the Court could not understand the "appreciation" expressed by the Security Council as intended to affirm the existence of such a right without also understanding it to be affirming that, in the view of the Security Council, there were two groups of States legally differentiated in the important sense that one group was entitled in law to use nuclear weapons against the other in certain circumstances, without the latter being correspondingly entitled in law to use such weapons against the former in any circumstances. The Court would need to pause before imputing such a view to the Security Council. In circumstances in which it was known that the existence of a right to use nuclear weapons was in contest, the "appreciation" expressed by the Security Council in its resolution can reasonably be understood as directed to the fact that the NWS had given "security assurances against the use of nuclear weapons to non-nuclear-weapon States . . . ", as stated in the resolution itself, without being intended to give recognition to the existence of a legal right of use by indirectly passing on the debated issue as to whether there was such a right.

An argument of some strength is based on the fact that, in paragraph 9 of its resolution, the Security Council reaffirmed "the inherent right, recognized under Article 51 of the Charter, of individual and collective self-defence if an armed attack occurs against a member of the United Nations, until the Security Council has taken measures necessary to maintain international peace and security". Although this statement did not refer to a right to use nuclear weapons, the argument is that, in the context in which it was made, it implied that, in the view of the Security Council, the inherent right of self-defence included a right to use nuclear weapons. It would not appear, however, that the correctness of any such implication of paragraph 9 of the resolution was accepted by those of the NNWS who spoke before the Security Council. *What Malaysia said was that that "paragraph sidesteps the question of the legality of the use of nuclear weapons because it justifies the use or threat of nuclear weapons in cases of 'self-defence'"*

(S/PV. 3514, 11 April 1995, p. 15). Thus, however much paragraph 9 may be understood as seeking to justify the threat or use of nuclear weapons in cases of self-defence, in the view of Malaysia the paragraph did not succeed in doing so but only side-stepped the question. Egypt associated itself with Indonesia as "speaking . . . on behalf of the non-aligned States"; the statement made by Indonesia does not suggest an intention to abandon the known position of that group of States on the subject of legality. India specifically recalled that at "the forty-ninth session of the General Assembly, the international community decided to seek an advisory opinion from the International Court of Justice on whether the threat or use of nuclear weapons is permissible under international law in any circumstances" (ibid., p. 6). India added: "One would hope that by offering a draft resolution of this kind, the nuclear-weapon States are not telling the non-members of the NPT that they, the nuclear-weapon States, are free to use nuclear weapons against them, because this would have implications which are too frightening to contemplate" (ibid). Hence, even if the resolution of the Security Council contained any implication that the Council considered the use of nuclear weapons to be lawful, the argument that the proponents of illegality accepted the correctness of that implication is not well founded.

Next, the matter may be looked at from the more general standpoint of the conduct of the proponents of illegality in relation to the security assurances. Did that conduct manifest acquiescence in the claim by the NWS to the existence of a right in law to use of nuclear weapons? In particular, was such an acquiescence demonstrated by the fact that the NNWS thought it necessary to obtain such assurances?

A reasonable appreciation of the position seems to be the following. The continuing, if temporary, possession of nuclear weapons by the NWS obviously presented risks to the NNWS. The sensible thing would be to obtain assurances against any threat or use. Malaysia and Zimbabwe submitted that, in like manner, non-aggression pacts "were the common currency of international relations well after the illegality of aggression had entered the body of customary law" (Joint answers by Malaysia and Zimbabwe to questions asked by Vice-President Schwebel on 3 November 1995, response to the second question). Realities may need to be dealt with in a practical way; but not every arrangement designed to deal with them accepts their legality. Especially is this so in international relations. When regard is also had to the power of the weapons concerned, the Court could find that there is not any contradiction between the position taken by the NNWS in the

General Assembly that the use of nuclear weapons is a crime, and the assurances which they accepted from States which nevertheless possessed such weapons that these would not be used against them. It is useful to remember Judge Alvarez's observation that "[r]eason, pushed to extremes, may easily result in absurdity" (*Anglo-Iranian Oil Company, I.C.J. Reports 1952*, p. 126, dissenting opinion). The practice of putting aside a legal problem in order to make progress towards a desirable goal is a familiar one in international relations. My understanding of the position taken by some of the NWS is that it was on this basis that they participated in certain negotiations in the field of humanitarian law.

*

It is also important to have in mind that bare proof of acts or omissions allegedly constituting State practice does not remove the need to interpret such acts or omissions. The fact that States may feel that realities leave them no choice but to do what they do does not suffice to exclude what they do from being classified as part of State practice, provided, however, that what they do is done in the belief that they were acting out of a sense of legal obligation. "The need for such a belief, i.e., the existence of a subjective element, is implied in the very notion of the *opinio juris sive necessitatis*" *(North Sea Continental Shelf Cases, I.C.J. Reports 1969*, p. 44.) Speaking of actions which could evidence an *opinio necessitatis juris*, Lauterpacht excepts conduct which "was not accompanied by any such intention" (Sir Hersch Lauterpacht, *The Development of International Law by the International Court* (London, 1958), p. 380). So intention is material. Whether it exists is to be determined not on a microscopic inspection of disjointed features of a large and shifting picture, but by looking at the picture as a whole. When the whole of the picture is regarded in the circumstances of this case, the Court could find that the matters relied on to evidence an acknowledgment by the proponents of illegality that there is a right in law to use nuclear weapons fall short of demonstrating an intention to make that acknowledgement.

*

I should add that I am not persuaded that Security Council resolution 255 (1968) of 19 June 1968, to which reference is made in paragraphs 59 and 61 of the Court's Advisory Opinion, takes the matter any further. The question remains whether the resolution was dealing with the objective fact that nuclear weapons existed and could in fact be used, or whether it was affirming, directly or indirectly, the existence of a legal right of use.

*   *

To sum up, putting at the highest all of the matters relied on by the proponents of legality, the Court could find that those matters do not suffice to cancel out the continuing assertion of the proponents of illegality that the threat or use of nuclear weapons is illegal. It would follow that the basic difficulties noticed above would remain. If, as I consider, a correct finding is that, on the law as it stood at the commencement of the nuclear age, a prohibitory rule then existed, that finding, as to what was the then law, cannot be contradicted by subsequent inconsistent State practice; the most that subsequent inconsistent State practice could do would be to generate a new rule rescinding or modifying the old rule. But the position taken by most of the NNWS would make it impossible to establish that the necessary *opinio juris* emerged to support the creation of a new rule having the effect of reversing the old, and more particularly if the latter had the status of *ius cogens*. The prior prohibitory rule would thus continue to the present time.

PART VI. CONCLUSION

A holding that there is a right in law to use nuclear weapons would bear a difficult relationship to the Court's finding that the "destructive power of nuclear weapons cannot be contained in either space or time. They have the potential to destroy all civilization and the entire ecosystem of the planet" (Advisory Opinion, para. 35). The affirmation of the existence of a right the exercise of which could yield such grim results would come as near as might be to a literal application of the maxim *fiat justitia ruat coelum*. Judge Carneiro's view was "that no judge nowadays can blindly follow the obsolete rule *fiat justitia, pereat mundus*" (*The Minquiers and Ecrehos* case, *I.C.J. Reports 1953*, p. 109, separate opinion). It would, at any rate, seem curious that a World Court should consider itself compelled by the law to reach the conclusion that a State has the legal right, even in limited circumstances, to put the planet to death. May it be that the maxim more properly attracted by its high mission is *fiat justitia ne pereat mundus*?

The danger of the maxim last referred to is that it could seduce the

Court into acting as a legislator. In the course of the proceedings, the Court was rightly reminded that it cannot do that. To use the words of the United States Military Tribunal in the List case, ". . . it is not our province to write international law as we would have it; we must apply it as we find it" (*List* case, *supra*, p. 1249). And thus, as Judge Lauterpacht remarked, "Reluctance to encroach upon the province of the legislature is a proper manifestation of judicial caution". However, as he added, "If exaggerated, it may amount to unwillingness to fulfil a task which is within the orbit of the functions of the Court as defined by its Statute" (*Admissibility of Hearings of Petitioners by the Committee on South West Africa, I.C.J. Reports 1956*, p. 57, separate opinion). The danger of legislating arises not only where a court essays to make law where there is none, but also where it fails to apply such law as exists; the failure may well be regarded as amounting to judicial legislation directed to repealing the existing law.

International law does indeed concern relations between sovereign States. However, as it has been remarked, sovereignty does not mean that those relations are between billiard balls which collide but do not cooperate. There is at work a process of cohesion-building. It is not, and possibly never will be, sufficiently advanced to attract the full force of Cicero's observation that "the solidity of a State is very largely bound up with its judicial decisions".[21] Nevertheless, the broad import of the statement is not altogether amiss: the role of the Court need not be overestimated; neither should its responsibility be misunderstood. There is disciplined room for recalling the obligations of international lawyers. As it was put by Jenks, "We are not dealing with the routine of the established certainties of life but must frequently come to grips with the great unsettled issues on which the future of the world depends".[22] The case at bar is the supreme illustration of this truth.

*

To recall what was said at the beginning of this opinion, the great unsettled issue on which the future of the world depends is how to reconcile the imperative need of a State to defend itself with the no less imperative need to ensure that, in doing so, it does not imperil the survival of the human species. Humanitarian law, it is said, must be read as being subject to an exception which allows a State to use nu-

---

[21]*Cicero, Selected Works*, tr. Michael Grant (London, 1960), p. 36.
[22]C. W. Jenks, *The Common Law of Mankind* (London, 1958), p. 416.

clear weapons in self-defence when its survival is at stake, that is to say, even if such use would otherwise breach that law, and this for the reason that no system of law obliges those subject to it to commit suicide. That is the argument which underlies the second part of sub-paragraph E of paragraph (2) of the operative paragraph of the Court's Advisory Opinion.

The implication of that part of the Court's holding is that, in the view of the Court, it is possible that the use of nuclear weapons could be lawful "in an extreme circumstance of self-defence, in which the very survival of a State would be at stake", and hence even if human-itarian law would otherwise be violated. What the Court so sought to leave on the basis of a possibility takes on a firmer aspect in the light of the "*Lotus*" case, as generally understood. In saying that it cannot definitively decide, the Court is saying that it cannot definitively say whether or not a prohibitory rule exists. If the Court is in a position in which it cannot definitively say whether or not a prohibitory rule ex-ists, the argument can be made that, on the basis of that case, the presumption is in favour of the right of States to act unrestrained by any such rule. Accordingly, the meaning of the Court's position would be that States have a right in law to use nuclear weapons. If this was not the intended result, the Court's holding was not well conceived.

Thus, however gross or excessive the suffering, the presence of the stated circumstances could create an exception to the application of humanitarian law, as indeed is visualised by the word "generally" in the first part of that subparagraph of the Court's holding. A law may, of course, provide for exceptions to its application. At the moment, however, there is nothing to suggest that humanitarian law provides for an exception to accommodate the circumstances visualized by the Court. It seems to me that to take the position that humanitarian law can be set aside in the stated circumstances would sit oddly with the repeated and correct submissions on the part of both sides to the argu-ment that the Court should apply the law and not make new law.

One further point. Despite variations in formulation and references to the concept of "vital security interests", an "extreme circumstance of self-defence, in which the very survival of a State would be at stake", as defined by the Court, is the main circumstance in which the proponents of legality advance a claim to a right to use nuclear weap-ons. This is so for the reason that, assuming that the use of nuclear weapons is lawful, the nature of the weapons, combined with the lim-itations imposed by the requirements of necessity and proportionality which condition the exercise of the right of self-defence, will serve to confine their lawful use to that "extreme circumstance". It follows that to hold that humanitarian law does not apply to the use of nuclear weapons in the main circumstance in which a claim to a right of use is advanced is to uphold the substance of the thesis that humanitarian law does not apply at all to the use of nuclear weapons. That view has long been discarded; as the Court itself recalls, the NWS themselves do not advocate it. I am not persuaded that that disfavoured thesis can be brought back through an exception based on self-defence.

*

*   *

And thus I return to the real meaning of the General Assembly's question. The essence of the question is whether the exercise of the right of self-defence can be taken to the point of endangering the survival of mankind. To this the Court responds that "in view of the current state of international law, and of the elements of fact at its disposal, the Court cannot conclude definitively whether the threat or use of nuclear weapons would be lawful or unlawful in an extreme circumstance of self-defence, in which the very survival of a State would be at stake". That is the material holding on which this opinion hinges. In so far as that holding suggests that there is a deficiency in the law, I do not think there is; in so far as it suggests that the facts are not sufficient to attract an application of the law, I am not able to agree. In my opinion, there was a sufficient legal and factual basis on which the Court could have proceeded to answer the General Assembly's question — one way or another. And hence my respectful dissent from its conclusion that it cannot.

(Signed) Mohamed SHAHABUDDEEN

[Original: English]   [Guyana]

DECLARATION OF JUDGE SHI JIUYONG

I have voted in favour of the operative paragraphs of the Advisory Opinion of the Court, because I am generally in agreement with its reasoning and conclusions.

However, I have reservations with regard to the role which the Court assigns to the policy of deterrence in determining *lex lata* on the use of nuclear weapons.

Thus, for instance, paragraph 67 of the Opinion states

"It [the Court] notes that it is a fact that a number of States adhered to that practice during the greater part of the Cold War and continued to adhere to it. Furthermore, the Members of the international community are profoundly divided on the matter of whether non-recourse to nuclear weapons over the past fifty years constitutes the expression of an *opinio juris*. Under these circumstances the Court does not consider itself able to find that there is such an *opinio juris*."

Then in the crucial paragraph 96 it is stated

"nor can it [the Court] ignore the practice referred to as 'policy of deterrence', to which an appreciable section of the international community adhered for many years".

In my view, "nuclear deterrence" is an instrument of policy which certain nuclear-weapon States use in their relations with other States and which is said to prevent the outbreak of a massive armed conflict or war, and to maintain peace and security among nations. Undoubtedly, this practice of certain nuclear weapon States is within the realm of international politics, not that of law. It has no legal significance from the standpoint of the formation of a customary rule prohibiting the use of nuclear weapons as such. Rather, the policy of nuclear deterrence should be an object of regulation by law, not *vice versa*. The Court, when exercising its judicial function of determining a rule of existing law governing the use of nuclear weapons, simply cannot have regard to this policy practice of certain States as, if it were to do so, it would be making the law accord with the needs of the policy of deterrence. The Court would not only be confusing policy with law, but also take a legal position with respect to the policy of nuclear deterrence, thus involving itself in international politics — which would be hardly compatible with its judicial function.

Also, leaving aside the nature of the policy of deterrence, this "appreciable section of the international community" adhering to the policy of deterrence is composed of certain nuclear weapon States and those States that accept the protection of the "nuclear umbrella". No doubt, these States are important and powerful members of the international community and play an important role on the stage of international politics. However, the Court, as the principal judicial organ of the United Nations, cannot view this "appreciable section of the international community" in terms of material power. The Court can only have regard to it from the standpoint of international law. Today the international community of States has a membership of over 185 States. The appreciable section of this community to which the Opinion refers by no means constitutes a large proportion of that membership, and the structure of the international community is built on the principle of sovereign equality. Therefore, any undue emphasis on the practice of this "appreciable section" would not only be contrary to the very principle of sovereign equality of States, but would also make it more difficult to give an accurate and proper view of the existence of a customary rule on the use of the weapon.

(*Signed*) SHI JIUYONG

[Original: English]   [China]

DECLARATION OF JUDGE VERESHCHETIN

The reply of the Court, in my view, adequately reflects the current legal situation and gives some indication for the further development of the international law applicable in armed conflict.

However, I find myself obliged to explain the reasons which have led me to vote in favour of paragraph 2E of the *dispositif*, which carries the implication of the indecisiveness of the Court and indirectly admits the existence of a "grey area" in the present regulation of the matter.

The proponents of the view that a court should be prohibited from declaring *non liquet* regard this prohibition as a corollary of the concept of the "completeness" of the legal system. Those among their number who do not deny the existence of gaps in substantive international law consider that it is the obligation of the Court in a concrete case to fill the gap and thus, by reference to a general legal principle or by way of judicial law-creation, to provide for the "completeness" of the legal system.

On the other hand, there is a strong doctrinal view that the alleged "prohibition" on a declaration of a *non liquet* "may not be fully sustained by any evidence yet offered" (J. Stone, *"Non Liquet* and the Function of Law in the International Community", *The British Year Book of International Law*, 1959, p. 145). In his book devoted specifically to the problems of lacunae in international law, L. Siorat comes to the conclusion that in certain cases a court is obliged to declare a *non liquet* (L. Siorat, *Le problème de lacunes en droit international* (Paris, 1958), p. 189.

In critically assessing the importance for our case of the doctrinal debate on the issue of *non liquet*, one cannot lose sight of the fact that the debate has concerned predominantly, if not exclusively, the admissibility or otherwise of *non liquet* in a contentious procedure in which the Court is called upon to pronounce a binding, definite decision settling the dispute between the Parties. Even in those cases, the possibility of declaring a *non liquet* was not excluded by certain authoritative publicists, although this view could not be convincingly supported by arbitral and judicial practice.

In the present case, however, the Court is engaged in advisory

procedure. It is requested not to resolve an actual dispute between actual Parties, but to state the law as it finds it at the present stage of its development. Nothing in the question put to the Court or in the written and oral pleadings by the States before it can be interpreted as a request to fill the gaps, should any be found, in the present status of the law on the matter. *On the contrary, several States specifically stated that the Court "is not being asked to be a legislator, or to fashion a régime for nuclear disarmament" (Samoa, CR 95/31, p. 34) and that "[t]he Court would be neither speculating nor legislating, but elucidating the law as it exists and is understood by it . . ." (Egypt, CR 95/23, p. 32; see also the oral statement of Malaysia, CR 95/27, p. 52).*

Even had the Court been asked to fill the gaps, it would have had to refuse to assume the burden of law-creation, which in general should not be the function of the Court. In advisory procedure, where the Court finds a lacuna in the law or finds the law to be imperfect, it ought merely to state this without trying to fill the lacuna or improve the law by way of judicial legislation. The Court cannot be blamed for indecisiveness or evasiveness where the law, upon which it is called to pronounce, is itself inconclusive. Even less warranted would be any allegation of the Court's indecisiveness or evasiveness in this particular Opinion, which gives an unequivocal, albeit non-exhaustive, answer to the question put to the Court.

In its reply the Court clearly holds that the threat or use of nuclear weapons would fall within the ambit of the prohibitions and severe restrictions imposed by the UN Charter and a number of other multilateral treaties and specific undertakings as well as by customary rules and principles of the law of armed conflict. Moreover, the Court found that the threat or use of nuclear weapons "would generally be contrary to the rules of international law applicable in armed conflict, and in particular the principles and rules of humanitarian law". It is plausible that by inference, implication or analogy, the Court (and this is what some States in their written and oral statements had exhorted it to do) could have deduced from the aforesaid a general rule comprehensively proscribing the threat or use of nuclear weapons, without leaving room for any "grey area", even an exceptional one.

The Court could not, however, ignore several important considerations, which debarred it from embarking upon this road. Apart from those which have been expounded in the reasoning part of the Opinion, I would like to add the following. The very States that called on the Court to display courage and perform its "historical mission", insisted that the Court should remain within its judicial function and should not act as a legislator, requested that the Court state the law as it is and not as it should be. Secondly, the Court could not but notice the fact that, in the past, all the existing prohibitions on the use of other weapons of mass destruction (biological, chemical), as well as special restrictions on nuclear weapons, had been established by way of specific international treaties or separate treaty provisions, which undoubtedly point to the course of action chosen by the international community as most appropriate for the total prohibition on the use and eventual elimination of weapons of mass destruction. And thirdly, the Court must be concerned about the authority and effectiveness of the "deduced" general rule with respect to the matter on which the States are so fundamentally divided.

Significantly, even such a strong proponent of the "completeness" of international law and the inadmissibility of non liquet *as H. Lauterpacht observes that, in certain circumstances, the*

> "apparent indecision [of the International Court of Justice], which leaves room for discretion on the part of the organ which requested the Opinion, may — both as a matter of development of the law and as a guide to action — be preferable to a deceptive clarity which fails to give an indication of the inherent complexities of the issue. In so far as the decisions of the Court are an expression of existing international law — whether customary or conventional — they cannot but reflect the occasional obscurity or inconclusiveness of a defective legal system." (H. Lauterpacht, The Development of International Law by the International Court, reprinted ed. (Cambridge, 1982), p. 152; emphasis added.)

In my view, the case in hand presents a good example of an instance where the absolute clarity of the Opinion would be "deceptive" and where on the other hand, its partial "apparent indecision" may prove useful "as a guide to action".

If I may be allowed the comparison, the construction of the solid edifice for the total prohibition on the use of nuclear weapons is not yet complete. This, however, is not because of the lack of building materials, but rather because of the unwillingness and objections of a sizeable number of the builders of this edifice. If this future edifice is to withstand the test of time and the vagaries of the international climate, it is the States themselves — rather than the Court with its limited building resources — that must shoulder

the burden of bringing the construction process to completion. At the same time, the Court has clearly shown that the edifice of the total prohibition on the threat or use of nuclear weapons is being constructed and a great deal has already been achieved.

The Court has also shown that the most appropriate means for putting an end to the existence of any "grey areas" in the legal status of nuclear weapons would be "nuclear disarmament in all its aspects under strict and effective international control". Accordingly, the Court has found that there exists an obligation of States to pursue in good faith and bring to a conclusion negotiations leading to this supreme goal.

(Signed) Vladlen S. VERESHCHETIN

[Original: English]   [Russian Federation]

DISSENTING OPINION OF JUDGE KOROMA

EDITOR'S OUTLINE OF KOROMA OPINION*

1. Court Could Have Ruled Definitively
2. UN Charter Articles 2.4 and 51
3. Elements of Fact
      Mayor of Hiroshima
      Mayor of Nagasaki
      Delegation of the Marshall Islands
4. Purpose of Advisory Opinions
5. Belligerent Reprisals
6. UN Charter Article 2.1
7. Genocide Convention
8. Right to Human Life: I.C.C.P.R. Article 6
9. Significance of This Opinion
10. Conclusion

*Editor's additions to original text are indicated by bracketed headings or boldface brackets.

It is a matter of profound regret to me that I have been compelled to append this Dissenting Opinion to the Advisory Opinion rendered by the Court, as I fundamentally disagree with its finding — secured by the President's casting vote — that:

> "in view of the current state of international law, and of the elements of fact at its disposal, the Court cannot conclude definitively **whether the threat or use of nuclear weapons would be lawful or unlawful in an extreme circumstance of self-defence, in which the very survival of a State would be at stake**".

This finding, in my considered opinion, is not only unsustainable on the basis of existing international law, but, as I shall demonstrate later, is totally at variance with the weight and abundance of material presented to the Court. The finding is all the more regrettable in view of the fact that the Court had itself reached a conclusion that:

"the threat or use of nuclear weapons would generally be contrary to the rules of international law applicable in armed conflict, and in particular the principles and rules of humanitarian law".

A finding with which I concur, save for the word "generally". It is my considered opinion based on the existing law and the available evidence that the use of nuclear weapons in any circumstance would be unlawful under international law. That use would at the very least result in the violation of the principles and rules of international humanitarian law, and would therefore be contrary to that law.

I am also unable to agree with various aspects of the reasoning which motivates the Advisory Opinion. Some of it, in my view, is not only untenable in law, but may even have the effect of potentially destabilizing the existing international legal order.

According to the material before the Court, it is estimated that more than 40,000 nuclear warheads exist in the world today with a total destructive capacity around a million times greater than that of the bomb which devastated Hiroshima. A single nuclear bomb detonated over a large city is said to be capable of killing more than 1 million people. These weapons, if used massively, could result in the annihilation of the human race and the extinction of human civilization. Nuclear weapons are thus not just another kind of weapon, they are considered the absolute weapon and are far more pervasive in terms of their destructive effects than any conventional weapon. A request for an advisory opinion asking for a determination about the lawfulness or otherwise of the use of such weapons is a matter which, in my considered opinion, this Court as a court of law and the guardian of legality in the United Nations system should be capable of making.

While it is admitted that the views of States are divided on the question of nuclear weapons, as well as about their possible consequences, views are also divided as to whether the Court should have been asked to render an opinion on the matter at all. However, the Court, having found that the General Assembly was competent to ask the question and in the absence of any "compelling reason" relating to propriety or to any issue that would compromise its judicial character, should have performed its judicial function in accordance with Article 38 of its Statute and determined the question, "in accordance with international law", by simultaneously applying international conventions, international custom as established rules recognized by States or as evidence of general practice accepted as law or the general principles of law recognized by all States, the judicial decisions of the Court and resolutions of international organizations, at a minimum as evidence of the law.In my view, the prevention of war, by the use of nuclear weapons, is a matter for international law and, if the Court is requested to determine such an issue, it falls within its competence to do so. Its decision can contribute to the prevention of war by ensuring respect for the law. The Court in the *Corfu Channel* case described as its function "the need to ensure respect for international law of which it is the organ" (*I.C.J. Reports 1949*, p. 35). The late Judge Nagendra Singh, a former Member and President of this Court, commenting on that statement, observed that it was made by the Court without reference to the United Nations Charter or to its own Statute. He observed that "the Court has thus to be conscious of this fact, as something inherent to its existence in relation to the law which it administers" ("The Role and Record of the International Court of Justice", p. 173). Today a system of war prevention exists in international law, and comprises the prohibition of the use of force, the collective security provisions of the United Nations Charter for the maintenance of international peace, the obligation to resort to peaceful means for the settlement of international disputes and the regulations on weapons prohibition, arms limitation and disarmament. The Court's Advisory Opinion in this case could have strengthened this regime by serving as a shield of humanity.

[1. Court Could Have Ruled Definitively]

In my view, it is wholly incoherent in the light of the material before the Court to say that it cannot rule definitively on the matter now before it in view of the current state of the law and because of the elements of facts at its disposal, for neither the law nor the facts are so imprecise or inadequate as to prevent the Court from reaching a definitive conclusion on the matter. On the other hand, the Court's findings could be construed as suggesting either that there is a gap, a lacuna, in the existing law or that the Court is unable to reach a definitive conclusion on the matter because the law is imprecise or its content insufficient or that it simply does not exist. It does not appear to me any new principles are needed for a determination of the matter to be made. All that was requested of the Court was to apply the existing law. A finding of *non liquet* is wholly unfounded in the present case. The Court has always taken the view that the burden of establishing the law is on the Court and not on the Parties. The Court has stated that:

> "there is no incompatibility with its judicial function in making a pronouncement on the rights and duties of the Parties under existing international law which would clearly be capable of having a forward reach . . . The possibility of the law changing is ever present: but that cannot relieve the Court from its obligation to render a judgment on the basis of the law as it exists at the time of its decision . . . " (*Fisheries Jurisdiction Case, I.C.J. Reports 1974*, p. 20.)

The *corpus juris* on the matter is not only considerable, but is sufficiently clear and precise for the Court to have been able to make a definitive finding. If the Court had applied the whole spectrum of the law, including international conventions, rules of customary international law, general principles of international law, judicial decisions, as well as resolutions of international organizations, there would have been no room for a purported finding of *non liquet*.

Furthermore, all States — both the nuclear-weapon and non-nuclear-weapon States — are agreed that the rules of international law applicable in armed conflict, particularly international humanitarian law, apply to the use of nuclear weapons. This law, which has been formulated and codified to restrict the use of various weapons and methods of warfare, is intended to limit the terrible effects of war. Central to it is the principle of humanity which above all aims to mitigate the effects of war on civilians and combatants alike. It is this law which also establishes a regime on the basis of which the methods and means of warfare are to be judged. Accordingly, it would seem apposite and justifiable for the effects of a conflict involving nuclear weapons — regarded as the ultimate weapon of mass destruction — to be judged against the standards of such a regime.

Despite its findings, the Court has itself recognized that the law of armed conflict, and in particular the principles and rules of humanitarian law — would apply to a conflict involving the use of nuclear weapons. It follows that the Court's finding that it cannot conclude definitively whether the threat or use of nuclear weapons would be lawful or unlawful in an extreme circumstance of self-defence, in which the very survival of a State would be at stake, is a contradiction and can at best be described as the identification of two principles, namely, the obligation to comply with the principles and rules of international law applicable in armed conflict and the right of a State to self-defence including when it considers its very survival to be at stake. [T]hese principles are not mutually exclusive and are recognized in international law. However, it has been argued that when the Court is faced with two competing principles or rights, it should jurisprudentially assign a priority to one of them and cause it to prevail. In the opinion of Sir Hersch Lauterpacht, even though the margin of preference for giving a priority to one principle over another may be small, yet, however tenuous, that margin must be decisive. He admits that judicial action along this line may in some respects be indistinguishable from judicial legislation. However, he argues, the Court "may have to effect a compromise — which is not a diplomatic but a legitimate judicial compromise — between competing principles of law", and concludes that:

> "there is no decisive reason why the Court should avoid at all cost some such outcome. It is in accordance with the true function of the Court that the dispute submitted to it should be determined by its own decision and not by the contingent operation of an attitude of accommodation on the part of the disputants. There is an embarrassing anticlimax, which is not legally irrelevant, in a situation in which the Court, after prolonged written and oral pleadings, is impelled to leave the settlement of the actual issue to . . . the parties." (*The Development of International Law by the International Court*, p. 146.)

[2. UN Charter Articles 2.4 and 51]

The suggestion that it should be left to individual States to determine whether or not it may be lawful to have recourse to nuclear weapons, is not only an option fraught with serious danger, both for the States that may be directly involved in conflict, and for those nations not involved, but may also suggest that such an option is not legally reprehensible. Accordingly, the Court, instead of leaving it to each State to decide whether or not it would be lawful or unlawful to use nuclear weapons in an extreme circumstance of "State survival", should have determined whether or not it is permissible to use nuclear weapons even in a case involving the survival of the state. **The question put to the Court is whether it is lawful to use nuclear weapons** and is not about the survival of the state, which is what the Court's reply turned on. If the Court had correctly interpreted the question this would not only have had the effect of declaring the law regarding the use of nuclear weapons but could well have deterred the use of such weapons. Regrettably, the Court refrained not only from performing its judicial function, but, by its "non-finding", appears to have made serious inroads into the present legal restraints relating to the use of nuclear weapons, while throwing the regime of self-defence into doubt by creating a new category called the "survival of the State", seen as constituting an exception to Articles 2, paragraph 4, and 51 of the United Nations Charter and to the principles and rules of humanitarian law. In effect, this kind of restraint would seem to be tantamount to judicial legislation at a time when the Court has itself — rightly in my view — recognized that it "cannot legislate", and, that

> "in the circumstances of the present case, *it is not* called upon *to do so*. Rather its task is to engage in its normal judicial function of ascertaining the existence or otherwise of legal principles and rules applicable to the threat or use of nuclear weapons." (Advisory Opinion, para. 18.)

However, just after reaffirming this self-denying ordinance, the Court went on to do just that by proclaiming that it cannot conclude definitively whether or not the threat or use of nuclear weapons would be "lawful or unlawful in an extreme circumstance of self-defence, in which the very survival of a State would be at stake", given the current state of international law and the elements of fact at its disposal. This finding, with respect, is not only untenable in law but legally superfluous. The right of self-defence is inherent and fundamental to all States. It exists within and not outside or above the law. To suggest that it exists outside or above the law is to render it probable that force may be used unilaterally by a State when it by itself considers its survival to be at stake. The right of self-defence is not a licence to use force; it is regulated by law and was never intended to threaten the security of other states.

Thus the Court's finding does not only appear tantamount to judicial legislation which undermines the regime of the non-use of force as enshrined in Article 2, paragraph 4, of the Charter, and that of self-defence as embodied in Article 51, but the doctrine of the survival of the State represents a throwback to the law before the adoption of the

United Nations Charter and is even redolent of a period long before that. Grotius, writing in the seventeenth century, stated that: "[t]he right of self-defence . . . has its origin directly, and chiefly, in the fact that nature commits to each his own protection" (Grotius, *De Jure Belli Ac Pacis*, bk. II, ch. I, pt. III, at 172 (Carnegie Endowment trans. 1925) (1646)). Thus, the Court's finding would appear to be tantamount to according to each State the exclusive right to decide for itself to use nuclear weapons when its survival is at stake as that State perceives it — a decision subjected neither to the law nor to third party adjudication. When Lauterpacht had to consider a similar situation following the conclusion of the Briand-Kellog Pact of 1928, according to which the participating States declared that a State claiming the right of self-defence "alone is competent to decide whether circumstances require recourse to war in self-defence", he found such a claim to be "self-contradictory in as much as it purports to be based on legal right and at the same time, it dissociates itself from regulations and evaluation of the law". While he acknowledged the right of self-defence as "absolute" in the sense that no law could disregard it, Lauterpacht however maintained that the right is "relative" in as much as it is presumably regulated by law. "It is regulated to the extent that it is the business of the Courts to determine whether, how far, and for how long, there was a necessity to have recourse to it" ("The Function of Law in the International Community", pp. 179-180).

As already stated, the Court's present finding represents a challenge to some of the fundamental precepts of existing international law including the proscription of the use of force in international relations and the exercise of the right of self-defence. That the Court cannot decide definitively whether the use of nuclear weapons would be lawful or unlawful when the survival of the State is at stake is a confirmation of the assertion that the survival of that State is not only not a matter for the law but that a State, in order to ensure its survival, can wipe out the rest of humanity by having recourse to nuclear weapons. In its historical garb "of the fundamental right of self-preservation", such a right was used in the past as a pretext for the violation of the sovereignty of other States. Such acts are now considered unlawful under contemporary international law. **The International Military Tribunal at Nuremburg in 1946 rejected the argument that the State involved had acted in self-defence and that every State must be the judge of whether, in a given case, it is entitled to decide whether to exercise the right of self-defence. The Tribunal held that "whether action taken under the claim of self-defence was in fact** aggressive or defensive must ultimately be subject to investigation or adjudication if international law is ever to be enforced" (*Judgment of the International Military Tribunal at Nuremburg, 1946, Trial of German Major War Criminals before the International Military Tribunal (1947)*, Vol. I, p. 208).

Similarly, this Court, in the *Nicaragua* case, rejected the assertion that the right of self-defence is not subject to international law. While noting that Article 51 of the United Nations Charter recognizes a "natural" or "inherent" right of self-defence, it stated that "it is hard to see how this can be other than of a customary nature, even if its present content has been confirmed by the Charter" (*I.C.J. Reports 1986*, p. 94). By its present findings, the Court would appear to be departing from its own jurisprudence by saying that it cannot determine conclusively whether or not it would be lawful for a State to use nuclear weapons.

Be that as it may, it is not as if the Court was compelled to reach such a conclusion, for the law is clear. The use of force is firmly and peremptorily prohibited by Article 2, paragraph 4, of the United Nations Charter. The regime of self-defence or the doctrine of "self-survival", as the Court would prefer to have it, is likewise regulated and subjected to that law. The right of self-defence by a State is clearly stipulated in Article 51 of the Charter, as follows:

"Nothing in the present Charter shall impair the inherent right of individual or collective self-defence if an armed attack occurs against a Member of the United Nations, until the Security Council has taken measures necessary to maintain international peace and security. Measures taken by Members in the exercise of this right of self-defence shall be immediately reported to the Security Council and shall not in any way affect the authority and responsibility of the Security Council under the present Charter to take at any time such action as it deems necessary in order to maintain or restore international peace and security."

Thus, the Article permits the exercise of that right subject to the conditions stipulated therein. Firstly, in order to exercise the right, a State must have been the victim of an armed attack and, while exercising such a right, it must observe the principle of proportionality. Secondly, the measure or measures taken in exercise of such a right must be reported to the Security Council and are to be discontinued as soon as the Security Council itself has taken measures necessary for the maintenance of international peace. Article 51 therefore envisages the ability of a State *lawfully* to defend itself against armed attack. The Court emphasized this when it stated that the right of self-defence under Article 51 is conditioned by necessity and proportionality and that these conditions would apply whatever the means of force employed. Moreover, self-defence must also meet the requirements of the law applicable in armed conflict, particularly the principles and rules of international humanitarian law.

The question therefore is not whether a State is entitled to exercise its right of self-defence in an extreme circumstance in which the very survival of that State would be at stake, but rather whether the use of nuclear weapons would be lawful or unlawful under any circumstance including an extreme circumstance in which its very survival was at stake — or, in other words, whether it is possible to conceive of consequences of the use of such weapons which do not entail an infringement of international law applicable in armed conflict, particularly international humanitarian law. As stated above, in terms of the law, the right of self-defence is restricted to the repulse of an armed attack and does not permit of retaliatory or punitive action. Nor is it an exception to the *jus in bello* (conduct of hostilities). Since, in the light of the law and the facts, it is inconceivable that the use of nuclear weapons would not entail an infringement of, at the very least, the law applicable in armed conflict, particularly humanitarian law, it follows that the use of such weapons would be unlawful. Nuclear weapons do not constitute an exception to humanitarian law.

Given these considerations, it is not legally sustainable to find, as the Court has done, that, in view of the present state of the law, it cannot conclude definitively whether the threat or use of nuclear weapons would be lawful or unlawful in an extreme circumstance of self-survival, for as it stated in the *Nicaragua* case:

> "the conduct of States should, in general, be consistent with
> . . . rules, and that instances of State conduct inconsistent with
> a given rule should generally have been treated as breaches of
> that rule, not as indications of the recognition of that rule"
> (*I.C.J. Report 1986*, p. 98).

Judge Mosler, a former member of this Court has in another context, stated .

> "*that law cannot recognise any act either of one member or of*

several members in concert, as being legally valid if it is directed against the very foundation of law". *(H. Mosler,* The International Society as a Legal Community *(1980), p. 18).*

The Court's finding is also untenable, for, and as already mentioned, the *corpus juris* on which it should have reached its conclusion does indeed exist, and in an ample and substantial form. The Court had itself taken cognizance of this when it noted that the "laws and customs of war" applicable to the matter before it had been codified in The Hague Conventions of 1899 and 1907, based upon the 1868 Declaration of St. Petersburg as well as the results of the Brussels Conference of 1874. The Court also recognized that "The Hague Law" and, more particularly, the Regulations Respecting the Laws and Customs of War on Land, do regulate the rights and duties of belligerent States in the conduct of their hostilities and limit the choice of methods and means of injuring the enemy in wartime. It found that the "Geneva Law" (the Conventions of 1864, 1906, 1929 and 1949), which protects the victims of war and aims to provide safeguards for disabled armed forces personnel and persons not taking part in the hostilities, is equally applicable to the issue before it. It noted that these two branches of law today constitute international humanitarian law which was codified in the 1977 Additional Protocols to the Geneva Conventions of 1949.

It observed that, since the turn of the century, certain weapons, such as explosive projectiles under 400 g, dum-dum bullets and asphyxiating gases, have been specifically prohibited, and that chemical and bacteriological weapons were also prohibited by the 1925 Geneva Gas Protocol. More recently, the Court found, the use of weapons producing "non-detectable fragments", of other types of mines, booby traps and other devices, and of incendiary weapons, was either prohibited or limited depending on the case by the Convention of 10 October 1980 on Prohibitions or Restrictions on the Use of Certain Conventional Weapons Which May Be Deemed to Be Excessively Injurious or to Have Indiscriminate Effects. Such prohibition, it stated, was in line with the rule that "the right of belligerents to adopt means of injuring the enemy is not unlimited" as stated in Article 22 of the 1907 Hague Regulations Respecting the Laws and Customs of War on Land. The Court further noted that the St. Petersburg Declaration had already condemned the use of weapons "which uselessly aggravate the suffering of disabled men or make their death inevitable" and that the aforementioned Regulations annexed to the Hague Convention IV of 1907, prohibit the use of "arms, projectiles, or material calculated to cause unnecessary suffering" (Article 23).

The Court also identified the cardinal principles constituting the fabric of international humanitarian law, the first of which is aimed at the protection of the civilian population and civilian objects and establishes the distinction between combatants and non-combatants. According to those principles, States are obliged not to make civilians the object of attack and must consequently not use weapons that are incapable of distinguishing between civilian and military targets. Secondly, it is prohibited to cause unnecessary suffering to combatants and, accordingly, it is prohibited to use weapons causing them needless harm or that uselessly aggravate their suffering. In this regard, the Court noted that States do not have unlimited freedom of choice in the weapons they can use.

The Court also considered applicable to the matter the Martens Clause, first enunciated in the Hague Convention of 1899 with respect to the laws and customs of war on land, a modern version of which has been codified in Article 1, paragraph 2, of Additional Protocol I of 1977, and reads as follows:

> "In cases not covered by this Protocol or by other international agreements, civilians and combatants remain under the protection and authority of the principles of international law derived from established custom, from the principles of humanity and from the dictates of public conscience."

The Court noted that the principles embodied in the Clause are principles and rules of humanitarian law and, together with the principle of neutrality, apply to nuclear weapons.

It was in the light of the foregoing that the Court recognized that humanitarian law does prohibit the use of certain types of weapons either because of their indiscriminate effect on combatants and civilians or because of the unnecessary and superfluous harm caused to combatants. The Court accordingly held that the principles and rules of international humanitarian law are obligatory and binding on all States as they also constitute intransgressible principles of customary international law.

With regard to the applicability of Additional Protocol I of 1977 to nuclear weapons, the Court recalled that even if not all States are parties to the Protocol, they are nevertheless bound by those rules in the Protocol which, when adopted, constituted an expression of the pre-existing customary law, such as, in particular, the Martens Clause, which is enshrined in Article I of the Protocol.

The Court observed that the fact that certain types of weapons were not specifically mentioned in the Convention does not permit the drawing of any legal conclusions relating to the substantive issues raised by the use of such weapons. It took the view that there can be no doubt that the principles and rules of humanitarian law, which are enshrined in the Geneva Conventions of 1949 and the Additional Protocols of 1977, are applicable to nuclear weapons. Even when it observed that the Conferences of 1949 and 1977 did not specifically address the question of nuclear weapons, the Court stated that it cannot be concluded from this that the established principles and rules of humanitarian law applicable in armed conflict do not apply to nuclear weapons, as such a conclusion would be incompatible with the intrinsically humanitarian character of the legal principles in question which permeate the entire law of armed conflict and apply to all forms of warfare and to all kinds of weapons.

The Court agreed with the submission that:

> "In general, international humanitarian law bears on the threat or use of nuclear weapons as it does of other weapons.
> International humanitarian law has evolved to meet contemporary circumstances, and is not limited in its application to weaponry of an earlier time. The fundamental principles of this law endure: to mitigate and circumscribe the cruelty of war for humanitarian reasons." (New Zealand, Written Statement, p. 15.)

The Court also observed that none of the States advocating the legality of the use of nuclear weapons under certain circumstances, including the "clean" use of smaller, low-yield, tactical nuclear weapons, had indicated that the principles of humanitarian law do not apply to nuclear weapons, noting that, for instance, the Russian Federation had recognized that "restrictions set by the rules applicable to armed conflicts in respect of means and methods of warfare definitely also extend to nuclear weapons"; that for the United States, "the United States has long shared the view that the law of armed conflict governs the use of nuclear weapons — just as it governs the use of conventional weapons"; while for the United Kingdom, "so far as the customary law of war is concerned, the United Kingdom has always accepted that the use of nuclear weapons is subject to the principles of the *jus in bello*".

[3. Elements of Fact]

With regard to the elements of fact advanced in its findings, the Court noted the definitions of nuclear weapons contained in various treaties and instruments, including those according to which nuclear explosions are "capable of causing massive destruction, generalized damage or massive poisoning" (Paris Accords of 1954), or the preamble of the Tlatelolco Treaty of 1967 which described nuclear weapons "whose terrible effects are suffered, indiscriminately and inexorably, by military forces and civilian population alike, [and which] constitute through the persistence of the radioactivity they release, an attack on the integrity of the human species and ultimately may even render the whole earth uninhabitable". It also took note of the fact that nuclear weapons release not only immense quantities of heat and energy, but also powerful and prolonged radiation; that the first two causes of damage are vastly more powerful than such causes of damage in other weapons of mass destruction, and that the phenomenon of radiation is said to be peculiar to nuclear weapons. These characteristics, the Court concluded, render nuclear weapons potentially catastrophic; their destructive power cannot be contained in either space or time, and they have the potential to destroy all civilization and the entire ecosystem of the planet.

With regard to the elements of fact, the Court noted that the radiation released by a nuclear explosion would affect health, agriculture, natural resources and demography over a wide area and that such weapons would be a serious danger to future generations. It further noted that ionizing radiation has the potential to damage the future environment, food and marine ecosystems, and to cause genetic defects and illness in future generations.

Also in this regard, the Government of Japan told the Court that the yields of the atomic bombs detonated in Hiroshima on 6 August 1945 and in Nagasaki on 9 August 1945 were the equivalent of 15 kilotons and 22 kilotons of TNT respectively. The bomb blast produced a big fireball, followed by extremely high temperatures of some several million degrees centigrade, and extremely high pressures of several hundred thousand atmospheres. It also emitted a great deal of radiation. According to the delegation, the fireball, which lasted for about 10 seconds, raised the ground temperature at the hypocentre to somewhere between 3,000 °C and 4,000 °C, and the heat caused the scorching of wood buildings over a radius of approximately 3 kilometres from the hypocentre. The number of houses damaged by the atomic bombs was

70,147 in Hiroshima and 18,409 in Nagasaki. People who were within 1,000 m of the hypocentre were exposed to the initial radiation of more than 3.93 Grays. It is estimated that 50 per cent of people who were exposed to more than 3 Grays die of marrow disorder within two months. Induced radiation was emitted from the ground and buildings charged with radioactivity. In addition, soot and dust contaminated by induced radiation was dispersed into the air and whirled up into the stratosphere by the force of the explosion, and this caused radioactive fallout back to the ground over several months.

According to the delegation, the exact number of fatalities was not known, since documents were scarce. It was estimated, however, that the number of people who had died by the end of 1945 amounted to approximately 140,000 in Hiroshima and 74,000 in Nagasaki. The population of the cities at that time was estimated at 350,000 in Hiroshima and 240,000 in Nagasaki. The number of people who died of thermal radiation immediately after the bomb blast, on the same day or within a few days, was not clear. However, 90 to 100 per cent of the people who were exposed to thermal radiation without any shield within 1 k of the hypocentre, died within a week. The early mortality rates for the people who were within 1.5 k to 2 k of the hypocentre were 14 per cent for people with a shield and 83 per cent for the people without a shield. In addition to direct injury from the bomb blast, death was caused by several interrelated factors such as being crushed or buried under buildings, injuries caused by splinters of glass, radiation damage, food shortages or a shortage of doctors and medicines.

Over 320,000 people who survived but were affected by radiation still suffer from various malignant tumours caused by radiation, including leukaemia, thyroid cancer, breast cancer, lung cancer, gastric cancer, cataracts and a variety of other after-effects. More than half a century after the disaster, they are still said to be undergoing medical examinations and treatment.

[Mayor of Hiroshima]

According to the Mayor of Hiroshima who made a statement before the Court, the atomic bomb which was detonated in Hiroshima produced an enormous destructive power and reduced innocent civilian populations to ashes. Women, the elderly and the newborn were said to have been bathed in deadly radiation. The Court was told that the dropping of the bomb unleashed a mushroom cloud and human skin was burned raw while other victims died in desperate agony. The Mayor further told the Court that when the bomb exploded, enormous pillars of flame leaped up towards the sky and a majority of the buildings crumbled, causing a large number of casualties, many of them fatal.

Later in his statement he described the unique characteristic of the atomic bombing as one whose enormous destruction was instantaneous and universal. Old, young, male, female, soldiers, civilians were all killed **indiscriminately**. *The entire city of Hiroshima, he said, had been exposed to thermal rays, shock-wave blast and radiation. The bomb purportedly generated heat that reached several million degrees centigrade. The fireball was about 280 metres in diameter, the thermal rays emanating from it were thought to have instantly charred any human being who was outdoors near the hypocentre. The witness further disclosed that according to documented cases, clothing had burst into flames at a distance of 2 kilometres from the hypocentre of the bomb; many fires were ignited simultaneously throughout the city; the entire city was carbonized and reduced to ashes. Yet another phenomenon was a shock-wave which inflicted even greater damage when it ricocheted off the ground and buildings. The blast wind which resulted had, he said, lifted and carried people through the air. All wooden buildings within a radius of 2 kilometres collapsed, while many well beyond that distance were damaged.*

The blast and thermal rays combined to burn to ashes or cause the collapse of approximately 70 per cent of the 76,327 dwellings in Hiroshima at the time. The rest were partially destroyed, half-bombed or damaged. The entire city was said to have been instantly devastated by the dropping of the bomb.

On the day the bomb was dropped, the witness further disclosed that there were approximately 350,000 people in Hiroshima, but it was later estimated that some 140,000 had died by the end of December 1945. Hospitals were said to be in ruins with medical staff dead or injured and with no medicines or equipment, and an incredible number of victims died, unable to receive sufficient treatment. Survivors developed fever, diarrhoea, haemorrhaging, and extreme fatigue, many died abruptly. Such was said to be the pattern of the acute symptoms of the atomic bomb disease. Other consequences were a widespread destruction of cells, loss of blood-producing tissue, and organ damage. The immune systems of survivors were weakened and such symptoms as hair loss were conspicuous. Other experiences recorded were an increase in leukaemia, cataracts, thyroid cancer, breast cancer, lung cancer and other cancers. As a result of the bombing, children exposed to radiation suffered mental and physical retardation. Nothing could be

done for these children medically and even unborn babies, the Mayor
stated, had been affected. He concluded by saying that exposure to high
levels of radiation continues in Hiroshima to this day.

[Mayor of Nagasaki]

The Mayor of Nagasaki, in his testimony, described effects on his
city that were similar to those experienced by Hiroshima as a result of
the atomic bombing which had taken place during the war. According
to the witness,

> *"The explosion of the atomic bomb generated an enormous*
> *fireball, 200 metres in radius, almost as though a small sun*
> *had appeared in the sky. The next instant, a ferocious blast and*
> *wave of heat assailed the ground with a thunderous roar. The*
> *surface temperature of the fireball was about 7,000 °C, and the*
> *heat rays that reached the ground were over 3,000 °C. The ex-*
> *plosion instantly killed or injured people within a two-*
> *kilometre radius of the hypocentre, leaving innumerable*
> *corpses charred like clumps of charcoal and scattered in the*
> *ruins near the hypocentre. In some cases not even a trace of*
> *the person's remains could be found. The blast wind of over*
> *300 metres per second slapped down trees and demolished*
> *most buildings. Even iron reinforced concrete structures were*
> *so badly damaged that they seemed to have been smashed by*
> *a giant hammer. The fierce flash of heat meanwhile melted*
> *glass and left metal objects contorted like strands of taffy, and*
> *the subsequent fires burned the ruins of the city to ashes. Na-*
> *gasaki became a city of death where not even the sounds of*
> *insects could be heard. After a while, countless men, women*
> *and children began to gather for a drink of water at the banks*
> *of nearby Urakami River, their hair and clothing scorched and*
> *their burnt skin hanging off in sheets like rags. Begging for*
> *help, they died one after another in the water or in heaps on*
> *the banks. Then radiation began to take its toll, killing people*
> *like a scourge of death expanding in concentric circles from*
> *the hypocentre. Four months after the atomic bombing, 74,000*
> *were dead and 75,000 had suffered injuries, that is, two-thirds*
> *of the city population had fallen victim to this calamity that*
> *came upon Nagasaki like a preview of the Apocalypse." (CR*
> *95/27.)*

[Delegation of the Marshall Islands]

The witness went on to state that even people who were lucky enough to survive continued to this day to suffer from the late effects unique to nuclear weapons. Nuclear weapons, he concluded, bring in their wake the indiscriminate devastation of civilian populations.

Testimony was also given by the delegation of the Marshall Islands which was the site of 67 nuclear weapons tests from 30 June to 18 August 1958, during the period of the United Nations Pacific Islands territories trusteeship. The total yield of those weapons was said to be equivalent to more than 7,000 bombs of the size of that which destroyed Hiroshima. Those nuclear weapon tests were said to have caused extensive radiation, induced illnesses, deaths and birth defects. Further on in the testimony, it was disclosed that human suffering and damage to the environment occurred at great distances, both in time and in geography, from the sites of detonations even when an effort was made to avoid or mitigate harm. The delegation went on to inform the Court that the unique characteristics of nuclear weapons are that they cause unnecessary suffering and include not only widespread, extensive, radioactive contamination with cumulative adverse effects, but also locally intense radiation with severe, immediate and long-term adverse effects, far-reaching blasts, heat, and light resulting in acute injuries and chronic ailments. Permanent, as well as temporary, blindness from intense light and reduced immunity from radiation exposures were said to be common and unavoidable consequences of the use of nuclear weapons, but which were uncommon or absent from the use of other destructive devices.

The delegation further disclosed that birth defects and extraordinarily prolonged and painful illnesses caused by the radioactive fallout inevitably and profoundly affected the civilian population long after the nuclear weapons tests had been carried out. Such suffering had affected generations born long after the testing of such weapons. It went on to say that, apart from the immediate damage at and near ground zero (where the detonation took place), the area experienced contamination of animals and plants and the poisoning of soil and water. As a consequence, some of the islands were still abandoned and in those that had recently been resettled, the presence of caesium in plants from the radioactive fallout rendered them inedible. Women on some of the other atolls in the islands who had been assured that their atolls were not affected by radiation, were said to have given birth to "monster babies". A young girl on one of these atolls was said to have no knees, three toes on each foot and a missing arm; her mother had not been born by 1954 when the tests started but had been raised on a contaminated atoll.

In the light of the foregoing the Court, as well as taking cognizance of the unique characteristics of nuclear weapons when used, reached the following conclusions; that nuclear weapons have a destructive capacity unmatched by any conventional weapon; that a single nuclear weapon has the capacity to kill thousands if not millions of human beings; that such weapons cause unnecessary suffering and superfluous injury to combatants and non-combatants alike; and that they are unable to distinguish between civilians and combatants. When recourse is had to such weapons, it can cause damage to generations unborn and produce widespread and long-term effects on the environment, particularly in respect of resources necessary for human survival. In this connection, it should be noted that the radioactive effects of such weapons are not only similar to the effects produced by the use of poison gas which would be in violation of the 1925 Geneva Gas Protocol, but are considered even more harmful.

The above findings by the Court should have led it inexorably to conclude that any use of nuclear weapons is unlawful under international law, in particular the law applicable in armed conflict including humanitarian law. However, instead of this, the Court found that:

"in view of the current state of international law, and of the elements of fact at its disposal, the Court cannot conclude definitively whether the threat or use of nuclear weapons would be lawful or unlawful in an extreme circumstance of self-defence, in which the very survival of a State would be at stake".

This finding that would appear to suggest that nuclear weapons when used in circumstaces of a threat to "State survival" — a concept invented by the Court — would constitute an exception to the corpus of humanitarian law which applies in all armed conflicts and makes no exception for nuclear weapons. In my considered opinion, the unlawfulness of the use of nuclear weapons is not predicated on the circumstances in which the use takes place, but rather on the unique and established characteristics of those weapons which under any circumstance would violate international law by their use. It is therefore most inappropriate for the Court's finding to have turned on the question of State survival when what is in issue is the lawfulness of nuclear weapons. Such a misconception of the question deprives the Court's finding of any legal basis.

On the other hand, if the Court had properly perceived the question and intended to give an appropriate reply, it would have found that an overwhelming justification exists on the basis of the law and the facts, which would have enabled it to reach a finding that the use of nuclear weapons in any circumstance would be unlawful. The Court's failure to reach this inevitable conclusion has compelled me to enter a vigor ous dissent to its main finding.

[4. Purpose of Advisory Opinions]

I am likewise constrained to mention various other, more general, misgivings with regard to the Advisory Opinion on the whole. While the purpose of the Court's advisory jurisdiction is to provide an authoritative legal opinion and to enlighten the requesting body on certain legal aspects of an issue with which it has to deal when discharging its functions, the device has also been used to secure authoritative interpretations of the provisions of the Charter or the constitutive instruments of specialized agencies, or to provide guidance to various organs of the United Nations in relation to their functions. Furthermore, although the Advisory Opinions of the Court are not legally binding and impose no legal obligations either upon the requesting body or upon States, such Opinions are nonetheless not devoid of effect as they remain the law "recognized by the United Nations" (*Admissibility of Hearings of Petitioners by the Committee on South West Africa, I.C.J. Reports 1956*, p. 23, Sep. Op. Judge Lauterpacht at p. 46). Accordingly, this Court has, on various occasions, used its advisory jurisdiction as a medium of participation in the work of the United Nations, helping the Organization to achieve its objectives. Advisory opinions have enabled the Court to contribute meaningfully to the development and crystallization of the law. For example, in the *Namibia* Advisory Opinion, the Court referred to the development "of international law in regard to the non-self-governing territories, as enshrined in the Charter of the United Nations" (*I.C.J. Reports 1971*, p. 31), which made the principle of self-determination applicable to such territories.

In its Advisory Opinion on the Western *Sahara*, the Court, citing the *Namibia* Opinion in relation to the principle of self-determination, stated that when questions are asked with reference to that principle, the Court

"must take into consideration the changes which have occurred in the supervening half-century, and its interpretation cannot remain unaffected by the subsequent development of law, through the Charter of the United Nations and by way of customary law. . . .

In this domain, as elsewhere, the *corpus juris gentium* has been considerably enriched, and this the Court, if it is faithfully to discharge its functions, may not ignore" (*I.C.J. Reports 1975*, p. 32).

The Court's Opinion in the case accordingly referred to Article 1 of the United Nations Charter and to the Declaration on the Granting of Independence to Colonial Countries and Peoples which, it said, "confirm and emphasize that the application of the right of self-determination requires a free and genuine expression of the will of the peoples concerned" (*I.C.J. Reports 1975*, p. 32). Moreover, the Court insisted that "the validity of the principle of self-determination, defined as the need to pay regard to the freely expressed will of peoples is not affected by the fact that in certain cases the General Assembly has dispensed with the requirement of consulting the inhabitants of a given territory" (*ibid.*, p. 33). It can therefore be observed that through the medium of its Advisory Opinions, the Court has rendered normative decisions which have enabled the United Nations to achieve its objectives, in some cases even leading to the peaceful settlement of disputes, and has either contributed to the crystallisation and development of the law or, with its imprimatur, affirmed the emergence of the law.

It is therefore to be regretted that, on this occasion, the Court would seem not only to have retreated from this practice of making its contribution to the development of the law on a matter of such vital importance to the General Assembly and to the international community as a whole but may, albeit unintentionally, have cast doubt on established or emerging rules of international law. Indeed, much of the approach of the Court in this Opinion is indicative of this attitude. When not looking for specific treaties or customary law rules supposed to regulate or prohibit the use of nuclear weapons, the Court has tended to declare either that it is not called upon to make a finding on the matter or that it is not necessary for it to take a position. For instance, regarding the matter of whether the principles and rules of humanitarian law are part of *jus cogens* as defined in Article 53 of the Vienna Convention on the Law of Treaties of 1969, the Court stated that there is no need for it to pronounce on the matter even though there is almost universal adherence to the fact that the Geneva Conventions of 1949 are declaratory of customary international law, and there is community

interest and consensus in the observance of and respect for their provisions. A pronouncement of the Court emphasizing their humanitarian
underpinnings and the fact that they are deeply rooted in the traditions
and values of member States of the international community and deserve universal respect and protection, and not to be derogated from
by States would assist in strengthening their legal observance especially in an era which has so often witnessed the most serious and
egregious violation of humanitarian principles and rules and whose
very *raison d'être* is irreconcilable with the use of nuclear weapons.
This has been part of the judicial function of the Court — the establishment of international legal standards for the community of States
and, in particular, for those that appear before it or are parties to its
Statute. In the establishment of such legal standards, the Court, in the
Reservations case, referred to the principles underlying the Convention
on the Prohibition of Genocide as principles which are recognized by
civilized nations "as binding on States, even without any conventional
obligation" (*I.C.J. Reports 1951*, p. 23). It also recognized the co-operation required by the Convention "in order to liberate mankind from
such an odious scourge . . . " (*ibid.*). The Court noted that the Convention was adopted for a purely humanitarian and civilizing purpose, "to
safeguard the very existence of certain human groups and, . . . to confirm and endorse the most elementary principles of humanity" (*ibid.*).
In the *Corfu Channel* case, the Court referred to "certain general and
well-recognized principles, namely: elementary considerations of humanity, even more exacting in peace than in war" (*I.C.J. Reports 1949*,
p. 22). Such pronouncements would undoubtedly have helped to foster
a proper sense of restraint within the international community. In the
Barcelona Traction case, the Court in discussing the obligations of
States towards the international community stated that such obligations
are *ergo omnes* and

> "derive, for example, in contemporary international law, from
> the outlawing of acts of aggression, and of genocide, as also
> from the principles and rules concerning the basic rights of the
> human person, including protection from slavery and racial
> discrimination. Some of the corresponding rights of protection
> have entered into the body of general international law . . . "
> (*I.C.J. Reports 1970*, p. 32).

In the case under consideration, the Court would appear to have
been all too reluctant to take any position of principle on a question
involving what the late Judge Nagendra Singh described as the most

important aspect of international law facing humanity today (Nagendra Singh, *Nuclear Weapons and International Law*, p. 17). Instead, the Court resolved the issue about the *jus cogens* character of some of the principles and rules of humanitarian law by saying that the request transmitted to it "does not raise the question of the character of the humanitarian law which would apply to the use of nuclear weapons". With respect they do. A pronouncement by the Court about the character of such rules while not guaranteeing their observance at all times, would nonetheless as they are related to human values already protected by positive legal principles which, taken together, reveal certain criteria of public policy. (See I. Brownlie, *Principles of Public International Law* (1990), p. 29.) H. Lauterpacht has also stated that among other reasons, that many of the provisions of the Geneva Conventions following as they do from "compelling considerations of humanity, are declaratory of universally binding international custom". (E. Lauterpacht, *International Law, being the Collected Papers of Hersch Lauterpacht*, p. 115 (E. Lauterpacht, ed., 1970)). The International Law Commission pointed out in its commentary on Article 50 (now 53) of the Vienna Convention of the Law of Treaties, that "it is not the form of a general rule of international law, but the particular nature of the subject-matter with which it deals that may . . . give it a character of *ius cogens*". Already in 1980, the Commission observed that "some of the rules of humanitarian law are, in the opinion of the Commission, rules which impose obligations of *jus cogens*".

[5. Belligerent Reprisals]

The Court also adopted the judicial policy of "non-pronouncement" on the question of belligerent reprisals — an issue most pertinent to the question before it — "save to observe that should the possibility to make such reprisals exist, it would, like self-defence, be governed *inter alia* by the principle of proportionality" (paras. 41-42). It is to say the least strange that the Court should refrain from pronouncing on the lawfulness or otherwise of belligerent reprisals, particularly if it would involve the use of nuclear weapons. Under contemporary international law, belligerent reprisals, if carried out with nuclear weapons, would grossly violate humanitarian law in any circumstance and international law in general. More specifically the Geneva Conventions prohibit such reprisals against a range of protected persons and objects as reaffirmed in Additional Protocol I of 1977. According to the Protocol, all belligerent parties are prohibited from carrying out belligerent reprisals. If nuclear weapons were used and given the characteristics of those weapons, their inability to discriminate between civilians and combatants and between civilian and military objectives, together with the likelihood of violations of the prohibition of unnecessary suffering and superfluous injuries to belligerents, such reprisals would at a minimum be contrary to established humanitarian law and would therefore be unlawful. The Court's "judicial restraint" on an issue of such crucial importance to the question before it contributes neither to the clarification of the law, let alone to its observance.

The Court's reluctance to take a legal position on some of the important issues which pertain to the question before it could also be discerned from what may be described as a "judicial odyssey" in search of a specific conventional or customary rule specifically authorizing or prohibiting the use of nuclear weapons, which only led to the discovery that no such specific rule exists. Indeed, if such a specific rule did exist, it is more than unlikely that the question would have been brought before the Court in its present form, if at all. On the other hand, the absence of a specific convention prohibiting the use of nuclear weapons should not have suggested to the Court that the use of such weapons might be lawful, as it is generally recognized by States that customary international law embodies principles which are applicable to the use of such weapons. Hence the futile quest for specific legal prohibition can only be attributable to an extreme form of positivism, which is out of keeping with the international jurisprudence — including that of this Court. The futility of such an enterprise was recognized by the British-American Claims Arbitral Tribunal in the *Eastern Extension, Australia and China Telegraph Company* case, where it was held that even if there were no specific rule of international law applicable to a case, it could not be said that there was no rule of international law to which resort might be had.

> "International law, as well as domestic law, may not contain, and generally does not contain, express rules decisive of particular cases; but the function of jurisprudence is to resolve the conflict of opposing rights and interests by applying, in default of any specific provision of law, the corollaries of general principles, and so to find — exactly as in the mathematical sciences — the solution of the problem. This is the method of jurisprudence; it is the method by which the law has been gradually evolved in every country, resulting in the

definition and settlement of legal relations as well between States as between private individuals." (*United Nations Arbitral Reports*, Vol. VI, p. 114.)

Such then has been the jurisprudential approach to issues before the Court. The Court has applied legal principles and rules to resolve the conflict of opposing rights and interests where no specific provision of the law exists, and has relied on the corollaries of general principles in order to find a solution to the problem. The Court's approach has not been restricted to a search for a specific treaty or rule of customary law specifically regulating or applying to a matter before it and, in the absence of such a specific rule or treaty, it has not declared that it cannot definitively conclude or that it is unable to reach a decision or make a determination on that matter. The Court has in the past — rightly in my view — not imposed such restrictions upon itself when discharging its judicial function to decide disputes in accordance with international law, but has referred to the principles of international law, to equity and to its own jurisprudence in order to define and settle the legal issues referred to it.

[6. UN Charter Article 2.1]

On the other hand, the search for specific rules led the Court to overlook or not fully to apply the principles of the United Nations Charter when considering the question before it. One such principle that does not appear to have been given its due weight in the Judgment of the Court is Article 2, paragraph 1, of the Charter of the United Nations, which provides that "The Organization is based on the principle of sovereign equality of all of its Members". The principle of sovereign equality of States is of general application. It presupposes respect for the sovereignty and territorial integrity of all States. International law recognizes the sovereignty of each State over its territory as well as the physical integrity of the civilian population. By virtue of this principle, a State is prohibited from inflicting injury or harm on another State. The principle is bound to be violated if nuclear weapons are used in a given conflict, because of their established and well-known characteristics. The use of such weapons would not only result in the violation of the territorial integrity of non-belligerent States by radioactive contamination, but would involve the death of thousands, if not millions, of the inhabitants of territories not parties to the conflict. This would be in violation of the principle as enshrined in the Charter, an aspect of the matter that would appear not to have been taken fully into consideration by the Court when making its findings.

[7. Genocide Convention]

I am likewise constrained to express my apprehension over some of the other findings in the Advisory Opinion with regard to respect for human rights and genocide, the protection of the natural environment and the policy of deterrence. With regard to genocide, it is stated that genocide would be considered to have been committed if a recourse to nuclear weapons resulted from an intent to destroy, in whole or in part, a national, ethnical, racial or religious group, as such. This reflects the text of the Genocide Convention. However, one must be mindful of the special characteristics of the Convention, its object and purpose, to which the Court itself referred in the *Reservations* case as being to condemn and punish

> "a crime under international law involving a denial of the right of existence of entire human groups, a denial which shocks the conscience of mankind and results in great losses to humanity and which is contrary to moral law and the spirit and aims of the United Nations";

while further pointing out

> "that the principles underlying the Convention are recognized by civilized nations as binding on States, even without any conventional obligation".

It further emphasized the co-operation required in order "to liberate mankind from such an odious scourge" and, given the humanitarian and civilizing purpose of the Convention, it referred to it as intended "to safeguard the very existence of certain human groups", and "to confirm and endorse the most elementary principles of morality". The Court cannot therefore view with equanimity the killing of thousands, if not millions, of innocent civilians which the use of nuclear weapons would make inevitable, and conclude that genocide has not been committed because the State using such weapons has not manifested any intent to kill so many thousands or millions of people. Indeed, under the Convention, the quantum of the people killed is comprehended as well. It does not appear to me that judicial detachment requires the Court from expressing itself on the abhorrent shocking consequences that a whole population could be wiped out by the use of nuclear weapons during an armed conflict, and the fact that this could tantamount to genocide, if the consequences of the act could have been foreseen. Such expression of concern may even have a preventive effect on the weapons being used at all.

[8. Right to Human Life: I.C.C.P.R. Article 6]

As to whether recourse to nuclear weapons would violate human rights, in particular the right to human life, the Court found that it was never envisaged that the lawfulness or otherwise of such weapons would be regulated by the International Covenant on Civil and Political Rights. While this is accepted as a legal position, it does seem to me that too narrow a view has been taken of the matter. It should be recalled that both human rights law and international humanitarian law have as their *raison d'être* the protection of the individual as well as the worth and dignity of the human person, both during peacetime or in an armed conflict. It is for this reason, to my mind, that the United Nations Charter, which was adopted immediately after the end of the Second World War in the course of which serious and grave violations of human rights had occurred, undertook to protect the rights of individual human beings whatever their race, colour or creed, emphasizing that such rights were to be protected and respected even during an armed conflict. It should not be forgotten that the Second World War had witnessed the use of the atomic weapon in Hiroshima and Nagasaki, resulting in the deaths of thousands of human beings. **The Second World War therefore came to be regarded as the period epitomizing gross violations of human rights. The possibility that the human rights of citizens, in particular their right to life, would be violated during a nuclear conflagration, is a matter which falls within the purview of the Charter and other relevant international legal instruments. Any activity which involves a terrible violation of the principles of the Charter deserves to be considered in the context of both the Charter and the other applicable rules. It is evidently in this context that the Human Rights Committee under the International Covenant on Civil and Political Rights adopted, in November 1984, a "general comment" on Article 6 of the Covenant (Right to Life), according to which the production, testing, possession, deployment and use of nuclear weapons ought to be prohibited and recognized as crimes against humanity. It is to be recalled that Article 6 of the Charter of the Nuremburg Tribunal defined crimes against humanity as "murder, extermination . . . , and other inhu-**

mane acts committed against any civilian population, before or during war . . . ". It follows that the Nuremburg principles are likewise pertinent to the matter just considered by the Court.

With regard to the protection and safeguarding of the natural environment, the Court reached the conclusion that existing international law does not prohibit the use of nuclear weapons, but that important environmental factors are to be taken into account in the context of the implementation of the principles and rules of law applicable in armed conflict. The Court also found that relevant treaties in relation to the protection of the natural environment could not have intended to deprive a State of the exercise of its right to self-defence under international law. In my view, what is at issue is not whether a State might be denied its right to self-defence under the relevant treaties intended for the protection of the natural environment, but rather that, given the known qualities of nuclear weapons when exploded as well as their radioactive effects which not only contaminate human beings but the natural environment as well including agriculture, food, drinking water and the marine ecosystem over a wide area, it follows that the use of such weapons would not only cause severe and widespread damage to the natural environment, but would deprive human beings of drinking water and other resources needed for survival. In recognition of this, the First Additional Protocol of 1977 makes provision for the preservation of objects indispensable to the survival of the civilian population, such as foodstuffs, agricultural produce, drinking water installations, etc. The Advisory Opinion should have considered the question posed in relation to the protection of the natural environment from this perspective, rather than giving the impression that the argument advanced was about denying a State its legitimate right of self-defence.

The Advisory Opinion considered that the fact of nuclear weapons not having been used for 50 years cannot be regarded as an expression of an *opinio juris*. The legal basis for such a recognition was not elaborated; it was more in the nature of an assertion. However, the Court was unable to find that the conviction of the overwhelming majority of States that the fact that nuclear weapons have not been used for the last 50 years has established an *opinio juris* in favour of the prohibition of such use, was such as to have a bearing on its Opinion. In this connection, the Court should have given due consideration and weight to the statements of the overwhelming majority of States together with the resolutions adopted by various international organizations on the use of nuclear weapons, as evidence of the emergence of an *opinio juris.*

In my view, it was injudicious for the Court to have appeared to give legal recognition to the doctrine of deterrence as a principle of international law. While it is legitimate for judicial notice should be taken of that policy, the Court should have realised that it has the potential of being declared illegal if implemented, as it would involve a nuclear conflict between belligerents with catastrophic consequences for the civilian population not only of the belligerent parties but those of States not involved in such a conflict, and could result in the violation of international law in general and humanitarian law in particular. It would therefore have been prudent for the Court to have refrained from taking a position on this matter, which is essentially non-legal.

[9. Significance of This Opinion]

Be that as it may, the Advisory Opinion cannot be considered as entirely without legal merit or significance. The positive findings it contains should be regarded as a step forward in the historic process of imposing legal restraints in armed conflicts. Some of those restraints as they relate to nuclear weapons have now found expression in the opinion of the Court. For the first time in its history, indeed in the history of any tribunal of similar standing, the Court has declared and confirmed that nuclear weapons are subject to international law; that a threat or use of force by means of nuclear weapons that is contrary to Article 2, paragraph 4, of the United Nations Charter, and that fails to meet the requirements of Article 51 is unlawful. The Court has also held that any threat or use of nuclear weapons that is incompatible with the requirements of international law applicable in armed conflict, particularly those of the principles of humanitarian law as well as specific obligations under the treaties or other undertakings, dealing expressly with nuclear weapons, would be unlawful. Inferentially, it is because recourse to nuclear weapons could not meet the aforementioned requirements that the Court has found "that the threat or use of nuclear weapons would generally be contrary to the rules of international law applicable in armed conflict, and in particular the principles and the rules of humanitarian law". This finding, though qualified, should be regarded as of normative importance, when taken together with the other conclusions reached by the Court. Among other things, it is a rejection of the argument that since humanitarian law pre-dated the invention of nuclear weapons, it could not therefore be applicable to those weapons. On the contrary, the Court has found that given the intrinsic character of the established principles and rules of humanitarian law, it does apply to them.

It is in the response to these juridical findings of both historic and normative importance that I have voted in favour of paragraphs 2A, 2C, 2D and 2F of the *dispositif*, but not without reservations with respect to paragraph 2C.

However, I have voted against paragraph B according to which the Court finds that there is in neither customary nor conventional international law any comprehensive and universal prohibition of the threat of nuclear weapons as such. Such a finding, in my view, is not in accordance with the law . At the very least, the use of nuclear weapons would violate the prohibition of the use of poison weapons as embodied in Article 23 *(a)* of the Hague Convention of 1899 and 1907 as well as the Geneva Gas Protocol of 1925 which prohibits the use of poison gas and/or bacteriological weapons. Because of its universal adherence, the Protocol is considered binding on the international community as a whole. Furthermore, the prohibition of the use of poison gas is now regarded as a part of customary international law binding on all States, and, the finding by the Court in Paragraph B cannot be sustained in the face of the Geneva Conventions of 1949 and the 1977 Additional Protocols thereto either. With regard to the Conventions, they are as of today binding on at least 186 states and their universal acceptance is said to be even greater than that of the United Nations Charter. Accordingly, those treaties are now recognized as a part of customary international law binding on all States. The Court in its Judgment in the *Nicaragua* case confirmed that the Conventions are a part of customary international law, when it stated that:

> "there is an obligation . . . in the terms of Article I of the Geneva Conventions, to 'respect' the Conventions and even 'to ensure respect' for them 'in all circumstances', since such an obligation does not derive only from the Conventions themselves, but from the general principles of humanitarian law to which the Conventions merely give specific expression" (*I.C.J. Reports 1986*, p. 114).

By reference to the humanitarian principles of international law, the Court recognized that the Conventions themselves are reflective of customary law and as such universally binding. The same reasoning applies to Additional Protocol I in particular, which constitutes a restatement and a reaffirmation of customary law rules based on the earlier Geneva and Hague Conventions. To date, 143 states have become parties to the Protocol, and the customary force of the provisions of the Protocol are not based on the formal status of the Protocol itself.

In the light of the foregoing conclusion, it cannot be maintained as the Court has done — that there is in neither customary nor conventional international law any comprehensive and universal prohibition of the threat or use of nuclear weapons as such. Such a finding is not consistent with its jurisprudence either as alluded to above.

I have however voted in favour of Paragraph F of the *dispositif* which stresses the obligation to pursue in good faith and bring to a conclusion negotiations leading to nuclear disarmament in all its aspects under strict and effective international control. I am of the view that the parties to the 1968 Treaty on the Non-Proliferation of Nuclear Weapons, realising the danger posed to all States by the proliferation of nuclear weapons, entered into a binding commitment to end the nuclear arms race at an early date and to embark on nuclear disarmament. The dangers that those weapons posed for humanity in 1968 are still current today, as is evident from the decision taken in 1995 by the States parties to the Treaty, to make it permanent. The obligation to eliminate those weapons remain binding on those States so as to remove the threat such weapons pose to violate the Charter or the principles and rules of humanitarian law. There is accordingly a correlation between the obligation of nuclear disarmament assumed by those States Parties to the Non-Proliferation Treaty and the obligations assumed by States under the United Nations Charter and under the law applicable in armed conflict, in particular international humanitarian law.

[10. Conclusion]

Despite this and some of the other normative conclusions reached by the Court in its Advisory Opinion, it is a matter of profound regret that on the actual question put to it, that is, whether it is permitted under international law to use nuclear weapons in any circumstances, the Court flinched and failed to reach the only and inescapable finding, namely, that in view of the established facts of the use of such weapons, it is inconceivable that there is any circumstance in which their use would not violate the principles and rules of international law applicable in armed conflict and, in particular, the principles and rules of humanitarian law. **By not answering the question and leaving it to**

States to decide the matter, the Court declined to the challenge to reaffirm the applicability of the rules of law and of humanitarian law in particular to nuclear weapons and to ensure the protection of human beings, of generations unborn and of the natural environment against the use of such weapons whose destructive power we have seen, is unable to discriminate between combatants and non-combatants, cannot spare hospitals or prisoner-of-war camps and can cause suffering out of all proportion to military necessity leaving their victims to die as a result of burns after weeks of agony, or to be afflicted for life with painful infirmities. The request by the General Assembly was for the Court, as the guarantor of legality, to affirm that because of these consequences, the use of nuclear weapons is unlawful under international law. A determination that this Court as a court of law should have been able to make.

In the absence of such a categoric and inescapable finding, I am left with no alternative but with deep regret to dissent from the Advisory Opinion.

                                                    (Signed) Abdul G. KOROMA
[Original: English]   [Sierra Leone]

SEPARATE OPINION OF JUDGE FLEISCHHAUER

EDITOR'S OUTLINE OF FLEISCHHAUR OPINION*

Humanitarian Law versus Inherent Right of Self-Defense
105 (2)D: Nuclear Weapons Subject to Law Evolved
    before Their Advent
¶ 105 (2)E 1
¶ 105 (2)E 2 and UN Charter Article 51
¶ 105 (2)E 2 and ¶¶ 95 and 96
Policy of Deterrence
Principle of Proportionality
Why I Supported ¶ 105 (2)F

---

* Editor's additions to original text are indicated by bracketed headings or boldface brackets.

[Humanitarian Law versus Inherent Right of Self-Defense]

I have voted in favour of all of the Court's Conclusions as contained in paragraph 105 of the Advisory Opinion, although these conclusions do not give a complete and clear-cut answer to the question asked of the Court by the General Assembly. In their incompleteness and vagueness the Court's Conclusions — and in particular their critical Point 2.E — rather reflect the terrible dilemma that confronts persons and institutions alike which have to deal with the question of the legality or otherwise of the threat or use of nuclear weapons in international law. At present, international law is still grappling with, and has not yet overcome, the dichotomy that exists between the international law applicable in armed conflict and, in particular, the rules and principles of humanitarian law, on the one side, with which principles and rules the use of nuclear weapons — as the Court says in paragraph 95 of its Opinion — seems scarcely reconcilable; and, on the other

side, the inherent right of self-defence which every State possesses as
a matter of sovereign equality. That basic right would be severely curtailed if for a State, victim of an attack with nuclear, chemical or bacteriological weapons or otherwise constituting a deadly menace for its
very survival, nuclear weapons were totally ruled out as an ultimate
legal option in collective or individual self-defence.

[¶ 105 (2)D: Nuclear Weapons Subject to Law Evolved before Their Advent]

1. In explaining my views more in detail, I would like to begin by
stating that, in my view, the Court is right in its reasoning that the
humanitarian rules and principles apply to nuclear weapons (para. 86)
and in its conclusion that

> "A threat or use of nuclear weapons should also be com-
> patible with the requirements of the international law applica-
> ble in armed conflict particularly those of the principles and
> rules of international humanitarian law . . . " (Point 2.D of the
> Conclusions.)

This is so, because of the intrinsically humanitarian character of
those rules and principles and in spite of the fact that they essentially
evolved much before nuclear weapons were invented. This finding is
also not altered by the fact that the Geneva Conferences, which were
held after the appearance on the international scene of nuclear weapons
and which adopted the four Geneva Conventions of 12 August 1949 on
the Protection of War Victims as well as the Protocol I of 8 June 1977
to those Conventions, did not address nuclear weapons specifically.
The same is true for other principles of the law applicable in armed
conflict, such as the principle of neutrality which likewise evolved
much before the advent of nuclear weapons.

[¶ 105 (2)E 1]

2. **The rules and principles of humanitarian law applicable in
armed conflict are expression of the — as the Court puts it (para.
95) — "overriding consideration of humanity" which is at the basis
of international law and which international law is expected to uphold and defend. The humanitarian rules and principles remind
States that whatever the weaponry used, notwithstanding the regrettable inevitability of civilian losses in times of war, civilians**

might never be the object of an attack. So far as combatants are concerned, weapons may not be used that cause unnecessary suffering. Similarly, the respect for the neutrality of States not participating in an armed conflict is a key element of orderly relations between States. The nuclear weapon is, in many ways, the negation of the humanitarian considerations underlying the law applicable in armed conflict and of the principle of neutrality. The nuclear weapon cannot distinguish between civilian and military targets. It causes immeasurable suffering. The radiation released by it is unable to respect the territorial integrity of a neutral State.

I therefore agree with the Court's finding in the first paragraph of Point 2.E of the Conclusions, to the effect that

> "the threat or use of nuclear weapons would generally be contrary to the rules of international law applicable in armed conflict, and in particular the principles and rules of humanitarian law".

[¶ 105 (2)E 2 and UN Charter Article 51]

3. As the Court rightly sees it, the answer to the question asked of it by the General Assembly does not lie alone in a finding that the threat or use of nuclear weapons would be contrary to the rules of international law applicable in armed conflict, and in particular the principles and rules of humanitarian law. Through the use of the word "generally" in the first paragraph of Point 2.E of the Conclusions and through the addition of the second paragraph to that Point, the Court points to qualifications that apply or may apply to its findings regarding irreconcilability between the use of nuclear weapons and humanitarian law. The word "generally" limits the finding as such; and according to the second paragraph,

> "in view of the current state of international law, and the elements of fact at its disposal, the Court cannot conclude definitively whether the threat or use of nuclear weapons would be lawful or unlawful in an extreme circumstance of self-defence, in which the very survival of a State would be at stake".

To end the matter with the simple statement that recourse to nuclear weapons would be contrary to international law applicable in armed conflict, and in particular the principles and rules of humanitarian law, would have meant that the law applicable in armed conflict, and in particular the humanitarian law, was given precedence over the inherent right of individual or collective self-defence which every State possesses as a matter of sovereign equality and which is expressly preserved in Article 51 of the Charter. That would be so because if a State is the victim of an all out attack by another State, which threatens the very existence of the victimized State, recourse to the threat or use of nuclear weapons in individual (if the victimized State is a nuclear-weapon State) or collective (if the victim is a non-nuclear-weapon State allied to a nuclear-weapon State) self-defence could be for the victimized State the last and only alternative to giving itself up and surrender. That situation would in particular exist if the attack is made by nuclear, bacteriological or chemical weapons. It is true that the right of self-defence as protected by Article 51 of the Charter is not weapon-specific (para. 39 of the Considerations of the Opinion). Nevertheless, the denial of the recourse to the threat or use of nuclear weapons as a legal option in any circumstance could amount to a denial of self-defence itself if such recourse was the last available means by way of which the victimized State could exercise its right under Article 51 of the Charter.

A finding that amounted to such a denial therefore would not, in my view, have been a correct statement of the law; there is no rule in international law according to which one of the conflicting principles would prevail over the other. The fact that the attacking State itself would act in contravention of international law, would not alter the situation. Nor would recourse to the Security Council, as mandated by Article 51, guarantee by itself an immediate and effective relief.

[¶ 105 (2)E 2 and ¶¶ 95 and 96]

4. It is true that the qualifying elements in Point 2.E of the Conclusions have been couched by the Court in hesitating, vague and halting terms. The first paragraph of Point 2.E does not explain what is to be understood by *"generally . . .* contrary to the rules of international law applicable in armed conflict" (emphasis added), and the wording of the second paragraph of Point 2.E avoids to take a position when it says that,

> "in view of the current state of international law, and of the elements of fact at its disposal, the Court cannot conclude definitively whether the threat or use of nuclear weapons would be lawful or unlawful in an extreme circumstance of self-de-

fence, in which the very survival of a State would be at stake".

Nor is the reasoning of the Court in the considerations of its Opinion leading up to the qualifications of the main finding in Point 2.E very clear. As far as the term "generally" in the first paragraph of Point 2.E of the Conclusions is concerned, the Court's explanations in paragraph 95 of its Opinion are limited to the statement

> "that it [i.e. the Court] does not have sufficient elements to enable it to conclude with certainty that the use of nuclear weapons would necessarily be at variance with the principles and rules of law applicable in armed conflict in any circumstance".

The considerations leading to the second paragraph of Point 2.E are contained in paragraph 96. They refer to Article 51 of the Charter, the State practice referred to as "policy of deterrence" and the reservations which certain nuclear-weapon States have appended to the undertakings they have given, notably under the Protocols to the Treaties of Tlatelolco and Rarotonga, and also under the declarations made by them in connection with the extension of the Treaty on the Non-Proliferation of Nuclear Weapons (para. 59 of the Opinion). The hesitating terms in which the Court has couched the qualifying elements in Point 2.E of the Conclusions witness, in my view, the legal and moral difficulties of the territory into which the Court has been led by the question asked of it by the General Assembly.

[Policy of Deterrence]

5. Nevertheless, the Court, by acknowledging in the considerations of its Opinion as well as in Point 2.E of the Conclusions the possibility of qualifying elements, made it possible for me to vote in favour of that particularly important point of its Conclusions. The Court could however — and in my view should — have gone further. My view on this is the following:

The Principles and rules of the humanitarian law and the other principles of law applicable in armed conflict, such as the principle of neutrality on the one side and the inherent right of self defence on the other, which are through the very existence of the nuclear weapon in sharp opposition to each other, are all principles and rules of law. None of these principles and rules is above the law, they are of equal rank in law and they can be altered by law. They are justiciable. Yet international law has so far not developed — neither in conventional nor in customary law — a norm on how these principles can be reconciled in the face of the nuclear weapon. As I stated above (para. 3 of this Separate Opinion), there is no rule giving prevalence of one over the other of these principles and rules. International politics have not yet produced a system of collective security of such perfection that it could take care of the dilemma, swiftly and efficiently.

In view of their equal ranking this means that, if the need arises, the smallest common denominator between the conflicting principles and rules has to be found. This means in turn that, although recourse to nuclear weapons is scarcely reconcilable with humanitarian law applicable in armed conflict as well as the principle of neutrality, recourse to such weapons could remain a justified legal option in an extreme situation of individual or collective self-defence in which the threat or use of nuclear weapons is the last resort against an attack with nuclear, chemical or bacteriological weapons or otherwise threatening the very existence of the victimized State.

The same result is reached if, in the absence of a conventional or a customary rule for the conciliation of the conflicting legal principles and rules, it is accepted that the third category of law which the Court has to apply by virtue of Article 38 of its Statute, i.e. the general principles of law recognized in all legal systems, contains a principle to the effect that no legal system is entitled to demand the self-abandonment, the suicide, of one of its subjects. Much can be said, in my view, in favour of the applicability of such a principle in all modern legal systems and consequently also in international law.

Whichever of the two lines of reasoning is followed, the result that the smallest common denominator, as I see it, is the guiding factor in the solution of the conflict created by the nuclear weapon between the law applicable in armed conflict and the right of self-defence, is confirmed by the important role played by the policy of deterrence during all the years of the Cold War in State practice of nuclear-weapon States as well as in the practice of non-nuclear-weapon States, supporting or tolerating that policy. Even after the end of the Cold War the policy of deterrence has not altogether been abandoned, if only in order to maintain the balance of power among nuclear-weapon States and in order to deter non-nuclear-weapon States from acquiring and threatening or using nuclear weapons. Nuclear-weapon States have found it necessary to continue beyond the end of the Cold War the reservations they have made to the undertakings they have given, notably to the Treaties of Tlatelolco and Rarotonga (para. 59 of the Opinion), and to add similar reservations under the declarations given by them in connection with the unlimited extension of the Non-Proliferation Treaty. These reservations are tolerated by the non-nuclear parties concerned as well as, in the case of the unlimited extension of the Non-Proliferation Treaty, by the Security Council. Of course, as the Court itself has stated (*North Sea Continental Shelf, Judgment, I.C.J. Reports 1969*, p. 3 at p. 44), not every act habitually performed or every attitude taken over a prolonged period of time by a plurality of States is a practice relevant for the determination of the state of the law. In the words of the Court:

"There are many international acts, e.g., in the field of ceremonial and protocol, which are performed almost invariably, but which are motivated only by considerations of courtesy, convenience or tradition, and not by any sense of legal duty." (*Ibid.*)

But the practice embodied in the policy of deterrence is based specifically on the right of individual or collective self-defence and so are the reservations to the guarantees of security. The States which support or which tolerate that policy and those reservations are aware of this. So was the Security Council when it adopted resolution 984 (1995). Therefore, the practice which finds expression in the policy of deterrence, in the reservations to the security guarantees and in their toleration, must be regarded as State practice in the legal sense.

[Principle of Proportionality]

6. For a recourse to nuclear weapons to be lawful, however, not only would the situation have to be an extreme one, but the conditions on which the lawfulness of the exercise of self-defence generally depends would also always have to be met. These conditions comprise, as the Opinion states *expressis verbis* (para. 41) that there must be proportionality. The need to comply with the proportionality principle must not *a priori* rule out recourse to nuclear weapons; as the Opinion states (para. 42): "The proportionality principle may thus not in itself exclude the use of nuclear weapons in all circumstances." The margin that exists for considering that a particular threat or use of nuclear weapons could be lawful is therefore extremely narrow.

The present state of international law does not permit a more precise drawing of the border line between unlawfulness and lawfulness of recourse to nuclear weapons.

[Why I Supported ¶ 105 (2)F]

7. In the long run the answer to the conflict which the invention of the nuclear weapon entailed between highest values and most basic needs of the community of States, can only lie in effective reduction and control of nuclear armaments and an improved system of collective security. This is why I have supported Point 2.F of the Conclusions of the Opinion on the existence of a general obligation of States to pursue in good faith and bring to a conclusion negotiations leading to nuclear disarmament in all its aspects under strict and effective international control — although this pronouncement goes, strictly speaking, beyond the question asked of the Court.

(*Signed*) Carl-August FLEISCHHAUER

[Original: English]   [Germany]

DECLARATION OF JUDGE HERCZEGH

According to Article 9 of the Statute of the International Court of Justice, "the representation of the main forms of civilization and of the principal legal systems of the world should be assured" in its membership. Accordingly, it is inevitable that differences of theoretical approach will arise between the members concerning the characteristic features of the system of international law and of its branches, the presence or absence of gaps in this system, and the resolution of possible conflicts between its rules, as well as on other more or less fundamental issues. The preparation of an advisory opinion on the very complicated question put by the General Assembly concerning the legality of the threat or use of nuclear weapons "in any circumstance" has highlighted the different conceptions of international law within the Court. The diversity of these conceptions prevented the Court from finding a more complete solution and therefore a more satisfactory result. The drafting of the reasons and the conclusions of the advisory opinion reflects these divergences. It must nevertheless be noted that the Court pronounced unanimously on several very important points.

In my view, however, in the present state of international law it would have been possible to formulate in the advisory opinion a more specific reply to the General Assembly's request, one less burdened with uncertainty and reluctance. In the fields where certain acts are not totally and universally prohibited "as such" the application of the general principles of law makes it possible to regulate the behaviour of subjects of the international legal order, obliging or authorizing them, as the case may be, to act or refrain from acting in one way or another. The fundamental principles of international humanitarian law, rightly emphasized in the reasons of the advisory opinion, categorically and unequivocally prohibit the use of weapons of mass destruction, including nuclear weapons. International humanitarian law does not recognize any exceptions to these principles.

I believe that the Court should have avoided any treatment whatsoever of the question of reprisals in time of armed conflict, for a detailed consideration, in my view, would have been beyond the scope of the request submitted by the General Assembly. As it happened, the Court saw fit to mention the question in its opinion, but it did so too briefly, risking subsequent hasty and unjustified interpretations.

The relations between points C and E in paragraph 105 of the advisory opinion are not entirely clear, and their respective contents are not absolutely coherent. According to point C, a threat or use of force by means of nuclear weapons must satisfy "all the requirements" of Article 51 of the Charter of the United Nations, concerning natural law and self-defence, whereas the second sentence of point E states that

> "the Court cannot conclude definitively whether the threat or use of nuclear weapons would be lawful or unlawful in an extreme circumstance of self-defence, in which the very survival of a State would be at stake".

In my view, it is not easy to reconcile this sentence with the earlier reference to "all the requirements" of Article 51 of the Charter. Paragraphs 40 and 41 of the opinion stated that the entitlement to resort to self-defence is subject to constraints and that there is "a specific rule . . . well established in international customary law" according to which "self-defence would warrant only measures which are proportional to the armed attack and necessary to respond to it". I think that the Court could have made this statement the subject of formal conclusions in paragraph 105 of the advisory opinion, thus rendering it more specific.

One of the many tasks assigned to the General Assembly — under Article 13 of the Charter of the United Nations — is "the progressive development of international law and its codification". The transformation, by means of codification, of general principles of law and customary rules into rules of treaty law would remove some of the weaknesses inherent in customary law and could certainly help to put an end to the disputes which led up to the request for an opinion addressed to the Court by the General Assembly as to the legality or illegality of the threat or use of nuclear weapons, pending complete nuclear disarmament under strict and effective international control.

I voted in favour of point E in paragraph 105 of the opinion, although I think that this point could have summarized more accurately the current state of international law with respect to the question of the threat or use of nuclear weapons "in any circumstance". In fact, to have voted against this point would have meant taking a negative position on certain essential conclusions — also stated in this opinion and alluded to in point E — which I fully endorse.

(Signed) Geza HERCZEGH

[Hungary]

[Original: French]

DECLARATION OF JUDGE FERRARI BRAVO

EDITOR'S OUTLINE OF FERRARI BRAVO OPINION*

For Deciding This Case, Not the WHO Case

Very First UN General Assembly Resolution: To Eliminate All Atomic Weapons

Cold War Stopped Concept of Illegality, Leading to Concept of Nuclear Deterrence

Importance of ¶ 104: One Must Evaluate Whole Reasoning of the Court

Nuclear Deterrence Has No Legal Force and Is Contrary to UN Charter

Gulf Separating UN Charter Arts. 2.4 and 51 Bridged by NNP Treaty Article VI

Humanitarian Law of Warfare: Protection of Civilian Population and Environment

Theory of Deterrence Is Not a Legal One

Element of Normative Imbalance Could Have Been Placed on Record Carefully

---

*Editor's additions to original text are indicated by bracketed headings or boldface brackets.

[For Deciding This Case, Not the WHO Case]

I have voted in favour of the Advisory Opinion on the legality of nuclear weapons because I think it is incumbent upon the International Court of Justice to do its best to answer the questions put to it by such principal organs of the United Nations as are entitled to seise the Court, particularly when such an answer may increase the likelihood of resolving a deadlock which, in the present case, has been perpetuated for over 50 years, casting a sombre, threatening shadow over the whole of mankind.

The Court, functioning as the principal judicial organ of the United

Nations (Art. 92 of the Charter), was set up to do just that — among other things — and does not have to ask itself whether its reply, given to the best of its ability, can contribute to the development of the situation. Neither does it have to justify itself if that reply is less than exhaustive. I accordingly subscribe fully to the reasons given in support of the Court's decision to allow the question put by the General Assembly.

In that regard, it is however necessary to point out that the matter appears in a quite different light when the Court is seised by a specialized agency of the United Nations, whose competence to make application to the Court is, for reasons of principle, clearly defined. I accordingly also voted in favour of the Opinion whereby the Court decided not to answer the question put to it by the World Health Organization, and consider my conduct to have been consistent. The Court is the principal judicial organ of the United Nations, but it is not the judicial organ of other international bodies whose right to seise the Court needs to be carefully restricted if the intention is to maintain a correct division of competences — and hence of effectiveness — among the international organizations, in a bid to prevent those political functions that the logic of the system has entrusted *only* to the United Nations from being usurped by other organizations which, to say the least, have neither the competence nor the structure to assume them.

*

* *

Having said this, I am however deeply dissatisfied with certain crucial passages of the decision as, to tell the truth, it strikes me as not very courageous and, what is more, difficult to read.

[Very First UN General Assembly Resolution: To Eliminate All Atomic Weapons]

More particularly, I regret that the Court should have arbitrarily divided into two categories the long succession of General Assembly resolutions which begins with resolution 1 (I) of 24 January 1946 and which, at least down to resolution 808 (IX), takes the form of a series of unanimously adopted resolutions. In my view these resolutions are fundamental, particularly the first of them, whose wording had already been determined in Moscow before the United Nations first came into being (for the history of the resolution and for the steps taken in Moscow with a view to entrusting the United Nations with the supervision of atomic energy to which, at that time, only the United States had the key, see *The United Nations in World Affairs, 1945-1947*, New York and London, 1947, p. 391 *et seq.*), and which could, at a pinch, be placed on the same footing as the provisions of the Charter. **As a matter of fact that resolution establishes — and in my view clearly establishes — the existence of an *actual undertaking* of a solemn nature to eliminate all atomic weapons whose presence in military arsenals was considered illegal. The resolution was worded as follows:**

> "5. In particular, the Commission shall make specific proposals: . . .
>
> (c) for the elimination from national armaments of atomic weapons and of all other major weapons adaptable to mass destruction;"

These ideas were repeated on several occasions in other General Assembly resolutions immediately after the founding of the United Nations (see for example resolution 41 (I) or resolution 191 (III)).

[Cold War Stopped Concept of Illegality, Leading to Concept of Nuclear Deterrence]

I am very well aware that the cold war which broke out shortly afterwards (and it does not fall to me to say who was responsible, although I would stress that responsibility did not lie with just one side), prevented the *development* of that concept of illegality (which was subsequently abandoned by the United States which had been its promoter), while giving rise to a whole series of arguments focusing on the concept of nuclear deterrence which has (and this is important, as we shall see) *no legal force*.

However, in my view [. . .] illegality already existed in advance of that time and any production of nuclear weapons had, as a consequence, to be *justified* in the light of that stigma of illegality which could not be effaced. It is, then, to be regretted that such a conclusion is not clearly apparent from the reasoning followed by the Court — a reasoning which, on the contrary, is often difficult to read, being tortuous and ultimately rather inadequate.

[Importance of ¶ 104: One Must Evaluate Whole Reasoning of the Court]

It is however important to acknowledge that there is still paragraph [104] *bis* of the Advisory Opinion, which introduces the operative part and whose importance is really crucial. It in fact suggests that the attentive reader should evaluate the whole of the reasoning given by the Court, take account of those parts of the reasoning which are not reflected in the various paragraphs of the operative part and, what is more, take account of the inevitable gaps in that reasoning. May its readers — and not only the academics — take heed of this advice while bearing in mind that an Advisory Opinion, in spite of the procedural similarities, is not a judgement of the Court. That is particularly true of the Advisory Opinion.

*

*   *

[Nuclear Deterrence Has No Legal Force and Is Contrary to UN Charter]

To be sure, there is no precise and specific rule that prohibits nuclear weapons and draws the fullest conclusions from that prohibition. The theory of deterrence, to which the Opinion makes no more than the barest reference (para. 97), would seem to have merited some further consideration. I have already said that, in my view, the idea of nuclear deterrence has no legal force and I would furthur add that the theory of deterrance, while creating a practice of nuclear-weapon States and their allies, is not able to create a legal practice which could serve as the basis for the creation of an international custom. One could go so far as to say that it is contrary to the law, if one thinks of the effect that it has had upon the Charter of the United Nations.

I will not go so far myself, but feel bound to point out that it is thanks to the doctrine of deterrence that the revolutionary scope of Article 2, paragraph 4, of the Charter has been reduced, while at the same time the scope of Article 51, which ran counter to it according to a traditional logic, has been extended as a whole series of conventional constructions have taken shape around that norm, as can be seen from the two systems governing respectively the Atlantic Alliance on the one hand and on the other the Warsaw Pact, while it was in existence. These are systems which are doubtless governed by legal rules but which proceed from an idea derived *essentially* from the political — and hence not legal — finding according to which the Security Council cannot function in the face of a conflict as major as the type of warfare which is the subject of the present Advisory Opinion would probably be.

[Gulf Separating UN Charter Articles 2.4 and 51 Bridged by NNP Treaty Article VI]

In this way, the gulf separating Article 2, paragraph 4, from Article 51 may be compared to a river which has grown wider, thanks largely to the tremendous rock of deterrence which has been thrown into it. This has occasioned a need to build a bridge across the river and, to that end, to make use of the materials currently available to us, namely, Article VI of the Nuclear Non-Proliferation Treaty.

I very much doubt whether these opinions are really shared by the Court, as the very condensed manner in which the Court has chosen to deal with deterrence is not such as to enable one clearly to understand whether this is really its view. However, it does not allow the exclusion of that possibility either.

In any case, this is in my view the fundamental reason why the Opinion of the Court is bound to include, in its final part, certain arguments based upon a clause of a treaty which cannot logically be given a place there as it is not of a universal character. Those arguments are, however, fully justified by the circumstances in which we now find ourselves, in which the N.P.T. would seem to be the only means whereby we can rapidly arrive at a solution capable of averting catastrophic consequences.

*

*   *

[Humanitarian Law of Warfare: Protection of Civilian Population and Environment]

In conclusion, I take the view that there is as yet no precise and specific rule prohibiting nuclear weapons and drawing the fullest consequences from that prohibition.

It is obvious that no such rule could have come into existence in the political situation that prevailed between 1945 and 1985. However,

I would point out that the whole of the rule-making production of the last 50 years, particularly with regard to the humanitarian law of armed conflict, is irreconcilable with the technological development of the construction of nuclear weapons. **Can one, for example, imagine that just as humanitarian law, an essential and increasingly significant part of the international law of warfare and (of late) of peace as well, is bringing into being a whole series of principles for the protection of the civilian population or the environment, that same international law should continue to accommodate the lawfulness of, for example, the use of the neutron bomb, which leaves the environment intact albeit . . . with the slight drawback that the people living in it are wiped out! If that is the case, it matters little whether a rule specific to the neutron bomb can be found, since it becomes *automatically* unlawful, being quite out of keeping with the majority of the rules of international law.**

This phenomenon is not new, as at every period in its development, since the beginning of the modern era, international law which is essentially a customary law — *and hence has come into being spontaneously* — has encountered situations in which the force of certain rules prevented contrary rules from being established or maintained.

All these considerations are unfortunately obscured, in the Court's Advisory Opinion, by its fear of engaging in a courageous analysis of the development over time of the General Assembly resolutions which, only from a certain period (around the 1960s), occasioned a clear-cut division between nuclear-weapon States (and their allies) and those States that were threatened by the bomb.

[Theory of Deterrence Is Not a Legal One]

I would point out once again that the fact that a rule prohibiting nuclear weapons began to take shape right at the beginning of the life of the United Nations does not mean that the development of that tendency and, as a consequence, the development of its propulsive force, were not cut short at the time at which the two principal Powers, both in possession of nuclear weapons, embarked on the cold war and developed a whole body of instruments — even treaties and conventions — that were focused upon the idea of deterrence. However, this only prevented the *implementation* of the prohibition (that could only be achieved by means of negotiations), whereas the prohibition as such — the "naked" prohibition, if I may express myself in such terms — has remained the same and still operates, at least at the level of the burden of proof, rendering it more difficult for the nuclear-weapon States to justify themselves by references to various applications of the theory of deterrence which, as I said before, *is not* a legal theory.

In other words, one must, by a legal instrument (the agreement) ward off the danger of an entity — the atomic weapon — which as such has nothing legal about it, without its being possible, in any given case, to verify whether the proposed solutions will hold good. Such a verification would require the explosion of the bomb. But would that verification still be meaningful in that event?

[Element of Normative Imbalance Could Have Been Placed on Record Carefully]

This element of normative imbalance between the reasons advanced by the nuclear-weapon States and those of the non-nuclear-weapon States should and could have been placed on record by the Court carefully, rather than in the somewhat contradictory manner in which it is perceived in the Advisory Opinion.

                                        (Signed) L. FERRARI BRAVO
[Original: French]   [Italy]

INDIVIDUAL OPINION OF JUDGE GUILLAUME

EDITOR'S OUTLINE OF GUILLAUME OPINION*
Unsatisfactory Situation Stems from Problems with Applicable Law
NGOs and Media Efforts to Affect the Court
¶ 105 (2)B and ¶ 105 (2)A
I Fully Endorse ¶ 105 (2)C; UN Charter Article 51; Opinion ¶¶ 58-59
Application of Customary International Law: Opinion ¶¶ 22, 78
Law of Neutrality
¶ 105 (2)E 1 and 2 Not Entirely Satisfactory
Right of Self-Defence; Legality of Deterrence
Jus in Bello; Tokyo District Court Opinion
¶ 105 (2)E 2 States Foundation of Policies of Deterrence
I Support ¶ 99 on Importance of Nuclear Non-Proliferation Treaty Article VI
Role of Judge Not to Take Place of Legislator

*Editor's additions to original text are indicated by bracketed headings or boldface brackets.

[Unsatisfactory Situation Stems from Problems with Applicable Law]

1. The advisory opinion given by the Court in this matter was the subject of serious reservations by a number of my colleagues and will probably be received with a chorus of criticism. I share some of the reservations but will not join in the chorus.

Of course the opinion has many imperfections. It deals too quickly with complex questions which should have received fuller and more balanced treatment, for example environmental law, the law of reprisals, humanitarian law and the law of neutrality. In these various areas of the Court, seeking to identify the custom in force, has taken hardly any account, whatever it may say on the matter, of practice and of the *opinio juris* of States, and too often it allowed itself to be guided by considerations falling more within the sphere of natural law than of positive law, and of *lex ferenda* rather than of *lex lata*. It also accorded excessive scope to the resolutions of the General Assembly of the United Nations. This confusion, aggravated by paragraph 104 of the opinion, was not without consequence for the wording adopted in the operative part. Indeed, this operative part, while ruling *ultra petita* with regard to nuclear disarmament, gives no answer on certain points which are only implicit in the question posed. In these circumstances it would be easy to condemn the Court. I will not do so, for this unsatisfactory situation ultimately stems less from the erring ways of the judge than from the applicable law.

[NGOs and Media Efforts to Affect the Court]

2. This being the case, the Court could have considered declining to respond to the request for an advisory opinion. This solution would have found some justification in the circumstances of the referral themselves. The opinion requested by the General Assembly of the United Nations (like indeed the one requested by the World Health Assembly) originated in a campaign conducted by an association called International Association of Lawyers Against Nuclear Arms (IALANA), which in conjunction with various other groups launched in 1992 a project entitled "World Court Project" in order to obtain from the Court a proclamation of the illegality of the threat or use of nuclear weapons. These associations worked very intensively to secure the adoption of the resolutions referring the question to the Court and to induce States hostile to nuclear weapons to make representations to the Court. Indeed, the Court and the judges received thousands of letters inspired by these groups, appealing both to the members' conscience and to the public conscience.

I am sure that the pressure brought to bear in this way did not influence the Court's deliberations but I wondered whether, in such circumstances, the requests for opinions could still be regarded as coming from the Assemblies which had adopted them or whether, on *prima facie* grounds, the Court should not have dismissed them as inadmissible. However, I dare to hope that Governments and intergovernmental institutions will still retain sufficient independence of decision to resist the powerful pressure groups which besiege them today with the support of the mass communication media. I also note that none of the States which appeared before the Court raised such an objection. In the circumstances I did not believe that it should be automatically accepted.

[¶ 105 (2)B and ¶ 105 (2)A]

3. Basically, I share the Court's opinion as stated in operative paragraph [¶ 105] 2B, to the effect that there is in neither customary nor conventional international law any comprehensive and universal prohibition of the threat or use of nuclear weapons as such. On the other hand, I find it hard to understand why, in operative paragraph 2A, the Court saw fit to state that "there is in neither customary nor conventional international law any specific authorization of the threat or use of nuclear weapons". This statement is not incorrect in itself but it is of no interest to the General Assembly of the United Nations since it stems from the view of the Court itself that "the illegality of the use of certain weapons as such does not result from an absence of authorization but, on the contrary, is formulated in terms of prohibition" (para. 52).

[I Fully Endorse ¶ 105 (2)C; UN Charter Article 51; Opinion ¶¶ 58-59]

4. In contrast, I fully endorse operative paragraph 2C, since States can obviously not have recourse to nuclear weapons, or indeed to any weapons, except under the conditions established by the Charter of the United Nations and in particular by its Article 51, concerning the right of individual or collective self-defence. States are moreover bound to respect the conventional rules specifically governing recourse to nuclear weapons which are summarized in paragraphs 58 and 59 of the opinion.

[Application of Customary International Law: Opinion ¶¶ 22, 78]

5. The application of customary humanitarian law to nuclear weapons raised much more difficult questions.

As the Court noted, customary law concerning the conduct of military operations derives mainly from the annex to the Hague Convention IV of 18 October 1907 respecting the Laws and Customs of War on Land. In view of the nature and antiquity of these provisions, it could be asked whether they were applicable to the use, and especially to the threat of use, of nuclear weapons. It seemed legitimate to have the gravest doubts on this latter point. But no nuclear-weapon State contested before the Court that this was the case, and the immense majority, if not all, of the other States was in agreement. The Court could do no more than take note of this consensus in paragraph 22 of its opinion.

These customary rules were summarized by the Court in three categories in paragraph 78 of the opinion: States do not have unlimited freedom of choice in the weapons they use; they must never use weapons which are incapable of distinguishing between civilian and military targets; and they are prohibited to use weapons likely to cause unnecessary suffering to combatants.

I fully subscribe to this analysis but I think that it should have been completed by a reference to the rules concerning the collateral damage which attacks on legitimate military objectives can cause to civilian populations. These rules originated in articles 23(g), 25 and 27 of the annex to the Hague Convention IV. They were the subject of new formulations in the draft convention on the rules of aerial warfare of 1923 and in the resolution adopted by the General Assembly of the League of Nations on 30 September 1938. They were clarified by the United States Nuremberg Military Tribunal in case No. 47. They were further clarified by the General Assembly of the United Nations in its resolution 2444 (XXIII) of 19 December 1968 concerning respect for human rights in armed conflicts, which was adopted unanimously and states:

> "That it is prohibited to launch attacks against the civilian Populations as such;
>
>   That distinction must be made at all times between persons taking part in the hostilities and members of the civilian population to the effect that the latter be spared as much as possible;".

Lastly, they were further developed by article 51 of Protocol I of 1977 Additional to the Geneva Conventions, which condemns attacks on military objectives which may be expected to cause "excessive" incidental damage to the civilian population.

Customary humanitarian law thus contains only one absolute prohibition: the prohibition of so-called "blind" weapons which are incapable of distinguishing between civilian targets and military targets. But nuclear weapons obviously do not necessarily fall into this category.

Furthermore, this law implies comparisons. The collateral damage caused to civilian populations must not be "excessive" in relation to "the military advantage anticipated". The suffering caused to combatants must not be "unnecessary", i.e. it must not cause, in the words of the Court itself, "a harm greater than that unavoidable to achieve legitimate military objectives" (para. 78).

Hence nuclear weapons could not be regarded as illegal by the sole reason of the suffering which they are likely to cause. Such suffering must still be compared with the "military advantage anticipated" or with the "military objectives" pursued.

With regard to nuclear weapons of mass destruction, it is clear however that the damage which they are likely to cause is such that their use could not be envisaged except in extreme cases.

6. The same reasoning holds good with respect to the law of neutrality since, on many occasions, it has been maintained or recognized that the legality of actions carried out by belligerents in neutral territory depends on the "military necessities", as the late Judge Ago noted in the light of a widespread practice described in the addendum to his eighth report to the International Law Commission on the responsibility of States (para. 50 and note 101).

[¶ 105 (2)E 1 and 2 Not Entirely Satisfactory]

7. In short, the Court should therefore have replied to the question on this point by stating that the threat or use of nuclear weapons is compatible with the law applicable in armed conflict only in certain extreme cases. The Court preferred, in operative paragraph 2E, to use a negative formula when it stated that such threat or use were "'generally prohibited". This wording is vague but it nevertheless implies that the threat or use of nuclear weapons are not prohibited "in any circumstance" by the law applicable in armed conflict, as indeed the Court pointed out in paragraph 95 of the opinion.

[Right of Self-Defense; Legality of Deterrence]

8. The Court added in paragraph 2E:

"However, in view of the current state of international law, and of the elements of fact at its disposal, the Court cannot conclude definitively whether the threat or use of nuclear weapons would be lawful or unlawful in an extreme circumstance of self-defence, in which the very survival of a State would be at stake".

Once again, this wording is not entirely satisfactory, and I therefore believe that it needs a little clarification.

None of the States which appeared before the Court raised the question of the relations between the right of legitimate self-defence recognized by Article 51 of the Charter and the principles and rules of the law applicable in armed conflict. All of them argued as if these two types of prescription were independent, in other words as if the *jus ad bellum* and the *jus in bello* constituted two entities having no relation with each other. In some parts of its opinion the Court even seemed to be tempted by such a construction. It may be wondered whether that is indeed the case of whether, on the contrary, the rules of the *jus ad bellum* do not provide any clarification of the rules of the *jus in bello*.

The right of self-defence proclaimed by the Charter of the United Nations is characterized by the Charter as natural law. But Article 51 adds that nothing in the Charter shall impair this right. The same applies *a fortiori* to customary law or treaty law. This conclusion is easily explained, for no system of law, whatever it may be, could deprive one of its subjects of the right to defend its own existence and safeguard its vital interests. Accordingly, international law cannot deprive a State of the right to resort to nuclear weapons if such action constitutes the ultimate means by which it can guarantee its survival. In such a case the State enjoys a kind of "ground for absolution" similar to the one which exists in all systems of criminal law.

The Court did indeed identify this problem when, in paragraph 96 of the opinion, it stated that it cannot

> "lose sight of the fundamental right of every State to survival, and thus its right to resort to self-defence, in accordance with Article 51 of the Charter, when its survival is at stake".

With this in mind, it pointed out in the same paragraph that "an appreciable section of the international community adhered for many years" to "the practice referred to as 'policy of deterrence'". It also stressed that States which adhered to this doctrine and this practice

> "have always, in concert with certain other States, reserved the right to use those weapons in the exercise of the right to self-defence against an armed attack threatening their vital security interests" (para. 66).

It also noted

> "the reservations which certain nuclear-weapon States have appended to the undertakings they have given, notably under the Protocols to the Treaties of Tlatelolco and Rarotonga, and also under the declarations made by them in connection with the extension of the Treaty on the Non-Proliferation of Nuclear Weapons, not to resort to such weapons" (para. 96).

Lastly, the Court observed that the reservations entered against these Protocols and the ones contained in the declarations had "met with no objection from the parties to the Tlatelolco or Rarotonga Treaties or from the Security Council" (para. 62). Indeed, it pointed out that the Security Council had noted with appreciation or welcomed the statements made in this connection (para. 45).

9. In these circumstances, the Court, in my view, ought to have carried its reasoning to its conclusion and explicitly recognized the legality of deterrence for defence of the vital interests of States. It did not do so explicitly, and that is why I was unable to support operative paragraph 2E. But it did so implicitly, and that is why I appended to the advisory opinion an individual opinion and not a dissenting one.

In operative paragraph 2E the Court decided in fact that it could not in those extreme circumstances conclude definitively whether the threat or use of nuclear weapons would be lawful or unlawful. In other words, it concluded that in such circumstances the law provided no guide for States. But if the law is silent in this case, States remain free to act as they intend.

10. International law rests on the principle of the sovereignty of States and thus originates from their consent. In other words, in the excellent language of the Permanent Court, "international law governs relations between independent States. The rules of law binding upon States therefore emanate from their own free will". (*Lotus, Judgment No. 9, 1927, C.P.J.I. series A, No. 10*, p. 18.)

The Court itself had occasion to draw the consequences of this principle in various forms in the case between Nicaragua and the United States. It pointed out that the principle of the sovereignty of States permits all States to decide freely on "the choice of a political, economic, social and cultural system, and the formulation of foreign policy" (*Case concerning Military and Paramilitary activities in and against Nicaragua, I.C.J. Reports 1986*, p. 108). It stated in particular that "in international law there are no rules, other than such rules as may be accepted by the State concerned, by treaty or otherwise, whereby the level of armaments of a sovereign State can be limited, and this principle is valid for all States without exception". *(Ibid.,* p. 135.)

[*Jus in Bello*; Tokyo District Court Opinion]

11. The constant practice of States is along these lines as far as the *jus in bello* is concerned. All the treaties concerning certain types of weapons are formulated in terms of prohibition. This is true, for example, of the 1967 Treaty for the Prohibition of Nuclear Weapons in Latin America, the 1975 Convention on the Prohibition of the Development, Production and Stockpiling of Bacteriological Weapons, the 1981 Convention on Prohibitions or Restrictions on the Use of Certain Conventional Weapons which may be Deemed to be Excessively Injurious, or the 1993 Convention on the Prohibition of the Development, Production, Stockpiling and Use of Chemical Weapons and their Destruction. Similarly, the draft convention annexed to resolutions 45/59 and 46/37 of the General Assembly of the United Nations is designed to achieve according to its own title "the prohibition of the use of nuclear weapons".

It will also be noted that the only national judgement, to my knowledge, to have pronounced on this point did so along the same lines. The Tokyo District Court stated in its judgement of 7 December 1963: "Of course, it is right that the use of a new weapon is legal as long as international law does not prohibit it". *(Japanese Annual of International Law,* 1964, No. 8, p. 235.)

Indeed, and as already pointed out, the Court itself recognized in this opinion the customary nature of such a principle when it stated that "the illegality of the use of certain weapons as such does not result from an absence of authorization but, on the contrary, is formulated in terms of prohibition" (para. 52).

[¶ 105 (2)E 2 States Foundation of Policies of Deterrence]

12. In these circumstances it follows implicitly but necessarily from paragraph 2E of the Court's opinion that States can resort to "the threat or use of nuclear weapons . . . in an extreme circumstance of self-defence, in which the very survival of a State would be at stake". This has always been the foundation of the policies of deterrence whose legality is thus recognized.

[I Support ¶ 99 on Importance of Nuclear Non-Proliferation Treaty Article VI]

13. Nuclear weapons are nevertheless "potentially catastrophic", and it is therefore understandable that the Court should have felt a need to stress in paragraph 99 of its opinion the great importance of article VI of the Treaty on the Non-Proliferation of Nuclear Weapons.

I fully approve of this reference and earnestly hope that the negotiations provided for by this text with regard both to nuclear disarmament and to conventional disarmament will be crowned with success. However, I would have preferred the Court to limit itself to dealing with this question in the reasons for its opinion. For I fear that by adopting operative paragraph 2F, in a formulation which attempts to summarize the obligations of States parties to the Treaty on the Non-Proliferation of Nuclear Weapons, without however doing so clearly, the Court may have ruled *ultra petita*.

[Role of Judge Not to Take Place of Legislator]

14. I should like solemnly to reaffirm in conclusion that it is not the role of the judge to take the place of the legislator. During the last two decades the international community has made considerable progress towards the prohibition of nuclear weapons. But this process has not been completed, and the Court must limit itself to recording the state of the law without being able to substitute its assessment for the will of sovereign States. It is the mark of the greatness of a judge to remain within his role in all humility, whatever religious, philosophical or moral debates he may conduct with himself.

(Signed) Gilbert GUILLAUME

[Original: French] [France]

DISSENTING OPINION OF JUDGE WEERAMANTRY

INDEX

Preliminary Observations on the Opinion of the Court

I. INTRODUCTION

1. Fundamental Importance of Issue before the Court
2. Submissions to the Court
3. Some Preliminary Observations on the United Nations Charter
4. The Law Relevant to Nuclear Weapons
5. Introductory Observations on Humanitarian Law
6. Linkage between Humanitarian Law and the Realities of War
7. The Limit Situation Created by Nuclear Weapons
8. Possession and Use
9. Differing Attitudes of States Supporting Legality
10. Importance of a Clarification of the Law

II. NATURE AND EFFECTS OF NUCLEAR WEAPONS

1. The Nature of the Nuclear Weapon
2. Euphemisms Concealing the Realities of Nuclear War
3. The Effects of Nuclear Weapons
    (a) Damage to the environment and the eco-system
    (b) Damage to future generations
    (c) Damage to civilian populations
    (d) The nuclear winter
    (e) Loss of life
    (f) Medical effects of radiation
    (g) Heat and blast

(*h*) Congenital deformities

(*i*) Transnational damage

(*j*) Potential to destroy all civilization

(*k*) The electro-magnetic pulse

(*l*) Damage to nuclear reactors

(*m*) Damage to food productivity

(*n*) Multiple nuclear explosions resulting from self-defence

(*o*) The "shadow of the mushroom cloud"

4. The Uniqueness of the Nuclear Weapon
5. The Differences in Scientific Knowledge between the Present Time and 1945
6. Do Hiroshima and Nagasaki Show that Nuclear War Is Survivable?
7. A Perspective from the Past

III. HUMANITARIAN LAW

1. Elementary Considerations of Humanity
2. Multicultural Background to the Humanitarian Laws of War
3. Outline of Humanitarian Law
4. Acceptance by States of the Martens Clause
5. The "Dictates of Public Conscience"
6. Impact of the United Nations Charter and Human Rights on "Considerations of Humanity" and "Dictates of Public Conscience"
7. The Argument that "Collateral Damage" Is Unintended
8. Illegality Exists Independently of Specific Prohibitions
9. The "*Lotus*" Decision
10. Specific Rules of the Humanitarian Laws of War

    (*a*) The prohibition against causing unnecessary suffering

    (*b*) The principle of discrimination

    (*c*) Respect for non-belligerent states

    (*d*) The prohibition against genocide

    (*e*) The prohibition against environmental damage

    (*f*) Human rights law

11. Juristic Opinion
12. The 1925 Geneva Gas Protocol
13. Article 23(a) of the Hague Regulations

IV. SELF-DEFENCE

1. Unnecessary Suffering
2. Proportionality/Error
3. Discrimination
4. Non-Belligerent States
5. Genocide
6. Environmental Damage
7. Human Rights

V. SOME GENERAL CONSIDERATIONS

1. Two Philosophical Perspectives
2. The Aims of War
3. The Concept of a "Threat of Force" under the United Nations Charter
4. Equality in the Texture of the Laws of War
5. The Logical Contradiction of a Dual Regime in the Laws of War
6. Nuclear Decision-Making

VI. THE ATTITUDE OF THE INTERNATIONAL COMMUNITY TOWARDS NUCLEAR WEAPONS

1. Universality of the Ultimate Goal of Complete Elimination
2. Overwhelming Majorities in Support of Total Abolition
3. World Public Opinion
4. Current Prohibitions
5. Partial Bans
6. Who Are the States Most Specially Concerned?
7. Have States, by Participating in Regional Treaties, Recognized the Use or Threat of Use of Nuclear Weapons as Legal?

VII. SOME SPECIAL ASPECTS

1. The Non-Proliferation Treaty
2. Deterrence
3. Reprisals
4. Internal Wars
5. The Doctrine of Necessity
6. Limited or Tactical or Batlefield Nuclear Weapons

VIII. SOME ARGUMENTS AGAINST THE GRANT OF AN ADVISORY OPINION
1. The Advisory Opinion Would Be Devoid of Practical Effects
2. Nuclear Weapons Have Preserved World Peace

IX. CONCLUSION
1. The Task before the Court
2. The Alternatives before Humanity

APPENDIX: COMPARISON OF THE EFFECTS OF BOMBS (Demonstrating Danger to Neutral States)

Preliminary Observations on the Opinion of the Court

(a) Reasons for dissent

My considered opinion is that the use or threat of use of nuclear weapons is illegal *in any circumstances whatsoever*. It violates the fundamental principles of international law, and represents the very negation of the humanitarian concerns which underlie the structure of humanitarian law. It offends conventional law and, in particular, the Geneva Gas Protocol of 1925, and Article 23*(a)* of the Hague Regulations of 1907. It contradicts the fundamental principle of the dignity and worth of the human person on which all law depends. It endangers the human environment in a manner which threatens the entirety of life on the planet.

I regret that the Court has not held directly and categorically that the use or threat of use of the weapon is unlawful *in all circumstances without exception*. The Court should have so stated in a vigorous and forthright manner which would have settled this legal question now and forever.

Instead, the Court has moved in the direction of illegality with some far-reaching pronouncements that strongly point in that direction, while making other pronouncements that are both less than clear and clearly wrong.

I have therefore been obliged to title this a Dissenting Opinion, although there are some parts of the Court's Opinion with which I agree, and which may still afford a substantial basis for a conclusion of illegality. Those aspects of the Court's Opinion are discussed below. They do take the law far on the road towards total prohibition. In this sense, the Court's Opinion contains positive pronouncements of significant value.

There are two of the six operative sections of the second part of the Opinion with which I profoundly disagree. I believe those two paragraphs state the law wrongly and incompletely, and I have felt compelled to vote against them.

However, I have voted in favour of paragraph 1 of the *dispositif*, and in favour of four out of the six items in paragraph 2.

(b) The positive aspects of the Court's Opinion

This Opinion represents the first decision of this Court, and indeed of any international tribunal, that clearly formulates limitations on nuclear weapons in terms of the United Nations Charter. It is the first such decision which expressly addresses the contradiction between nuclear weapons and the laws of armed conflict and international humanitarian law. It is the first such decision which expresses the view that the use of nuclear weapons is hemmed in and limited by a variety of treaty obligations.

In the environmental field, it is the first Opinion which expressly embodies, in the context of nuclear weapons, a principle of "prohibition of methods of warfare which not only are intended, but may also be expected to cause" widespread, long-term and severe environmental damage, and "the prohibition of attacks against the natural environment by way of reprisals" (para. 31).

In the field of nuclear disarmament, it also reminds all nations of their obligation to bring these negotiations to their conclusion in all their aspects, thereby ending the coninuance of this threat to the integrity of international law.

Once these propositions are established, one needs only to examine the effects of the use of nuclear weapons to conclude that there is no possibility whatsoever of a use or threat of use that does not offend these principles. This Opinion examines at some length the numerous unique qualities of the nuclear weapon which stand in flagrant contradiction of the basic values underlying the United Nations Charter, international law, and international humanitarian law. In the light of that information, it becomes demonstrably impossible for the weapon to comply with the basic postulates laid down by the Court, thus rendering them illegal in terms of the unanimous finding of the Court.

In particular, I would mention the requirement, in Article 2(4) of the Charter, of compliance with the Purposes of the United Nations. Those Purposes involve respect for human rights, and the dignity and worth of the human person. They also involve friendly relations among nations, and good neighbourliness (see Art. 1 (Purposes and Principles) read with the Preamble). The linkage of legality with compliance with these principles has now been judicially established. Weapons of warfare which can kill a million or a billion human beings (according to the estimates placed before the Court) show scant regard for the dignity and worth of the human person, or for the principle of good neighbourliness. They stand condemned upon the principles laid down by the Court.

Even though I do not agree with the entirety of the Court's Opinion, strong indicators of illegality necessarily flow from the unanimous parts of that Opinion. Further details of the total incompatibility of the weapons with the principles laid down by the Court appear in the body of this Opinion.

It may be that further clarification will be possible in the future.

I proceed now to make some comments on the individual paragraphs of Part 2 of the *dispositif*. I shall deal first with the two paragraphs with which I disagree.

(c) Particular comments on the final paragraph

(i) Paragraph 2(B) — (11 votes to 3)

Regarding paragraph 2(B), I am of the view that there are comprehensive and universal limitations imposed by treaty upon the use of nuclear weapons. Environmental treaties and, in particular, the Geneva Gas Protocol and Article 23(*a*) of the Hague Regulations, are among these. These are dealt with in my Opinion. I do not think it is correct to say that there are no conventional prohibitions upon the use of the weapon.

(ii) Paragraph 2(E) — (7 votes to 7. Casting vote in favour by the President)

I am in fundamental disagreement with both sentences contained within this paragraph.

I strongly oppose the presence of the word "*generally*" in the first sentence. The word is too uncertain in content for use in an Advisory Opinion, and I cannot assent to a proposition which, even by remotest implication, leaves open any possibility that the use of nuclear weapons would not be contrary to law in any circumstances whatsoever. I regret the presence of this word in a sentence which otherwise states the law correctly. It would also appear that the word "generally" introduces an element of internal contradiction into the Court's Opinion, for in paragraphs 2(C) and 2(D) of the Court's Opinion, the Court concludes that nuclear weapons must be consistent with the United Nations Charter, the principles of international law, and the principles of humanitarian law, and, such consistency being impossible, the weapon becomes illegal.

The word "generally" admits of many meanings, ranging through various gradations, from "as a general rule; commonly", to "universally; with respect to all or nearly all".[1] Even with the latter meaning, the word opens a window of permissibility, however narrow, which does not truly reflect the law. There should be no niche in the legal principle, within which a nation may seek refuge, constituting itself the sole judge in its own cause on so important a matter.

The main purpose of this Opinion is to show that, not *generally* but *always*, the threat or use of nuclear weapons would be contrary to the rules of international law and, in particular, to the principles and rules of humanitarian law. Paragraph 2(E) should have been in those terms, and the Opinion need have stated no more.

The second paragraph of 2(E) states that the current state of international law is such that the Court cannot conclude definitely whether the threat or use of the weapon would or would not be lawful in extreme circumstances of self defence. It seems self-evident to me that once nuclear weapons are resorted to, the laws of war (the *ius in bello*) take over, and that there are many principles of the laws of war, as recounted in

---

[1]*The Shorter Oxford English Dictionary*, 3rd ed., 1987, Vol. I, p. 840.

this Opinion, which totally forbid the use of such a weapon. The existing law is sufficiently clear on this matter to have enabled the Court to make a definite pronouncement without leaving this vital question, as though sufficient principles are not already in existence to determine it. All the more should this uncertainty have been eliminated in view of the Court's very definite findings as set out earlier.

(iii) Paragraph 2(A) — (Unanimous)

Speaking for myself, I would have viewed this unquestionable proposition as a preliminary recital, rather than as part of the *dispositif*.

(iv) Paragraph 2(C) — (Unanimous)

The positive features of this paragraph have already been noted. The Court, in this paragraph, has unanimously endorsed Charter-based pre-conditions to the legality of nuclear weapons, which are diametrically opposed to the results of the use of the weapon. I thus read paragraph 2(C) of the *dispositif* as rendering the use of the nuclear weapon illegal without regard [to] the circumstances in which the weapon is used — whether in aggression or in self-defence, whether internationally or internally, whether by individual decision or in concert with other nations. A unanimous endorsement of this principle by all the judges of this Court takes the principle of illegality of use of nuclear weapons a long way forward from the stage when there was no prior judicial consideration of legality of nuclear weapons by any international tribunal.

Those contending that the use of nuclear weapons was within the law argued strongly that what is not expressly prohibited to a state is permitted. On this basis, the use of the nuclear weapon was said to be a matter on which the state's freedom was not limited. I see the limitations laid down in paragraph 2(C) as laying that argument to rest.

(v) Paragraph 2(D) — (Unanimous)

This paragraph, also unanimously endorsed by the Court, lays down the further limitation of compatibility with the requirements of international law applicable in armed conflict, and particularly with the rules of international humanitarian law and specific treaty obligations.

There is a large array of prohibitions laid down here. My Opinion will show what these rules and principles are, and how it is impossible, in the light of the nature and effects of nuclear weapons, for these to be satisfied.

If the weapon is demonstrably contrary to these principles, it is unlawful in accordance with this paragraph of the Court's Opinion.

(vi) Paragraph 2(F) — (Unanimous)

This paragraph is strictly outside the terms of reference of the question. Yet, in the overall context of the nuclear weapons problem, it is a useful reminder of state obligations, and I have accordingly voted in favour of it.

The ensuing Opinion sets out my views on the question before the Court. Since the question posed to the Court relates only to use and threat of use, this Opinion does not deal with the legality of other important aspects of nuclear weapons, such as possession, vertical or horizontal proliferation, assembling or testing.

I should also add that I have some reservations in regard to some of the reasoning in the body of the Court's Opinion. Those reservations will appear in the course of this Opinion. In particular, while agreeing with the Court in the reasoning by which it rejects the various objections raised to admissibility and jurisdiction, I would register my disagreement with the statement in paragraph 14 of the Opinion (lines 23-25) that the refusal to give the World Health Organization the Advisory Opinion requested by it was justified by the Court's lack of jurisdiction in that case. My disagreement with that proposition is the subject of my Dissenting Opinion in that case.

I am of the view that in dealing with the question of reprisals (para. 46), the Court should have affirmatively pronounced on the question of the unlawfulness of belligerent reprisals. I do not agree also with its treatment of the question of intent towards a group as such in relation to genocide, and with its treatment of nuclear deterrence. These aspects are considered in this Opinion.

(vii) Paragraph 1 — (13 votes to 1)

One other matter needs to be mentioned before I commence the substantive part of this Dissenting Opinion. I have voted in favour of the first finding of the Court, recorded in item 1 of the *dispositif*, which follows from the Court's rejection of the various objections to admissibility and jurisdiction which were taken by the States arguing in favour of the legality of nuclear weapons. I strongly support the views expressed by the Court in the course of its reasoning on these matters, but I have some further thoughts upon these objections, which I have set out in my Dissenting Opinion in relation to the WHO Request, where also similar objections were taken. There is no need to repeat those observations in this Opinion, in view of the Court's conclusions. However, what I have stated on these matters in that Dissenting Opinion should be read as supplementary to this Opinion as well.

*

* *

I. INTRODUCTION

1. Fundamental Importance of Issue before the Court

I now begin the substantive part of this Opinion.

This case has from its commencement been the subject of a wave of global interest unparalleled in the annals of this Court. Thirty-five states have filed written statements before the Court and twenty-four have made oral submissions. A multitude of organizations, including several NGO's, have also sent communications to the Court and submitted materials to it; and nearly two million signatures have been actually received by the Court from various organizations and individuals from around 25 countries. In addition, there have been other shipments of signatures so voluminous that the Court could not physically receive them and they have been lodged in various other depositories. If these are also taken into account, the total number of signatures has been estimated by

the Court's Archivist at over three million?[2] The overall number of signatures, all of which could not be deposited in the Court, is well in excess of this figure. The largest number of signatures has been received from Japan, the only nation that has suffered a nuclear attack.[3] Though these organizations and individuals have not made formal submissions to the Court, they evidence a groundswell of global public opinion which is not without legal relevance, as indicated later in this Opinion.

The notion that nuclear weapons are inherently illegal, and that a knowledge of such illegality is of great practical value in obtaining a nuclear-free world, is not new. Albert Schweitzer referred to it, in a letter to Pablo Casals, as early as 1958 in terms of:

> "the most elementary and most obvious argument: namely, that international law prohibits weapons with an unlimitable effect, which cause unlimited damage to people outside the battle zone. This is the case with atomic and nuclear weapons. . . . The argument that these weapons are contrary to international law contains everything that we can reproach them with. It has the advantage of being a *legal argument*. . . . No government can deny that these weapons violate international law . . . and international law cannot be swept aside!"[4]

Though lay opinion has thus long expressed itself on the need for attention to the legal aspects, the matter has not thus far been the subject of any authoritative judicial pronouncement by an international tribunal. It was considered by the courts in Japan in the *Shimoda* case[5] but, until the two current requests for Advisory Opinions from this Court, there has been no international judicial consideration of the

---

[2]In a memorandum responding to an inquiry regarding the number of signatures received, the Archivist observes that "To be precise in this matter is to count the stars in the sky."

[3]The sponsors of a Declaration of Public Conscience from Japan have stated, in a communication to the Registrar, that they have stored in a warehouse in The Hague, 1,757,757 signatures, which the Court had no space to accommodate, in addition to the 1,564,954 actually deposited with the Court. Another source, based in Europe, has reckoned the declarations it has received, in connection with the current applications to the Court, at 3,691,899, of which 3,338,408 have been received from Japan.

[4]*Albert Schweitzer, Letters 1905-1965*, H.W. Bäher (ed.), J. Neugroschel (tr.), 1992, p. 280, letter to Pablo Casals dated 3 October 1958; emphasis added.

[5]*Shimoda v. The Japanese State*, (1963) *Japanese Annual of International Law*, pp. 212-252.

question. The responsibility placed upon the Court is thus of an extraordinarily onerous nature, and its pronouncements must carry extraordinary significance.This matter has been strenuously argued before the Court from opposing points of view. The Court has had the advantage of being addressed by a number of the most distinguished practitioners in the field of international law. In their submissions before the Court, they have referred to the historic nature of this Request by the General Assembly and the Request of the World Health Organization, which has been heard along with it. In the words of one of them, these Requests:

> "will constitute milestones in the history of the Court, if not in history *per se*. It is probable that these requests concern the most important legal issue which has ever been submitted to the Court" (Salmon, Solomon Islands, CR 95/32, p. 38).

In the words of another, "It is not every day that the opportunity of pleading for the survival of humanity in such an august forum is offered" (David, Solomon Islands, CR 95/32, p. 49).

It is thus the gravest of possible issues which confronts the Court in this Advisory Opinion. It requires the Court to scrutinize every available source of international law, quarrying deep, if necessary, into its very bedrock. Seams of untold strength and richness lie therein, waiting to be quarried. Do these sources contain principles mightier than might alone, wherewith to govern the mightiest weapon of destruction yet devised?

It needs no emphasis that the function of the Court is to state the law as it now is, and not as it is envisaged in the future. Is the use or threat of use of nuclear weapons illegal under presently existing principles of law, rather than under aspirational expectations of what the law should be? The Court's concern in answering this Request for an Opinion is with *lex lata* not with *lex ferenda*.

At the most basic level, three alternative possibilities could offer themselves to the Court as it reaches its decision amidst the clash of opposing arguments. If indeed the principles of international law decree that the use of the nuclear weapon is legal, it must so pronounce. The anti-nuclear forces in the world are immensely influential, but that circumstance does not swerve the Court from its duty of pronouncing the use of the weapons legal if that indeed be the law. A second alternative conclusion is that the law gives no definite indication one way or the other. If so, that neutral fact needs to be declared, and a new stimulus may then emerge for the development of the law. Thirdly, if legal rules or principles dictate that the nuclear weapon is illegal, the Court will so pronounce, undeterred again by the immense forces ranged on the side of the legality of the weapon. As stated at the very commencement, this last represents my considered view. **The forces ranged against the view of illegality are truly colossal. However, collisions with the colossal have not deterred the law on its upward course towards the concept of the rule of law. It has not flinched from the task of imposing constraints upon physical power when legal principle so demands. It has been by a determined stand against forces that seemed colossal or irresistible that the rule of law has been won. Once the Court determines what the law is, and ploughs its furrow in that direction, it cannot pause to look over its shoulder at the immense global forces ranged on either side of the debate.**

2. Submissions to the Court

Apart from submissions relating to the competence of the General Assembly to request this Opinion, a large number of submissions on the substantive law have been made on both sides by the numerous states who have appeared before the Court or tendered written submissions.

Though there is necessarily an element of overlap among some of these submissions, they constitute in their totality a vast mass of material, probing the laws of war to their conceptual foundations. Extensive factual material has also been placed before the Court in regard to the many ways in which the nuclear weapon stands alone, even among weapons of mass destruction, for its unique potential of damaging humanity and its environment for generations to come.

On the other hand, those opposing the submission of illegality have argued that, despite a large number of treaties dealing with nuclear weapons, no single clause in any treaty declares nuclear weapons to be illegal in specific terms. They submit that, on the contrary, the various treaties on nuclear weapons entered into by the international community, including the NPT in particular, carry a clear implication of the current legality of nuclear weapons in so far as concerns the nuclear powers. Their position is that the principle of the illegality of the use or threat of use of nuclear weapons still lies in the future, although considerable progress has been made along the road leading to that result. It is *lex ferenda* in their submission, and not yet of the status of *lex lata*. Much to be desired, but not yet achieved, it is a principle waiting to be born.

This Opinion cannot possibly do justice to all of the formal submissions made to the Court, but will attempt to deal with some of the more important among them.

3. Some Preliminary Observations on the United Nations Charter

It was only a few weeks before the world was plunged into the age of the atom that the United Nations Charter was signed. The subscribing nations adopted this document at San Francisco on 26 June 1945. The bomb was dropped on Hiroshima on 6 August 1945. Only forty days intervened between the two events, each so pregnant with meaning for the human future. The United Nations Charter opened a new vista of hope. The bomb opened new vistas of destruction.

Accustomed as it was to the destructiveness of traditional war, the world was shaken and awe-struck at the power of the nuclear bomb — a small bomb by modern standards. The horrors of war, such as were known to those who drafted the Charter, were thus only the comparatively milder horrors of World War II, as they had been experienced thus far. Yet these horrors, seared into the conscience of humanity by the most devastating conflict thus far in human history, were sufficient to galvanize the world community into action, for, in the words of the United Nations Charter, they had "brought untold sorrow to mankind". The potential to bring untold sorrow to mankind was within weeks to be multiplied several-fold by the bomb. Did that document, drafted in total unawareness of this escalation in the weaponry of war, have anything to say of relevance to the nuclear age which lay round the corner?

There are six keynote concepts in the opening words of the Charter which have intense relevance to the matter before the Court.

The Charter's very first words are "We, the peoples of the United Nations" — thereby showing that all that ensues is the will of the *peoples of the world*. Their collective will and desire is the very source of the United Nations Charter and that truth should never be permitted to recede from view. In the matter before the Court, the peoples of the world have a vital interest, and global public opinion has an important influence on the development of the principles of public international law. As will be observed later in this Opinion, the law applicable depends heavily upon "the principles of humanity" and "the dictates of public conscience", in relation to the means and methods of warfare that are permissible.

The Charter's next words refer to the determination of those peoples to save succeeding generations from the scourge of war. The only war they knew was war with non-nuclear weapons. That resolve would presumably have been steeled even further had the destructiveness and the intergenerational effects of nuclear war been known.

The Charter immediately follows those two key concepts with a third — the dignity and worth of the human person. This is recognized as the cardinal unit of value in the global society of the future. A means was about to reveal itself of snuffing it out by the million with the use of a single nuclear weapon.

The fourth observation in the Charter, succeeding hard on the heels of the first three, is the equal rights of nations large and small. This is an ideal which is heavily eroded by the concept of nuclear power.

The next observation refers to the maintenance of obligations arising from treaties and *other sources of international law* (emphasis added). The argument against the legality of nuclear weapons rests principally not upon treaties, but upon such "other sources of international law" (mainly humanitarian law), whose principles are universally accepted.

The sixth relevant observation in the preamble to the Charter is its object of promoting social progress and better standards of life in larger freedom. Far from moving towards this Charter ideal, the weapon we are considering is one which has the potential to send humanity back to the stone age if it survives at all.

It is indeed as though, with remarkable prescience, the founding fathers had picked out the principal areas of relevance to human progress and welfare which could be shattered by the appearance only six weeks away of a weapon which forever would alter the contours of war — a weapon which was to be described by one of its creators, in the words of ancient oriental wisdom, as a "shatterer of worlds".[6]

The Court is now faced with the duty of rendering an Opinion in regard to the legality of this weapon. The six cardinal considerations set out at the very commencement of the Charter need to be kept in constant view, for each of them offers guidelines not to be

---

[6]Robert Oppenheimer, quoting *The Bhagvadgita*. See Peter Goodchild and Robert Oppenheimer, *Shatterer of Worlds*, 1980.

lightly ignored.

4. The Law Relevant to Nuclear Weapons

As Oscar Schachter observes, the law relevant to nuclear weapons is "much more comprehensive than one might infer from the discussions of nuclear strategists and political scientists"[7]

1. The international law applicable generally to armed conflicts — the *jus in bello*, sometimes referred to as the "humanitarian law of war".
2. The *ius ad bellum* — the law governing the right of states to go to war. This law is expressed in the United Nations Charter and related customary law.
3. The *lex specialis* — the international legal obligations that relate specifically to nuclear arms and weapons of mass destruction.
4. The whole corpus of international law that governs state obligations and rights generally, which may affect nuclear weapons policy in particular circumstances.
5. National law, constitutional and statutory, that may apply to decisions on nuclear weapons by national authorities.

All of these will be touched upon in the ensuing Opinion, but the main focus of attention will be on the first category mentioned above.

This examination will also show that each one of the sources of international law, as set out in Article 38(1) of the Court's Statute, supports the conclusion that the use of nuclear weapons in any circumstances is illegal.

5. Introductory Observations on Humanitarian Law

It is in the department of humanitarian law that the most specific and relevant rules relating to this problem can be found.

Humanitarian law and custom have a very ancient lineage. They reach back thousands of years. They were worked out in many civilizations — Chinese, Indian, Greek, Roman, Japanese, Islamic, modern European, among others. Through the ages many

---

[7]Proceedings of the Canadian Conference on Nuclear Weapons and the Law, published as *Lawyers and the Nuclear Debate*, Maxwell Cohen and Margaret Gouin (eds.), 1988, p. 29.

religious and philosophical ideas have been poured into the mould in which modern humanitarian law has been formed. They represented the effort of the human conscience to mitigate in some measure the brutalities and dreadful sufferings of war. In the language of a notable declaration in this regard (the St. Petersburg Declaration of 1868), international humanitarian law is designed to "conciliate the necessities of war with the laws of humanity". In recent times, with the increasing slaughter and devastation made possible by modern weaponry, the dictates of conscience have prompted ever more comprehensive formulations.

It is today a substantial body of law, consisting of general principles flexible enough to accommodate unprecedented developments in weaponry, and firm enough to command the allegiance of all members of the community of nations. This body of general principles exists in addition to over 600 special provisions in the Geneva Conventions and their Additional Protocols, apart from numerous other conventions on special matters such as chemical and bacteriological weapons. It is thus an important body of law in its own right, and this case in a sense puts it to the test.

Humanitarian law is ever in continuous development. It has a vitality of its own. As observed by the 1945 Nuremberg Tribunal, which dealt with undefined "crimes against humanity" and other crimes, "[the law of war] is not static, but by continual adaptation follows the needs of a changing world".[8] Humanitarian law grows as the sufferings of war keep escalating. With the nuclear weapon, those sufferings reach a limit situation, beyond which all else is academic. Humanitarian law, as a living discipline, must respond sensitively, appropriately and meaningfully.

By their very nature, problems in humanitarian law are not abstract, intellectual inquiries which can be pursued in ivory-tower detachment from the sad realities which are their stuff and substance. Not being mere exercises in logic and black-letter law, they cannot be logically or intellectually disentangled from their terrible context. Distasteful though it be to contemplate the brutalities surrounding these legal questions, the legal questions can only be squarely addressed when those brutalities are brought into vivid focus.

The brutalities tend often to be hidden behind a veil of generalities

---

[8]22 *Trial of the Major War Criminals before the International Military Tribunal,* 1948, p. 464.

and platitudes — such as that all war is brutal or that nuclear weapons are the most devastating weapons of mass destruction yet devised. It is necessary to examine more closely what this means in all its stark reality. A close and unvarnished picture is required of the actual human sufferings involved, and of the multifarious threats to the human condition posed by these weapons. Then only can humanitarian law respond appropriately. Indeed, it is by turning the spotlight on the agonies of the battlefield that modern humanitarian law began. This Opinion will therefore examine the factual effects of nuclear weapons in that degree of minimum detail which is necessary to attract to these considerations the matching principles of humanitarian law.

6. Linkage between Humanitarian Law and the Realities of War

The 19th century tended to view war emotionally, as a glorious enterprise, and practically, as a natural extension of diplomacy. Legitimized by some philosophers, respected by nearly all statesmen, and glorified by many a poet and artist, its brutalities tended to be concealed behind screens of legitimacy, respectability and honour.

Henri Dunant's *Memory of Solferino*, written after a visit to the battlefield of Solferino in 1859, dragged the brutalities of war into public view in a manner which shook contemporary civilization out of its complacency and triggered off the development of modern humanitarian law. That spirit of realism needs to be constantly rekindled if the law is not to stray too far from its subject matter, and thus become sterile.

Dunant's historic account touched the conscience of his age to the extent that a legal response seemed imperative. Here is his description of the raw realities of war as practised in his time:

"Here is a hand-to-hand struggle in all its horror and frightfulness: Austrians and Allies trampling each other under foot, killing one another on piles of bleeding corpses, felling their enemies with their rifle butts, crushing skulls, ripping bellies open with sabre and bayonet. No quarter is given. It is a sheer butchery . . .

A little further on, it is the same picture, only made the more ghastly by the approach of a squadron of cavalry, which gallops by, crushing dead and dying beneath its horses' hoofs. One poor man has his jaw carried away; another his head shattered; a third, who could have been saved, has his chest beaten in.

Here comes the artillery, following the cavalry and going at full gallop. The guns crash over the dead and wounded, strewn pell-mell on the ground. Brains spurt under the wheels, limbs are broken and torn, bodies mutilated past recognition — the soil is literally puddled with blood, and the plain littered with human remains."

His description of the aftermath is no less powerful:

"The stillness of the night was broken by groans, by stifled sighs of anguish and suffering. Heart-rending voices kept calling for help. Who could ever describe the agonies of that fearful night?

When the sun came up on the twenty-fifth, it disclosed the most dreadful sights imaginable. Bodies of men and horses covered the battlefield: corpses were strewn over roads, ditches, ravines, thickets and fields: the approaches of Solferino were literally thick with dead."

Such were the realities of war, to which humanitarian law was the response of the legal conscience of the time. The nuclear weapon has increased the savagery a thousandfold since Dunant wrote his famous words. The conscience of our time has accordingly responded in appropriate measure, as amply demonstrated by the global protests, the General Assembly resolutions, and the universal desire to eliminate nuclear weapons altogether. It does not sit back in a spirit of scholarly detachment, drawing its conclusions from refined exercises in legal logic.

Just as it is through close contact with the raw facts of artillery and cavalry warfare that modern humanitarian law emerged, it is through a consideration of the raw facts of nuclear war that an appropriate legal response can emerge.

While we have moved from the cruelties of cavalry and artillery to the exponentially greater cruelties of the atom, we now enjoy a dual advantage, not present in Dunant's time — the established discipline of humanitarian law and ample documentation of the human suffering involved. Realities infinitely more awful than those which confronted Dunant's age of simpler warfare cannot fail to touch the legal conscience of our age.

Here is an eyewitness description from the first use of the weapon in the nuclear age — one of hundreds of such scenes which no doubt occurred simultaneously, and many of which have been recorded in contemporary documentation. The victims were not combatants, as was the case at Solferino:

> "It was a horrible sight. Hundreds of injured people who were trying to escape to the hills passed our house. The sight of them was almost unbearable. Their faces and hands were burnt and swollen; and great sheets of skin had peeled away from their tissues to hang down like rags on a scarecrow. They moved like a line of ants. All through the night they went past our house, but this morning they had stopped. I found them lying on both sides of the road, so thick that it was impossible to pass without stepping on them.
>
> "And they had no faces! Their eyes, noses and mouths had been burned away, and it looked like their ears had been melted off. It was hard to tell front from back. One soldier, whose features had been destroyed and was left with his white teeth sticking out, asked me for some water but I didn't have any. [I clasped my hands and prayed for him. He didn't say anything more.] His plea for water must have been his last words."[9]

Multiply this a thousand-fold or even a million-fold and we have a picture of just one of the many possible effects of nuclear war.

Massive documentation details the sufferings caused by nuclear weapons — from the immediate charring and mutilation for miles from the site of the explosion, to the lingering after-effects — the cancers and the leukaemias which imperil human health, the genetic mutations which threaten human integrity, the environmental devastation which endangers the human habitat, the disruption of all organization, which undermines human society.

The Hiroshima and Nagasaki experience were two isolated incidents three days apart. They tell us very little of the effects of multiple explosions that would almost inevitably follow in quick succession in the event of a nuclear war today (see section II.6 below). Moreover,

---

[9]*Hiroshima Diary: The Journal of a Japanese Physician, August 6-September 30, 1945*, by Michihiko Hachiya, M.D., translated and edited by Warner Wells, M.D., University of North Carolina Press, 1955, pp. 14-15.

fifty years of development have intervened, with bombs being available now which carry seventy or even seven hundred times the explosive power of the Hiroshima and Nagasaki bombs. The devastation of Hiroshima and Nagasaki could be magnified several-fold by just one bomb today, leave alone a succession of bombs.

7. The Limit Situation Created by Nuclear Weapons

Apart from human suffering, nuclear weapons, as observed earlier, take us into a limit situation. They have the potential to destroy all civilization — all that thousands of years of effort in all cultures have produced. It is true "the dreary story of sickened survivors lapsing into stone-age brutality is not an assignment that any sensitive person undertakes willingly"[10], but it is necessary to "contemplate the likely outcome of mankind's present course clearsightedly" (*ibid.*). Since nuclear weapons can destroy all life on the planet, they imperil all that humanity has ever stood for, and humanity itself.

An analogy may here be drawn between the law relating to the environment and the law relating to war.

At one time it was thought that the atmosphere, the seas and the land surface of the planet were vast enough to absorb any degree of pollution and yet rehabilitate themselves. The law was consequently very lax in its attitude towards pollution. However, with the realization that a limit situation would soon be reached, beyond which the environment could absorb no further pollution without danger of collapse, the law found itself compelled to reorientate its attitude towards the environment.

With the law of war, it is no different. Until the advent of nuclear war, it was thought that however massive the scale of a war, humanity could survive and reorder its affairs. With the nuclear weapon, a limit situation was reached, in that the grim prospect opened out that humanity may well fail to survive the next nuclear war, or that all civilization may be destroyed. That limit situation has compelled the law of war to reorientate its attitudes and face this new reality.

---

[10]"The Medical and Ecological Effects of Nuclear War" by Don G. Bates, Professor of the History of Medicine, McGill University, in (1983) 28 *McGill Law Journal*, p. 717.

8. Possession and Use

Although it is the use of nuclear weapons, and not possession, that is the subject of this reference, many arguments have been addressed to the Court which deal with possession and which therefore are not pertinent to the issues before the Court.

For example, the Court was referred, in support of the position that nuclear weapons are a matter within the sovereign authority of each state, to the following passage in *Military and Paramilitary Activities in and against Nicaragua*:

> "in international law, there are no rules, other than such rules as may be accepted by the State concerned, by treaty or otherwise, whereby the level of armaments of a sovereign State can be limited" (France, CR 95/23, p. 79; *I.C.J. Reports 1986*, p. 135; emphasis added).

This passage clearly relates to possession, not use.

Much was made also of the Nuclear Non-Proliferation Treaty, as permitting nuclear weapons to the nuclear weapons states. Here again such permission, if any, as may be inferred from that treaty relates to possession and not use, for nowhere does the NPT contemplate or deal with the use or threat of use of nuclear weapons. On questions of use or threat of use, the NPT is irrelevant.

9. Differing Attitudes of States Supporting Legality

There are some significant differences between the positions adopted by States supporting the legality of the use of nuclear weapons. Indeed, in relation to some very basic matters, there are divergent approaches among the nuclear States themselves.

Thus the French position is that

> "This criterion of proportionality does not itself rule out in principle the utilization, whether in response or as a matter of first use, of any particular weapon whatsoever, including a nuclear weapon, *provided that such use is intended to withstand an attack and appears to be the most appropriate means of doing so*" (French Written Statement, tr. p. 15; emphasis added).

According to this view, the factors referred to could, in a given case, even outweigh the principle of proportionality. It suggests that the governing criterion determining the permissibility of the weapon is whether it is the most appropriate means of withstanding the attack. The United States position is that:

> "Whether an attack with nuclear weapons would be dispro-portionate depends entirely on the circumstances, including the nature of the enemy threat, the importance of destroying the objective, the character, size and likely effects of the de-vice, and the magnitude of the risk to civilians" (United States Written Statement, p. 23).

The United States position thus carefully takes into account such cir-cumstances as the character, size and effects of the device and the magnitude of risk to civilians.

The position of the Russian Federation is that the "Martens clause" (see section III.4) is not working at all and that today the Martens clause may formally be considered inapplicable (Written Statement, p. 13).

The United Kingdom, on the other hand, while accepting the ap-plicability of the Martens clause, submits that the clause does not on its own establish the illegality of nuclear weapons (UK Written State-ment, p. 48, para. 3.58). The United Kingdom argues that the terms of the Martens clause make it necessary to point to a rule of customary law outlawing the use of nuclear weapons.

These different perceptions of the scope, and indeed of the very basis of the claim of legality on the part of the nuclear powers them-selves, call for careful examination in the context of the question ad-dressed to the Court.

10. The Importance of a Clarification of the Law

The importance of a clarification of the law upon the legality of nuclear weapons cannot be overemphasized.

On June 6, 1899, Mr. Martens (presiding over the Second Subcom-mission of the Second Commission of the Hague Conference), after whom the Martens clause has been named, (which will be referred to at some length in this Opinion), made the following observations in reply to the contention that it was preferable to leave the laws of war in a vague state. He said:

> "But is this opinion quite just? Is this uncertainty advanta-geous to the weak? Do the weak become stronger because the

duties of the strong are not determined? Do the strong become weaker because their *rights* are specifically defined and consequently limited? I do not think so. I am fully convinced that it is particularly in the interest of the weak that these rights and duties be defined. . . .

Twice, in 1874 and 1899, two great international Conferences have gathered together the most competent and eminent men of the civilized world on the subject. They have not succeeded in determining the laws and customs of war. They have separated, leaving utter vagueness for all these questions. . . .

To leave uncertainty hovering over these questions would necessarily be to allow the interests of force to triumph over those of humanity . . ."[11]

It is in this quest for clarity that the General Assembly has asked the Court to render an Opinion on the use of nuclear weapons. The nations who control these weapons have opposed this application, and so have some others. It is in the interests of all nations that this matter be clarified which, for one reason or another, has not been specifically addressed for the past fifty years. It has remained unresolved and has hung over the future of humanity, like a great question mark, raising even issues so profound as the future of human life upon the planet.

The law needs to be clearly stated in the light of State rights and obligations under the new world dispensation brought about by the United Nations Charter which, for the first time in human history, outlawed war by the consensus of the community of nations. Fifty years have passed since that epoch-making document which yet lay in the distant future when Martens spoke. Those fifty years have been years of inaction, in so far as concerns the clarification of this most important of legal issues ever to face the global community.

II. NATURE AND EFFECTS OF NUCLEAR WEAPONS

1. The Nature of the Nuclear Weapon

The matter before the Court involves the application of humanitar-

---

[11]J.B. Scott, "The Conference of 1899", *The Proceedings of the Hague Peace Conferences,* 1920, pp. 506-507; emphasis added.

ian law to questions of fact, not the construction of humanitarian law as an abstract body of knowledge.

The Court is inquiring into the question whether the use of nuclear weapons produces factual consequences of such an inhumane nature as to clash with the basic principles of humanitarian law. Both in regard to this Advisory Opinion and in regard to that sought by the World Health Organization, a vast mass of factual material has been placed before the Court as an aid to its appreciation of the many ways in which the effects of nuclear weapons attract the application of various principles of humanitarian law. It is necessary to examine these specific facts, at least in outline, for they illustrate, more than any generalities can, the unique features of the nuclear weapon.

Moreover, the contention that nuclear war is in some way containable renders essential a detailed consideration of the unique and irreversible nature of the effects of nuclear weapons.

2. Euphemisms Concealing the Realities of Nuclear War

It would be a paradox if international law, a system intended to promote world peace and order, should have a place within it for an entity that can cause total destruction of the world system, the millennia of civilization which have produced it, and humanity itself. A factor which powerfully conceals that contradiction, even to the extent of keeping humanitarian law at bay, is the use of euphemistic language — the disembodied language of military operations and the polite language of diplomacy. They conceal the horror of nuclear war, diverting attention to intellectual concepts such as self-defence, reprisals, and proportionate damage which can have little relevance to a situation of total destruction.

Horrendous damage to civilians and neutrals is described as collateral damage, because it was not directly intended; incineration of cities becomes "considerable thermal damage". One speaks of "acceptable levels of casualties", even if megadeaths are involved. Maintaining the balance of terror is described as "nuclear preparedness"; assured destruction as "deterrence", total devastation of the environment as "environmental damage". Clinically detached from their human context, such expressions bypass the world of human suffering, out of which humanitarian law has sprung.

As observed at the commencement of this Opinion, humanitarian law needs to be brought into juxtaposition with the raw realities of war if it is to respond adequately. Such language is a hindrance to this process.[12]

Both ancient philosophy and modern linguistics have clearly identified the problem of the obscuring of great issues through language which conceals their key content. Confucius, when asked how he thought order and morality could be created in the state, answered, "By correcting names". By this he meant calling each thing by its correct name.[13]

Modern semantics has likewise exposed the confusion caused by words of euphemism, which conceal the true meanings of concepts.[14] The language of nuclear war, rich in these euphemisms, tends to sidetrack the real issues of extermination by the million, incineration of the populations of cities, genetic deformities, inducement of cancers, destruction of the food chain, and the imperilling of civilization. The mass extinction of human lives is treated with the detachment of entries in a ledger which can somehow be reconciled. If humanitarian law is to address its tasks with clarity, it needs to strip away these verbal dressings and come to grips with its real subject-matter. Bland and disembodied language should not be permitted to conceal the basic contradictions between the nuclear weapon and the fundamentals of international law.

3. The Effects of the Nuclear Weapon

Before 1945 "the highest explosive effect of bombs was produced by TNT devices of about 20 tons".[15] The nuclear weapons exploded in Hiroshima and Nagasaki were more or less of the explosive power of 15 and 12 kilotons respectively, i.e., 15,000 and 12,000 tons of TNT (trinitrotoluene) respectively. Many of the weapons existing today and in process of being tested represent several multiples of the explosive

---

[12]This aspect is addressed in a volume of contemporary philosophical explorations of the problem of war, *The Critique of War*, Robert Ginsberg (ed.), 1969. See, in particular, Ch. 6, "War and the Crisis of Language" by Thomas Merton.

[13]Cited in Robert S. Hartman, "The Revolution Against War", in Ginsberg (ed.), *ibid.*, p. 324.

[14]"They serve to build these figments of hell into the system of power politics, and to dim the minds of the nuclear citizens." (*Ibid.*, p. 325.)

[15]N. Singh and E. McWhinney, *Nuclear Weapons and Contemporary International Law*, 1989, p. 29.

power of these bombs. Bombs in the megaton (equivalent to a million tons of TNT) and multiple megaton range are in the world's nuclear arsenals, some being even in excess of 20 megatons (equivalent to 20 million tons of TNT). A one-megaton bomb, representing the explosive power of a million tons of TNT, would be around 70 times the explosive power of the bombs used on Japan, and a 20-megaton bomb well over a thousand times that explosive power.

Since the mind is numbed by such abstract figures and cannot comprehend them, they have been graphically concretized in various ways. One of them is to picture the quantity of TNT represented by a single one-megaton bomb, in terms of its transport by rail. It has been estimated that this would require a train two hundred miles long.[16] When one is carrying death and destruction to an enemy in war through the use of a single one-megaton bomb, it assists the comprehension of this phenomenon to think in terms of a 200-mile train loaded with TNT being driven into enemy territory, to be exploded there. It cannot be said that international law would consider this legal. Nor does it make any difference if the train is not 200 miles long, but 100 miles, 50 miles, 10 miles, or only 1 mile. Nor, again, could it matter if the train is 1000 miles long, as would be the case with a 5-megaton bomb, or 4000 miles long, as would be the case with a 20-megaton bomb.

Such is the power of the weapon upon which the Court is deliberating — power which dwarfs all historical precedents, even if they are considered cumulatively. A 5-megaton weapon would represent more explosive power than all of the bombs used in World War II and a twenty-megaton bomb "more than all of the explosives used in all of the wars in the history of mankind" (ibid.).

The weapons used at Hiroshima and Nagasaki are "small" weapons compared with those available today and, as observed earlier, a one-megaton bomb would represent around 70 Hiroshimas and a 15-megaton bomb around 1000 Hiroshimas. Yet the unprecedented magnitude of its destructive power is only one of the unique features of the bomb. It is unique in its uncontainability in both space and time. It is unique as a source of peril to the human future. It is unique as a source of continuing danger to human health, even long after its use. Its infringement of humanitarian law goes beyond its being a weapon of mass

---

[16]Bates, op. cit., p. 719.

destruction[17] to reasons which penetrate far deeper into the core of humanitarian law.

Atomic weapons have certain special characteristics distinguishing them from conventional weapons, which were summarized by the United States Atomic Energy Commission in terms that:

"it differs from other bombs in three important respects: *first*, the amount of energy released by an atomic bomb is a thousand or more times as great as that produced by the most powerful TNT bombs; *secondly*, the explosion of the bomb is accompanied by highly penetrating and deleterious invisible rays, in addition to intense heat and light; and, *thirdly*, the substances which remain after the explosion are radio-active, emitting radiations capable of producing harmful consequences in living organisms".[18]

The following more detailed analysis is based on materials presented to the Court, which have not been contradicted at the hearings, even by the States contending that the use of nuclear weapons is not illegal. They constitute the essential factual foundation on which the legal arguments rest, and without which the legal argument is in danger of being reduced to mere academic disputation.

(a)   Damage to the environment and the eco-system[19]

The extent of damage to the environment, which no other weapon is capable of causing, has been summarized in 1987 by the World Commission on the Environment and Development in the following terms:

"The likely consequences of nuclear war make other threats to the environment pale into insignificance. Nuclear weapons represent a qualitatively new step in the development of warfare. One thermonuclear bomb can have an

---

[17]The Final Document of the First Special Session of the United Nations General Assembly devoted to Disarmament (1978) unanimously categorized nuclear weapons as weapons of mass destruction, a conclusion which was adopted by consensus (C 95/25, p. 17).

[18]*Effects of Atomic Weapons*, prepared by the US Atomic Energy Commission in co-operation with the Department of Defense, 1950, cited in Singh & McWhinney, *op. cit.*, p. 30.

[19]On environmental law, see further section III.10(*e*) below.

explosive power greater than all the explosives used in wars
since the invention of gunpowder. In addition to the destructive effects of blast and heat, immensely magnified by
these weapons, they introduce a new lethal agent — ionising radiation — that extends lethal effects over both space
and time."[20]

Nuclear weapons have the potential to destroy the entire eco-
system of the planet. Those already in the world's arsenals have the
potential of destroying life on the planet several times over.

Another special feature of the nuclear weapon, referred to at
the hearings, is the damage caused by ionizing radiation to conif-
erous forests, crops, the food chain, livestock and the marine eco-
system.

(b) Damage to future generations

The effects upon the eco-system extend, for practical purposes,
beyond the limits of all foreseeable historical time. The half-life of one
of the by-products of a nuclear explosion — plutonium 239 — is over
twenty thousand years. With a major nuclear exchange it would require
several of these "half-life" periods before the residuary radioactivity
becomes minimal. Half-life is "the period in which the rate of radioactive emission by a pure sample falls by a factor of two. Among
known radioactive isotopes, half lives range from about 10-7 seconds
to 1016 years". [21]

The following table gives the half-lives of the principal radioactive
elements that result from a nuclear test.[22]

Nucleid		Half-Life (in years)
Cesium	137	30.2
Strontium	90	28.6
Plutonium	239	24,100.0
Plutonium	240	6,570.0
Plutonium	241	14.4
Americium	241	432.0

---

[20]World Commission on Environment and Development ("the Brundtland
Commission"), *Our Common Future* (1987), p. 295, cited in CR 95/22, p. 55.

[21]*Encyclopedia Britannica Micropaedia*, 1992 ed., Vol. 9, p. 893.

[22]Source: *Radioecology*, Holm (ed.), 1995, World Scientific Publishing Co.

Theoretically, this could run to tens of thousands of years. At any level of discourse, it would be safe to pronounce that no one generation is entitled, for whatever purpose, to inflict such damage on succeeding generations.

This Court, as the principal judicial organ of the United Nations, empowered to state and apply international law with an authority matched by no other tribunal must, in its jurisprudence, pay due recognition to the rights of future generations. If there is any tribunal that can recognize and protect their interests under the law, it is this Court.

It is to be noted in this context that the rights of future generations have passed the stage when they were merely an embryonic right struggling for recognition. They have woven themselves into international law through major treaties, through juristic opinion and through general principles of law recognized by civilized nations.

Among treaties may be mentioned, the 1979 London Ocean Dumping Convention, the 1973 Convention on International Trade in Endangered Species, and the 1972 Convention Concerning the Protection of the World Cultural and Natural Heritage. All of these expressly incorporate the principle of protecting the natural environment for future generations, and elevate the concept to the level of binding state obligation.

Juristic opinion is now abundant, with several major treatises appearing upon the subject and with such concepts as intergenerational equity and the common heritage of mankind being academically well established.[23] Moreover, there is a growing awareness of the ways in which a multiplicity of traditional legal systems across the globe protect the environment for future generations. To these must be added a series of major international declarations commencing with the 1972 Stockholm Declaration on the Human Environment.

When incontrovertible scientific evidence speaks of pollution of the environment on a scale that spans hundreds of generations, this Court would fail in its trust if it did not take serious note of the ways in which the distant future is protected by present law. The ideals of the United Nations Charter do not limit themselves to the present, for they look forward to the promotion of social progress and better standards of life, and they fix their vision, not only on the present, but on "succeeding generations". This one factor of impairment of the envi-

---

[23]For further references, see Edith Brown Weiss, *In Fairness to Future Generations: International Law, Common Patrimony and Intergenerational Equity*, 1989.

ronment over such a seemingly infinite time span would by itself be
sufficient to call into operation the protective principles of international law which the Court, as the pre-eminent authority empowered to
state them, must necessarily apply.

(c)   Damage to civilian populations

This needs no elaboration, for nuclear weapons surpass all other
weapons of mass destruction in this respect. In the words of a well-
known study of the development of international law:

> "A characteristic of the weapons of mass destruction — the
> ABC weapons — is that their destructive effect cannot be lim-
> ited in space and time to military objectives. Consequently
> their use would imply the extinction of unforeseeable and in-
> determinable masses of the civilian population. This means
> also that their actual employment would be — even in the
> absence of explicit treaty provisions — contrary to interna-
> tional law, but it is also true that the problem of the weapons
> of mass destruction has grown out of the sphere of humanitar-
> ian law taken in the narrow sense and has become one of the
> fundamental issues of the peaceful coexistence of States with
> different social systems."[24]

d)   The nuclear winter

One of the possible after-effects of an exchange of nuclear weapons is the nuclear winter, a condition caused by the accumulation of
hundreds of millions of tons of soot in the atmosphere, in consequence
of fires in cities, in forests and the countryside, caused by nuclear
weapons. The smoke cloud and the debris from multiple explosions
blots out sunlight, resulting in crop failures throughout the world and
global starvation. Starting with the paper by Turco, Toon, Ackerman,
Pollack and Sagan (known as the TTAPS study after the names of its
authors) on "Nuclear Winter: Global Consequences of Multiple Nuclear Explosions",[25] an enormous volume of detailed scientific work
has been done on the effect of the dust and smoke clouds generated in

---

[24]Géza Herczegh, *Development of International Humanitarian Law*, 1984, p. 93.
"ABC weapons" refer to atomic, biological and chemical weapons.

[25]*Science*, December 23, 1983, Vol. 222, p. 1283.

nuclear war. The TTAPS study showed that smoke clouds in one hemisphere could within weeks move into the other hemisphere.[26] TTAPS and other studies show that a small temperature drop of a few degrees during the ripening season, caused by the nuclear winter, can result in extensive crop failure even on an hemispherical scale. Such consequences are therefore ominous for non-combatant countries also.

"There is now a consensus that the climatic effects of a nuclear winter and the resulting lack of food aggravated by the destroyed infrastructure could have a greater overall impact on the global population than the immediate effects of the nuclear explosions. The evidence is growing that in a post-war nuclear world Homo Sapiens will not have an ecological niche to which he could flee. It is apparent that life everywhere on this

---

[26]The movement of a cloud of dust particles from one hemisphere to another, with the resultant effects resembling those of a nuclear winter, are not futuristic scenarios unrelated to past experience. In 1815, the eruption of the Indonesian volcano, Tambora, injected dust and smoke into the atmosphere on a scale so great as to result in worldwide crop failure and darkness in 1816. *The Scientific American*, March 1984, p. 58, reproduced a poem, "Darkness", written by Lord Byron, thought to have been inspired by this year without a summer. At a hearing of the US Senate on the effects of nuclear war, in December 1983, the Russian physicist, Kapitza, drew attention to this poem, in the context of the effects of nuclear war, referring to it as one well-known to Russians through its translation by the novelist Ivan Turgenev. Here are some extracts, capturing with poetic vision the human despair and the environmental desolation of the post-nuclear scene:

> "A fearful hope was all the world contain'd;
> Forests were set on fire — but hour by hour
> They fell and faded — and the crackling trunks
> Extinguish'd with a crash — and all was black.
> The brows of men by the despairing light
> Wore an unearthly aspect, as by fits
> The flashes fell upon them; some lay down
> And hid their eyes and wept; ...
>
> ... The world was void,
> The populous and the powerful was a lump,
> Seasonless, herbless, treeless, manless, lifeless —
> A lump of death — a chaos of hard clay
> The rivers, lakes, and ocean all stood still,
> And nothing stirr'd within their silent depths;
> Ships sailorless lay rotting on the sea ... "

planet would be threatened."[27]

(e) Loss of life

The WHO estimate of the number of dead in the event of the use of a single bomb, a limited war and a total war vary from one million to one billion, with, in addition, a similar number of injured in each case.

Deaths resulting from the only two uses of nuclear weapons in war — Hiroshima and Nagasaki — were 140,000 and 74,000 respectively, according to the representative of Japan, out of total populations of 350,000 and 240,000 respectively. Had these same bombs been exploded in cities with densely-packed populations of millions, such as Tokyo, New York, Paris, London or Moscow, the loss of life would have been incalculably more.

An interesting statistic given to the Court by the Mayor of Nagasaki is that the bombing of Dresden by 773 British aircraft followed by a shower of 650,000 incendiary bombs by 450 American aircraft caused 135,000 deaths — a similar result to a single nuclear bomb on Hiroshima — a "small" bomb by today's standards.

(f) Medical effects of radiation

Nuclear weapons produce instantaneous radiation, in addition to which there is also radioactive fall-out.

> "It is well established that residual nuclear radiation is a feature of the fission or Atomic bomb as much as the thermonuclear weapon known as the 'fusion bomb' or H-bomb."[28]

Over and above the immediate effects just set out, there are longer term effects caused by ionizing radiation acting on human beings and on the environment. Such ionization causes cell damage and the changes that occur may destroy the cell or diminish its capacity to function.[29]

---

[27]Wilfrid Bach, "Climatic Consequences of Nuclear War", in *Proceedings of the Sixth World Congress of the International Physicians for the Prevention of Nuclear War (IPPNW)*, Cologne, 1986, published as *Maintain Life on Earth!*, 1987, p. 154.

[28]Singh & McWhinney, *op. cit.*, p. 123.

[29]Herbert Abrams, "Chernobyl and the Short-Term Medical Effects of Nuclear War", in *Proceedings of the IPPNW Congress, op. cit.*, p. 122.

After a nuclear attack the victim population suffers from heat, blast and radiation, and separate studies of the effects of radiation are complicated by injuries from blast and heat. Chernobyl has however given an opportunity for study of the effects of radiation alone, for:

"Chernobyl represents the largest experience in recorded time of the effects of whole body radiation on human subjects, uncomplicated by blast and/or burn."[30]

Apart from the long-term effects such as keloids and cancers, these effects include in the short-term anorexia, diarrhoea, cessation of production of new blood cells, haemorrhage, bone marrow damage, damage to the central nervous system, convulsions, vascular damage, and cardiovascular collapse.[31]

Chernobyl, involving radiation damage alone, in a comparatively lightly populated area, strained the medical resources of a powerful nation and necessitated the pouring in of medical personnel, supplies and equipment from across the Soviet Union — 5000 trucks, 800 buses, 240 ambulances, helicopters and special trains.[32] Yet the Chernobyl explosion was thought to be approximately that of a half-kiloton bomb (*ibid.*, p. 127) — about 1/25 of the comparatively "small" Hiroshima bomb, which was only 1/70 the size of a one-megaton bomb. As observed already, the nuclear arsenals contain multi-megaton bombs today.

The effects of radiation are not only agonizing, but are spread out over an entire lifetime. Deaths after a long life of suffering have occurred in Hiroshima and Nagasaki, decades after the nuclear weapon hit those cities. The Mayor of Hiroshima has given the Court some glimpses of the lingering agonies of the survivors — all of which is amply documented in a vast literature that has grown up around the subject. Indonesia made reference to Antonio Cassese's *Violence and Law in the Modern Age* (1988), which draws attention to the fact that "the quality of human suffering . . . does not emerge from the figures and statistics only . . . but from the account of survivors". These re-

---

[30]*Ibid.*, p. 120.
[31]*Ibid.*, pp. 122-125.
[32]*Ibid.*, p. 121.

cords of harrowing suffering are numerous and well known.[33]

Reference should also be made to the many documents received by the Registry in this regard, including materials from the *International Symposium: Fifty Years since the Atomic Bombing of Hiroshima and Nagasaki*. It is not possible in this Opinion even to attempt the briefest summary of the details of these sufferings.

The death toll from lingering death by radiation is still adding to the numbers. Over 320,000 people who survived but were affected by radiation suffer from various malignant tumours caused by radiation, including leukaemia, thyroid cancer, breast cancer, lung cancer, gastric cancer, cataracts and a variety of other after-effects more than half a century later, according to statistics given to the Court by the representative of Japan. With nuclear weapons presently in the world's arsenals of several multiples of the power of those explosions, the scale of damage expands exponentially.

As stated by WHO (CR 95/22, pp. 23-24), overexposure to radiation suppresses the body's immune systems and increases victims' vulnerability to infection and cancers.

Apart from an increase in genetic effects and the disfiguring keloid tumours already referred to, radiation injuries have also given rise to psychological traumas which continue to be noted among the survivors of Hiroshima and Nagasaki. Radiation injuries result from direct exposure, from radiation emitted from the ground, from buildings charged with radioactivity, and from radioactive fall-out back to the ground several months later from soot or dust which had been whirled up into the stratosphere by the force of the explosion.[34]

In addition to these factors, there is an immense volume of specific material relating to the medical effects of nuclear war. A fuller account of this medical material appears in my Dissenting Opinion on the WHO Request. That medical material should also be considered as incorporated in this account of the unique effects of the nuclear weapon.

---

[33]Among the internationally known contemporary accounts are John Hersey, *Hiroshima* (to which *The New Yorker* devoted its whole issue of 31 August 1946, and which has since appeared as a Penguin Classic, 1946); *Hiroshima Diary: The Journal of a Japanese Physician, August 6–September 30, 1945*, by Michihiko Hachiya, M.D., *op. cit.*); and *The Day Man Lost: Hiroshima, 6 August 1945* (Kodansha, 1972). They are all part of a voluminous documentation.

[34]Over the effects of radiation, see, generally, *Nuclear Radiation in Warfare*, 1981, by Professor Joseph Rotblat, the Nobel Laureate.

(g) Heat and blast

Nuclear weapons cause damage in three ways — through heat, blast and radiation. As stated by the WHO representative, while the first two differ quantitatively from those resulting from the explosion of conventional bombs, the third is peculiar to nuclear weapons. In addition to instantaneous radiation, there is also radioactive fall-out.

The distinctiveness of the nuclear weapon can also be seen from statistics of the magnitude of the heat and blast it produces. The representative of Japan drew our attention to estimates that the bomb blasts in Hiroshima and Nagasaki produced temperatures of several million degrees centigrade and pressures of several hundred thousand atmospheres. In the bright fireball of the nuclear explosion, the temperature and pressure are said indeed to be the same as those at the centre of the sun.[35] Whirlwinds and firestorms were created approximately 30 minutes after the explosion. From these causes 70,147 houses in Hiroshima and 18,400 in Nagasaki were destroyed. The blastwind set up by the initial shockwave had a speed of nearly 1000 miles per hour, according to figures given to the Court by the Mayor of Hiroshima.

The blast

"turns people and debris into projectiles that hurl into stationary objects and into each other. Multiple fractures, puncture wounds and the smashing of skulls, limbs and internal organs makes the list of possible injuries endless."[36]

(h) Congenital deformities

The intergenerational effects of nuclear weapons mark them out from other classes of weapons. As the delegation of the Solomon Islands put it, the adverse effects of the bomb are "virtually permanent — reaching into the distant future of the human race — if it will have a future, which a nuclear conflict would put in doubt" (CR 95/32, p. 36). Apart from damage to the environment which successive generations will inherit far into the future, radiation also causes genetic dam-

---

[35]Bates, *op. cit.*, p. 722. Cf. the reference in *The Bhagvadgita*, "brighter than a thousand suns", which was widely used by nuclear scientists — as in Robert Jungk, *Brighter than a Thousand Suns: A Personal History of the Atomic Scientist* (Penguin, 1982), and Oppenheimer's famous quote from the same source.

[36]*Ibid.*, p. 723.

age and will result in a crop of deformed and defective offspring, as proved in Hiroshima and Nagasaki (where those who were in the vicinity of the explosion — the *hibakusha* — have complained for years of social discrimination against them on this account), and in the Marshall Islands and elsewhere in the Pacific. According to the Mayor of Nagasaki:

"[T]he descendants of the atomic bomb survivors will have to be monitored for several generations to clarify the genetic impact, which means that the descendants will be forced to live in anxiety for generations to come" (CR 95/27, p. 43).

The Mayor of Hiroshima told the Court that children "exposed in their mothers' womb were often born with microcephalia, a syndrome involving mental retardation and incomplete growth" (*ibid.*, p. 29). In the Mayor's words:

"For these children, no hope remains of becoming normal individuals. Nothing can be done for them medically. The atom bomb stamped its indelible mark on the lives of these utterly innocent unborn babies" (*ibid.*, p. 30).

In Japan the social problem of *hibakusha* covers not only persons with hideous keloid growths, but also deformed children and those exposed to the nuclear explosions, who are thought to have defective genes which transmit deformities to their children. This is a considerable human rights problem, appearing long after the bomb and destined to span the generations.

Mrs. Lijon Eknilang, from the Marshall Islands, told the Court of genetic abnormalities never before seen on that island until the atmospheric testing of nuclear weapons. She gave the Court a moving description of the various birth abnormalities seen on that island after the exposure of its population to radiation. She said that Marshallese women

"give birth, not to children as we like to think of them, but to things we could only describe as 'octopuses', 'apples', 'turtles', and other things in our experience. We do not have Marshallese words for these kinds of babies because they were never born before the radiation came.

Women on Rongelap, Likiep, Ailuk and other atolls in the Marshall Islands have given birth to these 'monster babies'. . . . One woman on Likiep gave birth to a child with two heads.

... There is a young girl on Ailuk today with no knees, three toes on each foot and a missing arm ...

The most common birth defects on Rongelap and nearby islands have been 'jellyfish' babies. These babies are born with no bones in their bodies and with transparent skin. We can see their brains and hearts beating. .... Many women die from abnormal pregnancies and those who survive give birth to what looks like purple grapes which we quickly hide away and bury. ...

My purpose for travelling such a great distance to appear before the Court today, is to plead with you to do what you can not to allow the suffering that we Marshallese have experienced to be repeated in any other community in the world" *(CR 95/32, pp. 30-31).*

From another country which has had experience of deformed births, Vanuatu, there was a similar moving reference before the World Health Assembly, when that body was debating a reference to this Court on nuclear weapons. The Vanuatu delegate spoke of the birth, after nine months, of "a substance that breathes but does not have a face, legs or arms"[37]

(i) Transnational damage

Once a nuclear explosion takes place, the fall-out from even a single local detonation cannot be confined within national boundaries.[38] According to WHO studies, it would extend hundreds of kilometres downwind and the gamma ray exposure from the fall-out could reach the human body, even outside national boundaries, through radioactivity deposited in the ground, through inhalation from the air, through consumption of contaminated food, and through inhalation of suspended radioactivity. The diagram appended to this Opinion, extracted from the WHO Study, comparing the areas affected by conventional bombs and nuclear weapons, demonstrates this convincingly. Such is the danger to which neutral populations would be exposed.

All nations, including those carrying out underground tests, are in

---

[37]Record of the 13th Plenary Meeting, Forty-Sixth World Health Assembly, 14 May 1993, Doc. A46/VR/13, p. 11, furnished to the Court by WHO.

[38]See diagram appended from *Effects of Nuclear War on Health and Health Services*, World Health Organization, Geneva, 2nd ed., 1987, p. 16.

agreement that extremely elaborate protections are necessary in the case of underground nuclear explosions in order to prevent contamination of the environment. Such precautions are manifestly quite impossible in the case of the use of nuclear weapons in war — when they will necessarily be exploded in the atmosphere or on the ground. The explosion of nuclear weapons in the atmosphere creates such acknowledgedly deleterious effects that it has already been banned by the Partial Nuclear Test Ban Treaty, and considerable progress has already been made towards a Total Test Ban Treaty. If the nuclear powers now accept that explosions below ground, in the carefully controlled conditions of a test, are so deleterious to health and the environment that they should be banned, this ill accords with the position that above ground explosions in uncontrolled conditions are acceptable.

The transboundary effects of radiation are illustrated by the nuclear meltdown in Chernobyl which had devastating effects over a vast area, as the by-products of that nuclear reaction could not be contained. Human health, agricultural and dairy produce and the demography of thousands of square miles were affected in a manner never known before. On 30 November 1995, the United Nation's Under-Secretary-General for Humanitarian Affairs announced that thyroid cancers, many of them being diagnosed in children, are 285 times more prevalent in Belorus than before the accident, that about 375,000 people in Belorus, Russia and Ukraine remain displaced and often homeless — equivalent to numbers displaced in Rwanda by the fighting there — and that about 9 million people have been affected in some way.[39] Ten years after Chernobyl, the tragedy still reverberates over large areas of territory, not merely in Russia alone, but also in other countries such as Sweden. Such results, stemming from a mere accident rather than a deliberate attempt to cause damage by nuclear weapons, followed without the heat or the blast injuries attendant on a nuclear weapon. They represented radiation damage alone — only one of the three lethal aspects of nuclear weapons. They stemmed from an event considerably smaller in size than the explosions of Hiroshima and Nagasaki.

---

[39]*New York Times Service*, reported in *International Herald Tribune*, 30 November 1995.

(j) Potential to destroy all civilization

Nuclear war has the potential to destroy all civilization. Such a result could be achieved through the use of a minute fraction of the weapons already in existence in the arsenals of the nuclear powers.

As Former Secretary of State, Dr. Henry Kissinger, once observed, in relation to strategic assurances in Europe:

> "The European allies should not keep asking us to multiply strategic assurances that we cannot possibly mean, or if we do mean, we should not want to execute because if we execute, we risk the destruction of civilization."[40]

So, also, Robert McNamara, United States Secretary of Defense from 1961 to 1968, has written:

> "Is it realistic to expect that a nuclear war could be limited to the detonation of tens or even hundreds of nuclear weapons, even though each side would have tens of thousands of weapons remaining available for use? The answer is clearly no."[41]

Stocks of weapons may be on the decline, but one scarcely needs to think in terms of thousands or even hundreds of weapons. Tens of weapons are enough to wreak all the destructions that have been outlined at the commencement of this Opinion.

Such is the risk attendant on the use of nuclear weapons — a risk which no single nation is entitled to take, whatever the dangers to itself. An individual's right to defend his own interests is a right he enjoys against his opponents. In exercising that right, he cannot be considered entitled to destroy the village in which he lives.

(i) Social institutions

All the institutions of ordered society — judiciaries, legislatures, police, medical services, education, transport, communications, postal and telephone services, and newspapers —

---

[40]Henry A. Kissinger, "NATO Defense and the Soviet Threat", *Survival*, November/December 1979, p. 266 (address in Brussels), cited by Robert S. McNamara in "The Military Role of Nuclear Weapons: Perceptions and Misperceptions", (1983-1984) 62 *Foreign Affairs*, Vol. 1, p. 59; emphasis added.

[41]McNamara, *ibid.*, p. 71.

would disappear together in the immediate aftermath of a nuclear attack. The country's command centres and higher echelons of administrative services would be paralysed. There would be "social chaos on a scale unprecedented in human history".[42]

(ii) Economic structures

Economically, society would need to regress even beyond that of the Middle Ages to the levels of man's most primitive past. One of the best known studies examining this scenario summarizes the situation in this way:

> "The task . . . would be not to restore the old economy but to invent a new one, on a far more primitive level. . . . The economy of the Middle Ages, for example, was far less productive than our own, but it was exceedingly complex, and it would not be within the capacity of people in our time suddenly to establish a medieval economic system in the ruins of their twentieth-century one. . . . Sitting among the debris of the Space Age, they would find that the pieces of a shattered modern economy around them — here an automobile, there a washing machine — were mismatched to their elemental needs . . . . [T]hey would not be worrying about rebuilding the automobile industry or the electronics industry: they would be worrying about how to find nonradioactive berries in the woods, or how to tell which trees had edible bark."[43]

(iii) Cultural treasures

Another casualty to be mentioned in this regard is the destruction of the cultural treasures representing the progress of civilization through the ages. The importance of the protection of this aspect of civilization was recognized by the Hague Convention of 14 May 1954, for the protection of cultural property in the case of armed conflict, which decreed that cultural property is entitled to special protection. Historical monu-

---

[42]Bates, *op. cit.*, p. 726.

[43]Jonathan Schell, *The Fate of the Earth*, 1982, pp. 69-70, cited in Bates, *op. cit.*, p. 727.

ments, works of art or places of worship which constitute the cultural or spiritual heritage of peoples must not be the objects of any acts of hostility.

Additional Protocol II provides that cultural property and places of worship which constitute the cultural and spiritual heritage of peoples must not be attacked. Such attacks are grave breaches of humanitarian law under the Conventions and the Protocol. The protection of culture in wartime is considered so important by the world community that UNESCO has devised a special Programme for the Protection of Culture in Wartime. Whenever any cultural monuments were destroyed, there has been a public outcry and an accusation that the laws of war had been violated.

Yet it is manifest that the nuclear bomb is no respecter of such cultural treasures.[44] It will incinerate and flatten every object within its radius of destruction, cultural monument or otherwise.

Despite the blitz on many great cities during World War II, many a cultural monument in those cities stood through the war. That will not be the case after nuclear war.

That this is a feature of considerable importance in all countries can be illustrated from the statistics in regard to one. The number of listed monuments in the Federal Republic of Germany alone, in 1986, was around 1 million, of which Cologne alone had around 9,000 listed buildings.[45] A nuclear attack on a city such as Cologne would thus deprive Germany, in particular, and the world community in general, of a considerable segment of their cultural inheritance, for a single bomb would easily dispose of all 9,000 monuments, leaving none standing — a result which no wartime bombing in World War II could achieve.

Together with all other structures, they will be part of the desert of radioactive rubble left in the aftermath of the nuclear bomb. If the preservation of humanity's cultural inheritance is of any value to civilization, it is important to note that it will

---

[44]On state responsibility to protect the cultural heritage, see Article 5 of the World Heritage Convention, 1972 (The Convention for the Protection of the World Cultural and Natural Heritage).

[45]See Hiltrud Kier, "UNESCO Programme for the Protection of Culture in Wartime", in Documents of the Sixth World Congress of IPPNW, *op. cit.*, p. 199.

be an inevitable casualty of the nuclear weapon.

(k)   The electromagnetic pulse

Another feature distinctive to nuclear weapons is the electromagnetic pulse. The literature indicates that this has the effect of displacing electrons out of air molecules in the upper atmosphere and these electrons are then displaced by the earth's magnetic field. As they spin down and around the lines of magnetic force, they transmit a very sudden and intensive burst of energy — the electromagnetic pulse — which throws all electronic devices out of action. As these systems go haywire, all communication lines are cut, health services (among other essential services) disrupted and organized modern life collapses. Even the command and control systems geared for responses to nuclear attack can be thrown out of gear, thus creating a fresh danger of unintended release of nuclear weapons.

A standard scientific dictionary, *Dictionnaire Encyclopédique d'Électronique,* describes the effects of the electromagnetic pulse in the following terms:

> "Electromagnetic pulse, nuclear pulse; strong pulse of electromagnetic energy radiated by a nuclear explosion in the atmosphere; caused by collisions between the gamma rays emitted during the first nanoseconds of the explosion and the electrons in the molecules in the atmosphere; the electromagnetic pulse produced by a nuclear explosion of an average force at around 400 km. altitude can instantly put out of service the greater part of semiconductor electronic equipment in a large country, such as the United States, as well as a large part of its energy distribution networks, without other effects being felt on the ground, with military consequences easy to imagine." [Translation of the Registry.][46]

---

[46]Original French text: *"impulsion électromagnétique, impulsion nucléaire (forte impulsion d'énergie électromagnétique rayonnée par une explosion nucléaire dans l'atmosphère) (est due aux collisions entre les rayons gammas émis pendant les premières nanosecondes de l'explosion et les électrons des molécules de l'atmosphère) (l'impulsion électromagnétique produite par une explosion nucléaire de puissance moyenne à environ 400 km d'altitude peut mettre hors service instantanément la majeure partie des appareils électroniques à semi-conducteurs d'un pays grand comme les États-Unis et une grande partie de ses réseaux de distribution d'énergie sans que d'autres effets soient ressentis au sol, avec des conséquences militaires faciles à imaginer."* (Michel Fleutry, *Dictionnaire Encyclopédique d'Électronique (Anglais-*

An important aspect of the electromagnetic pulse is that it travels at immense speeds, so that the disruption of communication systems caused by the radioactive contamination immediately can spread beyond national boundaries and disrupt communication lines and essential services in neutral countries as well. Having regard to the dominance of electronic communication in the functioning of modern society at every level, this would be an unwarranted interference with such neutral states.

Another important effect of the electromagnetic pulse is the damage to electrical power and control systems from nuclear weapons — indeed electromagnetic pulse could lead to a core melt accident in the event of nuclear power facilities being in the affected area.[47]

(l) Damage to nuclear reactors

The enormous area of devastation and the enormous heat released would endanger all nuclear powers stations within the area, releasing dangerous levels of radioactivity apart from that released by the bomb itself. Europe alone has over 200 atomic power stations dotted across the continent, some of them close to populated areas. In addition, there are 150 devices for uranium enrichment.[48] A damaged nuclear reactor could give rise to:

"lethal doses of radiation to exposed persons 150 miles downwind and would produce significant levels of radioactive contamination of the environment more than 600 miles away".[49]

The nuclear weapon used upon any country in which the world's current total of 450 nuclear reactors is situated could leave in its wake a series of Chernobyls.

The effects of such radiation could include anorexia, cessation of production of new blood cells, diarrhoea, haemorrhage, damage to the bone marrow, convulsions, vascular damage and cardiovascular col-

---

Français), 1995, p. 250.)

[47]Gordon Thompson, "Nuclear Power and the Threat of Nuclear War", in Documents of the Sixth World Congress of IPPNW, *op. cit.*, p. 240.

[48]William E. Butler (ed.), *Control over Compliance with International Law*, 1991, p. 24.

[49]Bates, *op. cit.*, p. 720.

lapse.[50]

(m)   Damage to food productivity

Unlike other weapons, whose direct impact is the most devastating part of the damage they cause, nuclear weapons can cause far greater damage by their delayed after-effects than by their direct effects. The detailed technical study, *Environmental Consequences of Nuclear War*, while referring to some uncertainties regarding the indirect effects of nuclear war, states:

> "What can be said with assurance, however, is that the Earth's human population has a much greater vulnerability to the indirect effects of nuclear war, especially mediated through impacts on food productivity and food availability, than to the direct effects of nuclear war itself."[51]

The nuclear winter, should it occur in consequence of multiple nuclear exchanges, could disrupt all global food supplies.

After the United States tests in the Pacific in 1954, fish caught in various parts of the Pacific, as long as eight months after the explosions, were contaminated and unfit for human consumption, while crops in various parts of Japan were affected by radioactive rain. These were among the findings of an international Commission of medical specialists appointed by the Japanese Association of Doctors against A- and H-bombs.[52] Further:

> "The use of nuclear weapons contaminates water and food, as well as the soil and the plants that may grow on it. This is not only in the area covered by immediate nuclear radiation, but also a much larger unpredictable zone which is affected by the radio-active fall-out."[53]

(n)   Multiple nuclear explosions resulting from self-defence

If the weapon is used in self-defence after an initial nuclear attack, the eco-system, which had already sustained the impact of the first

---

[50]See Herbert Abrams, *op. cit.*, pp. 122-125.

[51]SCOPE publication 28, released at the Royal Society, London, on January 6, 1986, Vol. I, p. 481.

[52]As referred to in Singh & McWhinney, *op. cit.*, p. 124.

[53]*Ibid.*, p. 122.

nuclear attack, would have to absorb on top of this the effect of the retaliatory attack, which may or may not consist of a single weapon, for the stricken nation will be so ravaged that it will not be able to make fine evaluations of the exact amount of retaliatory force required. In such event, the tendency to release as strong a retaliation as is available must enter into any realistic evaluation of the situation. The ecosystem would in that event be placed under the pressure of multiple nuclear explosions, which it would not be able to absorb without permanent and irreversible damage. Capital cities with densely packed populations could be targeted. The fabric of civilization could be destroyed.

It is said of some of the most ruthless conquerors of the past that, after they dealt with a rebellious town, they ensured that it was razed to the ground with no sound or sign of life left in it — not even the bark of a dog or the purr of a kitten. If any student of international law were asked whether such conduct was contrary to the laws of war, the answer would surely be "Of course!". There would indeed be some surprise that the question even needed to be asked. In this age of higher development, the nuclear weapon goes much further, leaving behind it nothing but a total devastation, wrapped in eerie silence.

(o) The "shadow of the mushroom cloud"

As pointed out in the Australian submissions (CR 95/22, p. 49), the entire post-war generation lies under a cloud of fear — sometimes described as the "shadow of the mushroom cloud", which pervades all thoughts about the human future. This fear, which has hung like a blanket of doom over the thoughts of children in particular, is an evil in itself and will last so long as nuclear weapons remain. The younger generation needs to grow up in a climate of hope, not one of despair that at some point in their life, there is a possibility of their life being snuffed out in an instant, or their health destroyed, along with all they cherish, in a war to which their nation may not even be a party.

*

* *

This body of information shows that, even among weapons of mass destruction, many of which are already banned under international law, the nuclear weapon stands alone, unmatched for its potential to damage all that humanity has built over the centuries and all that humanity relies upon for its continued existence.

I close this section by citing the statement placed before the Court by Professor Joseph Rotblat, a member of the British team on the Manhattan Project in Los Alamos, a Rapporteur for the 1983 WHO investigation into the Effects of Nuclear War on Health and Health Services, and a Nobel Laureate. Professor Rotblat was a member of one of the delegations, but was prevented by ill health from attending the Court.

Here is a passage from his statement to the Court:

> "I have read the written pleadings prepared by the United Kingdom and the United States. Their view of the legality of the use of nuclear weapons is premised on three assumptions: a) that they would not necessarily cause unnecessary suffering; b) that they would not necessarily have indiscriminate effects on civilians; c) that they would not necessarily have effects on territories of third States. It is my professional opinion — set out above and in the WHO reports referred to — that on any reasonable set of assumptions their argument is unsustainable on all three points."
> (CR 95/32, Annex, p. 2.)

4. The Uniqueness of Nuclear Weapons

After this factual review, legal argument becomes almost superfluous, for it can scarcely be contended that any legal system can contain within itself a principle which permits the entire society which it serves to be thus decimated and destroyed — along with the natural environment which has sustained it from time immemorial.[54] The dangers are so compelling that a range of legal principles surges through to meet them.

It suffices at the present stage of this Opinion to outline the reasons for considering the nuclear weapon unique, even among weapons of mass destruction. Nuclear weapons:

1. cause death and destruction;
2. induce cancers, leukaemia, keloids and related afflictions;
3. cause gastro intestinal, cardiovascular and related afflictions;
4. continue for decades after their use to induce the health-

---

[54]See further, on this aspect, section V.1 below.

related problems mentioned above;

5. damage the environmental rights of future generations;
6. cause congenital deformities, mental retardation and genetic damage;
7. carry the potential to cause a nuclear winter;
8. contaminate and destroy the food chain;
9. imperil the eco-system;
10. produce lethal levels of heat and blast;
11. produce radiation and radioactive fall-out;
12. produce a disruptive electromagnetic pulse;
13. produce social disintegration;
14. imperil all civilization;
15. threaten human survival;
16. wreak cultural devastation;
17. span a time range of thousands of years;
18. threaten all life on the planet;
19. irreversibly damage the rights of future generations;
20. exterminate civilian populations;
21. damage neighbouring States;
22. produce psychological stress and fear syndromes

as no other weapons do

Any one of these would cause concern serious enough to place these weapons in a category of their own, attracting with special intensity the principles of humanitarian law. In combination they make the case for their application irrefutable. This list is by no means complete. However, to quote the words of a recent study:

"Once it becomes clear that all hope for twentieth century man is lost if a nuclear war is started, it hardly adds any meaningful knowledge to learn of additional effects."[55]

The words of the General Assembly, in its "Declaration on the Prevention of Nuclear Catastrophe" (1981), aptly summarize the entirety of the foregoing facts:

"all the horrors of past wars and other calamities that have befallen people would pale in comparison with what is inher-

---

[55]Bates, *op. cit.*, p. 721.

ent in the use of nuclear weapons, capable of destroying civilization on earth".[56]

Here then is the background to the consideration of the legal question with which the Court is faced. Apart from this background of hard and sordid fact, the legal question cannot be meaningfully addressed. Juxtapose against these consequences — so massively destructive of all the principles of humanity — the accepted principles of humanitarian law, and the result can scarcely be in doubt. As the ensuing discussion will point out, humanitarian principles are grotesquely violated by the consequences of nuclear weapons. This discussion will show that these effects of the nuclear weapon and the humanitarian principles of the laws of war are a contradiction in terms.

5. The Differences in Scientific Knowledge between the Present Time and 1945

On July 17, 1945, United States Secretary of War, Stimson, informed Prime Minister Churchill of the successful detonation of the experimental nuclear bomb in the New Mexican desert, with the cryptic message "Babies satisfactorily born".[57] A universe of knowledge has grown up regarding the effects of the bomb since that fateful day when the advent of this unknown weapon could, even cryptically, be so described.

True, much knowledge regarding the power of the bomb was available then, but the volume of knowledge now available on the effects of nuclear weapons is exponentially greater. In addition to numerous military studies, there have been detailed studies by WHO and other concerned organizations such as International Physicians for the Prevention of Nuclear War (IPPNW); the TTAPS studies on the nuclear winter; the studies of the Scientific Committee on Problems of the Environment (SCOPE); the International Council of Scientific Unions (ICSU); the United Nations Institute of Disarmament Research (UNIDIR); and literally hundreds of others. Much of this material has been placed before the Court or deposited in the Library by WHO and various States that have appeared before the Court in this matter.

Questions of knowledge, morality and legality in the use of nuclear

---

[56]Resolution 36/100 of 9 December 1981.

[57]Winston Churchill, *The Second World War*, Vol. 6, "Triumph and Tragedy", 1953, p. 63.

weapons, considered in the context of 1995, are thus vastly different from those questions considered in the context of 1945, and need a totally fresh approach in the light of this immense quantity of information. This additional information has a deep impact upon the question of the legality now before the Court.

Action with full knowledge of the consequences of one's act is totally different in law from the same action taken in ignorance of its consequences. Any nation using the nuclear weapon today cannot be heard to say that it does not know its consequences. It is only in the context of this knowledge that the question of legality of the use of nuclear weapons can be considered in 1996.

6. Do Hiroshima and Nagasaki Show that Nuclear War Is Survivable?

Over and above all these specific aspects of the rules of humanitarian law, and in a sense welding them together in one overall consideration, is the question of survivability of the target population — indeed, of the human race. Survivability is the limit situation of each individual danger underlying each particular principle of humanitarian law. The extreme situation that is reached if each danger is pressed to the limit of its potential is the situation of non-survivability. We reach that situation with nuclear war. In the fact that nuclear war could spell the end of the human race and of all civilization, all these principles thus coalesce.

A fact that obscures perception of the danger that nuclear war may well be unsurvivable is the experience of Hiroshima and Nagasaki. The fact that nuclear weapons were used in Japan and that that nation emerged from the war resilient and resurgent may lull the observer into a sense of false security that nuclear war is indeed survivable. International law itself has registered this complacency, for there is what may be described as an underlying subliminal assumption that nuclear war has been proved to be survivable.

It is necessary therefore to examine briefly some clear differences between that elementary scenario of a nuclear attack half a century ago and the likely characteristics of a nuclear war today.

The following differences may be noted:

    1. The bombs used in Hiroshima and Nagasaki were of not more than 15 kilotons explosive power. The bombs available for a future nuclear war will be many multiples of this

explosive power.

2. Hiroshima and Nagasaki ended the war. The limit of that nuclear war was the use of two "small" nuclear weapons. The next nuclear war, should it come, cannot be assumed to be so restricted, for multiple exchanges must be visualized.

3. The target country in Hiroshima and Nagasaki was not a nuclear power. Nor were there any other nuclear powers to come to its assistance. A future nuclear war, if it occurs, will be in a world bristling with nuclear weapons which exist, not for display, but for a purpose. The possibility of even a minute fraction of those weapons being called into service is therefore an ever present danger to be reckoned with in a future nuclear war.

4. Hiroshima and Nagasaki, important though they were, were not the nerve centres of Japanese government and administration. Major cities and capitals of the warring States are likely to be targeted in a future nuclear war.

5. Major environmental consequences such as the nuclear winter — which could result from a multiple exchange of nuclear weapons — could not result from the "small" bombs used in Hiroshima and Nagasaki. Hiroshima and Nagasaki thus do not prove the survivability of nuclear war.

They are, rather, a forewarning on a minuscule scale of the dangers to be expected in a future nuclear war. They remove any doubt that might have existed, had the question of the legality of nuclear weapons been argued on the basis of scientific data alone, without a practical demonstration of their effect on human populations.

Every one of the evils which the rules of humanitarian law are designed to prevent thus comes together in the questions of survival attendant on the future use of nuclear weapons in war.

7. A Perspective from the Past

This section of the present Opinion has surveyed in the broadest outline the effects of the bomb in the light of the known results of its use and in the light of scientific information available today. The non-conformity of the bomb with the norms of humanitarian law and, indeed, with the basic principles of international law seems upon this evidence to be self-evident, as more fully discussed later in this Opinion.

It adds a sense of perspective to this discussion to note that even before the evidence of actual use, and even before the wealth of scientific material now available, a percipient observer was able, while the invention of the nuclear bomb still lay far in the distance, to detect the antithesis between the nuclear bomb and every form of social order — which would of course include international law. H.G. Wells, in *The World Set Free*, visualized the creation of the bomb on the basis of information already known in 1913 resulting from the work of Einstein and others on the correlation of matter and energy. Projecting his mind into the future with remarkable prescience, he wrote in 1913:

"The atomic bombs had dwarfed the international issues to complete insignificance . . . we speculated upon the possibility of stopping the use of these frightful explosives before the world was utterly destroyed. For to us it seemed quite plain these bombs, and the still greater power of destruction of which they were the precursors, might quite easily shatter every relationship and institution of mankind."[58]

The power that would be unleashed by the atom was known theoretically in 1913. That theoretical knowledge was enough, even without practical confirmation, to foresee that the bomb could shatter every human relationship and institution. International law is one of the most delicate of those relationships and institutions.

It seems remarkable that the permissibility of the weapon under international law is still the subject of serious discussion, considering that the power of the bomb was awesomely demonstrated forty years after its consequences were thus seen as "quite plain", and that the world has had a further fifty years of time for reflection after that event.

III. HUMANITARIAN LAW

It could indeed be said that the principal question before the Court is whether the nuclear weapon can in any way be reconciled with the

---

[58]H.G. Wells, *The First Men in the Moon and the World Set Free*, the Literary Press, London, undated reprint of 1913 ed., p. 237. See, also, the reference to Wells in R.J. Lifton and Richard Falk, *Indefensible Weapons*, 1982, p. 59.

basic principles of humanitarian law.

The governance of nuclear weapons by the principles of humanitarian law has not been in doubt at any stage of these proceedings, and has now been endorsed by the unanimous opinion of the Court (para. 2(D)). Indeed, most of the States contending that the use of nuclear weapons is lawful have acknowledged that their use is subject to international humanitarian law.

Thus Russia has stated:

> "Naturally, all that has been said above does not mean that the use of nuclear weapons is not limited at all. Even if the use of nuclear weapons is in principle justifiable — in individual or collective self-defence — that use shall be made within the framework of limitations imposed by humanitarian law with respect to means and methods of conducting military activities. It is important to note that with respect to nuclear weapons those limitations are limitations under customary rather than treaty law." (Written Statement, p. 18.)

The United States states:

> "The United States has long taken the position that various principles of the international law of armed conflict would apply to the use of nuclear weapons as well as to other means and methods of warfare. This in no way means, however, that the use of nuclear weapons is precluded by the law of war. As the following will demonstrate, the issue of the legality depends on the precise circumstances, involved in any particular use of a nuclear weapon." (Written Statement, p. 21.)

So, also, the United Kingdom:

> "It follows that the law of armed conflict by which the legality of any given use of nuclear weapons falls to be judged includes all the provisions of customary international law (including those which have been codified in Additional Protocol I) and, where appropriate, of conventional law but excludes those provisions of Protocol I which introduced new rules into the law." (Written Statement, p. 46, para. 3.55.)

The subordination of nuclear weapons to the rules of humanitarian law has thus been universally recognized, and now stands judicially confirmed as an incontrovertible principle of international law.

It remains then to juxtapose the leading principles of humanitarian law against the known results of nuclear weapons, as already outlined. When the principles and the facts are lined up alongside each other, the total incompatibility of the principles with the facts leads inescapably to but one conclusion — that nuclear weapons are inconsistent with humanitarian law. Since they are unquestionably governed by humanitarian law, they are unquestionably illegal.

Among the prohibitions of international humanitarian law relevant to this case are the prohibitions against weapons which cause superfluous injury, weapons which do not differentiate between combatants and civilians, and weapons which do not respect the rights of neutral states.

A more detailed consideration follows.

1. "Elementary Considerations of Humanity"

This phrase gives expression to a core concept of humanitarian law. Is the conduct of a State in any given situation contrary to the elementary considerations of humanity? One need go no further than to formulate this phrase, and then recount the known results of the bomb as outlined above. The resulting contrast between light and darkness is so dramatic as to occasion a measure of surprise that their total incompatibility has even been in doubt.

One wonders whether, in the light of common sense, it can be doubted that to exterminate vast numbers of the enemy population, to poison their atmosphere, to induce in them cancers, keloids and leukaemias, to cause congenital defects and mental retardation in large numbers of unborn children, to devastate their territory and render their food supply unfit for human consumption - whether acts such these can conceivably be compatible with "elementary considerations of humanity". Unless one can in all conscience answer such questions in the affirmative, the argument is at an end as to whether nuclear weapons violate humanitarian law, and therefore violate international law.

President Woodrow Wilson, in an address delivered to a joint session of Congress on April 2, 1917, gave elegant expression to this concept when he observed:

"By painful stage after stage has that law been built up, with meager enough results, indeed, . . . but always with a clear view, at least, of what the heart and conscience of mankind demanded."[59]

In relation to nuclear weapons, there can be no doubt as to "what the heart and conscience of mankind" demand. As was observed by another American President, President Reagan, "I pray for the day when nuclear weapons will no longer exist anywhere on earth".[60] That sentiment, shared by citizens across the world — as set out elsewhere in this Opinion — provides the background to modern humanitarian law, which has progressed from the time when President Wilson described its results as "meager . . . indeed".

The ensuing portions of this Opinion are devoted to an examination of the present state of development of the principles of humanitarian law.

2. Multicultural Background to the Humanitarian Laws of War

It greatly strengthens the concept of humanitarian laws of war to note that this is not a recent invention, nor the product of any one culture. The concept is of ancient origin, with a lineage stretching back at least three millennia. As already observed, it is deep-rooted in many cultures — Hindu, Buddhist, Chinese, Christian, Islamic and traditional African. These cultures have all given expression to a variety of limitations on the extent to which any means can be used for the purposes of fighting one's enemy. The problem under consideration is a universal problem, and this Court is a universal Court, whose composition is required by its Statute to reflect the world's principal cultural traditions.[61] The multicultural traditions that exist on this important matter cannot be ignored in the Court's consideration of this question, for to do so would be to deprive its conclusions of that plenitude of universal authority which is available to give it added strength — the

---

[59]Address of the President of the United States at a Joint Session of the Two Houses of Congress, April 2, 1917, reprinted in (1917) 11 *American Journal of International Law*, Supp., p. 144. The President was speaking in the context of the indiscriminate German submarine attacks on shipping which he described as "a warfare against mankind".

[60]Speech of June 16, 1983, referred to by Robert S. McNamara, *op. cit.*, p. 60.

[61]I note in this context the sad demise of our deeply respected Latin American colleague, Judge Andrés Aguilar Mawdsley, six days before the hearings of the case commenced, thus reducing the Court to fourteen, and depriving its composition of a Latin American component.

strength resulting from the depth of the tradition's historical roots and the width of its geographical spread.[62]

Of special relevance in connection with nuclear weapons is the ancient South Asian tradition regarding the prohibition on the use of hyperdestructive weapons. This is referred to in the two celebrated Indian epics, the *Ramayana* and the *Mahabharatha*, which are known and regularly reenacted through the length and breadth of South and South East Asia, as part of the living cultural tradition of the region. The references in these two epics are as specific as can be on this principle, and they relate to a historical period around three thousand years ago.

The Ramayana[63] *tells the epic story of a war between Rama, prince of Ayodhya in India, and Ravana, ruler of Sri Lanka. In the course of this epic struggle, described in this classic in the minutest detail, a weapon of war became available to Rama's half-brother, Lakshmana, which could "destroy the entire race of the enemy, including those who could not bear arms".*

Rama advised Lakshmana that the weapon could not be used in the war

> *"because such destruction* en masse *was forbidden by the ancient laws of war, even though Ravana was fighting an unjust war with an unrighteous objective".[64]*

These laws of war which Rama followed were themselves ancient in his time. The laws of Manu forbade stratagems of deceit, all attacks on unarmed adversaries and non-combatants, irrespective of whether the war being fought was a just war or not.[65] The Greek historian Megasthenes[66] makes reference to the practice in India that warring

---

[62]As observed in a contemporary study of the development of international humanitarian law, there is evidence "of efforts made by every people in every age to reduce the devastation of war" (Herczegh, *op. cit.*, p. 14).

[63]*The Ramayana*, Romesh Chunder Dutt (tr.).

[64]See Nagendra Singh, "The Distinguishable Characteristics of the Concept of the Law as it Developed in Ancient India", in *Liber Amicorum for the Right Honourable Lord Wilberforce*, 1987, p. 93. The relevant passage of the *Ramayana* is *Yuddha Kanda (Sloka)*, VIII.39.

[65]*Manusmrti*, vii, pp. 91-92.

[66]*C*.350BC-*C*.290BC — ancient Greek historian and diplomat sent on embassies by Seleucus I to Chandragupta Maurya, who wrote the most complete account of India then known to the Greek world.

armies left farmers tilling the land unmolested, even though the battle raged close to them. He likewise records that the land of the enemy was not destroyed with fire nor his trees cut down.[67]

The Mahabharatha *relates the story of an epic struggle between the* Kauravas *and the* Pandavas. *It refers likewise to the principle forbidding hyperdestructive weapons when it records that:*

> "Arjuna, observing the laws of war, refrained from using the 'pasupathastra', a hyper-destructive weapon, because when the fight was restricted to ordinary conventional weapons, the use of extraordinary or unconventional types was not even moral, let alone in conformity with religion or the recognized laws of warfare."[68]

Weapons causing unnecessary suffering were also banned by the Laws of Manu *as, for example, arrows with hooked spikes which, after entering the body would be difficult to take out, or arrows with heated or poisoned tips.*[69]

The environmental wisdom of ancient Judaic tradition is also reflected in the following passage from Deuteronomy (20:19):

> "When you are trying to capture a city, do not cut down its fruit trees, even though the siege lasts a long time. Eat the fruit but do not destroy the trees. The trees are not your enemies." *(Emphasis added.)*

Recent studies of warfare among African peoples likewise reveal the existence of humanitarian traditions during armed conflicts, with moderation and clemency shown to enemies.[70] *For example, in some cases of traditional African warfare, there were rules forbidding the use of particular weapons and certain areas had highly developed systems of etiquette, conventions, and rules, both before hostilities com-*

---

[67]Megasthenes, *Fragments*, cited in N. Singh, *Juristic Concepts of Ancient Indian Polity*, 1980, pp. 162-163.

[68]*Mahabharatha, Udyog Parva*, 194.12, cited in Nagendra Singh, "The Distinguishable Characteristics of the Concept of Law as it Developed in Ancient India", *op. cit.*, p. 93.

[69]*Manusmriti*, VII.90, cited in N. Singh, *India and International Law*, 1973, p. 72.

[70]See Y. Diallo, *Traditions africaines et droit humanitaire*, Geneva, 1978, p. 16; and E. Bello, *African Customary Humanitarian Law*, ICRC, Geneva, 1980, both referred to in Herczegh, *op. cit.*, p. 14.

menced, during hostilities, and after the cessation of hostilities — including a system of compensation.[71]

In the Christian tradition, the Second Lateran Council of 1139 offers an interesting illustration of the prohibition of weapons which were too cruel to be used in warfare — the crossbow and the siege machine, which were condemned as "deadly and odious to God".[72] Nussbaum, in citing this provision, observes that, it "certainly appears curious in the era of the atomic bomb". There was a very early recognition here of the dangers that new techniques were introducing into the field of battle. Likewise, in other fields of the law of war, there were endeavours to bring it within some forms of control as, for example, by the proclamation of "Truces of God" — days during which feuds were not permitted which were expanded in some church jurisdictions to periods from sunset on Wednesday to sunrise on Monday.[73]

Gratian's Decretum *in the 12th century was one of the first Christian works dealing with these principles, and the ban imposed by the Second Lateran Council was an indication of the growing interest in the subject. However, in Christian philosophy, while early writers such as St. Augustine examined the concept of the just war* (jus ad bellum) *in great detail, the* ius in bello *was not the subject of detailed study for some centuries.*

Vitoria gathered together various traditions upon the subject, including traditions of knightly warfare from the age of chivalry; Aquinas worked out a well-developed doctrine relating to the protection of non-combatants; and other writers fed the growing stream of thought upon the subject.

In the Islamic tradition, the laws of war forbade the use of poisoned arrows or the application of poison on weapons such as swords or spears.[74] Unnecessarily cruel ways of killing and mutilation were expressly forbidden. Non-combatants, women and children, monks and places of worship were expressly protected. Crops and livestock were not to be destroyed[75] by anyone holding authority over territory. Prisoners were to be treated mercifully in accordance with such Qur'anic passages as "Feed for the love of Allah, the indigent, the orphan and

---

[71]Bello, *op. cit.*, pp. 20-21.

[72]Resolutions of the Second Lateran Council, Canon XXIX, cited by Nussbaum, *A Concise History of the Law of Nations*, 1947, p. 25.

[73]*Ibid.*, p. 26.

[74]See N. Singh, *India and International Law, op. cit.*, p. 216.

[75]*Qur'an*, II.205.

the captive".[76] *So well developed was Islamic law in regard to conduct during hostilities that it ordained not merely that prisoners were to be well treated, but that if they made a last will during captivity, the will was to be transmitted to the enemy through some appropriate channel.*[77]

The Buddhist tradition went further still, for it was totally pacifist, and would not countenance the taking of life, the infliction of pain, the taking of captives or the appropriation of another's property or territory in any circumstances whatsoever. Since it outlaws war altogether, it could under no circumstances lend its sanction to weapons of destruction — least of all to a weapon such as the nuclear bomb.

> "According to Buddhism there is nothing that can be called a 'just war' — which is only a false term coined and put into circulation to justify and excuse hatred, cruelty, violence and massacre. Who decides what is just and unjust? The mighty and the victorious are 'just', and the weak and the defeated are 'unjust'. Our war is always 'just' and your war is always 'unjust'. Buddhism does not accept this position."[78]

In rendering an Advisory Opinion on a matter of humanitarian law concerning the permissibility of the use of force to a degree capable of destroying all of humanity, it would be a grave omission indeed to neglect the humanitarian perspectives available from this major segment of the world's cultural traditions.[79]

Examples of the adoption of humanitarian principles in more recent history are numerous. For example, in the Crimean War in 1855, the banning of sulphur was proposed at the Siege of Sebastopol, but would not be permitted by the British Government, just as during the American Civil War the use of chlorine in artillery shells by the Union

---

[76]*Ibid.*, LXXVII.8; emphasis added.

[77]S.R. Hassan, *The Reconstruction of Legal Thought in Islam*, 1974, p. 177. See, generally, Majid Khadduri, *War and Peace in the Law of Islam*, 1955. For a brief summary of the Islamic law relating to war, see C.G. Weeramantry, *Islamic Jurisprudence: Some International Perspectives*, 1988, pp. 134-138.

[78]Walpola Rahula, *What the Buddha Taught*, 1959, p. 84.

[79]On Buddhism and international law, see, generally, K.N. Jayetilleke, "The Principles of International Law in Buddhist Doctrine", 120 *Recueil des Cours* (1967 I), pp. 441-567.

forces was proposed in 1862, but rejected by the Government.[80]

It is against such a varied cultural background that these questions must be considered and not merely as though they are a new sentiment invented in the 19th century and so slenderly rooted in universal tradition that they may be lightly overridden.

Grotius' concern with the cruelties of war is reflected in his lament that:

"when arms were once taken up, all reverence for divine and human law was thrown away, just as if men were thenceforth authorized to commit all crimes without restraint".[81]

The foundations laid by Grotius were broad-based and emphasized the absolute binding nature of the restrictions on conduct in war. In building that foundation, Grotius drew upon the collective experience of humanity in a vast range of civilizations and cultures.

Grotius' encyclopedic study of literature, from which he drew his principles, did not of course cover the vast mass of Hindu, Buddhist and Islamic literature having a bearing on these matters, and he did not have the benefit of this considerable supplementary source, demonstrating the universality and the extreme antiquity of the branch of law we call the *ius in bello*.

3. Outline of Humanitarian Law

Humanitarian principles have long been part of the basic stock of concepts embedded in the corpus of international law. Modern international law is the inheritor of a more than hundred-year heritage of active humanitarian concern with the sufferings of war. This concern has aimed at placing checks upon the tendency, so often prevalent in war, to break every precept of human compassion. It has succeeded in doing so in several specific areas, but animating and underlying all those specific instances are general principles of prevention of human suffering that goes beyond the purposes and needs of war.

The credit goes to the United States of America for one of the

---

[80]See L.S. Wolfe, "Chemical and Biological Warfare: Effects and Consequences" (1983), 28 *McGill Law Journal*, p. 735. See also, "Chemical Warfare" in *Encyclopedia Britannica*, 1959, Vol. 5, pp. 353-358.

[81]Grotius, *Prolegomena*, para. 28, tr. Whewell.

earliest initiatives in reducing humanitarian law to written form for the guidance of its armies. During the War of Secession, President Lincoln directed Professor Lieber to prepare instructions for the armies of General Grant — regulations which Mr. Martens, the delegate of Czar Nicholas II, referred to at the 1899 Peace Conference as having resulted in great benefit, not only to the United States troops but also to those of the Southern Confederacy. Paying tribute to this initiative, Martens described it as an example, of which the Brussels Conference of 1874 convoked by Emperor Alexander II, was "the logical and natural development". This conference in turn led to the Peace Conference of 1899, and in its turn to the Hague Conventions which assume so much importance in this case.[82]

The St. Petersburg Declaration of 1868 provided that "the only legitimate object which States should endeavour to accomplish during war is to weaken the military forces of the enemy" — and many subsequent declarations have adopted and reinforced this principle.[83] It gives expression to a very ancient rule of war accepted by many civilizations.[84]

The Martens clause, deriving its name from Mr. Martens, was by unanimous vote, inserted into the preamble to the Hague Convention II of 1899, and Convention IV of 1907, with respect to the Laws and Customs of War on Land. It provided that:

> "Until a more complete code of the laws of war has been issued, the high contracting Parties deem it expedient to declare that, *in cases not included in the Regulations adopted by them*, the inhabitants and the belligerents remain under the protection and the rule of the principles of the law of nations, as they result from the usages established among civilized peoples, from the laws of humanity and the dictates of the public conscience." (Emphasis added.)

Although the Martens clause was devised to cope with disagree-

---

[82]For Martens' speech, see *The Proceedings of the Hague Peace Conferences, op. cit.*, pp. 505-506.

[83]The Hague Regulations of 1899 and 1907, Art. 25; the Hague Convention (IX) of 1907, Art. 1; League of Nations Assembly Resolution of 30 September 1928; UNGA Resolutions 2444 (XXIII) of 19 December 1968, and 2675 (XXV) of 9 December 1970; Additional Protocol I to the 1949 Geneva Conventions, Arts. 48 & 51.

[84]See V.2 on "The Aims of War".

ments among the parties to the Hague Peace Conferences regarding the status of resistance movements in occupied territory, it is today considered applicable to the whole of humanitarian law.[85] It appears in one form or another in several major treaties on humanitarian law.[86] The Martens clause clearly indicates that, behind such specific rules as had already been formulated, there lay a body of general principles sufficient to be applied to such situations as had not already been dealt with by a specific rule.[87]

To be read in association with this is Article 22 of the 1907 Hague Regulations which provides that, "The right of belligerents to adopt means of injuring the enemy is not unlimited".

These were indications also that international law, far from being insensitive to such far-reaching issues of human welfare, has long recognized the pre-eminent importance of considerations of humanity in fashioning its attitudes and responses to situations involving their violation, however they may occur. These declarations were made, it is to be noted, at a time when the development of modern weaponry was fast accelerating under the impact of technology. It was visualized that more sophisticated and deadly weaponry was on the drawing boards of military establishments throughout the world and would continue to be so for the foreseeable future. These principles were thus meant to apply to weapons existing then as well as to weapons to be created in the future, weapons already known and weapons as yet unvisualized. They were general principles meant to be applied to new weapons as well as old.

The Parties to the Geneva Conventions of 1949 expressly recognized the Martens clause as a living part of international law — a proposition which no international jurist could seriously deny.

---

[85]See D. Fleck (ed.), *The Handbook of Humanitarian Law in Armed Conflicts*, 1995, p. 29.

[86]First Geneva Convention 1949, Art. 63, para. 4; Second Geneva Convention, Art. 62, para. 4; Third Geneva Convention, Art. 142, para. 4; Fourth Geneva Convention, Art. 158, para. 4; Inhumane Weapons Convention, 1980, Preamble, para. 5.

[87]At the last meeting of the Fourth Commission of the Peace Conference, on September 26, 1907, Mr. Martens summarized its achievements in terms that, "If from the days of antiquity to our own time people have been repeating the Roman adage '*Inter arma silent leges*', we have loudly proclaimed, '*Inter arma vivant leges*'. This is the greatest triumph of law and justice over brute force and the necessities of war." (J.B. Scott, "The Conference of 1907", *The Proceedings of the Hague Peace Conferences*, 1921, Vol. III, p. 914.)

As McDougal and Feliciano have observed:

"To accept as lawful the deliberate terrorization of the enemy community by the infliction of large-scale destruction comes too close to rendering pointless all legal limitations on the exercise of violence."[88]

International law has long distinguished between conventional weapons and those which are unnecessarily cruel. It has also shown a continuing interest in this problem. For example, the Convention on Prohibitions or Restrictions on the Use of Certain Conventional Weapons Which May be Deemed to be Excessively Injurious or to Have Indiscriminate Effects, 1980, dealt in three separate Protocols with such weapons as those which injure by fragments, which in the human body escape detection (Protocol I); Mines, Booby Traps and Other Devices (Protocol II); and Incendiary Weapons (Protocol III).

If international law had principles within it strong enough in 1899 to recognize the extraordinary cruelty of the "dum dum" or exploding bullet as going beyond the purposes of war [89], and projectiles diffusing asphyxiating or deleterious gases as also being extraordinarily cruel[90], it would cause some bewilderment to the objective observer to learn that in 1996 it is so weak in principles that, with over a century of humanitarian law behind it, it is still unable to fashion a response to the cruelties of nuclear weapons as going beyond the purposes of war. At the least, it would seem passing strange that the expansion within the body of a single soldier of a single bullet is an excessive cruelty which international law has been unable to tolerate since 1899, and that the incineration in one second of a hundred thousand civilians is not. This astonishment would be compounded when that weapon has the capability, through multiple use, of endangering the entire human species and all civilization with it.

Every branch of knowledge benefits from a process of occasionally stepping back from itself and scrutinizing itself objectively for anomalies and absurdities. If a glaring anomaly or absurdity becomes apparent and remains unquestioned, that discipline is in danger of being seen

---

[88]M.S. McDougal and F.P. Feliciano, *Law and Minimum World Public Order: The Legal Regulation of International Coercion*, 1961, p. 657.

[89]International Declaration Respecting Expanding Bullets, signed at The Hague, 29 July 1899.

[90]International Declaration Respecting Asphyxiating Gases, signed at The Hague, 29 July 1899.

as floundering in the midst of its own technicalities. International law is happily not in this position, but if the conclusion that nuclear weapons are illegal is wrong, it would indeed be.

As will appear from the ensuing discussion, international law is not so lacking in resources as to be unable to meet this unprecedented challenge. Humanitarian law is not a monument to uselessness in the face of the nuclear danger. It contains a plethora of principles wide enough, deep enough and powerful enough to handle this problem.

Humanitarian law has of course received recognition from the jurisprudence of this Court (for example, *Corfu Channel, I.C.J. Reports 1949*, p. 22; *Border and Transborder Armed Actions (Nicaragua v. Honduras), I.C.J. Reports 1988*, p. 114), but this Court has not so far had occasion to examine it in any depth. This case offers it the opportunity par excellence for so doing.

4. Acceptance by States of the Martens Clause

The Martens clause has commanded general international acceptance. It has been incorporated into a series of treaties, as mentioned elsewhere in this Opinion, has been applied by international judicial tribunals, has been incorporated into military manuals[91], and has been generally accepted in international legal literature as indeed encapsulating in its short phraseology the entire philosophy of the law of war.

At the Krupp Trial (1948), it was described as:

"a general clause, making the usages established among civilised nations, the laws of humanity and the dictates of the public conscience into the legal yardstick to be applied if and when the specific provisions of the Convention and the Regulations annexed to it do not cover specific cases occurring in warfare, or concomitant to warfare".[92]

The clause has been described by Lord Wright as furnishing the keynote to the Hague Regulations which particularize a great many war crimes,

"leaving the remainder to the governing effect of that sovereign clause which does really in a few words state the whole animating and motivating principle of the law of war, and in-

---

[91]See section III.10 (a), *infra*.
[92]*Law Reports of Trials of War Criminals*, Vol. 10, p. 133.

deed of all law, because the object of all law is to secure as far as possible in the mutual relations of the human beings concerned the rule of law and of justice and of humanity".[93]

The Martens clause has thus become an established and integral part of the corpus of current customary international law. International law has long passed the stage when it could be debated whether such principles had crystallized into customary international law. No state would today repudiate any one of these principles.

A generally accepted test of recognition of rules of customary international law is that the rule should be "so widely and generally accepted, that it can hardly be supposed that any civilized State would repudiate it".[94] While no state today would repudiate any one of these principles, what seems to be in dispute is the application of those principles to the specific case of nuclear weapons which, for some unarticulated reason, seem to be placed above and beyond the rules applicable to other weapons. If humanitarian law regulates the lesser weapons for fear that they may cause the excessive harm which those principles seek to prevent, it must *a fortiori* regulate the greater. The attempt to place nuclear weapons beyond the reach of these principles lacks the support not only of the considerations of humanity, but also of the considerations of logic.

These considerations are also pertinent to the argument that customary law cannot be created over the objection of the nuclear weapon States (United States Written Statement, p. 9).[95] The general principles of customary law applicable to the matter commanded the allegiance of the nuclear weapon States long before nuclear weapons were invented. It is on those general principles that the illegality of nuclear weapons rests.

It seems clear that if the principles are accepted and remain undisputed, the applicability of those principles to the specific case of nu-

---

[93]Foreword by Lord Wright to the last volume of the *Law Reports of Trials of War Criminals*, Vol. 15, p. xiii. See, further, the discussion of the Martens clause in Singh & McWhinney, *op. cit.*, pp. 46 *et seq.*, referring, *inter alia*, to the two passages cited above.

[94]*West Rand Central Gold Mining Co., Ltd. v. R* (1905), 2 KB, p. 407.

[95]On this aspect, see further section VI.6, *infra*.

clear weapons cannot reasonably be in doubt.

5. The "Dictates of Public Conscience"

This phraseology, stemming from the Martens clause, lies at the heart of humanitarian law. The Martens clause and many subsequent formulations of humanitarian principles recognize the need that strongly held public sentiments in relation to humanitarian conduct be reflected in the law.

The phrase is, of course, sufficiently general to pose difficulties in certain cases in determining whether a particular sentiment is shared widely enough to come within this formulation.

However, in regard to the use or threat of use of nuclear weapons, there is no such uncertainty, for on this issue the conscience of the global community has spoken, and spoken often, in the most unmistakable terms. Resolutions of the General Assembly over the years are not the only evidence of this. Vast numbers of the general public in practically every country, organized professional bodies of a multinational character[96], and many other groupings across the world have proclaimed time and again their conviction that the public conscience dictates the non-use of nuclear weapons. Across the world, presidents and prime ministers, priests and prelates, workers and students, and women and children have continued to express themselves strongly against the bomb and its dangers. Indeed, this conviction underlies the conduct of the entire world community of nations when, for example, in the NPT, it accepts that all nuclear weapons must eventually be got rid of. The recent Non-Proliferation Review Conference of 1995 reconfirmed this objective. The work currently in progress towards a total test ban treaty reconfirms this again.

Reference is made in the next section (section VI.6) to the heightening of public sensitivity towards humanitarian issues, resulting from the vast strides made by human rights law ever since the United Nations Charter in 1945.

---

[96]See, on these organizations, section VI.3 below.

General Assembly resolutions on the matter are numerous.[97] To cite just one of them, Resolution 1653(XVI) of 1961 declared that:

"The use of nuclear and thermo-nuclear weapons is contrary to the spirit, letter and aims of the United Nations and, as such, a direct violation of the Charter of the United Nations."

and asserted, with more specific reference to international law, that such use was "contrary to the rules of international law and to the laws of humanity". In addition, the "threat" to use nuclear weapons, and not merely their actual use, has been referred to by the General Assembly as prohibited.[98]

Nuclear weapons have been outlawed by treaty in numerous areas of planetary space — the sea-bed, Antarctica, Latin America and the Caribbean, the Pacific, and Africa, not to speak of outer space. Such universal activity and commitment would be altogether inconsistent with a global acceptance of the compatibility of these weapons with the general principles of humanity. They point rather to a universal realization that there is in them an element which deeply disturbs the public conscience of this age.

As has been well observed in this regard:

"in this burgeoning human rights era especially, respecting an issue that involves potentially the fate of human civilization itself, it is not only appropriate but mandated that the legal expectations of all members of human society, official and

---

[97]Resolution 1653 (XVI) of 24 November 1961 ("Declaration on the Prohibition of the Use of Nuclear and Thermo-nuclear Weapons"); resolution 2936 (XXVII) of 29 November 1972 ("Non-Use of Force in International Relations and Permanent Prohibition of the Use of Nuclear Weapons"); resolution 33/71B of 14 December 1978 ("Non-Use of Nuclear Weapons and Prevention of Nuclear War"); resolution 34/83G of 11 December 1979 ("Non-Use of Nuclear Weapons and Prevention of Nuclear War"); resolution 36/92I of 9 December 1981 ("Non-Use of Nuclear Weapons and Prevention of Nuclear War"); resolution 44/117C of 15 December 1989 ("Convention on the Prohibition of the Use of Nuclear Weapons"); resolution 45/59B of 4 December 1990 ("Convention on the Prohibition of the Use of Nuclear Weapons"); resolution 46/37D of 6 December 1991 ("Convention on the Prohibition of the Use of Nuclear Weapons"). See, also, e.g., resolution 36/100 of 9 December 1981 ("Declaration on the Prevention of Nuclear Catastrophe"), paragraph 1 ("States and statesmen that resort first to the use of nuclear weapons will be committing the gravest crime against humanity").

[98]Resolution 2936 (XXVII) of 29 November 1972 ("Non-Use of Force in International Relations and Permanent Prohibition of the Use of Nuclear Weapons"), preambular paragraph 10.

non-official, be duly taken into account".[99]

It is a truism that there is no such thing as a unanimous opinion held by the entire world community on any principle, however lofty. Yet it would be hard to find a proposition so widely and universally accepted as that nuclear weapons should not be used. The various expressions of opinion on this matter "are expressive of a far-flung community consensus that nuclear weapons and warfare do not escape the judgment of the humanitarian rules of armed conflict".[100]

The incompatibility between "the dictates of public conscience" and the weapon appears starkly, if one formulates the issues in the form of questions that may be addressed to the public conscience of the world, as typified by the average citizen in any country.

Here are a few questions, from an extensive list that could be compiled:

Is it lawful for the purposes of war to induce cancers, keloid growths or leukaemias in large numbers of the enemy population?

Is it lawful for the purposes of war to inflict congenital deformities and mental retardation on unborn children of the enemy population?

Is it lawful for the purposes of war to poison the food supplies of the enemy population?

Is it lawful for the purposes of war to inflict any of the above types of damage on the population of countries that have nothing to do with the quarrel leading to the nuclear war?

Many more such questions could be asked.

If it is conceivable that any of these questions can be answered in the affirmative by the public conscience of the world, there may be a case for the legality of nuclear weapons. If it is not, the case against nuclear weapons seems unanswerable.

---

[99]Burns H. Weston, "Nuclear Weapons and International Law: Prolegomenon to General Illegality", (1982-1983) 4 *New York Law School Journal of International and Comparative Law*, p. 252 and authorities therein cited.

[100] *Ibid.*, p. 242.

6. Impact of the United Nations Charter and Human Rights on Considerations of Humanity and "Dictates of Public Conscience"[101]

The enormous developments in the field of human rights in the post-war years, commencing with the Universal Declaration of Human Rights in 1948, must necessarily make their impact on assessments of such concepts as "considerations of humanity" and "dictates of the public conscience". This development in human rights concepts, both in their formulation and in their universal acceptance, is more substantial than the developments in this field for centuries before. The public conscience of the global community has thus been greatly strengthened and sensitized to "considerations of humanity" and "dictates of public conscience". Since the vast structure of internationally accepted human rights norms and standards has become part of common global consciousness today in a manner unknown before World War II, its principles tend to be invoked immediately and automatically whenever a question arises of humanitarian standards.

This progressive development must shape contemporary conceptions of humanity and humanitarian standards, thus elevating the level of basic expectation well above what it was when the Martens clause was formulated.

In assessing the magnitude of this change, it is helpful to recall that the first movement towards modern humanitarian law was achieved in a century (the 19th century) which is often described as the "Clausewitzean century" for the reason that, in that century, war was widely regarded as a natural means for the resolution of disputes, and a natural extension of diplomacy. Global sentiment has moved an infinite distance from that stance, for today the United Nations Charter outlaws all resort to force by States (Art. 2(4)), except in the case of self-defence (Art. 51). The Court's Opinion highlights the importance of these articles, with far-reaching implications which this Opinion has addressed at the very outset (see "Preliminary Observations"). There is a firm commitment in Article 2(3) that all members shall settle their international disputes by peaceful means, in such manner that international peace and security, *and justice*, are not endangered. This totally altered stance regarding the normalcy and legitimacy of war has undoubtedly heightened the "dictates of public conscience" in our time.

---

[101]See, also, Section III.10(f), *infra*.

Charter provisions bearing on human rights, such as Articles 1, 55, 62 and 76, coupled with the Universal Declaration of 1948, the twin Covenants on Civil and Political Rights and Economic, Social and Cultural Rights of 1966, and the numerous specific conventions formulating human rights standards, such as the Convention against Torture — all of these, now part of the public conscience of the global community, make the violation of humanitarian standards a far more developed and definite concept than in the days when the Martens clause emerged. Indeed, so well are human rights norms and standards ingrained today in global consciousness, that they flood through into every corner of humanitarian law.

Submissions on these lines were made to the Court (for example, by Australia, CR 95/22, p. 25) in presentations which drew attention further to the fact that the General Assembly has noted the linkage between human rights and nuclear weapons when it condemned nuclear war "as a violation of the foremost human right — the right to life".[102]

Parallel to the developments in human rights, there has been another vast area of development — environmental law, which has likewise heightened the sensitivity of the public conscience to environmentally related matters which affect human rights. As observed by the International Law Commission in its consideration of state responsibility, conduct gravely endangering the preservation of the human environment violates principles "which are now so deeply rooted in the conscience of mankind that they have become particularly essential rules of general international law".[103]

7. The Argument that "Collateral Damage" Is Unintended

It is not to the point that such results are not directly intended, but are "by-products" or "collateral damage" caused by nuclear weapons. Such results are known to be the necessary consequences of the use of the weapon. The author of the act causing these consequences cannot in any coherent legal system avoid legal responsibility for causing

---

[102]GA Res. 38/75 of 15 December 1983 ("Condemnation of nuclear war"), operative para. 1.

[103]Report of the International Law Commission on the work of its twenty-eighth session, *Yearbook of the International Law Commission, 1976*, Vol. II, Part II, p. 109, para. 33.

them, any less than a man careering in a motor vehicle at a hundred and fifty kilometres per hour through a crowded market street can avoid responsibility for the resulting deaths on the ground that he did not intend to kill the particular persons who died.

The plethora of literature on the consequences of the nuclear weapon is so much part of common universal knowledge today that no disclaimer of such knowledge would be credible.

8. Illegality Exists Independently of Specific Prohibitions

Much of the argument of States opposing illegality was based on the proposition that what is not expressly prohibited to a State is permitted. Some practical illustrations would be of assistance in testing this proposition.

  (a) If tomorrow a ray were invented which would immediately incinerate all living things within a radius of 100 miles, does one need to wait for an international treaty specifically banning it to declare that it offends the basic principles of the *ius in bello* and cannot therefore be legitimately used in war? It would seem rather ridiculous to have to await the convening of an international conference, the drafting of a treaty, and all the delays associated with the process of ratification, before the law can treat such a weapon as illegal.

  (b) The fallacy of the argument that what is not expressly prohibited is permitted appears further from an illustration used earlier in this Opinion. The argument advanced would presuppose that, immediately prior to the treaties outlawing bacteriological weapons, it was legal to use warheads packed with the most deadly germs wherewith to cause lethal epidemics among the enemy population. This conclusion strains credibility and is tenable only if one totally discounts the pre-existing principles of humanitarian law.

The fact that no treaty or declaration expressly condemns the weapon as illegal does not meet the point that illegality is based upon principles of customary international law which run far deeper than any particular weapon or any particular declaration. Every weapon proscribed by international law for its cruelty or brutality does not need to be specified any more than every implement of torture needs to be specified in a general prohibition against torture. It is the principle that is the subject of customary international law. The *particular* weapon or implement of torture becomes relevant only as an application of undisputed *principles* — principles which have been more than once described as being such that no civilized nation would deny them.

It will always be the case that weapons technologists will from time to time invent weapons based on new applications of technology, which are different from any weapons known before. One does not need to wait until some treaty specifically condemns that weapon before declaring that its use is contrary to the principles of international law.

If, as is indisputably the case, the Martens clause represents a universally accepted principle of international law, it means that beyond the domain of express prohibitions, there lies the domain of the general principles of humanitarian law. It follows that "If an act of war is not expressly prohibited by international agreements by customary law, this does not necessarily mean that it is actually permissible".[104]

It is self-evident that no system of law can depend for its operation or development on specific prohibitions *ipsissimis verbis.* Any developed system of law has, in addition to its specific commands and prohibitions, an array of general principles which from time to time are applied to specific items of conduct or events which have not been the subject of an express ruling before. The general principle is then applied to the specific situation and out of that particular application a rule of greater specificity emerges.

A legal system based on the theory that what is not expressly prohibited is permitted would be a primitive system indeed, and international law has progressed far beyond this stage. Even if domestic systems could function on that basis — which indeed is doubtful — international law, born of generations of philosophical thinking, cannot. Modern legal philosophy in many jurisdictions has exposed the untenability of this view in regard to domestic systems and, *a fortiori,* the same applies to international law. As a well-known text on jurisprudence observes:

> "The rules of every legal order have an enveloping blanket
> of principles and doctrines as the earth is surrounded by air,
> and these not only influence the operation of rules but some-
> times condition their very existence."[105]

---

[104]D. Fleck, *op. cit.*, p. 28, basing this principle on the Martens clause.
[105]Dias, *Jurisprudence*, 4th ed., 1976, p. 287.

More to the point than the question whether any treaty speaks of the *illegality* of nuclear weapons is whether any single provision of any treaty or declaration speaks of the *legality* of nuclear weapons. The fact is that, though there is a profusion of international documents dealing with many aspects of nuclear weapons, not one of these contains the shred of a suggestion that the *use* or *threat of use* of nuclear weapons is legal. By way of contrast, the number of international declarations which expressly pronounce against the legality or the use of nuclear weapons is legion. These are referred to elsewhere in this Opinion.

The general principles provide both nourishment for the development of the law and an anchorage to the mores of the community. If they are to be discarded in the manner contended for, international law would be cast adrift from its conceptual moorings. "The general principles of law recognised by civilised nations" remains law, even though indiscriminate mass slaughter *through the nuclear weapon*, irreversible damage to future generations *through the nuclear weapon*, environmental devastation *through the nuclear weapon*, and irreparable damage to neutral states *through the nuclear weapon* are not expressly prohibited in international treaties. If the italicized words are deleted from the previous sentence, no one could deny that the acts mentioned therein are prohibited by international law. It seems specious to argue that the principle of prohibition is defeated by the absence of particularization of the weapon.

The doctrine that the sovereign is free to do whatever statute does not expressly prohibit is a long-exploded doctrine. Such extreme positivism in legal doctrine has led humanity to some of its worst excesses. History has demonstrated that power, unrestrained by principle, becomes power abused. Black-letter formulations have their value, but by no stretch of the imagination can they represent the totality of the law.

With specific reference to the laws of war, it would also set at nought the words of the Martens clause, whose express terms are that, "Until a more complete code of the laws of war has been issued, the High contracting Parties . . . declare that, *in cases not included in the Regulations adopted by them . . .*" (emphasis added), the humanitarian principles it sets out would apply.

Thus, by express agreement, if that indeed were necessary, the wide range of principles of humanitarian law contained within customary international law would be applicable to govern this matter, for which no specific provision has yet been made by treaty.

9. The *"Lotus"* Decision

Much of the argument based on the absence of specific illegality was anchored to the *"Lotus"* decision. In that case, the Permanent Court addressed its inquiry to the question:

> "whether or not under international law there is a principle which would have prohibitcd Turkey, in the circumstances of the case before the Court, from prosecuting Lieutenant Demons" *(P.C.I.J., Series A, No. 10*, p. 21).

In the absence of such a principle or of a specific rule to which it had expressly consented, it was held that the authority of a State could not be limited.

Indeed, even within the terms of the *"Lotus"* case, these principles become applicable, for, in relation to the laws of war, there is the express acceptance by the nuclear powers that the humanitarian principles of the laws of war should apply. Apart from the nuclear powers, some other powers who have opposed a finding of illegality before this Court (or not adopted a clear-cut position in regard to the present Request), were also parties to the Hague Convention, e.g., Germany, The Netherlands, Italy and Japan.

The *"Lotus"* case was decided in the context of a collision on the high seas, in time of peace, between the Lotus, flying the French flag and a vessel flying the Turkish flag. Eight Turkish sailors and passengers died and the French officer responsible was sought to be tried for manslaughter in the Turkish courts. This was a situation far removed from that to which the humanitarian laws of war apply. Such humanitarian law was already a well established concept at the time of the *"Lotus"* decision, but was not relevant to it. It would have been furthest from the mind of the Court deciding that case that its dictum, given in such entirely different circumstances, would be used in an attempt to negative all that the humanitarian laws of war had built up until that time — for the interpretation now sought to be given to the *"Lotus"* case is nothing less than that it overrides even such well-entrenched principles as the Martens clause, which expressly provides that its humanitarian principles would apply "in cases not included in the Regulations adopted by them".

Moreover, at that time, international law was generally treated in two separate categories — the laws of peace and the laws of war — a distinction well recognized in the structure of the legal texts of that time. The principle the *"Lotus"* court was enunciating was formulated entirely within the context of the laws of peace.

It is implicit in *"Lotus"* that the sovereignty of other States should be respected. One of the characteristics of nuclear weapons is that they violate the sovereignty of other countries who have in no way consented to the intrusion upon their fundamental sovereign rights, which is implicit in the use of the nuclear weapon. It would be an interpretation totally out of context that the *"Lotus"* decision formulated a theory, equally applicable in peace and war, to the effect that a State could do whatever it pleased so long as it had not bound itself to the contrary. Such an interpretation of *"Lotus"* would cast a baneful spell on the progressive development of international law.

It is to be noted also that just four years earlier, the Permanent Court, in dealing with the question of state sovereignty, had observed in *Nationality Decrees Issued in Tunisia and Morocco (Advisory Opinion, P.C.I.J., Series B, No. 4)* (1923) that the sovereignty of states would be proportionately diminished and restricted as international law developed (pp. 121-125, p. 127, p. 130). In the half century that has elapsed since the *"Lotus"* case, it is quite evident that international law — and the law relating to humanitarian conduct in war — have developed considerably, imposing additional restrictions on state sovereignty over and above those that existed at the time of the *"Lotus"* case. This Court's own jurisprudence in the *Corfu Channel* case sees customary international law as imposing a duty on all States so to conduct their affairs as not to injure others, even though there was no prohibition *ipsissimis verbis* of the particular act which constituted a violation of the complaining nation's rights. This Court cannot in 1996 construe *"Lotus"* so narrowly as to take the law backward in time even beyond the Martens clause.

10. Specific Rules of the Humanitarian Law of War

There are several interlacing principles which together constitute the fabric of international humanitarian law. Humanitarian law reveals not a paucity, but rather an abundance of rules which both individually and cumulatively render the use or threat of use of nuclear weapons illegal.

The rules of the humanitarian law of war have clearly acquired the status of *ius cogens*, for they are fundamental rules of a humanitarian character, from which no derogation is possible without negating the basic considerations of humanity which they are intended to protect. In the words of Roberto Ago, the rules of jus cogens include:

"the fundamental rules concerning the safeguarding of peace, and notably those which forbid recourse to force or threat of *force; fundamental rules of a humanitarian nature* (prohibition of genocide, slavery and racial discrimination, *protection of essential rights of the human person in time of peace and war*); the rules prohibiting any infringement of the independence and sovereign equality of States; the rules which ensure to all members of the international community the enjoyment of certain common resources (high seas, outer space, etc.)"[106]

The question under consideration is not whether there is a prohibition in peremptory terms of nuclear weapons specifically so mentioned, but whether there are basic principles of a *ius cogens* nature which are violated by nuclear weapons. If there are such principles which are of a *ius cogens* nature, then it would follow that the weapon itself would be prohibited under the *ius cogens* concept.

As noted at the commencement of Part III, most of the States which support the view that the use of nuclear weapons is lawful acknowledge that international humanitarian law applies to their use, and that such use must conform to its principles. Among the more important of the relevant principles of international law are:

1. the prohibition against causing unnecessary suffering;

2. the principle of proportionality;

3. the principle of discrimination between combatants and non-combatants;

4. the obligation to respect the territorial sovereignty of non-belligerent states;

5. the prohibition against genocide and crimes against humanity;

6. the prohibition against causing lasting and severe damage to the environment;

7. human rights law

---

[106](1971-III) *Recueil des Cours*, p. 324, fn. 37; emphasis added. See, also, the detailed study of various peremptory norms in the international law of armed conflict, in Lauri Hannikainen, *Peremptory Norms (Jus Cogens) in International Law*, 1988 pp. 596-715, where the author finds that many of the principles of the humanitarian law of war are *ius cogens*.

(a) The prohibition against causing unnecessary suffering

The Martens clause, to which reference has already been made, gave classic formulation to this principle in modern law, when it spelt out the impermissibility of weapons incompatible with "the laws of humanity and the dictates of public conscience".

The prohibition against cruel and unnecessary suffering, long a part of the general principles of humanitarian law, has been embodied in such a large number of codes, declarations, and treaties as to constitute a firm and substantial body of law, each document applying the general principles to a specific situation or situations.[107] They illustrate the existence of overarching general principles transcending the specific instances dealt with.

The principle against unnecessary suffering has moreover been incorporated into standard military manuals. Thus the British *Manual of Military Law,* issued by the War Office in 1916, and used in World War I, reads:

"IV The Means of Carrying on War

39. The first principle of war is that the enemy's powers of resistance must be weakened and destroyed. The means that may be employed to inflict injury on him are not however unlimited [footnote cites Hague Rules 22, 'Belligerents have not an unlimited right as to the choice of means of injuring the enemy']. They are in practice definitely restricted by international conventions and declarations, and also by the customary rules of warfare. And, moreover, there are the dictates of morality, civilization and chivalry, which ought to be obeyed.

*

*   *

42. It is expressly forbidden to employ arms, projectiles or material calculated to cause unnecessary suffering [Hague

---

[107]Examples are the Lieber Code of 1863 (adopted by the United States for the Government of Armies in the Field); the Declaration of St. Petersburg of 1868; the Hague Conventions of 1899 and 1907; the Protocol for the Prohibition of the Use in War of Asphyxiating, Poisonous or Other Gases, and of Bacteriological Methods of Warfare of 1925; the Hague Rules of Air Warfare of 1923; the Nuremberg Charter of 1945; and the four Geneva conventions of 1949.

Rules 23(e)]. Under this heading might be included such weapons as lances with a barbed head, irregularly shaped bullets, projectiles filled with broken glass and the like; also the scoring of the surface of bullets, the filing off the end of their hard case, and smearing on them any substance likely to inflame or wound. The prohibition is not, however, intended to apply to the use of explosives contained in mines, aerial torpedoes, or hand-grenades." (Pp. 242-243.)

Such was the Manual the British forces used in World War I, long before the principles of humanitarian warfare were as well entrenched as they now are.[108]

As early as 1862, Franz Lieber accepted the position that even military necessity is subject to the law and usages of war, and this was incorporated in the instructions for the army.[109] Modern United States War Department Field Manuals are in strict conformity with the Hague Regulations and expressly subject military necessity to "the customary and conventional laws of war".[110]

The facts set out in Part II of this Opinion are more than sufficient to establish that the nuclear weapon causes unnecessary suffering going far beyond the purposes of war.

An argument that has been advanced in regard to the principle regarding "unnecessary suffering" is that, under Article 23(*e*) of the 1907 Hague Regulations, it is forbidden, "To employ arms, projectiles, or material *calculated* to cause unnecessary suffering" (emphasis added). The nuclear weapon, it is said, is not *calculated* to cause suffering, but suffering is rather a part of the "incidental side effects" of nuclear weapons explosions. This argument is met by the well-known legal principle that the doer of an act must be taken to have *intended* its natural and foreseeable consequences (see section III.7, *supra*.). It is, moreover, a literal interpretation which does not take into account the spirit and underlying rationale of the provision — a method of interpretation particularly inappropriate to the construction of a humanitarian instrument. It may also be said that nuclear weapons are indeed deployed "in part with a view to utilising the destructive effects

---

[108]On the importance of validity of military manuals, see, Singh & McWhinney, *op. cit.*, p. 59.

[109]General Orders 100, *Instructions for the Government of the Armies of the United States in the Field*, s. 14.

[110]Singh & McWhinney, *op. cit.*, p. 59.

of radiation and fall-out".[111]

(b) The principle of discrimination

The principle of discrimination originated in the concern that weapons of war should not be used indiscriminately against military targets and civilians alike. Non-combatants needed the protection of the laws of war. However, the nuclear weapon is such that non-discrimination is built into its very nature. A weapon that can flatten a city and achieve by itself the destruction caused by thousands of individual bombs, is not a weapon that discriminates. The radiation it releases over immense areas does not discriminate between combatant and non-combatant, or indeed between combatant and neutral states.

Article 48 of the First Protocol of 1977 Additional to the Geneva Conventions of 1949 repeats as a "Basic Rule" the well-accepted rule of humanitarian law:

> "In order to ensure respect for and protection of the civilian population and civilian objects, the Parties to the conflict shall *at all times* distinguish between the civilian population and combatants and between civilian objects and military objectives and accordingly shall direct their operations only against military objectives." (Emphasis added.)

The rule of discrimination between civilian populations and military personnel is, like some of the other rules of ius *in bello, of ancient vintage and shared by many cultures. We have referred already to the ancient Indian practice that Indian peasants would pursue their work in the fields, in the face of invading armies, confident of the protection afforded them by the tradition that war was a matter for the combatants.[112] This scenario, idyllic though it may seem, and so out of tune with the brutalities of war, is a useful reminder that basic humanitarian principles such as discrimination do not aim at fresh standards unknown before.*

The protection of the civilian population in times of armed conflict has for long been a well-established rule of international humanitarian law. Additional Protocol I to the Geneva Convention (1949) provides by Article 51(5)(*b*) that the "indiscriminate attacks" which it prohibits

---

[111]Ian Brownlie, "Some Legal Aspects of the Use of Nuclear Weapons" (1965), 14 *International and Comparative Law Quarterly*, p. 445.

[112]Nagendra Singh, fn. 67, *supra*.

include:

> "an attack which may be expected to cause incidental loss of civilian life, injury to civilians, damage to civilian objects, or a combination thereof, which would be excessive in relation to the concrete and direct military advantage anticipated".

So, also, Article 57(2)(*b*) prohibits attacks when:

> "the attack may be expected to cause incidental loss of civilian life, injury to civilians, damage to civilian objects or a combination thereof, which would be excessive in relation to the concrete and direct military advantage anticipated".

The many facets of this rule were addressed in the resolution of the International Law Institute, passed at its Edinburgh Conference in 1969[113] which referred to them as prohibited by existing law as at that date. The acts described as prohibited by existing law included the following:

> "[A]ll attacks for whatsoever motive or by whatsoever means for the annihilation of any group, region or urban centre with no possible distinction between armed forces and civilian populations or between military objectives and non-military objects".[114]
>
> "[A]ny action whatsoever designed to terrorize the civilian population" (para. 6).
>
> "[T]he use of all weapons which, by their nature, affect indiscriminately both military objectives and non-military objects, or both armed forces and civilian populations. In particular, it prohibits the use of weapons the destructive effect of which is so great that it cannot be limited to specific military objectives or is otherwise uncontrollable . . ., as well as of 'blind' weapons" (para. 7).

(c) Respect for non-belligerent states

When nuclear weapons are used their natural and foreseeable consequence of irreparable damage to non-belligerent third parties is a

---

113On the eminent juristic support for this proposition, see Section III.11, *infra.*

114(1969) 53 *Annuaire de l'IDI*, Vol. II, p. 377, para. 8; Iran, CR 95/26, p. 47, fn. 45.

necessary consideration to be taken into reckoning in deciding the permissibility of the weapon. It is not merely a single non-belligerent state that might be irretrievably damaged, but the entire global community of states. The uncontainability of radiation extends it globally. The enormous area of damage caused by nuclear weapons, as compared with the most powerful conventional weapons, appears from the diagram appended to this Opinion, which is taken from WHO studies. When wind currents scatter these effects further, it is well established by the TTAPS and other studies that explosions in one hemisphere can spread their deleterious effects even to the other hemisphere. No portion of the globe — and therefore no country — could be free of these effects.

The argument of lack of intention has been addressed in this context as well. In terms of this argument, an action directed at an enemy State is not intended to cause damage to a third party, and if such damage in fact ensues, it is not culpable. This argument has already been dealt with in an earlier section of this Opinion, when it was pointed out that such an argument is untenable (see section III.7). The launching of a nuclear weapon is a deliberate act. Damage to neutrals is a natural, foreseeable and, indeed, inevitable consequence. International law cannot contain a rule of non-responsibility which is so opposed to the basic principles of universal jurisprudence.

(d) The prohibition against genocide[115]

The Court's treatment of the relevance of genocide to the nuclear weapon is, in my view, inadequate (para. 26 of the Opinion).

Nuclear weapons used in response to a nuclear attack, especially in the event of an all-out nuclear response, would be likely to cause genocide by triggering off an all-out nuclear exchange, as visualized in Section IV (*infra*.). Even a single "small" nuclear weapon, such as those used in Japan, could be instruments of genocide, judging from the number of deaths they are known to have caused. If cities are targeted, a single bomb could cause a death toll exceeding a million. If the retaliatory weapons are more numerous, on WHO's estimates of the effects of nuclear war, even a billion people, both of the attacking state and of others, could be killed. This is plainly genocide and, whatever the circumstances, cannot be within the law.

When a nuclear weapon is used, those using it must know that it

---

[115]See, further, section III.10(f) below on human rights law.

will have the effect of causing deaths on a scale so massive as to wipe out entire populations. Genocide, as defined in the Genocide Convention (Art. II), means any act committed with intent to destroy, in whole or in part, a national, ethnical, racial or religious group, as such. Acts included in the definition are killing members of the group, causing serious bodily or mental harm to members of the group, and deliberately inflicting on the group conditions of life calculated to bring about its physical destruction in whole or in part.

In discussions on the definition of genocide in the Genocide Convention, much play is made upon the words "as such". The argument offered is that there must be an intention to target a particular national, ethnical, racial or religious group qua such group, and not incidentally to some other act. However, having regard to the ability of nuclear weapons to wipe out blocks of population ranging from hundreds of thousands to millions, there can be no doubt that the weapon targets, in whole or in part, the national group of the State at which it is directed.

Nuremberg held that the extermination of the civilian population in whole or in part is a crime against humanity. This is precisely what a nuclear weapon achieves.

(e) The prohibition against environmental damage

The environment, the common habitat of all member states of the United Nations, cannot be damaged by any one or more members to the detriment of all others. Reference has already been made, in the context of dictates of public conscience (section III.6, *supra.*), to the fact that the principles of environmental protection have become "so deeply rooted in the conscience of mankind that they have become particularly essential rules of general international law".[116] The International Law Commission has indeed classified massive pollution of the atmosphere or of the seas as an international crime.[117] These aspects have been referred to earlier.

Environmental law incorporates a number of principles which are violated by nuclear weapons. The principle of intergenerational equity and the common heritage principle have already been discussed. Other

---

[116]Report of the International Law Commission on the work of its 28th Session, *Yearbook of the International Law Commission*, 1976, Vol. II, Part II, p. 109, para. 33.

[117]Draft Article 19(3) (*d*) on "State Responsibility" of the International Law Commission, *ibid.*, p. 96.

principles of environmental law, which this Request enables the Court to recognize and use in reaching its conclusions, are the precautionary principle, the principle of trusteeship of earth resources, the principle that the burden of proving safety lies upon the author of the act complained of, and the "polluter pays principle", placing on the author of environmental damage the burden of making adequate reparation to those affected.[118] There have been juristic efforts in recent times to formulate what have been described as "principles of ecological security" — a process of norm creation and codification of environmental law which has developed under the stress of the need to protect human civilization from the threat of self-destruction.

One writer[119], in listing eleven such principles, includes among them the "Prohibition of Ecological Aggression", deriving this principle *inter alia* from such documents as the 1977 Convention on the Prohibition of Military or Any Other Hostile Use of Environmental Modification Techniques which entered into force on 5 October 1978 (1108 *UNTS*, p. 151), and the United Nations General Assembly resolution "Historical responsibility of States for the preservation of nature for present and future generations" (GA Res. 35/8 of 30 October 1980).

The same writer points out that, "Under Soviet (now Russian) legal doctrine, the deliberate and hostile modification of the environment — ecocide — is unlawful and considered an international crime".[120]

Another writer, drawing attention to the need for a co-ordinated, collective response to the global environmental crisis and the difficulty of envisioning such a response, observes:

> "But circumstances are forcing just such a response; if we cannot embrace the preservation of the earth as our new organizing principle, the very survival of our civilization will be in doubt."[121]

---

[118]See the references to these principles in my Dissenting Opinion in *Request for an Examination of the Situation in accordance with Paragraph 63 of the Court's Judgment of 20 December 1974 in the Nuclear Tests (New Zealand v. France) Case, I.C.J. Reports 1995*, pp. 339-347.

[119]A. Timoshenko, "Ecological Security: Global Change Paradigm", (1990) 1 *Columbia Journal of International Environmental Law and Policy*, p. 127.

[120]Timoshenko, *supra*.

[121]A. Gore, *Earth in the Balance: Ecology and the Human Spirit*, 1992, p. 295, cited in Guruswamy, Palmer and Weston, *International Environmental Law and World Order*, 1994, p. 264.

Here, forcefully stated, is the driving force behind today's environmental law — the "new organizing principle" of preservation of the earth, without which all civilization is in jeopardy.

A means already at work for achieving such a co-ordinated collective response is international environmental law, and it is not to be wondered at that these basic principles ensuring the survival of civilization, and indeed of the human species, are already an integral part of that law.

The same matter is put in another perspective in an outstanding study, already referred to:

"The self-extinction of our species is not an act that anyone describes as sane or sensible; nevertheless, it is an act that, without quite admitting it to ourselves, we plan in certain circumstances to commit. Being impossible as a fully intentional act, unless the perpetrator has lost his mind, it can come about only through a kind of inadvertence — as a 'side effect' of some action that we do intend, such as the defense of our nation, or the defense of liberty, or the defense of socialism, or the defense of whatever else we happen to believe in. To that extent, our failure to acknowledge the magnitude and significance of the peril is a necessary condition for doing the deed. We can do it only if we don't quite know what we're doing. If we did acknowledge the full dimensions of the peril, admitting clearly and without reservation that any use of nuclear arms is likely to touch off a holocaust in which the continuance of all human life would be put at risk, extinction would at that moment become not only 'unthinkable' but also undoable." [122]

These principles of environmental law thus do not depend for their validity on treaty provisions. They are part of customary international law. They are part of the *sine qua non* for human survival.

Practical recognitions of the principle that they are an integral part of customary international law are not difficult to find in the international arena. Thus, for example, the Security Council, in resolution 687 of 1991, referred to Iraq's liability "under international law . . . for environmental damage" resulting from the unlawful invasion of Kuwait. This was not a liability arising under treaty, for Iraq was not a party to either the 1977 ENMOD Convention, nor the 1977 Protocols,

---

[122]Jonathan Schell, *The Fate of the Earth, op. cit.*, p. 186.

nor any other specific treaty dealing expressly with the matter. Iraq's liability to which the Security Council referred in such unequivocal terms was clearly a liability arising under customary international law.[123]

Nor are these principles confined to either peace or war, but cover both situations, for they proceed from general duties, applicable alike in peace and war.[124]

The basic principle in this regard is spelt out by Article 35(3) of the 1977 Additional Protocol I to the Geneva Convention in terms prohibiting:

"methods or means of warfare which are intended, or may be expected, to cause widespread, long-term and severe damage to the natural environment".

Article 55 prohibits:

"the use of methods or means of warfare which are intended or may be expected to cause such damage to the natural environment and thereby to prejudice the health or survival of the population".

The question is not whether nuclear weapons were or were not intended to be covered by these formulations. It is sufficient to read them as stating undisputed principles of customary international law. To consider that these general principles are not explicit enough to cover nuclear weapons, or that nuclear weapons were designedly left unmentioned and are therefore not covered, or even that there was a clear understanding that these provisions were not intended to cover nuclear weapons, is to emphasize the incongruity of prohibiting lesser weapons of environmental damage, while leaving intact the infinitely greater agency of causing the very damage which it was the rationale of the treaty to prevent.

If there are general duties arising under customary international law, it clearly matters not that the various environmental agreements do not specifically refer to damage by nuclear weapons. The same principles apply whether we deal with belching furnaces, leaking reac-

---

[123] A submission to this effect was made by the Solomon Islands in the hearings before the Court — Sands, CR 95/32, p. 71.

[124] See, for example, the phraseology of Principle 21 of the Stockholm Declaration and Principle 2 of the Rio Declaration, referring to the duties of States to prevent damage to the environment of other States.

tors or explosive weapons. The mere circumstance that coal furnaces or reactors are not specifically mentioned in environmental treaties cannot lead to the conclusion that they are exempt from the incontrovertible and well established standards and principles laid down therein.

Another approach to the applicability of environmental law to the matter before the Court is through the principle of good neighbourliness, which is both impliedly and expressly written into the United Nations Charter. This principle is one of the bases of modern international law, which has seen the demise of the principle that sovereign states could pursue their own interests in splendid isolation from each other. A world order in which every sovereign state depends on the same global environment generates a mutual interdependence which can only be implemented by co-operation and good neighbourliness.

The United Nations Charter spells this out as "the general principle of good-neighbourliness, due account being taken of the interests and well-being of the rest of the world, in social, economic, and commercial matters" (Art. 74). A course of action that can destroy the global environment will take to its destruction not only the environment, but the social, economic and commercial interests that cannot exist apart from that environment. The Charter's express recognition of such a general duty of good neighbourliness makes this an essential part of international law.

This Court, from the very commencement of its jurisprudence, has supported this principle by spelling out the duty of every State not to "allow knowingly its territory to be used for acts contrary to the rights of other States" (*Corfu Channel, I.C.J. Reports 1949*, p. 22).

The question of State responsibility in regard to the environment is dealt with more specifically in my Dissenting Opinion on the WHO Request, and that discussion must be regarded as supplementary to the discussion of environmental considerations in this Opinion. As therein pointed out, damage to the environment caused by nuclear weapons is a breach of State obligation, and this adds another dimension to the illegality of the use or threat of use of nuclear weapons.

(f) Human rights law[125]

This Opinion has dealt in Section III.3 with the ways in which the

---

[125]See, also, Section III.6, *supra*.

development of human rights in the post-war years has made an impact on "considerations of humanity and "dictates of public conscience".

Concentrating attention more specifically on the rights spelt out in the Universal Declaration of Human Rights, it is possible to identify the right to dignity (Preamble and Art. 1), the right to life, the right to bodily security (Art. 3), the right to medical care (Art. 25(1)), the right to marriage and procreation (Art. 16(1)), the protection of motherhood and childhood (Art. 25(2)), and the right to cultural life (Art. 27(1)), as basic human rights which are endangered by nuclear weapons.

It is part of established human law doctrine that certain rights are non-derogable in any circumstances. The right to life is one of them. It is one of the rights which constitute the irreducible core of human rights.

The preamble to the Declaration speaks of recognition of the inherent dignity of all members of the human family as the foundation of freedom, justice and peace in the world. Article 1 follows this up with the specific averment that "All human beings are born free and equal in dignity and rights". Article 6 states that everyone has the right to recognition everywhere as a person before the law. The International Covenant on Civil and Political Rights made this right more explicit and imposed on States the affirmative obligation of protecting it by law. Article 6(i) states, "Every human being has the inherent right to life. This right shall be protected by law". States parties to the Covenant expressly assumed the responsibility to implement the provisions of the Covenant.

The European Convention for the Protection of Human Rights and Fundamental Freedoms (1950, Art. 2) and the American Convention of Human Rights (1969, Art. 4) likewise confirm the right to life. It is one of the non-derogable rights and an integral part of the irreducible core of human rights.

It has been argued that the right to life is not an absolute right and that the taking of life in armed hostilities is a necessary exception to this principle. However, when a weapon has the potential to kill between one million and one billion people, as WHO has told the Court, human life becomes reduced to a level of worthlessness that totally belies human dignity as understood in any culture. Such a deliberate action by an State is, in any circumstances whatsoever, incompatible with a recognition by it of that respect for basic human dignity on which world peace depends, and respect for which is assumed on the part of all member States of the United Nations.

This is not merely a provision of the Universal Declaration on Human Rights and other human rights instruments, but is fundamental Charter law as enshrined in the very preamble to the United Nations Charter, for one of the ends to which the United Nations is dedicated is "to reaffirm faith in fundamental human rights, in the *dignity and worth* of the human person" (emphasis added). No weapon ever invented in the long history of man's inhumanity to man has so negatived the dignity and worth of the human person as has the nuclear bomb.

Reference should also be made to the General Comment of the United Nations Human Rights Committee entitled "The Right to Life and Nuclear Weapons"[126]which endorsed the view of the General Assembly that the right to life is especially pertinent to nuclear weapons.[127] Stating that nuclear weapons are among the greatest threats to life and the right to life, it carried its view of the conflict between nuclear weapons and international law so far as to propose that their use should be recognized as crimes against humanity.

All of these human rights follow from one central right — a right described by René Cassin as "the right of human beings to exist" (CR 95/32, p. 64, and see fn. 20). This is the foundation of the elaborate structure of human rights that has been painstakingly built by the world community in the post-war years.

Any endorsement of the legality of the use, in any circumstances whatsoever, of a weapon which can snuff out life by the million would tear out the foundations beneath this elaborate structure which represents one of the greatest juristic achievements of this century. That structure, built upon one of the noblest and most essential concepts known to the law, cannot theoretically be maintained if international law allows this right to any State. It could well be written off the books.

11. Juristic Opinion

It would be correct to say that the bulk of juristic opinion is of the view that nuclear weapons offend existing principles of humanitarian law. Juristic opinion is an important source of international law and there is no room in this Opinion for a citation of all the authorities. It will suffice, for present purposes, to refer to a resolution already noted in an earlier part of this discussion — the resolution adopted by the

---

[126]Gen. C 14/23, reproduced in M. Nowak, *United Nations Covenant on Civil and Political Rights*, 1983, p. 861.

[127]GA Res. 38/75, "Condemnation of Nuclear War", first operative paragraph.

Institute of International Law in 1969, at its Edinburgh Session, at a time when juristic writing on nuclear arms had not reached its present level of intensity and was in fact quite scarce.

The finding of the Institute, already cited (see section III.10(*b*), *supra.*), that *existing* international law prohibits, in particular, the use of weapons whose destructive effect "is so great that it cannot be limited to specific military objectives or is otherwise uncontrollable . . ., as well as of 'blind' weapons"[128], was adopted by 60 votes, with one against and two abstentions. Those voting in favour included Charles De Visscher, Lord McNair, Roberto Ago, Suzanne Bastid, Erik Castrén, Sir Gerald Fitzmaurice, Wilfred Jenks, Sir Robert Jennings, Charles Rousseau, Grigory Tunkin, Sir Humphrey Waldock, José Maria Ruda, Oscar Schachter and Kotaro Tanaka, to select a few from an illustrious list of the most eminent international lawyers of the time.

12. The 1925 Geneva Gas Protocol

Quite independently of the various general principles that have been invoked in the discussion thus far, there is a conventional basis on which it has been argued that nuclear weapons are illegal. It is for this reason that I have voted against paragraph 2(B) of the *dispositif* which holds that there is not, in conventional international law, a comprehensive and universal prohibition of the threat or use of nuclear weapons as such. I refer, in particular, to the Protocol for the Prohibition of the Use in War of Asphyxiating, Poisonous or Other Gases and of Bacteriological Methods of Warfare, June 17, 1925 (commonly referred to as the Geneva Gas Protocol). It is so comprehensive in its prohibition that, in my view, it clearly covers nuclear weapons, which thus become the subject of conventional prohibition. There is considerable scholarly opinion favouring this view. [129] Moreover, if radiation

---

128(1969) 53 *Annuaire de l'IDI*, Vol. II, p. 377, para. 7.

129See Burns H. Weston, *op. cit.*, p. 241; E. Castrén, *The Present Law of War and Neutrality*, 1954, p. 207; G. Schwarzenberger, *The Legality of Nuclear Weapons*, 1958, pp. 37-38; N. Singh, *Nuclear Weapons and International Law*, 1959, pp. 162-166; Falk, Meyrowitz and Sanderson, "Nuclear Weapons and International Law", (1980) 20 *Indian Journal of International Law*, p. 563; Julius Stone, *Legal Controls of International Conflict*, 1954, p. 556; Spaight, *Air Power and War Rights*, 3rd ed., 1947, pp. 275-276; H. Lauterpacht (ed.) in *Oppenheim's International Law*, Vol. 2, 7th ed., 1952, p. 348.

is a poison, it is caught up also by the prohibition on poison weapons contained in Article 23(a) of the Hague Regulations. The rule against poisonous weapons has indeed been described as "The most time-honoured special prohibition on the subject of weapons and instruments of war".[130] It is a rule recognized from the remotest historical periods and in a wide spread of cultures.

The Geneva Gas Protocol was drafted in very wide terms. It prohibits "the use in war of asphyxiating, poisonous, or other gases and of all analogous liquids, *materials* or *devices*" (emphasis added).

If this Protocol is to be applicable to nuclear weapons, it must be shown:

(1) that radiation is *poisonous*; and

(2) that it involves the contact of *materials* with the human body.

If both these questions are answered in the affirmative, the damage to the human body caused by radiation would be covered by the terms of the Protocol.

(i) Is radiation poisonous?

Poison is generally defined as a substance which, of its own force, damages health on contact with or absorption by the body.[131] The discussion of the effects of radiation in Section II.3(e) above can leave one in no doubt that the effects of radiation are that it destroys life or damages the functions of the organs and tissues.

Schwarzenberger points out that if introduced into the body in sufficiently large doses, radiation produces symptoms indistin-

---

[130]Singh & McWhinney, *op. cit.*, p. 120.

[131]*The McGraw-Hill Dictionary of Scientific and Technical Terms* defines poison as "A substance that in relatively small doses has an action that either destroys life or impairs seriously the functions of organs and tissues." (2nd ed., 1978, p. 1237.) The definition of poison in the *Oxford English Dictionary* is that poison is: "Any substance which, when introduced to or absorbed by a living organism, destroys life or injures health, irrespective of mechanical means or direct thermal changes. Particularly applied to a substance capable of destroying life by rapid action, and when taken in a small quantity. Fig. phr. to hate like poison. But the more scientific use is recognized in the phrase slow poison, indicating the accumulative effect of a deleterious drug or agent taken for a length of time." (Vol. XII, p. 2, 1989 ed.)

guishable from poisoning.[132]

Once it is established that radioactive radiation is a poison, it is also covered by the prohibition on poison weapons contained in the Hague Regulations already referred to. It poisons, indeed in a more insidious way than poison gas, for its effects include the transmission of genetic disorders for generations.

The NATO countries have themselves accepted that poisoning is an effect of nuclear weapons, for Annex II to the Protocol on Arms Control of the Paris Agreements of 23 October 1954, on the accession of the Republic of Germany to the North Atlantic Treaty, defines a nuclear weapon as any weapon:

> "designed to contain or utilise, nuclear fuel or radioactive isotopes and which, by explosion or other uncontrolled nuclear transformation . . . is capable of mass destruction, mass injury or *mass poisoning*" (emphasis added).

(ii) Does radiation involve contact of the body with "materials"?

The definitions of poison speak of it in terms of its being a "substance". The Geneva Gas Protocol speaks of "materials" which are poisonous. It is necessary therefore to know whether radiation is a "substance" or a "material", or merely a ray such as a light ray which, when it impinges on any object, does not necessarily bring a substance or material in contact with that object. If it is the former, it would satisfy the requirements of the Geneva Gas Protocol.

The definition of "radioactive" in the *Shorter Oxford Dictionary* is as follows: "Capable (as radium) of emitting spontaneously rays consisting of *material particles* travelling at high velocities".[133]

---

[132]*The Legality of Nuclear Weapons, op. cit.*, p. 35. He remarks very severely that they "inflict death or serious damage to health in, as Gentili would have put it, a manner more befitting demons than civilised human beings". The reference is to Gentili's observation that, though war is struggle between men, the use of such means as poison makes it "a struggle of demons" (*De Jure Belli Libri Tres* (1612), Book II, Ch. VI, p. 161, tr. J.C. Rolfe.

[133]3rd ed., 1987, Vol. II, p. 1738.

Scientific discussions[134]draw a distinction between the spectrum of electromagnetic radiations that have zero mass when (theoretically) at rest, such as radio waves, microwaves, infrared rays, visible light, ultraviolet rays, x-rays, and gamma rays, and the type of radiation that includes such particles as electrons, protons and neutrons which have mass. When such forms of particulate matter travel at high velocities, they are regarded as radiation.

The ionizing radiation caused by nuclear weapons is of the latter kind. It consists inter alia of a stream of particles[135]coming into contact with the human body and causing damage to tissues. In other words, it is a material substance that causes damage to the body and cannot fall outside the prohibition of poisonous weapons prohibited by the Geneva Gas Protocol.

The question whether radiation is a "material" seems thus beyond doubt. In the words of Schwarzenberger:

"the words 'all analogous liquids, materials or devices' are so comprehensively phrased as to include any weapons of an analogous character, irrespective of whether they were known or in use at the time of the signature of the Protocol. If the radiation and fall-out effects of nuclear weapons can be likened to poison, all the more can they be likened to poison gas . . . "[136]

There has been some discussion in the literature of the question whether the material transmitted should be in gaseous form as the provision in question deals with materials "analogous" to gases. It is to be noted in the first place that the wording of the provision itself takes the poisons out of the category of *gases* because it speaks also of analogous *liquids, materials*, and even devices. However, even in terms of *gases*, it is clear that the distinction between solids, liquids and gases has never been strictly applied in military terminology to the words "gas". As Singh and McWhinney point out, in strict scientific language, mustard gas

---

[134]See *Encyclopedia Britannica Macropaedia*, Vol. 26, pp. 471 ff. on "Radiation".

[135]The definitions of radiation in the *McGraw-Hill Dictionary of Physics and Mathematics* (1978, p. 800) is "a stream of particles, . . . or high energy photons, or a mixture of these".

[136]Singh & McWhinney, *op. cit.*, p. 38.

is really a liquid and chlorine is really a gas, but in military terminology both are categorized as gas.[137]

The case that nuclear weapons are covered by the Geneva Gas Protocol seems therefore to be irrefutable. Further, if indeed radioactive radiation constitutes a poison, the prohibition against it would be declaratory of a universal customary law prohibition which would apply in any event whether a State is party or not to the Geneva Protocol of 1925.[138]

Yet another indication, available in terms of the Geneva Gas Protocol, is that the word "devices" would presumably cover a nuclear bomb, irrespective of the question whether radiation falls within the description of "analogous materials".

Nuclear weapons, being unknown at the time of the documents under consideration, could not be more specifically described, but are covered by the description and intent of the Protocol and the Hague Regulations.

It has been submitted by the United States that:

> **"This prohibition was not intended to apply, and has not been applied, to weapons that are designed to kill or injure by other means, even though they may create asphyxiating or poisonous byproducts." (Written Statement, p. 25.)**

If, in fact, radiation is a major by-product of a nuclear weapon — as indeed it is — it is not clear on what jurisprudential principle an exemption can thus be claimed from the natural and foreseeable effects of the use of the weapon. Such "byproducts" are sometimes described as collateral damage but, collateral or otherwise, they are a major consequence of the bomb and cannot in law be taken to be unintended, well known as they are.

Besides, such an argument involves the legally unacceptable contention that if an act involves both legal and illegal consequences, the former justify or excuse the latter.

---

[137]*Ibid.*, p. 126.

[138]See, to this effect, Schwarzenberger, *op. cit.*, pp. 37-38, in relation to chemical and bacteriological weapons.

13. Article 23(*a*) of the Hague Regulations

The foregoing discussion demonstrates that radiation is a poison. Using the same line of reasoning, it follows that there is also a clear contravention of Article 23(*a*) of the Hague Regulations which frames its prohibition in unequivocal terms.[139] No extended discussion is called for in this context, and it is well accepted that the categorical prohibition against poisoning therein contained is one of the oldest and most widely recognized laws of war. Since "the universally accepted practice of civilised nations has regarded poison as banned", the prohibition contained in Article 23(*a*) has been considered as binding even on States not parties to this conventional provision.

> "Thus, apart from purely conventional law, the customary position based on the general principles of law would also bar the use in warfare of poisonous substances as not only barbarous, inhuman and uncivilised, but also treacherous."[140]

IV. SELF-DEFENCE

Self-defence raises probably the most serious problems in this case. The second sentence in paragraph 2(E) of the *dispositif* states that, in the current state of international law and of the elements of fact at its disposal, the Court cannot conclude definitively whether the threat or use of nuclear weapons would be lawful or unlawful in an extreme circumstance of self-defence, in which the very survival of a state would be at stake. I have voted against this clause as I am of the view that the threat or use of nuclear weapons would not be lawful in any circumstances whatsoever, as it offends the fundamental principles of the *ius in bello*. This conclusion is clear and follows inexorably from well-established principles of international law.

If a nation is attacked, it is clearly entitled under the United Nations Charter to the right of self-defence. Once a nation thus enters into the domain of the *ius in bello*, the principles of humanitarian law apply to the conduct of self-defence, just as they apply to the conduct of any other aspect of military operations. We must hence examine what prin-

---

[139]See Singh & McWhinney, *op. cit.*, pp. 127 and 121.
[140]*Ibid.*, p. 121.

ciples of the *ius in bello* apply to the use of nuclear weapons in self-defence.

The first point to be noted is that the use of *force* in self-defence (which is an undoubted right) is one thing and the use of *nuclear weapons* in self-defence is another. The permission granted by international law for the first does not embrace the second, which is subject to other governing principles as well.

All of the seven principles of humanitarian law discussed in this Opinion apply to the use of nuclear weapons in self-defence, just as they apply to their use in any aspect of war. Principles relating to unnecessary suffering, proportionality, discrimination, non-belligerent states, genocide, environmental damage and human rights would all be violated, no less in self-defence than in an open act of aggression. The *ius in bello* covers all use of force, whatever the reasons for resort to force. There can be no exceptions, without violating the essence of its principles.

The state subjected to the first attack could be expected to respond in kind. After the devastation caused by a first attack, especially if it be a nuclear attack, there will be a tendency to respond with any nuclear firepower that is available.

Robert McNamara, in dealing with the response to initial strikes, states:

> *"But under such circumstances, leaders on both sides would be under unimaginable pressure to avenge their losses and secure the interests being challenged. And each would fear that the opponent might launch a larger attack at any moment. Moreover, they would both be operating with only partial information because of the disruption to communications caused by the chaos on the battlefield (to say nothing of possible strikes against communication facilities). Under such conditions, it is highly likely that rather than surrender, each side would launch a larger attack, hoping that this step would bring the action to a halt by causing the opponent to capitulate."* [141]

With such a response, the clock would accelerate towards global catastrophe, for a counter-response would be invited and, indeed, could be automatically triggered off.

It is necessary to reiterate here the undoubted right of the state that

---

[141]McNamara, *op. cit.*, pp. 71-72.

is attacked to use all the weaponry available to it for the purpose of repulsing the aggressor. Yet this principle holds only *so long as such weapons do not violate the fundamental rules of warfare embodied in those rules*. Within these constraints, and for the purpose of repulsing the enemy, the full military power of the state that is attacked can be unleashed upon the aggressor. While this is incontrovertible, one has yet to hear an argument in any forum, or a contention in any academic literature, that a nation attacked, for example, with chemical or biological weapons is entitled to use chemical or biological weapons in self-defence, or to annihilate the aggressor's population. It is strange that the most devastating of all the weapons of mass destruction can be conceived of as offering a singular exception to this most obvious conclusion following from the bedrock principles of humanitarian law.

That said, a short examination follows of the various principles of humanitarian law which could be violated by self-defence.

1. Unnecessary Suffering

The harrowing suffering caused by nuclear weapons, as outlined earlier in this Opinion, is not confined to the aggressive use of such weapons. The lingering sufferings caused by radiation do not lose their intensity merely because the weapon is used in self-defence.

2. Proportionality/Error

The principle of proportionality may on first impressions appear to be satisfied by a nuclear response to a nuclear attack. Yet, viewed more carefully, this principle is violated in many ways. As France observed:

> "The assessment of the necessity and proportionality of a response to attack depends on the nature of the attack, its scope, the danger it poses and the adjustment of the measures of response to the desired defensive purpose." (CR 95/23, pp. 82-83.)

For these very reasons, precise assessment of the nature of the appropriate and proportionate response by a nation stricken by a nuclear attack becomes impossible.[142] If one speaks in terms of a nuclear response to a nuclear attack, that nuclear response will tend, as already

---

[142]On this, see further Section II.3(n), *supra.*, and Section VII.6, *infra.*

noted, to be an all-out nuclear response which opens up all the scenarios of global armageddon which are so vividly depicted in the literature relating to an all-out nuclear exchange.

Moreover, one is here speaking in terms of measurement — measurement of the intensity of the attack and the proportionality of the response. But one can measure only the measurable. With nuclear war, the quality of measurability ceases. Total devastation admits of no scales of measurement. We are in territory where the principle of proportionality becomes devoid of meaning.

It is relevant also, in the context of nuclear weapons, not to lose sight of the possibility of human error. However carefully planned, a nuclear response to a nuclear attack cannot, in the confusion of the moment, be finely graded so as to assess the strength of the weapons of attack, and to respond in like measure. Even in the comparatively tranquil and leisured atmosphere of peace, error is possible, even to the extent of unleashing an unintentional nuclear attack. This has emerged from studies of unintentional nuclear war.[143] The response, under the stress of nuclear attack, would be far more prone to accident.

According to the *Bulletin of the Atomic Scientists*:

> "Top decision-makers as well as their subordinate information suppliers rely on computers and other equipment which have become even more complex and therefore more vulnerable to malfunction. Machine failures or human failures or a combination of the two could, had they not been discovered within minutes, have caused unintended nuclear war in a number of reported cases."[144]

The result would be all-out nuclear war.

Here again there is confirmation from statesmen, who have had much experience in matters of foreign and military policy, that all-out nuclear war is likely to ensue. Robert McNamara observes:

> *"It is inconceivable to me, as it has been to others who have studied the matter, that 'limited' nuclear wars would remain limited — any decision to use nuclear weapons would imply a high probability of the same cataclysmic consequences as a*

---

[143]For example, *Risks of Unintentional Nuclear War*, United Nations Institute of Disarmament Research (UNIDIR), 1982.

[144]June 1982, Vol. 38, p. 68.

total nuclear exchange." [145]

Former Secretary of State, Dr. Kissinger, has also written to the same effect:

"Limited war is not simply a matter of appropriate military forces and doctrines. It also places heavy demands on the discipline and subtlety of the political leadership and on the confidence of the society in it. For limited war is psychologically a much more complex problem than all-out war. . . . An all-out war will in all likelihood be decided so rapidly — if it is possible to speak of decision in such a war — and the suffering it entails will be so vast as to obscure disputes over the nuances of policy." [146]

He proceeds to observe:

"Limited nuclear war is not only impossible, according to this line of reasoning, but also undesirable. For one thing, it would cause devastation in the combat zone approaching that of thermonuclear war in severity. We would, therefore, be destroying the very people we were seeking to protect." [147]

It is thus no fanciful speculation that the use of nuclear weapons in self defence would result in a cataclysmic nuclear exchange. That is a risk which humanitarian law would consider to be totally unacceptable. It is a risk which no legal system can sanction.

3. Discrimination

As already observed earlier in this Opinion, nuclear weapons violate the principle of discrimination between armed forces and civilians. True, other weapons also do, but the intensity of heat and blast, not to speak of radiation, are factors which place the nuclear weapon in a class apart from the others. When one speaks of weapons that count their victims by hundreds of thousands, if not millions, principles of discrimination ceases to have any legal relevance.

---

[145]*Op. cit.*, p. 72.
[146]Henry Kissinger, *Nuclear Weapons and Foreign Policy*, 1957, p. 167.
[147]*Ibid.*, p. 175.

4. Non-Belligerent States

One of the principal objections to the use of nuclear weapons in self-defence occurs under this head.

Self-defence is a matter of purely internal jurisdiction only if such defence can be undertaken without clearly causing damage to the rights of non-belligerent states. The moment a strategy of self-defence implies damage to a non-belligerent third party, such a matter ceases to be one of purely internal jurisdiction. It may be that the act of self-defence inadvertently and unintentionally causes damage to a third State. Such a situation is understandable and sometimes does occur, but that is not the case here.

5. Genocide

The topic of genocide has already been covered.[148] Self-defence, which will, as shown in the discussion on proportionality, result in all probability in all-out nuclear war, is even more likely to cause genocide than the act of launching an initial strike. If the killing of human beings, in numbers ranging from a million to a billion, does not fall within the definition of genocide, one may well ask what will.

No nation can be seen as entitled to risk the destruction of civilization for its own national benefit.

6. Environmental Damage

Similar considerations exist here, as in regard to genocide. The widespread contamination of the environment may even lead to a nuclear winter and to the destruction of the eco-system. These results will ensue equally, whether the nuclear weapons causing them are used in aggression or in self-defence.

International law relating to the environment, in so far as it concerns nuclear weapons, is dealt with at greater length in my Dissenting Opinion on the World Health Organization Request, and the discussion in that Opinion should be considered as supplementary to the above discussion.

---

[148]See Section III.10(d), *supra*.

7. Human Rights

All the items of danger to human rights as recounted earlier in this Opinion would be equally operative whether the weapons are used in aggression or in self-defence.

*

* *

The humanitarian principles discussed above have long passed the stage of being merely philosophical aspirations. They are the living law and represent the highwatermark of legal achievement in the difficult task of imposing some restraints on the brutalities of unbridled war. They provide the groundrules for military action today and have been forged by the community of nations under the impact of the sufferings of untold millions in two global cataclysms and many smaller wars. As with all legal principles, they govern without distinction all nations great and small.

It seems difficult, with any due regard to the consistency that must underlie any credible legal system, to contemplate that all these hard-won principles should bend aside in their course and pass the nuclear weapon by, leaving that unparalleled agency of destruction free to achieve on a magnified scale the very evils which these principles were designed to prevent.

*

* *

Three other aspects of the argument before the Court call for brief mention in the context of self-defence.

The United Kingdom relied (Written Statement, para. 3.40) on a view expressed by Judge Ago in his addendum to the Eighth Report on State Responsibility, to the effect that:

"The action needed to halt and repulse the attack may well have to assume dimensions disproportionate to those of the attack suffered. What matters in this respect is the result to be achieved by the 'defensive' action, and not the forms, substance and strength of the action itself."[149]

Ago is here stressing that the defensive action must always be related to its purpose, that of halting and repelling the attack. As he observes, in the same paragraph:

"The requirement of the *proportionality* of the action taken in self-defence . . . concerns the relationship between that action and its purpose, namely, . . . that of halting and repelling the attack." (Emphasis added.)

That purpose is to halt and repulse the attack, not to exterminate the aggressor, or to commit genocide of its population. His reference to forms, substance and strength is expressly set out by him, within the context of this purpose, and cannot be read as setting at nought all the other requirements of humanitarian law such as those relating to damage to neutral states, unnecessary suffering, or the principle of discrimination. The statement of so eminent a jurist cannot be read in the sense of neutralizing the classic and irreducible requirements of the *ius in bello* — requirements which, moreover, had received massive endorsement from the Institute of International Law over which he was later to preside with such distinction. **The Edinburgh Session of 1969 adopted by a majority of 60 to 1, with 2 abstentions, the resolution[150] prohibiting weapons affecting indiscriminately both military and non-military objects, both armed forces and civilian populations, and weapons designed to terrorize the civilian population.** Ago himself was a member of that majority.

The second submission calling for attention is the suggestion that Security Council resolution 984(1995) (UK Written Statement, para. 3.42 and Annex D) in some way endorses the view that the use of nuclear weapons, in response to an armed attack, should not be regarded as necessarily unlawful.

A careful perusal of the resolution shows that it reassures the non-nuclear-weapon States that the Security Council and the nuclear-weapon States will act immediately in the event that such States are victims of nuclear aggression. It *avoids any mention whatsoever* of the measures to be adopted to protect the victim. Had such been the intention, and had such use of nuclear weapons been legal, this was the

---

[149]*Yearbook of the International Law Commission*, 1980, Vol. II, Part I, p. 69, para. 121.

[150]Already noted in Section III.11, *supra*.

occasion par excellence for the Security Council to have said so.

For the sake of completeness, it should here be pointed out that, even if the Security Council had expressly endorsed the use of such weapons, it is this Court which is the ultimate authority on questions of legality, and that such an observation, even if made, would not prevent the Court from making its independent pronouncement on this matter.

The third factor calling for mention is that much of the argument of those opposing illegality seems to blur the distinction between the *ius ad bellum* and the *ius in bello*. Whatever be the merits or otherwise of resorting to the use of force (the province of the *ius ad bellum*), when once the domain of force is entered, the governing law in that domain is the *ius in bello*. The humanitarian laws of war take over and govern all who participate, assailant and victim alike. The argument before the Court has proceeded as though, once the self-defence exception to the use of force comes into operation, the applicability of the *ius in bello* falls away. This supposition is juristically wrong and logically untenable. The reality is, of course, that while the *ius ad bellum* only opens the door to the use of force (in self-defence or by the Security Council), whoever enters that door must function subject to the *ius in bello*. The contention that the legality of the use of force justifies a breach of humanitarian law is thus a total non-sequitur.

*

*   *

Upon a review therefore, no exception can be made to the illegality of the use of nuclear weapons merely because the weapons are used in self-defence.

Collective self-defence, where another country has been attacked, raises the same issues as are discussed above.

Anticipatory self-defence — the pre-emptive strike before the enemy has actually attacked — cannot legally be effected by a nuclear strike, for a first strike with nuclear weapons would axiomatically be prohibited by the basic principles already referred to. In the context of non-nuclear weaponry, all the sophistication of modern technology and the precise targeting systems now developed would presumably be available for this purpose.

V. SOME GENERAL CONSIDERATIONS

1. Two Philosophical Perspectives

This Opinion has set out a multitude of reasons for the conclusion that the resort to nuclear weapons for any purpose entails the risk of the destruction of human society, if not of humanity itself. It has also pointed out that any rule permitting such use is inconsistent with international law itself.

Two philosophical insights will be referred to in this section — one based on rationality, and the other on fairness.

In relation to the first, all the postulates of law presuppose that they contribute to and function within the premiss of the continued existence of the community served by that law. Without the assumption of that continued existence, no rule of law and no legal system can have any claim to validity, however attractive the juristic reasoning on which it is based. That taint of invalidity affects not merely the particular rule. The legal system, which accommodates that rule, itself collapses upon its foundations, for legal systems are postulated upon the continued existence of society. Being part of society, they must themselves collapse with the greater entity of which they are a part. This assumption, lying at the very heart of the concept of law, often recedes from view in the midst of the nuclear discussion.

Without delving in any depth into philosophical discussions of the nature of law, it will suffice for present purposes to refer briefly to two tests proposed by two preeminent thinkers about justice of the present era — H.L.A. Hart and John Rawls.

Hart, a leading jurist of the positivistic school, has, in a celebrated exposition of the minimum content of natural law, formulated this principle pithily in the following sentence:

"We are committed to it as something presupposed by the terms of the discussion; for our concern is with social arrangements for continued existence, not with those of a suicide club."[151]

His reasoning is that:

"there are certain rules of conduct which any social organiza-

---

[151]H.L.A. Hart, *The Concept of Law*, 1961, p. 188; emphasis added.

tion must contain if it is to be viable. Such rules do in fact constitute a common element in the law and conventional morality of all societies which have progressed to the point where these are distinguished as different forms of social control." [152]

International law is surely such a social form of control devised and accepted by the constituent members of that international society — the nation states.

Hart goes on to note that:

"Such universally recognized principles of conduct which have a basis in elementary truths concerning human beings, their natural environment, and aims, may be considered the minimum content *of Natural Law, in contrast with the more grandiose and more challengeable constructions which have often been proffered under that name."* [153]

Here is a recognized minimum accepted by positivistic jurisprudence which questions some of the more literal assumptions of other schools. We are down to the common denominator to which all legal systems must conform.

To approach the matter from another standpoint, the members of the international community have for the past three centuries been engaged in the task of formulating a set of rules and principles for the conduct of that society — the rules and principles we call international law. In so doing, they must ask themselves whether there is a place in that set of rules for a rule under which it would be legal, for whatever reason, to eliminate members of that community or, indeed, the entire community itself. Can the international community, which is governed by that rule, be considered to have given its acceptance to that rule, whatever be the approach of that community — positivist, natural law, or any other? Is the community of nations, to use Hart's expression, a "suicide club"?

This aspect has likewise been stressed by perceptive jurists from the non-nuclear countries who are alive to the possibilities facing their countries in conflicts between other States in which, though they are not parties, they can be at the receiving end of the resulting nuclear

---

[152]*Ibid.*
[153]*Ibid.*, p. 189; emphasis added.

devastation. Can international law, which purports to be a legal system for the entire global community, accommodate any principles which make possible the destruction of their communities?

> "No legal system can confer on any of its members the right to annihilate the community which engenders it and whose activities it seeks to regulate. In other words, there cannot be a *legal* rule, which *permits* the threat or use of nuclear weapons. In sum, nuclear weapons are an unprecedented event which calls for rethinking the self-understanding of traditional international law. Such rethinking would reveal that the question is not whether one interpretation of existing laws of war prohibits the threat or use of nuclear weapons and another permits it. Rather, the issue is whether the debate can take place at all in the world of law. The question is in fact one which cannot be legitimately addressed by law at all since it cannot tolerate an interpretation which negates its very essence. The end of law is a rational order of things, with survival as its core, whereas nuclear weapons eliminate all hopes of realising it. In this sense, nuclear weapons are unlawful by definition."[154]

The aspect stressed by Hart that the proper end of human activity is survival is reflected also in the words of Nagendra Singh, a former President of this Court, who stated, in his pioneering study of nuclear weapons, that:

> "it would indeed be arrogant for any single nation to argue that to save humanity from bondage it was thought necessary to destroy humanity itself . . . No nation acting on its own has a right to destroy its kind, or even to destroy thousands of miles of land and its inhabitants in the vain hope that a crippled and suffering humanity — a certain result of nuclear warfare — was a more laudable objective than the loss of human dignity, an uncertain result which may or may not follow from the use of nuclear weapons."[155]

---

[154]B.S. Chimni, "Nuclear Weapons and International Law: Some Reflections", in *International Law in Transition: Essays in Memory of Judge Nagendra Singh*, 1992, p. 142; emphasis added.

[155]Nagendra Singh, *Nuclear Weapons and International Law*, 1959, p. 243.

Nagendra Singh expressed the view, in the same work, that "resort to such weapons is not only incompatible with the laws of war, but irreconcilable with international law itself" (p. 17).

Another philosophical approach to the matter is along the lines of the "veil of ignorance" posited by John Rawls in his celebrated study of justice as fairness.[156]

If one is to devise a legal system under which one is prepared to live, this exposition posits as a test of fairness of that system that its members would be prepared to accept it if the decision had to be taken behind a veil of ignorance as to the future place of each constituent member within that legal system.

A nation considering its allegiance to such a system of international law, and not knowing whether it would fall within the group of nuclear nations or not, could scarcely be expected to subscribe to it if it contained a rule by which legality would be accorded to the use of a weapon by others which could annihilate it. Even less would it consent if it is denied even the right to possess such a weapon and, least of all if it could be annihilated or irreparably damaged in the quarrels of others to which it is not in any way a party.

One would indeed be in a desirable position in the event that it was one's lot to become a member of the nuclear group but, if there was a chance of being cast into the non-nuclear group, would one accept such a legal system behind a veil of ignorance as to one's position? Would it make any difference if the members of the nuclear group gave an assurance, which no one could police, that they would use the weapon only in extreme emergencies? The answers to such questions cannot be in doubt. By this test of fairness and legitimacy, such a legal system would surely fail.

Such philosophical insights are of cardinal value in deciding upon the question whether the illegality of use would constitute a minimum component of a system of international law based on rationality or fairness. By either test, widely accepted in the literature of modern jurisprudence, the rule of international law applicable to nuclear weapons would be that their use would be impermissible.

Fundamental considerations such as these tend to be overlooked in discussions relating to the legality of nuclear weapons. On matter so intrinsic to the validity of the entire system of international law, such perspectives cannot be ignored.

---

[156]John Rawls, *A Theory of Justice*, 1972.

2. The Aims of War

War is never an end in itself. It is only a means to an end. This was recognized in the St. Petersburg Declaration of 1968, already noted (in section III.3 on humanitarian law), which stipulated that the weakening of the military forces of the enemy was the only legitimate object of war. Consistently with this principle, humanitarian law has worked out the rule, already referred to, that "The right of belligerents to adopt means of injuring the enemy is not unlimited" (Art. 22 of the Hague Rules, 1907).

All study of the laws of war becomes meaningless unless it is anchored to the ends of war, for thus alone can the limitations of war be seen in their proper context. This necessitates a brief excursus into the philosophy of the aims of war. Literature upon the subject has existed for upwards of twenty centuries.

Reference has already been made, in the context of hyperdestructive weapons, to the classical Indian tradition reflected in India's greatest epics, the *Ramayana* and the *Mahabharatha*. The reason behind the prohibition was that the weapon went beyond the purposes of war.

This was precisely what Aristotle taught when, in Book VII of Politics, *he wrote that, "War must be looked upon simply as a means to peace".*[157] *It will be remembered that Aristotle was drawing a distinction between actions that are no more than necessary or useful, and actions which are good in themselves. Peace was good in itself, and war only a means to this end. Without the desired end, namely peace, war would therefore be meaningless and useless. Applying this to the nuclear scenario, a war which destroys the other party is totally lacking in meaning and utility, and hence totally lacks justification.* Aristotle's view of war was that it is a temporary interruption of normalcy, with a new equilibrium resulting from it when that war inevitably comes to an end.

The philosophy of the balance of power which dominated European diplomacy since the Peace of Utrecht in 1713 presupposed not the elimination of one's adversary, but the achievement of a workable balance of power in which the vanquished had a distinct place. Even the extreme philosophy that war is a continuation of the processes of diplomacy which Clausewitz espoused, presupposed the continuing existence, as a viable unit, of the vanquished nation.

---

[157]Aristotle, *Politics,* tr. John Warrington, Heron Books, 1934, p. 212.

The United Nations Charter itself is framed on the basic principle that the use of force is outlawed (except for the strictly limited exception of self defence), and that the purpose of the Charter is to free humanity from the scourge of war. Peace between the parties is the outcome the Charter envisages and not the total devastation of any party to the conflict.

Nuclear weapons render these philosophies unworkable. The nuclear exchanges of the future, should they ever take place, will occur in a world in which there is no monopoly of nuclear weapons. A nuclear war will not end with the use of a nuclear weapon by a single power, as happened in the case of Japan. There will inevitably be a nuclear exchange, especially in a world in which nuclear weapons are triggered for instant and automatic reprisal in the event of a nuclear attack.

Such a war is not one in which a nation, as we know it, can survive as a viable entity. The spirit that walks the nuclear wasteland will be a spirit of total despair, haunting victors (if there are any) and vanquished alike. We have a case here of methodology of warfare which goes beyond the purposes of war.

3. The Concept of a "Threat of Force" under the United Nations Charter

The question asked by the General Assembly relates to the use of force and the threat of force. Theoretically, the use of force, even with the simplest weapon, is unlawful under the United Nations Charter. There is no purpose therefore in examining whether the use of force with a nuclear weapon is contrary to international law. When even the use of a single rifle is banned, it makes little sense to inquire whether a nuclear weapon is banned.

The question of a threat of force, within the meaning of the Charter, needs some attention. To determine this question, an examination of the concept of threat of force in the Charter becomes necessary.

Article 2(4) of the United Nations Charter outlaws threats against the territorial integrity or political independence of any State. As reaffirmed in the Declaration on Principles of International Law Concerning Friendly Relations 1970:

> "Such a threat or use of force constitutes a violation of international law and the Charter of the United Nations and shall never be employed as a means of settling international issues." (GA Res. 2625(XXV).)

Other documents confirming the international community's understanding that threats are outside the pale of international law include the 1965 Declaration on the Inadmissibility of Intervention in the Domestic Affairs of States and the Protection of Their Independence and Sovereignty (GA Res. 2131(XX)), and the 1987 Declaration on the Enhancement of the Principle of Non-Use of Force (GA Res. 42/22, para. 2).

It is to be observed that the United Nations Charter draws no distinction between the use of force and the threat of force. Both equally lie outside the pale of action within the law.

Numerous international documents confirm the prohibition on the threat of force without qualification. Among these are the 1949 Declaration on Essentials of Peace (GA Res. 290(IV)); the 1970 Declaration on the Strengthening of International Security (GA Res. 2734(XXV)); and the 1988 Declaration on the Prevention and Removal of Disputes and Situations Which May Threaten International Peace and Security and on the Role of the United Nations in this Field (GA Res. 43/51). The Helsinki Final Act (1975) requires participating States to refrain from the threat or use of force. The Pact of Bogota (the American Treaty on Pacific Settlement) is even more specific, requiring the contracting parties to "refrain from the threat or the use of force, or from any other means of coercion for the settlement of their controversies . . .".

The principle of non-use of threats is thus as firmly grounded as the principle of non-use of force and, in its many formulations, it has not been made subject to any exceptions. If therefore deterrence is a form of threat, it must come within the prohibitions of the use of threats.

A more detailed discussion follows in Section VII.2 of the concept of deterrence.

4. Equality in the Texture of the Laws of War

There are some structural inequalities built into the current international legal system, but the substance of international law — its corpus of norms and principles — applies equally to all. Such equality of all those who are subject to a legal system is central to its integrity and legitimacy. So it is with the body of principles constituting the corpus of international law. Least of all can there be one law for the powerful and another law for the rest. No domestic system would accept such a principle, nor can any international system which is premised on a concept of equality.

In the celebrated words of the United States Chief Justice John Marshall in 1825, "No principle of general law is more universally acknowledged than the perfect equality of nations. Russia and Geneva have equal rights".[158] *As with all sections of the international legal system, the concept of equality is built into the texture of the laws of war.*

Another anomaly is that if, under customary international law, the *use of* the weapon is legal, this is inconsistent with the denial, to 180 of the United Nation's 185 members, of even the right to *possession of* this weapon. Customary international law cannot operate so unequally, especially if, as is contended by the nuclear powers, the use of the weapon is essential to their self-defence. Self-defence is one of the most treasured rights of States and is recognized by Article 51 of the United Nations Charter as the inherent right of every member State of the United Nations. It is a wholly unacceptable proposition that this right is granted in different degrees to different members of the United Nations family of nations.

De facto inequalities always exist and will continue to exist so long as the world community is made up of sovereign States, which are necessarily unequal in size, strength, wealth and influence. But a great conceptual leap is involved in translating *de facto* inequality into inequality *de jure*. It is precisely such a leap that is made by those arguing, for example, that when the Protocols to the Geneva Conventions did not pronounce on the prohibition of the use of nuclear weapons, there was an implicit recognition of the legality of their use by the nuclear powers. Such silence meant an agreement not to deal with the question, not a consent to legality of use. The "understandings" stipulated by the United States and the United Kingdom that the rules established or newly introduced by the 1977 Protocol Additional to the four 1949 Geneva Conventions would not regulate or prohibit the use of nuclear weapons do not undermine the basic principles which antedated these formal agreements and received expression in them. They rest upon no conceptual or juristic reason that can make inroads upon those principles. It is conceptually impossible to treat the silence of these treaty provisions as overruling or overriding these principles.

Similar considerations apply to the argument that treaties imposing

---

158*The Antelope* case, [1825] 10 *Wheaton*, p. 122. Cf. Vattel, "A dwarf is as much a man as a giant is; a small republic is no less a sovereign state than the most powerful Kingdom." (*Droit des Gens*, tr. Fenwick in *Classics of International Law*, S. 18.)

partial bans on nuclear weapons must be interpreted as a current acceptance, by implication, of their legality.

This argument is not well founded. Making working arrangements within the context of a situation one is powerless to avoid is neither a consent to that situation, nor a recognition of its legality. It cannot confer upon that situation a status of recognition of its validity. Malaysia offered in this context the analogy of needle exchange programmes to minimize the spread of disease among drug users. Such programmes cannot be interpreted as rendering drug abuse legal (Written Comments, p. 14). What is important is that, amidst the plethora of resolutions and declarations dealing with nuclear weapons, there is not one which sanctions the use of such weapons for any purpose whatsoever.

A legal rule would be inconceivable that some nations alone have the right to use chemical or bacteriological weapons in self-defence, and others do not. The principle involved, in the claim of some nations to be able to use nuclear weapons in self-defence, rests on no different juristic basis.

Another feature to be considered in this context is that the community of nations is by very definition a voluntarist community. No element in it imposes constraints upon any other element from above. Such a structure is altogether impossible except on the basic premise of equality. Else "the danger is very real that the law will become little more than the expression of the will of the strongest".[159]

If the corpus of international law is to retain the authority it needs to discharge its manifold and beneficent functions in the international community, every element in its composition should be capable of being tested at the anvil of equality. Some structural inequalities have indeed been built into the international constitutional system, but that is a very different proposition from introducing inequalities into the corpus of substantive law by which all nations alike are governed.

It scarcely needs mention that whatever is stated in this section is stated in the context of the total illegality of the use of nuclear weapons by any powers whatsoever, in any circumstances whatsoever. That is the only sense in which the principle of equality which underlies international law can be applied to the important international problem of nuclear weapons.

---

[159]Weston, *op. cit.*, p. 254.

5. The Logical Contradiction of a Dual Regime in the Laws of War

If humanitarian law is inapplicable to nuclear weapons, we face the logical contradiction that the laws of war are applicable to some kinds of weapons and not others, while both sets of weapons can be simultaneously used. One set of principles would apply to all other weapons and another set to nuclear weapons. When both classes of weapons are used in the same war, the laws of armed conflict would be in confusion and disarray.

Japan is a nation against which both sets of weapons were used, and it is not a matter for surprise that this aspect seems first to have caught the attention of Japanese scholars. Professor Fajita, in an article to which we were referred, observed:

"*this separation of fields of regulation between conventional and nuclear warfare will produce an odd result not easily imaginable, because conventional weapons and nuclear weapons will be eventually used at the same time, and in the same circumstances in a future armed conflict*".[160]

Such a dual regime is inconsistent with all legal principle, and no reasons of principle have ever been suggested for the exemption of nuclear weapons from the usual regime of law applicable to all weapons. The reasons that have been suggested are only reasons of politics or of expediency, and neither a Court of law nor any body of consistent juristic science can accept such a dichotomy.

It is of interest to note in this context that even nations denying the illegality of nuclear weapons per se instruct their armed forces in their military manuals that nuclear weapons are to be judged according to the same standards that apply to other weapons in armed conflict.[161]

6. Nuclear Decision-Making

A factor to be taken into account in determining the legality of the use of nuclear weapons, having regard to their enormous potential for global devastation, is the process of decision-making in regard to the use of nuclear weapons.

A decision to use nuclear weapons would tend to be taken, if taken

---

[160](1982) 3 *Kansai University Review of Law and Political Science*, p. 77.
[161]See Burns H. Weston, *op. cit.*, p. 252, fn. 105.

at all, in circumstances which do not admit of fine legal evaluations. It will in all probability be taken at a time when passions run high, time is short and the facts are unclear. It will not be a carefully measured decision, taken after a detailed and detached evaluation of all relevant circumstances of fact. It would be taken under extreme pressure and stress. Legal matters requiring considered evaluation may have to be determined within minutes, perhaps even by military rather than legally trained personnel, when they are in fact so complex as to have engaged this Court's attention for months. The fate of humanity cannot fairly be made to depend on such a decision.

Studies have indeed been made of the process of nuclear decision-making and they identify four characteristics of a nuclear crisis.[162] These characteristics are:

1. **The shortage of time for making crucial decisions. This is the fundamental aspect of all crises;**

2. **The high stakes involved and, in particular, the expectation of severe loss to the national interest;**

3. **The high uncertainty resulting from the inadequacy of clear information, e.g., what is going on?, what is the intent of the enemy?; and**

4. **The leaders are often constrained by political considerations, restricting their options.**

If such is the atmosphere in which leaders are constrained to act, and if they must weigh the difficult question whether it is legal or not in the absence of guidelines, the risk of illegality in the use of the weapon is great.

The weapon should in my view be declared illegal in *all* circumstances. If it is legal in some circumstances, however improbable, those circumstances need to be specified (or else a confused situation is made more confused still).

---

[162]See Conn Nugent, "How a Nuclear War Might Begin", in Proceedings of the Sixth World Congress of the International Physicians for the Prevention of Nuclear War, *op. cit.*, p. 117.

VI. THE ATTITUDE OF THE INTERNATIONAL COMMUNITY TOWARDS NUCLEAR WEAPONS

Quite apart from the importance of such considerations as the conscience of humanity and the general principles of law recognized by civilized nations, this section becomes relevant also because the law of the United Nations proceeds from the will of the peoples of the United Nations; and ever since the commencement of the United Nations, there has not been an issue which has attracted such sustained and widespread attention from its community of members. Apartheid was one of the great international issues which attracted concentrated attention until recently, but there has probably been a deeper current of continuous concern with nuclear weapons, and a universally shared revulsion at their possible consequences. The floodtide of global disapproval attending the nuclear weapon has never receded and no doubt will remain unabated so long as those weapons remain in the world's arsenals.

1. The Universality of the Ultimate Goal of Complete Elimination

The international community's attitude towards nuclear weapons has been unequivocal — they are a danger to civilization and must be eliminated. The need for their complete elimination has been the subject of several categorical resolutions of the General Assembly, which are referred to elsewhere in this Opinion.

The most recent declaration of the international community on this matter was at the 1995 Non-Proliferation Treaty Review Conference which, in its "Principles and Objectives for Nuclear Non-Proliferation and Disarmament", stressed "the ultimate goals of the complete elimination of nuclear weapons and a treaty on general and complete disarmament". This was a unanimous sentiment expressed by the global community and a clear commitment by every nation to do all that it could to achieve the complete elimination of these weapons.

The NPT, far from legitimizing the possession of nuclear weapons, was a treaty for their liquidation and eventual elimination. Its preamble unequivocally called for the liquidation of all existing stockpiles and their elimination from national arsenals. Such continued possession as it envisaged was not absolute but subject to an overriding condition — the pursuit in good faith of negotiations on effective measures relating to the cessation of the nuclear arms race at an early date. Inherent in this condition and in the entire treaty was not the acceptance of nuclear weapons, but their condemnation and repudiation. So it was when the NPT entered into force on 5 March 1970 and so it was when the NPT Review and Extension Conference took place in 1995.[163]

The NPT Review Conference of 1995 was not new in the universality it embodied or in the strength of the commitment it expressed, but merely a reiteration of the views expressed in the very first resolution of the United Nations in 1945. From the formation of the United Nations to the present day, it would thus be correct to say that there has been a universal commitment to the elimination of nuclear weapons — a commitment which was only a natural consequence of the universal abhorrence of these weapons and their devastating consequences.

2. Overwhelming Majorities in Support of Total Abolition

This view, which cannot be more clearly expressed than it has been in numerous pronouncements of the General Assembly, provides a backdrop to the consideration of the applicable law, which follows.

It is beyond dispute that the preponderant majority of States oppose nuclear weapons and seek their total abandonment.

The very first resolution of the General Assembly, adopted at its Seventeenth Plenary Meeting on 24 January 1946, appointed a Commission whose terms of reference were, *inter alia*, to make specific proposals "for the elimination from national armaments of atomic weapons and of all other major weapons adaptable to mass destruction".

In 1961, at Belgrade, the Non-aligned Heads of State made a clear pronouncement on the need for a global agreement prohibiting all nuclear tests. The non-aligned movement, covering 113 countries from Asia, Africa, Latin America and Europe, comprises within its territories not only the vast bulk of the world's population, but also the bulk of

---

[163]Article 4 of Decision number 2 on the Principles and Objectives for Nuclear Non-Proliferation and Disarmament, adopted by that Conference, stipulated as an obligation of States Parties which was inextricably linked to the extension of the treaty, the following goal, *inter alia*: "The determined pursuit by the nuclear-weapon States of systematic and progressive efforts to reduce nuclear weapons globally, with the ultimate goals of eliminating those weapons" (para. 4(*c*)). Also the Conference on Disarmament was to complete the negotiations for a Comprehensive Nuclear-Test-Ban Treaty no later than 1996 (para. 4(*a*)).

the planet's natural resources and the bulk of its bio-diversity. It has pursued the aim of the abolition of nuclear weapons and consistently supported a stream of resolutions[164] in the General Assembly and other international forums pursuing this objective. The massive majorities of States calling for the Non-Use of Nuclear Weapons can leave little doubt of the overall sentiment of the world community in this regard.

States appearing before the Court have provided the Court with a list of United Nations resolutions and declarations indicating the attitude towards these weapons of the overwhelming majority of that membership. Several of those resolutions do not merely describe the use of nuclear weapons as a violation of international law, but also assert that they are a crime against humanity.

Among these latter are the resolutions on Non-Use of Nuclear Weapons and Prevention of Nuclear War, passed by the General Assembly to this effect in 1978, 1979, 1980 and 1981, were passed with 103, 112, 113 and 121 votes respectively in favour, with 18, 16, 19 and 19 respectively opposing them, and 18, 14, 14 and 6 abstentions respectively. These can fairly be described as massive majorities (see Appendix IV of Malaysian Written Comments).

Resolutions setting the elimination of nuclear weapons as a goal are legion. One State (Malaysia) has, in its Written Comments, listed no less than 49 such resolutions, several of them passed with similar majorities and some with no votes in opposition and only 3 or 4 abstentions. For example, the resolution on Conclusion of effective international arrangements to assure non-nuclear weapon States against the use or threat of use of nuclear weapons of 1986 and 1987 were passed with 149 and 151 votes in favour, none opposed and 4 and 3 abstentions respectively. Such resolutions, adopting a goal of complete elimination, are indicative of a global sentiment that nuclear weapons are inimical to the general interests of the community of nations.

The declarations of the world community's principal representative organ, the General Assembly, may not themselves make law, but when repeated in a stream of resolutions, as often and as definitely as they have been, provide important reinforcement to the view of the impermissibility of the threat or use of such weapons under customary international law. Taken in combination with all the other manifestations of global disapproval of threat or use, the confirmation of the

---

[164]See fn. 97, *supra*.

position is strengthened even further. Whether or not some of the General Assembly resolutions are themselves "law making" resolutions is a matter for serious consideration, with not inconsiderable scholarly support for such a view.[165]

Although the prime thrust for these resolutions came from the non-aligned group, there has been supportive opinion for the view of illegality from states outside this group. Among such states contending for illegality before this Court are Sweden, San Marino, Australia and New Zealand. Moreover, even in countries not asserting the illegality of nuclear weapons, opinion is strongly divided. *For example, we were referred to a resolution passed by the Italian Senate, on 13 July 1995, recommending to the Italian Government that they assume a position favouring a judgment by this Court condemning the use of nuclear weapons.*

It is to be remembered also that, of the 185 member States of the UN, only five have nuclear weapons and have announced policies based upon them. From the standpoint of the creation of international custom, the practice and policies of five states out of 185 seem to be an insufficient basis on which to assert the creation of custom, whatever be the global influence of those five. As was stated by Malaysia:

> "If the laws of humanity and the dictates of the public conscience demand the prohibition of such weapons, the five nuclear-weapon States, however powerful, cannot stand against them." (CR 95/27, p. 56.)

In the face of such a preponderant majority of States' opinions, it is difficult to say there is no *opinio juris* against the use or threat of use of nuclear weapons. Certainly it is impossible to contend that there is an *opinio juris* in favour of the legality of such use or threat.

3. World Public Opinion

Added to all these official views, there is also a vast preponderance of public opinion across the globe. Strong protests against nuclear weapons have come from learned societies, professional groups, religious denominations, women's organizations, political parties, student federations, trade unions, NGO's and practically every group in which

---

[165]For example, Brownlie, *Principles of Public International Law*, 4th ed., 1990, p. 14, re resolution 1653(XVI) of 1961, which described the use of nuclear and thermo-nuclear weapons as such a "law-making resolution".

public opinion is expressed. Hundreds of such groups exist across the world. The names that follow are merely illustrative of the broad spread of such organizations: International Physicians for the Prevention of Nuclear War (IPPNW); Medical Campaign Against Nuclear Weapons; Scientists Against Nuclear Arms; People for Nuclear Disarmament; International Association of Lawyers against Nuclear Arms (IALANA); Performers and Artists for Nuclear Disarmament International; Social Scientists Against Nuclear War; Society for a Nuclear Free Future; European Federation against Nuclear Arms; The Nuclear Age Peace Foundation; Campaign for Nuclear Disarmament; Children's Campaign for Nuclear Disarmament. They come from all countries, cover all walks of life, and straddle the globe.

The millions of signatures received in this Court have been referred to at the very commencement of this Opinion.

4. Current Prohibitions

A major area of space on the surface of the planet and the totality of the space above that surface, and of the space below the ocean surface, has been brought into the domain of legal prohibition of the very presence of nuclear weapons. Among treaties accomplishing this result are the 1959 Antarctic Treaty, the 1967 Treaty of Tlatelolco in respect of Latin America and the Caribbean, the 1985 Treaty of Rarotonga in regard to the South Pacific, and the 1996 Treaty of Cairo in regard to Africa. In addition, there is the Treaty prohibiting nuclear weapons in the atmosphere and outer space, and the 1971 Treaty on the Prohibition of the Emplacement of Nuclear Weapons and Other Weapons of Mass Destruction on the Seabed and the Ocean Floor and in the Subsoil Thereof (see CR 95/22, p. 50). The major portion of the total area of the space afforded for human activity by the planet is thus declared free of nuclear weapons — a result which would not have been achieved but for universal agreement on the uncontrollable danger of these weapons and the need to eliminate them totally.

5. Partial Bans

The notion of partial bans and reductions in the levels of nuclear arms could not, likewise, have achieve their current results but for the existence of such a globally shared sentiment. Important among these measures are the Partial Test Ban Treaty of 1963 prohibiting the testing of nuclear weapons in the atmosphere, and the Nuclear Non-Proliferation Treaty of 1968. These treaties not only prohibited even the testing of nuclear weapons in certain circumstances, but also provided against the horizontal proliferation of nuclear weapons by imposing certain legal duties upon both nuclear and non-nuclear states. The Comprehensive Test Ban Treaty, now in the course of negotiation, aims at the elimination of all testing. The START agreements (START I and START II) aim at considerable reductions in the nuclear arsenals of the United States and the Russian Federation reducing their individual stockpiles by around 2000 weapons annually.

6. Who Are the States Most Specially Concerned?

If the nuclear States are the States most affected, their contrary view is an important factor to be taken into account, even though numerically they constitute a small proportion (around 2.7%) of the United Nations' membership of 185 States.

This aspect of their being the States most particularly affected has been stressed by the nuclear powers.

One should not however rush to the assumption that in regard to nuclear weapons the nuclear states are necessarily the states most concerned. The nuclear states possess the weapons, but it would be unrealistic to omit a consideration of those who would be affected once nuclear weapons are used. They would also be among the States most concerned, for their territories and populations would be exposed to the risk of harm from nuclear weapons no less than those of the nuclear powers, if ever nuclear weapons were used. This point was indeed made by Egypt in its presentation (CR 95/23, p. 40).

For probing the validity of the proposition that the nuclear States are the States most particularly affected, it would be useful to take the case of nuclear testing. Suppose a metropolitan power were to conduct a nuclear test in a distant colony, but with controls so unsatisfactory that there was admittedly a leakage of radioactive material. If the countries affected were to protest, on the basis of the illegality of such testing, it would be strange indeed if the metropolitan power attempted to argue that because it was the owner of the weapon, it was the State most affected. Manifestly, the States at the receiving end were those most affected. The position can scarcely be different in actual warfare, seeing that the radiation from a weapon exploding above ground cannot be contained within the target State. It would be quite legitimate for the neighbouring States to argue that they, rather than the owner of the bomb, are the States most affected.

This contention would stand, quite independently of the protests of the State upon whose territory the weapon is actually exploded. The relevance of this latter point is manifest when one considers that of the dozens of wars that have occurred since 1945, scarcely any have been fought on the soil of any of the nuclear powers. This is a relevant circumstance to be considered when the question of states most concerned is examined.

A balanced view of the matter is that no one group of nations — nuclear or non-nuclear — can say that its interests are most specially affected. Every nation in the world is specially affected by nuclear weapons, for when matters of survival are involved, this is a matter of universal concern.

7. Have States, by Participating in Regional Treaties Recognized Nuclear Weapons as Lawful?

The United States, the United Kingdom and France have in their written statements taken up the position that by signing a regional treaty such as the Treaty of Tlatelolco prohibiting the use of nuclear weapons in Latin America and the Caribbean, the signatories indicated by implication that there is no general prohibition on the use of nuclear weapons.

The signatories to such treaties are attempting to establish and strengthen a non-proliferation regime in their regions, not because they themselves do not accept the general illegality of nuclear weapons, but because the pro-nuclear states do not.

The position of the regional states is made quite clear by the stance they have adopted in the numerous General Assembly resolutions wherein several of them, e.g., Costa Rica, have voted on the basis that the use of nuclear weapons is a crime against humanity, a violation of the United Nations Charter and/or a violation of international law.

Indeed, the language of the Treaty itself gives a clear indication of the attitude of its subscribing parties to the weapon, for it describes it as constituting "an attack on the integrity of the human species", and states that it "ultimately may even render the whole earth uninhabitable".

VII. SOME SPECIAL ASPECTS

1. The Non-Proliferation Treaty

An argument has been made that the NPT, by implication, recognizes the legality of nuclear weapons, for all participating States accept without objection the possession of nuclear weapons by the nuclear powers. This argument raises numerous questions, among which are the following.

(i)   As already observed, the NPT has no bearing on the question of *use* or *threat of use* of nuclear weapons. Nowhere is the power given to use weapons, or to threaten their use.

(ii)   The Treaty was dealing with what may be described as a "winding-down situation". The reality was being faced by the world community that a vast number of nuclear weapons was in existence and that they might proliferate. The immediate object of the world community was to wind down this stockpile of weapons.

       As was stressed to the Court by some States in their submissions, the Treaty was worked out against the background of the reality that, whether or not the world community approved of this situation, there were a small number of nuclear states and a vast number of non-nuclear states. The realities were that the nuclear states would not give up their weapons, that proliferation was a grave danger and that everything possible should be done to prevent proliferation, recognizing at the same time the common ultimate goal of the elimination of nuclear weapons.

(iii)   As already observed, an acceptance of the inevitability of a situation is not a consent to that situation, for accepting the existence of an undesirable situation one is powerless to prevent, is very different to consenting to that situation.

(iv)   In this winding-down situation, there can be no hint that the right to possess meant also the right of use or threat of use. If there was a right of possession, it was a temporary and qualified right until such time as the stockpile could be wound down.

(v)   The preamble to the Treaty makes it patently clear that its object is:

"the cessation of the manufacture of nuclear weapons, the liquidation of all existing . . . stockpiles, and the elimination from national arsenals of nuclear weapons and the means of their delivery".

That Preamble, which, it should be noted, represents the unanimous view of all parties, nuclear as well as non-nuclear, describes the use of nuclear weapons in war as a "the devastation that would be visited upon all mankind".

These are clear indications that, far from acknowledging the legitimacy of nuclear weapons, the Treaty was in fact a concentrated attempt by the world community to whittle down such possessions as there already were, with a view to their complete elimination. Such a unanimous recognition of and concerted action towards the elimination of a weapon is quite inconsistent with a belief on the part of the world community of the legitimacy of the continued presence of the weapon in the arsenals of the nuclear powers.

(vi) Even if possession be legitimized by the treaty, that legitimation is temporary and goes no further than possession. The scope and the language of the treaty make it plain that it was a temporary state of possession *simpliciter* and nothing more to which they, the signatories, gave their assent — an assent given in exchange for the promise that the nuclear powers would make their utmost efforts to eliminate those weapons which *all* signatories considered so objectionable that they must be eliminated. There was here no recognition of a *right*, but only of a fact. The legality of that fact was not conceded, for else there was no need to demand a *quid pro quo* for it — the *bona fide* attempt by all nuclear powers to make every effort to eliminate these weapons, whose objectionability was the basic premise on which the entire treaty proceeded.

2. Deterrence

Deterrence has been touched upon in this Opinion in the context of the NPT. Yet, other aspects also merit attention, as deterrence bears upon the threat of use, which is one of the matters on which the Court's Opinion is sought.

(i) Meaning of deterrence

Deterrence means in essence that the party resorting to deterrence is intimating to the rest of the world that it means to use nuclear power against any State in the event of the first State being attacked. The concept calls for some further examination.

(ii) Deterrence — from what?

Deterrence as used in the context of nuclear weapons is deterrence from an act of war — not deterrence from *actions which one opposes.*[167]

One of the dangers of the possession of nuclear weapons for purposes of deterrence is the blurring of this distinction and the use of the power the nuclear weapon gives for purposes of deterring unwelcome actions on the part of another state. The argument of course applies to all kinds of armaments, but a *fortiori* to nuclear weapons. As Polanyi observes, the aspect of deterrence that is most feared is the temptation to extend it beyond the restricted aim of deterring war to deterring unwelcome actions (*ibid.*).

It has been suggested, for example, that deterrence can be used for the protection of a nation's "vital interests". What are vital interests, and who defines them? Could they be merely commercial interests? Could they be commercial interests situated in another country, or a different area of the globe?

Another phrase used in this context is the defence of "strategic interests". Some submissions adverted to the so-called "sub-strategic deterrence", effected through the use of a low-yield "warning shot" when a nation's vital interests are threatened (see, for example, Malaysia's submission in CR 95/27, p. 53). This Opinion will not deal with such types of deterrence, but rather with deterrence in the sense of self-defence against an act of war.

(iii) The degrees of deterrence

Deterrence can be of various degrees, ranging from the concept of maximum deterrence, to what is described as a minimum or near-minimum deterrent strategy.[168] Minimum nuclear deter-

---

[167]John Polanyi, *Lawyers and the Nuclear Debate, op. cit.*, p. 19.
[168]R.C. Karp (ed.), *Security Without Nuclear Weapons? Different Perspectives*

rence has been described as:

> "nuclear strategy in which a nation (or nations) maintains the minimum number of nuclear weapons necessary to inflict unacceptable damage on its adversary even after it has suffered a nuclear attack".[169]

The deterrence principle rests on the threat of massive retaliation, and as Professor Brownlie has observed:

> "If put into practice this principle would lead to a lack of proportion between the actual threat and the reaction to it. Such disproportionate reaction does not constitute self-defence as permitted by Article 51 of the United Nations Charter." [170]

In the words of the same author, "the prime object of deterrent nuclear weapons is ruthless and unpleasant retaliation — they are instruments of terror rather than weapons of war".[171]

Since the question posed is whether the use of nuclear weapons is legitimate in *any* circumstances, minimum deterrence must be considered.

(iv) Minimum deterrence

One of the problems with deterrence, even of a minimal character, is that actions perceived by one side as defensive can all too easily be perceived by the other side as threatening. Such a situation is the classic backdrop to the traditional arms race, whatever be the type of weapons involved. With nuclear arms it triggers off a nuclear arms race, thus raising a variety of legal concerns. Even minimum deterrence thus leads to counter-deterrence, and to an ever ascending spiral of nuclear armament testing and tension. If, therefore, there are legal objections to deterrence, those objections are not removed by that deterrence being minimal.

---

on Non-Nuclear Security, 1992, p. 251.

[169]*Ibid.*, p. 250, citing Hollins, Powers and Sommer, *The Conquest of War: Alternative Strategies for Global Security*, 1989, pp. 54-55.

[170]"Some Legal Aspects of the Use of Nuclear Weapons", *op. cit.*, pp. 446-447.

[171]*Ibid.*, p. 445.

(v) The problem of credibility

Deterrence needs to carry the conviction to other parties that there is a real intention to use those weapons in the event of an attack by that other party. A game of bluff does not convey that intention, for it is difficult to persuade another of one's intention unless one really has that intention. Deterrence thus consists in a real intention[171] to use such weapons. If deterrence is to operate, it leaves the world of make-believe and enters the field of seriously-intended military threats.

Deterrence therefore raises the question not merely whether the threat of use of such weapons is legal, but also whether *use* is legal. Since what is necessary for deterrence is assured destruction of the enemy, deterrence thus comes within the ambit of that which goes beyond the purposes of war. Moreover, in the split second response to an armed attack, the finely graded use of appropriate strategic nuclear missiles or "clean" weapons which cause minimal damage does not seem a credible possibility.

(vi) Deterrence distinguished from possession

The concept of deterrence goes a step further than mere possession. Deterrence is more than the mere accumulation of weapons in a storehouse. It means the possession of weapons in a state of readiness for actual use. This means the linkage of weapons ready for immediate take-off, with a command and control system geared for immediate action. It means that weapons are attached to delivery vehicles. It means that personnel are ready night and day to render them operational at a moment's notice. There is clearly a vast difference between weapons stocked in a warehouse and weapons so readied for immediate action. Mere possession and deterrence are thus concepts which are clearly distinguishable from each other.

(vii) The legal problem of intention

For reasons already outlined, deterrence becomes not the stor-

---

[171]For further discussion of the concept of intention in this context, see *Just War, Nonviolence and Nuclear Deterrence*, D.L. Cady and R. Werner (eds.), 1991, pp. 193-205.

age of weapons with intent to terrify, but a stockpiling with *intent to use*. If one intends to use them, all the consequences arise which attach to *intention* in law, whether domestic or international. One *intends* to cause the damage or devastation that will result. The intention to cause damage or devastation which results in total destruction of one's enemy or which might indeed wipe it out completely clearly goes beyond the purposes of war.[172] Such intention provides the mental element implicit in the concept of a threat.

However, a secretly harboured intention to commit a wrongful or criminal act does not attract legal consequences, unless and until that intention is followed through by corresponding conduct. Hence such a secretly harboured intention may not be an offence. If, however, the intention is announced, whether directly or by implication, it then becomes the criminal act of threatening to commit the illegal act in question.

Deterrence is by definition the very opposite of a secretly harboured intention to use nuclear weapons. Deterrence is not deterrence if there is no communication, whether by words or implication, of the serious intention to use nuclear weapons. It is therefore nothing short of a *threat* to use. If an act is wrongful, the threat to commit it and, more particularly, a publicly announced threat, must also be wrongful.

(viii) The temptation to use the weapons maintained for deterrence

Another aspect of deterrence is the temptation to use the weapons maintained for this purpose. The Court has been referred to numerous instances of the possible use of nuclear weapons of which the Cuban Missile Crisis is probably the best known. A study based on Pentagon documents, to which we were referred, lists numerous such instances involving the possibility of nuclear

---

[172]For the philosophical implications of deterrence, considered from the point of view of natural law, see Cady & Werner, *op. cit.*, pp. 207-219. See, also, John Finnis, Joseph Boyle and Germain Grisez, *Nuclear Deterrence, Morality and Realism* (1987). Other works which present substantially the same argument are Anthony Kenny, *The Logic of Deterrence* (1985), and *The Ivory Tower* (1985); Roger Ruston, *Nuclear Deterrence—Right or Wrong?* (1981), and "Nuclear Deterrence and the Use of the Just War Doctrine" in Blake and Pole (eds.), *Objections to Nuclear Defense* (1984).

use from 1946 to 1980.[173]

(ix) Deterrence and sovereign equality

This has already been dealt with. Either all nations have the right to self-defence with any particular weapon or none of them can have it — if the principle of equality in the right of self-defence is to be recognized. The first alternative is clearly impossible and the second alternative must then become, necessarily, the only option available.

The comparison already made with chemical or bacteriological weapons highlights this anomaly, for the rules of international law must operate uniformly across the entire spectrum of the international community. No explanation has been offered as to why nuclear weapons should be subject to a different regime.

(x) Conflict with the St. Petersburg principle

As already observed, the Declaration of St. Petersburg, followed and endorsed by numerous other documents (see section III.3, *supra*.) declared that weakening the military forces of the enemy is the only legitimate object which States should endeavour to accomplish during war (on this aspect, see section V.2, *supra*). Deterrence doctrine aims at far more — it aims at the destruction of major urban areas and centres of population and even goes so far as "mutually assured destruction". Especially during the Cold War, missiles were, under this doctrine, kept at the ready, targeting many of the major cities of the contending powers. Such policies are a far cry from the principles solemnly accepted at St. Petersburg and repeatedly endorsed by the world community.

3. Reprisals

The Court has not in its Opinion expressed a view in regard to the acceptance of the principle of reprisals in the corpus of modern international law. I regret that the Court did not avail itself of this opportunity to confirm the unavailability of reprisals under international law

---

[173]Michio Kaku and Daniel Axelrod, *To Win a Nuclear War*, 1987, p. 5; CR 95/27, p. 48.

at the present time, whether in time of peace or in war.

I wish to make it clear that I do not accept the lawfulness of the right to reprisals as a doctrine recognized by contemporary international law.

Does the concept of reprisals open up a possible exception to the rule that action in response to an attack is, like all other military action, subject to the laws of war?

The Declaration concerning Principles of Friendly Relations and Co-operation among States (Res. 2625(XXV) of 1970) categorically asserted that "States have a duty to refrain from acts of reprisal involving the use of force".

Professor Bowett puts the proposition very strongly in the following passage:

> *"Few propositions about international law have enjoyed more support than the proposition that, under the Charter of the United Nations, the use of force by way of reprisals is illegal. Although, indeed, the words 'reprisals' and 'retaliation' are not to be found in the Charter, this proposition was generally regarded by writers and by the Security Council as the logical and necessary consequence of the prohibition of force in Article 2(4), the injunction to settle disputes peacefully in Article 2(3) and the limiting of permissible force by states to self-defense."* [174]

While this is an unexceptionable view, it is to be borne in mind, further, that nuclear weapons raise special problems owing to the magnitude of the destruction that is certain to accompany them. In any event, a doctrine evolved for an altogether different scenario of warfare can scarcely be applied to nuclear weapons without some re-examination. Professor Brownlie addresses this aspect in the following terms:

> "In the first place, it is hardly legitimate to extend a doctrine related to the minutiae of the conventional theatre of war to an exchange of power which, in the case of the strategic and deterrent uses of nuclear weapons, is equivalent to the total of war effort and is the essence of the war aims." [175]

---

[174] D. Bowett, "Reprisals Involving Recourse to Armed Force", (1972) 66 *American Journal of International Law*, p. 1, quoted in Weston, Falk & D'Amato, *International Law and World Order*, 1980, p. 910.

[175] "Some Legal Aspects of the Use of Nuclear Weapons", *op. cit.*, p. 445.

These strong legal objections to the existence of a right of reprisal are reinforced also by two other factors — the conduct of the party indulging in the reprisals and the conduct of the party against whom the reprisals are directed.

The action of the party indulging in the reprisals needs to be a measured one, for its only legitimate object is as stated above. Whatever tendency there may be to unleash all its nuclear power in anger or revenge needs to be held strictly in check. It is useful to note in this connection the observation of Oppenheim who, after reviewing a variety of historical examples, concludes that:

> "reprisals instead of being a means of securing legitimate warfare may become an effective instrument of its wholesale and cynical violation in matters constituting the very basis of the law of war".[176]

The historical examples referred to relate, *inter alia*, to the extreme atrocities sought to be justified under the principle of retaliation in the Franco-German War, the Boer War, World War I and World War II.[177] They all attest to the brutality, cynicism and lack of restraint in the use of power which it is the object of the laws of war to prevent. Such shreds of the right to retaliation as might have survived the development of the laws of war are all rooted out by the nature of the nuclear weapon, as discussed in this Opinion.

If history is any guide, the party indulging in reprisals will in practice use such "right of reprisal" — if indeed there is such a right — in total disregard of the purpose and limits of retaliation — namely, the limited purpose of ensuring compliance with the laws of war.

Turning next to the conduct of the party against whom the right is exercised — a party who already has disregarded the laws of war — that party would only be stimulated to release all the nuclear power at its disposal in response to that retaliation — unless, of course, it has been totally destroyed.

In these circumstances, any invitation to this Court to enthrone the legitimacy of nuclear reprisal for a nuclear attack is an invitation to enthrone a principle that opens the door to arbitrariness and lack of

---

[176]*Ibid.*, Vol. II, p. 565.
[177]*Ibid*, pp. 563-565.

restraint in the use of nuclear weapons.

The sole justification, if any, for the doctrine of reprisals is that it is a means of securing legitimate warfare. With the manifest impossibility of that objective in relation to nuclear weapons, the sole reason for this alleged exception vanishes. *Cessante ratione legis, cessat ipsa lex.*

4. Internal Wars

The question asked of the Court relates to the use of nuclear weapons in *any* circumstances. The Court has observed that it is making no observation on this point. It is my view that the use of the weapon is prohibited in *all* circumstances.

The rules of humanity which prohibit the use of the weapon in external wars do not begin to take effect only when national boundaries are crossed. They must apply internally as well.

Article 3 which is common to the four Geneva Conventions applies to all armed conflicts of a non-international character and occurring in the territory of one of the Powers parties to the Convention. Protocol II of 1977 concerning internal wars is couched in terms similar to the Martens clause, and refers to "the principles of humanity and to the dictates of public conscience".

Thus international law makes no difference in principle between internal and external populations.

Moreover, if nuclear weapons are used internally by a State, it is clear from the foregoing analysis of the effects of nuclear weapons that the effects of such internal use cannot be confined internally. It will produce widespread external effects, as Chernobyl has demonstrated.

5. The Doctrine of Necessity

Does the doctrine of necessity offer a principle under which the use of nuclear weapons might be permissible in retaliation for an illegitimate act of warfare?

There is some support for the principle of necessity among the older writers, especially those of the German school[178], who expressed this doctrine in terms of the German proverb "*Kriegraeson geht vor*

---

[178]See the list of German authors cited by Oppenheim (ed.), *op. cit.*, Vol. II, p. 231, fn. 6.

Kriegsmanier" ("necessity in war overrules the manner of warfare"). However, some German writers did not support this view and in general it did not have the support of English, French, Italian and American publicists.[179]

According to this doctrine, the laws of war lose their binding force when no other means, short of the violation of the laws of war, will offer an escape from the extreme danger caused by the original unlawful act.

However, the origins of this principle, such as it is, go back to the days when there were no *laws* of war, but rather *usages* of war, which had not yet firmed into laws accepted by the international community as binding.

The advance achieved in recognition of these principles as binding laws, ever since the Geneva Convention of 1864, renders untenable the position that they can be ignored at the will, and in the sole unilateral judgment, of one party. Even well before World War I, authoritative writers such as Westlake strenuously denied such a doctrine[180] and, with the new and extensive means of destruction — particularly submarine and aerial — which emerged in World War I, the doctrine became increasingly dangerous and inapplicable. With the massive means of destruction available in World War II, the desuetude of the doctrine was even further established.

Decisions of war crimes tribunals of that era attest to the collapse of that doctrine, if indeed it had ever existed. The case of the *Peleus (War Crimes Reports,* i (1946), pp. 1-16) relating to submarine warfare, decided by a British military court; the *Milch* case (*War Crimes Trials,* 7 (1948), pp. 44, 65), decided by the United States Military Tribunal at Nuremberg; and the *Krupp* case (*War Crimes Trials,* 10 (1949), p. 138), where the tribunal addressed the question of grave economic necessity, are all instances of a judicial rejection of that doctrine in no uncertain terms.[181]

The doctrine of necessity opens the door to revenge, massive devastation and, in the context of nuclear weapons, even to genocide. To the extent that it seeks to override the principles of the laws of war, it has no place in modern international law.

---

[179]*Ibid.,* p. 232.

[180]Westlake, *International Law,* 2nd ed., 1910 1913, pp. 126-128; *The Collected Papers of John Westlake on Public International Law,* L. Oppenheim (ed.), 1914, p. 243.

[181]See, on these cases, Oppenheim, *op. cit.,* pp. 232-233.

In the words of a United States scholar:

"[W]here is the military necessity in incinerating entire urban populations, defiling the territory of neighboring and distant neutral countries, and ravaging the natural environment for generations to come . . . ? . . . If so, then we are witness to the demise of Nuremberg, the triumph of *Kreigraison*, the virtual repudiation of the humanitarian rules of armed conflict . . . The very meaning of 'proportionality' becomes lost, and we come dangerously close to condoning the crime of genocide, that is, a military campaign directed more towards the extinction of the enemy than towards the winning of a battle or conflict."[182]

6. Limited or Tactical or Battlefield Nuclear Weapons

Reference has already been made to the contention, by those asserting legality of use, that the inherent dangers of nuclear weapons can be minimized by resort to "small" or "clean" or "low yield" or "tactical" nuclear weapons. This factor has an important bearing upon the legal question before the Court, and it is necessary therefore to examine in some detail the acceptability of the contention that limited weapons remove the objections based upon the destructiveness of nuclear weapons.

The following are some factors to be taken into account in considering this question.

(i)   no material has been placed before the Court demonstrating that there is in existence a nuclear weapon which does not emit radiation, does not have a deleterious effect upon the environment, and does not have adverse health effects upon this and succeeding generations. If there were indeed a weapon which does not have any of the singular qualities outlined earlier in this Opinion, it has not been explained why a conventional weapon would not be adequate for the purpose for which such a weapon is used. We can only deal with nuclear weapons as we know them.

---

[182]Burns H. Weston, "Nuclear Weapons versus International Law: A Contextual Reassessment" (1983) 28 *McGill Law Journal*, p. 578.

(ii) the practicality of small nuclear weapons has been contested by high military[183] and scientific[184] authority.

(iii) reference has been made (see Section IV, *supra.*), in the context of self defence, to the political difficulties, stated by former American Secretaries of State, Robert McNamara and Dr. Kissinger, of keeping a response within the ambit of what has been described as a limited or minimal response. The assumption of escalation control seems unrealistic in the context of nuclear attack.

(iv) with the use of even "small" or "tactical" or "battlefield" nuclear weapons, one crosses the nuclear threshold. The state at the receiving end of such a nuclear response would not know that the response is a limited or tactical one involving a small weapon and it is not credible to posit that it will also be careful to respond in kind, i.e., with a small weapon. The door would be opened and the threshold crossed for an all-out nuclear war.

The scenario here under consideration is that of a limited nuclear response to a nuclear attack. Since, as stated above:

(a) the "controlled response" is unrealistic; and

(b) a "controlled response" by the nuclear power making the first attack to the "controlled response" to its first strike is even more unrealistic,

the scenario we are considering is one of all-out nuclear war, thus rendering the use of the controlled weapon illegitimate.

The assumption of a voluntary "brake" on the recipient's full-scale use of nuclear weapons is, as observed earlier in this Opinion, highly fanciful and speculative. Such fanciful speculations provide a very unsafe assumption on which to base the future of humanity.

(v) As was pointed out by one of the States appearing before the Court:

---

[183]General Colin Powell, *A Soldier's Way*, 1995, p. 324): "No matter how small these nuclear payloads were, we would be crossing a threshold. Using nukes at this point would mark one of the most significant military decisions since Hiroshima. . . . I began rethinking the practicality of those small nuclear weapons."

[184]See *Bulletin of the Atomic Scientists*, May 1985, p. 35, at p. 37, referred to in Malaysian Written Comments, p. 20.

> *"it would be academic and unreal for any analysis to seek to demonstrate that the use of a single nuclear weapon in particular circumstances could be consistent with principles of humanity. The reality is that if nuclear weapons ever were used, this would be overwhelmingly likely to trigger a nuclear war."* (Australia, Gareth Evans, CR 95/22, pp. 49-50.)

(vi) in the event of some power readying a nuclear weapon for a strike, it may be argued that a pre-emptive strike is necessary for self-defence. However, if such a pre-emptive strike is to be made with a "small" nuclear weapon which by definition has no greater blast, heat or radiation than a conventional weapon, the question would again arise why a nuclear weapon should be used when a conventional weapon would serve the same purpose.

(vii) the factor of accident must always be considered. Nuclear weapons have never been tried out on the battlefield. Their potential for limiting damage is untested and is as yet the subject of theoretical assurances of limitation. Having regard to the possibility of human error in high scientific operations — even to the extent of the accidental explosion of a space rocket with all its passengers aboard — one can never be sure that some error or accident in construction may deprive the weapon of its so-called "limited" quality. Indeed, apart from fine gradations regarding the size of the weapon to be used, the very use of any nuclear weapons under the stress of urgency is an area fraught with much potential for accident.[185] The UNIDIR study, just mentioned, emphasizes the "very high risks of escalation once a confrontation starts" (p. 11).

(viii) there is some doubt regarding the "smallness" of tactical nuclear weapons, and no precise details regarding these have been placed before the Court by any of the nuclear powers. Malaysia, on the other hand, has referred the Court to a US law forbidding "research and development which could lead to the production . . . of a low-yield nuclear weapon" (Written Comments, p. 20),

---

[185]See the UNIDIR Study, *Risks of Unintentional Nuclear War, supra.*

which is defined as having a yield of less than five kilotons (Hiroshima and Nagasaki were 15 and 12 kilotons, respectively.[186]
Weapons of this firepower may, in the absence of evidence to the
contrary, be presumed to be fraught with all the dangers attendant on nuclear weapons, as outlined earlier in this Opinion.

(ix) It is claimed a weapon could be used which could be precisely
aimed at a specific target. However, recent experience in the
Gulf War has shown that even the most sophisticated or "small"
weapons do not always strike its intended target with precision.
If there should be such error in the case of nuclear weaponry,
the consequence would be of the gravest order.

(x) *Having regard to WHO estimates of deaths ranging from one
million to one billion in the event of a nuclear war which could
well be triggered off by the use of the smallest nuclear weapon,
one can only endorse the sentiment which Egypt placed before
us when it observed that, having regard to such a level of casualties:*

> *"even with the greatest miniaturization, such speculative
> margins of risk are totally abhorrent to the general prin-
> ciples of humanitarian law" (CR 95/23, p. 43).*

(xi) Taking the analogy of chemical or bacteriological weapons, no
one would argue that because a small amount of such weapons
will cause a comparatively small amount of harm, therefore
chemical or bacteriological weapons are not illegal, seeing that
they can be used in controllable quantities. If, likewise, nuclear
weapons are generally illegal, there could not be an exception
for "small weapons".

If nuclear weapons are intrinsically unlawful, they cannot
be rendered lawful by being used in small quantities or in
smaller versions. Likewise, if a state should be attacked with
chemical or bacteriological weapons, it seems absurd to argue
that it has the right to respond with small quantities of such
weapons. The fundamental reason that all such weapons are not
permissible, even in self-defence, for the simple reason that

---

[186]National Defense Authorization Act for Fiscal Year (FY) 1944, *Public Law*,
103-160, 30 November 1993.

their effects go beyond the needs of war, is common to all these weapons.

(xii) Even if — and it has not been so submitted by any State appearing before the Court — there is a nuclear weapon which *totally* eliminates the dissemination of radiation, and which is not a weapon of mass destruction, it would be quite impossible for the Court to define those nuclear weapons which are lawful and those which are unlawful, as this involves technical data well beyond the competence of the Court. The Court must therefore speak of legality in general terms.

The Court's authoritative pronouncement that *all* nuclear weapons are not illegal (i.e., that *every* nuclear weapon is not illegal) would then open the door to those desiring to use, or threaten to use, nuclear weapons to argue that any particular weapon they use or propose to use is within the rationale of the Court's decision. No one could police this. The door would be open to the use of whatever nuclear weapon a state may choose to use.

It is totally unrealistic to assume, however clearly the Court stated its reasons, that a power desiring to use the weapon would carefully choose those which are within the Court's stated reasoning.

VIII. SOME ARGUMENTS AGAINST THE GRANT OF AN ADVISORY OPINION

1. The Advisory Opinion Would Be Devoid of Practical Effects

It has been argued that, whatever may be the law, the question of the use of nuclear weapons is a political question, politically loaded, and politically determined. This may be, but it must be observed that, however political be the question, there is always value in the clarification of the law. It is not ineffective, pointless and inconsequential.

It is important that the Court should assert the law as it is. A decision soundly based on law will carry respect with it by virtue of its own inherent authority. It will assist in building up a climate of opinion in which law is respected. It will enhance the authority of the Court in that it will be seen to be discharging its duty of clarifying and developing the law, regardless of political considerations.

The Court's decision on the illegality of the apartheid regime had little prospect of compliance by the offending government, but helped to create the climate of opinion which dismantled the structure of apartheid. Had the Court thought in terms of the futility of its decree, the end of apartheid may well have been long delayed, if it could have been achieved at all. The clarification of the law is an end in itself, and not merely a means to an end. When the law is clear, there is a greater chance of compliance than when it is shrouded in obscurity.

The view has indeed been expressed that, in matters involving "high policy", the influence of international law is minimal. However, as Professor Brownlie has observed in dealing with this argument, it would be "better to uphold a prohibition which may be avoided in a crisis than to do away with standards altogether".[187]

I would also refer, in this context, to the perceptive observations of Albert Schweitzer, cited at the very commencement of this Opinion, on the value of a greater public awareness of the illegality of nuclear weapons.

The Court needs to discharge its judicial role, declaring and clarifying the law as it is empowered and charged to do, undeterred by considerations that pertain to the political realm, which are not its concern.

2. Nuclear Weapons Have Preserved World Peace

It was argued by some States contending for legality that such weapons have played a vital role in support of international security over the last fifty years, and have helped to preserve global peace.

Even if this contention were correct, it makes little impact upon the legal considerations before the Court. The threat of use of a weapon which contravenes the humanitarian laws of war does not cease to contravene those laws of war merely because the overwhelming terror it inspires has the psychological effect of deterring opponents. This Court cannot endorse a pattern of security that rests upon terror. *In the dramatic language of Winston Churchill, speaking to the House of Commons in 1955, we would then have a situation where, "Safety will*

---

[187]"Some Legal Aspects of the Use of Nuclear Weapons", *op. cit.*, p. 438; emphasis added.

be the sturdy child of terror and survival the twin brother of annihila-
tion". A global regime which makes safety the result of terror and can
speak of survival and annihilation as twin alternatives makes peace
and the human future dependent on terror. This is not a basis for world
order which this Court can endorse. This Court is committed to uphold
the rule of law, not the rule of force or terror, and the humanitarian
principles of the laws of war are a vital part of the international rule
of law which this Court is charged to administer.

A world order dependent upon terror would take us back to the
state of nature described by Hobbes in *The Leviathan,* with sovereigns
"in the posture of Gladiators; having their weapons pointing and their
eyes fixed on one another . . . which is a posture of Warre".[188]

As international law stands at the threshold of another century,
with over three centuries of development behind it, including over one
century of development of humanitarian law, it has the ability to do
better than merely re-endorse the dependence of international law on
terror, thus setting the clock back to the state of nature as described by
Hobbes, rather than the international rule of law as visualized by
Grotius. As between the widely divergent world views of those near
contemporaries, international law has clearly a commitment to the
Grotian vision; and this case has provided the Court with what future
historians may well describe as a "Grotian moment" in the history of
international law. I regret that the Court has not availed itself of this
opportunity. The failure to note the contradictions between deterrence
and international law may also help to prolong the "posture of Warre"
described by Hobbes, which is implicit in the doctrine of deterrence.

However, conclusive though these considerations be, the weakness
of the argument that deterrence is valuable in that it has preserved
world peace does not end here. It is belied by the facts of history. It is
well documented that the use of nuclear weapons has been contemplated more than once during the past fifty years. Two of the best
known examples are the Cuban Missile Crisis (1962) and the Berlin
Crisis (1961). To these, many more could be added from well re-
searched studies upon the subject.[189] The world has on such occasions
been hovering on the brink of nuclear catastrophe and has, so to speak,
held its breath. In these confrontations, often a test of nerves between

---

188Thomas Hobbes, *The Leviathan,* James B. Randall (ed.), Washington Square
Press, 1970, p. 86.

189For example, *The Nuclear Predicament: A Sourcebook,,* D. U. Gregory (ed.),
1982.

those who control the nuclear button, anything could have happened, and it is humanity's good fortune that a nuclear exchange has not resulted. **Moreover, it is incorrect to speak of the nuclear weapon as having saved the world from wars, when well over 100 wars, resulting in 20 million deaths, have occurred since 1945.**[190] **Some studies have shown that since the termination of World War II, there have been armed conflicts around the globe every year, with the possible exception of 1968**[191]**, while more detailed estimates show that in the 2,340 weeks between 1945 and 1990, the world enjoyed a grand total of only three that were truly war-free.**[192]

It is true there has been no global conflagration, but the nuclear weapon has not saved humanity from a war-torn world, in which there exist a multitude of flashpoints with the potential of triggering the use of nuclear weapons if the conflict escalates and the weapons are available. Should that happen, it would bring "untold sorrow to mankind" which it was the primary objective of the United Nations Charter to prevent.

IX. CONCLUSION

1. The Task before the Court

Reference has been made (in section VI.4 of this Opinion) to the wide variety of groups that have exerted themselves in the anti-nuclear cause — environmentalists, professional groups of doctors, lawyers, scientists, performers and artists, parliamentarians, women's organizations, peace groups, students, federations. They are too numerous to mention. They come from every region and every country.

There are others who have maintained the contrary for a variety of reasons.

Since no authoritative statement of the law has been available on the matter thus far, an appeal has now been made to this Court for an Opinion. That appeal comes from the world's highest representative

---

[190]Ruth Sivard, in *World Military and Social Expenditures, World Priorities* (1993, p. 20), counts 149 wars and 23 million deaths during this period.

[191]See Charles Allen, *The Savage Wars of Peace: Soldiers' Voices 1945-1989*, 1989.

[192]Alvin and Heidi Toffler, *War and Anti-War: Survival at the Dawn of the 21st Century*, 1993, p. 14.

organization on the basis that a statement by the world's highest judicial organization would be of assistance to all the world in this all-important matter.

This Request thus gives the International Court of Justice a unique opportunity to make a unique contribution to this unique question. The Opinion rendered by the Court has judicially established certain important principles governing the matter for the first time. Yet it does not go to the full extent which I think it should have.

In this Opinion I have set down my conclusions as to the law. While conscious of the magnitude of the issues, I have focused my attention on the law as it is — on the numerous principles worked out by customary international law, and humanitarian law in particular, which cover the particular instances of the damage caused by nuclear weapons. As stated at the outset, my considered opinion on this matter is that the use or threat of use of nuclear weapons is incompatible with international law and with the very foundations on which that system rests. I have sought in this Opinion to set out my reasons in some detail and to state why the use or threat of use of nuclear weapons is absolutely prohibited by existing law — in *all circumstances and without reservation.*

It comforts me that these legal conclusions accord also with what I perceive to be the moralities of the matter and the interests of humanity.

2. The Alternatives before Humanity

To conclude this Opinion, I refer briefly to the Russell-Einstein Manifesto, issued on 9th July 1955. Two of the most outstanding intellects of this century, Bertrand Russell and Albert Einstein, each of them specially qualified to speak with authority of the power locked in the atom, joined a number of the world's most distinguished scientists in issuing a poignant appeal to all of humanity in connection with nuclear weapons. That appeal was based on considerations of rationality, humanity and concern for the human future. Rationality, humanity and concern for the human future are built into the structure of international law.

International law contains within itself a section which particularly concerns itself with the humanitarian laws of war. It is in the context of that particular section of that particular discipline that this case is set. It is an area in which the concerns voiced in the Russell-Einstein manifesto resonate with exceptional clarity.

Here are extracts from that appeal:

"No one knows how widely such lethal radioactive particles may be diffused, but the best authorities are unanimous in saying that a war with H-bombs might possibly put an end to the human race . . .

. . . We appeal, as human beings, to human beings: Remember your humanity, and forget the rest. If you can do so, the way lies open to a new Paradise; if you cannot, there lies before you the risk of universal death."

Equipped with the necessary array of principles with which to respond, international law could contribute significantly towards rolling back the shadow of the mushroom cloud, and heralding the sunshine of the nuclear-free age.

No issue could be fraught with deeper implications for the human future, and the pulse of the future beats strong in the body of international law. This issue has not thus far entered the precincts of international tribunals. Now that it has done so for the first time, it should be answered — convincingly, clearly and categorically.

(*Signed*) Christopher Gregory WEERAMANTRY

[Original: English]   [Sri Lanka]

APPENDIX: COMPARISON OF THE EFFECTS OF BOMBS
(Demonstrating Danger to Neutral States)

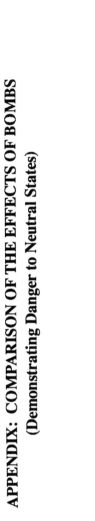
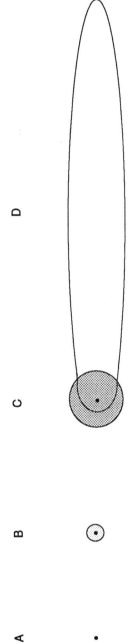

A — Lethal area from the blast wave of the blockbusters used in Second World War
B — Lethal area from the blast wave of the Hiroshima bomb
C — Lethal area from the blast wave of a 1-Mt bomb
D — Lethal area for fall-out radiation from a 1-Mt bomb

WHO 83896

INDIVIDUAL OPINION OF JUDGE RANJEVA

EDITOR'S OUTLINE OF RANJEVA OPINION*
Illegality of Nuclear Weapons Affirmed for First Time: ¶ 105 (2)E 1
Rule of Law Appears to Precede the Fact
¶ 105 (2)E 2
Legal Character of Question Asked
Who Requests Answer Matters
Advisory Opinion Is Different
¶ 105 (2)E 2
¶ 105 (2)C and ¶ 105 (2)E 2 Should Be Read Together

*Editor's additions to original text are indicated by bracketed headings or boldface brackets.

I voted for the whole of the operative part, in particular the first clause of paragraph E, since this opinion confirms the principle of the illegality of the threat or use of nuclear weapons, although I consider that the second clause of paragraph E raises problems of interpretation which may impair the clarity of the rule of law.

*

*　　*

[Illegality of Nuclear Weapons Affirmed for First Time: ¶ 105 (2)E 1]

The illegality of the threat or use of nuclear weapons will have been affirmed, for the first time, in the international jurisprudence inaugurated by this advisory opinion requested by the General Assembly of the United nations. If the first clause of the operative paragraph E had been worded differently, it would have kept alive the doubt about the justification of this principle of positive law, for a superficial comparison of the two preambular paragraphs A and B could have led to error. To have regarded the statements contained in these paragraphs as of equal weight would presumably have excluded either an affirmative or a negative answer to the question put in the resolution referring the matter to the Court. The Court's true answer is given in paragraph E, more in the first clause thereof, while paragraph 104 of the reasons provides the key to the reading of the reasons and the operative part in the sense that this paragraph E cannot be detached from paragraphs A, C, D and F. In my view, the adverb "generally" means: in the majority of cases and in the doctrine; its grammatical function is to determine with emphasis the statement made in the main proposition. By using a determinative adverb the opinion dismisses any other interpretation which could have resulted from the use of a dubitative adverb such as "apparently", "perhaps" or "no doubt". Lastly, the conditional mood of the verb "to be" used in making this statement expresses two ideas: on the one hand a probability, a qualification which can be more easily asserted than some other qualification; and on the other hand a supposition about the future which it is hoped will never come about. These reasons producing the conclusion of the illegality of the threat or use of nuclear weapons, merely confirm, in my view, the state of positive law.

The absence of a direct and specific reference to nuclear weapons cannot be used to justify the legality, even indirect, of the threat or use of nuclear weapons. The wording of the first clause of operative paragraph E excludes any limitation to the general principle of illegality. On the assumption that the intention is to assign a dubitative value to the adverb "generally", no conclusion implying modification of the scope of the illegality could withstand legal analysis. When "generally" is taken as an adverb of quantity, the natural meaning of the word excludes any temptation to infer an idea of legality, which is contrary to the fundamental principle stated. The use of the adverb "generally" is due only to an indirect appeal by the Court for the consequences of the analyses contained in paragraphs 70, 71 and 72 of the reasons to be drawn by those to whom the opinion is addressed. In other words, the current law,which the opinion has stated, wants consolidation. The absence of a specific reference to nuclear weapons raises in fact considerations of diplomatic, technical or political opportuneness rather than juridical considerations. It would thus seem useful to analyze the international practice in terms of law, in order to confirm this interpretation.

Three facts deserve attention. Firstly, there has been no repetition of the precedents of Hiroshima and Nagasaki since 1945 even though the spectre of the nuclear threat has been widely debated; on the other hand, the effects of nuclear power, in general and of nuclear weapons in particular, are such as to challenge the very foundations of humanitarian law and the law of armed conflict. Secondly, no declaration of the legality of nuclear weapons in principle has been recorded; there is no need to emphasize the fact that it is in the form of a justification of an exception to a principle accepted as being established in law, in this case the illegality of the threat or use of nuclear weapons, that the nuclear-weapon States attempt to present the reasons for their attitude. Thirdly and lastly, the consistently guarded and even hostile attitude of the General Assembly towards nuclear weapons and the continuous development of nuclear awareness have resulted in the steady tightening of the juridical mesh of the regime governing nuclear weapons, the control of which belongs increasingly less to the discretionary power of their possessors, in order to arrive at juridical situations of prohibition.

Two observations are prompted by this account of the facts. Firstly, the principle of the illegality of the threat or use of nuclear weapons has taken shape gradually in positive law. An exhaustive inventory of the relevant legal instruments and acts reveals the catalytic effect of the principle that nuclear weapons, should be regarded as unlawful. The study of the positive law cannot be limited therefore, to stating purely and simply the current state of the law as the Permanent International Court of Justice stressed in the case *Nationality Decrees issued in Tunis and Morocco*, the question of conformity with international law depends on the evolution of thinking and of international relations. Legal realism argues for acceptance of the notion that the juridical awareness of nuclear questions depends on the evolution of attitudes and knowledge, while one fact remains permanent: the final objective — disarmament. The same catalytic effect can be seen in the evolution of the law of the Charter of the United Nations. The examples of the law of decolonization and of the law of Article 2, paragraph 4, show that, originally, to regard the relevant principles as falling within the sphere of juridical prolegomena amounted to a legal heresy. And can these same arguments be maintained today? Cannot questions also be asked about the advent of an ecological and environmental order which would tend to superimpose itself on the nuclear order and which is being elaborated in the order of positive law? There is no longer any permissible doubt about the illegality of the threat or use of nuclear weapons. But for some States the difficulty stems from the fact that this principle has not been consolidated in treaties, a question raised by the second observation.

Secondly, does the silence on the specific case of nuclear weap-

ons with respect to a legal regime for their use truly exclude the customary illegality of the threat or use of nuclear weapons? There can be no doubt that in a matter of such importance for peace and the future of mankind, the treaty solution remains the best means of achieving general disarmament and nuclear disarmament in particular. But the characteristic consensualism of international law cannot be limited either to a technicality of contractual or conventional engineering or to formalization by majority vote of the rules of international law. The law of nuclear weapons is one of the branches of international law which is inconceivable without n minimum of ethical requirements expressing the values to which the members of the international community as a whole subscribe. The survival of mankind and of civilization is one of these values. It is not a question of substituting a moral order for the legal order of positive law in the name of some higher or revealed order. The moral requirements are not direct and positive sources of prescriptions or obligations but they do represent a framework for the scrutiny and questioning of the techniques and rules of conventional and consensual engineering. On the great issues of mankind the requirements of positive law and of ethics make common cause, and nuclear weapons, because of their destructive effects, are one such issue. In these circumstances, is illegality a matter of *opinio juris*? To this question the Court gives an answer which some would consider dubitative, whereas an answer in the affirmative, in my view, cannot be questioned and prevails.

[Rule of Law Appears to Precede the Fact]

Traditionally, when an *opinio juris* is sought the fact precedes the law: the analysis of the facts determines the application of the rule of law. But can this hold good in the present consultative procedure: the Court is in fact requested to go back to the first principles which provide the foundation of the normative rule (see Part II below) before saying whether the combined interpretation of the relevant rules results in the legality or illegality of the threat or use of nuclear weapons. In other words, the Court is dealing with a case in which the rule of law appears to precede the fact. The Court is rightly very rigorous and very demanding when it is considering sanctioning the juridical consolidation of a practice by way of an *opinio juris*. But does not the Court's increasingly frequent reference to the principles stated in the Charter and to the resolutions and legal instruments of international organizations indicate a solution of continuity? The recognition of the customary nature of the principles contained in Article 2, paragraph 4, of the Charter and in the case *Military and Paramilitary Activities in and against Nicaragua* constitutes in fact a significant break with the earlier practice. Does not the repeated proclamation of principles, regarded up to now as merely moral but of such importance that the irreversible nature of their acceptance appears definitive, constitute the advent of a constant and uniform practice? It is on the basis of these concrete considerations that such important principles as the prohibition of genocide, the right to decolonization, the prohibition of the use of force, and the theory of implicit jurisdictions have been incorporated in customary law. In the present case it is this conviction, constantly affirmed and never denied in principle in the facts, which indicates the incorporation of the principle of the illegality of the threat or use of nuclear weapons in customary law.

*

*   *

[¶105 (2)E 2]

The second clause of paragraph E might prompt one to wonder whether the Court did not try to avoid giving a clear answer to the basic question addressed to it by the General Assembly. Much of the argumentation of the reasons for the opinion is designed to establish that international law would not prohibit the threat or use of nuclear weapons. Thus, the problem is to decide whether in its handling of the General Assembly's request the Court has not based its position on a postulate: the equality of treatment to be accorded both to the principle of legality and to the principle of illegality. This difficulty, in my view, leads to an examination of the essential purpose of the question put, followed by an examination of the second clause of paragraph E.

The natural meaning of the words used in the General Assembly resolution defines the purpose of the question: does international law authorize the threat or use of nuclear weapons in any circumstance? Does the opinion answer this question honestly when it speaks simultaneously, and most importantly on the same footing, of "the illegality"?

In my view, the structure of the question implied a comprehensive analysis of the law governing nuclear weapons within the framework of the limits set the purpose of the question.

Several delegations were uncomfortable with the structure of the General Assembly's question, partly because the question was unprecedented and partly because of the scope of the matters dealt with in the first section of the operative part of the opinion.

[Legal Character of Question Asked]

Firstly, the legal character of the question amply justifies the Court's positive reaction to the General Assembly's request. But the Court's judicial reply would appear enigmatic or even incoherent if the Court had not previously provided the key to its reading. The opinion ought to have developed the meaning of its implicit interpretation of the notion of "legal question". The preparatory materials of the San Francisco Conference have little to say about the attempts to define this notion. Can we take it that its meaning is to be found in the data directly available to the mind or should we view this silence as the expression of the jurist's unease when he has to grapple with the notion of "question" as such.

The context of the present consultative procedure is unique in the history of the universal jurisdiction. The General Assembly's request has no connection whatsoever with an international dispute or with a dispute born of a difference of interpretation of a written and specific rule. The Court's task is in fact a complex one in the present case. The final conclusion, or to use the language of the theater, the dénouement, is for the Court to pronounce on the conformity or non-conformity of an act, decision or fact with a higher normative rule; but in order to do this the Court must first determine the presence or absence of general and objective prescriptions (paragraphs A and B) and then justify the legal nature of the principles thus identified and stated. In other words, to parody Levi Strauss, the General Assembly is requesting the Court to try to answer questions which no one asks. The inherent difficulty of this kind of question lies in the scope of the reply which the Court wishes to give both in the reasons and in the operative part (see para. 104). In this case, as pointed out above, the Court gave equal treatment of the different aspects of the problem of legality and illegality, devoting particular attention to the question of the absence of a prohibition on use.

Litteris verbis, resolution 49/75 does not request a legal opinion on the prohibition of the threat or use of nuclear weapons. The General Assembly invites the Court to go back to the first principles and to the most general propositions which explain or may call into question the interpretation that, in the absence of accepted rules as such which prohibit such acts, discretionary freedom would be the norm. There was obviously no lack of criticism of the structure of the question. The arguments put forward to support the idea that the question was a bad one were based on two main grounds: first, the obvious or absurd nature of the question, for the reply is not in doubt: no rule authorizes in international law the threat or use of nuclear weapons; second, such a question, which these critics regard as apparently valid, would run the risk of leading to inadmissible conclusions in view of the judicial nature of the Court. By seeing fit on the one hand to respond to the General Assembly's request (last section of the operative part) and on the other hand not to reformulate the terms of the question (see para. 20), notwithstanding the slight difference between the English and French versions of the text, the Court rejected the sophistry of fear of innovation. Such a question does not amount to the questioning or a request for amendment of positive law; nor was the Court asked to depart from its judicial function, for:

> "The Court . . . as an international judicial organ, is deemed to take judicial notice of international law, and is therefore required in a case falling under Article 53 of the Statute, as in any other case, to consider on its own initiative all rules of international law which may be relevant to the settlement of the dispute. It being the duty of the Court itself to ascertain and apply the relevant law in the given circumstances of the case, the burden of establishing or proving rules of international law . . . lies within the judicial knowledge of the Court." (*I.C.J. Reports 1974*, p. 9, para. 17, and p. 181, para. 18.)

These considerations facilitate a better understanding of the meaning of the notion of *legal question* and of the method followed by the Court in reply to the General Assembly's question, which does not in fact amount to a request or question which would restrict the Court's reply to one alternative.

By addressing exhaustively all the aspects of the problem, the opinion invests the legal question with a broad dimension. A question represents a subject, a matter on which the knowledge of the relevant rule lacks certainty. This uncertainty results from the inflationary proliferation of contradictory propositions having a link to the subject submitted to the Court. The Court is then invited to impose order on them by identifying the propositions clad in the sanction of juridical normativity and by explaining, in terms of an *opinio juris*, the normative status of various propositions. It is obvious that the outcome of such a consultation cannot avoid producing a proposition of a general character.

[Who Requests Answer Matters]

Secondly, the decision to accept the General Assembly's request for an opinion, the subject of the first section of the operative part, confirms the Court's liberal interpretation of the right of access of authorized international institutions to the consultative procedure. The case of the request for an opinion submitted by the World Health Organization will in all probability remain unusual, if not unique. Intrinsically, the purpose of WHO resolution 46/40 could not give rise to criticism, since each institution is the judge of its own competence. But when the question establishes a link of conditionality between the Court's reply, if any, and the performance of the preventive functions of primary health care, the specialized agency has substituted a link of conditionality for the link of connectivity envisaged by the Charter, the Statute and the relevant instruments of the World Health Organization. The fact that the purpose of the question can be detached from the Organization's functions did not allow the Court, in conformity with the rules of its own competence, to exercise its consultative function. This connection to today's opinion is not without interest; it is evident that the same majority of States wanted to obtain from the General Assembly confirmation of a request for a consultative opinion which contained defects capable of justifying a decision by the Court not to reply. By referring to the WHO request, the General Assembly revived memories of Article 14 of the Covenant of the League of Nations. In the absence of a joinder of decisions, since each request is dealt with separately, the Court confirmed the magnitude of the possible scope of the request for a consultative opinion submitted by the General Assembly. Nevertheless, the limits of the access to the consultative procedure are constituted by the legal nature of the purpose of the question put. On the other hand, there is no effect on the well-established legal precedent that a request seeking to obtain by the consultative method the amendment of positive law amounts to a political question.

[Advisory Opinion Is Different]

The conditions in which the Court discharged its task expose it to the criticism that the professionals of judicial law will not fail to raise against the whole of the second section of the operative part of the opinion. The judicial reply *stricto sensu* is found in paragraph E; in fact, its purpose is to declare the conformity or non-conformity of a pre-established rule. However, orbiting around this judicial conclusion are a number of propositions whose purpose is to state the justification or the questioning of the question which lead to the true conclusion. This circumductory structure of the operative part combined with the wording of paragraph E poses the problem of the actual consistency of the judicial conclusion in the advisory opinion of the Court. It is regrettable that the inherent difficulties of the very subject of nuclear weapons were not taken advantage of by the Court in order to exercise its judicial function more clearly and state the principle of illegality more clearly by dividing the two clauses of paragraph E into two separate paragraphs. A quick reading of the whole of the text of the opinion (reasons and operative part) can give the impression of a Court setting itself up as a servant of legal consultation. But on this question the Court was not requested to carry out legal analyses whose use would be left to the discretion of the various parties. The exercise of its consultative function imposes on the Court the duty to state the law on the question put by the author of the request; the optional character attached to the normative scope of an opinion does not however have the consequence of changing the nature of the Court's judicial function. Its "dictum" constitutes the interpretation of the rule of law in question, and to violate the operative part of the "dictum" amounts to a failure to fulfil the obligation to respect the law. It is always the case that, unlike a contentious procedure concerning a dispute over subjective rights, the statement of the law in a consultative procedure can necessarily not be limited to the alternatives of permitted/prohibited; although complicated, the positive law must be stated with clarity, a quality wanting in the second clause of paragraph E.

*

*   *

[¶ 105 (2)E 2]

In my view, the second clause of paragraph E causes difficulties of interpretation because of the problem of its intrinsic coherence in relation to the rules of the law of armed conflict themselves, although its positive dimension must be emphasized: the principle that the exercise of legitimate self-defence is subject to the rule of law.

Paragraph E deals with the law of armed conflict and with humanitarian law the second branch of law applicable to the threat or use of nuclear weapons (see para, 34). The law of armed conflict is a matter of written law, while the so-called Martens principle performs a residual function.

Two consequences flow from this: firstly, this law of armed conflict be interpreted as containing lacunae capable of justifying a reluctant or at least doubtful attitude; secondly, nuclear weapons cannot be used outside the context of the law of armed conflict. Since no State supported the principle of a regime of non-law, the use of these weapons must be in conformity, from the standpoint of the law, with the rules governing such conflict. In these circumstances and on such an important question, there cannot be any doubt about the validity of the principle of illegality in the law of armed conflict.

With regard to the substance of the law of armed conflict, the second clause of operative paragraph E introduces the possibility of an exception to the rules of the law of armed conflict by introducing a notion hitherto unknown in this branch of international law: the "extreme circumstance of self-defence, in which the very survival of a State would be at stake". Two criticisms must be offered. Firstly, the Court makes an amalgamation of the rules of Charter of the United Nations on the one hand and the law of named conflict and specifically the rules of humanitarian law on the other; whereas paragraph E deals only with the law of armed conflict, and the right of self-defence belongs in paragraph C. Rigorousness and clarity were necessary, failing a paragraph E *bis* separate from paragraph E and the attachment of the notion of "extreme circumstance of self-defence" to the more general problem of self-defence dealt with in paragraph C. Paragraph C covers all the cases of the right to use force by reference to the provisions of the Charter (Articles 2 and 4 and Article 51). *A priori* nothing prohibits an interpretation giving precedence to the rules of self-defence, including nuclear self-defence, over the rules of humanitarian law, a difficulty which lends consequentially to the second criticism. Secondly, the criticism is addressed to the acceptance of this concept of "extreme circumstance of self-defence, in which the very survival of a State would be at stake". There is no doubt that the meaning of this concept is expressed in the normal meaning of the words, but this observation is not sufficient for the purposes of legal qualification.

The principal difficulty of the interpretation of clause 2 of paragraph E lies in the true nature of the exception of "extreme circumstance of self-defence" to the application of humanitarian law and the law of armed conflict. Neither the legal precedents of the Court or of any other jurisdiction nor the doctrine offer any authority to confirm the existence of a distinction between the general case of application of the rules of the law of armed conflict and the exceptional case exempting a belligerent from fulfilling the obligations imposed by those rules.

If such a rule must exist, it can be deduced only from the intention of the States authors of and parties to these instruments. The fact that the case of nuclear weapons was deliberately not addressed during the negotiation and conclusion of the major conventions on the law of armed conflict has been repeatedly stressed. Accordingly, it is difficult to see how these plenipotentiaries could envisage exceptions of such importance to the principles governing the law of armed conflict. These principles were intended to be applied in all cases of conflict without any particular consideration of the status of the parties to the conflict — whether they were victims or aggressors. If an exceptional authorization had been envisaged, the authors of these instruments could have referred to it, for example by incorporating limits or exceptions to their universal application.

The distinction proposed by the Court would certainly be difficult to apply and in the end would only render even more complicated a problem which is already difficult to handle in law. 0. Schachter has drawn up an inventory of the cases in which, quite apart from any question of aggression, a State has claimed the privilege of self-defence:

"1. The use of force to rescue political hostages believed to face imminent danger of death or injury;

2. The use of force against officials or installations in a foreign state believed to support terrorist acts directed against nationals of the state claiming the right of defense;

3. The use of force against troops, planes, vessels, or installations believed to threaten imminent attack by a state with declared hostile intent;

4. The use of retaliatory force against a government or military force so as to deter renewed attacks on the state taking such action;

5. The use of force against a government that has provided arms or technical support to insurgents in a third state;

6. The use of force against a government that has allowed its territory to be used by military forces of a third state considered to be a threat to the state claiming self-defense;

7. The use of force in the name of collective defense (or counterintervention) against a government imposed by foreign forces and faced with large-scale military resistance by many of its people." (O. Schachter, "Self-defense over the rule of law", *A.J.I.L.*, 1989, p. 271.)

The question is to decide which category the case of an extreme circumstance of self-defence, in which the very survival of a State is at stake , must be placed in order to justify recourse to the ultimate weapon and the paralysis of the application of the rules of humanitarian law and the law applicable in armed conflict. This question must be answered with a negative assertion: the obligation of each belligerent to respect the rules of humanitarian law applicable in armed conflict is in no way limited to the case of self-defence; the obligation exists independently of the status of aggressor or victim. Furthermore, no evidence of the existence of a "clean nuclear weapon" was presented to the Court, and States merely argued that there was indeed a problem of compatibility between the legality of the use of nuclear weapons and the rules of humanitarian law. In my view, these criticisms strip the exception of "extreme circumstance of self-defence" of all logical and juridical foundation.

[¶105 (2)C and ¶ 105 (2)E 2 Should Be Read Together]

However, the respect in which I hold the Court prompts me to acknowledge that the principal judicial organ of the United Nations was not unaware of these criticisms or of the reproaches which the professionals of the juridical and judicial worlds would certainly offer. But I still believe that the close interrelationship of all the elements of this decision requires that the second clause of paragraph E should be read in the light of paragraph C. It must be acknowledged that in the final analysis the Court does affirm that the exercise of legitimate self-defence cannot be envisaged outside the framework of the rules of law. Paragraphs C and E define the prior legal constraints on the exercise of this right under such conditions that, in the light of paragraphs C, D and E, the legality of its exercise is more than improbable in actuality. The most important element, however, is the ordering of the legal guarantees. Paragraph E leaves open in these extreme circumstances the question of legality or illegality; it thus sets aside the possibility of creating predefined or predetermined blocks of legality or illegality.

A reply can be envisaged only in *concreto* in the light of the conditions of the preceding paragraphs C and D. This conclusion must be emphasized, for if the Court had addressed only one of the alternatives, the solution of indirect legality, the second clause would have nullified the purpose of the first clause. By addressing the two branches of the question the Court opens the way to a debate on illegality and legality in the eyes of international law, as the Nuremberg Tribunal had already stated:

> "Whether action taken under the claim of self-defense was in fact aggressive or defensive must ultimately be subject to investigation or adjudication if international law is ever to be enforced." (O. Schachter, ibid., p. 262.)

This complicated construction definitely limits the unilateral exercise of legitimate self-defence. Moreover, by reserving its definitive reply, therefore in principle, the Court is creating a possible sphere of competence which had been inconceivable hitherto owing to the effect of the combined mechanism of unilateral qualification and the right of veto. The difficulty of the terms of the problem did not, however, induce the Court to agree to assert the primacy of the requirements of the survival of a State over the obligation to respect the rules of international humanitarian law applicable in armed conflict.

In conclusion, if the two clauses of paragraph E had appeared as separate paragraphs, I would have voted without hesitation in favour of the first clause and, if the provisions of the Statute and the Rules of the Court so allowed, I would have abstained on the second clause. The joinder of these two proposals caused me to vote in all conscience in favour of the whole, for the essential element of the law is safe and the prohibition of nuclear weapons is a question of the responsibility of all and everyone, the Court having made its modest contribution by questioning each subject and actor of international life on the basis of the law. I hope that no jurisdiction will ever have to rule on the basis of the second clause of paragraph E.

(*Signed*) Raymond RANJEVA

[Madagascar]

[Original: French]

DISSENTING OPINION OF JUDGE HIGGINS

EDITOR'S OUTLINE OF HIGGINS OPINION*

1. I Voted for ¶ 105 (2)A, B, C, D and F, Not for E
4. The Requirement of Proportionality and the Exercise of Self-Defense
8. The Law of Armed Conflict
14. Balancing of Necessity and Humanity
18. What Military Necessity Would Justify Use of Nuclear Weapons?
20. The Principle of Proportionality
22. Foreseeability and Intent
23. Discriminating between Civilian and Military Targets
24. All Nuclear Weapons Are Not Monolithic in Their Effects
25. ¶ 105 (2)E 1
27. ¶ 105 (2)E 2
36. ¶ 105 (2)E Pronounces a *Non Liquet*
41. Not Clear How Best to Protect against Unimaginable Suffering

*Editor's additions to original text are indicated by bracketed headings or boldface brackets.

[I Voted for 105 (2)A, B, C, D and F, Not for E]

1. I agree with all that the Court has to say as to why it must render this Opinion and much that it has to say on the substance of the question put to it. I have also voted in favour of paragraphs 2A, 2B, 2C, 2D and 2F of the *dispositif*. The first four of these findings are in a sense stepping stones to the heart of the matter, which is to be found in paragraph 2E. I have, with regret, been unable to vote for what the Court there determines.

2. In the first part of its Opinion the Court has rejected suggestions that it should in its discretion decline to give the Opinion on the

grounds that the question is not legal, or is too vague, or would require the Court to make scenarios, or would require it to "legislate". But at paragraph 96 of its Opinion, and in paragraph 2E of its *dispositif*, the Court effectively pronounces a *non liquet* on the key issue on the grounds of uncertainty in the present state of the law, and of facts. I find this approach inconsistent.

3. I agree with most of the legal reasoning that sustains paragraphs 2A, 2B, 2C and 2D. Although paragraph C is negatively formulated, it is clear from the Court's analysis that neither the Charter provisions, nor customary international law, nor treaty law, make the threat or use of nuclear weapons unlawful *per se*.

[The Requirement of Proportionality and the Exercise of Self-Defense]

4. In its Judgment on *Military and Paramilitary Activities* the Court confirmed the existence of a rule of proportionality in the exercise of self-defence under customary international law. It there noted that the Charter "does not contain any specific rule whereby self-defence would warrant only measures which are proportional to the armed attack and necessary to respond to it" (*I.C.J. Reports 1986*, para. 176). Importantly, in the present Opinion the Court makes clear (paras. 40-41) that notwithstanding the absence of specific mention of proportionality in Article 51, this requirement applies equally to the exercise of self-defence under the Charter.

5. In the *Military and Paramilitary Activities* case the terms used by the Court already made clear that the concept of proportionality in self-defence limits a response to what is needed to reply to an attack. This is consistent with the approach of Professor Ago (as he then was), who had made clear in the Addendum to his Eighth Report on State Responsibility that the concept of proportionality referred to was that which was proportionate to repelling the attack, and not a requirement of symmetry between the mode of the initial attack and the mode of response (A/CN.4/318/Adds.5-7, para. 121, *YBILC* (1980), Vol. II, Part One, p. 69.)

6. Paragraph 2E states in its first part that the threat or use of nuclear weapons would generally be contrary to the rules of international law applicable in armed conflict, in particular the principles and

rules of humanitarian law; and in its second part that the Court cannot conclude whether a threat or use of nuclear weapons *in extremis* in self-defence, where a State's very survival was at stake, would be lawful or unlawful.

7. I have not been able to vote for these findings for several reasons. It is an essential requirement of the judicial process that a court should show the steps by which it reaches its conclusions. I believe the Court has not done so in respect of the first part of paragraph 2E. The findings in a judicial *dispositif* should be clear. I believe paragraph 2E is unclear in its meaning (and one may suspect that this lack of clarity is perhaps regarded as a virtue). I greatly regret the *non liquet* offered in the second part of paragraph 2E. And I believe that in that second sentence the Court is declining to answer a question that was in fact never put to it.

[The Law of Armed Conflict]

8. After finding that the threat or use of nuclear weapons is not prohibited *per se* by reference to the Charter or treaty law, the Court moves to see if it is prohibited *per se* by reference to the law of armed conflict (and especially humanitarian law).

9. It is not sufficient, to answer the question put to it, for the Court merely briefly to state the requirements of the law of armed conflict (including humanitarian law) and then simply to move to the conclusion that the threat or use of nuclear weapons is generally unlawful by reference to these principles and norms. The Court limits itself to affirming that the principles and rules of humanitarian law apply to nuclear weapons. It finds in paragraph 95, by reference to "the unique characteristics of nuclear weapons" that their use is "scarcely reconcilable" with the requirements of humanitarian law and "would generally be contrary" to humanitarian law (*dispositif*, para. 2E). At no point in its Opinion does the Court engage in the task that is surely at the heart of the question asked: the systematic application of the relevant law to the use or threat of nuclear weapons. It reaches its conclusions without the benefit of detailed analysis. An essential step in the judicial process — that of legal reasoning — has been omitted.

10. What in my view the Court should have done is to explain, elaborate and apply the key elements of humanitarian law that it iden-

tifies. I agree with the Court that certain general principles emanating from the treaties on the law of armed conflict and on humanitarian law are binding, either as continuing treaty obligations or as prescriptions of customary international law. These principles stem from a variety of uncontested sources (by which I mean they are in no way dependent upon the provisions of Additional Protocol I to the Geneva Conventions of 1949 nor upon any views held as to the application of those provisions to nuclear weapons). Particular reference may be made to the St. Petersburg Declaration of 11 December 1868 and to the Regulations, annexed to the Hague Convention IV, 1907, Articles 22 and 23 *(e)*. The Court recalls that the Regulations annexed to Hague Convention IV were in 1946 held by the Nuremberg Military Tribunal to have become part of customary international law by 1939. (Opinion, para. 80.)

11. The legal principle by which parties to an armed conflict do not have an unlimited choice of weapons or of methods of warfare cannot of itself give the answer to the question before the Court. Its purpose is to ensure that weapons, both in the context of their use, and in the methods of warfare, must comply with the other substantive rules.

12. It is not permitted in the choice of weapons to cause unnecessary suffering to enemy combatants, nor to render their death inevitable, nor to aggravate their sufferings when disabled. Equally, the Report of the International Military Commission in St. Petersburg of 1868 made clear that harm to civilians as a means of securing victory over the enemy was not a legitimate right of war; and that even in seeking to disable the military not every method was lawful. There has been, in many of the written and oral submissions made to the Court, a conflation of these two elements. But the Court itself makes clear, in paragraph 78 of its Opinion, that the prohibitions against means of conflict that cause unnecessary suffering is directed towards the fulfilment of the second, progressive, limb — namely, that even in seeking to disable the military forces of the enemy, there is a limitation upon the means that may be employed. These provisions are not directed at the protection of civilians, — other provisions serve that purpose. It is in any event absolutely prohibited to attack civilians, whether by nuclear or other weapons. Attack upon civilians does not depend for its illegality upon a prohibition against "superfluous injury" or aggravating the sufferings of men already disabled.

13. If then the "unnecessary suffering" provision does not operate as a generalized prohibition, but is rather directed at the protection of combatants, we must ask whether it still does not follow that the appalling primary effects of a nuclear weapon — blast waves, fires, radiation or radioactive fallout — cause extensive unnecessary suffering? These effects indeed cause horrendous suffering. But that is not necessarily "unnecessary suffering" as this term is to be understood within the context of the 1868 and 1907 law, which is directed at the limitation of means against a legitimate target, military personnel.

[Balancing of Necessity and Humanity]

14. The background to Article 23 *(a)* of the Hague Regulations was the celebrated provision in Article 22 (which opens a Chapter on the means of injuring the enemy) that the means of injuring the enemy is not unlimited. A certain level of violence is necessarily permissible in the exercise of self-defence; humanitarian law attempts to contain that force (and illegal uses of force too), by providing a "balancing" set of norms. It is thus unlawful to cause suffering and devastation which is in excess of what is required to achieve these legitimate aims. Application of this proposition requires a balancing of necessity and humanity. This approach to the proper understanding of "unnecessary suffering" has been supported, *inter alia,* by the Netherlands (Request for an Advisory Opinion on the Legality of the use by a State of Nuclear Weapons, Written Statement (Art. 66, para. 2, of the Statute), para. 27; United Kingdom, *ibid.,*paras. 36 ff. and Oral Statement (CR 95/34); United States, *ibid.*, para. 25; and New Zealand, Request for an Advisory Opinion on the Legality of the Threat or use of Nuclear Weapons, Written Statement, para. 69).

15. Subsequent diplomatic practice confirms this understanding of "unnecessary suffering" as established in the 1907 Regulations. In the Lucerne Conference of Governmental Experts on the use of Certain Conventional Weapons of 1974, the Experts were agreed both what was meant by "suffering" and by "unnecessary". As to the latter:

"This involved some sort of equation between, on the one hand, the degree of injury or suffering inflicted (the humanitarian aspect) and, on the other, the degree of necessity underlying the choice of a particular weapon (the military aspect)." (Conference Report, published by ICRC, 1975, para. 23.)

They were in accord that the concept entailed a "balancing" or "equation" rather than a prohibition against a significant degree or even a vast amount of suffering. Any disagreement rather lay in whether, on the military necessity side of the equation, all that was permitted was to put enemy personnel *hors de combat*, or whether it was permitted also to attack enemy material, lines of communication and resources (*ibid.*, para. 25).

16. It is this understanding of the principle that explains why States have been able to move to a specific prohibition of dum-dum bullets, whereas certain weapons that cause vastly greater suffering have neither been the subject of specific prohibitions, nor, in general State practice, been regarded as clearly prohibited by application of the "unnecessary suffering" principle. The status of incendiary projectiles, flamethrowers, napalm, high velocity weapons — all especially repugnant means of conducting hostilities — have thus remained contested.

17. The prohibition against unnecessary suffering and superfluous injury is a protection for the benefit of military personnel that is to be assessed by reference to the necessity of attacking the particular military target. The principle does not stipulate that a legitimate target is not to be attacked if it would cause great suffering.

[What Military Necessity Would Justify Use of Nuclear Weapons?]

18. There remains unanswered the crucial question: *what* military necessity is so great that the sort of suffering that would be inflicted on military personnel by the use of nuclear weapons would ever be justified? That question, in turn, requires knowing the dimensions of the suffering of which we speak and the circumstances which occasion it. It has been suggested that suffering could be relatively limited in the tactical theatre of war. The Court rightly regards that evidence as uncertain. If the suffering is of the sort traditionally associated with the use of nuclear weapons — blast, radiation, shock, together with risk of escalation, risk of spread through space and time — then only the most extreme circumstances (defence against untold suffering or the obliteration of a State or peoples) could conceivably "balance" the equation between necessity and humanity.

19. To show how it reached its findings in paragraph 2E of the *dispositif*, the Court should, after analysing the provisions of humanitarian law concerning the protection of combatants, then systematically have applied the humanitarian rules and principles as they apply to the protection of civilians. The major legal issues in this context which it might have been expected the Court would address are these: does the prohibition against civilians being the object of attack preclude attack upon a military target if it is realized that collateral civilian casualties will be unavoidable? And in the light of the answer to the above question, what then is meant by the requirements that a weapon must be able to discriminate between civilian and military targets and how will this apply to nuclear weapons?

[The Principle of Proportionality]

20. For some States making submissions to the Court, the large number of civilian victims was said *itself to show* that the collateral damage is excessive. But the law of armed conflict has been articulated in terms of a broad prohibition — that civilians may not be the object of armed attack — and the question of numbers or suffering (provided always that this primary obligation is met) falls to be considered as part of the "balancing" or "equation" between the necessities of war and the requirements of humanity. Articles 23 *(g)*, 25 and 27 of the Annex to the Fourth Hague Convention have relevance here. The principle of proportionality, even if finding no specific mention, is reflected in many provisions of Additional Protocol I to the Geneva Conventions of 1949. Thus even a legitimate target may not be attacked if the collateral civilian casualties would be disproportionate to the specific military gain from the attack. One is inevitably led to the question of whether, if a target is legitimate and the use of a nuclear weapon is the only way of destroying that target, any need can ever be so necessary as to occasion massive collateral damage upon civilians.

21. It must be that, in order to meet the legal requirement that a military target may not be attacked if collateral civilian casualties would be excessive in relation to the military advantage, the "military advantage" must indeed be one related to the very survival of a State or the avoidance of infliction (whether by nuclear or other weapons of mass destruction) of vast and severe suffering on its own population; and that no other method of eliminating this military target be available.

[Foreseeability and Intent]

22. It is said that collateral damage to civilians, even if proportionate to the importance of the military target,must never be intended. "One's intent is defined by what one chooses to do, or seeks to achieve through what one chooses to do." (Finnis, Boyle and Grisez, *Nuclear Deterrence, Morality and Idealism* (1987), at pp. 92-93.) This closely approximates to the legal doctrine of foreseeability, by which one is assumed to intend the consequences of one's actions. Does it follow that knowledge that in concrete circumstances civilians will be killed by the use of a nuclear weapon is tantamount to an intention to attack civilians? In law, analysis must always be contextual and the philosophical question here put is no different for nuclear weapons than for other weapons. The duty not to attack civilians as such applies to conventional weapons also. Collateral injury in respect of these weapons has always been accepted as not constituting "intent", provided always that the requirements of proportionality are met.

[Discriminating between Civilian and Military Targets]

23. Very important also in the present context is the requirement of humanitarian law that weapons may not be used which are incapable of discriminating between civilian and military targets.

[All Nuclear Weapons Are Not Monolithic in Their Effects]

24. The requirement that a weapon be capable of differentiating between military and civilian targets is not a general principle of humanitarian law specified in the 1899, 1907 or 1949 law, but flows from the basic rule that civilians may not be the target of attack. There has been considerable debate, as yet unresolved, as to whether this principle refers to weapons which, because of the way they are commonly used, strike civilians and combatants indiscriminately (*Weapons that May Cause Unnecessary Suffering or Have Indiscriminate Effects*, Report of the Work of Experts, published by the ICRC, 1973) or whether it refers to whether a weapon "having regard to [its] effects in time and space" can "be employed with sufficient or with predictable accuracy against the chosen target" (Conference of Government Experts on the Use of Certain Conventional Weapons (Lucerne, 1974), Report published by the ICRC, 1975, pp. 10-11, para. 31; see also Kalshoven "Arms, Armaments and Interpretation of Law", *Receuil des Cours*,

1985, II, at p. 236). For this concept to have a separate existence, distinct from that of collateral harm (with which it overlaps to an extent), and whichever interpretation of the term is chosen, it may be concluded that a weapon will be unlawful *per se* if it is incapable of being targeted at a military objective only, even if collateral harm occurs. Notwithstanding the unique and profoundly destructive characteristics of all nuclear weapons, that very term covers a variety of weapons which are not monolithic in all their effects. To the extent that a specific nuclear weapon would be incapable of this distinction, its use would be unlawful.

[105 (2)E 1]

25. I do not consider it juridically meaningful to say that the use of nuclear weapons is "generally contrary to the rules of international law applicable in armed conflict, and in particular the principles and rules of humanitarian law". What does the term "generally" mean? Is it a numerical allusion, or is it a reference to different types of nuclear weapons, or is it a suggestion that the rules of humanitarian law cannot be met save for exceptions? If so, where is the Court's analysis of these rules, properly understood, and their application to nuclear weapons? And what are any exceptions to be read into the term "generally"? Are they to be linked to an exceptional ability to comply with humanitarian law? Or does the term "generally", especially in the light of paragraph 96, suggest that if a use of nuclear weapons in extreme circumstances of self-defence were lawful, that might *of itself* exceptionally make such a use compatible with the humanitarian law? The phraseology of paragraph 2E of the *dispositif* raises all these questions and answers none of them.

26. **There is a further reason why I have been unable to vote for paragraph 2E of the *dispositif*. It states a negative consequence of humanitarian law and (unspecified) possible exceptions. The role of humanitarian law (in contrast to treaties of specific weapon prohibition) is to prescribe legal requirements of conduct rather than to give "generalized" answers about particular weapons. I do not, however, exclude the possibility that such a weapon could be unlawful by reference to the humanitarian law, if its use could never comply with its requirements — no matter what specific type within that class of weapon was being used and no matter where it might be used. We may believe that, in the present stage of weapon**

development, there may be very limited prospects of a State being able to comply with the requirements of humanitarian law. But that is different from finding the use of nuclear weapons "generally unlawful".

[¶ 105 (2)E 2]

27. The meaning of the second sentence of paragraph 2E of the *dispositif*, and thus what the two sentences of paragraph 2E of the *dispositif* mean when taken together, is unclear. The second sentence is presumably not referring to self-defence in those exceptional circumstances, implied by the word "generally", that might allow a threat or use of nuclear weapons to be compatible with humanitarian law. If, as the Court has indicated in paragraph 42 (and operative paragraph 2C), the Charter law does not *per se* make a use of nuclear weapons illegal, and if a specific use complied with the provisions of Article 51 *and* was also compatible with humanitarian law, the Court can hardly be saying in the second sentence of paragraph 2E that it knows not whether such a use would be lawful or unlawful.

28. Therefore it seems the Court is addressing the "general" circumstances that it envisages — namely that a threat or use of nuclear weapons violates humanitarian law — and that it is addressing whether in *those* circumstances a use of force *in extremis* and in conformity with Article 51 of the Charter, might nonetheless be regarded as be lawful, or not. The Court answers that it does not know.

29. What the Court has done is reach a conclusion of "incompatibility in general" with humanitarian law; and then effectively pronounce a *non liquet* on whether a use of nuclear weapons in self-defence when the survival of a State is at issue might still be lawful, even were the particular use to be contrary to humanitarian law. Through this formula of non-pronouncement the Court necessarily leaves open the possibility that a use of nuclear weapons contrary to humanitarian law might nonetheless be lawful. This goes beyond anything that was claimed by the nuclear weapons States appearing before the Court, who fully accepted that any lawful threat or use of nuclear weapons would have to comply with both the *jus ad bellum* and the *jus in bello* (see para. 86).

30. That the formula chosen is a *non liquet* cannot be doubted,

because the Court does not restrict itself to the inadequacy of facts and argument concerning the so-called "clean" and "precise" weapons. I share the Court's view that it has not been persuasively explained in what circumstances it might be essential to use any such weaponry. Nor indeed may it be assumed that such types of weapons (perhaps to be used against submarines, or in deserts) can suffice to represent for a nuclear weapon State all that is required for an effective policy of deterrence.

31. The formula in the second part of paragraph 2E refers also to "the current state of international law" as the basis for the Court's *non liquet*. I find it very hard to understand this reference. Paragraph F of the *dispositif*, and the final paragraphs of the Court's Opinion, indicate that the Court hopes for a negotiated and verified total disarmament, including nuclear disarmament. But it cannot be the absence of this goal which means that international law has no answer to give on the use of nuclear weapons in self-defence. International law does not simply consist of total prohibitions. Nor can it be that there is no substantive law of self-defence upon which the Court may offer advice — this, all said and done, is one of the most well developed areas of international law.

32. Can the reference to "the current state of international law" possibly refer to humanitarian law? This is one of the many elements that is unclear. This aspect appears to have been disposed of already in the first part of paragraph E. In any event, humanitarian law too is very well developed. The fact that its principles are broadly stated and often raise further questions that require a response can be no ground for a *non liquet*. It is exactly the judicial function to take principles of general application, to elaborate their meaning and to apply them to specific situations. This is precisely the role of the International Court, whether in contentious proceedings or in its advisory function.

33. Perhaps the reference to "the current state of international law" is a reference to perceived tensions between the widespread acceptance of the possession of nuclear weapons (and thus, it may be presumed, of the legality of their use in certain circumstances) as mentioned by the Court in paragraphs 67 and 96 on the one hand, and the requirements of humanitarian law on the other. If so, I believe this to be a false dichotomy. The pursuit of deterrence, the shielding under the nuclear umbrella, the silent acceptance of

reservations and declarations by the nuclear powers to treaties prohibiting the use of nuclear weapons in certain regions, the seeking
of possible security assurances — all this points to a significant
international practice which is surely relevant not only to the law
of self-defence but also to humanitarian law. If a substantial number of States in the international community believe that the use of
nuclear weapons might *in extremis* be compatible with their duties
under the Charter (whether as nuclear powers or as beneficiaries
of "the umbrella" or security assurances) they presumably *also* believe that they would not be violating their duties under humanitarian law.

34. Nothing in relevant statements made suggests that those States
giving nuclear assurances or receiving them believed that they would
be violating humanitarian law, — but decided nonetheless to act in
disregard of such violation. In sum, such weight as may be given to
the State practice just referred to has a relevance for our understanding
of the complex provisions of humanitarian law as much as for the
provisions of the Charter law of self-defence.

35. For all of these reasons, I am unable to see why the Court
resorts to the answer it does in the second part of paragraph 2E of the
dispositif.

[¶ 105 (2)E Pronounces a *Non Liquet*]

36. It is also, I think, an important and well-established principle
that the concept of *non liquet* — for that is what we have here — is no
part of the Court's jurisprudence.

37. The Court has, of course, on several occasions, declined to
answer a question even after it has established its jurisdiction. Reasons
of propriety (Art. 65 of the Statute; and the *Monetary Gold,* and *Northern Cameroons* cases) or important defects in procedure (the *Asylum*
case, the *Haya de la Torre* case) have been given. But "[in] none of
these cases is the *non-liquet* due . . . to deficiencies in the law"
(Rosenne, *The Law and Practice of the International Court,* 2nd rev.
ed., p. 100).

38. This unwelcome formulation ignores sixty-five years of proud
judicial history and also the convictions of those who went before us.

Former President of the International Court, Judge Elias, reminds us that there are what he terms "useful devices" to assist if there are difficulties in applying the usual sources of international law. In his view these "preclude the Court from pleading *non liquet* in any given case" (Elias, *The International Court of Justice and Some Contemporary Problems,* 1983, p. 14).

39. The learned editors of the 9th Edition of *Oppenheim's International Law* remind us:

"there is [not] always a clear and specific legal rule readily applicable to every international situation, but that every international situation is capable of being determined *as a matter of law*" (Jennings and Watts, Vol. I, p. 13).

40. Nor is the situation changed by any suggestion that the problem is as much one as "antimony" or clashes between various elements in the law as much as alleged "vagueness" in the law. Even were there such an "antimony" (which, as I have indicated above, I doubt), the judge's role is precisely to decide which of two or more competing norms is applicable in the particular circumstances. The corpus of international law is frequently made up of norms that, taken in isolation, appear to pull in different directions — for example, States may not use force/States may use force in self-defence; *pacta sunt servanda*/States may terminate or suspend treaties on specified grounds. It is the role of the judge to resolve, in context, and on grounds that should be articulated, why the application of one norm rather than another is to be preferred in the particular case. As these norms indubitably exist, and the difficulties that face the Court relate to their application, there can be no question of judicial legislation.

[Not Clear How Best to Protect against Unimaginable Suffering]

41. One cannot be unaffected by the knowledge of the unbearable suffering and vast destruction that nuclear weapons can cause. And one can well understand that it is expected of those who care about such suffering and devastation that they should declare its cause illegal. It may well be asked of a judge whether, in engaging in legal analysis of such concepts as "unnecessary suffering", "collateral damage" and "entitlement to self-defence", one has not lost sight of the real human circumstances involved. The judicial lode-

star, whether in difficult questions of interpretation of humanitarian law, or in resolving claimed tensions between competing norms,
must be those values that international law seeks to promote and
protect. In the present case, it is the physical survival of peoples
that we must constantly have in view. We live in a decentralized
world order, in which some States are known to possess nuclear
weapons but choose to remain outside of the non-proliferation
treaty system; while other such non-parties have declared their intention to obtain nuclear weapons; and yet other States are believed clandestinely to possess, or to be working shortly to possess
nuclear weapons (some of whom indeed may be party to the NPT).
It is not clear to me that either a pronouncement of illegality in all
circumstances of the use of nuclear weapons or the answers formulated by the Court in paragraph 2E best serve to protect mankind
against that unimaginable suffering that we all fear.

                                              (*Signed*) Rosalyn HIGGINS
[Original: English]   [United Kingdom]

DISSENTING OPINION OF JUDGE ODA

TABLE OF CONTENTS

Paragraphs

PART I. INTRODUCTORY REMARKS — MY OPPOSITION TO THE COURT'S DECISION TO RENDER AN OPINION IN RESPONSE TO THE REQUEST UNDER GENERAL ASSEMBLY RESOLUTION 49/75K IN THIS CASE

(1) The Inadequacy of the Question Put by the General Assembly in the Resolution as the Request for Advisory Opinion   2-5

(2) The Lack of a Meaningful Consensus of the Member States of the United Nations on the Request Drafted without Any Adequate Statement of Reasoning   6-14

Table I

PART II. ONE ASPECT OF NUCLEAR DISARMAMENT — THE UNSUCCESSFUL EFFORTS OVER A LONG PERIOD TO BRING ABOUT A CONVENTION "PROHIBITING THE USE OR THREAT OF USE OF NUCLEAR WEAPONS UNDER ANY CIRCUMSTANCES" AS AN IMMEDIATE BACKGROUND TO THE REQUEST TO THE COURT

(1) Declaration for the Non-Use or the Prohibition of Nuclear Weapons   15-19

Table II

Paragraphs

(2) The 1982-1995 Resolutions on the Convention on
the Prohibition 20-25 of the Use of Nuclear Weap-
ons   20-25

Table III

**PART III. ANOTHER ASPECT OF NUCLEAR
DISARMAMENT — NUCLEAR DISARMA-
MENT IN THE PERIOD OF THE COLD WAR
AND THE ROAD TO THE CONCLUSION OF
THE NON-PROLIFERATION TREATY**

(1) The Nuclear Arms Race and the Control of Nuclear Weapons in the Period of the Cold War; the
Emergence of the Non-Proliferation Treaty   26-33

(2) Perpetuation of the NPT Régime   34-41

Table IV

(3) Significance of the NPT Régime in the Period of
the Still Valid Doctrine of Nuclear Deterrence   42

Table V

PART IV. CONCLUDING REMARKS

(1) Re-Examination of the General Assembly's Request for the Court's Advisory Opinion   43-46

(2) Role of the Advisory Function and the Discretion
of the Court to Decline to Render an Advisory
Opinion   47-51

(3) Conclusions   52-54

**PART V. SUPPLEMENTARY OBSERVATIONS
ON MY POSITION AS REGARDS PARAGRAPH
2 OF THE OPERATIVE PART OF THE PRES-
ENT ADVISORY OPINION**

I. INTRODUCTORY REMARKS — MY OPPOSITION TO THE COURT'S DECISION TO RENDER AN OPINION IN RESPONSE TO THE REQUEST UNDER GENERAL ASSEMBLY RESOLUTION 49/75K IN THIS CASE

1. As the only Judge who voted against paragraph (1) of the operative part of the Court's Opinion, I would like to state my firm conviction that the Court, for reasons of judicial propriety and economy, should have exercised its discretionary power to refrain from rendering an opinion in response to the request for advisory opinion submitted by the United Nations General Assembly under its resolution 49/75K of 15 December 1994. I am sorry to have to say that the conclusions the Court has now reached do not appear to me to constitute substantive or substantial answers to the questions that the General Assembly wanted to raise by means of its resolution and occasion doubts about the credibility of the Court.

(1) *The Inadequacy of the Question Put by the General Assembly in the Resolution as the Request for Advisory Opinion*

2. (*The request laid down in resolution 49/75K*) The question put to the Court by the General Assembly, under resolution 49/75K within the framework of the agenda item: "General and complete disarmament", reads strangely. It is worded as follows:

> "Is the threat or use of nuclear weapons in any circumstance permitted under international law?" ([T]he French text reads: "Est-il permis en droit international de recourir à la menace ou à l'emploi d'armes nucléaires en toute circonstance?")

The Court's Opinion points out the difference between the English and the French texts of the Request and states that "[t]he Court finds it unnecessary to pronounce on the possible divergences" (Court's Opinion, para. 20). We should, however, note that the resolution which originated in draft resolution A/C.1/49/L.36 (original: English), prepared and introduced by Indonesia (on behalf of the States Members of the United Nations that are members of the Movement of Non-Aligned Countries), was originally drafted in English and that, in the First Committee at the 49th Session (1994) which took up this draft resolution, the content of this original English text was not questioned by any delegate. Moreover, it would seem that the francophone delegates raised no question about the text of the French translation, as far as the verbatim records indicate. I shall therefore proceed with my analysis based on the English text.

3. (*The request was presented to the Court, not so much in order to ascertain its opinion as to seek the endorsement of an alleged legal axiom*) When putting this question to the Court, the General Assembly — or those States which took the initiative in drafting the Request — clearly *never* expected that it would give an answer in the *affirmative* stating that: "*Yes*, the threat or use of nuclear weapons *is* permitted under international law in any circumstance [or, in all circumstances]". If this is true, it follows that, in fact, the General Assembly *only* expected the Court to state that: "*No*, the threat or use of nuclear weapons is *not* permitted under international law *in any circumstance*". The General Assembly, by asking the question that it did, wished to obtain nothing more than the Court's *endorsement* of the latter conclusion.

Since the Court was simply asked in this instance to give an opinion endorsing what is, in the view of the General Assembly, a legal axiom to the effect that "the threat or use of nuclear weapons is not permitted under international law in any circumstance", I wonder if the Request really does fall within the category of a request for advisory opinion within the meaning of Article 96(1) of the Charter of the United Nations. In the history of the advisory function of the Court, a simple endorsement or approval of what either the General Assembly or the Security Council believed to be a correct legal axiom has never been asked for in the form of a request for advisory opinion.

The drafting of the question put by the General Assembly seems to have been extremely singular. The Court has, however, reformulated the question to read, as indicated: "[the] real objective [of the question] is clear: to determine the legality or illegality of the *threat or use of nuclear weapons*" (Court's Opinion, para. 20) (emphasis added) and, furthermore, has implicitly reformulated the question to read: if nuclear weapons are not totally prohibited, under what circumstances is the threat or use of nuclear weapons considered to be lawful or permissible?

4. (*The lack of clarity as regards the concept of a "threat" in connection with nuclear weapons*) I would like further to point out that the words "the threat of nuclear weapons" are not clearly defined in the Request and may not have been understood in an unequivocal

manner by the member States which supported the resolution. An important point seems to be overlooked in the Request, namely a possibility that nuclear weapons may well be considered to constitute a "threat" merely by being in a State's possession or being under production by a State, considering that the phrase "*threat or use* of nuclear weapons" (emphasis added) was first used in the Request while the phrase "the use *or threat of use* of nuclear weapons" (emphasis added) had long been employed in the United Nations resolutions. In my view it was quite possible, at the time of the Request, for some member States of the United Nations to consider that the actual "possession" or "production" of nuclear weapons constituted a "threat". In other words, the Request might have been prepared by some States who strongly upheld the straightforward notion of the illegality of nuclear weapons as whole.

5. (*Political history of the Request*) What actually gave rise to this inaptly phrased and inadequately understood Request? I shall engage in a detailed analysis of this question and would like to stress one point, namely that, in spite of the Court's view that "regard [should] *not* [be had] to the origins or to the political history of the request, or to the distribution of votes in respect of the adopted resolution" (Court's Opinion, para. 16) (emphasis added), it appears to me pertinent and essential to examine why and under what circumstances the present Request was submitted to the Court under resolution 49/75K in 1994 and by whom — within the Organization of the United Nations or outside of it — this Request was initiated. It is for this reason that I will engage in an analysis of the history of the Request and the way in which some relevant decisions were taken by the General Assembly.

(2) *The Lack of a Meaningful Consensus of the Member States of the United Nations on the Request Drafted without Any Adequate Statement of Reasoning*

6. (*Preliminary attempt in 1993*) It was not until 1994 that the General Assembly raised the question of what was the *existing international law* concerning nuclear weapons generally, despite the fact that the discovery, development and possession of nuclear weapons, as well as the threat of their use, had for the previous fifty years, since 1945, consistently been a matter of profound political concern to the international community.

However, prior to the adoption of resolution 49/75K by the General Assembly at its 49th Session (1994), the idea of requesting the Court's opinion on the existing international law concerning nuclear weapons had been suggested at the 48th Session (1993) under the agenda item: "General and complete disarmament" (an item dating back to the 26th Session (1971) of the General Assembly), when, in the First Committee, Indonesia introduced on 9 November 1993 a draft resolution on behalf of the Movement of Non-Aligned Countries: "Request for an advisory opinion from the International Court of Justice on the legality of the threat or use of nuclear weapons" (A/C.1/48/L.25).

In fact a request for an advisory opinion of the Court had already been made by the WHO (WHA46.60) just a few months previously — a fact that was mentioned in the preambular paragraph of that Indonesian draft resolution. On 19 November 1993 the sponsors of that draft resolution decided not to press for action on it, but without giving any explanation for that decision. A draft resolution with a similar content was, however, once again brought before the General Assembly in the following year at its 49th Session (1994).

7. (*The movement of non-aligned countries*)   Relevant to this was one of the decisions made at the Eleventh Ministerial Conference of the Movement of Non-Aligned Countries which was convened in Cairo in May/June 1994. The Conference covered an extremely wide range of subjects and its Final Document on "Disarmament and international security" read:

> "69. The Ministers *decided to retable and put to the vote* the resolution seeking an advisory opinion from the International Court of Justice on the legality of *the use and threat of use of nuclear weapons* during the forty-ninth Session of the General Assembly." (A/49/287; S/1994/894.) (Emphasis added.)

The circumstances under which the Conference reached this particular decision were not clear from the documentation available.

The same decision of the non-aligned countries was repeated by the meeting of the Ministers of Foreign Affairs and Heads of Delegation of the Movement of Non-Aligned Countries to the 49th session (1994) of the General Assembly held at the United Nations Headquarters on 5 October 1994 (A/49/532; S/1994/1179: para. 34).

8. (*Non-governmental organization*)   I would also point to another factor. The idea behind the resolution whereby the General As-

sembly (and also the WHO) requested advisory opinions, had previously been advanced by a handful of non-governmental organizations (NGOs) which initiated a campaign for the *total prohibition* of nuclear weapons but failed to persuade the States' delegations in the forum of the General Assembly, which has done no more during a period of more than ten years than to pass repeated resolutions suggesting a convention on the prohibition of the use or threat of use of nuclear weapons (*cf.* paras. 21-24, below). Some NGOs seem to have tried to compensate for the vainness of their efforts by attempting to get the principal judicial organ of the United Nations to determine the *absolute illegality* of nuclear weapons, in a bid to persuade the member States of the United Nations to press for their immediate and complete prohibition in the political forum.

A statement made by an observer from the International Physicians for the Prevention of Nuclear War at the World Health Assembly in 1993 appears to shed light on what was behind the movement towards the attempt to get the International Court of Justice to render an advisory opinion on the matter in response to a request from the World Health Organization if not from the United Nations General Assembly. The observer stated that "WHO would be right to seek an opinion on the matter from the International Court of Justice".

An observer from the World Federation of Public Health Associations informed the World Health Assembly that

"it [itself] had unanimously adopted a resolution on nuclear weapons and public health which, *inter alia*, urged the World Health Assembly to request an advisory opinion from the International Court of Justice on the legal status of the use of nuclear weapons, so as to remove the cloud of legal doubt under which the nuclear powers continued their involvement with such weapons, as well as to provide the legal basis for the gradual creation of a nuclear-free world."

This matter is referred to in my Separate Opinion appended to the Court's Opinion in response to the request of the WHO.

Another document of interest is an essay in a newsletter of the World Government of World Citizens, a part of which reads as follows:

"The threat to humanity's existence posed by nuclear weapons has encouraged humans the world over to consider new strategies for influencing their governments. One of these initiatives — the movement to *'illegalize' nuclear weapons* —

*may increase participation in new governing structures being
created to address global problems. The World Court Project
is thus taking its place in the forefront of the antinuclear movement. . . .*

To crystallize a united front against nuclear weaponry,
several nongovernmental organizations (NGOs) . . . have established a World Court Project. These NGOs have *successfully lobbied the 'non-aligned' members of the United Nations
General Assembly* and the U.N.'s World Health Organization
(WHO) to establish, according to customary international law,
the illegality of nuclear weapons." (*World Citizen News,* Vol.
IX, No. 6, December/January 1996.) (Emphasis added.)

This gives the impression that the Request for an advisory opinion
which was made by the General Assembly in 1994 originated in ideas
developed by some NGOs.

9. (*The Indonesian draft resolution in the 49th Session*)   In the
First Committee at the 49th Session (1994), some States' representatives made various kinds of reference, in the general debate on all
disarmament and international security agenda items that was held in
the period 17-20 October 1994, to the earlier decisions of the Non-
Aligned Movement as referred to [in] paragraph 7 above.

While Benin was opposed to

"any initiative which could be counter-productive and which
might necessitate a legal ruling from the International Court
of Justice on questions which are essentially political in nature, such of those of the legality of the use or a threat of the
use of nuclear weapons" (A/C.1/49/PV.3, p. 22),

the United Arab Emirates, Zimbabwe, Namibia, Tanzania and Malaysia
were in favour of such an initiative (A/C.1/49/PV.5-7).

In that situation, Indonesia, on behalf of the members of the Movement of Non-Aligned Countries, introduced on 9 November 1994 a
draft resolution on "Request for an advisory opinion from the International Court of Justice on the legality of the threat or use of nuclear
weapons" (A/C.1/49/L.36) to the First Committee (A/C.1/49/PV.15, p.
7). This draft resolution, which proposed that the General Assembly
should

"*[d]ecide[s],* pursuant to Article 96, paragraph 1, of the Charter, to request the International Court of Justice urgently to render its advisory opinion on the following question: 'Is the threat or use of nuclear weapons in any circumstance permitted under international law?'"

and which was practically identical to the 1993 text (A/C.1/48/L.25) proposed by Indonesia (which however did not press for action at the 48th Session (1993)) (see para. 6, above), became the subject of discussion at the First Committee on 17 and 18 November 1994.

In fact, the text of this question put to the Court, which was originally a part of the Indonesian draft, seems simply to have been copied, though not in exactly the same terms, from the General Assembly resolutions on a "Convention on the prohibition of nuclear weapons and prevention of nuclear war" (which have been adopted as a matter of routine and without being subjected to any substantive discussions in every session of the General Assembly since 1982) with a accompanying draft convention reading:

"The States Parties to this Convention solemnly undertake not to *use or threaten to use nuclear weapons under any circumstances.*" (Article 1.) (Emphasis added.)

(See, e.g., General Assembly resolution 48/76B and Table III, 1-12).

10. (*For and against the Indonesian draft*)   While Malaysia gave its support to this draft resolution by stating that:

"In the present post-cold-war climate, the legal opinion of the International Court of Justice could make an important contribution to the realization of a nuclear-weapons-free world. It could not replace nuclear disarmament initiatives, but it could provide the *legal and moral* parameters within which such initiatives could succeed" (A/C.1/49/PV.22, p. 4) (emphasis added),

Senegal, Chile and Benin asked for the postponement of the discussions in order to have more time for consultations before voting (*ibid.*, pp. 4-6).

The United States, asserting that

"it is even harder to fathom the purpose of a draft resolution requesting such an opinion from the International Court of Justice this year, when further steps to control and eliminate nuclear weapons are being taken, negotiated or contemplated",

urged its colleagues to abstain or to vote against this draft resolution (*ibid.*, p. 6).

Morocco appealed that no action should be taken on the draft resolution since "the consensus on this subject among the Movement of Non-Aligned Countries ha[d] been seriously eroded" (A/C.1/49/PV.24, p. 5). Germany, representing the European Union, was opposed to the draft resolution for the reason that

> "[this] resolution would do nothing to help the ongoing consideration of the questions by the International Court of Justice and might adversely affect the standing of both the First Committee and the Court itself. It could also have wider adverse implications on non-proliferation goals which we all share"

and regretted having failed to convince its sponsors to withdraw it (*ibid.*, p. 6). Hungary immediately echoed the same position.

After Indonesia and Colombia had expressed their opposition to the motion submitted by Morocco for no action on the resolution, this motion was put to the vote and rejected by a recorded vote of 45 in favour, 67 against with 15 abstentions (*ibid.*, p. 7).

Prior to the voting on the Indonesian draft resolution, Russia took the view that

> "the question of the advisability of the use of nuclear weapons is above all a political, not a legal problem . . . Since the Charter of the United Nations and the statutes of the International Court of Justice came into force, nuclear weapons have been considered in States' doctrines not so much as a means of warfare but as a deterrent to war, especially global conflicts. They are therefore different from other weapons, in that they have a political function in the world today" (*ibid.*).

France stated that

> "Trying to utilize for partisan purposes so respected an international institution as the International Court of Justice entails a very serious responsibility: that of putting at risk the credibility of the Court by leading it away from its mission. Indeed, who can seriously believe that the question posed is a legal one? It is, as we all know, a purely political issue . . . Need I recall that, for the first time since the invention of

nuclear weapons, the entire international community is engaged in multilateral negotiations on a universal and verifiable treaty on a comprehensive nuclear-test ban, and that important progress on this issue has already been achieved at Geneva?" (*ibid.*, p. 8)

The United Kingdom stated that:

"the draft resolution . . . risks being seen as a deliberate attempt to exert political pressure over the Court to prejudice its response . . . Secondly, this draft resolution can do nothing to further the various positive diplomatic efforts under way in the field of nuclear disarmament, arms control and non-proliferation, notably on a comprehensive test-ban treaty . . . Thirdly, this draft resolution can do nothing to further global peace and security . . . Fourthly, this draft resolution risks serving the interests of those who wish to distract attention from the destabilizing accumulation of conventional arms and from clandestine programmes aimed at acquiring weapons of mass destruction and developing delivery systems" (*ibid.*).

Germany (on behalf of the European Union) again pointed out that the European Union and its own country could not support the draft resolution (*ibid.*). Malta expressed its opposition and stated that

"[w]ithin the Non-Aligned Movement, to which we belong, we raised the question of withdrawal of the draft resolution. Unfortunately, our request was not acted upon by the Movement" (*ibid.*).

The United Arab Emirates stated that it would not participate in the voting (*ibid.*, p. 9), and Benin once again expressed its support of the motion presented by Morocco (*ibid.*).

On the other hand, Iran and Mexico gave support to the draft resolution (*ibid.*).

11. (Adoption of the Indonesian draft) The draft resolution proposed by Indonesia (on behalf of the Movement of Non-Aligned Countries) was adopted by the First Committee on 7 December 1994, as a result of a recorded vote of 77 votes in favour, 33 against with 21 abstentions (*ibid.*, p. 13).

After the voting, Canada, which had abstained from voting, stated that

"Canada is . . . concerned that the process of seeking an advisory opinion of the International Court could have a negative impact on certain of these ongoing negotiations by diverting attention from them" (*ibid.*).

Australia, which also abstained from the voting, explained that

"we are concerned that seeking an advisory opinion from the International Court of Justice on this issue could have an adverse rather than a positive effect on efforts to advance the process of nuclear disarmament. On the whole, we believe the question is unsuitable for adjudication. It certainly goes beyond a definable field of judicial inquiry and enters into the wider realms of policy and security doctrines of States." (*ibid.*, p. 14.)

Sweden, which had also abstained from the voting, expressed the opinion that "the use of nuclear weapons would not comply with international law" and desired that "the legal situation be clarified as soon as possible by the Court" while stating, however, that that view was simply based on a report of the Swedish Parliament (*ibid.*).

To continue the explanation of votes, Chile stated that it had voted in favour of the draft resolution, as it felt that it should be guided by the majority orientation of the Movement of Non-Aligned Countries (A/C.1/49/PV.25, p. 1), and Japan gave an explanation of its abstention from the voting, saying that

"in the present international situation, pursuing the question of the legality of the use of nuclear weapons may simply result in confrontation between countries. Japan therefore believes that it is more appropriate to steadily promote realistic and specific disarmament measures" (*ibid.*).

China declared that it had not participated in the vote on the draft resolution, hoping that

"in the further promotion of nuclear disarmament and the prevention of nuclear war the General Assembly, the First Committee, the Disarmament Commission and the Conference on Disarmament, which have already played an important role, will continue to do so" (*ibid.*, p. 4).

12. (*My general views on the discussions in the First Commit-*

tee)   I would like to point out that, in spite of the support for the draft resolution proposed by Indonesia, hardly any explanation was given by any delegate backing the resolution as to why the *lex lata* concerning the "threat or use of nuclear weapons" should, as of 1994, require clarification by the International Court of Justice. No positive argument in support of the Request was heard from any delegate who favoured the Indonesian proposal. Rather, the statements made in the First Committee by a number of those delegates appear for the most part to have been no more than appeals for the elimination of nuclear weapons.

In addition, the substance of the question or the wording of that question to be asked of the Court, i.e., "[i]s the threat or use of nuclear weapons in any circumstance permitted under international law?" was scarcely considered by any of the member States in the General Assembly. The questions of what would constitute the "threat" of nuclear weapons, as opposed to the "threat of use" (a phrase employed in many United Nations resolutions) and whether the "threat" would imply the "possession" or "production" of nuclear weapons, together with the question of what was meant by "any circumstance", were not raised by any delegate in the First Committee. However, it remains a fact that the Indonesian draft resolution was adopted by a majority in the First Committee.

13. (*Plenary meeting*)   The draft resolution adopted by the First Committee on 7 December 1994 by 77 votes in favour, 33 against with 21 abstentions (as stated in para. 11, above) was taken up at the Plenary Meeting on 15 December 1994 and was adopted by a recorded vote of 78 in favour, 43 against with 38 abstentions as resolution 49/75K (Table I). France, Russia, the United Kingdom and the United States were among the opposing States, and China did not participate in the voting. Except for New Zealand and San Marino, there were no other countries in favour of the resolution in the category of West European and Other countries.

14. (*Conclusion*)   I have thus demonstrated that the "question", which itself appears to me to be inadequate as a request for an advisory opinion of the Court under Article 96(1) of the Charter of the United Nations (as explained in para. 3, above), was drafted without any adequate statement of reasoning in support of any real need to ask the Court to rule on the "legality or illegality" of the "threat or use" (if not the "use or threat of use") of nuclear weapons or, in more general

terms, of nuclear weapons themselves. It is certain that the Request did not reflect a meaningful consensus of the member States of the United Nations or even of its Non-Aligned Members.

TABLE I

(Note: the nuclear-weapon States under the NPT are underlined; "R" denotes recorded vote)

Voting on the 1994 Resolution Requesting the Court's Advisory Opinion

The 49th Session (1994)

A/C.1/49/L.36: Sponsored by: Indonesia (on behalf of the States Members of the United Nations that are members of the Movement of Non-Aligned Countries)

A/RES/49/75K: adopted on 15 December 1994 by R78-43-38

> For: (78) (*names of States not reproduced*)
>
> Against: (43) Albania, Andorra, Argentina, Belgium, Benin, Bulgaria, Cambodia, Comoros, Côte d'Ivoire, Czech Republic, Denmark, Djibouti, Estonia, Finland, France, Gabon, Georgia, Germany, Greece, Hungary, Iceland, Israel, Italy, Latvia, Luxembourg, Malta, Mauritania, Monaco, Netherlands, Poland, Portugal, Republic of Korea, Romania, Russian Federation, Senegal, Slovakia, Slovenia, Spain, Tajikistan, The FYR of Macedonia, Turkey, United Kingdom, United States
>
> Abstaining: (38) Antigua and Barbuda, Armenia, Australia, Austria, Azerbaijan, Bahrain, Belarus, Belize, Cameroon, Canada, Central African Republic, Chile, Croatia, Dominica, Eritrea, Ghana, Guinea, Ireland, Jamaica, Japan, Kazakhstan, Kyrgyzstan, Liechtenstein, Lithuania, Maldives, Micronesia (Fed. States of), Niger, Norway, Republic of Moldova, Swaziland, Sweden, Togo, Trinidad and Tobago, Tunisia, Turkmenistan, Ukraine, Uzbekistan, Vanuatu

Note: China was absent from the voting

II. ONE ASPECT OF NUCLEAR DISARMAMENT — THE UNSUCCESSFUL EFFORTS OVER A LONG PERIOD TO BRING ABOUT A CONVENTION "PROHIBITING THE USE OR THREAT OF USE OF NUCLEAR WEAPONS UNDER ANY CIRCUMSTANCES" AS AN IMMEDIATE BACKGROUND TO THE REQUEST TO THE COURT

(1) *Declaration on the Non-Use or the Prohibition of Nuclear Weapons*

15. (*Immediate background of the Request*)   While the General Assembly resolution requesting an advisory opinion of the Court was prepared by Indonesia on behalf of the Non-Aligned Movement in 1994, as mentioned in paragraph 9 above, the following circumstances are noted as its immediate background.

The prohibition of the use of nuclear weapons had been an earnest desire of a group of some member States of the United Nations and had been presented to the General Assembly throughout a long period extending over several decades. A review of the development of the idea of that prohibition in the United Nations General Assembly may reveal the background to resolution 49/75K and is extremely useful when one evaluates that resolution, despite the Court's opinion, to a part of which I have already referred in paragraph 5 above, which states:

> "once the Assembly has asked, by adopting a resolution, for an advisory opinion on a legal question, the Court, in determining whether there are any compelling reasons for it to refuse to give such an opinion, will not have regard to the origins or to the political history of the request, or to the distribution of votes in respect of the adopted resolution" (Court's Opinion, para. 16).

16. (*The 1961 Declaration on the prohibition of the use of nuclear weapons*)   The General Assembly in its 16th Session (1961), when passing resolution 1653 (XVI) entitled "Declaration on the prohibition of the use of nuclear and thermo-nuclear weapons", declared that

> "the use of nuclear and thermo-nuclear weapons is . . . a direct violation of the Charter of the United Nations; . . . is contrary to the rules of international law and to the laws of humanity; [and] . . . is a war directed . . . against mankind in general"

and that

> "[a]ny State using nuclear and thermo-nuclear weapons is to be considered as violating the Charter of the United Nations, as acting contrary to the laws of humanity and as committing a crime against mankind and civilization."

This resolution originated from the draft resolution (A/C.1/L.292), sponsored by some 12 States, and introduced by Ethiopia. After it had been subjected to extensive discussion, both for and against, in the First Committee, the Plenary Meeting adopted the part comprising the above-mentioned declaration by a recorded vote of 56 in favour, 19 against, with 26 abstentions. The Resolution as a whole, itself comprising the declaration, was adopted by a recorded vote of 55 in favour, 20 against, with 26 abstentions on 24 November 1961 (Table II, 1).

The resolution, however, did nothing more than request the Secretary-General of the United Nations to consult member States in order to ascertain the possibility of convening a special conference for signing a convention on the prohibition of the use of nuclear weapons.

17. (*The first special disarmament session*)   Nearly two decades elapsed in which no practical action was taken to implement the 1961 resolution. Being "[a]larmed by the threat to the very survival of mankind posed by the existence of nuclear weapons and the continuing arms race," the General Assembly held in May/June 1978 its first session devoted to disarmament, that is, the Tenth Special Session (*GAOR*, 10th Sp. Sess., suppl. 4; A/S-10/2). The General Assembly at this first special disarmament session adopted a "Final Document" covering nearly 130 paragraphs including a programme of action, in which it was stated that "[a] convention should be concluded prohibiting the development, production, stockpiling and use of radiological weapons" (*ibid.*, para. 76). Among a number of proposals put forth at this special session for consideration, there was a draft resolution submitted by Ethiopia and India: "Non-use of nuclear weapons and prevention of nuclear war", the intention of which was to have the General Assembly declare that:

> "(a) *The use of nuclear weapons* will be a violation of the

Charter of the United Nations and a crime against humanity;

(b) *The use of nuclear weapons* should therefore be prohibited, pending nuclear disarmament" (*ibid.*, para.
125(z); A/S-10/AC.1/L.11) (emphasis added).

In that special session neither this nor any other particular resolution
was adopted.

18. (*The 1978 resolution on "Non-use of nuclear weapons and
prevention of nuclear war"*)   Ever since the 33rd Session (1978), that
is, a regular session which was held a few months later, the General
Assembly has included on its agenda an item entitled: "Review of the
implementation of the recommendations and decisions adopted by the
General Assembly at its tenth special session" (the item which has
appeared at every session of the General Assembly down to the present
day).

A draft resolution (A/C.1/33/L.2), submitted by some 34 States and
introduced by India, entitled "Non-use of nuclear weapons and prevention of nuclear war" (which was practically identical to the one submitted by Ethiopia and India at the first special disarmament session,
as mentioned in para. 17, above) was adopted at the Plenary Meeting
on 14 December 1978 by a recorded vote of 103 in favour, 18 against
with 18 abstentions as resolution 33/71B (Table II, 2).

Under this 1978 resolution, which followed the spirit of the 1961
Declaration, the General Assembly declared that

"*[t]he use of nuclear weapons* will be a violation of the Charter of the United Nations and a crime against humanity [and]
should therefore be *prohibited*, pending nuclear disarmament"
(emphasis added).

and requested all States to submit proposals concerning the *non-use* of
nuclear weapons and avoidance of nuclear war in order that the question of an international convention on the subject might be discussed
at a subsequent session.

It may be noted that the idea of the *prohibition of the use of nuclear
weapons* was introduced here for the first time as a part of the declaration in a General Assembly resolution.

19. (*The 1980 and 1981 resolutions*)   Thereafter, and at the 35th

(1980) and the 36th (1981) sessions, practically identical draft resolutions, including declarations which were similar to the 1978 resolution, prepared by almost the same States (between 20 and 30 in number) were introduced by India and adopted with a similar vote, almost the same countries being against each time and almost the same countries abstaining each time (Table II, 3 and 4).

It should be pointed out, however, that the expression reading the "threat of use" of nuclear weapons and the idea that not only the "use" but also, in parallel, the "threat of use" of nuclear weapons should be prohibited was introduced only in 1980 for the first time. No explanation was given by the sponsoring State nor did any discussion take place in the General Assembly meetings on what would constitute the "threat of use" of nuclear weapons or, more particularly, on whether the "possession" or the "production" of nuclear weapons would constitute a "threat of use".

TABLE II

*(Note: the nuclear-weapon States under the NPT are underlined;
"R" denotes recorded vote)*

Voting on the UN Declarations Relating
to the Use of Nuclear Weapons

1. **The 1961 "Declaration on the Prohibition of the Use of Nuclear Weapons and Thermo-Nuclear Weapons"**

The 16th Session (1961)
A/C.1/L.292 and Add. 1-3: Sponsored by: (12) Ceylon, Ethiopia, Ghana, Guinea, Indonesia, Liberia, Libya, Nigeria, Somalia, Sudan, Togo, Tunisia
A/RES/1653 (XVI): adopted on 24 November 1961 by R55-20-26
> For: (55) USSR (*names of other States not reproduced*)
> Against: (20) Australia, Belgium, Canada, China, Costa Rica, France, Greece, Guatemala, Ireland, Italy, Luxembourg, Netherlands, New Zealand, Nicaragua, Portugal, South Africa, Spain, Turkey, United Kingdom, United States
> Abstaining: (26) Argentina, Austria, Bolivia, Brazil, Chile, Colombia, Denmark, Ecuador, El Salvador, Federation of Malaya,

Finland, Haiti, Honduras, Iceland, Iran, Israel, Norway, Pakistan, Panama, Paraguay, Peru, Philippines, Sweden, Thailand, Uruguay, Venezuela

2. The 1978 Resolution on "Non-Use of Nuclear Weapons and Prevention of Nuclear War"

The 33rd Session (1978)

A/C.1/33/L.2: Sponsored by: (34) Algeria, Argentina, Cyprus, Ethiopia, India, Indonesia, Malaysia, Nigeria and Yugoslavia, with the later addition of Angola, Barbados, Bhutan, Bolivia, Burundi, Colombia, the Congo, Cuba, Ecuador, Egypt, Guinea, Jordan, Liberia, Madagascar, Mali, Mauritius, Morocco, Peru, Romania, Senegal, Sri Lanka, Syrian Arab Republic, the United Republic of Cameroon, Uruguay, Zaire

A/RES/33/71B: adopted on 14 December 1978 by R103-18-18

For: (103) China (*names of other States not reproduced*)

Against: (18) Australia, Belgium, Canada, Denmark, France, Germany (Fed. Rep.), Greece, Iceland, Ireland, Italy, Luxembourg, Netherlands, New Zealand, Norway, Portugal, Turkey, United Kingdom, United States

Abstaining: (18) Austria, Bulgaria, Byelorussian SSR, Czechoslovakia, El Salvador, Finland, Gabon, German Democratic Republic, Hungary, Israel, Japan, Mongolia, Nicaragua, Poland, Spain, Sweden, Ukrainian SSR, USSR

3. The 1980 resolution on "Non-Use of Nuclear Weapons and Prevention of Nuclear War"

The 35th Session (1980)

A/C.1/35/L.22: Sponsored by: (24) Algeria, Angola, Argentina, the Congo, Ethiopia, India, Indonesia, Jamaica, Madagascar, Nigeria, Peru, Romania, Sri Lanka, Uruguay, Yugoslavia and Zaire with the later additions of Bhutan, Costa Rica, Cyprus, Ecuador, Egypt, Malaysia, Qatar, Yemen

A/RES/35/152D: adopted on 12 December 1980 by R112-19-14

For: (112) China (*names of other States not reproduced*)

Against: (19) Australia, Belgium, Denmark, France, Germany (Fed. Rep.), Greece, Iceland, Ireland, Israel, Italy, Japan, Luxembourg, Netherlands, New Zealand, Norway, Portugal, Turkey, United Kingdom, United States

Abstaining: (14) Austria, Bulgaria, Byelorussian SSR, Canada, Czechoslovakia, German Democratic Republic, Hungary, Malawi, Mongolia, Poland, Spain, Sweden, Ukrainian SSR, USSR

4. **The 1981 Resolution on "Non-Use of Nuclear Weapons and Prevention of Nuclear War"**

The 36th Session (1981)

A/C.1/36/L.29: Sponsored by: (30) Algeria, Argentina, the Bahamas, Barbados, Bhutan, Colombia, Cyprus, Ecuador, Egypt, Ethiopia, India, Indonesia, Jamaica, Jordan, Madagascar, Malaysia, Nigeria, Peru, Romania, Yemen, Yugoslavia with the later additions of Bangladesh, Congo, Ghana, Guinea, Mali, Niger, Qatar, Rwanda, Sri Lanka

A/RES/36/92I: adopted on 9 December 1981 by R121-19-6

> For: (121) <u>China</u>, <u>USSR</u> (*names of other States not reproduced*)
>
> Against: (19) Australia, Belgium, Canada, Denmark, <u>France</u>, Germany (Fed. Rep.), Iceland, Ireland, Italy, Japan, Luxembourg, Netherlands, New Zealand, Norway, Portugal, Spain, Turkey, <u>United Kingdom</u>, <u>United States</u>
>
> Abstaining: (6) Austria, Comoros, Finland, Greece, Israel, Sweden

(2) *The 1982-1995 Resolutions on the Convention on the Prohibition of the Use of Nuclear Weapons*

20. (*The second special disarmament session*)   The General Assembly, which was not satisfied with the development of disarmament so far, held, in June/July 1982, its second session devoted to disarmament, that is, the Twelfth Special Session, and approved the "Report of its *Ad Hoc* Committee" (*GAOR*, 12th Sp. Sess., Suppl. 6; A/S-12/32) as the "Concluding Document" of that session in which reference was made to a draft resolution proposed by India (among various draft resolutions put forward in that session). The Indian draft read:

> "*The General Assembly,* . . .
>
> *Decides* to adopt an international convention . . . , *prohibiting the use or threat of use* of nuclear weapons *under any circumstances*, pending nuclear disarmament." (A/S-12/32, para. 20; A/S-12/AC.1/L.4.) (Penultimate and final emphasis added.)

The draft of the "Convention on the Prohibition of the Use of Nuclear Weapons" was annexed to this draft resolution which read:

"The States Parties to this Convention . . .

Convinced that *any use* of nuclear weapons constitutes a violation of the Charter of the United Nations and a crime against humanity,

Convinced that this Convention would be a step towards the complete elimination of nuclear weapons leading to general and complete disarmament under strict and effective international control,

Determined to continue negotiations for the achievement of this goal,

Article 1. The States Parties to this Convention solemnly undertake *not to use or threaten to use nuclear weapons under any circumstances.*" (Emphasis added.)

In fact this draft resolution with the annexed draft of the Convention originally submitted by India at this special disarmament session was subsequently put forward by India during each regular session of the General Assembly from 1982 to 1995, inclusive, as explained below.

21. (*The 1982 resolution on "Convention on the prohibition of the use of nuclear weapons"*) The 37th Session (1982) of the General Assembly which met a few months after the second special disarmament session, that is, in the fall of 1982, included on its agenda item: "Review and implementation of the Concluding Document of the Twelfth Special Session of the General Assembly".[1] Some twenty States presented a draft resolution (A/C.1/37/L.4), which was introduced by India in the First Committee. This draft resolution, after some minor revisions by the sponsoring States, was adopted by the Plenary Meeting on 13 December 1982 as resolution 37/100C: "Convention on the prohibition of the use of nuclear weapons" as a result of a recorded vote of 117 in favour, 17 against with 8 abstentions (Table III, 1).

---

[1]This agenda item remains until the present day at every session of the General Assembly but with the addition of sub-item "convention on prohibition of the use of nuclear weapons: Report of the Committee on Disarmament" from the 38th Session until the 42nd Sessions, inclusive. From the 43rd Session the sub-item simply referred to the convention on the prohibition of the use of nuclear weapons without making any mention of the Report of the Committee on Disarmament.

The resolution read:

"The General Assembly,

Reaffirming the declaration that *the use of nuclear weapons* would be a violation of the Charter of the United Nations and a crime against humanity . . .

1. *Requests* the Committee on Disarmament to undertake, on a priority basis, negotiations with a view to achieving agreement on an international convention prohibiting the *use or threat of use of nuclear weapons under any circumstances,* taking as a basis the text of the annexed draft Convention . . ." (third and final emphasis added).

The draft Convention, which had been included in the Indian draft resolution submitted to the second special disarmament session (as quoted in paragraph 20 above) was annexed to this resolution.

The resolution certainly originated in the Indian draft proposal at the second special disarmament session of that year but, unlike that original Indian proposal, which would have led *the General Assembly itself to decide to adopt an international convention,* it requested that *negotiations should be undertaken in the Committee on Disarmament* (known presently as the Conference on Disarmament) in Geneva with a view to achieving agreement on an international convention "prohibiting the use or threat of use of nuclear weapons under any circumstances".

22. (*The phrase "the use or threat of use of nuclear weapons under any circumstances"*)   The phrase "*the use or threat of use* of nuclear weapons *under any circumstances*" (emphasis added) was first used in a General Assembly resolution in 1982. However, there was no discussion of the phrase in the General Assembly. Furthermore, that phrase was initially used in the context of a possible prohibition in a future international convention.

It is important to note that the wording of the question in the Request presented to the Court that reads: "Is the *threat* or use of nuclear weapons *in any circumstance* permitted under international law?" (emphasis added), which seems to have originated in the phrase used in a twelve-year old (1982) General Assembly resolution, is in fact different in that the question in the 1994 Request singles out the "threat" of nuclear weapons and leaves open the possibility that this "threat" —

not the "threat of use"- might be interpreted as meaning the "possession" or the "production" of those weapons. It is even more important to note that the phrase "threat of use" in the 1982 resolution was used in a quite different context, as I explained above, namely, with respect to a convention to be agreed upon in future.

23. (*From 1983 to 1995*)   In the 38th Session (1983), the General Assembly, "noting with regret that the Committee on Disarmament, during its session in 1983, was not able to undertake [such] negotiations", reiterated its request to the Conference on Disarmament[2] in Geneva

"to commence negotiations, as a matter of priority, in order to achieve agreement on an international convention prohibiting the *use or threat of use* of nuclear weapons under any circumstances, taking as a basis the text of [the annexed draft Convention which was identical to that of 1982]"[3] (emphasis added).

In every session of the General Assembly since 1982 until 1995 (37th-50th Sessions), under the same agenda item as referred to in paragraph 21 above, practically the same States presented practically identical draft resolutions with the attached draft convention which did not change at all during a fourteen-year period (which draft resolutions were invariably introduced by India) and these draft resolutions were adopted as a result of practically the same voting (Table III, 1-14). In fact, while the number of sponsoring States remained almost steady, the number of States which took a negative position on the resolution increased.

24. (*Repetition of resolutions with the same content*)   The *request* of the General Assembly in New York that the Conference on Disarmament in Geneva should undertake negotiations and the General Assembly's *regret* that the Conference had failed to do so during the previous year, were repeated at every subsequent session down to the

---

[2]From 7 February 1984, the date of commencement of its annual session, the Committee on Disarmament was to be known as the Conference on Disarmament.

[3]The wording "as a matter of policy" was dropped since the 49th Session (1994) and the word "possible" was added so that it read "as a possible basis" since the 48th Session (1993).

50th Session (1995) in practically the same wording.[4] The repetition of the same resolutions during this period of over fourteen sessions appears to indicate that the Conference on Disarmament (formerly the Committee on Disarmament) was never able to or never attempted to negotiate to achieve agreement on an international convention "prohibiting the use or threat of use of nuclear weapons under any circumstances". In other words *the cumulation of resolutions have not produced any noticeable effect.*

25. (*Motive behind the Request for advisory opinion*)   It appears that the 1994 Request for advisory opinion, particularly in view of the drafting of its text referring to "*the threat or use* of nuclear weapons in any circumstance" (emphasis added), was prompted by a group of practically the same States which, since 1982, had been sponsoring the resolutions calling for the conclusion of "an international convention prohibiting the *use or threat of use* of nuclear weapons under any circumstances" (emphasis added) (resolutions referred to in Table III, 1-14), without any meaningful discussion on what was meant by the expressions "threat or use of nuclear weapons" or "any circumstances". I consider it likely that the "threat" of nuclear weapons would, in the view of some of those States which sponsored the resolution, comprehend the "production" and the "possession" of nuclear weapons.

Now the Request, by purporting to ask whether "the *threat or use* of nuclear weapons [is] in any circumstance *permitted* under international law" (emphasis added), was in fact attempting to secure the Court's endorsement of an alleged legal axiom — the *threat* (which may imply the possession or the production) *or use* of nuclear weapons is *not permitted* under international law *in any circumstance* — in order to produce a breakthrough, thus laterally achieving agreement on the Convention which would establish the illegality of nuclear weapons themselves. It is to me quite clear that this Request was prepared and adopted with highly political motives which do not correspond to any genuine legal mandate of a judicial institution. This certainly does not accord with the role that the advisory function of the Court has, in essence, to play under Article 96(1) of the Charter of the United Nations.

---

[4]In the resolutions of the 48th and 49th Session, the preambular part, as quoted in the test, was simplified to read "was not able to undertake negotiations on this subject".

TABLE III

(Note: the nuclear-weapon States under the NPT are underlined;
"R" denotes recorded vote)

Voting on the 1982-1995 Resolutions on "Convention on the Prohibition of the Use of Nuclear Weapons"

1. The 37th Session (1982)

A/C.1/37/L.4 and Rev. 1: Sponsored by: (20) Algeria, Argentina, Bahamas, Bangladesh, Bhutan, Congo, Cyprus, Ecuador, Egypt, Ethiopia, Ghana, Guyana, Indonesia, Jamaica, Madagascar, Mali, Nigeria, Romania, Yugoslavia, Zambia

A/RES/37/100C: adopted on 13 December 1982 by R117-17-8

> For: (117) China, USSR *(names of other States not reproduced)*
>
> Against: (17) Australia, Belgium, Canada, Denmark, France, Germany (Fed. Rep.), Iceland, Italy, Luxembourg, Netherlands, New Zealand, Norway, Portugal, Spain, Turkey, United Kingdom, United States
>
> Abstaining: (8) Austria, Finland, Greece, Guatemala, Ireland, Israel, Japan, Paraguay

2. The 38th Session (1983)

A/C.1/38/L.55: Sponsored by: (16) Algeria, Argentina, Bahamas, Bangladesh, Bhutan, Congo, Ecuador, Egypt, Ethiopia, India, Indonesia, Madagascar, Nigeria, Romania, Yugoslavia, with the later addition of Viet Nam

A/RES/38/73G: adopted on 16 December 1983 by R126-17-6

> For: (126) China, USSR *(names of other States not reproduced)*
>
> Against: (17) Australia, Belgium, Canada, Denmark, France, Germany (Fed. Rep.), Iceland, Italy, Luxembourg, Netherlands, New Zealand, Norway, Portugal, Spain, Turkey, United Kingdom, United States
>
> Abstaining: (8) Austria, Greece, Ireland, Israel, Japan, Philippines

3. The 39th Session (1984)

A/C.1/39/L.50: Sponsored by: (14) Algeria, Argentina, Bahamas, Bangladesh, Bhutan, Ecuador, Egypt, Ethiopia, India, Indonesia, Madagascar, Romania, Viet Nam, Yugoslavia

A/RES/39/63H: adopted on 12 December 1984 by R128-17-5

> For: (128) China, USSR *(names of other States not reproduced)*

Against: (17) Australia, Belgium, Canada, Denmark, <u>France</u>, Germany (Fed. Rep.), Iceland, Italy, Luxembourg, Netherlands, New Zealand, Norway, Portugal, Spain, Turkey, <u>United Kingdom</u>, <u>United States</u>

Abstaining: (5) Austria, Greece, Ireland, Israel, Japan

4. The 40th Session (1985)

A/C.1/40/L.26: Sponsored by: (15) Algeria, Argentina, Bahamas, Bangladesh, Bhutan, Ecuador, Egypt, Ethiopia, India, Indonesia, Madagascar, Nigeria, Romania, Viet Nam, Yugoslavia

A/RES/40/151F: adopted on 16 December 1985 by R126-17-6

For: (126) <u>China</u>, USSR (*names of other States not reproduced*)

Against: (17) Australia, Belgium, Canada, Denmark, <u>France</u>, Germany (Fed. Rep.), Iceland, Italy, Luxembourg, Netherlands, New Zealand, Norway, Portugal, Spain, Turkey, <u>United Kingdom</u>, <u>United States</u>

Abstaining: (6) Austria, Greece, Grenada, Ireland, Israel, Japan

5. The 41st Session (1986)

A/C.1/41/L.49: Sponsored by: (13) Algeria, Argentina, Bangladesh, Bhutan, Ecuador, Egypt, Ethiopia, India, Indonesia, Madagascar, Romania, Viet Nam, Yugoslavia

A/RES/41/60F: adopted on 3 December 1986 by R132-17-4

For: (132) <u>China</u>, <u>USSR</u> (*names of other States not reproduced*)

Against: (17) Australia, Belgium, Canada, Denmark, <u>France</u>, Germany (Fed. Rep.), Iceland, Italy, Luxembourg, Netherlands, New Zealand, Norway, Portugal, Spain, Turkey, <u>United Kingdom</u>, <u>United States</u>

Abstaining: (4) Greece, Ireland, Israel, Japan

6. The 42nd Session (1987)

A/C.1/42/L.28: Sponsored by: (13) Algeria, Argentina, Bangladesh, Bhutan, Ecuador, Egypt, Ethiopia, India, Indonesia, Romania, Yugoslavia, with the later additions of Madagascar, Viet Nam

A/RES/42/39C: adopted on 30 November 1987 by R135-17-4

For: (135) <u>China</u>, <u>USSR</u> (*names of other States not reproduced*)

Against: (17) Australia, Belgium, Canada, Denmark, <u>France</u>, Germany (Fed. Rep.), Iceland, Italy, Luxembourg, Netherlands, New Zealand, Norway, Portugal, Spain, Turkey, <u>United King-</u>

dom, United States

Abstaining: (4) Greece, Ireland, Israel, Japan

7. The 43rd Session (1988)

A/C.1/43/L.55: Sponsored by: (14) Algeria, Argentina, Bangladesh, Bhutan, Ecuador, Egypt, Ethiopia, India, Indonesia, Madagascar, Romania, Viet Nam,Yugoslavia, with the later addition of Malaysia

A/RES/43/76E: adopted on 7 December 1988 by R133-17-4

> For: (133) China, USSR (names of other States not reproduced)
>
> Against: (17) Australia, Belgium, Canada, Denmark, France, Germany (Fed. Rep.), Iceland, Italy, Luxembourg, Netherlands, New Zealand, Norway, Portugal, Spain, Turkey, United Kingdom, United States
>
> Abstaining: (4) Greece, Ireland, Israel, Japan

8. The 44th Session (1989)

A/C.1/44/L.39: Sponsored by: (12) Algeria, Bangladesh, Bhutan, Ecuador, Egypt, India, Indonesia, Malaysia, Romania, Viet Nam,Yugoslavia, with the later addition of Madagascar

A/RES/44/117C: adopted on 15 December 1989 by R134-17-4

> For: (134) China, USSR (names of other States not reproduced)
>
> Against: (17) Australia, Belgium, Canada, Denmark, France, Germany (Fed. Rep.), Iceland, Italy, Luxembourg, Netherlands, New Zealand, Norway, Portugal, Spain, Turkey, United Kingdom, United States
>
> Abstaining: (4) Greece, Ireland, Israel, Japan

9. The 45th Session (1990)

A/C.1/45/L.25: Sponsored by: (14) Afghanistan, Algeria, Argentina, Bangladesh, Bhutan, Ecuador, Egypt, Ethiopia, India, Indonesia, Madagascar, Malaysia, Viet Nam,Yugoslavia

A/RES/45/59B: adopted on 4 December 1990 by R125-17-10

> For: (125) China, USSR *(names of other States not reproduced)*
>
> Against: (17) Australia, Belgium, Canada, Denmark, France, Germany, Iceland, Italy, Luxembourg, Netherlands, New Zealand, Norway, Portugal, Spain, Turkey, United Kingdom, United States
>
> Abstaining: (10) Bulgaria, Czechoslovakia, Greece, Hungary, Ireland, Israel, Japan, Liechtenstein, Poland, Romania

10. The 46th Session (1991)

A/C.1/46/L.20: Sponsored by: (15) Afghanistan, Algeria, Bangladesh, Bhutan, Ecuador, Egypt, Ethiopia, India, Indonesia, Madagascar, Malaysia, Viet Nam, Yugoslavia, with the later additions of Bolivia, Lao People's Democratic Republic

A/RES/46/37D: adopted on 6 December 1991 by R122-16-22

For: (122) China, USSR (*names of other States not reproduced*)

Against: (16) Australia, Belgium, Canada, Denmark, France, Germany, Italy, Luxembourg, Netherlands, New Zealand, Norway, Portugal, Spain, Turkey, United Kingdom, United States

Abstaining: (22) Albania, Argentina, Austria, Bulgaria, Czechoslovakia, Estonia, Finland, Greece, Hungary, Iceland, Ireland, Israel, Japan, Latvia, Liechtenstein, Lithuania, Marshall Islands, Poland, Republic of Korea, Romania, Samoa, Sweden

11. The 47th Session (1992)

A/C.1/47/L.33: Sponsored by: (15) Algeria, Bangladesh, Bolivia, Costa Rica, Ecuador, Egypt, Ethiopia, India, Indonesia, Lao People's Democratic Republic, Madagascar, Malaysia, Vietnam, with the later additions of Bhutan, Democratic People's Republic of Korea

A/RES/47/53C: adopted on 9 December 1992 by R126-21-21

For: (126) China, USSR (names of other States not reproduced)

Against: (21) Australia, Belgium, Bulgaria, Canada, Czechoslovakia, Denmark, France, Germany, Hungary, Iceland, Italy, Luxembourg, Netherlands, New Zealand, Norway, Poland, Portugal, Spain, Turkey, United Kingdom, United States

Abstaining: (21) Armenia, Austria, Estonia, Finland, Greece, Ireland, Israel, Japan, Latvia, Liechtenstein, Lithuania, Malta, Marshall Islands, Republic of Korea, Republic of Moldova, Romania, Samoa, San Marino, Slovenia, Solomon Islands, Sweden

12. The 48th Session (1993)

A/C.1/48/L.13 and Rev. 1 and 2: Sponsored by: (20) Algeria, Bangladesh, Bhutan, Bolivia, Colombia, Costa Rica, Democratic People's Republic of Korea, Ecuador, Egypt, Ethiopia, India, Indonesia, Lao People's Democratic Republic, Madagascar, Malaysia, Mexico, Vietnam, with the later additions of Haiti, Honduras, Sudan

A/RES/48/76B: adopted on 16 December 1993 by R120-23-24

For: (120) China (*names of other States not reproduced*)

Against: (23) Andorra, Belgium, Bulgaria, Canada, Czech Republic, Denmark, Finland, France, Germany, Hungary, Iceland, Italy, Luxembourg, Monaco, Netherlands, Norway, Poland, Portugal, Slovakia, Spain, Turkey, United Kingdom, United States

Abstaining: (24) Albania, Argentina, Armenia, Australia, Austria, Estonia, Georgia, Greece, Ireland, Israel, Japan, Latvia, Liechtenstein, Lithuania, Malta, Marshall Islands, New Zealand, Republic of Korea, Republic of Moldova, Romania, Russian Federation, Slovenia, Sweden, The FYR Macedonia

13. The 49th Session (1994)

A/C.1/49/L.31: Sponsored by: (20) Bangladesh, Bhutan, Bolivia, Colombia, Democratic People's Republic of Korea, Ecuador, Egypt, Ethiopia, Honduras, India, Indonesia, the Lao People's Democratic Republic, Madagascar, Malaysia, Mexico, Myanmar, Sudan, Viet Nam, with the later additions of Costa Rica, Haiti

A/RES/49/76E: adopted on 15 December 1994 by R115-24-31

For: (115) China (names of other States not reproduced)

Against: (24) Andorra, Belgium, Canada, Czech Republic, Denmark, Finland, France, Germany, Greece, Hungary, Iceland, Italy, Luxembourg, Monaco, Netherlands, Norway, Poland, Portugal, Romania, Slovakia, Spain, Turkey, United Kingdom, United States

Abstaining: (31) Albania, Argentina, Armenia, Australia, Austria, Belarus, Bulgaria, Croatia, Estonia, Fiji, Georgia, Ireland, Israel, Japan, Kazakhstan, Latvia, Liechtenstein, Lithuania, Malta, Marshall Islands, Micronesia (Federated States of), New Zealand, Republic of Korea, Republic of Moldova, Russian Federation, Samoa, Slovenia, Sweden, Tajikistan, The FYR Macedonia, Ukraine

14. The 50th Session (1995)

A/C.1/50/L.47: Sponsored by: Bangladesh, Belize, Bhutan, Bolivia, Botswana, Brunei Darussalam, Colombia, Democratic People's Republic of Korea, Ecuador, Egypt, Ethiopia, Haiti, India, Indonesia, Iran (Islamic Republic of), Kenya, Lao People's Democratic Republic, Madagascar, Malawi, Malaysia, Mexico, Micronesia (Federated States of), Myanmar, Nepal, Nigeria, Philippines, Sudan, Vietnam

A/RES/50/71E: adopted on 12 December 1995 by R108-27-28

For: (108) China (*names of other States not reproduced*)

Against: (27) Andorra, Belgium, Bulgaria, Canada, Czech Republic,
        Denmark, Finland, France, Germany, Greece, Hungary, Ice-
        land, Italy, Latvia, Lithuania, Luxembourg, Monaco, Nether-
        lands, Norway, Poland, Portugal, Romania, Slovakia, Spain,
        Turkey, United Kingdom, United States
Abstaining: (28) Afghanistan, Albania, Antigua and Barbuda, Argen-
        tina, Armenia, Australia, Austria, Bahamas, Barbados, Belarus,
        Croatia, Equatorial Guinea, Estonia, Georgia, Ireland, Israel,
        Japan, Liechtenstein, Malta, New Zealand, Republic of Korea,
        Republic of Moldova, Russian Federation, Slovenia, Sweden,
        The FYR Macedonia, Ukraine, Uzbekistan

III. ANOTHER ASPECT OF NUCLEAR DISARMAMENT
— NUCLEAR DISARMAMENT IN THE PERIOD OF
THE COLD WAR AND THE ROAD TO THE CONCLUSION
OF THE NON-PROLIFERATION TREATY

(1) *The Nuclear Arms Race and the Control of Nuclear Weapons in the Period of the Cold War; the Emergence of the Non-Proliferation Treaty*

(a) Development of Nuclear Disarmament

26. (*Arms race between the United States and the Soviet Union*) After the success of the first nuclear weapons test by the Soviet Union in 1949 and the first test of hydrogen bombs by the United States in 1952, and even with the participation of France, the United Kingdom and later China in the group of States in possession of nuclear weapons, these weapons remained a source of friction between the United States and the Soviet Union in the post-war period known as the Cold War. However, in parallel to the arms race between them, the United States and the Soviet Union, which were themselves fully aware of the catastrophic effects of nuclear weapons once actually used, recognized that some restraints would be needed.

In their search for the means of achieving restraints on the quantity of strategic nuclear weapons or even the freezing of these weapons, the United States and the Soviet Union made the Joint Statement of Agreed Principles for Disarmament Negotiations (UN Doc. A/4879) in 1961. The plan included a gradual process of elimination and suspension of the production of weapons of mass destruction — such as nuclear weapons — and marked the beginning of the negotiation between the two countries of the Strategic Arms Limitation Talks (SALT I) in 1969, which was ended by the conclusion of the 1972 Anti-Ballistic Missile (ABM) Treaty, and was followed by SALT II in 1972. The Treaty on the Limitation of Strategic Offensive Arms (SALT II Treaty) was concluded in 1979 but has never been ratified. Negotiations within the framework of the Strategic Arms Reduction Talks (START) commenced in 1982.

27. (*Committee and later Conference on Disarmament (CD) in Geneva*) With the agreement of the United States and the Soviet Union and with the endorsement of the United Nations under resolution 1722 (XVI) on "Question of disarmament", the Eighteen-Nations Committee on Disarmament (ENDC) was set up in Geneva in 1961, composed of an equal number of States in each "bloc" — that is, five on each side, together with eight additional non-aligned countries — as a forum for global disarmament. The ENDC became the Conference of the Committee on Disarmament (CCD) with the membership of twenty-six States (which was increased to thirty-one in 1975) in 1969, and, pursuant to the decision of the 1978 first special disarmament session of the United Nations General Assembly (the conference being then composed of forty States, including all five nuclear-weapon States), changed its name to the Committee on Disarmament. This has, since 1984, been in existence as the Conference on Disarmament (CD), an organ of disarmament negotiations.

28. (*Partial Test-Ban Treaty*) In an international context that included the Cuban missile crisis in October 1962 and with the agreement of the United States and the Soviet Union, the Treaty Banning Nuclear Weapon Tests in the Atmosphere, in Outer Space and Under Water (Partial Test-Ban Treaty (PTBT)), with the United States, the Soviet Union and the United Kingdom as the original parties, was signed in Moscow on 5 August 1963. The signatories agreed:

"to prohibit, to prevent, and not to carry out any nuclear weapon test explosion, or any other nuclear explosion . . . in the atmosphere; beyond its limits, including outer space; or under water, including territorial waters or high seas" (Art.1) (*UNTS*, Vol. 480, p. 43).

This treaty was to be of unlimited duration and was open for signature to all States. Ninety-nine States have, as of 1 January 1995, ratified or acceded to it and five have only signed it. The complete banning of all nuclear tests, including underground tests, has still not been finally achieved at this writing, while negotiations on the Comprehensive Nuclear-Test-Ban Treaty are at present in progress.

29. (*The 1978 first special disarmament session of the United Nations*)   The United Nations General Assembly has from the outset, and with the close collaboration of the ENDC in Geneva, adopted, in parallel with bilateral negotiations between the United States and the Soviet Union related to nuclear weapons, a number of resolutions concerning nuclear weapons, one of which was the 1961 resolution 1653 (XVI) in 1961 concerning the "Declaration on the prohibition of the use of nuclear weapons", to which I referred in paragraph 16, above (see Table I). This 1961 resolution, which met some strong opposition and reservations, has, however, for long been regarded as one of the leading objectives to be achieved for nuclear disarmament and has led to the regular succession of resolutions aiming at the Convention on the prohibition of the use of nuclear weapons which, however, has not yet borne any fruit (see paras. 20-25, above).

Considering the issues of nuclear disarmament as a problem of global peace and security, the first special session devoted to disarmament (Tenth Special Session) of the General Assembly was held in May/June 1978 to lay the foundation of an international disarmament strategy which would aim at a general and complete disarmament under effective international control (*cf.* para. 17, above).

The Final Document of this special session set out various principles, including the primary responsibility of nuclear-weapon States for nuclear disarmament, the observance of an acceptable balance of mutual responsibilities and obligations for nuclear- and non-nuclear-weapon States, the consideration of proposals designed to secure the avoidance of the use of nuclear weapons and the prevention of nuclear wars, and the non-proliferation of nuclear weapons.

A programme of action in that Final Document indicated that the ultimate goal should be the complete elimination of nuclear weapons and for this purpose it encouraged, among other things, the cessation of nuclear-weapon testing by all States within the framework of an effective nuclear disarmament process, the giving of assurances to non-nuclear-weapon States of their intent to refrain from any use or threat of use of nuclear weapons, and the encouragement of the establishment of nuclear-weapon-free zones on the basis of arrangements freely arrived at among the States of the regions concerned.

In response to this final document of the first special disarmament session, the General Assembly has, since its 33rd Session in 1978, placed the "Review of the implementation of the recommendations and decisions of the tenth special session" on its agenda at every session down to the present day.

30. (*The 1982 second special disarmament session of the General Assembly*) Although the General Assembly had noted that developments since 1978 had not lived up to the hopes engendered by that special disarmament session, it held the second special disarmament session (the Twelfth Special Session) in 1982 to review the implementation of the recommendations and decisions adopted by the General Assembly at its previous disarmament session in 1978 (*cf.*, para. 20 above). The Concluding Document, that is, the Report of the *Ad hoc* Committee, was adopted at this special disarmament session (A/S-12/32).

Ever since the 37th Session (1982) held late in the same year, the General Assembly has had on its agenda at every session down to the present day an item entitled "Review and implementation of the Concluding Document of the Twelfth Special Session of the General Assembly". Under this agenda item, the General Assembly adopted at its 37th Session (1982) various resolutions concerning nuclear disarmament among which a resolution entitled "Convention on the prohibition of the use of nuclear weapons" was to be noted (as stated in paragraphs 21-22, above). The General Assembly repeated an almost identical resolution from 1982, over a period of fourteen sessions, until 1995 (see para. 23, above). The number of sponsoring States did not increase, but opposition to the resolution grew and abstentions from the voting became more numerous. In fact this resolution had no impact on any occasion when it was passed, so that the General Assembly had to repeat at every session its regret that no result had been achieved in the previous year. There has never been any discussion of substance, either at the United Nations in New York or at the Conference on Disarmament in Geneva, in relation to the Convention prohibiting the use or threat of use of nuclear weapons under any circumstances.

(b) Separation Between Nuclear-Weapon States and Non-Nuclear-Weapon States

31. (*The non-proliferation treaty*)   In the atmosphere of detente which was brought about by the conclusion in 1963 of the Partial Test-Ban Treaty (PTBT), the United States and the Soviet Union became concerned with the prevention of the proliferation of nuclear weapons beyond those States which already possessed them. The United States and the Soviet Union jointly submitted the draft of the Treaty on the Non-Proliferation of Nuclear Weapons (Non-Proliferation Treaty (NPT)) in July 1968 in Geneva where, with the participation of the non-nuclear weapon States, the multilateral negotiations had been conducted. The Non-Proliferation Treaty, with the agreement of the United States, the Soviet Union and the United Kingdom, was opened to all States for signature in three cities: London, Moscow and Washington (*UNTS*, Vol. 729, p. 161). It became effective on 5 March 1970 after its ratification by all three original member States and the deposit of the instruments of ratification of forty other signatory States (China and France ratified the Treaty only in 1992).

This Treaty clearly distinguished between, on the one hand, the *nuclear-weapon States*, defined as those which prior to 1 January 1967 had manufactured and exploded a nuclear weapon or other nuclear device, and which would undertake not to transfer nuclear weapons to non-nuclear-weapon States or to assist, encourage or induce any of them to manufacture or acquire nuclear weapons (Article I), and, on the other hand, the *non-nuclear-weapon States* which would not receive the transfer of nuclear weapons or other nuclear explosive devices and would not manufacture them or otherwise acquire them (Article II). The Treaty imposed, however, on all the States Parties, whether nuclear-weapon States or non-nuclear-weapon States, the obligation to pursue negotiations in good faith with a view to the taking of effective measures relating to the cessation of the nuclear arms race and to nuclear disarmament (Article VI). It is also to be noted that, at the First Special Disarmament Session of the General Assembly in 1978, the five nuclear-weapon States gave assurances to the non-nuclear-weapon States which were Parties to the Treaty, undertaking not to use nuclear weapons against them.

The balance of power, as far as nuclear weapons are concerned, would be maintained between the nuclear-weapon and the non-nuclear-weapon States by this seemingly unequal treaty, which in fact reflected the reality of the international relations in the 1970s and 1980s. Up to the end of 1979, 111 States had become Parties to the Treaty and at the end of 1989, 138 States were Parties. To date, the Treaty has received 182 ratifications.

Twenty-five years after the entry into force of that Treaty, in 1995, a Conference was to be convened to decide, by a majority of the Parties to it, whether the Treaty should continue in force indefinitely or should be extended for an additional fixed period or periods (Article X(2)).

32. (*Nuclear Free Zone — Treaty of Tlatelolco*) The Non-Proliferation Treaty recognized the right to any group of States to conclude regional treaties in order to assure the total absence of nuclear weapons in their respective territories (Article VII).

The Treaty for the Prohibition of Nuclear Weapons in Latin America (later the words "and the Caribbean" were added) (the Treaty of Tlatelolco) was signed on 14 February 1967 by 14 Latin American States (with 7 additional States signing subsequently) and became effective on 22 April 1968 (*UNTS*, Vol. 634, p. 281). This Treaty is drawn up to be of a permanent nature and to remain in force indefinitely (Article 30), and is currently valid among 30 States in the region.

The five nuclear-weapon States would be bound to compliance with this Treaty by their acceptance of Additional Protocol II by which the nuclear-weapon States would "undertake not to use or threaten to use nuclear weapons against the Contracting Parties of the Treaty" (Article 3). The United Nations General Assembly in its resolutions adopted in successive sessions (resolution 2286 (XXII); 2456 (XXIII); etc.) welcomed this Treaty with special satisfaction and invited the five nuclear-weapon States to sign and ratify this Additional Protocol, by which they would become bound by the Treaty. In fact, the five nuclear-weapon States had successively signed and ratified Additional Protocol II by the end of the 1970s but accompanied their actions by declarations whereby some attached reservations.

33. (*Treaty of Rarotonga*) Following the Treaty of Tlatelolco covering the Latin American region, the South Pacific Nuclear Free Zone Treaty (Treaty of Rarotonga) was signed by eight States at the South Pacific forum on 6 August 1985 (with the later addition of one signature), to provide for the abandonment of instruments of nuclear explosion, the prevention of their placement by nuclear-weapon States and the prevention of testing (*UNTS*, Registration no. 24592 of 2 January 1987). This Treaty became effective on 11 December 1986 and is of a permanent nature, remaining in force indefinitely (Article 13) and

currently valid among 12 States in the region.

Protocol 2, which was aimed at securing the agreement of the five nuclear-weapon States "not to use or threaten to use" any nuclear explosive device against the Parties to the Treaty (Article 1), had by 1988 been signed and ratified by China and the Soviet Union, to which instrument they appended respectively some reservations. Signature by France, the United Kingdom and the United States had to wait until March 1996.

(2) *Perpetuation of the NPT Régime*

(a) Non-Proliferation Treaty

34. (*End of the Cold War*)   The collapse of régimes in eastern Europe, which commenced with the destruction of the Berlin Wall in November 1989 and the dissolution of the Soviet Union and which led to the end of the Cold War, had a very strong impact on the question of nuclear weapons at the end of the 1980s and beginning of the 1990s.

35. (*Expectation of the comprehensive test-ban treaty*)   Since the conclusion of the Partial Test-Ban Treaty in 1963, the complete banning of all nuclear explosion tests has been the most important political task — in Geneva in particular — and it became, with the approach of 1995, a most essential matter for the nuclear-weapon States to achieve the indefinite extension of the Non-Proliferation Treaty, thus perpetuating that treaty's régime. When the Conference on the Review of the Non-Proliferation Treaty broke down in 1990 due to the conflict concerning the Comprehensive Nuclear-Test-Ban Treaty (CTBT), the spotlight fell upon that latter Treaty. The nuclear-weapon States had become aware that, if they were to succeed in bringing about the indefinite extension of the Non-Proliferation Treaty, they would have to give up any planned tests of nuclear weapons.

In 1991 the "Comprehensive Nuclear-Test-Ban Treaty" was included for the first time as a consolidated and independent agenda item of the General Assembly and a proposal sponsored by 45 States was adopted on 6 December 1991 by 147 States in favour, 2 against and 4 abstentions, and became the resolution 46/29 entitled "Comprehensive Nuclear-Test-Ban Treaty" (Table IV, 1). The United States and France were against, and China and the United Kingdom abstained. This resolution required all States to do their utmost to achieve the total prohibition of nuclear weapon tests and asked the Conference on

Disarmament to proceed with negotiations.

36. (*Negotiations in Geneva*) The real negotiations in Geneva started in 1992 and late in that year the United Nations General Assembly adopted resolution 47/47 — which was pratically identical to the previous resolution — on 9 December 1992 by 159 votes in favour, 1 against and 4 abstentions (Table IV, 2). It was noted that, although the United States voted against, France, because of the modification to its national policy, no longer voted against it but abstained. The United States had likewise changed its policy with the start of President Clinton's term of office in January 1993 as well as in consideration of the fact that it would soon be time for the extension of the Non-Proliferation Treaty. Thus, the draft resolution on "Comprehensive Nuclear-Test-Ban Treaty" in 1993 was sponsored by 157 States, including the United States, and adopted without being put to the vote as resolution 48/70 (Table IV, 3).

In fact, through the CTBT negotiations at the Conference on Disarmament in Geneva in 1994 there began to be a real hope that the Treaty could be drafted. At the 49th Session of the General Assembly in 1994, the resolution on the same subject, which was sponsored for the first time by all five nuclear-weapon States, was adopted on 15 December 1994, again without being put to the vote, as resolution 49/70. That resolution called upon the participants in the Conference on Disarmament to negotiate intensively as a high priority and to conclude a universal treaty for a comprehensive ban of nuclear tests, which would contribute to nuclear disarmament and the prevention of the proliferation of nuclear weapons in all their aspects (Table IV, 4).

It was stated that, in order to have an effective implementation of Article VI of the Non-Proliferation Treaty, as referred to in paragraph 31 above, the completion by the Conference on Disarmament of the negotiation on the CTBT was expected by no later than 1996. In 1995 the General Assembly at its 50th Session again adopted resolution 50/65 on "Comprehensive Nuclear-Test-Ban Treaty" without its being put to the vote (Table IV, 5) and the CTBT will, it is hoped, be concluded in 1996.

(b) Indefinite Extension of the Non-Proliferation Treaty

37. (*Convocation of the conference*) In spite of the fact that the 1968 Non-Proliferation Treaty has certainly been seen as unequal, the monopoly of nuclear weapons by a limited number of States and the prevention of the proliferation of nuclear weapons beyond those States

has for some time been the linchpin of the doctrine of nuclear deterrence. Under this Treaty, a conference would be convened in 1995 to decide whether the treaty should continue in force indefinitely or should be extended for an additional fixed period or periods (Article X(2)). The General Assembly at its 47th Session (1992) adopted by a recorded vote of 168 votes in favour to none against with no abstentions (India later advised the Assembly that it had intended to abstain) resolution 47/52A by which it took note of the decision of the Parties to the Treaty to form the preparatory committee for this 1995 Review and Extension Conference, which would meet in May 1993, and requested the possible assistance of the Secretary-General. Pursuant to the decision of the preparatory committee the Review and Extension Conference was held in April/May 1995 in New York.

38. (*Security assurances given by the nuclear States*)   In order to perpetuate the NPT régime, it was necessary for the nuclear-weapon States to give some assurances to the non-nuclear-weapon States concerning the use of these weapons. Prior to the Conference in April/May 1995, the five nuclear-weapons States proceeded early in April 1995 to make their respective statements, in which they gave security assurances of their intent to refrain from any use of nuclear weapons against the non-nuclear-weapon States that are Parties to the Non-Proliferation Treaty. The Security Council in its resolution 984 (1995) on 11 April 1995, which it adopted unanimously, "[took] note with appreciation of the statements" made by the five nuclear-weapon States. The assurances given by the nuclear-weapon States were more or less identical, stating that "[each State] will not use nuclear weapons against non-nuclear-weapon States Parties to the NPT" (S/1995/261, the Russian Federation; 262, the United Kingdom; 263, the United States; 264, France) except that China gave the assurance that it would "not . . . be the first to use nuclear weapons at any time or under any circumstances" and that "[it] undertakes not to use or threaten to use nuclear weapons against non-nuclear weapon States or nuclear-weapon free zones at any time or under any circumstances" (S/1995/265). In fact, a similar security assurance had also been given five years previously, in 1990.

39. (*The indefinite extension of the NPT*)   One hundred and seventy-five member States participated and ten non-member States sent observers. The Conference decided that, "the Treaty [should] continue in force indefinitely" (Decision 3) as a majority existed among States party to the Treaty for its indefinite extension, in accordance with Ar-

ticle X, paragraph 2. The nuclear-weapon States, while looking forward as far as possible to nuclear disarmament and the non-use of nuclear weapons, did not alter their positions. On the other hand the non-nuclear-weapon States, while expressing their appreciation of the efforts made by the nuclear-weapon States to promote nuclear disarmament, were agreed that the nuclear-weapon States, given their privileged status, would continue to remain the only States to hold nuclear weapons. That decision of the Conference was noted by the General Assembly in its resolution 50/70Q on "1995 Review and extension conference of the parties to the treaty on the non-proliferation of nuclear weapons" on 12 December 1995 by a recorded vote of 161 in favour, none against with the abstention of only India and Israel.

It can, then, be said that the NPT régime has thus been firmly established in the international community.

40. (*Nuclear free zone treaties*) Following the Treaties of Tlatelolco and Rarotonga, some further treaties have been concluded to expand the non-nuclear weapon zones pursuant to Article VII of the Non-Proliferation Treaty.

In South-East Asia in December 1995 a Treaty of the Non-Nuclear Regions was signed in Bangkok on the occasion of the Conference of the Heads of State of the Association of South-East Asian Nations (ASEAN) by ten States in that area and this Treaty should remain in force indefinitely. The Protocol was opened for signature to the five nuclear-weapon States. It is reported that China and the United States declined to sign the Protocol for the reason that the Treaty covered the exclusive economic zone and the continental shelf in the region.

In Africa, where South Africa gave up its nuclear weapons, the establishment of a nuclear free zone became a reality and the United Nations General Assembly at its 49th Session (1994) adopted resolution 49/138 on "Establishment of an African nuclear-weapon-free zone" requesting the Secretary-General to work in consultation with the Organization of African Unity (OAU) on the text of a treaty on an African Nuclear-Weapon-Free Zone. In June 1995, after the extension of the Non-Proliferation Treaty was decided, the Conference of Heads of States of the OAU adopted the African Nuclear-Weapon-Free Zone Treaty (the Treaty of Pelindaba) which was signed by 42 African States on 11 April 1996 in Cairo. China, France, the United Kingdom and the United States signed Protocol I at the same time by which they undertook not to use or threaten to use nuclear weapons against the Parties to the Treaty. The Treaty is of unlimited duration and should remain in force indefinitely.

41. (*Conclusion*)   One can conclude from the above that, on the one hand, the NPT régime which presupposes the possession of nuclear weapons by the five nuclear-weapon States has been firmly established and that, on the other, they have themselves given security assurances to the non-nuclear weapon States by certain statements they have made in the Security Council. In addition, those nuclear-weapon States, in so far as they adhere to the Protocols appended to the respective nuclear-free zone treaties, are bound not to use or threaten to use nuclear weapons against States Parties to those respective treaties.

This reality should not be overlooked. It is most unlikely that those nuclear-weapon States will use those weapons, even among themselves, but the possibility of the use of those weapons cannot be totally excluded in certain special circumstances. That is the meaning of the Non-Proliferation Treaty. It is generally accepted that this NPT régime is a necessary evil in the context of international security, where the doctrine of nuclear deterrence continues to be meaningful and valid.

TABLE IV

(Note: the nuclear-weapon States under the NPT are underlined;
"R" denotes recorded vote)

General Assembly Resolutions on "Comprehensive Nuclear-Test-Ban Treaty"

1. The 46th Session (1991)

A/C.1/46/L.4: Sponsored by: (45) USSR (*names of other States not reproduced*)

A/RES/46/29: adopted on 6 December 1991 by R147-2-4

   For: (147) USSR (*names of other States not reproduced*)
   Against: (2) France, United States
   Abstaining: (4) China, Micronesia (Federated States), Israel, United Kingdom

2. The 47th Session (1992)

A/C.1/47/L.37: Sponsored by: (99) the Russian Federation (names of other

States not reproduced)
A/RES/47/47: adopted on 9 December 1992 by R159-1-4
   For: (159) Russian Federation (*names of other States not reproduced*)
   Against: (1) United States
   Abstaining: (4) China, France, Israel, United Kingdom

3. The 48th Session (1993)

A/C.1/48/L.40: Sponsored by: (159) Russian Federation, United States (*names of other States not reproduced*)
A/RES/48/70: adopted without a vote on 16 December 1993

4. The 49th Session (1994)

A/C.1/49/L.22/Rev. 1: Sponsored by: (87) China, France, Russian Federation, United Kingdom, United States (*names of other States not reproduced*)
A/RES/49/70: adopted without a vote on 15 December 1994

5. The 50th Session (1995)

A/C.1/50/L.8/Rev. 1: Sponsored by: (91) France, Russian Federation, United Kingdom, United States (*names of other States not reproduced*)
A/RES/50/65: adopted without a vote on 12 December 1995

(3) *Significance of the NPT Régime in the Period of the Still Valid Doctrine of Nuclear Deterrence*

42. (*Ultimate goal of elimination of nuclear weapons*)   The resolution sponsored and introduced by Japan and entitled "Nuclear disarmament with a view to the ultimate elimination of nuclear weapons" was adopted on 15 December 1994 as resolution 49/75H at the 49th Session (1994) by a recorded vote of 163 in favour, none against and 8 abstentions (Table V, 1). In that resolution, the General Assembly "urge[d] States not parties to the Treaty on the Non-Proliferation of Nuclear Weapons to accede to it at the earliest possible date" and "call[ed] upon the nuclear-weapon States to pursue their efforts for nuclear disarmament with the *ultimate objective of the elimination of nuclear weapons* in the framework of general and complete disarmament" (emphasis added).

After it was determined in May 1995 that the NPT was to be indefinitely extended, the General Assembly at its 50th Session (1995) adopted on 12 December 1995, by 154 votes in favour, none against and 10 abstentions, resolution 50/70C by which the General Assembly "[c]all[ed] for the determined pursuit by the nuclear-weapon States of systematic and progressive efforts to reduce nuclear weapons globally, with the *ultimate goal of eliminating those weapons,* and by all States of general and complete disarmament under strict and effective international control" (emphasis added) (Table V, 2).

It is to be noted that another resolution similarly entitled "Nuclear disarmament" which proposed "effective nuclear disarmament measures with a view to the total elimination of [nuclear] weapons *within a time-bound framework*" (emphasis added) was adopted on the same day as resolution 50/70P but met strong opposition as reflected in a recorded vote of 103 in favour, 39 against and 17 absentions (Table V, 3).

TABLE V

(Note: the nuclear-weapon States under the NPT are underlined; "R" denotes recorded vote)

General Assembly Resolutions on"Nuclear Disarmament with a View to the Ultimate Elimination of Nuclear Weapons"

1. The 49th Session (1994)

A/C.1/49/L.33/Rev. 1:
   Sponsored by: Japan A/RES/49/75H: adopted on 15 December 1994 by R163-0-8
      For: (163) China, Russian Federation (*names of other States not reproduced*)
      Against: (0)
      Abstaining: (8) Brazil, Cuba, Democratic People's Republic of Korea, France, India, Israel, United Kingdom, United States

2. The 50th Session (1995)

A/C.1/50/L.17/Rev. 2: Sponsored by: Japan, with the later additions of Australia, Austria, Belgium, Canada, Denmark, Finland, Germany, Iceland, Ireland, Italy, Malta, Netherlands, New Zealand, Norway, Poland, Spain, Sweden, Venezuela

A/RES/50/70C: adopted on 12 December 1995 by R154-0-10

> For: (154) France, Russian Federation, United Kingdom, United States (*names of other States not reproduced*)
>
> Against: (0)
>
> Abstaining: (10) Algeria, Brazil, China, Cuba, Democratic People's Republic of Korea, India, Iran, Israel, Myanmar, Pakistan

General Assembly Resolution on "Nuclear Disarmament"

3. The 50th Session (1995)

A/C.1/50/L.46/Rev. 1: Sponsored by: Algeria, Angola, Bangladesh, Cambodia, Colombia, Cuba, Democratic People's Republic of Korea, Ecuador, Egypt, Fiji, Ghana, India, Indonesia, Iran (Islamic Republic), Iraq, Kenya, Malaysia, Marshall Islands, Mauritius, Mexico, Mongolia, Myanmar, Nigeria, Pakistan, Papua New Guinea, Philippines, Samoa, Sri Lanka, Sudan, Thailand, United Republic of Tanzania, Viet Nam, Zimbabwe

A/RES/50/70P: adopted on 12 December 1995 by R106-39-17

> For: (106) China (*names of other States not reproduced*)
>
> Against: (39) Albania, Andorra, Argentina, Austria, Belgium, Bulgaria, Canada, Czech Republic, Denmark, Estonia, Finland, France, Germany, Greece, Hungary, Iceland, Ireland, Israel, Italy, Latvia, Liechtenstein, Lithuania, Luxembourg, Malta, Monaco, Netherlands, Norway, Poland, Portugal, Republic of Moldova, Romania, Slovakia, Slovenia, Spain, Sweden, The Former Yugoslav Republic of Macedonia, Turkey, United Kingdom, United States
>
> Abstaining: (17) Antigua and Barbuda, Armenia, Australia, Azerbaijan, Bahamas, Belarus, Benin, Croatia, Cyprus, Equatorial Guinea, Georgia, Japan, Kazakstan, New Zealand, Republic of Korea, Russian Federation, Ukraine

IV. CONCLUDING REMARKS

(1) *Re-examination of the General Assembly's Request for the Court's Advisory Opinion*

43. (*Re-examination of the Request*) I have shown, firstly, that the Request contained in General Assembly resolution 49/75K and that reads: "Is the threat or use of nuclear weapons permitted in any circumstance under international law?" was, in fact, nothing more than a request to the Court to endorse what, in the view of those that framed it, is a legal axiom that the threat or use of nuclear weapons is *not* permitted under international law in any circumstance, and so cannot be considered as a request for advisory opinion in the real sense as laid down by Article 96(1) of the Charter of the United Nations.

In the second place, I maintain that the Request contains an element of uncertainty as regards the meaning of the phrase "threat or use of nuclear weapons", as opposed to "the use or threat of use of nuclear weapons", and provides no clarification of the concept of "threat", leading one to raise the question of whether or not the possession or the production of nuclear weapons should be included as an object of the Request. In my view there was sufficient reason to believe that, in view of the background to the drafting, the absolute illegality of nuclear weapons themselves was in the mind of some States.

Thirdly, as can be seen from the *travaux preparatoires* of the Request, the adoption of that resolution was far from representing a consensus of the General Assembly (*cf.*, para. 6-14, above).

44. (*Standstill of the movement towards an agreement on the convention prohibiting the use of nuclear weapons*) In the development of nuclear disarmament in the forum of the United Nations, the movement aiming at the conclusion of a treaty to totally prohibit the "use or threat of use of nuclear weapons" was at a standstill for more than ten years, that is, from 1982 to 1994. Support for such repeated resolutions on disarmament within the United Nations General Assembly in New York did not increase but rather decreased (see Table III, above), and the Conference on Disarmament in Geneva made no attempt to respond favourably to those resolutions nor did it commence negotiations in order to achieve agreement on such a convention.

Against the background of that situation, a group of States stimulated by a few NGOs attempted to achieve a breakthrough by obtaining the Court's endorsement of an alleged legal axiom in order to move towards a worldwide anti-nuclear weapons convention. I have no doubt that the Request was prepared and drafted — not in order to ascertain the status of existing international law on the subject but to try to promote the total elimination of nuclear weapons — that is to say, with highly *political* motives. This reason, among others, explains why, in 1994, resolution 49/75K, although passed at the General Assembly with the support of 78 States, did meet with 43 objections while 38 States abstained from the voting.

45. (*The reality of the NPT régime*) The reality of international society is far removed from the desires expressed by that group of States which supported resolution 49/75K. In the period of the Cold War, the monopoly of nuclear weapons by five States and the prevention of proliferation beyond that restricted circle, were regarded as essential and indispensable conditions for the maintenance of international peace and security, as proved by the conclusion of the Non-Proliferation Treaty in 1968 which clearly distinguished between the five nuclear-weapon States and the non-nuclear-weapon States. The doctrine, or strategy, of nuclear deterrence, however it may be judged and criticized from different angles and in different ways, was made a basis for the NPT régime which has been legitimized by international law, both conventional and customary, during the past few decades.

The situation has remained unchanged down to the present day, even in the post-Cold-War period. The term of the 1968 Non-Proliferation Treaty was extended indefinitely in 1995. In such an international climate in which nuclear disarmament is incomplete and general and complete disarmament chimerical, a total prohibition of these weapons would have been seen as a rejection of the legal basis on which that Treaty was founded. If the total prohibition of nuclear weapons was the driving force behind the Request, then the question put under resolution 49/75K could only have been raised in defiance of the then legitimately existing NPT régime.

There is another point which should not be overlooked. As a matter of fact the nuclear-weapon States have tended to undertake not to use or threaten to use nuclear weapons against the States in some specific regions covered by the nuclear-free-zone treaties and these five nuclear-weapon States, early in 1995, gave security assurances through statements made in the Security Council in which they undertook not to use or threaten to use these weapons against the non-nuclear-weapon States. In other words, if legal undertak-

ings are respected, there is little risk of the use of nuclear weapons at present by the five declared nuclear-weapon States. Under such circumstances there was, in 1994, no imminent need to raise the question of the legality or illegality of nuclear weapons.

46. (*Caricature of the advisory procedure*) In the climate in which the NPT régime was about to be legitimized for an indefinite term, and at a time when there was no probability of the use of nuclear weapons by the five nuclear-weapon States, the General Assembly on the same day, 15 December 1994, was asked, under resolution 49/76E on a "Convention on the prohibition of the use of nuclear weapons", to request the Conference on Disarmament in Geneva to prepare such a convention (without much expectation of success), and was also asked to adopt two other resolutions under the same agenda item "General and complete disarmament" — one, resolution 49/75H, aimed at the *ultimate elimination* of nuclear weapons and the other, resolution 49/75K, requesting from the Court the endorsement of the illegality of nuclear weapons under contemporary international law. This is highly contradictory. There was no need and no rational justification, under the circumstances prevailing in 1994, for the request for advisory opinion by the General Assembly to the Court concerning the legality or illegality of the threat or use of nuclear weapons. This was simply, in my view, a caricature of the advisory procedure.

(2) *Role of the Advisory Function and the Discretion of the Court to Decline to Render an Advisory Opinion*

47. (*Function of the advisory opinion*) The International Court of Justice is competent not only to function as a judicial organ but also to give advisory opinions. However, the advisory function is a questionable function of any judicial tribunal and was not exercised by any international tribunal prior to the Permanent Court of International Justice, which first introduced it amidst uncertainty and controversy. The advisory function has now been incorporated into the role of the International Court of Justice in parallel with its contentious function, but continues to be regarded as an exception and to be seen as an incidental function of the Court. This is the reason why, as distinct from the exercise of its contentious jurisdiction, the Court has discretion in exercising its advisory function, as stated in Article 65 of the Statute, which provides that "the Court *may* give an advisory opinion . . . "

(emphasis added).

48. (*One refusal to render an advisory opinion in the period of the Permanent Court*)   The Permanent Court once declined to give an opinion but not because it exercised its discretionary power in so doing. In the period of the Permanent Court, the advisory function played a relatively important role in settling inter-State disputes (as in contentious cases), and in cases involving an inter-State dispute, the consent of the States in dispute was required for an advisory opinion to be rendered. The *Eastern Carelia* case in 1923 was very important in this respect and was the only case in which the Permanent Court declined to render an advisory opinion. In that case, which was related to the interpretation of a declaration concerning the autonomous status of Eastern Carelia in the 1920 Dorpat Peace Treaty between Finland and Russia, Finland first appealed to the Council of the League of Nations to ask the Court for an advisory opinion. Russia, which was not a member of the League of Nations, opposed that move. Further to proceedings before the Court in which Russia was not represented, the Court, when declining to deliver an advisory opinion, indicated its unwillingness to take the matter any further under the circumstances and invoked a well-established principle of international law to the effect that "no State can, without its consent, be compelled to submit its disputes with other States either to mediation or to arbitration, or to any other kind of pacific settlement" (*P.C.I.J., Series B, No. 5*, p. 27).

In all the advisory cases in the period of the Permanent Court which involved inter-State disputes and which followed the *Eastern Carelia* case, the consent of the State concerned was secured in advance or there was at least a guarantee that neither party to the dispute would object to the proceedings. In the circumstances, the precedent of the *Eastern Carelia* case as dealt with by the previous Court is of no relevance to the present case.

49. (*Advisory function in the International Court of Justice*)   Of the twenty advisory opinions that the International Court of Justice has rendered to date, twelve were given in response to requests made pursuant to General Assembly resolutions.

There have been seven cases, all in the early period of the Court, in which it dealt simply with the interpretation of the United Nations Charter itself or with matters concerning the functions of the United Nations, i.e., *Conditions of Admission of a State to Membership in the*

United Nations (Article 4 of Charter) (1948); *Reparation for Injuries Suffered in the Service of the United Nations* (1949); *Competence of the General Assembly for the Admission of a State to the United Nations* (1950); *Effect of Awards of Compensation Made by the United Nations Administrative Tribunal* (1954); *Voting Procedure on Questions relating to Reports and Petitions concerning the Territory of South West Africa* (1955); *Admissibility of Hearings of Petitioners by the Committee on South West Africa* (1956) and the case concerning *Certain Expenses of the United Nations* (1962).

Unlike the previous Court, which dealt mostly with inter-State disputes even in the context of advisory cases, the present Court has on only a few occasions been asked to give an advisory opinion on a matter related to an inter-State dispute, i.e., in the cases concerning the *Interpretation of Peace Treaties with Bulgaria, Hungary and Romania* (1950) and the *Western Sahara* (1975). On some occasions the Court has dealt with disputes between international organizations and States, such as the *South West Africa* case (1950) and the *Applicability of the Obligation to Arbitrate under Section 21 of the United Nations Headquarters Agreement of 26 June 1947* case (1988).

50. (*Legal questions of a general nature*)   In fact, during the life of the present Court, there has only been one case in which a legal question of a general nature was dealt with and that was the one concerning *Reservations to the Convention on the Prevention and Punishment of the Crime of Genocide* (1951) in which the meaning of reservations attached to a multilateral convention was questioned. In that case, however, the request to the Court arose from circumstances of practical necessity, and it was asked to focus upon the question of whether

> "the reserving State [can] be regarded as being a party to the [Genocide] Convention while still maintaining its reservation if the reservation is objected to by one or more of the Parties of the Convention but not by others" (*I.C.J. Reports 1951*, p. 16)

and to render an opinion on the meaning of the reservation attached to a multilateral convention and, more particularly, on the concrete question of the interpretation and application of the Genocide Convention. This fact makes that case quite different from the present case in which no issues of a practical nature are in dispute and there is no need to specify the legality or illegality of the threat or use of nuclear weapons, as I explained in paragraph 45, above.

51. (*Declining to render an advisory opinion*) If one looks at this practice, it can be seen that no request for an advisory opinion concerning a legal question of a general nature, where that question is unrelated either to a concrete dispute or to a concrete problem awaiting a practical solution, has ever been submitted to the Court. It is true that the present Court, even though given a discretionary power to render or to decline to render an advisory opinion, has in the past had no occasion to decline to render an opinion in response to a request from the General Assembly. The fact is however that, in the past, the Court has never received any requests which could reasonably have been refused in the given circumstances. In this connection it is irrelevant to argue, in the present context, that "[t]he Court . . . is mindful that it should not, in principle, refuse to give an advisory opinion" and that "[t]here has been no refusal, based on the discretionary power of the Court, to act upon a request for advisory opinion in the history of the present Court" (Court's Opinion, para. 14).

(3) *Conclusions*

52. (*Judicial propriety*) Under the circumstances and considering the discretionary competence of the Court in declining to render an advisory opinion, the Court should, in my view, for the reason of *judicial propriety*, have dismissed the Request raised under resolution 49/75K. Moreover, in the event, it seems to me that the elementary or equivocal conclusions reached by the Court in the present Opinion do not constitute a real response to the Request, and I am afraid that this unimpressive result may cause some damage to the Court's credibility.

53. (*Judicial economy*) In addition, I would like to explain why I consider that the Request should have been dismissed in the present case, on account of considerations of *judicial economy*. There are any number of questions which could be brought to the Court as requiring legal interpretation or the application of international law in general terms in fields such as the law of the sea, law of humanitarian and human rights, environmental law, etc. If the Court were to decide to render an opinion — as in the present case — by giving a response to a legal question of a general nature as to whether a specific action would or would not be in conformity with the application of treaty law or of customary law — a question raised in the absence of any practical

need — this could in the long run mean that the Court could be seised of a number of hypothetical cases of a general nature and would eventually risk its main function — to settle international disputes on the basis of law — to become a consultative or even a legislative organ.

If the flood-gates were thus opened for any legal question of a general nature which would not require immediate solution, in circumstances where there was no practical dispute or need, then the Court could receive many cases of an academic or intellectual nature with the consequence that it would be the less able to exercise its real function as a judicial institution. I have expressed my concern at an abuse of the right to request an advisory opinion in my separate opinion appended to the Court's Opinion rendered today in response to the Request from the World Health Assembly, in terms which I would like to repeat:

> "I am personally very much afraid that if encouragement is given or invitations are extended for a greater use of the advisory function of the Court — as has recently been advocated on more than one occasion by some authorities — it may well be seised of more requests for advisory opinions which may in essence be unnecessary and over-simplistic. I firmly believe that the International Court of Justice should primarily function as a judicial institution to provide solutions to inter-State disputes of a contentious nature and should neither be expected to act as a legislature (although new developments in international law may well be achieved through the jurisprudence of the Court) or to function as an organ giving legal advice (except that the Court may give opinions on legal questions which arise within the scope of activities of the authorized international organizations) in circumstances in which there is no conflict or dispute concerning legal questions between States or between States and international organizations."

54. (*My personal appeal*)   In concluding this exposition of my position against the Court's rendering an opinion in the present case, I would emphasize that I am among the first to hope that nuclear weapons can be totally eliminated from the world as proposed in General Assembly resolutions 49/75H and 50/70C, which were adopted at the General Assembly without there being one single objection. However, a decision on this matter is a function of

political negotiations among States in Geneva or New York and is not one which concerns our judicial institution here at The Hague, where an interpretation of *existing international law* can only be given in response to a genuine need.

V. SUPPLEMENTARY OBSERVATIONS ON MY POSITION AS REGARDS PARAGRAPH 2 OF THE OPERATIVE PART OF THE PRESENT ADVISORY OPINION

55. While I take the position that the Court should have declined to render an advisory opinion, I proceeded nonetheless to cast my vote on all of the sub-paragraphs in its operative part in view of the rule that no Judge may abstain from the voting on the operative part of any decision of the Court. I have done so although, in my view, the statements listed in paragraph 2 may not be interpreted as constituting replies to the question posed by resolution 49/75K while sub-paragraph F, in particular, concerns a matter which, in my view, should not be advanced in the operative part of the Advisory Opinion as it simply reproduces Article VI of the Non-Proliferation Treaty. However, I did vote in favour of all the sub-paragraphs A to F — apart from the sub-paragraph E — as I can accept the statements made in each one of them. The equivocations of sub-paragraph E prove my point that it would have been prudent for the Court to decline from the outset to give any opinion at all in the present case. The fact that the Court could only come to such an equivocal conclusion hardly serves to enhance its credibility.

(Signed) Shigeru ODA

[Original: English] [Japan]

The Anti-nuclear Movement Grew
by the Thousands

Protest in New York City. Photo by Richard Laird.

Anti-war rally in Moscow's Central Park during the Month of Actions Against Threat of Nuclear War, June 1984. Photos courtesy of FPG.

Credit: UN Photo 167960

PART FOUR

THE OPINION ON ILLEGALITY OF NUCLEAR WEAPONS IS BEING ENFORCED

Ann Fagan Ginger

We have a right to ask whether, how, and when the July 8, 1996, opinion of the International Court of Justice will be enforced.

People who enjoy sports and can handicap horses, or can discuss the fine points of a player's ERA, or Gs and As or changes in the latest GNP,[1] will enjoy all the nuances in the answers to the questions about enforcement of the World Court opinion. People who enjoy chess, word games, drama, court cases or genealogy charts will find the answers fascinating. And anyone concerned about the possible future of the world will find the answers are critical to that future.

People have a duty to listen to the answers, even if they cannot be given accurately in one page and cannot easily be translated into numbers. We are learning that the numbers showing rising and falling stock market prices do not accurately measure the health of the economy any more than the security of a nation can be measured accurately by the size of the military forces on alert and the value of the weapons they command. So we need to analyze the words and phrases in the Court's opinion.

People who take the time to work for peace are usually people who also are taking the time to work for a living, to raise a family, to participate in their local unions and professional organizations and in their local communities. They may also care about their own health and the health of their environment. Busy people hate to have to learn a new language and a new set of procedures in order to be effective in working for peace. Since working for peace is often the last project we undertake, we think that learning the players and laws and procedures to work for peace is an added burden.

To save a little time in analyzing the Court opinion, in this Part Four we will consider:

1. Why We Are Actually Very Lucky
2. Who Asked Whom to Do What?
3. Why Did the Court Decide/Not Decide as It Did?
4. The Duty to Inform about the Opinion
5. Actions by Governments and Leaders Obeying the Opinion
6. Decisions by Courts Enforcing the Opinion
7. Actions by Military Officers (Retired) to Enforce the Opinion
8. Actions by the General Assembly to Enforce the Opinion
9. How the Opinion Moved from Non-Binding Advisory to Enforcement
10. Actions by NPT Treaty Parties at UN PrepComm for 2000 Review Conference
11. The Ultimate Judges on Any Issue
12. The Last Word
13. The Very Last Word

1. Why We Are Actually Very Lucky

Looked at in a certain way, we are extremely lucky to be living in the century that has made the greatest progress in peace work of any previous era — pushed by also having made the greatest steps to be able to destroy all life.

The United Nations has a system of operation just as a business does, or a government, or an army or a family. The UN has a structure with officials selected by various means to carry out various tasks and forbidden to act in certain ways. This structure is different from the structures of other governments and of military machines and businesses and families. It is a structure that has worked for more than fifty years.

The problems with the structure of the UN are more obvious, and certainly more publicized, than the problems with the structure of various national governments, corporations and military machines and families. The problems with the UN certainly are based on much smaller budgets than the budgets for the U.S. civilian government, the U.S. military and multinational corporations. (The late Prof. Frank Newman was fond of repeating the figure that the U.S. spends more money on military marching bands than its total dues to the United Nations.)

We must consider the problems faced by the World Court judges in this case and how they resolved them even if it requires us to learn UN procedures and parlance and the differences between the UN court, the International Court of Justice, and the courts of countries like the United States with which some people are more familiar. This is appropriate in this UN Decade of International Law.

2. Who Asked Whom to Do What?

Judges on a court were asked to study whether the law made by courts and treaties up to that point had clearly decided that the threat or use of nuclear weapons is legal or illegal. They were asked to answer the question by a congress or legislative body consisting of delegates from nuclear weapons states, non-nuclear weapons states and anti-nuclear weapons states, that is, the General Assembly of the United Nations, which had not been able to agree unanimously on what the law about nuclear weapons is or should be or how to enforce whatever law there is. The national and multinational corporations engaged in nuclear weapons production, mining, storage and transportation were not open participants in this proceeding.

As soon as the decision was issued, some governments took steps to enforce it. Parliamentary leaders, judges and concerned citizens also acted at the local and national levels in several countries, at the regional level and at the United Nations. They acted on a clear understanding that each nation must obey this international law if it is going to insist that its people obey their national law.

Governments acted because peoples all over the world are demanding that the nations carry out their duty, clearly enunciated by the World Court in a unanimous decision, to urgently negotiate to conclusion for the complete abolition of nuclear weapons. No governments openly and officially condemned the decision or started a public campaign to reject it, which was the experience after the U.S. Supreme Court handed down its decisions in the famous desegregation case of *Brown v. Board of Education.*[2]

Most people want to know why the judges voted as they did before they find out what actions have been taken to enforce the opinion.

3. Why Did the Court Decide/Not Decide as It Did?

To understand this opinion of the World Court, put yourself in the position of the judges on the International Court of Justice. If you are asked a question, you think about who asked the question. If the question is very important and you know that you do not have the power to enforce whatever answer you give, you must think about your answer in a different way than if you are asked a question and you know you have the power to enforce the answer. The parent of a young child answers a question in a different way than the parent of a teen-ager; a grandparent answers a question by a child about a grandchild in a different way than either of the others.

If a person, or a Court, gives an answer to a question that is not popular with an important person or country and the court does not have the power to enforce that answer, that answer is not helpful. It is not, in fact, an answer to the question, but rather an invitation to a second question: "Says who?" or "Says you?" or "Prove it!"

As we enter the twenty-first century, it pays us to look back over the past millennium and the past century at the steps we have made as a world of peoples to keep other peoples, and ourselves, from killing each other and from threatening to kill each other in world wars, the Cold War and in so-called internal or regional wars.

We will find that there has been an exponential increase in the methods we have discovered to kill ourselves and each other, and in the horrible agony we have learned to inflict before mass deaths.

We will also find that we have stopped the use of dum-dum bullets and have taken steps to stop the use of explosive projectiles, asphyxiating gases and land mines. (Opinion ¶ 76) We have strengthened the right to be a conscientious objector to war in many countries. We have created Nuclear Weapons Free Zones in many cities of the world and in several regions.

These steps all involved the use of words on pieces of paper argued over by lawyers, generals, heads of states and corporations. Ultimately, heads of state signed treaties that legislative bodies ratified. Presidents ordered military officers to obey these treaties and they ordered foot soldiers to obey them. Weapons manufacturers could not ignore these treaties. They were not forgotten by the people who had written and signed and ratified them. Even in the midst of crises, the words in the treaties were remembered. In many instances, they affected decisions not to use certain weapons against certain peoples under certain circumstances.

The judges in the World Court told the heads of state and the legislative bodies who ratify treaties that the question they asked about the legality or illegality of nuclear weapons has an answer. The Court held that the bodies that must provide that answer are the legislators and heads of state who write and sign and consent to treaties, not the judges who write opinions. The Court said, in effect, that the method for enforcing the treaty language must also be negotiated and agreed to by the heads of state with the power to change the practices of armies and of corporations.

The judges on the World Court who wanted to take the next step and issue a simple decision that the threat or use of nuclear weapons is now illegal could not find eight votes for that proposition. If they had found eight votes, there is no way to predict exactly how the five known and official nuclear weapons states would have responded to that decision, or how the governments of would-be nuclear weapons states would have responded.

The judges who wanted to decide that the threat or use of nuclear weapons can be legal could not find eight votes for that proposition. If they had found eight votes, there is reason to believe that several non-nuclear weapons states would have immediately stepped up their efforts to become nuclear weapons states, and that the many anti-nuclear weapons states would have rejected that decision and formed a negative view of the World Court.

Instead, the Court wrote the two sentences in ¶ 105 (2)E. However, the seeming hole they left in these two sentences actually faces the impervious steel wall they constructed when they ruled unanimously that nuclear weapons can only be used legally if they obey the humanitarian laws of war, which everyone agreed they can never do. (Discussed in Part One, paragraph 10.)

Nay-sayers who insist that the opinion is "only an advisory opinion" have a problem. The United States refused to abide by a *binding* decision of the same Court handed down in a *contentious* suit, *Nicaragua v. United States*,[3] even though the United States had benefited from the fact that Iran *had* abided by the Court's binding opinion in an earlier, parallel suit by the United States in *United States v. Iran*.[4] So whether a decision of the World Court is defined as "binding" or "nonbinding" does not determine whether it can be enforced in the face of a refusal to obey the decision by a nation with veto power in the Security Council. And whether a decision is "advisory" or not likewise does not determine whether it can be enforced.[5]

4. The Duty to Inform about the Opinion

The media in many of the nuclear weapons states did not give the

World Court opinion a banner headline. In fact, many major newspapers in the largest cities in the largest nuclear weapons state, the United States, did not print the story anywhere in their daily or Sunday papers. National radio and television news did not give coverage to the story, either on commercial or public stations. Yet the right to freedom of the press in the constitutions of many countries and in UN treaties includes the right of the people to read and to know.

There is no record of discussion or debate on the opinion in the Congressional Record of actions by the Congress in the United States or in the comparable records of the proceedings of many national parliaments. There is no record of discussions or debates on the opinion in the annual meetings of corporations engaged in manufacturing, mining, transporting, or other aspects of nuclear weapons production and maintenance. Bar associations, chambers of commerce, and colleges of law, business, diplomacy and international relations did not immediately present discussions on the opinion. No statements on the opinion were issued by the heads of the United States, the United Kingdom, France, Russia or China, the nuclear weapons states, and the media did not ask them to comment on the opinion.

5. Actions by Governments and Leaders Obeying the Opinion[6]

Government leaders in several nations read the World Court opinion and immediately took some steps toward enforcing it. The first steps are described here as this book goes to press. They suggest other actions governmental and non-governmental agencies are planning in many regions of the world.

United Kingdom: In the Debates on the Defence Estimates in October 1996, Jerome Corbyn MP, Lord Carver (former Chief of Defence Staff) and Lord Jenkins raised for the first time the issue of nuclear disarmament and the British Government's response to the World Court decision in the Commons and in the House of Lords. People are pushing the new Labor Government to support enforcement of the opinion.

Canada: Ottawa's former disarmament ambassador completed a round of national consultations and Foreign Affairs Minister Lloyd Axworthy put questions on his Department's Home Page on the Internet on what Canada's response should be to the opinion that led to a consensus opposing nuclear weapons for Canada. Axworthy then instructed his Commons Foreign Affairs Committee to undertake a review of the issues of nuclear weaponry and Canada's membership in

NATO (which "protects" Canada with the U.S. nuclear arsenal).

Norway: The governing Norwegian Labour Party adopted a platform demanding "a treaty on a time-bound elimination of nuclear weapons" following the opinion.

Australia: The government established the Canberra Commission on the Elimination of Nuclear Weapons in 1995, which issued a detailed report in August 1996, finding that "nuclear weapons pose an intolerable threat to all humanity and its habitat," and calling for "taking nuclear forces off alert" and for the "removal of warheads from delivery vehicles."[7]

United States: U.S. Congressman Major Owens released an open letter to President Clinton calling for the United States to join negotiations leading to the establishment of a Nuclear Weapons Convention.

U.S. Congresswoman Eleanor Holmes Norton introduced the Nuclear Disarmament and Economic Conversion Act as H.R. 827 in February 1997, requiring the U.S. government to disable and dismantle all its nuclear weapons and to redirect its resources to address human needs.[8]

The City Council in Oakland, California, which administers a nuclear free zone ordinance, governs the site of the University of California Board of Regents, who administer Livermore and Los Alamos Nuclear Weapons Laboratories. The Council adopted a resolution February 22, 1997, to support the Abolition 2000 campaign, and to declare that day "Nuclear Abolition Day," based in part on the unanimous decision of the Court in ¶ 105 (2)F that "There exists an obligation to pursue . . . to a conclusion negotiations leading to nuclear disarmament in all its aspects . . ."[9]

In November 1997, U.S. President Clinton signed a Presidential Decision Directive rewriting the guidelines for U.S. use of nuclear weapons to require the Pentagon to focus its strategic planning on deterring the use of nuclear weapons rather than on winning a nuclear war outright. The guidelines reflect a new recognition of the totally destructive character of nuclear weapons, although they apparently do not mention the ICJ opinion or conform to it.

European Parliament: On March 13, 1997, the European Parliament called on all its members to support negotiations leading to establishment of a Nuclear Weapons Convention.

Central Asia: Kazakstan, Kyrgyzstan, Tajikistan, Turkmenistan and Uzbekistan signed the Almaty Declaration on December 28, 1997, initiating steps to establish a Nuclear Weapons Free Zone in Central Asia. This initiative was welcomed by Egypt, Australia, New Zealand,

Canada and the Kyrgyz Republic.

Tahiti: Five hundred people marched through the streets of Pape-ete in January, 1997, to celebrate the first anniversary of the end of nuclear weapons testing in the Pacific which came about at least in part due to decisions by the World Court in *New Zealand v. France,* mentioned in ¶ 32[10], and to issue the Moorea Declaration to supplement the Abolition 2000 Foundation statement for the unconditional abolition of nuclear weapons:

> "Colonized and indigenous peoples have, in large part, borne the brunt of this nuclear devastation — from the mining of uranium and the testing of nuclear weapons on indigenous land, to the dumping, storage and transport of plutonium and nuclear wastes, and the theft of land for nuclear infrastructure.
>
> " . . . [I]ndigenous and colonized people must be central to [the process of abolishing nuclear weapons]. This can only happen if and when they are able to participate in decisions relating to the nuclear weapons cycle . . . The inalienable right to self-determination, sovereignty and independence is crucial in allowing all peoples of the world to join in the common struggle to rid the planet forever of nuclear weapons." [11]

6. Decisions by Courts Enforcing the Opinion

In September 1996, a Police Court judge in Beringen, Belgium, adjourned the proceedings against two peace activists who were charged with climbing into the nuclear weapons base at Kleine Brogel after one stated in his defense that their action aimed to expose the illegality of nuclear weapons and quoted the verdict of the International Court of Justice.

On September 10, 1996, the Sheriffs Court at Balloch, Scotland, UK, acquitted 13 protesters who stopped a convoy carrying Trident nuclear warheads to Coulport after the defendants cited the World Court decision.[12]

In September 1996, a jury in Wisconsin, U.S.A., acquitted two nuclear protesters charged with sabotage against a U.S. Navy communications system (Extremely Low-Frequency transmitter) after they defended their actions based on the opinion of the World Court.[13]

Lawyers and activists indicate that these cases are early examples of a practice that will become common of using the opinion whenever nuclear weapons protesters participate in actions to convince legislators, administrators, or the military to stop all use of nuclear weapons.[14]

These decisions followed the precedent set by the first court to rule on the illegality of nuclear weapons in war in *Shimoda v. The State (Japan)*, a case worth study in regions where it is not known.[15]

7. Actions by Military Officers (Retired) to Enforce the Opinion

General Lee Butler, USAF (Retired) presented a joint statement by 60 top generals and admirals from 17 nations addressed to U.S. President Clinton and Russian President Yeltsin on December 4, 1996 which was published in leading newspapers as an advertisement. The former Commander-in-Chief of U.S. Strategic Air Command (1991), the Supreme Allied Commander in Europe (1965-74), the Vice-Chair Joint Chiefs of U.S. Staff (1994-96), and 15 other U.S. retired officers of the USA, USN and USAF were able to join 18 Russian retired officers and the other signatories in a post-Cold War statement. They concluded that the World Court opinion and the present circumstances, including the signatures of virtually every nation on the Nuclear Non-Proliferation Treaty of 1970, condition "government at all levels to create and respond to every opportunity for shrinking arsenals, cutting infrastructure and curtailing modernization." They issued a call to the five nuclear powers and three undeclared nuclear nations "to begin moving toward abolition by negotiating new treaties and removing all nuclear warheads from missiles," based on their first-hand work with nuclear weapons and participation in wars.[16]

8. Actions by the General Assembly to Enforce the Opinion

The General Assembly on December 10, 1996, discussed and adopted a resolution that welcomes the ICJ opinion and

- "Underlines the unanimous conclusion of the Court that there exists an obligation to pursue in good faith and bring to a conclusion negotiations leading to nuclear disarmament in all its aspects under strict and effective international control;. . .

- "Calls upon all States to fulfill that obligation immediately by commencing multilateral negotiations in 1997 leading to an early conclusion of a nuclear-weapons convention prohibiting the development, production, testing, deployment, stockpiling, transfer, threat or use of nuclear weapons and providing for their elimination;

- "Decides to include in the provisional agenda of its fifty-second session an item entitled 'Follow-up to the Advisory Opinion of the International Court of Justice on the Legality of the Threat or Use of Nuclear Weapons'."

The General Assembly took this action in response to a report by the First Committee on General and Complete Disarmament as part M. of a 20-part resolution on all aspects of disarmament and peacekeeping, from A. (Treaty on Non-Proliferation of Nuclear Weapons for 2000 Review Conference) to T. (Status of the Convention on the Prohibition of the Development, Production, Stockpiling and Use of Chemical Weapons and on their Destruction).[17]

In the vote on December 9, 1997, 35 nations shifted from their votes in the General Assembly not to send the nuclear weapons question to the Court:

To Ask Court (12/15/94)		Change	To Conclude Treaty (12/9/96)	
Yes	79	+35	Yes	115
No	43	-21	No	22
Abstaining	38	-6	Abstaining	32
Absent	18	-9	Absent	9
	178			178

The vote to send the question to the World Court had been Yes 79 and Not Yes 99. After the opinion, the vote on concluding a treaty was Yes 115 to Not Yes 63. Almost two-thirds of the General Assembly voted Yes on this resolution. The General Assembly adopted a stronger resolution by a similar vote on November 21, 1997; it appears in Part Five.

9. How the Opinion Moved from Non-Binding Advisory to Enforcement

The action of the UN General Assembly on December 10, 1996, the day before Human Rights Day, constituted the first step by the United Nations to enforce the opinion of the World Court.

This approach is similar to the approach that moved the Universal Declaration of Human Rights of 1948 from a General Assembly resolution to become customary international law. The Declaration was adopted as a "declaration," not as a "treaty." Its provisions are now written into a series of treaties that most of the nations of the world have ratified. Nations are making periodic reports to UN committees of experts, as required by these treaties, on their efforts to enforce rights set forth in the Declaration.[18] The list and definitions of human rights in the Declaration are now also written into the constitutions and laws of many nations.

In 1994 the General Assembly had asked the Court for a non-binding advisory opinion on the legality or illegality of nuclear weapons. The opinion was advisory in that it was not based on a lawsuit by one nation against another nation, i.e., a contentious suit. The General Assembly had asked the Court to state the law on a specific subject, which the Court did in ¶¶ 10-105.

In 1996 the General Assembly acknowledged the law set forth in the opinion and took steps to cause all member nations to abide by the Court's ruling. To put it another way: The World Court unanimously concluded that:

> "There exists an obligation to pursue in good faith and bring to a conclusion negotiations leading to nuclear disarmament in all its aspects under strict and effective international control." (¶ 105 (2)F)

The World General Assembly, by two-thirds voting Yes, called on all states to fulfill this obligation immediately.

By voting for this resolution, two-thirds of the nations stated publicly that they welcome the World Court opinion, underline its unanimous conclusion, and call upon all member nations to fulfill their obligation under it.

The Court played its role by providing the authoritative interpretation of binding law. The fact that each nation has not yet signed its name to a binding treaty to implement this Court decision does not change the content or weight of the law announced by the Court.

10. Actions by NPT Treaty Parties at UN PrepComm[19] for 2000 Review Conference

One hundred forty-eight nations attended the Preparatory Committee Meeting for the 2000 Review Conference of the Nuclear Non-Proliferation Treaty Parties in April 1997, as did 100 NGOs. The fact of the World Court opinion was clearly in the air. Mexico repeatedly stated its views about the importance of nuclear disarmament and the need to take into account new developments such as the World Court opinion.

The Non-Aligned Movement of 111 nations in Africa, Asia and Central and South America made a statement underlining the importance of balancing the obligations and responsibilities of the nuclear-weapon states (NWS) and non-nuclear weapon states (NNWS). The Movement (NAM) called on countries to accept the NNP Treaty without delay and place their nuclear facilities under full-scope International Atomic Energy Agency safeguards. NAM welcomed the participation of NGOs, which could make a positive contribution to the attainment of these objectives. NAM gave priority to legally binding negative security assurances to non-nuclear weapon states, a fissile materials production ban (fissban), and elimination of nuclear arsenals to be pursued through the establishment of an ad hoc committee in the Conference on Disarmament (CD), among other items.

Britain, France and the United States felt called upon to list the ways in which they have reduced their arsenals and curtailed fissile material production. The United Kingdom said that when the U.S. and Russian arsenals are cut down to the hundreds, the UK would be prepared to join talks on nuclear disarmament. France said its participation in international negotiations on nuclear arsenals is not relevant now in light of the nuclear capacities of Russia and the U.S.

The group of international lawyers, scientists and disarmament experts participating with NGOs presented an overview of the proposed model nuclear weapons convention, including:

- General obligations
- Agency to implement
- Verification
- Compliance and enforcement
- Individual responsibility
- Phases for elimination

NGOs[20] made many specific proposals in the sessions open to them, including a deep cuts program to reduce nuclear forces of weapon states to immobilized, multilaterally monitored arsenals of 100-200 warheads each as a final trial stage before complete elimination, and listed main steps to be taken.

The Preparatory Committee scheduled further meetings: April 28-May 8, 1998, in Geneva; April 12-23, 1999, in New York; and Review Conference: April 24-May 19, 2000, in New York.[21]

In other words, the meeting ended in success after many moments when it was not clear that progress could be made.

11. The Ultimate Judges on Any Issue

In the end, after many centuries or millennia, individual men began to obey a law that said they did not have life-and-death power over their women and children. In the end, individual tribes began to obey a law that said the genocide of any people is illegal as well as immoral. In the end, peoples of the world are learning to trade with each other in goods, not in exchanges of weapons. Today many leaders of the U.S. government and of the military/indutrial complex, who sometimes acted as if they thought the U.S. was the emperor of the world after Hiroshima and Nagasaki, no longer hold that view.

Today more and more practicing lawyers from many countries want to be associated with lawyers from other countries in the UN in order to discuss and work together on issues of peace and international law. Although the idea for a UN Bar Association, proposed by the National Lawyers Guild and welcomed by President Roosevelt in 1944,[22] has not yet materialized, the end of the Cold War and the opportunity to help enforce the World Court decision on nuclear weapons can be a goad in that direction. Seven hundred NGOs on six continents have endorsed the Abolition 2000 statement calling for the complete elimination of nuclear weapons through negotiations on a nuclear weapons abolition convention building on the illegality of the threat or use of nuclear weapons, as set forth in the ICJ opinion.[23]

At the same time, the arms trade is increasing, non-nuclear weapons are becoming more deadly, and the use of labor power, creative thought and energy to produce weapons is destroying the economic, social, educational and physical environment.

General Butler, from his years in the U.S. military, concludes that:

> "It falls unavoidably to us to work painfully back through
> the tangled moral web of the frightful 50-year-gauntlet, born
> of the hellish confluence of two unprecedented historical cur-
> rents, the bipolar collision of ideology and the unleashing of
> the power of the atom."[24]

Professor Roger Clark, from his years teaching and practicing international law, concludes that:

> "The decision of the Court, binding or not binding, is not
> a wand to wash away the stockpile of nuclear weaponry that

could eliminate us all several times over. It is, however, surely a call to go urgently and with gusto to the next stage — the final negotiation for a comprehensive treaty aimed at total abolition."[25]

Commander Robert Green, of the UK Royal Navy, Retired, concludes that:

"With this remarkable decision, I could never have used a nuclear weapon legally. This places a duty on the military to review their whole attitude toward nuclear weapons, which are now effectively in the same category as chemical and biological weapons."[26]

12. The Last Word

The last word on many questions is about money. After discussing law and military and humanitarian affairs, the bottom line for many governments and peoples is: can our nation afford to continue to threaten or to use nuclear weapons?

The U.S. Nuclear Weapons Cost Study Project of the Brookings Institution and the Center for Defense Information estimate that the U.S. Pentagon spends **$67.4 million every day** to prepare to fight a nuclear war, which comes to **$24.6 billion for fiscal 1997.** The money goes toward maintaining, improving and controlling the existing arsenal and toward retaining the capability to produce new weapons. An additional $8 billion is being spent annually on waste management, environmental remediation, dismantlement and disposition activities. These figures are higher than they were in 1996 after President Clinton announced a push for a test ban treaty in 1995. Astronomical figures can also be estimated of expenditures by the other known nuclear weapons and would-be nuclear weapons states.

The Project of the Brookings Institution and the Center study these costs on a continuing basis. Their final total — for the U.S. building of the bomb; delivering, commanding, controlling and defending the bomb; retiring and dismantling the bomb; and legacies and managment of the bomb — is three trillion nine hundred billion dollars ($3,900,000,000,000).[27]

These figures are being weighed against the cuts in social services and education and in actual wages paid civilian workers as a result of bills passed by the U.S. Congress and parliaments in other nuclear weapons states, and in would-be nuclear weapons states. Many parents and grandparents are weighing these costs against the militarization of society and the feeling of hopelessness they see in their children and grandchildren. They are moving toward not doing business with corporations engaged in any way in the nuclear weapons industry. They are moving from considering some of their actions "civil disobedience" to "civil obedience" of the World Court opinion.

13. The Very Last Word

The history of this case proves that people can affect the course of law and of history: individual people, associations of lawyers and doctors and other non-governmental organizations, and some government officials and military officers. The next article in Part Four gives the details on the work around this case.

Lawyers, litigants, judges, legislators and administrators have an obligation to start using this opinion in every appropriate case, statute, regulation and budget. The military and all corporations in the military/industrial complex have an obligation, and a need, to start using this opinion in every corporate and military plan to shake off their image as an enveloping military/industrial kudzu.

We can all insist that our governments carry out their obligation to support the action of the General Assembly to enforce the World Court opinion. This will involve each governmental organization, each weapons manufacturing and mining corporation, each military command, and all of the bodies and agencies of the United Nations.

If this opinion is not enforced, we will each lose a great deal. We can lose our lives in a nuclear weapons accident or attack. We will certainly lose a sense of security, knowing that such an accident or attack is possible. We will lose the sense of security that comes from knowing that opinions of the world's court are being enforced. We will be left with the sense of immorality that comes from spending so much money on arms that we cannot spend enough to help people injured in the natural disasters over which we have no control. And we will be left with the sense of insecurity that comes from spending money on arms instead of on the peaceful needs of all the peoples of the world.

The process of working to enforce this opinion will resemble the process of working to enforce the U.S. Supreme Court opinion in *Brown v. Board of Education* and the process of working to carry out the work of the Truth and Reconciliation Commissions in South Africa.

The process of enforcing desegregation in the United States and of ending apartheid in South Africa is liberating for the peoples of the United States and of South Africa. The process of moving elected officials to obey this decision of the World Court can be liberating for people all over the world. The possibility of abolishing nuclear weapons is awesome.

NOTES

[1] Earned Run Average of a baseball player, Goals and Assists of a soccer player, or Gross National Product of a nation.

[2] Described in Mitchell Franklin, "Interposition Interposed: I and II," 21 *Law in Transition* 1 (1961), p. 77.

[3] Merits, *I.C.J. Reports 1986* 14 (June 27).

[4] *I.C.J. Reports 1980* 3 (May 24).

[5] It must be noted that it is not possible to know what the final outcome of the Nicaragua litigation would have been if Nicaragua, under newly elected President Chamorro, had not withdrawn the petition to the Court to determine the issue of economic reparations. See Augusto Zamora, "*Nicaragua v. U.S.*, The World Court Case: An Historic Decision," 49 *Lawyers Guild Practitioner* 14 (1992). Joaquin Tacsan argued that the decision was effective in shaping a peace process, "The Dynamics of International Law in Conflict Resolution" (1992).

[6] Where not stated explicitly, the source in this and the next section is the World Court Project, Lawyers' Committee on Nuclear Policy, 666 Broadway, Room 625, New York, NY 10012, USA. For information on the Court decision in the WHO case, the source is the International Physicians for the Prevention of Nuclear War; e-mail: ippnwbos@igc.apc.org.

[7] ISBN D 462 25090 1.

[8] 105th Congress 1st Session House Bill H.R. 827.

[9] Oakland City Council Resolution No. 73299 C.M.S. "RESOLVED . . . the City of Oakland calls for all nuclear weapons to be taken off of alert status, for all nuclear warheads to be separated from their delivery vehicles, and for the Nuclear Weapon States to agree to unconditional no first use of these weapons; and . . . for the termination of all nuclear weapons research, devel-

opment and testing activities; and . . . to begin negotiations immediately on a Nuclear Weapons Convention which sets a timetable for the elimination of all nuclear weapons; and . . . urges that these negotiations be completed by the year 2000 . . . ." (Copy on file at Meiklejohn Institute, Box 673, Berkeley, CA 94701, USA.)

The City of Oakland has protested some shipments of nuclear materials through its city streets. It is in the same earthquake fault zone as the U.S. nuclear weapons facility at Livermore Nuclear Weapons Laboratory.

[10]Order of 22 September 1995, *I.C.J. Reports 1995*, p. 306.

[11]Abolition 2000 Global Network Office, P.O. Box 220, Point Hueneme, CA 93044, USA; e-mail: pmeidell@igc.apc.org.

[12]World Court Project, *op. cit.* (note 6).

[13]*Wisconsin v. Howard-Hastings*, Ashland Co. Cir. Ct., September 1996, in *Christian Science Monitor*, September 20, 1996.

[14]For cases raising the issue of the illegality of nuclear weapons filed before the World Court opinion, *see Human Rights & Peace Law Docket: 1945-1993*, Ann Fagan Ginger (ed.), Meiklejohn Institute, 1995.

[15]*The Japanese Annual of International Law*, Vol. 8 (1964), p. 212, discussed in Shahabuddeen § III.1.

[16]General Lee Butler, "The General's Bombshell: What Happened When I Called for Phasing Out the U.S. Nuclear Arsenal," *Washington Post*, January 12, 1997, C1-2.

[17]A/RES/51/45, 10 January 1997.

[18]*See* Ginger, "The Energizing Effect of Enforcing a Human Rights Treaty," 42 *DePaul L. Rev. (1993), p. 1341.*

[19]UN language includes many abbreviations: NPT (nations that have signed the Nuclear Non-Proliferation Treaty), CD (Conference on Disarmament), NWS (Nuclear Weapons States), NNWS (Non-Nuclear Weapons States), Prep-Comm (Preparatory Committee).

[20]For descriptions of NGOs in the U.S. concerned about nuclear weapons issues, see *Human Rights Organizations & Periodicals Directory*, published biennially by Meiklejohn Civil Liberties Institute, Box 673, Berkeley, CA 94701, USA.

[21]From the reports by Rebecca Johnson, *Disarmament Intelligence Rev.*, 24 Colverstone Crescent, London E8 2LH, UK. (Tel. +41-171-503-5557.)

[22]Quoted in *The National Lawyers Guild: From Roosevelt through Reagan,* Ann Fagan Ginger and Eugene M. Tobin (eds.), 1988, pp. 58-59.

[23]Abolition 2000, *op. cit.* (note 11).

[24]Butler, *op. cit.*, p. C2.

[25]State University of New Jersey, Rutgers School of Law, Camden, NJ, in "Over the Atlantic Again," 9 July 1996, p. 14.

[26]Press Communique, "World Court Declares Nuclear Weapons Threat and Use Illegal," World Court Project, July 8, 1996.

[27]"Historical and Proposed Spending for Nuclear Weapons Research, Development, Testing, and Production—1948-2003," U.S. Nuclear Weapons Cost Study Project, Brookings Institution, 1715 Massachusetts Avenue, NW, Washington D.C. 20036-2188, and the Center for Defense Information, 1500 Massachusetts Avenue, NW, Washington D.C. 20005.

THE WORLD COURT PROJECT: HOW A CITIZEN NETWORK CAN INFLUENCE THE UNITED NATIONS

Kate Dewes and
Commander Robert Green RN (Retired)*

Introduction

The World Court Project (WCP) is an international citizens' initiative which has succeeded in persuading the UN to use Article 96 of the UN Charter to request the International Court of Justice (ICJ) at The Hague, or World Court, for its first-ever advisory opinion on the legal status of nuclear weapons.

This paper surveys how a loose network of individual activists and Non-Governmental Organizations (NGOs) made use of the UN system to help the UN use its own judicial organ to stimulate nuclear disarmament. Adopting an anecdotal approach, the authors trace the WCP's evolution through primary source material and interviews with some of the key players. Particular emphasis is given to events in Aotearoa (New Zealand) and the United Kingdom (UK), drawing on the authors' personal experience.

World Court Project Origins

Government Initiatives. The question of banning nuclear weapons was implicit in the inaugural resolution adopted by the UN,[1] which was tabled by the five permanent members of the newly formed Security Council. This led to the U.S. Baruch Plan, rejected by the USSR in December 1946 because, whilst effectively allowing the U.S. to maintain its nuclear monopoly, it would have placed control of nuclear know-how and materials in the hands of an international authority

---

*See biographies at end of this paper.

dominated by Western interests.[2]

The Soviets produced a counter-proposal which was nothing less than a draft Nuclear Weapons Convention on the lines of the now widely acclaimed Chemical Weapons Convention. After hard U.S. lobbying they were outvoted, and the first attempt to bring nuclear weapons within the law collapsed.

In 1949 at the Diplomatic Conference which agreed to the four Geneva Conventions, the USSR again tabled/presented[3] a proposal to outlaw nuclear weapons: but Cold War pressures froze it out.[4] Nevertheless, since 1961 the overwhelming majority of states have regularly voted in the UNGA that the use of nuclear weapons would be a crime against humanity.[5]

NGO Initiatives. On 5 September 1945, barely a month after Hiroshima, the International Committee of the Red Cross (ICRC) alerted National Red Cross Societies to the grave problems which the use of this new weapon of mass destruction posed for it. This followed logically from its growing concern since 1918 to protect civilians from aerial warfare. During the Second World War the ICRC had repeatedly called upon all belligerents to restrict attacks to those against military objectives and to spare civilians — to no avail. It was the realization that combatants were far better protected by law than civilians, yet civilians were suffering more casualties, which led the ICRC to draw up the 1949 Geneva Conventions and urge the signatory states "to take . . . all steps to reach an agreement on the prohibition of atomic weapons . . . "[6] The ICRC's next attempt was an ill-fated initiative to devise the first rules for civilians exposed to weapons of mass destruction. Known as "The Draft Rules," they were published for the 1957 ICRC Conference in New Delhi, and included the statement: "The general principles of the law of war apply to nuclear and similar weapons."

Dr. Keith Suter describes[7] how the conference folded in acrimony after a dispute between the Communist and Taiwanese Chinese factions as to which should represent China. The ICRC tried to raise the Draft Rules again at its Vienna conference in 1965, but overlooked an important lesson: that the development of law occurs after an armed conflict, not during one (Vietnam). It is widely accepted that the WCP has benefited from the end of the Cold War.

The Draft Rules, without the reference to nuclear weapons, were incorporated in a resolution[8] adopted at the UN human rights conference in Teheran in 1968. This forced the issue of strengthening the international humanitarian laws of war onto the UN agenda.

Suter recounts the initiative, persistence and skill of one man, acting on behalf of an NGO, Sean MacBride, then Secretary-General of the International Commission of Jurists. A former Irish Foreign Affairs Minister, Deputy UN Secretary-General and human rights lawyer, he was awarded the Nobel Peace Prize in 1974 while President of the International Peace Bureau (IPB). MacBride drafted a resolution which ultimately became the 1977 Additional Protocols to the 1949 Geneva Conventions. Using his unique contacts and access, he persuaded the Indian government to propose the resolution in Teheran, then helped lobby other delegations and UN officials; and the resolution was adopted.[9] In so doing, he pioneered some of the methods used by the WCP, and prepared the ground for it.

Suter argues that the lawlessness of belligerents in World War II was a consequence of the lack of any serious attempt to update the law of armed conflicts from 1914 to 1968.[10]

World Court Project Gestation

In 1969 MacBride wrote about prohibiting nuclear weapons under international law.[11] However, he had excluded the reference to nuclear weapons from his Tehran resolution almost certainly because of its sensitivity with the U.S. This is borne out by Suter's conclusion that the ICRC failed to get any of the Draft Rules accepted in Vienna in 1965 because it overreached itself and was too radical.[12] It was left to MacBride to pick up the baton and not repeat the error.

Suter ends with the following prophetic words for the WCP:

". . . If war is too serious to be left to generals, then this book has shown that the law of armed conflict is too serious to be left to international lawyers. Disarmament negotiations, by the same token, are too important to be left to the negotiators. NGOs should seek to be involved in one way or another at all stages of the work."[13]

When the two Additional Protocols were agreed to in 1977, the U.S., UK and France took care to lodge "understandings," or reservations, excluding nuclear weapons from Protocol I which applied to international conflicts.[14] Thus the anomalous legal position of nuclear weapons was sustained, despite the fact that in 1963 in the *Shimoda* case in Japan, the court had ruled that the use of nuclear weapons by the U.S. against Japan had been illegal.[15]

In 1973 Australia and NZ had taken France to the World Court in

connection with its plans to continue atmospheric nuclear tests in the
South Pacific. When the Court issued orders insisting that France cease
testing pending resolution of the case, France argued that the Court
lacked jurisdiction and refused to appear or file pleadings. After conducting two more tests, France had then announced that it had finished
that phase of research, and would only test underground. The Court
majority seized on this to evade ruling on whether it had jurisdiction,
let alone on the substance of the case, and dropped it. Nonetheless, NZ
set an important precedent in asking for a declaratory judgement that
causing nuclear pollution to other countries was unlawful.[16]

In 1981 the IPB organized a major symposium on nuclear deterrence, which coincided with publication of a comprehensive UN study
on nuclear weapons.[17] At that time a growing number of international
lawyers began to write about nuclearism and international law.[18] The
revived debate among U.S. lawyers had led in 1982 to the formation
of the Lawyers' Committee on Nuclear Policy (LCNP).

A year earlier, 140 West German judges and prosecutors had
formed a group called "Judges and Prosecutors for Peace" who challenged the legal status of nuclear weapons and protested against sta-
tioning NATO's Pershing 2 and Cruise missiles on West German soil.
Encouraged by this, in 1983 Petra Kelly instigated a Tribunal against
First Strike and Mass Destructive Weapons in Nuremberg. A year later
in the Netherlands, 20,000 plaintiffs took the government to court for
its decision to allow Cruise missile deployments in violation of international law. Although it failed, it broke new ground. Meanwhile, in
the UK the Greenham Common women began to couple direct action
to prevent deployment of Cruise missiles with legal self-defence based
on the criminality of nuclearism under international and hence also
domestic law.[19]

In the Pacific, Belau had decided to enshrine nuclear-free status in
its constitution on achieving independence in 1979. Vanuatu went nuclear-free by statute in 1983, as did the Solomon Islands later that year.
Jo Vallentine was elected as Senator for the Nuclear Disarmament
Party in the Australian government in 1984. Around this time, moves
were made to get Australia, NZ, the Philippines, Japan and Ireland
declared nuclear-free; and visits by nuclear-armed warships to these
countries plus Sweden, Denmark and Norway met with strong chal-
lenges from "peace squadron" actions in most of them.

All this helped to prompt the Six Nation Initiative. Launched in
1984 by the leaders of Mexico, Argentina, Greece, India and Tanzania,
it resulted in the Stockholm Declaration. At the Third UN Special Ses-

sion on Disarmament in 1988, Swedish Prime Minister Carlsson said that this

> " . . . stressed that all states have the responsibility to uphold the rule of law in international relations. Those who possess nuclear weapons have a crucial role . . . One important step would be to prohibit the use of nuclear weapons. And I believe that the time has come to explore the possibility of such a step . . ."

Mexico had played an important role in securing the 1967 Treaty for Prohibition of Nuclear Weapons in Latin America (the Tlatelolco Treaty). In 1980 Olaf Palme had founded the Independent Commission on Disarmament and Security Issues. Their 1982 report stated: "There can be no hope of victory in a nuclear war, the two sides would be united in suffering and destruction. They can only survive together."

Meanwhile, the UN Human Rights Committee issued a powerful condemnation of nuclear weapons. Citing Article 6 of the International Covenant on Civil and Political Rights (1966), the Committee's General Comment 14 (23) ended as follows:

> "The production, testing, possession, deployment and use of nuclear weapons should be prohibited and recognized as crimes against humanity. The Committee accordingly, in the interest of mankind, calls upon all States, whether Parties to the Covenant or not, to take urgent steps, unilaterally and by agreement, to rid the world of this menace."

MacBride's work came to fruition in 1985 when he chaired the London Nuclear Warfare Tribunal, which the UK Ecology Party initiated following Petra Kelly's 1983 example and organized with Lawyers for Nuclear Disarmament. The tribunal, which included U.S. international law expert Professor Richard Falk, concluded that "current and planned (nuclear) weapons developments, strategies and deployments violate the basic rules and principles of international law."[20]

MacBride followed this up with a Lawyers' Appeal calling for the prohibition of nuclear weapons. Launched in 1987, it declared that the use of a nuclear weapon would constitute a violation of international law and human rights, and a crime against humanity. His hope was to present it to the UN General Assembly "which is empowered to request the International Court of Justice to give an opinion as to the validity of our Declaration."[21] Sadly he died in 1988; but by 1992 it had been signed by 11,000 lawyers from 56 countries.

In 1987 the LCNP co-sponsored with the Association of Soviet Lawyers an International Conference on Nuclear Weapons and International Law, a first. Some of the speakers were to become key players in the WCP. It was decided to form the International Association of Lawyers Against Nuclear Arms (IALANA). Two years later it held a World Congress at The Hague, at which it adopted a Declaration which included an appeal to UN members to "take immediate steps towards obtaining a resolution by the United Nations (General) Assembly under Article 96 of the United Nations Charter, requesting the International Court of Justice to render an advisory opinion on the illegality of the use of nuclear weapons."

The Aotearoa/New Zealand Initiative[22]

Meanwhile, in 1986 Falk was invited by the NZ Foundation for Peace Studies to speak on nuclearism and international law. A Labour government had been elected in 1984 with a mandate to outlaw nuclear weapons and propulsion. Falk encouraged the peace movement to study the ingredients of previous social movements which, at their outset, had seemed impractical and unlikely to succeed: the campaigns against slavery, royalism, colonialism and infanticide. He suggested building on the "embryonic" structures that were already in place for global reform, such as the international groups of physicians, lawyers and ecologists who sought arms reductions. He added:

> "Another important source to tap is the women's movement with its creative contribution of feminine consciousness. This includes positive images of authority, order and power that do not rest on a hierarchy of violence and patriarchal systems that we have become accustomed to. Similarly we can draw on perspectives on society offered by indigenous peoples of diverse cultures."[23]

Falk suggested that the government use the World Court to clarify its obligations, if any, under the ANZUS Treaty with regard to hosting port visits by U.S. nuclear-powered and armed vessels. Although the government did not take up the suggestion, Falk's ideas alerted some peace campaigners to the idea.[24]

A few months later, retired Christchurch magistrate Harold Evans compiled the opinions of six leading international jurists, including Falk, Edward St. John and Christopher Weeramantry (now Vice-President of the World Court), into an Open Letter. In March 1987, Evans sent it to the Prime Ministers of Australia and NZ three months before the nuclear-free bill became law. In it he challenged them to sponsor a UN resolution to seek a World Court opinion on "the legality or otherwise of nuclear weaponry." Hawke rejected the idea, but Lange showed interest. Evans followed it up with appeals to all 71 UN member states with diplomatic representation in Canberra and Wellington. Some indicated support.

Within Aotearoa/New Zealand a dialogue with government and officials ensued, strongly backed by the newly formed Public Advisory Committee on Disarmament and Arms Control (PACDAC), tasked with advising the government on the implementation of the nuclear-free legislation. Among its members were Dr. Robin Briant, Chair of International Physicians for the Prevention of Nuclear War (IPPNW) in NZ, and Kate Dewes. In 1988 a NZ-sponsored resolution supporting the WCP was adopted at IPPNW's World Congress. In May 1988, Dewes was one of two NGO members of the NZ government delegation to the Third UN Special Session on Disarmament (UNSSOD III) in New York. She had worked on peace issues with Evans since 1979, and organized Falk's Christchurch visit. She said:

> "We strongly urge all nations and peace groups to support a move by jurists in NZ and other countries to have the International Court of Justice give an advisory opinion on whether or not nuclear arms are illegal. The symbolic power of such a ruling would be immense . . ."

While in New York, she shared Evans' Open Letter with LCNP, IPB representatives and key diplomats from India, Mexico, Sweden and Australia. Her meetings with Rikhi Jaipal (former Indian UN Ambassador and Chair of the Conference on Disarmament), and Swedish Disarmament Ambassador Maj Britt Theorin heralded their critical role in later years. Jaipal advised that, as early as 1981, Indira Gandhi had looked closely at the illegality question with support from Nagendra Singh (the World Court judge and later its President) and other Indian lawyers. Jaipal said it was vital to get an advisory opinion, and then to build it into a legally binding treaty.[25] In later correspondence, he gave astute guidance on the text of the resolution, and how to lobby the UNGA.[26]

In March 1989, the new Minister of Disarmament, Fran Wilde, confirmed that the government would not co-sponsor the resolution but would "keep it on the table." PACDAC was reassured that the illegality issue would be included in the updated UN Study on Nuclear Weapons.

The Group of Governmental Experts producing this was chaired by
Theorin and included NZ's Director of Disarmament. NGOs within the
South Pacific region were encouraged to provide inputs to the report.
Both Evans and St. John submitted vital documentation for the section
on illegality.[27] At its annual conference in Brighton, UK, in September
1989, the IPB endorsed Evans' strategy. IALANA followed a few
weeks later at its World Congress at The Hague.

In March 1991, another Aotearoa citizen arrived at the UN in New
York, representing NGOs worldwide opposing the Gulf War. Alyn
Ware, then a 29-year-old kindergarten teacher and peace educator, ap-
proached several UN missions and found strong support for the WCP
idea. He was given guidance by Dr. Kennedy Graham, a former NZ
diplomat who was now Secretary-General of Parliamentarians for
Global Action (PGA). Costa Rica began redrafting an earlier resolution
from Evans, with the intention of co-sponsoring it at the 1992 UNGA.
PGA printed articles on the idea by Vallentine[28] and Swedish lawyer
Stig Gustaffson, which went to over 600 MPs in over 40 countries.

Three months later Dewes and IPB Secretary-General Colin Archer
found similar support in Geneva missions. The idea was seen as non-
discriminatory; supportive of the UN Decade of International Law; it
complemented moves for nuclear-free zones in Africa and the Middle
East; and it would strengthen efforts to secure a Convention on Prohibition of Use of Nuclear Weapons. However, at least 50 states, including some neutral ones, would be needed to co-sponsor the resolution
in order to withstand the expected severe pressure from the nuclear
weapon states.[29]

UK: Declarations of Public Conscience

Encouraged by this support, Dewes then visited UK where she
helped mobilize a strong network already working on the idea. Robert
Green attended a follow-up meeting in London in October 1991 at
which WCP(UK) was launched.

Keith Mothersson, a legal scholar and anti-nuclear activist, pioneered many innovative ideas, including a key aspect of the WCP's
success: harnessing the public conscience and the law. In "From Hiroshima to The Hague," a guide to the WCP, published by the IPB in
1992, he proposed invoking the de Martens clause from the 1907
Hague Convention as an individual Declaration of Public Conscience.[30] This idea was developed into a leaflet with a text ready for
signature. MacBride had mentioned the de Martens clause in his Tehe-

ran resolution. Following his lobbying, Swedish MPs began referring to it in speeches. Falk and other supportive lawyers took it up, and IALANA incorporated it in their Hague Declaration at their inaugural World Congress in 1989.

The concept of ordinary citizens separately signing personal declarations on a question of international law was novel. Not only did it link the de Martens clause with the custodians of the public conscience for the first time: it also empowered them to exercise it. Only World Court judges can decide the legal status of nuclear weapons; but ordinary citizens now had a way to express whether they think nuclear weapons are right or wrong — and these decisions should be linked.

Moreover, the intention was somehow to present them to the World Court — although this began as just a vague hope, since only governments and UN agencies are entitled to submit evidence to it. Falk encouraged the WCP to try, citing such declarations as quasi-legal evidence of public concern and support. Along with letters of endorsement from NGOs, prominent people and institutions, these would all help to put "psycho-political pressure" on the judges to counter inevitable opposing pressures from the nuclear weapon states — all an accepted part of the juridical process.

WCP(UK) set up a pilot scheme to test public reaction in November 1991. Once people understood what the WCP was, and that this was not just another petition, they began to sign with enthusiasm. The idea quickly spread to countries with active anti-nuclear movements, including Aotearoa, Australia, Canada, France, Germany, Ireland, Japan, Netherlands, Norway, Sweden and the U.S. Declarations were translated into nearly 40 languages.

The World Court Project Is Born

Article 96 of the UN Charter states that, in addition to the General Assembly or Security Council, other UN organs and specialized agencies may also request advisory opinions of the Court on legal questions arising within the scope of their activities.

In February 1992, Dr. Erich Geiringer of IPPNW(NZ) had begun to explore the possibility of getting IPPNW to spearhead a request to the WHO's annual assembly because the doctors could use that forum most effectively. Also Ware approached UNICEF, which was sympathetic but declined involvement.

During the international WCP launch that took place in Geneva in May 1992, the Zimbabwe Foreign Minister announced his gov-

ernment's support: the first to do so. IALANA published a legal memo
by Dr. Nicholas Grief, which summarized the legal case against the
threat or use of nuclear weapons.[31]

An International Steering Committee was formed of representatives of the IPB, IPPNW and IALANA, plus the authors. Ware returned to New York as a volunteer with LCNP, now the U.S. affiliate of IALANA, and later became its Executive Director.

The steering committee focused on promoting an empowerment plan to help mobilize groups globally in support of the WCP. By 1994 over 700 organizations had signed on, including many City Councils, Greenpeace International and the Anglican Communion of Primates, while some 200,000 individual Declarations of Conscience had been collected, plus letters of support from Gorbachev and Archbishop Tutu.

The WHO Breakthrough

In 1993 IPPNW masterminded a resolution in the annual assembly of the WHO, co-sponsored by 22 states. It asked the World Court: "In view of the health and environmental effects, would the use of nuclear weapons by a State in war or other armed conflict be a breach of its obligations under international law including the WHO Constitution?" Arguments by the NATO nuclear weapon states and their allies that the WHO lacked the competence to ask the question were countered by the fact that the WHO had been investigating the health and environmental effects of nuclear weapons since 1981.

IPPNW fielded a strong lobbying team of Swedish and NZ doctors, including George Salmond, a former NZ Director General of Health. They prepared comprehensive background papers, countered misinformation and answered questions as they were raised in committees. Hilda Lini, Vanuatu's Health Minister, proved a successful lobbyist on the inside. Her speech, a powerful mix of passion and facts delivered from the point of view of a South Pacific Island woman and mother, apparently swayed the female U.S. Surgeon General. This split the Health and State Department groups in the U.S. delegation, which helped to blunt its counter-lobbying. On 14 May 1993, the resolution was passed by 73 votes to 40, with 10 abstentions. After some delay, the question was received by the Court in September 1993.

The Court invited entitled states to make submissions on the WHO question. Thirty-five submissions were received, which the Court's President remarked was an unusually large total and reflected the degree of concern in the international community about the issue.

Only five non-nuclear states (Australia, Finland, Germany, Italy, the Netherlands) made submissions echoing the rejectionist line taken by the NATO nuclear weapon states and Russia (China did not make a submission). Of the remainder, 22 argued that any nuclear weapon use would be illegal, one (Ireland) wanted the question answered, and three (NZ, Japan, Norway) were "on the fence."

WCP Challenges Legality of Nuclear Deterrence

A major objection to the WHO resolution by the NATO nuclear states, and the Australian and NZ governments, was that the UN was the correct forum for the WCP issue. Accordingly LCNP members approached several UN missions in New York following the WHO success. Led by Zimbabwe's Foreign Minister, the Non-Aligned Movement (NAM) — 111 of the UN's 185 member states — agreed to table [present] a more ambitious resolution at the 1993 UN disarmament session. This resolution asked the World Court urgently to render its advisory opinion on the question: "Is the threat or use of nuclear weapons in any circumstance permitted under international law?" The nuclear weapon states correctly perceived it as threatening their privileged status as permanent members of the UN Security Council.

The last week of October 1993 saw a struggle in the UNGA's First Committee. Zimbabwe, backed by a determined group of South Pacific states, lobbied hard, helped by a WCP team which included Lini and Maori elder Pauline Tangiora. The presence of two indigenous women from the South Pacific had a powerful impact on the diplomats of small island states within that region.

Theorin was on the Swedish delegation and played a vital role as the link between the activists and ambassadors — many of whom were long-time personal friends who trusted her opinion. She also wrote to all members of PGA and Women Parliamentarians for Peace, alerting them to the resolution and suggesting parliamentary questions about their government's support for the resolution.

NGO delegations quietly lobbied diplomats in the UN corridors, the Delegates' Lounge and missions. They showed them newspaper articles from Ireland[32] and Aotearoa[33] reporting probable government support; a supportive letter from the newly elected Canadian Prime Minister; evidence that the Italian Foreign Affairs Committee had passed a binding resolution requiring the government to support the NAM resolution if it got to a vote; and other indications of cracks in the Western line. The NZ and Australian NGOs challenged their diplomats directly about their governments' role in leaning on South Pacific states not to support the resolution.

After some crucial lobbying by Vanuatu, the resolution was introduced reluctantly by the NAM Chair, Indonesia. Peggy Mason, Canada's Disarmament Ambassador, described the reaction: "Hysteria is not too strong a word to describe the nuclear weapon states' point of view around here."[34] The U.S., UK and France sent delegations to many NAM capitals threatening trade and aid cuts if the resolution was not withdrawn. Theorin said: "During my 20 years' experience as a UN delegate, I have never seen such supreme power politics openly being used as during the fall of 1993."[35] On 19 November the NAM consensus buckled, and Indonesia announced that action had been deferred.

In May 1994, the NAM Foreign Ministers meeting in Cairo decided not just to re-table the resolution, but to put it to a vote. Benin — under heavy French pressure — decided to oppose it; and the NAM duly re-tabled it in the First Committee on 9 November.

The UK and France enlisted Germany, as President of the European Union at the time, to present a broader front of support for their intense opposition to the resolution, and to diffuse accusations of pressure on NAM capitals. The UK claimed that the resolution risked "being seen as a deliberate attempt to exert pressure over the Court to prejudice its response (to the WHO question) . . . (it) can do nothing to further global peace and security."[36] The French showed signs of hysteria: "It is a blatant violation of the UN Charter. It goes against the law. It goes against reason . . ."[37]

The NAM were not deflected. On 18 November 1994 in the First Committee, Morocco tabled (presented) a resolution for no action to be taken. This was defeated by 67 votes to 45, with 15 abstentions (including NZ) and 57 states not voting. The WCP resolution was then adopted by 77 votes to 33, with 21 abstentions and 53 not voting. China did not vote; Ukraine abstained; and the normally compliant Western caucus of non-nuclear states collapsed. By abstaining, Canada and Norway broke ranks with NATO, Japan and Australia with the U.S., and Ireland with the European Union along with two prospective neutral non-NATO members, Sweden and Austria.

The most serious insubordination, however, was that Aotearoa voted for it. As a Security Council member at the time and the only Western state to do so, this undid at a stroke the progress made by the U.S. to lure the one such state with nuclear-free legislation back under Washington's control. The government conceded that public opinion forced it to vote for the resolution and withstand Western pressure to abstain. There had been frequent public visits by both U.S. and UK high-level military and diplomatic personnel during 1994.

The common factor in this breakdown in Western cohesion was the strength of public support for the WCP. In the run-up to the vote, several hundred individual letter-writers worldwide were mobilized to fax Prime Ministers personally with expressions of gratitude, and encouraging them to withstand any coercion by the nuclear states. In one instance, a UN ambassador who had just received new instructions to abstain because of pressure was shown a letter from his Prime Minister replying to a WCP correspondent which stated that his government's support for the resolution would stand. The ambassador decided to ignore his latest instructions.

Resolutions adopted by the First Committee go to the General Assembly for confirmation in a final plenary session. Normally this is only a formality, and the voting pattern shows little change. However, a UK representative told Ware that the NATO nuclear weapon states intended to "kill" the WCP resolution. The WCP responded by launching a new faxing campaign, adjusted to capitals of supportive states which had abstained or not voted.

In the plenary session on 15 December 1994, the NATO nuclear weapon states tried again with a resolution for no action to be taken. It was defeated, but by a margin which was more than halved, from 22 votes to 10. France then tried to have the word "urgently" removed: but the motion was defeated by just five votes. This was crucial because, without it, consideration of the question by the Court could have been delayed, perhaps for years. Moreover, the process at the Court was strengthened by enabling the Court to consider both questions simultaneously.

In the final vote, the resolution was adopted by 78 votes to 43, with 38 abstentions and 25 not voting. The majority only fell by nine, and the "yes" total actually increased by one. China did not vote, which was embarrassing for the other nuclear states. Apparently it even considered supporting the resolution, but backed off when its UN mission was advised that "threat" implied possession.

William Epstein, a distinguished disarmament adviser at the UN, described it as "the most exciting night in the UN for thirty years." Yet there was almost no coverage in the major Western newspapers and other news media despite strenuous efforts by the WCP.

Next Steps at the World Court

Because the UNGA request was for an opinion to be made "urgently," the Court decided to consider both questions simultaneously and followed its timetable for the WHO question. Governments were invited to make written submissions by 20 September 1995, and oral proceedings were held at The Hague from 30 October to 15 November 1995. Forty-three governments and the WHO made written submissions, and 22 and the WHO made oral statements — the biggest participation in an ICJ case. The Court gave its decision on 8 July 1996.[38]

The World Court and Citizens' Evidence

On 10 June 1994, the World Court Registrar received a citizens' delegation representing over 700 NGOs which had endorsed the WCP. The delegation presented a unique collection of documents, including:

- 170,000 Declarations of Public Conscience;

- a sample of the 100 million signatures to the Appeal from Hiroshima and Nagasaki;

- 11,000 signatures to the MacBride Lawyers' Appeal Against Nuclear Weapons;

- material surveying 50 years of citizens' opposition to nuclear weapons.

Accepting these into the Court's archive, the Registrar undertook to draw the judges' attention to them when considering the questions. He took care to point out that only entitled states and UN agencies are allowed to submit evidence to the Court; and that therefore these documents had not been accepted as legal evidence. This is the first time that the Court had accepted material from a citizens' delegation, which sets a precedent for NGOs in future cases.

The Unique Nature of the World Court Project

The WCP was not a conventional NGO. A loose umbrella network, its international core comprises an unprecedented, non-hierarchical coalition of IPB, IPPNW and IALANA. These respected NGOs were working on a common cause with short-term, achievable goals. They were supported by leading members of society such as doctors, lawyers (including judges), politicians (including ex-prime ministers), Nobel Peace Prize winners and religious leaders (including Archbishops). An important reason for such wide backing was a sense that this was a project which might be really effective. Also using the legal arm of the UN was not only novel and exciting, but placed opposition to nuclear weapons on the right side of the law.

Unlike earlier initiatives, which were Eurocentric and male-dominated, the WCP was truly international. There was a strong input from African, Latin American, Asian and South Pacific countries. Although the ISC core was Western, white and middle class, it had links with other regions, and women and indigenous peoples played an important part in the network.

The ISC was able to mobilize movements in key "middle" (non-nuclear but Western-orientated) countries such as Ireland, Germany, Sweden, Aotearoa, Canada, Japan and Australia. This helped to build and then sustain support within the NAM, and frighten the Western bloc. In Japan a draft submission on the WHO question was leaked to WCP campaigners because it echoed the nuclear weapon states' line that nuclear weapon use might be legal in some circumstances. After a public outcry, a revised text was submitted which acknowledged that the use of nuclear weapons would violate "the humanitarian principle upon which international law is based."[39]

Factors common to WCP success in these "middle" countries were accessibility to key decision-makers and politicians; media access and interest; and friendships between politicians and leading members of IPB, IPPNW and IALANA.

Within the NAM, support was gained from visits to UN missions of Latin American, African, Arab, Asian and South Pacific states. Strong anti-nuclear sentiment in the latter region was translated into a feeling that the WCP offered a way for small states to confront the nuclear states successfully. In addition, visits were made to the South Pacific Forum in 1992, and key capitals in Latin America. Visits by WCP(UK) to London Embassies/High Commissions proved fruitful. Following one, Ukraine was the first state to make a submission to the Court on the WHO question, which encouraged others.[40]

Meanwhile, a public education campaign was conducted using the limited resources and energy available. Apart from promoting Declarations of Public Conscience, parallel WCP launches to focus media attention were organized in UK, Aotearoa, Canada, India, Malaysia and Zimbabwe. The ISC compiled a register of prominent endorsers which was used for publicity. In UK, where a more formal coordinating committee had been formed of representatives from the most active NGOs, supporters were encouraged to establish local WCP groups. Public ceremonies to hand over Declarations to prominent politicians or officials were arranged in several countries: these included an international handover in New York in October 1993 to the UN Head of Disarmament, and then at The Hague before delivering them to the Court the following June.

Use was made of national parliamentary systems: keeping governments under pressure by frequent questions; snap debates in the more responsive systems; meetings with foreign affairs select committees, key ministers, and leaders of political parties. A major effort was made to gain public support from MPs, who were asked to send it in writing to the Prime Minister. Even some sympathetic NZ government MPs asked questions of their own ministers.

The lobby teams at the WHO's 1993 assembly and UNGA forced a degree of accountability from politicians and even diplomats. In 1988, NZ Foreign Minister Russell Marshall was reprimanded by his Prime Minister David Lange for making a speech in Geneva supporting nuclear deterrence. In his defence, Marshall said: "I tried to be all things to all people . . . was I thinking I could get away with it because people at home will be too busy to see it?"[41]

In Aotearoa the WCP used the Official Information Act to request release of ministry briefing papers on voting tactics in the UN, and the text of the submission to the World Court. If denied, there is recourse to the Ombudsman.

Conclusion

The World Court Project caught the post-Cold War revival of disarmament momentum, including agreement over the Chemical Weapons Convention and progress toward a Comprehensive Test Ban Treaty. The breakup of the USSR forced the nuclear weapon States to acknowledge that nuclear proliferation was the greatest threat to world security. Doubts grew about the effectiveness of nuclear deterrence. The acrimonious review and extension of the NPT and subsequent Chinese and French testing kept the nuclear issue at the top of the international agenda.

The loose umbrella network of NGOs with an informal steering group seems to have been effective, and offers flexible applications. The campaign helped to empower ordinary citizens to learn about and then participate in the UN system through their governments.

NOTES

[1]On 24 January 1946, the UN General Assembly unanimously adopted Resolution 1(I) to establish an international Atomic Energy Commission, which included a clause "for the elimination from national armaments of atomic weapons and of all other weapons of mass destruction."

[2]A detailed account of the Baruch Plan is given by Elliott L Meyrowitz, *Prohibition of Nuclear Weapons: The Relevance of International Law* (Dobbs Ferry, NY: Transnational Publishers, 1990), Chapter IV.

[3]In New Zealand, to "table" is to put on the table or present for discussion. It has the opposite meaning in the United States, where to "table" is to kill a motion.

[4]International Committee of the Red Cross (ICRC), *Commentary on the Additional Protocols of 8 June 1977 to the Geneva Conventions of 12 August 1949* (Geneva: Martinus Nijhoff Publishers, 1987), paragraph 1839.

[5]As evidenced by the votes on UNGA resolutions 1653 (XVI) of 1961, 33/71B of 1978, 34/83G of 1979, 35/152D of 1980, 36/92I of 1981, 45/59B of 1990, 46/37D of 1991, and 47/53C of 1992. 47/53C was adopted by 125 votes for, 21 against, with 22 abstentions and 16 not voting.

[6]ICRC Appeal to the High Contracting Parties Signatory to the Geneva Conventions for the Protection of the Victims of War: Atomic Weapons and Non-Directed Missiles, Geneva, April 5, 1950.

[7]Dr. Keith Suter, *An International Law of Guerrilla Warfare: The Global Politics of Law-Making* (London: Frances Pinter, 1984), p. 93.

[8]*Ibid.*, pp. 30-31.

[9]*Ibid.*, pp. 28-35.

[10]*Ibid.*, pp. 39-41.

[11]He submitted a memorandum to an International Conference on Chemical and Biological Warfare in London on 21-23 November 1969. Entitled, "The Humanitarian Laws of Armed Conflict," on page 7 he wrote: "The (1925) Geneva (Gas) Protocol was drawn up before the discovery of atomic power, and today the damage which indiscriminate use of such energy could cause is out of all proportion to military requirements. There is of course the view that no use of nuclear weapons can be justified, and that the total prohibition of such weapons in warfare should form a separate convention or part of a non-proliferation treaty."

[12]Suter, *op. cit.*, p. 95.

[13]*Ibid.*, p. 184.

[14]ICRC, *Commentary on the Additional Protocols, op. cit.*, paragraph 1845.

[15]Meyrowitz, *Prohibition of Nuclear Weapons, op. cit.*, pp. 60-62.

[16]Keith Mothersson, *From Hiroshima to the Hague* (Geneva: IPB, 1992), p. 51.

[17]Comprehensive Study on Nuclear Weapons, Report of the Secretary-General A/45/373, 18 September 1990 (UN publication, Sales No. E.81.I.11).

[18]Richard Falk, Elliott Meyrowitz and Jack Sanderson, "Nuclear Weapons and International Law," 541 *Indian Journal of International Law* (1980).

[19]Mothersson, *From Hiroshima to the Hague, op cit.*, pp. 24-28.

[20]*The Bomb and the Law*, London Nuclear Warfare Tribunal, Summary Report (Alva and Gunnar Myrdal Foundation, Munkbron 11, S-111 28 Stockholm, Sweden, 1989), p. D3.

[21]Letter from Sean MacBride to Harold Evans, 13 July 1987.

[22]The names Aotearoa and New Zealand are used interchangeably. Aotearoa is the original Maori name; New Zealand is the European name. Both are official.

[23]*Christchurch Press*, 20 June 1986.

[24]Harold Evans, "The World Court Project on Nuclear Weapons and International Law," *New Zealand Law Journal*, July 1993, p. 1.

[25]Dewes notes from meeting with Jaipal and NZ diplomats, June 1988.

[26]Letter from Jaipal to Dewes, 18 May 1991.

[27]Comprehensive Study on Nuclear Weapons, Report of the Secretary-General A/45/373, *op. cit.*, pp. 130-131.

[28]Senator Jo Vallentine, "Nuclear Weapons: The Legal Case for Prohibition," *Parliamentarians for Global Action Newsletter*, June 1991, p. 7.

[29]Report of meetings with missions by Dewes and Archer, July 1991.

[30]One of the first Russian writers on international law, Frederic de Martens (1845-1909) helped draft the 1907 Hague Convention, including the clause in the preamble.

[31]Nicholas Grief, *The World Court Project on Nuclear Weapons and International Law* (Aletheia Press, P.O. Box 1178, Northampton, MA 01061, USA, 1993).

[32]Colin Boland, "Move to Outlaw Use of Nuclear Weapons," *Irish Times*, 21 October 1993: "Brian Lenihan, Chair of the Committee on Foreign Affairs, said he was very much in favour of subjecting such weapons to some form of rule of law and he felt the committee should support it."

[33]Brendon Burns, "Government Supports Christchurch Man's Move," *Christchurch Press*, 29 September 1993: "Mr. Graham, Minister of Justice and Disarmament, said there was little doubt New Zealand would vote for a resolution at the UNGA to have the World Court rule on the issue."

[34]Miguel Marin Bosch, Mexico's UN Ambassador in Geneva, who was also there, said: "What is at the heart of this debate is that it detonates a rethinking of the whole nuclear business, which in turn forces a rethinking of the whole Cold War power structure . . . Look at France. This whole debate is driving the French crazy. The French government thinks that their legitimacy comes from having nuclear weapons. Take their nukes and their Security Council veto, and what are they? A little more than Italy and less than Germany." Richard Butler, Australia's UN Ambassador, commented: "There is no post-Cold War order. The first step to getting there is the elimination of nuclear weapons." (Mark Schapiro, "Mutiny on the Nuclear Bounty," *The Nation*, 27 December 1993.)

[35]Speech at WCP Implications Seminar, Episcopal Church Center, New York, NY, 19 April 1995.

[36]UK Explanation of Vote on Draft Resolution A/C.1/49/L.36 "Requests for an Advisory Opinion from ICJ on Legality of Nuclear Weapons," Agenda Item 62, 18 November 1994.

[37]Explanation of Vote by H.E.M., Gerard Errera, Representative of France to the Conference on Disarmament, on 49th UNGA—First Committee, "Advisory Opinion of the International Court of Justice on the Legality of the Use or the Threat of Use of Nuclear Weapons," Agenda Item 62, 18 November 1994.

[38]International Court of Justice Communique No. 95/4, 2 February 1995.

[39]"Tokyo Alters Stance on Nuclear Weapons," *Japan Times*, 9 June 1994.

[40]Letter to Green from Embassy of Ukraine, 20 May 1994.

[41]Interview by Dewes with Marshall, 19 July 1994.

About the Authors

Kate Dewes taught Peace Studies at the University of Canterbury in Christchurch, NZ, for ten years, served on the Public Advisory Committee on Disarmament and Arms Control which monitors implementation of the NZ Nuclear Free Act, and co-chaired the Labour Party Policy Committee on Foreign Affairs and Defence. She was elected vice-president of the International Peace Bureau in 1997. A pioneer of the World Court Project (WCP), she was on its International Steering Committee. She is completing her Ph.D. at the University of New England, Australia. For fifteen years she ran the NZ Peace Foundation's South Island regional office from her home.

Robert Green served in the UK Royal Navy from 1962-82. As a Fleet Air Arm Observer, he flew in Buccaneer carrier-borne nuclear strike aircraft (1968-72), then in anti-submarine helicopters equipped with nuclear depth-bombs (1972-77). On promotion to Commander, he spent 1978-80 in the Ministry of Defence as Personal Staff Officer to the Assistant Chief of Naval Staff (Policy), who was closely involved in the replacement for the Polaris ballistic missile submarine system. As Staff Officer (Intelligence) to Commander-in-Chief Fleet at Northwood HQ, he was in charge of round-the-clock intelligence support for Polaris and the rest of the Fleet. He took voluntary redundancy in the 1981 defence review and was released after the Falklands War. The Gulf War and breakup of the USSR caused him to speak out against nuclear weapons. He became UK Chair of the WCP in 1991 and was on its International Steering Committee.

Dewes and Green are now co-coordinators to the NZ Peace Foundation's new Disarmament and Security Center.

The Movement Grows Everywhere

NH Clam Shell Alliance in Rocky Flats, Colorado, where triggers for nuclear bombs are manufactured.

Delegation from Japan at Annual Demonstration in Denver and Rocky Flats, Colorado. (Banner reads "Human Beings Must Live.") Photos by Mary Fagan Bates.

Credit: UN Photo 150404/Milton Grant

The
Movement
Becomes
History

The Movement appeals to UN General Assembly,
blocking First Avenue entrance, June 1982.

September 1979 demonstration in New York City's Central Park. Photos courtesy of FPG.

PART FIVE

Appendices

STUDY GUIDE

I. THE FACTS

1. Effects of nuclear weapons
   Effects on people of tests and of use in 1945
   Effects on people of tests since 1945
   Effects on people of threat of use today
      On military personnel
         In nuclear weapons states
         In non-nuclear weapons states
      On civilians
         In nuclear weapons states
         In non-nuclear weapons states
      On children
         In nuclear weapons states
         In non-nuclear weapons states
   Effects on environment
      In nuclear weapons test states
      In nuclear weapons manufacturing states
      In non-nuclear weapons states
      Globally
   Effects on economy
      In nuclear weapons states
      In non-nuclear weapons states
      In would-be nuclear weapons states
      On global economy
   Effects on political process
      Lobbying by military/industrial complex
      Organizing/lobbying by anti-nuclear weapons movement
      Organizing/lobbying by UN supporters
   Effects on culture and morality
      In nuclear weapons states
      In would-be nuclear weapons states
      In anti-nuclear weapons states
2. Examples of use and threats of use of nuclear weapons
   World War II
   Korean War
   Cuban missile crisis

Cold War

Vietnam War

Persian Gulf War

3. Effects of nuclear weapons: projections

Impossibility of storing nuclear waste products safely as long as necessary

Possibility of developing smaller, "cleaner," "tactical," "battle-field," "theatre" nuclear weapons in the future

On the future of the globe

On future generations

QUESTIONS FOR DISCUSSION

I. THE FACTS

1. What has happened to people who reside near nuclear weapons test sites in the United States, in the Pacific Ocean, in Russia, in China and in other nations?

1. The judges heard graphic descriptions of the effects of nuclear weapons on the peoples of several nations and areas. They were presented with statistics on the destructive capacity of current nuclear weapons stockpiles of 5,000 times more than the capacity of all weapons that caused 40-50 million deaths in World War II (Shahabuddeen, pt. 3). Is it helpful to spend many pages in a legal opinion describing the medical results of nuclear weapons that were used in Hiroshima and Nagasaki in 1945 and in tests in many regions since 1945?

1. Should a legal opinion include a mathematical or physics equation, as Judge Weeramantry's does?

2. Does Judge Schwebel convince you that the threat by the U.S. to the Iraqi government to use nuclear weapons just before Desert Storm was the reason Saddam Hussain did not use chemical or biological weapons? What did Judge Guillaume (in his ¶ 12), and Judge Shi think of the policy of nuclear deterrence?

3. Why did Judge Weeramantry say the Court can only deal with existing weapons?

3. As to limited tactical battlefield nuclear weapons: Was there evidence before the Court that they exist or can be produced?

3. Would such "clean nuclear bombs" violate the "humanitarian laws of war"?

STUDY GUIDE

II. THE ISSUE

  4. The question

  5. Authority of General Assembly to ask for opinion

     Nature of advisory opinion

     Urgency of request

     Different from authority of UN agencies (like the WHO) to ask for opinion

     Different from power of U.S. Supreme Court

III. THE HISTORY

  6. Limitations on war/weapons before 1945

     Philosophers/religious leaders

     Treaties arising out of many wars; Hague law

     Development of customary law

          Humanitarian laws of war forbid weapons that

               Kill civilians

               Kill people in neutral nations

               Kill the environment

               Cause unnecessary suffering

          Weapons used in response must obey rule of proportionality

          Jus in bello/Jus ad bello

          Martens/de Martens clause

     International Permanent Court of Justice opinions

     Example: Banning dum-dum bullets

  7. Limitations on war/weapons since UN founded

     UN Charter Articles 2.3, 2.4, 51, 2.1

     General Assembly Resolutions

     Security Council Resolutions

     Geneva law

     UN treaties

     International Court of Justice opinions

     National negative and positive security assurances

     National policies on first use

  8. Nuclear non-proliferation treaties

     Effects of treaty review conference process

QUESTIONS FOR DISCUSSION

II. THE ISSUE

5. Could an anti-nuclear weapons state have brought a case in the International Court of Justice against one or all of the nuclear weapons states, charging them with violating international law and UN law in the manufacture, stockpiling, transporting, testing and threatening to use nuclear weapons? What arguments would be made against filing such a suit?

5. Why did the International Court of Justice issue an advisory opinion in answer to a question by the General Assembly instead of taking a contentious case brought by one nation against another nation in which the issue was the legality of nuclear weapons?

5. Can the U.S. Supreme Court issue an advisory opinion in answer to a question from the U.S. Congress? If not, why not?

5. What are the differences between General Assembly resolutions and acts of the U.S. Congress?

III. THE HISTORY

6. What is the "humanitarian law of war"? Does it supersede military law or "military necessity"?

6. Why do the opinions use so many Latin phrases? (See Glossary for definitions.)

6. What does the law include in forbidding "endangering the environment"?

7. What are negative and positive security assurances? How do they relate to self-defense? How do they relate to a policy of first use?

STUDY GUIDE

IV. THE COURT

9. Predecessor Court
10. Composition of Court
11. Authority to hear and issue advisory opinions
12. Procedure for hearing and deciding
13. Effectiveness of previous decisions and opinions
    In settling disputes between nations
    In enforcing sanctions against recalcitrant nations
    In clarifying the functions of UN specialized agencies

V. THE CASE

14. Procedure for getting the case to the Court
    Actions of General Assembly
    Actions of NGOs
    Petitions of millions of people from many nations
15. The participants in the case
    Nuclear weapons states
    Anti-nuclear weapons states
    Would-be (or not admitted) nuclear weapons states
    Counsel and scholars presenting briefs, oral arguments

VI. THE DECISION TO DECIDE THE CASE

16. Argument against deciding
    No power to decide: Oda, J.
17. Argument for deciding
    Non liquet wrong: Higgins, J.
    Proper role of the Court

QUESTIONS FOR DISCUSSION

IV. THE COURT

10. How are the judges appointed to the International Court of Justice? How long are the terms of ICJ judges — for life, as in the U.S. Supreme Court, or for a term of years? What nations, if any, have always been entitled to select a member of the ICJ?

10. Does each judge on the ICJ represent his/her country on the Court? Does each judge vote as the political leaders of his/her nation would vote? If not, how does each judge decide how to vote?

11. The International Court of Justice is the highest court in the UN system. Does it hear appeals from other agencies in the UN system, or from national supreme courts?

13. What power does the ICJ have to enforce its opinions?

13. Is this the same kind of power the U.S. Supreme Court has to enforce its opinions, or does the Supreme Court have more power?

V. THE CASE

14. Since the General Assembly had passed resolutions on the illegality of nuclear weapons, why did the General Assembly have to ask the International Court of Justice for an opinion on whether nuclear weapons are illegal?

14. The General Assembly had passed several resolutions that nuclear weapons are illegal. Did the U.S., UK, France, Russia and China vote for these resolutions?

14. If not, how could the resolutions have been passed? Does the General Assembly give veto power to the nuclear weapons states?

14. What role did NGOs play in causing the delegates to the General Assembly to vote to bring the issue of the illegality of nuclear weapons to the ICJ?

VI. THE DECISION TO DECIDE THE CASE

16. Does the Court have the power to make law if the law is not now clear? Should it make law?

16. Discuss Judge Oda's statement (his ¶ 45) that "there is little risk of the use of nuclear weapons at present by the five declared nuclear-weapon States . . . [since] these five . . . States, early in 1995, gave security assurances through statements made in the Security Council . . . not to use or threaten to use these weapons against the non-nuclear-weapon States."

17. Should the role of the ICJ be to *pronounce* what the law is, as Judge Weeramantry says, or should the ICJ limit its opinions to *enunciating* what the law is now, as the majority voted?

17. Discuss Judge Guillaume's ¶ 14 that the role of the judge and the Court is not to take the place of the legislature.

STUDY GUIDE

VII. THE LEGAL QUESTIONS

18. Existing treaties or laws prohibit nuclear weapons
    Nuclear Non-Proliferation Treaty
    Regional treaties
19. Right of sovereignty/self-defense against attacks; deterrents:
    military necessity
20. Law of reprisal
21. Humanitarian laws of war
22. Survival of a nation//Global survival
23. Legality of projected smaller, "cleaner," "tactical," "battlefield,"
    "theatre" nuclear weapons

VIII. THE EXISTING LAW

24. Case law/precedent
    Customary international law
    Lotus case
    Shimoda case
    Corfu Channel case
    Other decisions/opinions of International Court of Justice
25. UN Charter law
26. Treaty law
    International/UN treaties
    Regional treaties

IX. THE DECISION/OPINION

27. ¶ 104
28. ¶ 105 (1) by 13-1
29. ¶ 105 (2)A unanimously
30. ¶ 105 (2)B by 11-3
31. ¶ 105 (2)C unanimously
32. ¶ 105 (2)D unanimously
33. ¶ 105 (2)E 1 by 7-7 by the President's casting vote
34. ¶ 105 (2)E 2 by 7-7 by the President's casting vote
35. ¶ 105 (2)F unanimously

QUESTIONS FOR DISCUSSION

VII. THE LEGAL QUESTIONS

19. What is the meaning of "sovereignty" and "sovereign nation" today in the era of globalization?

19. Are there any sets of facts that might cause the World Court to rule that a nuclear weapon state was justified in using nuclear weapons to repel an attack because the very life of the nation was at stake?

19. How could nuclear weapon states justify the use of nuclear weapons that violate the humanitarian laws of war even in their self-defense?

20. What is the difference between retaliation and reprisal? Does this difference matter in deciding on the legality or illegality of nuclear weapons use?

VIII. THE EXISTING LAW

24. Discuss the facts and decisions in the *Lotus* case, *Shimoda* case, *Corfu Channel* case.

IX. THE DECISION/OPINION

28-35. Discuss the statements by Judges Bedjaoui (his ¶ 24) and Vereshchetin (closing ¶) that the Opinion is a guide to action.

35. What duty does each nation now have to prevent the threat or use of nuclear weapons?

35. What roles do the Court and the General Assembly and the Security Council play as international governmental entities in the UN system in preventing the threat or use of nuclear weapons?

35. Discuss Judge Ferrari Bravo's statement that the Nuclear Non-Proliferation Treaty bridges UN Charter Art. 2.4 and Art. 51 and Judge Guillaume's paragraph 13 on NNPT Art. VI and the Opinion ¶ 99.

35. Discuss Judge Vereshchetin's statement that the building materials are now available to construct a solid edifice for the total prohibition of nuclear weapons and that nations, not the ICJ, must bring the construction to completion.

35. What did Judge Fleischhauer mean when he said, in his ¶ 7, that the invention of nuclear weapons led to a conflict the solution to which can only lie in effective reduction and control of nuclear weapons and an improved system of collective security, as in ¶ 105 (2)F?

35. Why did Judge Schwebel say he voted for ¶ 105 (2)F in response to the question put by the General Assembly and then write: "If it applies to States not party to the Nuclear Non-proliferation Treaty, . . . it would not be a conclusion that could easily be reconciled with the fundamentals of international law" ?

35. Why did Judges Schwebel, Fleischhauer and Vereshchetin say that ¶ 105 (2)F goes beyond the question asked of the ICJ?

STUDY GUIDE

X. THE INDIVIDUAL OPINIONS

36. Declaration by Bejaoui, President from Algeria
37. Declaration by Fleischhauer from Germany
38. Declaration by Herczegh from Hungary
39. Declaration by Ranjeva from Madagascar
40. Declaration by Shi from China
41. Declaration by Vereshchetein from Russian Federation
42. Declaration by Ferrari Bravo from Italy
43. Dissent by Schwebel, Vice-President from U.S.A.
44. Dissent by Guillaume from France
45. Dissent by Higgins from U.K.
46. Dissent by Oda from Japan
47. Dissent by Shahabuddeen from Guyana
48. Dissent by Koroma from Sierra Leone
49. Dissent by Weeramantry from Sri Lanka

XI. ENFORCING THE DECISION

50. General Assembly action on transmittal of opinion
51. Actions of Preparatory Committee for 2000 Review Conference
    of the Nuclear Non-Proliferation Treaty
52. Actions of UN bodies and agencies
53. Actions of parliamentary bodies and members
54. Actions of heads of state
55. Actions of national military leaders
56. Actions of Non-Governmental Organizations
57. Actions of corporations manufacturing nuclear weapons
58. Actions of the media in reporting on the court's opinion
    In the United States
    In other nuclear weapons states
    In anti-nuclear weapons states
    In would-be nuclear weapons states
    In newsletters of corporations, NGOs, labor unions, churches,
    etc.
59. Actions of scholars analyzing and discussing the opinion
60. Actions of committed individuals

QUESTIONS FOR DISCUSSION

X. THE INDIVIDUAL OPINIONS

36-49. Why were the judges so careful to discuss points in the Court opinion with which they agreed and disagreed and to discuss points in the opinions of the other judges with whom they agreed and with whom they disagreed?

36. Why did Judge Bedjaoui first say that the Court could go no further than it did (in his ¶ 17), then say that the Court meant that nuclear weapons can never be used, even in self-defense (in his ¶ 22), and then say (in his ¶ 23) that the important thing is for nation states to carry out ¶ 105 (2)F?

40. Why did Judge Shi from China vote that nuclear weapons are illegal, since he is from a country that possesses nuclear weapons?

40. Why did Judge Shi, from the country with the largest population in the world, emphasize the principle of sovereign equality of countries and the importance of not giving undue emphasis to the nuclear weapon states and the nuclear-weapon umbrella states?

41. Why did Judge Vereshchetin from Russia vote that nuclear weapons are illegal, since he is also from a country that possesses nuclear weapons?

43. How did Judge Schwebel from the U.S. explain his vote for ¶ 105 (2)D on nuclear weapons being governed by the humanitarian laws of war?

43. How did Judge Schwebel from the United States explain his vote against ¶ 105 (2)E 1 and 2?

45. Discuss Opinion ¶ 86 and Judge Higgins' paragraph 29 that the nuclear weapons states who appeared before the Court "fully accepted that any lawful threat or use of nuclear weapons would have to comply with both the *jus ad bellum* and the *jus in bello*." Consider Judge Guilaume's ¶ 11.

45. What did Judge Higgins mean by the last sentence of her opinion?

47. Discuss Judge Shahabuddeen's statement (in his ¶ 2) that the preservation of the human species and of civilization constitutes the ultimate purpose of a legal system and of international law.

48 and 43. Discuss Judge Koroma's and Judge Schwebel's arguments on the limitations on the right of self-defense.

XI. ENFORCING THE DECISION

50. What actions, if any, did the General Assembly take after it received a formal copy of the International Court of Justice opinion?

52. What can individuals do to strengthen government officials in their work for the Preparatory Committee in preparing for the 2000 Re-

(continued over)

view Conference in light of the opinion and the Abolition 2000 campaign?

53-57. Find stories on recent actions by governmental bodies, NGOs and concerned individuals against nuclear weapons in newspapers and magazines, on TV and radio, and in organizational newsletters, and ask local reporters and writers to join in discussions of the Court's opinion.

GLOSSARY OF LATIN AND LEGAL WORDS AND PHRASES*

(Prepared with the inspired help of Professor John Quigley, Ohio State University College of Law, and Professor Pamela Vaughn, Classics Department, San Francisco State University)

advisory opinion • opinion on a legal question asked of the Court by UN organs or UN specialized agencies, not an opinion on a case brought by one state against another; not binding in law, although it may establish principles of law that are followed in subsequent opinions and cases

a fortiori • it follows; because one ascertained fact exists, therefore another, which is included in or analogous to it, which is less improbable, must also exist

a priori reasoning • reasoning not based on anything

arguendo • as a matter of argument or illustration

bis • twice, duplicate

black-letter law • law that everyone agrees is absolutely binding

bona fide • in or with good faith

cessante ratione legis; cessat ipso lex • the reason for the law

---

*Black's Law Dictionary, the customary source for definitions used by U.S. lawyers, judges and law students, does not include translations into English of many Latin phrases concerning the laws of war and peace used frequently by many of the 14 judges of the International Court of Justice. Words and phrases are spelled as they are in the opinions, which is not always consistent.

ending; the law itself also ends

consideranda • considering

convention • an international treaty

Corfu Channel **case rule, 1949** • the International Court of Justice
held a nation's obligations are based on elementary considerations
of humanity, even more exacting in peace than in war

corpus juris gentium • the body of law of nations

Court finds • the specific decision of the Court follows

covenant • an international treaty

de facto • existing as a matter of fact

dehors • foreign to, unconnected with

de jure • existing as a matter of law

dicta/dictum • word(s) of a judge that are part of a Court opinion
but are not binding, for example, because they go beyond the question presented

dispositif • the operative provisions of the judgment of the Court

ecocide • destruction of an ecosystem

erga omnes • a type of international obligation owed to the international community generally (e.g., *Barcellona Traction* case, ICJ
1970)

ex hypothesi • upon the theory or facts assumed, by definition

expressis verbis • in clear words, stated specifically, not left to
inference

fiat justitia ne pereat mundus • let justice be done lest the world
end

fiat justitia pereat mundus • let justice be done though the world

perish

fiat justitia ruat coelum ● let justice be done though the heavens fall

First Committee ● of the UN General Assembly with jurisdiction over political and security issues

hibakusha ● people injured in the Hiroshima and Nagasaki nuclear bombings

hors de combat ● out of the combat

hortus conclusus ● fruit of the conclusion in the civil law

hypotheses non fingo ● proposition going beyond actual data — or — I do not form hypotheses

ICRC ● International Committee of the Red Cross/Red Crescent

in concreto ● in concrete terms

in extremis ● in a desperate situation

instruments ● legal documents, a state act in writing

instrumentum ● a larger document or "envelope" containing certain pre-existing customary rules of international law

inter alia ● among other things

inter arma silent leges ● in time of war the laws are silent

inter arma vivant leges ● let law thrive in time of war

ipsissimis verbis ● in the identical words

ipso facto ● by the fact itself, by the mere fact

juridical prolegomena ● prefatory observations, introduction giving the fundamental points

jus ad bellum ● the law governing going to war, including self-defense — or — the right to resort to war

jus cogens ● peremptory norm or rule of general international law from which no derogation is permitted (Vienna Convention on the Law of Treaties, Art. 64)

jus in bello ● the laws and customs of war in wartime; law governing the conduct of war/armed conflict, e.g., whether a means of warfare is lawful

just war ● righteous war to right a wrong received when one sovereign violated a natural-law-based norm guaranteeing something to the other state

"Kriegraeson geht vor Kriegsmanier" ● military necessity takes precedence in deciding how to carry out a war

lacunae ● gaps or blanks in writing

lex ferenda ● an instrument, such as a treaty, that makes new law

lex lata ● customary law as it exists

lex specialis ● an applicable treaty, e.g., to be used in deciding a case between two states

litteris verbis ● literal words, verbatim

***Lotus* case rule, 1927** ● the Permanent Court of International Justice held: "Behavior not expressly forbidden by international law is authorized by this fact alone." (Bedjaoui, para. 14)

Martens Clause/de Martens Clause, 1899 ● in cases not covered by treaty law, inhabitants and belligerents remain under the principles of the law of nations resulting from usages among civilized peoples, humanitarian law and the dictates of the public conscience (from Hague Convention)

maxim ● an established principle

non-derogable right ● right to be free from torture that states must observe even during a state of emergency

non liquet doctrine ● an international tribunal should not decline to decide a case where rules are not available for determinations because of gaps or lacunae in national law

nullum crimen sine lege ● no one shall be held guilty of any penal offense on account of an act or omission that did not constitute a penal offense under national or international law when it was committed

NWS ● Nuclear Weapons States

NNWS ● Non-Nuclear Weapons States

opinio juris/opinio juris sive necessitatis ● a general practice accepted as law (ICJ Statute 38(1)(b))

pacta sunt servanda ● every treaty in force is binding upon the parties and must be performed by them in good faith (Vienna Convention, Art. 26)

Permanent Court of International Justice ● established by the League of Nations in 1920, succeeded by the International Court of Justice of the United Nations in 1945

plenipotentiaries ● ministers, envoys

procedural law ● method of enforcing rights; legal rules on how, where, when and by whom issues shall be decided

protocol ● a document amending or supplemental to another treaty

que group qua such group ● the group like the one we talked about

quid pro quo ● this for that

ratified/ratification ● act by a state approving of a treaty

realpolitik ● practical politics based on material factors without theoretical, ethical or moralistic objectives

reservation ● a unilateral statement by a state when signing, ratifying a treaty that purports to exclude or modify the legal effect of certain provisions in their application to that state but only within bounds (Vienna Convention, Art. 2)

right of reprisal "est limités par les experiences
    de l'humanite" ● a doctrine (pre-UN Charter law), allowing a state victim of unlawful military force to undertake an equivalent act of military force against the perpetrator (Shah, p. 23)

San Francisco Conference ● founding conference of the United Nations in 1945

seise ● legal variant of seize

simpliciter ● simply, without ceremony

sine qua non ● without which, indispensable

stricto sensu ● in the strict sense

substantive law ● creates, defines and regulates rights

ultra petita ● beyond what is sought, required or petitioned for

understandings ● statements made by signatory governments to clarify their interpretation of specific provisions in treaties

UNESCO ● United Nations Educational, Scientific and Cultural Organization

WCP ● World Court Project

WHO ● World Health Organization

TEXTS OF RELEVANT DOCUMENTS

Charter of the United Nations

**June 26, 1945, 59 Stat. 1031, T.S. 993, 3 Bevans 1153,
entered into force Oct. 24, 1945.**

Excerpts

Preamble

WE THE PEOPLES OF THE UNITED NATIONS DETERMINED

to save succeeding generations from the scourge of war, which twice in our lifetime has brought untold sorrow to mankind, and

to reaffirm faith in fundamental human rights, in the dignity and worth of the human person, in the equal rights of men and women and of nations large and small, and

to establish conditions under which justice and respect for the obligations arising from treaties and other sources of international law can be maintained, and

to promote social progress and better standards of life in larger freedom,

AND FOR THESE ENDS

to practice tolerance and live together in peace with one another as good neighbors, and

to unite our strength to maintain international peace and security, and

to ensure by the acceptance of principles and the institution of methods, that armed force shall not be used, save in the common interest, and

to employ international machinery for the promotion of the economic and social advancement of all peoples,

HAVE RESOLVED TO COMBINE OUR EFFORTS TO ACCOMPLISH THESE AIMS

CHAPTER I

Purposes and Principles

Article 1

The Purposes of the United Nations are:

1. To maintain international peace and security, and to that end: to take effective collective measures for the prevention and removal of threats to the peace, and for the suppression of acts of aggression or other breaches of the peace, and to bring about by peaceful means, and in conformity with the principles of justice and international law, adjustment or settlement of international disputes or situations which might lead to a breach of the peace;

2. To develop friendly relations among nations based on respect for the principle of equal rights and self-determination of peoples, and to take other appropriate measures to strengthen universal peace;

3. To achieve international cooperation in solving international problems of an economic, social, cultural, or humanitarian character, and in promoting and encouraging respect for human rights and for fundamental freedoms for all without distinction as to race, sex, language, or religion; and

4. To be a center for harmonizing the actions of nations in the attainment of these common ends.

Article 2

The Organization and its Members, in pursuit of the Purposes stated in Article 1, shall act in accordance with the following Principles.

1. The Organization is based on the principle of the sovereign equality of all its Members.

2. All Members, in order to ensure to all of them the rights and benefits resulting from membership, shall fulfill in good faith the obligations assumed by them in accordance with the present Charter.

3. All Members shall settle their international disputes by peaceful means in such a manner that international peace and security, and justice, are not endangered.

4. All Members shall refrain in their international relations from the threat or use of force against the territorial integrity or political independence of any state, or in any other manner inconsistent with the Purposes of the United Nations.

5. All Members shall give the United Nations every assistance in any action it takes in accordance with the present Charter, and shall refrain from giving assistance to any state against which the United

Nations is taking preventive or enforcement action.

6. The Organization shall ensure that states which are not Members of the United Nations act in accordance with these Principles so far as may be necessary for the maintenance of international peace and security.

CHAPTER II
Membership

Article 4

1. Membership in the United Nations is open to all other peace-loving states which accept the obligations contained in the present Charter and, in the judgment of the Organization, are able and willing to carry out these obligations.

2. The admission of any such state to membership in the United Nations will be effected by a decision of the General Assembly upon the recommendation of the Security Council.

CHAPTER IV
The General Assembly

Article 10

The General Assembly may discuss any questions or any matters within the scope of the present Charter or relating to the powers and functions of any organs provided for in the present Charter, and, except as provided in Article 12, may make recommendations to the Members of the United Nations or to the Security Council or to both on any such questions or matters.

Article 11

1. The General Assembly may consider the general principles of cooperation in the maintenance of international peace and security, including the principles governing disarmament and the regulation of armaments, and may make recommendations with regard to such principles to the Members or to the Security Council or to both.

2. The General Assembly may discuss any questions relating to the maintenance of international peace and security brought before it by any Member of the United Nations, or by the Security Council, or by a state which is not a Member of the United Nations in accordance with Article 35, paragraph 2, and, except as provided in Article 12, may make recommendations with regard to any such questions to the state or states concerned or to the Security Council or to both. Any such question on which action is necessary shall be referred to the Security

Council by the General Assembly either before or after discussion.

3. The General Assembly may call the attention of the Security Council to situations which are likely to endanger international peace and security.

4. The powers of the General Assembly set forth in this Article shall not limit the general scope of Article 10.

Article 17

1. The General Assembly shall consider and approve the budget of the Organization.

2. The expenses of the Organization shall be borne by the Members as apportioned by the General Assembly.

3. The General Assembly shall consider and approve any financial and budgetary arrangements with specialized agencies referred to in Article 57 and shall examine the administrative budgets of such specialized agencies with a view to making recommendations to the agencies concerned.

CHAPTER V

The Security Council

Article 24

1. In order to ensure prompt and effective action by the United Nations, its Members confer on the Security Council primary responsibility for the maintenance of international peace and security, and agree that in carrying out its duties under this responsibility the Security Council acts on their behalf.

2. In discharging these duties the Security Council shall act in accordance with the Purposes and Principles of the United Nations. The specific powers granted to the Security Council for the discharge of these duties are laid down in Chapters VI, VII, VIII, and XII.

Article 26

In order to promote the establishment and maintenance of international peace and security with the least diversion for armaments of the world's human and economic resources, the Security Council shall be responsible for formulating, with the assistance of the Military Staff Committee referred to in Article 47, plans to be submitted to the Members of the United Nations for the establishment of a system for the regulation of armaments.

CHAPTER VII

Action with Respect to Threats to the Peace, Breaches of the Peace, and Acts of Aggression

Article 41

The Security Council may decide what measures not involving the use of armed force are to be employed to give effect to its decisions, and it may call upon the Members of the United Nations to apply such measures. These may include complete or partial interruption of economic relations and of rail, sea, air, postal, telegraphic, radio, and other means of communication, and the severance of diplomatic relations.

Article 42

Should the Security Council consider that measures provided for in Article 41 would be inadequate or have proved to be inadequate, it may take such action by air, sea, or land forces as may be necessary to maintain or restore international peace and security. Such action may include demonstrations, blockade, and other operations by air, sea, or land forces of Members of the United Nations.

Article 51

Nothing in the present Charter shall impair the inherent right of individual or collective self-defense if an armed attack occurs against a Member of the United Nations, until the Security Council has taken measures necessary to maintain international peace and security. Measures taken by Members in the exercise of this right of self-defense shall be immediately reported to the Security Council and shall not in any way affect the authority and responsibility of the Security Council under the present Charter to take at any time such action as it deems necessary in order to maintain or restore international peace and security.

CHAPTER IX

International Economic and Social Co-Operation

Article 55

With a view to the creation of conditions of stability and well-being which are necessary for peaceful and friendly relations among nations based on respect for the principle of equal rights and self-determination of peoples, the United Nations shall promote:

a. higher standards of living, full employment, and conditions of economic and social progress and development;

b. solutions of international economic, social, health, and related problems; and international cultural and educational co-operation; and

c. universal respect for, and observance of, human rights and fundamental freedoms for all without distinction as to race, sex, language, or religion.

Article 56

All Members pledge themselves to take joint and separate action in cooperation with the Organization for the achievement of the purposes set forth in Article 55.

CHAPTER X

The Economic and Social Council

Article 62

1. The Economic and Social Council may make or initiate studies and reports with respect to international economic, social, cultural, educational, health, and related matters and may make recommendations with respect to any such matters to the General Assembly, to the Members of the United Nations, and to the specialized agencies concerned.

2. It may make recommendations for the purpose of promoting respect for, and observance of, human rights and fundamental freedoms for all.

3. It may prepare draft conventions for submission to the General Assembly, with respect to matters falling within its competence.

4. It may call, in accordance with the rules prescribed by the United Nations, international conferences on matters falling within its competence.

CHAPTER XI

Declaration Regarding Non-Self-Governing Territories

Article 74

Members of the United Nations also agree that their policy in respect of the territories to which this Chapter applies, no less than in respect of their metropolitan areas, must be based on the general principle of good-neighborliness, due account being taken of the interests and well-being of the rest of the world, in social, economic, and commercial matters.

CHAPTER XII
International Trusteeship System
Article 76

The basic objectives of the trusteeship system, in accordance with the Purposes of the United Nations laid down in Article 1 of the present Charter, shall be:

a. to further international peace and security;

b. to promote the political, economic, social, and educational advancement of the inhabitants of the trust territories, and their progressive development towards self-government or independence as may be appropriate to the particular circumstances of each territory and its peoples and the freely expressed wishes of the peoples concerned, and as may be provided by the terms of each trusteeship agreement;

c. to encourage respect for human rights and for fundamental freedoms for all without distinction as to race, sex, language, or religion, and to encourage recognition of the interdependence of the peoples of the world; and

d. to ensure equal treatment in social, economic, and commercial matters for all Members of the United Nations and their nationals and also equal treatment for the latter in the administration of justice without prejudice to the attainment of the foregoing objectives and subject to the provisions of Article 80.

CHAPTER XIV
The International Court of Justice
Article 92

The International Court of Justice shall be the principal judicial organ of the United Nations. It shall function in accordance with the annexed Statute which is based upon the Statute of the Permanent Court of International Justice and forms an integral part of the present Charter.

Article 93

1. All Members of the United Nations are ipso facto parties to the Statute of the International Court of Justice.

2. A state which is not a Member of the United Nations may become a party to the Statute of the International Court of Justice on conditions to be determined in each case by the General Assembly upon the recommendation of the Security Council.

Article 94

1. Each Member of the United Nations undertakes to comply with the decision of the International Court of Justice in any case to which it is a party.

2. If any party to a case fails to perform the obligations incumbent upon it under a judgment rendered by the Court, the other party may have recourse to the Security Council, which may, if it deems necessary, make recommendations or decide upon measures to be taken to give effect to the judgment.

Article 95

Nothing in the present Charter shall prevent Members of the United Nations from entrusting the solution of their differences to other tribunals by virtue of agreements already in existence or which may be concluded in the future.

Article 96

1. The General Assembly or the Security Council may request the International Court of Justice to give an advisory opinion on any legal question.

2. Other organs of the United Nations and specialized agencies, which may at any time be so authorized by the General Assembly, may also request advisory opinions of the Court on legal questions arising within the scope of their activities.

Treaty on the Non-Proliferation of Nuclear Weapons (1968)

**U.N.T.S. No. 10485, Vol. 729, pp. 169-175, entered into force
5 March 1970**

Excerpts

The States concluding this Treaty, hereinafter referred to as the "Parties to the Treaty",

Considering the devastation that would be visited upon all mankind by a nuclear war and the consequent need to make every effort to avert the danger of such a war and to take measures to safeguard the security of peoples,

Believing that the proliferation of nuclear weapons would seriously enhance the danger of nuclear war,

In conformity with resolutions of the United Nations General Assembly calling for the conclusion of an agreement on the prevention of wider dissemination of nuclear weapons,

Undertaking to co-operate in facilitating the application of International Atomic Energy Agency safeguards on peaceful nuclear activities,

Expressing their support for research, development and other efforts to further the application, within the framework of the International Atomic Energy Agency safeguards system, of the principle of safeguarding effectively the flow of source and special fissionable materials by use of instruments and other techniques at certain strategic points,

Affirming the principle that the benefits of peaceful applications of nuclear technology, including any technological by-products which may be derived by nuclear-weapon States from the development of nuclear explosive devices, should be available for peaceful purposes to all Parties to the Treaty, whether nuclear-weapon or non-nuclear-weapon States,

Convinced that, in furtherance of this principle, all Parties to the

Treaty are entitled to participate in the fullest possible exchange of scientific information for, and to contribute alone or in co-operation with other States to, the further development of the applications of atomic energy for peaceful purposes,

Declaring their intention to achieve at the earliest possible date the cessation of the nuclear arms race and to undertake effective measures in the direction of nuclear disarmament,

Urging the co-operation of all States in the attainment of this objective,

Recalling the determination expressed by the Parties to the 1963 Treaty banning nuclear weapon tests in the atmosphere, in outer space and under water in its Preamble to seek to achieve the discontinuance of all test explosions of nuclear weapons for all time and to continue negotiations to this end,

Desiring to further the easing of international tension and the strengthening of trust between States in order to facilitate the cessation of the manufacture of nuclear weapons, the liquidation of all their existing stockpiles, and the elimination from national arsenals of nuclear weapons and the means of their delivery pursuant to a Treaty on general and complete disarmament under strict and effective international control,

Recalling that, in accordance with the Charter of the United Nations, States must refrain in their international relations from the threat or use of force against the territorial integrity or political independence of any State, or in any other manner inconsistent with the Purposes of the United Nations, and that the establishment and maintenance of international peace and security are to be promoted with the least diversion for armaments of the world's human and economic resources,

Have agreed as follows:

Article I

Each nuclear-weapon State Party to the Treaty undertakes not to transfer to any recipient whatsoever nuclear weapons or other nuclear explosive devices or control over such weapons or explosive devices directly, or indirectly; and not in any way to assist, encourage, or induce any non-nuclear-weapon State to manufacture or otherwise acquire nuclear weapons or other nuclear explosive devices, or control over such weapons or explosive devices.

Article II

Each non-nuclear-weapon State Party to the Treaty undertakes not to receive the transfer from any transferor whatsoever of nuclear weapons or other nuclear explosive devices or of control over such weapons or explosive devices directly, or indirectly; not to manufacture or otherwise acquire nuclear weapons or other nuclear explosive devices; and not to seek or receive any assistance in the manufacture of nuclear weapons or other nuclear explosive devices.

Article III

1. Each non-nuclear-weapon State Party to the Treaty undertakes to accept safeguards, as set forth in an agreement to be negotiated and concluded with the International Atomic Energy Agency in accordance with the Statute of the International Atomic Energy Agency and the Agency's safeguards system, for the exclusive purpose of verification of the fulfilment of its obligations assumed under this Treaty with a view to preventing diversion of nuclear energy from peaceful uses to nuclear weapons or other nuclear explosive devices. Procedures for the safeguards required by this Article shall be followed with respect to source or special fissionable material whether it is being produced, processed or used in any principal nuclear facility or is outside any such facility. The safeguards required by this Article shall be applied on all source or special fissionable material in all peaceful nuclear activities within the territory of such State, under its jurisdiction, or carried out under its control anywhere.

2. Each State Party to the Treaty undertakes not to provide: (a) source or special fissionable material, or (b) equipment or material especially designed or prepared for the processing, use or production of special fissionable material, to any non-nuclear-weapon State for peaceful purposes, unless the source or special fissionable material shall be subject to the safeguards required by this Article.

3. The safeguards required by this Article shall be implemented in a manner designed to comply with Article IV of this Treaty, and to avoid hampering the economic or technological development of the Parties or international co-operation in the field of peaceful nuclear activities, including the international exchange of nuclear material and equipment for the processing, use or production of nuclear material for peaceful purposes in accordance with the provisions of this Article and the principle of safeguarding set forth in the Preamble of the Treaty.

4. Non-nuclear-weapon States Party to the Treaty shall conclude agreements with the International Atomic Energy Agency to meet the requirements of this Article either individually or together with other States in accordance with the Statute of the International Atomic Energy Agency. Negotiation of such agreements shall commence within 180 days from the original entry into force of this Treaty. For States depositing their instruments of ratification or accession after the 180-day period, negotiation of such agreements shall commence not later than the date of such deposit. Such agreements shall enter into force not later than eighteen months after the date of initiation of negotiations.

Article IV

1. Nothing in this Treaty shall be interpreted as affecting the inalienable right of all the Parties to the Treaty to develop research, production and use of nuclear energy for peaceful purposes without discrimination and in conformity with Articles I and II of this Treaty.

2. All the Parties to the Treaty undertake to facilitate, and have the right to participate in, the fullest possible exchange of equipment, materials and scientific and technological information for the peaceful uses of nuclear energy. Parties to the Treaty in a position to do so shall also co-operate in contributing alone or together with other States or international organizations to the further development of the applications of nuclear energy for peaceful purposes, especially in the territories of non-nuclear-weapon States Party to the Treaty, with due consideration for the needs of the developing areas of the world.

Article V

Each Party to the Treaty undertakes to take appropriate measures to ensure that, in accordance with this Treaty, under appropriate international observation and through appropriate international procedures, potential benefits from any peaceful applications of nuclear explosions will be made available to non-nuclear-weapon States Party to the Treaty on a non-discriminatory basis and that the charge to such Parties for the explosive devices used will be as low as possible and exclude any charge for research and development. Non-nuclear-weapon States Party to the Treaty shall be able to obtain such benefits, pursuant to a special international agreement or agreements, through an appropriate international body with adequate representation of non-nuclear-weapon States. Negotiations on this subject shall commence as soon as possible after the Treaty enters into force. Non-nuclear-weapon

States Party to the Treaty so desiring may also obtain such benefits pursuant to bilateral agreements.

Article VI

Each of the Parties to the Treaty undertakes to pursue negotiations in good faith on effective measures relating to cessation of the nuclear arms race at an early date and to nuclear disarmament, and on a treaty on general and complete disarmament under strict and effective international control.

Article VII

Nothing in this Treaty affects the right of any group of States to conclude regional treaties in order to assure the total absence of nuclear weapons in their respective territories.

Article VIII

1. Any Party to the Treaty may propose amendments to this Treaty. The text of any proposed amendment shall be submitted to the Depositary Governments which shall circulate it to all Parties to the Treaty. Thereupon, if requested to do so by one-third or more of the Parties to the Treaty, the Depositary Governments shall convene a conference, to which they shall invite all the Parties to the Treaty, to consider such an amendment.

2. Any amendment to this Treaty must be approved by a majority of the votes of all the Parties to the Treaty, including the votes of all nuclear-weapon States Party to the Treaty and all other Parties which, on the date the amendment is circulated, are members of the Board of Governors of the International Atomic Energy Agency. The amendment shall enter into force for each Party that deposits its instrument of ratification of the amendment upon the deposit of such instruments of ratification by a majority of all the Parties, including the instruments of ratification of all nuclear-weapon States Party to the Treaty and all other Parties which, on the date the amendment is circulated, are members of the Board of Governors of the International Atomic Energy Agency. Thereafter, it shall enter into force for any other Party upon the deposit of its instrument of ratification of the amendment.

3. Five years after the entry into force of this Treaty, a conference of Parties to the Treaty shall be held in Geneva, Switzerland, in order to review the operation of this Treaty with a view to assuring that the purposes of the Preamble and the provisions of the Treaty are being realised. At intervals of five years thereafter, a majority of the Parties

to the Treaty may obtain, by submitting a proposal to this effect to the Depositary Governments, the convening of further conferences with the same objective of reviewing the operation of the Treaty.

Article IX

1. This Treaty shall be open to all States for signature. Any State which does not sign the Treaty before its entry into force in accordance with paragraph 3 of this Article may accede to it at any time.

2. This Treaty shall be subject to ratification by signatory States. Instruments of ratification and instruments of accession shall be deposited with the Governments of the United Kingdom of Great Britain and Northern Ireland, the Union of Soviet Socialist Republics and the United States of America, which are hereby designated the Depositary Governments.

3. This Treaty shall enter into force after its ratification by the States, the Governments of which are designated Depositaries of the Treaty, and forty other States signatory to this Treaty and the deposit of their instruments of ratification. For the purposes of this Treaty, a nuclear-weapon State is one which has manufactured and exploded a nuclear weapon or other nuclear explosive device prior to 1 January, 1967.

4. For States whose instruments of ratification or accession are deposited subsequent to the entry into force of this Treaty, it shall enter into force on the date of the deposit of their instruments of ratification or accession.

Article X

1. Each Party shall in exercising its national sovereignty have the right to withdraw from the Treaty if it decides that extraordinary events, related to the subject matter of this Treaty, have jeopardized the supreme interests of its country. It shall give notice of such withdrawal to all other Parties to the Treaty and to the United Nations Security Council three months in advance. Such notice shall include a statement of the extraordinary events it regards as having jeopardized its supreme interests.

2. Twenty-five years after the entry into force of the Treaty, a conference shall be convened to decide whether the Treaty shall continue in force indefinitely, or shall be extended for an additional fixed period or periods. This decision shall be taken by a majority of the Parties to the Treaty.

General Assembly Resolution

Fifty-second session   21 November 1997
Agenda item 71, para. 0

GENERAL AND COMPLETE DISARMAMENT
[on the report of the First Committee] A/52/600

Excerpt

Advisory Opinion of the International Court of Justice on the Legality of the Threat or Use of Nuclear Weapons

The General Assembly,

Recalling its resolutions 49/75 K of 15 December 1994, and 51/45 of 10 December, 1996,

Convinced that the continuing existence of nuclear weapons poses a threat to all humanity and that their use would have catastrophic consequences for all life on Earth, and recognizing that the only defence against a nuclear catastrophe is the total elimination of nuclear weapons and the certainty that they will never be produced again,

Mindful of the solemn obligations of States parties, undertaken in Article VI of the Treaty on the Non-Proliferation of Nuclear Weapons, [1] particularly to pursue negotiations in good faith on effective measures relating to cessation of the nuclear arms race at an early date and to nuclear disarmament,

Recalling also the Principles and Objectives for Nuclear Non-Proliferation and Disarmament adopted at the 1995 Review and Extension Conference of the Parties to the Treaty on the Non-Proliferation of Nuclear Weapons, [2] and in particular the objective of determined pur-

---

[1] United Nations, *Treaty Series* Vol. 729, No. 10485.

[2] *1995 Review and Extension Conference of the Parties to the Treaty on the Non-Proliferation of Nuclear Weapons, Final Document, Part I* (NPT/CONF. 1995/32 (Part I)), annex, decision 2.

suit by the nuclear-weapon States of systematic and progressive efforts to reduce nuclear weapons globally, with the ultimate goal of eliminating those weapons,

Recalling also the adoption of the Comprehensive Nuclear Test Ban Treaty in its resolution 50/245 of 10 September 1996,

Recognizing with satisfaction that the Antarctic Treaty [3] and the treaties of Tlatelolco, [4] Rarotonga, [5] Bangkok [6] and Polindaba [7] are gradually freeing the entire southern hemisphere and adjacent areas covered by those treaties from nuclear weapons,

Noting the efforts by the States possessing the largest inventories of nuclear weapons to reduce their stockpiles of such weapons through bilateral and unilateral agreements or arrangements, and calling for the intensification of such efforts to accelerate the significant reduction of nuclear-weapon arsenals,

Recognizing the need for a multilaterally negotiated and legally binding instrument to assure non-nuclear-weapon States against the threat or use of nuclear weapons,

Reaffirming the central role of the Conference on Disarmament as the single multilateral disarmament negotiating forum, and regretting the lack of progress in disarmament negotations, particularly nuclear disarmament, in the Conference on Disarmament during its 1997 session,

Emphasizing the need for the Conference on Disarmament to commence negotiation on a phased programme for the complete elimination of nuclear weapons with a specified framework of time,

Desiring to achieve the objective of a legally binding prohibition of the development, production, testing, deployment, stockpiling, threat or use of nuclear weapons and their destruction under effective international control,

Recalling the advisory opinion of the International Court of Justice on the Legality of the Threat or Use of Nuclear Weapons, [8] issued on 8 July 1996,

---

[3] United Nations, *Treaty Series*, Vol. 402, No. 5778.

[4] Treaty for the Prohibition of Nuclear Weapons in Latin America and the Caribbean.

[5] South Pacific Nuclear Free Zone Treaty.

[6] Treaty on the South-East Asia Nuclear-Weapon-Free Zone.

[7] African Nuclear-Weapon-Free Zone Treaty.

[8] A/51/218, annex.

1. *Underlines once again* the unanimous conclusion of the International Court of Justice that there exists an obligation to pursue in good faith and bring to a conclusion negotiations leading to nuclear disarmament in all its aspects under strict and effective international control;

2. *Calls once again upon* all States to immediately fulfil that obligation by commencing multilateral negotiations in 1998 leading to an early conclusion of a nuclear weapons convention prohibiting the development, production, testing, deployment, stockpiling, transfer, threat or use of nuclear weapons and providing for their elimination;

3. *Requests* all States to inform the Secretary-General of the efforts and measures they have taken on the implementation of the present resolution and nuclear disarmament, and requests the Secretary-General to apprise the General Assembly of that information at its fifty-third session;

4. *Decides* to include in the provisional agenda of its fifty-third session the item entitled "Followup to the advisory opinion of the International Court of Justice on the *Legality of the Threat or Use of Nuclear Weapons*".

Convention on the Prevention and Punishment
of the Crime of Genocide

78 U.N.T.S. 277, entered into force January 12, 1951

Excerpts

Article 1

The Contracting Parties confirm that genocide, whether committed in time of peace or in time of war, is a crime under international law which they undertake to prevent and to punish.

Article 2

In the present Convention, genocide means any of the following acts committed with intent to destroy, in whole or in part, a national, ethnical, racial or religious group, as such:

(a) Killing members of the group;

(b) Causing serious bodily or mental harm to members of the group;

(c) Deliberately inflicting on the group conditions of life calculated to bring about its physical destruction in whole or in part;

(d) Imposing measures intended to prevent births within the group;

(e) Forcibly transferring children of the group to another group.

Article 3

The following acts shall be punishable:

(a) Genocide;

(b) Conspiracy to commit genocide;

(c) Direct and public incitement to commit genocide;

(d) Attempt to commit genocide;

(e) Complicity in genocide.

Article 4

Persons committing genocide or any of the other acts enumerated in article III shall be punished, whether they are constitutionally responsible rulers, public officials or private individuals.

International Covenant on Civil and Political Rights

U.N.T.S. No. 14668, Vol. 999 (1976), p. 171

Excerpt

Article 6

1. Every human being has the inherent right to life. This right shall be protected by law. No one shall be arbitrarily deprived of his life.

TABLE OF CASES

(Numbers at end of main numbered entries indicate page
numbers where referred to in this volume.)

1. *Anglo-Iranian Oil Company, I.C.J. Reports 1952*   165

2. *Antelope* case, 10 *Wheaton* (U.S.) 122 (1825)   343

3. *Applicability of Article VI, Section 22, of the Convention on the
   Privileges and Immunities of the United Nations, Advisory Opinion, I.C.J. Reports 1989*   34-35

4. *Applicability of the Obligation to Arbitrate under Section 21 of the
   United Nations Headquarters Agreement of 26 June 1947 case
   (1988)*   450

5. *Application for Review of Judgement No. 158 of the United Nations Administrative Tribunal, Advisory Opinion, I.C.J. Reports
   1973*   33, 35

6. *Asylum* case (20 November, 1950 and 27 November, 1950), *I.C.J.
   Reports 1950*   400

   Australia. *See* 16, 36

7. *Barcelona Traction, Light and Power Co. Ltd., I.C.J. Reports
   1970*   149, 196

8. *Brown v. Board of Education*, 347 U.S. 483 (1954), 349 U.S. 294
   (1955)   20, 457, 469

9. *Bulgaria, Hungary and Romania, Interpretation of Peace Treaties
   with, First Phase; Advisory Opinion, I.C.J. Reports 1950*   34, 36,
   450

   Cameroon, Northern. *See* 35

10. *Certain Expenses of the United Nations (Article 17, paragraph 2,
    of the Charter), Advisory Opinion, I.C.J. Reports 1962*   33-35,
    450

    China. *See* 16

11. *Competence of the General Assembly for the Admission of a State*

to the United Nations, Advisory Opinion, I.C.J. Reports 1950 33, 450

12. *Conditions of Admission of a State to Membership in the United Nations (Article 4 of the Charter), Advisory Opinion, 1948, I.C.J. Reports 1947-1948* 33, 36, 134, 449

13. *Continental Shelf (Libyan Arab Jamahiriya/Malta), Judgment, I.C.J. Reports 1985* 58

14. *Corfu Channel*, Merits, *I.C.J. Reports 1949* 64, 87, 147-48, 178, 196, 297, 308, 319

15. *Eastern Carelia, Status of, 1923, P.C.I.J., Series B, No. 5* 35, 449

16. *Eastern Extension, Australia and China Telegraph Company* case, British-American Claims Arbitral Tribunal, *United Nations Arbitral Reports*, Vol. VI 198

17. *Effect of Awards of Compensation Made by the United Nations Administrative Tribunal, Advisory Opinion, I.C.J. Reports 1954* 36, 450

Egypt. *See* 55

18. *Fisheries, I.C.J. Reports 1951* 135

19. *Fisheries Jurisdiction Case (United Kingdom v. Iceland, Federal Republic of Germany v. Iceland); I.C.J. Reports 1974* 150, 179, 382

France. *See* 31, 36-37

Germany, Federal Republic of. *See* 19

20. *Genocide, Reservations to the Convention on the Prevention and Punishment of the Crime of; Advisory Opinion, I.C.J. Reports 1951* 34, 134, 196, 200, 450

21. *Haya de la Torre* case (13 June 1951), *I.C.J. Reports 1951,* 400

Honduras. *See* 32

Hungary. *See* 9

Iceland. *See* 19

Iran. *See* 1, 48

Italy. *See* 31

Japan. *See* 40

22. *Krupp* case, United States Military Tribunal, Nuremberg, *Annual Digest and Reports on Public International Law Cases*, 1948   149, 160, 297-98, 364

23. Legality of the Threat or Use of Nuclear Weapons, 1996

Advisory Opinion 7

¶ 3   8, 218-19
¶ 6   15
¶ 14   242, 451
¶ 16   407
¶ 18   181
¶ 20   382, 405-06
¶ 22   228
¶ 26   314
¶ 29   11
¶ 30   11, 462
¶ 31   238
¶ 32   12, 384
¶ 33   12
¶ 35   12, 124-25, 166
¶ 36   124-25
¶ 39   210
¶ 40   11, 216, 390
¶ 41   213, 216, 390
¶ 42   213, 398
¶ 45   231
¶ 46   109, 242
¶ 47   11
¶ 52   227, 232
¶ 58   6, 227
¶ 59   6, 211, 213, 227
¶ 59(c)   162
¶ 62   231
¶ 66   230
¶ 67   170, 399
¶ 70   377
¶ 71   129-30, 377

¶ 72   377
¶ 76   458
¶ 78   8, 12, 227-29 392
¶ 79   87
¶ 80   392
¶ 83   117, 155
¶ 85   153
¶ 86   138, 143, 148, 153, 208, 398
¶ 88   126
¶ 91   12
¶ 92   12-13, 138
¶ 93   13
¶ 94   8, 11-12
¶ 92   12-13, 138
¶ 95   11-13, 207-08, 211, 229, 391
¶ 96   8, 170, 211, 230-31, 390, 397, 399
¶ 97   11, 221-24
¶ 98   11
¶ 99   8, 233
¶ 100   8
¶ 104   116, 221, 226, 377, 381
dispositif,
¶ 105   16, 203-07, 216
(1)   243, 405-16
(2)A   11, 110, 115, 203-04, 227, 241, 377, 381, 389-90, 453

¶ 105 (2)B   110, 114, 204, 227, 239, 322, 381, 389-90, 453
(2)C   11, 110, 115, 203-04, 216, 227, 240-42, 377, 385, 387-88, 389-90, 398, 453
(2)D   12-13, 110, 115, 203-04, 208, 240-41, 286, 377, 387-90, 453
(2)E   13, 15, 80, 116, 128, 172-75, 207, 216-17, 229-32, 239-41, 377, 383-84, 389-91, 395, 453
(2)E, part 1   13, 101, 113, 177, 208-09, 376, 388, 397
(2)E, part 2   13, 82, 85-87, 102, 113, 152, 168, 176, 193, 209-13, 232, 240-41, 327, 380, 384-88, 391, 398-402
(2)F   1, 12, 16, 110, 115-16, 204-05, 214, 233, 242, 377, 389, 399, 453, 465

24. *Legality of the Use by a State of Nuclear Weapons in Armed Conflict* (Request for Advisory Opinion by WHO)   19, 27, 35, 67-68, 158, 218-19, 268, 332, 383, 452

Libyan Arab Jamahiriya. *See* 13

25. *List* case, *Trials of War Criminals before the Nuremberg Military Tribunals under Control Council Law No. 10* (Washington, 1950), Vol XI   160, 167

26. *Lotus* case, *Judgment No. 9, 1927, P.C.I.J., Series A, No. 10*   39, 84-85, 114, 128, 130-37, 150, 168, 231, 307-08

Maine, Gulf of. *See* 28

Malta. *See* 13

27. *Marbury v. Madison*, 1 Cranch (U.S.) 137 (1803)   20

28. *Maritime Delimitation of the Gulf of Maine Area, I.C.J. Reports 1984*   133, 150

29. *Milch* case (United States Military Tribunal at Nuremberg), *War Crimes Trials*, 7 (1948)   364

30. *Minquiers and Ecrehos* case, *I.C.J. Reports 1953*   166

31. *Monetary Gold (Italy v. France, United Kingdom and United States), I.C.J. Reports 1954*   400

Morocco. *See* 45

Namibia. *See* 43

New Zealand. *See* 37

32. *(Nicaragua v. Honduras), Border and Transborder Armed Actions*; *I.C.J. Reports 1988,*   297

33. *(Nicaragua v. United States of America), Military and Paramilitary Activities in and against Nicaragua*; Merits, *I.C.J. Reports 1986*   39, 47, 117, 135, 148, 183-84, 204, 231, 255, 297, 380, 390, 459

34. *North Sea Continental Shelf Cases, Judgment, I.C.J. Reports 1969*   155, 165, 213

35. *Northern Cameroon* case *(Republic of Northern Cameroon v. United Kingdom)*, 1963, dismissed, *I.C.J. Reports 1963*   150, 400

36. *Nuclear Tests (Australia v. France), Judgment of 20 December 1974, I.C.J. Reports 1974*   73

37. *Nuclear Tests* case (*New Zealand v. France*), Order of 22 September 1995 (re Court's Judgment of 20 December 1974), *I.C.J. Reports 1995*   44, 316, 462

Nuremburg. *See* 22, 25, 29, 47, 49-50

38. *Peleus* case (British military court), *War Crimes Reports*, i (1946)   364

39. *Reparation for Injuries Suffered in the Service of the United Nations, I.C.J. Reports 1949*   135, 450

Romania. *See* 9

40. *Shimoda v. The Japanese State*, Judgement, 7 December 1963, *Japanese Annual of International Law*, Vol. 8, 1964   136-44, 153, 232, 244, 463

South Africa. *See* 43

41. *South West Africa, Admissibility of Hearings of Petitioners by the Committee on*; *I.C.J. Reports 1956*   167, 194, 450

42. *South West Africa, International Status of*, *I.C.J. Reports 1950*   134, 450

43. *(South West Africa) notwithstanding Security Council Resolution 276 (1970), Legal Consequences for States of the Continued Presence of South Africa in Namibia; Advisory Opinion, I.C.J. Reports 1971*   20, 35-36, 139, 194

44. *South West Africa (1955), Voting Procedure on Questions relating to Reports and Petitions concerning the Territory of*   450

45. *Tunisia and Morocco, Nationality Decrees Issued in; Advisory Opinion, P.C.I.J., Series B, No. 4* (1923)   308, 378

46. *UNESCO, Judgments of the Administrative Tribunal of the ILO upon Complaints Made against; Advisory Opinion, I.C.J. Reports 1956*   34-35

United Kingdom. *See* 1, 19, 31, 35

United Nations. *See* 3-5, 10-12, 17, 39

47. United States Nuremberg Military Tribunal, case No. 47   228

48. *United States v. Iran, I.C.J. Reports 1980*   459

United States. *See also* 31, 33

49. *War Criminals before the International Military Tribunal (1947),*

Trial of German Major; Judgment of the International Military Tribunal at Nuremberg, 1946, Vol. I   182-83

50. *War Criminals before the International Military Tribunal, Trial of the Major,* 1948, Vol. 22   250

51. *War Criminals, Law Reports of Trials of,* Vol 10 (1949)   364

52. *War Criminals, Trial of the Major,* 1946, Nuremberg, 1947, Vol. 1   64

53. *West Rand Central Gold Mining Co., Ltd. v. R* (1905), 2 KB   298

54. *Western Sahara, Advisory Opinion, I.C.J. Reports 1975*   33, 35, 194-95, 450

55. *WHO and Egypt, Interpretation of the Agreement of 25 March 1951 between the; Advisory Opinion, I.C.J. Reports 1980*   33-34, 158

56. *Wisconsin v. Howard-Hastings,* Ashland Co. Cir. Ct., September 1996   462, 471

TABLE OF TREATIES, RESOLUTIONS, CONVENTIONS AND CHARTERS

(Includes Accords, Agreements, Conferences, Covenants, Declarations, Documents, Pacts, Protocols, Regulations, Rules and Statutes; numbers at end of main numbered entries refer to page numbers in this volume.)

1. African Nuclear-Weapon-Free Zone Treaty (Treaty of Pelindaba; Treaty of Cairo), 1996   58, 97, 123, 351, 441

   Air Warfare. *See* 44

2. Almaty Declaration to establish a Nuclear Weapons Free Zone in Central Asia   461

3. Antarctic Treaty of December 1959   52-53, 56, 351

4. Anti-Ballistic Missile (ABM) Treaty, 1972 (US-USSR)   123, 433

5. ANZUS Treaty   478

6. Asphyxiating Gases, International Declaration Respecting, 1899 (Hague Convention II)   51, 149, 185, 204, 294, 310, 396

7. Asphyxiating, Poisonous or Other Gases, and of Bacteriological Methods of Warfare; Protocol for the Prohibition of the Use in War of, 17 June 1925 (Geneva Gas Protocol)   51, 143, 185, 193, 204, 237, 239, 296, 310, 322-26, 489

8. Atlantic Charter   80

9. Atmosphere, in Outer Space and Under Water (Partial Test-Ban Treaty); Treaty Banning Nuclear Weapon Tests in the, 1963 (*UNTS*, Vol. 480, p. 43), Article 1   53, 272, 433

10. Austria, State Treaty for the Re-establishment of an Independent and Democratic, 1955   52

11. Bacteriological (Biological) and Toxic Weapons and on Their Destruction; Convention on the Prohibition of the Development,

Production and Stockpiling of, (Resolution 2826 (XXVI, Annex), 1972   26, 52, 232

12. Bogotá (the American Treaty on Pacific Settlement), Pact of   342

Briand-Kellogg Pact. *See* 56

13. British War Office in 1916 Military Law, Manual of; issued by the 310-11

Cairo Treaty. *See* 1

14. Canberra Commission on Elimination of Nuclear Weapons, 1995   461

Central Asia. *See* 2

15. Chemical Weapons and on Their Destruction; Convention on the Prohibition of the Development, Production, Stockpiling and Use of, 1993, (A/47/27)   26, 52, 109, 232, 464, 474

16. Civil and Political Rights, International Covenant on, 1966 303.   Article 4   40; Article 6   40, 201-02; Article 6, para. 1, 40

17. Colonial Countries and Peoples, Declaration on the Granting of Independence to   195

18. Conventional Weapons, Lucerne Conference of Government Experts on the Use of Certain, 1974   393, 396

19. Conventional Weapons Which May Be Deemed to Be Excessively Injurious or to Have Indiscriminate Effects, Convention on Prohibitions or Restrictions on the Use of Certain, 1980   62, 185, 232, 296.   Amendments, 1996   62

20. Cultural and Natural Heritage, Convention for the Protection of the World, 1972, Article 5   263

Cultural Property. *See* 43

Cultural Rights. *See* 24

21. Disarmament, Tenth Special Session of the General Assembly on the subject of, 1978 (GAOR, 10th Sp. Sess., suppl. 4; A/S-10/2), Final Document   122

22. Disputes and Situations Which May Threaten International Peace and Security and on the Role of the United Nations in this Field,

Declaration on the Prevention and Removal of, United Nations General Assembly Resolution 43/51, 1988   342

23. Dorpot Peace Treaty, 1920   449

24. Economic, Social and Cultural Rights, International Covenant on, United Nations General Assembly Resolution 2200A(XXI), 1966   303

25. Endangered Species, Convention on International Trade in, 1973   263

26. Environment in Times of Armed Conflict, United Nations General Assembly Resolution on the Protection of the, 47/37, 1992   44, 48

Environment. *See also* 20, 48

27. Environmental Modification Techniques (ENMOD Convention), Convention on the Prohibition of Military or Any Other Hostile Use of, 18 May 1977 (1108 *UNTS*, p. 151)   37, 42, 316

European Convention. *See* 50

28. Expanding Bullets, International Declaration Respecting, 1899 296

Force, Non-use of. *See* 68

29. Friendly Relations and Co-operation among States (United Nations General Assembly Resolution 2625 (XXV), Declaration Concerning Principles of   73

30. Geneva Convention of 1864   185, 364

31. Geneva Convention I of 1949   90, 185, 187, 195

32. Geneva Conventions for the Protection of War Victims, 1949   64, 87, 204

33. Geneva Conventions of 1949 (I-IV), Article 3 (common to all 4)   148, 295, 310, 363, 396, 474

34. Geneva Conventions of 1949, Additional Protocols of 1977   90, 185, 187, 197, 202, 204-05, 312, 317, 343, 363, 475

   Additional Protocol I of 1977 (Martens clause)   65-66, 109, 186, 208, 392, 395, 475

Article 1, para. 2   63
Article 35, paras. 1-3   42,
   137,142,318
Additional Protocol II of 1977   66

Geneva Gas Protocol. *See* 7

Article 51   228, 312
Article 55   318
Article 57(2)(b)   313

35. Geneva Law   64, 185, 197, 250

36. Genocide, Convention on the Prevention and Punishment of the Crime of, 1948, Article II   41, 65, 129, 196, 200

37. Germany into the North Atlantic Treaty Organization, Agreement of Paris on the entry of the Federal Republic of, 1954, Protocol No. III on Control of Armaments, Annex II, Article 1(a)   123

38. Germany, Treaty on the Final Settlement with respect to, 1990   52

39. Hague Convention (IV) Respecting the Laws and Customs of War on Land, 1907; Regulations annexed thereto, Preamble   185, 227, 396

(Martens clause)   65, 67, 137, 145, 147, 149, 256-57, 294-95, 297, 299, 305-06, 310, 480-81, 490

Article 22   63, 185, 295,
   340, 392-93
Article 23   63, 185, 392
Article 23(a)   51, 204, 237,
   239, 323, 327, 393

Article 23(e)   311
Article 23(g)   228, 395
Article 25   228, 395
Article 27   228, 395

40. Hague Convention (V) Respecting the Rights and Duties of Neutral Powers and Persons in Case of War on Land, 1907,   65, 67, 126-27, 186

41. Hague Convention (VIII), 1907   148

42. Hague Convention (XIII) Respecting the Rights and Duties of Neutral Powers in Naval War, 1907, Article 1   68

43. Hague Convention for the Protection of Cultural Property in the Case of Armed Conflict, 1954   274-75

44. Hague Conventions of 1899 and 1907   62, 185

45. Hague Law   62, 64, 87, 185, 294, 307

46. Hague Rules of Air Warfare of 1923   310

47. Helsinki Conference, Final Act, 1975   342

48. Human Environment, Stockholm Declaration on the, 1972, Principle 21   42, 263, 318

49. Human Rights, American Convention of, 1969, Article 4   320

50. Human Rights and Fundamental Freedoms, European Convention for the Protection of, 1950 Article 2   320

51. Human Rights Conference, Teheran, 1968   474

52. Human Rights, Universal Declaration of, 1948   302-03, 320-21, 464-65

   Preamble 18, 320   Articles 25(1)-25(2)   320
   Articles 1 and 3   320   Article 27(1)   320
   Articles 6 and 16(1)   320

   Human Rights. *See also* 96

53. International Court of Justice, Article 106   28

54. International Court of Justice Statute, Article 9   119, 215

   Article 38   103, 177-78, 212   Article 65   400, 448
   Article 38, para. 1   249   Article 65, para. 1   31, 34
   Article 38, para. 1(d)   141   Article 65, para. 2   27
   Article 53   382-83   Article 66, paras. 1-2, 4
   Article 55   80   27

55. Italian Senate Resolution, 1995   350

56. Kellogg-Briand Pact of 1928   182

   Latin America. *See* 81

57. Lausanne Convention of 1923, Article 15   84

58. Law of Treaties, Vienna Convention on the, 1969
       Article 26   73; Article 53   65, 195, 197

   Laws and Customs of War on Land. *See* 39

59. League of Nations, Covenant of the, Article 14   383

60. Lieber Code of 1863 (adopted by the United States for the Government of Armies in the Field)   310

London Convention. *See* 84

Lucerne Convention. *See* 18

61. Maritime Neutrality, Convention on, 1928, Preamble   68

62. Martens/de Martens Clause   65, 67, 137, 145-50, 152, 256-57, 294-95, 297, 299, 305-06, 310, 480-81, 490

63. McCloy-Zorin Accords, 1961, Fifth Principle   122

64. Military Tribunal Charter, International, 1945   65

65. Missiles Treaty, Intermediate-Range and Shorter-Range, 1987 (US-USSR)   124

66. Movement of Non-Aligned Countries, 11th Ministerial Conference, 1944. Final document on Disarmament and International Security   408, 412-14

Naval War. *See* 42

Neutral/Non-Aligned Powers. *See* 40, 42, 66

67. Non-Proliferation of Nuclear Weapons (NPT), Treaty on the, 1968 (*UNTS*, Vol. 729, p. 161)   8, 52, 55-58, 71, 94-96, 410, 151, 157-58, 205, 211, 213, 231, 255, 351, 354-60, 104, 436, 442-43, 447, 463-64

First Preamble 120, 122	Article VII 92, 441
Articles I-II 92, 436	Aricles VIII-IX 92
Articles III-V 92	Article X 93
Article VI 71, 73, 92, 110, 116, 222, 233, 436, 453	Article X(2) 440

Fourth Review Conference of the Parties
Final document of the Review and Extension Conference of the parties to the Treaty on the Non-Proliferation of Nuclear Weapons, 1995: "Principles and Objectives for Nuclear Non-Proliferation and Disarmament"   26, 74, 94, 205, 347-48, 446
Decision No. 2, Preamble, para. 1   122

68. Non-Use of Force, Declaration on the Enhancement of the Principle of, (United Nations General Assembly Resolution 42/22, para. 2, 1987)   342

69. North Atlantic Treaty Organization   123, 324

70. Nuclear Catastrophe, Declaration on the Prevention of, (United Nations General Assembly Resolution 36/100, 1981)   281

71. Nuclear Disarmament   443-44
    UN General Assembly Resolutions 50/70C and 50/70P, 1995   444-45

72. Nuclear Disarmament and Economic Conversion Act, H.R. 827 (1997)   461

73. Nuclear Free Zone Laws
    Belau Constitutution, 1979   476
    Oakland, California, U.S. Ordinance, 1997   461
    Solomon Islands Statute, 1983   476
    Vanuatu Statute, 1983   476

74. Nuclear Free Zone Treaty (Treaty of Raratonga), South Pacific, 1985 (*UNTS*, Registration No. 24592, 2 January 1987)   52-55, 57, 71, 97, 123, 211, 213, 231, 351, 437-38, 441

    Nuclear Free Zone Treaties. *See also* 1-2, 79

75. Nuclear Test-Ban Treaty, Comprehensive (CTBT), 1991   348, 352, 438
    United Nations General Assembly Resolutions

46/29 1991 438, 442	49/70 1994 439, 443
47/47 1992 439,443	50/65 1995 439, 443
47/52A 1992 440	50/70Q 1995 441
48/70 1993 439, 443	

76. Nuclear Test-Ban Treaty, Partial, 1963   272, 351, 436

77. Nuclear Test-Ban Treaty, Total   272

78. Nuclear War, Agreement on the Prevention of, 1973 (US-USSR)   123-24

79. Nuclear-Weapon-Free Zone, Treaty on the Southeast Asia, 1995, Protocol   58, 97, 123, 441

80. Nuclear Weapons Convention   461, 474

81. Nuclear Weapons in Latin America, Treaty of Tlatelolco for the Prohibition of, 1967 (*UNTS*, Vol. 634, p. 281)   52-53, 56-57, 71,

97, 144, 157, 188, 211, 213, 231-32, 351, 353, 437, 441, 477
    Article 1 53, 239   Additional Protocol II 53-54,
    Article 30 437   97, 123, 157, 437
                       Article 3 53, 437

82. Nuclear Weapons, United Nations General Assembly Resolutions
  on Use of 349

    1 (I), 1946 5, 151, 219,   36/100, 1981, para. 1
    348   300
    41 (I), 0101, para. 5,   37/100C, 1982 423, 427,
    1946 122, 220   435
    191 (III), 1948 220   38/73G, 1983 427
    808A (IX), 1954 72, 219   38/75, 1983, para. 1 151
    1653 (XVI), 1961 25,   39/63H, 1984 427
    59, 61, 98-99, 130, 300,   40/151F, 1985 428
    417-22, 434, 489   41/60F, 1986 428
    1722 (XVI), 1961 122,   42/39C, 1987 428
    433   43/76E, 1988 429
    2028 (XX), 1965, para.   44/117C, 1989 300, 429
    2(b) 158   45/59B, 1990 25, 232,
    2123 (XX), 1965 342   300, 429, 489
    2286 (XXII), 1967 437   46/29, 1991 438
    2444 (XXIII), 1968 228   46/37D, 1991 25, 232,
    2456 (XXIII), 1968 437   300, 430, 489
    2625 (XXV), 1970 341,   47/53C, 1992 130, 430,
    361   489
    2734 (XXV), 1970 342   48/76B, 1993 411, 430,
    2936 (XXVII), 1972   482
    300   49/75H, 1994 448, 452
    33/71B, 1978 25, 129,   49/75K, 1994 (Request
    300, 419, 489   for this Advisory Opin-
    34/83G, 1979 25, 300,   ion) 25, 50, 381, 405,
    489   407-11, 446-48, 451,
    35/8, 1980 316   453, 479, 484-88
    35/152D, 1980 25, 489   49/76E, 1994 431, 448
    36/92I, 1981 25, 98,   50/70C, 1995 452
    300, 489   50/71E, 1995 431

  Nuclear Weapons. *See also* 14, 67, 91, 99

83. Nuremberg Tribunal, Charter of the, 1945 65, 310
    Article 6 201

84. Ocean Dumping Convention, London, 1979   263

Ocean Floor. *See* 91

85. Outer Space, including the Moon and Other Celestial Bodies; Treaty on Principles Governing the Activities of States in the Exploration and Use of, 1967   52-53

Outer Space Tests. *See* 9

Pacific Settlement. *See* 12

86. Paris Accords of 1954 (Protocol on Arms Control)   188, 324

Paris Agreement. *See* 37

87. Peace, Declaration on Essentials of, United Nations General Assembly Resolution 290 (IV), 1949   342

Peace. *See also* 22-23, 100

Pelindaba Treaty. *See* 1

Raratonga Treaty. *See* 74

88. Red Cross, International Conference of the, XXth, Resolution XXVIII, 1965   138, 474
        Report, 1975   393-94, 396

89. Rio Declaration of 1992, Principles 2 and 24   42, 318

90. St. Petersburg Declaration of 1868   61-63, 185, 250, 294, 310, 340, 360, 392

91. Sea-Bed and the Ocean Floor and in the Subsoil Thereof, Treaty on the Prohibition of the Emplacement of Nuclear Weapons and Other Weapons of Mass Destruction on the, 1971   52, 351

Social Rights. *See* 24

South Pacific Treaty. *See* 74

Southeast Asia Treaty. *See* 79

Stockholm Declaration. *See* 48

92. Strategic Arms Reduction Talks (START I and START II), 1982   352, 433

93. Strategic Offensive Arms (SALT), Treaty on the Limitation of, 1979 (US-USSR)   124, 433

Test Ban Treaties, Nuclear. *See* 9, 74-75

Tlatelolco Treaty. *See* 81

94. Torture, Convention Against   303

Toxic Weapons. *See* 11

95. Truth and Reconciliation Commission   469

Under Water Tests. *See* 9

96. United Nations Charter, 1945   4, 18, 60, 68, 80, 108, 112, 173, 178, 201, 204-05, 238, 240, 247-49, 257, 263, 299-300, 319, 321, 341-42, 383, 385, 400

Preamble 119, 247-48
Article 1   195, 303
Article 2   385
Article 2, paras. 1-3   73, 199, 302, 361
Article 2, para. 4   11, 46, 48-49, 102, 115, 121, 180-87, 203, 221-22, 239, 302, 341, 361, 380
Article 4   134, 385
Articles 10-11   32
Article 13   32, 216
Article 42   46
Article 51   11, 46-48, 54-
55, 96, 102, 115, 158-63, 180-87, 203, 210-11, 216, 221-22, 227, 230, 302, 343, 357, 385, 398
Article 55   303
Article 62   303
Article 74   319
Article 76   303
Article 92   219
Article 96, paras. 1-2, 26, 31-32, 406, 415, 426, 446, 473, 478, 481
Chapter VII   46, 49

97. United Nations Decade of International Law (United Nations General Assembly Resolution 44/23)   480

98. United Nations General Assembly Resolutions

96 (I), 1946   129
2444 (XXIII), 1968   137
49/10, 1994   158

99. United Nations Human Rights Committee, "The Right to Life and Nuclear Weapons"; General Comment of the, Gen. C   14/23 321, 447

100. United Nations Secretary-General Report: "An Agenda for Peace" (A/47277-S/24111)   26

101. United Nations Security Council Resolutions

    255 (1968) 57, 165   984 (1995) 56-57, 73, 94,
    687 (1991) 317   156, 160, 213, 334, 440
    808 (1993) 64   984 (1995), paras. 1-3, 7, 9
                                95, 162-64

102. United States in the Field, Instructions for the Government of the Armies of the; General Orders 100, 1862   311

103. U.S. National Defense Authorization Act for Fiscal Year 1944, Public Law, 103-160, 1993   368

104. U. S. Senate, Hearings on the Global Proliferation of Weapons of Mass Destruction, 1996   107-08

105. United States War Department Field Manuals   311

United States. *See also* 12, 60

Vienna Convention. *See* 58

War on Land. *See* 39-40

War Victims. *See* 32

106. World Health Organization, Assembly of the; Resolution 46/40, 1993   26, 383

107. World Health Organization Constitution   26-27

108. Yugoslavia Since 1991, Humanitarian Law Committed in the Territory of the Former; International Tribunal for the Prosecution of Persons Responsible for Serious Violations of International, Statute, (United Nations Security Council Resolution 827, 1993)   64

INDEX

ABC weapons 264
Abdullah, Dató Mohtar 29
Abi-saabrn, George 29, 148
Abolition 2000 461-62, 467
Accident 2
Advisory Opinion 7, 26, 459
Africa/African, traditional 9-10,
 288, 300
Aggression 101, 115, 241, 332
Ago, Roberto 126, 308, 322, 330-
 31, 390
Ailuk 270
Alamogordo 112
Allah 291
Allen, Charles 372
Allies 96, 251
Alvarez, J. 147
Americium 241 262
Anorexia 267, 277
Answer, complete 38
Aotearoa/New Zealand. *See* New
 Zealand
Apartheid 370
Aquinas 291
Argentina 476
Aristotle 340
Arjuna 290
Armaments, possession of 140
Armed attack 95-96, 163, 183-84,
 187, 193, 201, 203, 208-09, 228-
 29, 274, 390, 392
Arms race 92, 205, 357, 404, 432
Asia 9
Asphyxiating gases 51, 62, 143,
 185, 323, 458
Assistance, immediate 96
Association of Soviet Lawyers 478
Assured destruction 258, 358

Atomic bombs 122, 188-91, 266
Atomic power station/stations 277
Australia 29, 414, 461, 475-76,
 479, 481, 483-84, 487
Austria/Austrians 251, 484
Authority, legal 98
Axelrod, Daniel 360
Axworthy, Lloyd 460
Aziz, Tariq 107-10

Ba'ath regime 104
Bacon, Francis 154
Bacteriological weapons. *See* Weap-
 ons, bacteriological
Baghdad 106, 108
Baker, James A. 104-10
Balance of power 340
Baruch Plan 473
Bastid, Suzanne 322
Bedjaoui, Mohammed 13, 15-16,
 74-76
Beernaert, M. 149
Belarus 7, 272
Belau 476
Belgium 462
Belligerents 48, 62, 67, 109, 126,
 128, 145, 185, 197, 203, 229,
 294, 310, 340, 386-87
Benin 411, 484
Berlin Crisis of 1961 371
Bhagvadgita, The 248, 269
Biological agents/weapons 104-
 06, 109, 125, 174
Birth abnormalities 2, 120, 190-
 93, 270-71
Blast/blastwind 188-92, 234, 269,
 367, 393-94
Bodily security, right to 320

Boer War 362
Bombs, comparative effects of 260
Bone marrow damage 267, 277
Booby traps 62, 185, 296
Bosch, Miguel Marin 491
Bosnia and Herzegovina 27, 158
Bowett, Professor D. 361
Bravo, Luigi Ferrari 74-76
Briant, Robin 479
Brookings Institution 468
Brownlie, Professor Ian 312, 350, 357, 361, 370
Brussels Conference of 1874 62, 185
Buddhist/Buddhist tradition 10, 288, 292-93
Bulletin of the Atomic Scientists 330, 366
Burden of proof 39
Burundi 27
Bush, President George 104-05
Butler, General Lee 463, 467

California 461
Campaign for Nuclear Disarmament 351
Canada 413, 460, 462, 481, 483-84, 487
Cancers 9, 189-90, 253, 259, 267-68, 272, 287
Captive 292
Cardiovascular collapse 9, 267, 277-78
Carlsson, Prime Minister 477
Carver, Lord 460
Casals, Pablo 244
Cassese, Antonio 267
Cassin, René 321
Castrén, Eric 322
Casualties, acceptable levels/number of 69, 100, 104, 258, 395
Center for Defense Information 468
Central nervous system 267
Cesium 137 262
Chernobyl 2, 266-67, 272, 277

Children 41, 189-92, 270-71, 291, 320
Children's Campaign for Nuclear Disarmament 351
Chile 411, 414
China 7, 54-55, 96, 162, 414-15, 432, 436, 438, 441, 460, 474, 483-85, 488
Chinese/Chinese civilization 10, 249, 288
Chlorine 292
Christian/Christian tradition 288, 291
Churchill, Winston 282, 370
Cicero 167
Civil disobedience 462, 469
Civilian population 69, 90, 100, 123, 140, 143, 148, 152, 179, 186, 192, 198, 202-03, 208, 223, 228, 234, 256, 258, 264, 280, 287, 312-13, 334, 385, 396
Civilized society 119
Clark, Roger 467
Clausewitz/Clausewitzean century 302, 340
Clinton, President Bill 461, 463, 468
Cloud of fear 279
Cold War 59, 81, 170, 212, 223, 404, 432, 438, 447, 474
Collateral damage 144, 235, 258, 401
Collective security 178
Collective self-defence 46, 95-96, 212, 227, 335
Cologne 275
Colombia 412
Colonialism 478
Colonized peoples 462
Combatants 12, 63, 69-70, 86, 90, 143-44, 148, 152, 179, 186, 193, 198, 206, 228, 287, 309, 312, 392-93, 395-96
Common heritage principle 315
Common sense 287
Communication systems 277

Compelling reasons 35
Conflict resolution 3
Confucius 259
Congenital deformities 9, 235, 287
Conscientious objections 458
Consent, principles of 39
Conventional prescription 51
Convulsions 267, 277
Corporations 456-57, 459
Costa Rica 30, 470
Counterforce use 100
Countervalue use 99
Crimean War 292
Crimes against humanity 25, 98,
    109, 129-30, 161, 201, 250, 315,
    418-19, 423, 477
Crop/crop failures 264, 291
Crossbow 291
Cruise missiles 476
Cuban missile crisis of 1962 371
Cultural life, right to 320
Cultural tradition 10, 293
Czar Nicholas II 294

de Brichambaut, Marc Perrin 29
deCuéllar, Javier Pérez 120
de Martens clause. *See* Martens
    clause
DeVisscher, Judge 134, 322
Death toll 100, 120, 150, 189-91,
    266, 268
Declaration of Public Conscience
    247, 482, 486-87
Declarations, hypothetical 36
Decolonization, law of/right to
    380
Deleterious gases 51
Denmark 476
Desert Storm 106-08
Deterrence, policy of 16, 49, 59,
    71, 91, 93, 109, 124, 170-71,
    200, 203, 211-12, 221, 223, 229-
    30, 232, 243, 258, 357-58, 371,
    399, 461
Deuteronomy 290
Devastation 15, 46, 253, 259,

261, 313, 324, 359, 364, 393,
    462, 434
Diarrhoea 267
Dignity, right to 338
Disarmament/disarmament negotia-
    tions 37, 71-73, 76, 87-88, 92-
    93, 110, 116, 122, 378-79, 399,
    403, 411, 413-14, 417, 419, 425,
    432-33, 438, 444, 446, 464
Discrimination between combatants
    and non-combatants 63, 69, 143-
    44, 198, 206, 228, 280, 309, 328
Discrimination, principle of 100,
    235
Dispute, specific 36
Dum-dum bullets 62, 142, 185,
    394, 458
Dunant, Henri 251-52
Duties, legal/of the strong 213,
    257
D'Amato, Professor Anthony 361

Ecocide/damage to eco-system 9,
    261, 316, 332
Ecological security 316, 378
Economic aspects 5
Economic paths/power 49, 91
Ecuador 27
Edinburgh Conference in 1969
    140
Egypt 27-29, 164, 352, 368, 441,
    461
Einstein, Albert 16, 88, 285, 373
Einstein Manifesto/Russell-Einstein
    Manifesto 373
Eisenhower, Dwight D. 6
Ekeus, Rolf 108-10
Eknilang, Lijon 270
Electrical power systems 277
Electro-magnetic pulse 9, 235, 276
Elias, Judge 401
Emperor Alexander II 294
Energy distribution networks 276
Environment/environmental/natural
    11, 42-44, 152, 206, 223, 246,
    261, 318, 337, 365, 455, 467

Environmental damage 9, 12, 18, 238, 253, 258, 263, 277-78, 328, 332, 482

Environmental law 3, 42-44, 225, 303, 319, 378, 451

Epstein, William 485

Ethics/ethical requirements 379

Ethiopia 418

Ethnic groups/ethnical 41, 200, 315

Europe 9

European civilization, modern 249

European Federation Against Nuclear Arms 351

European Parliament 461

European Union 484

Evans, Gareth 29, 367

Evans, Harold 478, 480

Extremely Lo-Frequency transmitter 462

Eyewitness description 252

Fact, questions of 8

Fairness 336, 339

Falk, Richard 19, 285, 322, 477-78, 481

Fascism 18

Feuds 291

Finland 27, 36, 449, 483

Finlay, Judge 135

First strike weapons 335

Fish 278

Fitzmaurice, Sir Gerald 147, 322

Flamethrowers 125, 394

Fleischhauer, Carl-August 74-76

Food chain 9, 259

Food productivity 235

France 7, 27, 29, 36, 54, 307, 329, 353, 415, 432, 436, 439, 441, 460, 466, 475-76, 481, 484-85, 488

Franck, James 5

Franco-German War 362

French position 54, 255

French text 38

Fusion bomb 266

Galvez, Sergio Gonzales 29

Gamma ray exposure 271, 276

Gas 103, 323

Gases, asphyxiating 51, 143

Gastro intestinal afflictions 9

Generations, future/unborn/to come 9, 11, 45, 234, 248, 263, 306, 365

Genetic defects, deformities & mutations 9, 45, 120, 150, 188, 192, 253, 259, 268-70

Geneva conventions 63, 91

Geneva Law. See Table of Treaties

Genocide 41, 129, 152, 196, 200-01, 242, 309, 314-15, 328, 332, 365, 450, 467

Germany 27, 29, 36, 275, 307, 324, 412-13, 481, 483, 487

Global effects 412

Global starvation 264

Good faith 73, 92, 110, 140, 175, 205, 436

Good neighborliness 239, 319

Gorbachev, Mikhail 482

Graham, Kennedy 480

Grandparents 458

Gratian 291

Greece 476

Greek civilization 249

Green, Robert 468

Greenham Common women 476

Grief, Nicholas 482

Griffith, Gavan 29

Gros, Judge 150

Grotius 182, 293, 371

Guerrero, Judge 134

Guillaume, Gilbert 15, 74-76

Gulf War 106-07, 368

Gustaffson, Stig 480

H-bomb 266, 432

Hague Law See Table of Treaties

Hart, H.L.A. 336-338

Health 106, 120, 150, 189-90, 267-68, 277

Heat 69, 124, 188-92, 234, 261, 269, 367

Helsinki Conference   73
Haemorrhage   267, 277
Herczegh, Géza   74-76, 264
Herodotus   131
Hibakusha   270
Higgins, Rosalyn   15, 74-76
High seas   69, 309, 434
Hillgenberg, Harmut   29
Hindu culture   10, 288, 293
Hiraoka, Takashi   29
Hiroshima   2, 5, 29, 80, 121, 177,
   188-90, 201, 235, 247, 253, 259-
   60, 467, 474, 480, 486
Hiroshima bomb: differences from
   present bombs   177, 266-67,
   272, 368, 377
Hobbes, Thomas   371
Homeless   272
Hsu Mo, Judge   134
Human rights in peace time   40,
   309
Human rights law   235, 273, 299,
   477
Humanitarian laws of war   1, 8,
   12, 37, 45, 67-70, 75, 98, 113,
   115-16, 167, 173, 179, 181, 184,
   186-87, 195, 197, 205, 207, 211,
   227-28, 240, 242, 247-49, 251,
   258, 288, 294, 298, 307, 365,
   368, 370, 373, 387-88, 391
Humanity, principle of/elementary
   considerations of   10, 69, 146,
   148, 155, 161, 177, 247, 287,
   293, 295, 299, 307, 320, 363,
   394, 418, 487
Hussein, Saddam   105

ICJ accessible   28
ICJ procedure   25, 31
ICJ public sittings   28
Immorality issue   5
Independent Commission on Disar-
   mament and Security Issues   477
India   27, 164, 419, 423, 440-41,
   476, 479
Indian civilization   249

Indigenous peoples   462, 478, 483
Indigent   291
Indirect effects   278
Individual self-defence   46, 95-96,
   212, 227, 241
Indonesia   29, 164, 267, 405, 408,
   411-12, 417, 484
Infanticide   478
Intent/intend/intention/intentional
   41, 358-59
International Association of Lawyers Against Nuclear Arms   6,
   226, 351, 478-80
International Committee of the Red
   Cross/Red Crescent   121
International community   71-72,
   74, 83, 91, 118, 122, 125, 132-
   33, 139-40, 146, 156, 161, 164,
   174, 195-96, 204, 230, 232, 246,
   248, 257, 299, 309, 337, 342,
   347, 379, 388, 400, 413, 447
International Council of Scientific
   Unions   282
International Court of Justice   2-3,
   8-9, 102, 164, 174, 218, 399, 408-
   09, 448, 473, 475-78, 452, 480-
   81, 483, 485-86, 488, 473, 475-
   78, 480-81, 483, 485-86, 488
International crime   147, 230
International environmental
   law   316
International humanitarian law   1,
   12, 15, 61-62, 64, 66, 75, 86-87,
   90, 99, 101, 103, 184-87, 201,
   205, 208, 238-39, 245, 248, 286,
   337, 373
International law in armed conflict
   1, 113, 115, 124, 126, 128, 137-
   38, 143, 173, 179-80, 184, 242,
   378, 384-85, 387, 389-92, 397
International Law Commission
   303, 315
International law, contemporary 38,
   110, 112, 196-97
International law, conventional   11
International law, customary   11,

38, 47, 58, 60-61, 63-64, 67, 69,
74, 86-87, 97-98, 114, 116, 142,
145-46, 148, 150, 152, 155, 174,
186, 196, 198, 204-05, 227, 249,
256, 286, 298, 318, 343, 380,
390, 392, 399, 407, 418, 448, 453
International peace and security
94-95, 178, 183, 282, 346, 351,
409, 479
International Peace Bureau 6
International Physicians for the Pre-
vention of Nuclear War 6, 282,
346, 351, 409, 479
Invasion 96
Ionising radiation 2, 188, 262, 324
Iran, Islamic Republic of 27, 29,
103, 413
Iran-Iraq War 103-04, 106
Iraq/Iraqi 103-06, 108-09, 317
Ireland 27, 476, 481, 483-84, 487
Irreparable damage 313
Islamic civilization/tradition 249,
288, 291, 293
Islamic law 10, 292
Ismael, Tan Sri Ragali 29
Israel 106, 441
Italy 27, 29, 307, 483
Itoh, Iccho 29

Jaipal, Rikhi 479
Japan 5-6, 9, 27, 244, 266, 268-
69, 307, 314, 414, 443, 463, 475-
76, 481, 483, 487
Japan note of protest 5
Japanese Association of Doctors
against A- and H-bombs 278
Japanese civilization 249
Jellyfish babies 2, 271
Jenkins, Lord 460
Jenks, Wilfred 167, 322
Jennings, Sir Robert 322
Jiuyong, Shi 14
Jordan 106
Judaic 10
Judges and Prosecuters for
Peace 476

Jurisdiction, decline to exercise 31
Jurisdiction, lack of 35
Jurisdiction to give reply 31
Just war 292

Kaku, Michio 360
Kapitza 265
Kardarisman, Johannes B.S. 29
Karp, R.C. 356-57
Kauravas 290
Kawamura, Takekazu 29
Kazakhstan 7, 461
Kelly, Petra 476-77
Keloid growths 9, 267, 270, 287
Khaldun, Ibn 119
Kissinger, Henry 273, 331, 366
Korea, People's Republic of 27
Koroma, Abdul G. 8, 74-76
Kurdish citizens 103
Kuwait 103-04, 106, 108
Kyrgyztan 461-62

Labor unions 3
Lakshmana 289
Lange, David 488
Latin America 9, 56, 58, 157,
300, 353, 437
Lauterpecht, Sir Hersch 102, 105,
153, 165, 180
Law in armed conflict, applicable
in 69-71, 109, 177, 179-80,
184, 193, 203, 205, 207, 209-10,
213, 222, 230, 238, 249
Law-making 37, 149, 220, 390,
426
Laws of peace 307
Laws of war 44, 118, 148, 153,
173, 187, 246, 257, 247, 294,
297, 291, 307, 311, 327, 334-35,
342, 345, 365, 384-85, 387, 389,
395, 398
Lawyers 4, 13, 167
Lawyers' Appeal 477, 486
Lawyers for Nuclear Disarmament 477
League of Nations 2, 35

Leanza, Umberto 29
Legal principle 90, 101, 113, 143,
    174, 197, 240, 380, 385, 392,
    406, 409, 426, 446
Legal question 32, 117-18, 140,
    165-66, 172, 198-99, 147, 152,
    208, 241, 244-45, 250, 339, 357-
    59, 365, 370, 378, 381-82, 395,
    414, 417, 450-52
Lesotho 27
Leukemias 9, 189, 253, 268, 287
Lieber, Franz 311
Life, loss of 41, 234, 266
Likiep 270
Limit situation 254
Lincoln, Abraham 294
Lini, Hilda 482-83
Livestock 291
Logic 298
London 266
London Nuclear Warfare Tribunal
    477
Lotus case 114, 128, 130, 135,
    150, 168

MacBride, Sean 147, 475, 477,
    480
Mahahharatha 289-90, 340
Majeed, Hussein Kamel
    Hassan 109-10
Malaysia 27, 29, 163-64, 344,
    349, 356, 367, 410, 487
Manhattan Project 280
Manu, laws of 289
Marriage, right to 320
Marshall Islands 27, 30, 126, 192,
    270
Marshall, John 343
Marshall, Russell 488
Martens clause 65, 67, 137, 149,
    295, 298-99, 384
Martens, Frederic de 294, 297
Mason, Peggy 484
Mawdsley, Andres Aguilar 288
McNair, Lord 134, 322
McNamara, Robert 273, 328, 366

Media 460
Medical Campaign Against Nuclear
    Weapons 351
Medical care, right to 320
Medical effects 234
Megasthenes 290
Mendlovitz, Saul 19
Mental retardation 9, 287
Mexico 27, 29, 413, 465, 476-77,
    479
Meyrowitz, Eliott L. 322, 486
Middle Ages 274
Military Leaders Against Nuclear
    Weapons 463
Military necessity/objective 8, 44,
    140, 229, 389, 393-94,
Military-industrial complex 19,
    467, 469
Mines 62, 185, 296, 311, 458
Mississippi 6
Monks 291
Monster babies 2, 192, 270
Morality/moral order 200
Morocco 412, 484
Moscow 219, 266, 436
Motherhood, right to 320
Mothersson, Keith 480
Multicultural background 235, 288
Mushroom cloud 235, 279, 374
Mutual Assured Destruction 16

Nagasaki 2, 5, 29, 188-89, 191,
    201, 235, 253, 259-60, 266-67,
    272, 368, 377, 467, 486
Namibia 164
Napalm 125, 394
National groups 41, 200, 315
National Lawyers Guild 467
NATO 324, 461, 476
Natural law 226, 230, 337
Nauru 27, 28, 126
Necessity, doctrine/principle of
    11, 47, 113, 168, 184, 389, 393-
    94
Necessity, military 206
Negative security assurances 55

Netherlands   27, 36, 307, 393,
    476, 481, 483
Neutral states   12, 67, 126, 131,
    149, 287, 229, 312, 365
Neutrality, law/principles of   50,
    61, 67-68, 70, 152, 186, 208-09,
    212, 225, 258
Neutron bomb   223
New York   266
New Zealand   27, 29, 67, 161,
    415, 433, 461, 473, 475-76, 479,
    481, 483-84, 487-88
Newman, Frank   456
Nicaragua   231
Non-aligned movement   410, 414,
    417, 466, 483, 487
Non-belligerent states   235, 328,
    332
Non-combatants   63, 86, 186, 193,
    206, 253, 265, 291, 312, 396
Non-derogable rights   320
Non-governmental organizations
    (NGOs)   3, 243, 409-10, 469,
    473-88
Non liquet   389, 391, 398, 401
Non-Nuclear-Weapon State
    (NNWS)   18, 48, 55, 57-58, 92-
    93, 95-96, 121, 154-55, 159-64,
    166, 179, 212, 224, 434, 436,
    440, 442, 447, 468
Non-radioactive berries   274
Norton, Eleanor Holmes   461
Norway   461, 476, 481, 483-84
NPT Review and Extension Confer-
    ence of 1995   465-66
Nuclear accident   469
Nuclear age   118
Nuclear Age Peace Foundation
    351
Nuclear attack   269, 341, 366, 469
Nuclear decision-making   241, 345
Nuclear deterrence   14, 155, 170,
    220, 396, 404, 442, 476
Nuclear disarmament   1, 11-12,
    16, 32, 129, 173, 175, 205, 214,
    238-40

Nuclear missiles, mass production
    of   81
Nuclear pollution   15, 476
Nuclear preparedness   258
Nuclear reactors   235
Nuclear scientists   5
Nuclear submarine   399
Nuclear terror   3
Nuclear umbrella   91, 155-56,
    171, 399
Nuclear war   269, 284, 338
Nuclear-weapon-free zones   54,
    56, 58, 97, 123, 162, 434, 437,
    440-41, 458, 461, 474, 476, 480
Nuclear Weapon State (NWS)   2,
    9-10, 14, 18, 53, 55-58, 60, 92,
    95, 112, 121, 124, 155-56, 161-
    62, 164, 169-70, 179, 223, 228,
    231, 255, 278, 399, 434, 437-38,
    447, 468, 482-85
Nuclear weapons abolition   463,
    470
Nuclear weapons acquisition   57,
    97
Nuclear weapons battlefield   119,
    365
Nuclear weapons, clean use of   8,
    70, 86, 119, 387, 399
Nuclear weapons cost   468-69
Nuclear weapons deployment   52,
    57, 91, 93, 97, 155, 201
Nuclear weapons industry   3, 8
Nuclear weapons internal use   50,
    241
Nuclear weapons labs   461
Nuclear weapons, limited/low-
    yield/smaller   69-70, 104, 236,
    365-66, 368
Nuclear weapons maintenance   91,
    468
Nuclear weapons manufacture   51,
    57, 91, 97, 201, 242, 420, 425,
    446
Nuclear weapons monopoly   474
Nuclear weapons, possession/stock-
    piles of   9, 18, 49, 52, 54, 57,

93, 97, 155, 164, 177, 201, 223, 242, 255, 402, 407, 420, 425, 446
Nuclear weapons, prohibition of/recourse to　8, 15, 114, 117, 131, 370
Nuclear weapons protestors　462
Nuclear weapons research　18
Nuclear weapons, tactical　47, 119, 365
Nuclear weapons testing　2, 9, 18, 44, 53, 57, 97, 201, 242, 357, 462, 476, 488
Nuclear weapons threat　9, 11, 13, 26, 33, 53, 58, 61, 66, 75, 80, 83, 85, 88, 90-91, 93-95, 97-98, 103, 108, 113-16, 155, 159, 164, 166, 173, 176, 193, 207, 209-10, 212, 226-27, 231, 237, 242, 246, 358, 376, 78, 380, 390, 398, 415, 420, 424
Nuclear weapons unique characteristics　45, 70, 124-25, 192, 242, 257, 391
Nuclear weapons use　9, 11, 13, 18, 25-26, 33, 37-45, 47-54, 58-61, 67-71, 75, 83-85, 91, 94-98, 101-03, 112-17, 125-30, 136, 149-55, 159-62, 164, 166, 168-69, 173-74, 176, 179, 187, 192-93, 201, 207, 209-12, 226-32, 237-41, 245-46, 255, 261, 273, 299-322, 335, 369, 376-78, 380, 390-98, 406, 415, 446, 477
Nuclear winter　3, 9, 12, 234, 264
Nuclearism　476, 478
Nuremberg Tribunal　64, 147, 250, 315, 388, 392, 476

Octopuses　270
Oda, Shigeru　75-76
Opinio juris　94, 97, 117, 379, 382
Opinion enforcement　455-70
Opinion, lay　244
Opinion, positive aspects of　238
Oppenheim, L.　146, 362, 401
Oppenheimer, Robert　112, 248,

269
Orphan　291
Outer space　300, 309, 433
Owens, Major　461

Pacific Island　2
Pacific Ocean　8, 278, 300
Pacifist　292
Palme, Olaf　479
Pandavas　290
Parents　2-3, 458
Paris　266
Partial bans　236
Pasupathastra　290
Pellet, Alain　29
People for Nuclear Disarmament　351
Peoples of the world　247
Performers & Artists for Nuclear Disarmament International　351
Permanent Court of International Justice　35, 133, 378
Permitted, use of word　38
Pershing 2 missiles　476
Persian Gulf War. *See* Gulf War
Petitions　8
Philippines　29, 133, 476
Pictet, M. Jean　147
Plutonium 239　262
Plutonium 240　262
Plutonium 241　262
Poison gas　51, 143-44, 204, 287, 323
Poison weapons/arrows　51, 291, 325
Polanyi, John　352
Political aspects　5, 33, 49, 412, 426, 447
Political independence　25, 46, 49
Political question　369-70, 383, 453
Polluter pays principle　316
Pollution　254, 263
Possession, right to　39, 339, 358
Potential to destroy civilization　119, 125, 132, 139, 150, 235

Powell, Colin L. 104, 107, 366
Power, discretionary 35
Practical assistance 35
Precautionary principle 316
Preemptive strike 335, 367
Press, freedom of 460
Procedure, advisory 172
Procedure, contentious 36, 383
Procreation, right of/procreate,
    right to 320
Proliferation, horizontal 242
Proliferation, vertical 242
Proportionality/proportionate 11-
    12, 43, 47-48, 99-100, 109, 113,
    152, 168, 183-84, 197, 206, 213,
    255, 258, 308, 328, 330, 365,
    389-90, 395-96
Psychological traumas 10
Public conscience 63, 125, 143,
    146, 148, 150-51, 186, 226, 235,
    247, 252, 288, 294, 299, 347,
    363, 480
Publicizing of Opinion 18

Qatar 27, 30
Qur'anic passages 291

Racial discrimination 196, 309
Racial groups 41, 200, 315
Radiation/radioactive fall-out/iso-
    topes 2, 9, 45, 69, 100, 120,
    123-24, 126, 188-89, 192, 202,
    209, 261, 266, 268, 275, 277,
    323, 365, 367, 393-94
Rama 289
Ramayana 289, 340
Ranjeva, Raymond 74-76
Ravana 289
Rawls, John 336, 339
Read, Judge 134
Reagan, Ronald 288
Religious groups 41, 200, 291,
    315
Reprisal/reprisals 44, 238, 242,
    258, 341
Retaliatory attack 105, 107, 279

Right to life 40, 320
Right to know 460
Rocky Flats 2
Roman civilization 249
Rongelap 270
Roosevelt, Franklin D. 467
Rotblat, Joseph 268
Rousseau, Charles 322
Royalism 478
Ruda, José Maria 322
Russell-Einstein Manifesto 373
Russia 54, 272, 412, 415, 449,
    460, 466, 483
Russian Federation 7, 27, 30, 67,
    187, 256, 352, 440
Rwanda 272

Sahara 194
St. Augustine 291
St. John, Edward 478-80
St. Petersburg principle 8. See
    also Table of Treaties
Salmond, George 482
Samoa 28, 30, 133
San Marino 28, 30, 415
Sanderson, Jack 322, 490
Schachter, Oscar 322
Schell, Jonathan 274, 318
Schwarzenberger, G. 322-26
Schwarzkopf, Gen. Norman 106
Schwebel, Stephen M. 15, 74-76,
    90-110
Schweitzer, Albert 244, 370
Scientific Committee on Problems
    of the Environment 282
Scientists Against Nuclear Arms
    351
Scotland 462
Second Lateran Council of 1139
    291
Secretary-General 64, 76, 418, 440
Security Council 47-49, 55-58,
    64, 73, 91, 94-96, 103, 106-08,
    160, 162-63, 165, 183, 210, 213,
    221, 231, 317-18, 334, 406, 440,
    442

Security interests, vital   18, 59, 113
Self-defence, legitimate   11, 47, 50, 69, 71, 76, 101-02, 116, 128, 131, 168-69, 176, 179, 181, 193, 213, 241, 258, 278, 327, 332, 335, 366, 368, 376, 385, 387-88, 390-91, 393, 398, 401
Self-defense, right of   13, 43, 46-48, 53-54, 59, 70, 87, 95, 103, 109, 113, 157-60, 163, 180, 182-83, 197, 202, 208-09, 211-18, 229, 232, 343, 357, 360-61, 401
Self-determination   462
Senegal   411
Serres, Michel
Shahabuddeen, Mohamed   74-76, 110
Shi, Judge   74-76
Shockwave   394
Siege machine   291
Siege of Sebastopol   292
Singh, Nagendra   177, 196, 312, 322, 338-39, 479
Sivard, Ruth   372
Slavery   196, 309, 478
Social disintregration   9
Social Scientists Against Nuclear War   351
Society for a Nuclear Free Europe 351
Solomon Islands   28, 30, 160, 245, 269, 476
South Africa   16, 441, 469-70
South Asian tradition   289
Southeast Asia   289, 441
Southeast Asia Nuclear-Weapon-Free Zone   58, 97, 123, 474
South Pacific   58, 437, 475-76, 482
South Pacific Nuclear-Weapon-Free Zone   53-54, 97, 437
Sovereign rights, territorial   67, 157, 194-95, 199, 208
Sovereignty, principles of   14, 38, 83-84, 130, 132-35, 158, 167, 171, 180, 182, 210, 231, 233, 255, 306, 308, 319, 462
Soviet Union   54-55, 122-23, 432, 436, 438
Space Age   274
Sri Lanka   289
State, heads of   458-59
State practice   90
State survival   385, 387, 391, 398
Stimson, Henry   282
Stockholm Declaration   476
Stone, J.   150, 322
Strontium 90   262
Substantive law   246
Successive resolutions 94
Suffering, unnecessary   125, 137, 142, 144
Sulphur   292
Survival/Survivability   15, 102, 116, 118, 122, 232, 245, 247, 251, 257, 273, 283, 318, 336, 338, 371-72, 379
Suter, Keith   474-75
Sweden   28, 272, 414, 476, 479, 481, 483, 487
Szilard, Leo   5

Tahiti 462
Taiwanese Chinese   474
Tajikistan 461
Tanaka, Kotaro   322
Tangiora, Pauline   483
Tanzania   410, 476
Target, civilian   99, 228, 389, 392, 395-96
Target, military   12, 99, 185, 228, 389, 395-96
Territorial integrity   25, 46, 49, 209
Terrorizement   109, 296, 313, 371, 386
Theorin, Maj Britt   479-80, 483-84
Threat of force   11, 75, 341
Toffler, Alvin and Heidi   372
Tokyo   141, 266
Torture   305
Toxins/toxic weapons   52

Transborder damage 67, 126
Transborder incursions/transbound-
  ary effects 67, 126, 272
Transnational corporations 3
Transnational damage 126, 235
Treaty law 50, 60, 136, 286, 458
Trials of nuclear weapons protes-
  tors 462
Trident 462
Truces of God 291
Trusteeship of earth resources 316
Truth and Reconciliation Commis-
  sion 469
TTAPS 264
Tunkin, Grigory 322
Turgenev, Ivan 265
Turkey 84, 307
Turkmenistan 461
Tutu, Archbishop 482

UK Ecology Party 477
Ukraine 7, 272, 484, 487
UN Decade of International
  Law 26, 457, 480
UN dues 459
UN GA First Committee 483-85
UN General Assembly 1, 4-5, 7,
  9, 12, 16, 25-28, 31, 35, 37-38,
  40, 44, 59-61, 72, 74, 85-86, 93,
  97, 112, 121, 129, 151, 195, 206-
  07, 209, 211, 219, 226, 246, 252,
  257, 300, 303, 347, 376, 378,
  380-81, 403-06, 408-09, 414-15,
  435, 438, 446-47, 451, 477-78,
  485-86
UN Human Rights Committee 477
UN Human Rights Conference, Te-
  heran 1968 474
UN Institute of Disarmament Re-
  search 282, 330, 367
UN Secretary General 26, 27, 120
UN Security Council 9, 31
UN Under-Secretary-General for
  Humanitarian Affairs 272
UNESCO 275
UNGA vote 7

UNICEF 481
Union of Soviet Socialist Republics
  473-74, 488
United Arab Emirates 410, 413
United Kingdom of Great Britain
  and Northern Ireland 7, 28, 30,
  36, 53-55, 67, 69, 93, 187, 256,
  286, 333, 353, 413, 415, 432,
  436, 438, 440-41, 460, 466, 473,
  475, 480, 484
United Nations head of disarmament 488
United Nations organs and agencies 4, 26, 34, 218-19, 263,
  382, 387, 409, 448, 452, 456
United Nations Security Council
  483-84
United States 2, 7-8, 28, 30, 36,
  53-55, 67, 96, 106-07, 122-23,
  148, 187, 220, 231, 276, 286,
  293, 352-53, 411, 415, 432-33,
  436, 438-41, 457, 460-62, 466-
  67, 469-70, 473-75, 481-85
United States Atomic Energy Commission 261
United States Civil War/War of Se-
  cession 292, 294
United States courts 457, 469
United States Military Tribunal at
  Nuremberg 167
United States Pentagon 468
Unlawful attack 48
Unnecessary suffering 12, 63, 90,
  142-45, 186, 192-93, 198, 209,
  228, 235, 250-52, 254, 258, 267,
  311, 328-29, 280, 389, 392-94,
  396, 401
"Urgently" defined 7, 27
U.S. Department of Defense 3, 5,
  311
U.S. Department of Education 3
U.S. Department of Energy 3
U.S. Department of Justice 3
U.S. Department of State 3
U.S. Supreme Court 17

Use of force   44, 46, 99
Uzbekistan   461

Valencia-Ospina, Eduardo
Vallentine, Jo   476
Vanuatu   271, 476, 482, 484
Vascular damage   267, 277
Vereshchetin, Vladlen S.   14, 74-76
Victim State   56, 96, 101
Vitoria   291
Volcano Tambora   265
Votes, distribution of   37

Waldock, Sir Humphrey   322
War crimes   297
War, laws of   62-64
War prevention   178, 458
Ware, Alyn   480-82, 485
Weapons, bacteriological   52, 62,
   104, 106, 122, 185, 204, 208,
   212, 250, 304, 360, 368
Weapons, blind   313
Weapons, chemical   52, 62, 104-
   06, 109, 122, 124, 174, 185, 208,
   212, 250, 304, 360, 368, 464, 468
Weapons, conventional   66, 311
Weapons, high velocity   70, 103,
   264, 394
Weapons, incendiary   296
Weapons manufacturers   458, 460
Weapons of mass destruction   246,
   324, 369, 395, 413, 433
Weapons, prohibited   458
Weeramantry, Christopher Gregory
   8, 10, 74-76, 292, 478
Weiss, Edith Brown   263
Weiss, Peter   19
Wells, H. G.   285
West German/West Germany   476
Weston, Burns H.   19, 301, 322,
   345, 365
Wilde, Fran   479
Wilson, Woodrow   287
Woman/Women   189, 191, 291,
   476, 478
Women Parliamentarians for Peace

483
World Commission on the Environ-
   ment and Development   261
World Court. *See* International
   Court of Justice
World Court Project   6, 473
World Federation of Public Health
   Associations   409
World Government of World Citi-
   zens   409
World Health Assembly   226, 271,
   409, 452
World Health Organization (WHO)
   2, 19, 27-28, 67, 158, 219, 242-
   43, 255, 258, 266, 268, 271, 314,
   319, 332, 368, 383, 409-09, 481-
   82, 484, 486-88
World public opinion   236, 350
World War   143, 310, 362
World War II/Second World War
   201, 247, 260, 275, 362, 364,
   474-75
Worth of the human person   123,
   239, 248, 253, 309
Wright, Lord   298

Yeltsin, President Boris   463
Yugoslavia   34

Zarif, Mohammad J.   29
Zimbabwe   30, 164, 410, 481,
   483, 487